HEARING THE MOTET

Essays on the Motet of the
Middle Ages and Renaissance

EDITED BY

DOLORES PESCE

OXFORD UNIVERSITY PRESS
New York   Oxford

Oxford University Press

Oxford   New   York
Athens   Auckland   Bangkok   Bogotá   Buenos Aires   Calcutta
Cape Town   Chennai   Dar es Salaam   Delhi   Florence   Hong Kong   Istanbul
Karachi   Kuala Lumpur   Madrid   Melbourne   Mexico City   Mumbai
Nairobi   Paris   São Paulo   Singapore   Taipei   Tokyo   Toronto   Warsaw

and associated companies in
Berlin   Ibadan

First published in 1997 by Oxford University Press, Inc.
198 Madison Avenue, New York, New York 10016

First issued as an Oxford University Press paperback, 1998

Oxford is a registered trademark of Oxford University Press

Library of Congress Cataloging-in-Publication Data
Hearing the motet : essays on the motet of the Middle Ages and Renaissance / edited by Dolores
Pesce.
      p.   cm.
"This collection of essays . . . grew out of a conference, Hearing the Motet, held at Washing-
ton University in February 1994" —Introd.
Includes bibliographical references and index.
ISBN 0-19-509709-2; ISBN 0-19-512905-9 (pbk.)
1. Motet—500–1400—Congresses.   2. Motet—15th century—Congresses.   3. Motet—16th
century—Congresses.   I. Pesce, Dolores.
ML 3275.H4   1996
782.2′6′092—dc20   96-33653

1 3 5 7 9 8 6 4 2

Printed in the United States of America
on acid-free paper

HEARING THE MOTET

To my husband, Bill

Acknowledgments

The organization and presentation of the conference from which many of these papers derive would have been impossible without the generous financial support of the administration of Washington University Faculty of Arts and Sciences, as well as the Music Department and the Medieval-Renaissance Studies Program. I would like to thank Ruth Steiner, Don Randel, Cristle Collins Judd, and James Haar for chairing the sessions at the conference, and the student conference coordinators, Robyn Reso and Sarah Stoycos, for their unflagging assistance.

A number of individuals have been instrumental in preparing this volume for publication. Maribeth Payne of Oxford University Press encouraged and supported the project from the outset; Soo Mee Kwon, her assistant, and Cynthia L. Garver, who served as production manager, launched and produced the book with precision and care. A special thanks is owed by all of us to Bonnie Blackburn, who, through her thoughtful comments and insightful suggestions, went beyond her role as copy editor. I am also indebted to James Doering, Craig Monson, Hon-Lun Yang, and the office staff of the Washington University Music Department for special assistance of various kinds.

Contents

Contributors   xii

Introduction
    DOLORES PESCE   3

Conference Introductory Remarks
    JAMES HAAR   12

1. The Polyphonic Progeny of an *Et gaudebit*:
   Assessing Family Relations in the
   Thirteenth-Century Motet
      REBECCA A. BALTZER   17

2. Beyond Glossing: The Old Made New in
   Mout me fu grief/Robin m'aime/Portare
      DOLORES PESCE   28

3. Which Vitry? The Witness of the Trinity
   Motet from the *Roman de Fauvel*
      ANNE WALTERS ROBERTSON   52

4. Polyphony of Texts and Music in the
   Fourteenth-Century Motet: *Tribum que*
   non abhorruit/Quoniam secta latronum/Merito
   hec patimur and Its "Quotations"
      MARGARET BENT   82

5. Du Fay and the Cultures of Renaissance
   Florence
   ROBERT NOSOW   104

6. For Whom the Bell Tolls: Reading and
   Hearing Busnoys's *Anthoni usque limina*
   ROB C. WEGMAN   122

7. Love and Death in the Fifteenth-Century
   Motet: A Reading of Busnoys's *Anima mea
   liquefacta est/Stirps Jesse*
   PAULA HIGGINS   142

8. Obrecht as Exegete: Reading *Factor orbis*
   as a Christmas Sermon
   M. JENNIFER BLOXAM   169

9. Conflicting Levels of Meaning and
   Understanding in Josquin's *O admirabile
   commercium* Motet Cycle
   RICHARD SHERR   193

10. Josquin, Good King René, and *O bone et
    dulcissime Jesu*
    PATRICK MACEY   213

11. Miracles, Motivicity, and Mannerism: Adrian
    Willaert's *Videns Dominus flentes sorores
    Lazari* and Some Aspects of Motet
    Composition in the 1520s
    JOSHUA RIFKIN   243

12. Lasso as Historicist: The Cantus-Firmus Motets
    JAMES HAAR   265

13. Tonal Compass in the Motets of Orlando
    di Lasso
    DAVID CROOK   286

14. Palestrina as Reader: Motets from the Song
    of Songs
    JESSIE ANN OWENS   307

15. On William Byrd's *Emendemus in melius*
JOSEPH KERMAN   329

16. Byrd, the Catholics, and the Motet:
The Hearing Reopened
CRAIG MONSON   348

Index of Names   375

Contributors

REBECCA A. BALTZER — Professor, University of Texas at Austin

MARGARET BENT — Fellow of All Souls College, Oxford

M. JENNIFER BLOXAM — Professor, Williams College

DAVID CROOK — Associate Professor, University of Wisconsin-Madison

JAMES HAAR — Professor Emeritus, University of North Carolina at Chapel Hill

PAULA HIGGINS — Associate Professor, University of Notre Dame

JOSEPH KERMAN — Professor Emeritus, University of California at Berkeley

PATRICK MACEY — Associate Professor, Eastman School of Music, University of Rochester

CRAIG MONSON — Professor, Washington University

ROBERT NOSOW — A 1993–94 Fellow at Villa I Tatti, Florence

JESSIE ANN OWENS — Professor, Brandeis University

DOLORES PESCE — Professor, Washington University

JOSHUA RIFKIN — Director, The Bach Ensemble

ANNE WALTERS ROBERTSON — Professor, University of Chicago

RICHARD SHERR — Professor, Smith College

ROB C. WEGMAN — Assistant Professor, Princeton University

HEARING THE MOTET

Introduction

This collection of essays about the motet of the Middle Ages and Renaissance grew out of a conference, "Hearing the Motet," held at Washington University in February 1994. This gathering offered scholars and performers working in one or both of these periods the opportunity to share their ideas about this repertory and to discover where their findings intersected and diverged. The conference generated a lively interchange that I hope will continue through the availability of these papers in print. The volume additionally includes a few chapters by scholars who did not participate in the conference, but whose work illustrates a vital approach to the motet today.

The title *Hearing the Motet* reflects an increasing concern among scholars and performers with bringing to light the diverse ways in which these works may have been heard in their own time. This quest involves investigations of different sorts: examining the social-historical situation that may have prompted the creation of a motet, whether a patron's commission or an ideological response on the composer's part; discovering the performance context and function of a motet, particularly with respect to the liturgy; reading the texts to uncover dual meanings possibly shared only by the composer and a select audience; reading the music to discover the attractiveness and innovative spirit it offered in its own time; and reading text and music together to uncover the ways in which composers made them serve one another to yield what can rightfully be called "music-poetic" creations.

In carrying out these investigations, the authors in many cases expand on traditional musicological methods. For instance, several essays present style analysis in the service of chronological dating of a piece, but supplement it with newly uncovered critical data on the composer or text under consideration. Several authors explore the significance of a chant used in a motet; they proceed beyond the most obvious liturgical connection, searching out more precise answers in relevant local liturgies and supplementary iconographic evidence. One author, prompted by her new understanding of an upper-voice text, examines a fourteenth-century motet and uncovers multiple layers of structure in addition to the expected isorhythmic skeleton. In a majority of cases, these expansions upon tried and true musicological methods involve increased focus on the texts.

The volume's chapters also offer a number of newer approaches akin to recent work in literary criticism. One chapter presents a feminist rereading of a fifteenth-century motet based on the Song of Songs. Various authors ask us to consider the new historicists' view that a given symbol can have multiple meanings and that meaning is construed in different ways by different people.[1] For the motet, the symbols can be musical and/or textual. A number of authors use this concept of shifting, unstable meanings to assist the modern hearer in finding a historical, liturgical, and conceptual framework outside his/her own and closer to the interpretive community of the time in which the motet was written. Furthermore, the authors suggest that diverse contemporary audiences could have responded differently to a given motet, that multiple interpretations were possible. They reread, and might even have misread, a given motet. Accordingly, some of the essays provide multiple readings of the motet in lieu of a "definitive" one.

Sometimes the various methodologies are juxtaposed in different chapters, at other times intermingled in one. The volume is organized chronologically, beginning with two chapters on the thirteenth-century motet and concluding with two chapters on the late sixteenth-century works of William Byrd. In between appear fresh investigations into the music of Philippe de Vitry, Du Fay, Busnoys, Obrecht, Josquin des Prez, Willaert, Lasso, and Palestrina.

In his introductory remarks, first presented at the conference, James Haar outlines the difficulties in defining the motet, given that it is not limited "by period, genre, form, style, textual language, or performance medium." Haar provocatively raises issues that are addressed later in the volume: How often in the fifteenth and sixteenth centuries did patrons provide not only the general subject, but also the specific idea or *invenzione* for a motet? Can we assume that composers alone knew the secrets of their art, that they did not intend to share the "meaning" of a motet with others?

The chapter by Rebecca Baltzer and my own focus on thirteenth-century motets, for Baltzer one of the largest complexes of motets built on a single clausula, and for me a single motet characterized by its borrowing of preexisting materials. Baltzer examines the *Et gaudebit* motets to explain how the earliest form was changed numerous times, through the addition of new music and new texts. Despite the liturgical designation of *Et gaudebit* for the Ascension, many of the texts attached to the motet treat the Virgin. Whereas in the past she and others have theorized that thirteenth-century motets with text not associated with feasts were performed outside of the liturgy, Baltzer newly asserts that these Marian motet versions were in fact performed in connection with the Ascension at Notre Dame cathedral in Paris. She first reviews evidence linking the *Et gaudebit* clausula and its early motet versions to Paris.

Her interpretation is further grounded in evidence that the clergy at Notre Dame cathedral in Paris viewed the Virgin as having an essential role in salvation that could be revealed within their cathedral.

The importance of the Virgin also surfaces in the portion of my chapter dealing with the texts of *Mout me fu grief/Robin m'aime/Portare*. Its upper-voice texts present courtly and pastoral love poetry in which a woman plays a central role. Though the tenor melody *Portare* is found most often in connection with feasts of the Holy Cross, I note its appearance with a Marian text in some chant sources, and provide evidence, both liturgical and iconographic, that the concepts of Christ on the Cross and Mary with Child were linked in late thirteenth-century France. From this vantage point, I argue that the motet's composer may have intended the tenor *Portare* to carry both Christological and Marian resonances that would have in different ways played off the sentiments of human love described in the upper voices.

I also ask for a reconsideration of how preexisting materials function in this late thirteenth-century motet, which uses a rondeau from Adam de la Halle's *Le Jeu de Robin et Marion* as its middle voice and snippets from another motet in its top voice, as well as the chant segment *Portare* in its tenor. I argue that the motet's composer achieved a calculated tonal design directed not by the tenor, as we tend to expect, but instead by the borrowed rondeau melody, which brings about changes in the other two voices. I liken the process of modifying the inherited chant to what happened in medieval textual practice— a creative rewriting of authority. This theme of a composer's willingness to alter a chant or even to select it in response to other materials resurfaces in Margaret Bent's study of a Fauvel motet and in Richard Sherr's essay on Josquin des Prez.

Anne Robertson takes a new approach to support the attribution to Philippe de Vitry of a motet in the *Roman de Fauvel*, *Firmissime fidem/Adesto sancta trinitas/Alleluia Benedictus es*. She argues that a trained medieval musician would likely have used a chant version indigenous to the locales where he lived and worked. Accordingly, she compares the *Alleluia Benedictus es* as it appears in *Firmissime fidem* to some 70 versions found in Paris and northern France, concluding that the motet version originated in Arras. Robertson then adds significantly to our biography of Vitry by demonstrating the likelihood that he originated from Vitry-en-Artois, near Arras. As to *Firmissime fidem's* connections with the *Roman de Fauvel*, Robertson suggests how the motet's non-Parisian tenor would have fit into the *Roman's* plan in which earthly and heavenly characters receive different music. She thus claims that by "hearing" a motet tenor in this new, intense way, we learn something about its own origin, the motet composer's life, and the motet's function within a larger artistic creation.

Robertson also devotes a portion of her study to unveiling the thoroughgoing numerical construction of this motet, musically and textually, a plan that emanates from the chant's "Trinitarian" allusion. This very aspect of the Fauvel motets—musical symbolism—returns as a focus of Margaret Bent's article.

Bent discusses the Fauvel motet *Tribum que non abhorruit/Quoniam secta latronum/Merito hec patimur* as an example of how a fourteenth-century work could offer a rich sampling of "semantic, structural, and sonic counterpoint" of both texts and music. Having identified an Ovidian letter as the source for a couplet within its duplum text, Bent illustrates how this quotation infiltrates both upper-voice texts, including verbal repetitions and the way in which the Golden Section is realized. Given the couplet's importance, she concludes that the composer may have chosen it at least as early as, or before, the Genesis source of the motet tenor. Bent also uncovers in the work a large-scale structure in addition to its isorhythmic pattern; it involves the number three that is so essential to the texts and to the music on a micro-level. Finally, she reveals in *Tribum/Quoniam* the quotation of the beginning of another Fauvel motet, *Garrit Gallus/In nova fert*, which itself contains a quotation of another Ovidian line. In view of this network of allusions and some historical data, Bent speculates on further meanings of *Tribum/Quoniam*.

Robert Nosow's study of Du Fay offers an analysis of two motets written during the composer's employment in the Papal Chapel in Florence during the 1420s and 1430s, *Mirandas parit* and *Gaude virgo mater Christi*. Nosow's analyses support his contention that Du Fay applied different musical styles to texts of a different sort: *Mirandas parit*, constructed in quantitative meter with classical vocabulary and allusions, and *Gaude virgo*, composed in accentual verse as an address to the Virgin, but without specific liturgical associations. The broader-reaching implication is that Du Fay was responding to different segments of Florentine society in both the choice of texts and the accompanying styles—in the first case, to the wave of secular humanism associated with the Medici and, in the second, to the lay piety that gave rise to confraternities, construction of family chapels, and possession of prayer books. Nosow argues that the two motets would thus have been heard in very different ways and contexts by their respective audiences.

The broad issue of an interpretive community provides the backdrop for Rob C. Wegman's study of Busnoys's *Anthoni usque limina* and its "hearing" by a medieval audience and one today. Wegman suggests that we should consider an array of possible meanings related to liturgical function, general medieval religious beliefs, and the circumstances of Busnoys's life in the 1460s and 1470s. He argues that the work is understandable as a personal votive offering by Busnoys to his name saint, Anthony, possibly related to a dire situation in Busnoys's own life, yet simultaneously as expressing a communal sensibility about disease, death, and dying. With respect to the latter, the issue of confraternities raised by Robert Nosow surfaces again.

Paula Higgins addresses another Busnoys motet, *Anima mea/Stirps Jesse*, in a reading that links it to dramatic historical events in the French royal court in 1445–46, a revision of the previously considered compositional date of 1468. After establishing Busnoys's use in *Anima mea* of a segment from the Song of Songs that many consider "an erotic dream sequence," Higgins draws attention to the life of Marguerite d'Ecosse, wife of Louis XI, who died at the age of 21 after she had been defamed by insinuations of infidelity by Louis's courtier, Jamet de Tillay. In suggesting that Busnoys may have had this event in mind when he composed the motet, Higgins draws on internal evidence from another Busnoys work, the song *Bel acueil*, and previous connections she has made between Busnoys and Marguerite's literary circle. Higgins thus offers a new feminist reading of *Anima mea/Stirps Jesse*.

While Robert Nosow asks us to consider Du Fay as a composer who responded to a new Renaissance cultural view, Jennifer Bloxam invites us to view a composer of a slightly later generation, Obrecht, as someone who based his Christmas motet *Factor orbis* on the model of a medieval sermon. Scholars and performers have long puzzled over Obrecht's intent in this monumental five-part motet for the vigil of Christmas, characterized by its profusion of texts and melodies. In her new approach, Bloxam examines the methods, structures, and goals of medieval preaching in the late fifteenth century when Obrecht lived, which she then offers as a compelling analytic context for hearing *Factor orbis*. Bloxam begins by outlining the exposure Obrecht likely had to the type of sermon that dominated the pulpit from the thirteenth into the early sixteenth centuries, the university or thematic sermon. In her analogies between the structure and methods of the sermon and the motet, Bloxam compares such features as Obrecht's inclusion of a text anticipating the Final Judgment with a device common to Advent sermons, in which the First Coming serves as an allegory for the Second Coming; and the joyful vernacular exclamations within the motet are likened to an audience's vernacular response to the Latin sermon. Bloxam's analysis brings us once again to the Virgin, who becomes the focus at the end of the motet, justified by the fact that the Gospel reading on the vigil of Christmas dwelt on the Virgin birth of Christ. Her hearing of this motet in relationship to medieval preaching offers a valuable new methodology to scholars studying the continuation of medieval ways of doing things in later times.

Richard Sherr's chapter on Josquin's *O admirabile commercium* motet cycle serves as a pivotal point in the volume since many of the issues previously raised coalesce here. Whereas Baltzer concluded that the thirteenth-century *Et gaudebit* motets were performed at the Ascension despite their Marian upper-voice texts, Sherr argues that the *O admirabile commercium* motets based on antiphons for the Feast of the Circumcision would have been heard in multiple venues, specifically the liturgy for the Circumcision and a Commemorative Office of the Virgin. The central point of Sherr's study is that the antiphon texts harbor ambiguities and multiple meanings that shift the attention between the Incarnation of Christ and Mary. Thus the possibility for Christological/ Marian interpretations mentioned earlier in my essay reappears. Furthermore, Josquin played the part of musical exegete by using transpositions of the chant, text underlay, and word repetition to enhance the shifting textual subject. Whereas Bloxam concludes that Obrecht, in modeling his motet on a sermon, followed an expected path of textual elaboration, Sherr suggests that Josquin may have played the part of radical exegete who "misread" his texts for dramatic effect.

Patrick Macey's chapter directs us to another Josquin work, the motet *O bone et dulcissime Jesu*, and offers varied evidence to support a revised dating and historical circumstance for its creation. By studying the provenance of its text, Macey concludes that Josquin may have written *O bone et dulcissime Jesu* for René d'Anjou, known as Good King René, sometime between 1477 and the king's death in 1480. Macey bolsters his argument by noting stylistic similarities between *O bone* and *Misericordias domini*, the latter probably also commissioned by a royal patron, Louis XI of France, sometime between 1480 and 1483. To James Haar's opening question, "Did patrons provide more than the general subject of a motet?", Macey responds that these two works, and a third, *Miserere mei, deus*, are Josquin's musical testaments which "aptly express the sentiments of three of [his] patrons as they approached the end of their days."

Joshua Rifkin turns in his chapter to a topic that he has addressed elsewhere, motivicity, a compositional phenomenon that becomes increasingly prominent in the later fifteenth and early sixteenth centuries. After defining what motivicity is and is not, and alluding to its use by Josquin, Mouton, and others, Rifkin settles into a discussion of how Adrian Willaert carries this approach to new lengths in his motet *Videns Dominus*. Rifkin goes so far as to describe what Willaert achieves as "a shaking up [of] an entire texture" through details of motivicity—varied repetition, irregular transpositions, and obscured articulations. Then, just as Robert Nosow viewed Du Fay as responding to the new Renaissance cultures in fifteenth-century Florence, Rifkin suggests that Willaert's musical art might find an analog in the mannerism of Italian visual arts around 1530. In both arts, he claims, one finds a self-conscious attempt to distort the classical features of inherited models.

James Haar offers quite a different view of Orlando di Lasso and his relationship to earlier music. Working from Jessie Ann Owens's concept of short-term historical awareness, Haar suggests that composers active in the middle third of the sixteenth century engaged in a practice genuinely historicist in intent—the use of cantus firmi within their motets in the manner of Willaert and Rore preceding them. Of Lasso's 15 motets using separately texted cantus firmi, Haar distinguishes instances where the composer seemed faithful to the old tradition, but more often used it as an appendage to his own style. He notes that these motets, in addition to illustrating Lasso's historicist intent, reveal a particular textual feature: a number of the cantus firmi texts are epigrammatic, some used historically as mottos. In one case we know the recipients of the motet and the nature of the commission under which Lasso composed it. This combined evidence leads Haar to speculate upon the likelihood that Lasso wrote these motets for specific patrons, offering a complementary view to Patrick Macey's study of Josquin.

David Crook takes a different approach to Lasso's music. Beginning with the observation that Lasso turned from early chromatic experiments to a tamer tonal language, Crook systematically outlines what he calls the "normative tonal compass" used in Lassos's motets. He shows that Lasso breached his own norm in only limited cases, and then always to mirror or highlight the sense of the text being set—instances that his listeners would have heard as meaningful tonal excursions. Crook's distinctive approach to tonal organization will offer a useful tool to scholars of sixteenth-century music. Another valuable aspect of

Crook's chapter is the complementary view it presents to James Haar's assessment of Lasso as historicist. Crook explains the limited tonal compass of Lasso's motets as a "neo-Guidonian diatonic," and speculates that Lasso may have sought his tonal guidelines in an earlier repertory as a response to the humanist-inspired historicism of sixteenth-century thought.

With Jessie Ann Owens's chapter on Palestrina and his motet settings of the Song of Songs, we encounter again the issue of composer as exegete. Owens first puts into perspective Palestrina's turn to this rich love poetry by documenting the widespread contemporary exegesis on this book of the Bible, refuting along the way the claim of some scholars that Palestrina was in fact composing "madrigals" acceptable to the Church. She then offers a rationale for the composer's choice of texts from within the Song of Songs, as well as an analysis of his text-setting in one motet, *Quam pulchra es*. Whereas Sherr suggests that Josquin played significantly on the ambiguities of the texts he set, Owens argues that Palestrina mildly "reread" the Song of Songs' syntactic structure to bring out meanings of his choosing. Finally, she speculates on what Palestrina meant in his dedication to the Song of Songs settings when he spoke of a "music somewhat livelier than I have been accustomed to use in ecclesiastical melodies."

The volume includes a revised version of Joseph Kerman's 1963 analysis of William Byrd's *Emendemus in melius*. Because this article has long offered students one model of how to approach a Renaissance motet, I have considered it appropriate to include it in this volume of current methodologies. Kerman analyzes aspects of *Emendemus in melius*'s texture, melody, harmony, rhythm, and dissonance (with a revised view of its tonality), and he then deftly reveals Byrd's reading of the text served by these musical elements. His chapter concludes with a historical reckoning of when and why Byrd turned to Lenten texts such as "Emendemus in melius" and suggests a musical model for this specific work. Through his discussion of musical modeling and influences Kerman focuses our attention on one more way in which an audience may have "heard" a motet.

Finally, in his study of the "political" vocabulary of William Byrd's motets from the *Gradualia* and *Cantiones sacrae*, Craig Monson revisits Byrd's connections with Catholic sympathizers in the 1580s and the composer's use of specific rhetoric to reflect the plight of persecuted Catholics. Examining the language of books and pamphlets published from the 1570s through the early 1600s, chiefly as part of the Jesuit "mission," Monson explores the extent to which the composer and Jesuit missionaries shared a common rhetoric. Perhaps even more striking, Monson suggests that certain of Byrd's motets, which have never been singled out as political, may also have served the Catholic cause. We gain a portrait of a composer offering his art to foster a larger communal spirit, and, more significantly, evidence that it was heard in that way by some of its listeners.

As a whole, the volume revises our view of the medieval and Renaissance motet in several ways. Many of the chapters contribute to a more balanced understanding of the motet as a "music-poetic" creation. These essays testify that motet texts from the thirteenth through sixteenth centuries abound in rich verbal meanings, explicit or implied, and that the composers, through their musical settings, "read" their texts and brought them to life in a new and creative way. We see a varied music-textual interaction, whether reacting to classical meter or numerical allusions, writing an analog to a medieval sermon, or highlighting "gallows texts." On the other hand, in at least two chapters it is argued that composers did concern themselves with aspects of the music viewed largely apart from the text. The composer of *Mout me fu grief/Robin m'aime/ Portare* realized a cohesive tonal design directed by a borrowed rondeau melody; Willaert in *Videns Dominus* carried to a "distorting" extreme the very compositional techniques that served unifying functions in other contexts.

A number of the chapters offer concrete evidence or speculations on the specific make-up of the audiences for their respective motets. Some of the *Et gaudebit* motets described by Rebecca Baltzer were heard by those attending Notre Dame cathedral; Robert Nosow speculates that Du Fay wrote *Mirandas parit* and *Gaude virgo* for a Florentine audience of secular humanists and lay pietists, respectively; Craig Monson suggests that Byrd's motets spoke especially to Jesuits and their supporters in late sixteenth-century England. Nosow and Monson in particular imply that the respective audiences for their motets would have been acutely tuned in to the verbal rhetoric contained within them. Would the audiences for other repertories represented in the volume have been so primed?

Here we return to James Haar's introductory query on whether we can continue to believe that a composer may have written complicated meanings into a motet without intending to share them. Robertson, Sherr, and I all argue that the motets we discuss carried either veiled or dual meanings tied to their respective chants. Robertson believes that a trained musician would have recognized the version of *Alleluia Benedictus es* in Vitry's *Firmissime fidem* as non-Parisian and accordingly would have understood its symbolic role in the *Roman de Fauvel*. I suggest that certain listeners to the motet *Mout me fu grief* may have interpreted it in relationship to a Christological and/or Marian association of the chant segment *Portare*. In a similar vein, Sherr argues that the dual Christological/Marian meanings of the *O admirabile commercium* chant texts were exploited by Josquin in his motet settings, and that contemporary audiences would have recognized his masterful handling of the shifting subject.

What these three and other essays in the volume suggest is that there was no secret art—that the most complicated of messages was to be shared, even if with only a select audience. As remarked earlier, a motet may well have communicated different messages to different audiences. Not incidentally, James Haar reminds us that some of the manuscripts in which motets appear were intended for repeated reading and study, making a "close" reading possible in their own time, just as it is possible for us today.[2] Margaret Bent readily agrees that intelligent contemporary appreciation of the complexities of music-textual interaction she has uncovered in the Fauvel motet *Tribum/Quoniam* must have depended upon some reflection outside of the performance.

Some of the essays offer new details within certain composers' biographies, specifically Vitry, Busnoys, Josquin, and Byrd. As importantly, the combined essays provide an emerging profile of the motet composer himself as a "reader" in the broadest sense of the culture around him—of someone who knew liturgical practice, sometimes in more than one locale, who knew biblical literature and its exegetical traditions, who moved in social contexts such as humanist gatherings or political-religious dissenters, who understood numerical symbolism and classical allusions, who wrote subtle *memorie* for patrons, and who found musical models (real and theoretical) to emulate or "distort." Whereas some of these tendencies are more apparent in the Middle Ages and some more so in the Renaissance, the essays suggest a continuity of concerns, that composers within this four-century span faced similar challenges in creating the motet repertory.

This volume of essays invites the reader to experience anew some motets that are well known from performances and recordings, and some lesser-known examples for the first time. In a few cases, the authors' readings offer performers a specific guide to new interpretations of the repertory; in others, they may engender a new approach, whether intended or not. For performers and listeners alike, we offer these essays as stimuli for continued fruitful "hearing of the motet."

NOTES

1. Robert Darnton provides a lucid illustration of how this ethnographic approach to symbols can benefit historians' understanding of a given historical event. See "The Symbolic Element in History," *Journal of Modern History* 58/1–2 (1986): 218–34.

2. In the last ten years in particular, studies in literary history and in language development have suggested the importance of author and reader relationships. Particularly cogent is the monograph by Martin Nystrand, *The Structure of Written Communication: Studies in Reciprocity between Writers and Readers* (Orlando, Fla.: Academic Press, 1986). He claims that "texts are explicit not just because of what they say but also because of a range of devices . . . which accompany the text and cue readers as to its interpretation" and that "in fact, almost all writers in actual rhetorical situations address very particular readers about whom they know something" (104–5). In an overview of studies on orality and reading, D. H. Green suggests that we have missed a mode of reception, namely the private reader. Referring to the work of Günter Scholz on the reading reception of vernacular literature, Green says: "Scholz is guilty of ignoring what I should term the intermediate mode of reception, widespread in the Middle Ages, in which a work was composed with an eye to public recital from a written text, but also for the occasional private reader. One of the pointers to this intermediate mode is the formula 'to hear or to read,' originally at home in classical Latin literature, but also to be found in medieval Latin literature, in legal practice, and in the various vernaculars." See D. H. Green, "Orality and Reading: The State of Research in Medieval Studies," *Speculum* 65/2 (1990): 277. Other writers who offer useful viewpoints on author/reader relationships are Walter J. Ong, Paul Zumthor, and Eric A. Havelock. See their contributions in *New Literary History* 14/1 (autumn 1984).

Conference Introductory Remarks

The motet has an immensely long history, extending from the early thirteenth century to the present. We are met here to take up problems connected with the first half of this eight-century span. The unifying thread in the conference is that we will all be talking about motets; so it would be natural for me to begin by offering a definition, an answer to the question "Motetus quid est?" Natural, perhaps; but not prudent. A word that does not limit the subject by period, genre, form, style, textual language, or performance medium is resistant to precise definition.[1] In place of hazarding anything of my own, I will offer the well-known words of Johannes de Grocheio on the subject: "The motet is music made for several voices, having multiple texts or a varied arrangement of syllables, harmoniously consonant in all respects."[2]

This is true, if not particularly helpful, for the whole period under discussion here. Grocheio does not go much further, though he does distinguish motet from organum and hocket. Moreover:

> This music should not be performed in the presence of ordinary people, for they will not pay heed to its subtleties nor be delighted by its sound, but should be [heard] in the presence of the educated and of those who seek out the subtleties of art. Thus it is to be sung at festive gatherings of the latter, whereas the song called *rotundellus* is meant for festivals of ordinary laymen.[3]

Elitist art, then; I give you fair warning.[4]

In its long history, the motet touches on nearly every aspect of sacred and secular musical culture. It is at first linked with Mass and Office polyphony through its troping of discant clausulae and its subsequent use of chant tenors. Quite early on it has connections with secular song, both monophonic and polyphonic. It is not, in its early history, intended for liturgical use but rather for the *festa* mentioned by Grocheio, probably and in many cases certainly not religious in character; but it may also be linked, text permitting, with extraliturgical devotional practices. By the early fourteenth century the motet is touching the "outside world" in works of formal ceremonial intent, built on texts containing political or moralizing messages, even doctrinal commentary. In the fourteenth and for much of the fifteenth century the motet exemplifies what might be called quadrivial culture, using arithmetic and the ancient science of harmonics in textual-musical schemes of a complexity of design and depth of allegorical reference we are only now beginning to sort out. At the same time we see, with particular clarity in the motets of Machaut, evidence of what might be called proto-humanist culture in manipulations of textual form and layering of classical reference.

In these linkages the motet, in origin a parasitic genre, is often the borrower of textual and musical features. It can be the lender as well: there are motet-chansons as well as chanson motets in the fifteenth century; the organizing principles we know under the rather inadequate label of isorhythm are surely important in the development of the cyclic Mass; chanson, madrigal, and motet have important reciprocal relationships in the sixteenth century. At times, in the period from ca. 1270 to ca. 1430 and again in the later sixteenth century, the motet is of prime importance to the contemporaries and descendants of Grocheio's *litterati*. Sometimes, as in its beginnings and again in the later fifteenth and early sixteenth centuries, it plays a more secondary role; but throughout the period to be considered here and for more than a century after it, the motet is something to be reckoned with.

Earlier study of the motet concentrated on features of musical style. There is still much to do here, as several papers—those of Dolores Pesce, Anne Walters Robertson, Joshua Rifkin, and Robert Nosow in particular—will show. To say that the music is only half of a motet is to put simply the fact that serious study of the text is of enormous importance. Recent work on fourteenth-century motet texts, by David Howlett, Kevin Brownlee, and others, has shown us new ways of approaching Grocheio's "multiple texts" (*plura dictamina*); Wulf Arlt and Margaret Bent join these with exciting musical analyses that give the texts and the "varied arrangement of syllables" (*multimodam discretionem syllabarum*) their proper role in the structure and allegorical significance of compositions now seen to have far more delicately contrived character than was once thought.[5] And Andrew Wathey's new study of the circulation in non-musical sources of Philippe de Vitry's motet texts shows us that these, like much fourteenth-century chanson and madrigal poetry, were considered important in their own right.[6] It will thus come as no surprise that all the authors not thus far mentioned are here concerned in serious ways with motet texts—their choice, their "reading" by the composer, their effect and affect on the listener.

The new importance accorded the words in recent work on the motet is changing our view of the composer, now seen as a much more active reader, rereader, or "misreader" of the texts chosen, even if not, as in the cases of Vitry and Machaut, their author. We are now all agreed that if the cyclic Mass can be studied primarily for its music, its unchanging text more often than not set in response to generally observed conventions, the motet simply must be approached as an amalgam of text and music. There are of course special problems here, notably in cases of contrafact texts. As we make studies of this kind, old generalizations begin to wither; for example, the notion that the tenor cantus firmus was seldom related in meaning to the texts of the upper voices is now being refuted, as is the idea that text in pre-sixteenth-century motets was casually if not haphazardly sprinkled over the notes.

In connection with composition, choice, and disposition of texts I think it should be kept in mind that highly educated and sophisticated motet composers such as Machaut and Philippe de Vitry must have been in the minority even in the fourteenth century. In the next century composition became more and more the province of church musicians who may have had less expert knowledge of and experience with verbal rhetoric, and who did not usually write their own texts. I hope my voice will not be drowned in a chorus of no's if I say that Dufay might be the last composer who could work easily in the old quadrivial-rhetorical mode, and even he abandoned it in part in his later career. We should remember that much music in the fifteenth and sixteenth centuries was written on commission, just as most paintings were done to order. In the visual arts the patron, or a person of learning associated with her/him, supplied not only the general subject but the *invenzione* or iconographic program for the work; the painter or sculptor might and doubtless often did modify this program as it was carried out, but did not normally initiate it. Should we allow for this in music, even at the risk of taking away a little of the glory we are now giving altogether to composers?

The title of this conference is "Hearing the Motet." To hear in the fullest sense is to understand, and that we are certainly trying to do. The kind of study we are about to share in the results of can only be achieved through close reading of verbal and musical texts. We are prepared to do just this; were the contemporary "hearers" (in the full sense) of the motet so prepared and so motivated?

We know from the recently published correspondence of Spataro and other musician-theorists that, in the early sixteenth century at any rate, details of musical structure if not meaning could be very closely scrutinized.[7] Some sources, such as the Paris Fauvel manuscript and the Machaut manuscripts, were surely intended for repeated reading and study as well as for performance.[8] In the fifteenth century musical manuscripts intended for reading like books tended to be chansonniers; but in the sixteenth century there were motet collections of works by Rore and Lasso that are not only sumptuous but were intended for study, and were even provided with textual commentary.[9] I think we can no longer be content with the view that composers of religious music were satisfied if God knew the secrets of their art and cared not whether men perceived them. We need to study the motet's sources, textual and musical, not just the convenient modern editions, to see whether they could have offered and can still offer clues to some of the kinds of meaning we will shortly be instructed about. Let us then begin to "hear" the motet.

NOTES

1. For a discussion of the motet, including considerations of etymology, see Rolf Dammann, "Geschichte der Begriffsbestimmung Motette," *Archiv für Musikwissenschaft* 16 (1959): 337–77.

2. Ernst Rohloff, *Die Quellenhandschriften zum Musiktraktat des Johannes de Grocheio*, Media latinitas 2 (Leipzig: Deutscher Verlag für Musik, 1972), 144. The Latin text is "Motetus vero est cantus ex pluribus compositus, habens plura dictamina vel multimodam discretionem syllabarum, utrobique harmonialiter consonans."

3. Ibid. The Latin is "Cantus autem iste non debet coram vulgaribus propinari, eo quod eius subtilitatem non [anim]advertunt nec in eius auditu delectantur, sed coram litteratis et illis, qui subtilitates artium sunt quaerentes. Et solet in eorum festis decantari ad eorum decorationem, quemadmodum cantilena, quae dicitur rotundellus, in festis vulgarium laicorum."

4. "Elitist" is perhaps too easy a word; it stands here for "those with appropriate educational background," meaning chiefly clerics, and perhaps university students. For a challenging discussion of Grocheio's remarks, and of medieval "audiences" in general, see Christopher Page, "Johannes de Grocheio, the *Litterati* and Verbal *Subtilitas* in the Ars Antiqua Motet," chap. 3 in *Discarding Images: Reflections on Music and Culture in Medieval France* (Oxford: Clarendon Press, 1993).

5. See Margaret Bent and David Howlett, "Subtiliter alternare: The Yoxford Motet O amicus/Precursoris," in *Studies in Medieval Music: Festschrift for Ernest H. Sanders*, ed. Peter M. Lefferts and Brian Seirup, = *Current Musicology* 45–47 (1990): 43–84; Wulf Arlt, "*Triginta denariis*: Musik und Text in einer Motette des *Roman de Fauvel* über dem Tenor Victimae paschali laudes," in *Pax et sapientia: Studies in Text and Music of Liturgical Tropes and Sequences, in Memory of Gordon Anderson*, Acta Universitatis Stockholmiensis, Studia latina (Stockholm: Almqvist and Wiksell, 1986), 97–113; Kevin Brownlee, "Machaut's Motet 15 and the *Roman de la Rose*: The Literary Context of *Amours qui a le pouoir/Faus samblant m'a deceü/Vidi Dominum*," *Early Music History* 10 (1991): 1–14; Margaret Bent, "Deception, Exegesis and Sounding Number in Machaut's Motet 15," *Early Music History* 10 (1991): 15–27. For cogent analytical discussion of fourteenth-century compositional practice, see the work of Daniel Leech-Wilkinson, particularly his *Compositional Procedure in the Four-part Isorhythmic Motets of Philippe de Vitry and His Contemporaries*, Outstanding Dissertations in Music from British Universities, 2 vols. (New York: Garland, 1989).

6. Andrew Wathey, "The Motets of Philippe de Vitry and the Fourteenth-Century Renaissance," *Early Music History* 12 (1993): 119–50.

7. *A Correspondence of Renaissance Musicians*, ed. Bonnie J. Blackburn, Edward E. Lowinsky, and Clement A. Miller (Oxford: Clarendon Press, 1991).

8. The *Roman de Fauvel* survives in a number of manuscripts without music. For the one containing the music, see *Le Roman de Fauvel in the Edition of Mesire Chaillou de Pesstain: A Reproduction in Facsimile of the Complete Manuscript, Paris, Bibliothèque Nationale fonds français 146*, with an introduction by Edward H. Roesner, François Avril, and Nancy Freeman Regalado (New York: Broude Brothers, 1990). Machaut is known to have collected and in part at least supervised the copying of his music; for the central manuscripts, see "Sources," in *The New Grove Dictionary of Music and Musicians*, ed. Stanley Sadie, 20 vols. (London: Macmillan, 1980), 17:661–63.

9. For manuscripts of motets by Rore and Lasso, two magnificently decorated col-

lections each containing a volume of music and one of commentary, see *Kataloge bayerischer Musiksammlungen*, ed. Bayerische Staatliche Bibliotheken, 5/1: *Katalog der Musikhandschriften. Chorbücher und Handschriften in chorbüchartiger Notierung*, ed. Martin Bente, Marie Louise Göllner, Helmut Hell, and Bettina Wackernagel (Munich: G. Henle, 1989), 54–58.

The Polyphonic Progeny of an *Et gaudebit*

Assessing Family Relations in the Thirteenth-Century Motet

When seeking a useful way to begin at the beginning, so to speak, in our consideration of the motet in the Middle Ages and the Renaissance, I decided to choose a clausula-based motet complex that exemplified as many different types of thirteenth-century motets as possible. The motet complex whose various texts are numbered 315–21 in Ludwig and Gennrich's catalogues, all built on a single *Et gaudebit* clausula from the Ascension *Alleluia Non vos relinquam* (M24), is perhaps the most widely traveled in the thirteenth century.[1] The verse of the Alleluia, which comes from John 14:18, is a statement made by Christ to his disciples: "Non vos relinquam orphanos, vado et venio ad vos *et gaudebit* cor vestrum" (I will not leave you orphans; I go away, and I come to you, and your heart shall rejoice).

The source clausula, *Et gaudebit* no. 2, appears in two manuscripts, the Florence and St. Victor manuscripts. In F it is the first of several *Et gaudebit* settings in the collection of separate clausulae in fascicle 5, beginning on system 5 of fol. 161ᵛ and continuing on 162ʳ.[2] It is no. 15 among the StV clausulae, found on folios 289ᵛ–290ʳ, with the incipit of the vernacular text *Al cor ai une alegrance* written in the margin beside the music.[3] In motet form the music appears in 10 manuscripts: Ch, F, Ma, W2 three times, ArsB, LoC, Hu, Cl, Mo, and Ba (see the list of manuscripts and their sigla in Table 1.1).[4] With a total of six Latin and two vernacular texts for upper voices, it exemplifies nearly all the types of motets composed in the Ars Antiqua: a Latin three-voice conductus motet (in Châlons), an early Latin double motet (in F), a reduced Latin two-voice motet (in ArsB, LoC, and Hu), two additional two-voice Latin contrafacts (in W2), an additional Latin double motet (in Ma and Ba, but, as is usually the case, with the tenor omitted in Madrid), a vernacular double motet (in W2), a bilingual double motet (in Mo 3), and a bilingual triple motet (in Cl); all are itemized in Table 1.2. The only significant type not represented in this complex is the two-voice French motet.

TABLE 1.1 Manuscripts and their sigla

ArsB	Paris, Bibliothèque de l'Arsenal, MS 3517–3518 (Gautier de Coincy)
Ba	Bamberg, Staatliche Bibliothek, MS Lit.115 (olim Ed.IV.6)
Bes	Besançon, Bibliothèque Municipale, MS I, 716 (index of a lost collection)
Ch	Châlons-sur-Marne, Archives Départementales, MS 3.J.250
Cl	Paris, Bibliothèque Nationale, MS nouv. acq. fr. 13521 (La Clayette)
F	Florence, Biblioteca Medicea-Laurenziana, MS Pluteus 29.1
Hu	Burgos, Monasterio de las Huelgas, MS without shelf number
LoC	London, British Library, Add. MS 30091
Ma	Madrid, Biblioteca Nacional, MS 20486 (olim Hh 167)
Mo	Montpellier, Bibliothèque Interuniversitaire, Section Médecine, MS H.196
PaXV	Paris, Bibliothèque Nationale, MS fr. 2193 (Gautier de Coincy)
StV	Paris, Bibliothèque Nationale, MS lat. 15139 (St. Victor)
W2	Wolfenbüttel, Herzog August Bibliothek, codex guelf. 1099 Helmstad. (Heinemann no. 1206)

Of the eight texts for this motet complex listed in Table 1.2C, five belong to the motetus. It has four different Latin texts, nos. 315, 317, 320, and 321 (two of them Marian), and one vernacular text, no. 319. The main triplum melody which first appears in the Latin double motet in the Florence manuscript has one Latin text, no. 316, and one French text, no. 318. The latter is a pastourelle that appears first in the double motet in W2; I should add that this genre of text looms much larger in the motet than it does in the trouvère repertory—the idea of the narrator riding out into the countryside and encountering a rustic maiden seems to have seized the fancy (or rather, the fantasy) of clerical composers of polyphony much more than it did the trouvères themselves, who probably had better romantic adventures about which to write poetry.

A unique melody for the triplum, sung with the same Marian text *O quam sancta* (no. 317) as its motetus, appears in the fragmentary conductus motet found in the Châlons-sur-Marne manuscript. And lastly, a unique triplum melody and text (*O Maria, mater pia*, no. 317a) are included in the four-voice bilingual motet that occurs in the La Clayette manuscript, with the French pastourelle triplum (no. 318) here moved up to the quadruplum part. In sum, the two triplum texts, *Ypocrite pseudopontifices* (no. 316) and *El mois d'avril* (no. 318), each appear in three motets, and text 317, *O quam sancta*, appears in six of the ten motets on this *Et gaudebit* clausula. The text of *O quam sancta* is found without music in a Gautier de Coincy manuscript, Paris, B.N. français 2193; and there was at least one more motet copy in the thirteenth century, because *O quam sancta* is the ninth motet listed in the Besançon index to a lost motet collection; we do not know what triplum went with it. *O quam sancta* is also cited by the theorists Lambertus and Anonymous VII, so

TABLE 1.2 Motets on *Et gaudebit* no. 2

A. Clausula Sources

2v clausula in **F**, 161ᵛ–162ʳ
2v clausula in **StV**, 289ᵛ–290ʳ, with incipit of 319 in margin

B. Motet Types and Locations

The 2v Latin motet: W2, 187ᵛ–188ᵛ
   Mot   Virgo virginum regina (321)   (= unicum text)

The 2v Latin motet: W2, 188ᵛ–189ʳ
   Mot   Memor tui creatoris (320)   (= unicum text)

The 2v Latin motet: ArsB, 117ʳ–117ᵛ; LoC, 3ᵛ–4ᵛ; Hu, 94ᵛ
   Mot   O quam sancta, quam benigna (317)

The 3v conductus motet: Ch, 6ʳ–6ᵛ (beginning and end missing)
   Tr   O quam sancta, quam benigna (317)
   Mot   O quam sancta, quam benigna (317)   (= unicum music)

The Latin double motet: F, 411ᵛ–413ʳ
   Tr   Ypocrite pseudopontifices (316)
   Mot   Velut stelle firmamente (315)   (= unicum text)

The Latin double motet (with tenor omitted): Ma, 132ʳ–133ʳ
   Tr   Ypocrite pseudopontifices (316)
   Mot   O quam sancta, quam benigna (317)

The Latin double motet: Ba, 47ʳ–48ᵛ
   Tr   Ypocrite pseudopontifices (316)
   Mot   O quam sancta, quam benigna (317)

The vernacular double motet: W2, 195ʳ–197ʳ
   Tr   El mois d'avril qu'ivers va departant (318)
   Mot   Al cor ai une alegrance (319)   (= unicum text [but see StV])

The 3v bilingual motet: Mo 3, 63ᵛ–66ʳ
   Tr   El mois d'avril qu'iver va departant (318)
   Mot   O quam sancta, quam benigna (317)

The 4v bilingual motet: Cl, 380ᵛ–381ᵛ
   Qu   El mois d'avril qu'ivers va departant (318)
   Tr   O Maria, mater pia, vite via (317a)   (= unicum music and text)
   Mot   O quam sancta, quam benigna (317)

C. Motet Texts and Subjects

315	*Velut stelle firmamente*	On good priests
316	*Ypocrite pseudopontifices*	On bad priests
317	*O quam sancta, quam benigna*	Marian
317a	*O Maria, mater pia, vite via*	Marian
318	*El mois d'avril qu'iver va departant*	Pastourelle
319	*Al cor ai une alegrance*	Secular love
320	*Memor tui creatoris*	Admonitio
321	*Virgo virginum regina*	Marian

it clearly figured as part of the most widely known version of this motet.[5] It deserves to be quoted in full:

> O quam sancta, quam benigna / fulget mater salvatoris, / laude plena, virgo digna, / archa Noe, Iacob scala, vasculum pudoris, / aula redemptoris, / tocius fons dulcoris, / angelorum gaudium, / lactans Dei filium, / regem omnium. / Audi, salus gentium, / preces supplicantium! / Ave, virgo, Iesse virga nobilis, / super omnes venerabilis! / Spes unica, succurre miseris! / Inebrians animas fons es admirabilis, / que tuos numquam mori deseris; / O anima, ex sordibus vilis / hanc Mariam virginem expostula, / ut sit pro te sedula / exorare filium / propicium, / una spes fidelium. / O genitrix, *gaude* in filio! *Gaudens* ego *gaudebo* in Domino.[6]

> (O how holy, O how kind, shines the mother of the Savior, a worthy maiden, full of praise, Noah's Ark, Jacob's ladder, vessel of modesty, the palace of the Redeemer, the font of all sweetness, the joy of the angels, who gave suck to the Son of God, the King of All. Hear, salvation of the peoples, the prayers of your suppliants! Hail, Virgin, noble rod of Jesse, venerable beyond all others! Our one hope, aid us wretched ones! You are the awesome font which fills souls to overflowing, you who never abandon your people to die. O my soul, despicable in your filth, call on this Virgin Mary, that on your behalf she plead constantly with her Son to be kind, she who is the one hope of the faithful. O mother, rejoice in your Son! Rejoicing, I shall rejoice in the Lord.)

There are other indications than the number of copies that this motet complex was held in unusually high esteem in the thirteenth century. First, it includes one of only three double motets to appear in the Florence manuscript, and it has the only double motet (even without its tenor) found in the Madrid manuscript. In the third motet fascicle in W2, which consists primarily of French double motets *not* in liturgical order, this motet is the second one in the fascicle, and just like the first one two folios earlier, it begins with an illuminated initial, not just a flourished one. Last, the three-voice bilingual motet version was chosen to begin fascicle 3 in the Montpellier manuscript, where the double-page opening is decorated with historiated initials and bas-de-page scenes. Clearly this motet was given unusual prominence, evident not only by the number of extant copies but also by where they are placed. What factors prompted such treatment?

The clausula—the only one found in both the Florence and the St. Victor manuscripts—is in the classic style of Perotin, with a fifth-mode tenor and a first-mode duplum that extend to 140 ternary longs, the equivalent of seventy 6/8 measures in transcription. Thus it is one of the longest clausulae in the repertory, and it swings along through two tenor statements with the duplum phrases sometimes coordinated and other times sharply overlapped with those of the tenor. Ernest Sanders did not hesitate to attribute this clausula to Perotin, and I see no reason to disagree with that attribution.[7]

A second factor in the prominence of this motet complex is that one and possibly two of the texts may be the work of Philip the Chancellor (d. 1236). Peter Dronke suggested a decade ago that the triplum text Y*pocrite pseudopon-*

tifices (no. 316), which first appears in the F double motet, could well be a work of Philip the Chancellor.[8] Its harsh tone of moral outrage at the corruption of bishops (and possibly popes, since *pontifex* can mean both), is, in both sentiment and wording, characteristic of a number of Philip's securely attributed poems. In a recent dissertation on Philip and his role in the music of the Notre-Dame school, Thomas Payne also nominated the Latin motetus text *Velut stelle firmamente*, which appears only in F, for inclusion in Philip's oeuvre.[9] The motet as a whole seems to contrast good prelates—those in the trenches, so to speak—with their superiors, who are full of greed and hypocrisy.[10] It is unusual as early as the Florence manuscript to find a double motet with a sixth-mode triplum that in effect stratifies the rhythms of the voices in the threefold manner we associate more with the later thirteenth century.[11] This triplum melody, which evidently replaced the unique triplum of the conductus motet in the Châlons-sur-Marne manuscript, appears in all subsequent three- and four-voice versions of this motet; once created, it had significant staying power.

Three manuscript copies drop the triplum part entirely and include the Marian motetus text that first appeared in Châlons, *O quam sancta*: the two-voice motets in ArsB, LoC, and Las Huelgas. But two more versions without a triplum and with contrafact Latin texts are in W2. One (*Memor tui creatoris*) is an "exhortation to cleanse the mind by good works," in Gordon Anderson's words.[12] Immediately prior to this motet in W2 is a Marian contrafact version, *Virgo, virginum regina*—one Marian motetus (*O quam sancta*) was evidently not enough. *Virgo* is a text of praise and petition to the Virgin, one that sounds all the usual themes about Mary's role in history and in salvation.

We might speculate that several manuscripts dropped the triplum of this motet because their editor/scribes did not want the harsh polemic in the Latin text of Philip the Chancellor. Yet at least two manuscripts offer a Latin double motet version that retains the original motetus text, the Marian *O quam sancta*, and pairs it with Philip's virulent attack on the clerical hierarchy. In this texting it appears in the rather early Madrid manuscript (though minus its tenor), and once again in a later but somewhat conservative manuscript, the Bamberg codex.

But there is possibly one way in which these seemingly unrelated texts do connect. One of the roles of the Virgin in the Christian scheme of things is her function as a type of the Church.[13] This is explicitly acknowledged in the text of *O quam sancta* when it speaks of Mary as the "palace of the Redeemer," *aula redemptoris* (in l. 5). Just as Mary is both the palace of the Redeemer, in that she bore Christ, and, through her intercession, the sinner's best hope of salvation, the Church is the house of God and the gate of Heaven—the "domus dei et porta celi." And when the house of God was defiled by a clerical hierarchy who were hypocritical, deceitful, and false, so was the Virgin herself defiled, a situation in which a polemical attack upon corruption as a call for remedy is justifiable.

The last three motets in Table 1.2B have vernacular texts. The early double motet in W2 has the French pastourelle text *El mois d'avril* in the triplum

EXAMPLE 1.1 The four-voice bilingual motet in La Clayette (mm. 1–12)

EXAMPLE 1.1   (*continued*)

and a Frenchified Provençal text (*Al cor ai une alegrance*), also dealing with secular love, in the motetus. The latter text appears only in W2, though its textual incipit is written in the margin by the clausula in the St. Victor manuscript. The three-voice bilingual motet that begins fascicle 3 of the Montpellier manuscript has the French pastourelle text *El mois d'avril* in the triplum over the Latin Marian text *O quam sancta* in the motetus. When a cleric's mind wandered from contemplation of the Virgin, did it stray to imagine himself in a pastoral encounter?

The final motet is the four-voice example in La Clayette, with a newly added Marian triplum, *O Maria, mater pia*, that is unique to this copy. The text begins with praise to the Virgin, *in medias res* addresses the listener and urges repentance and devotion to the Virgin, and petitions her help to achieve salvation. When we look at the music given as Example 1.1, we find that the newly composed voice begins by largely doubling the quadruplum; in the fourth measure it doubles the motetus. In measure 5 there are direct clashes with the quadruplum, but by measure 7 it is essentially doubling the quadruplum again. After this somewhat rocky beginning, it finds a suitable niche between the motetus and quadruplum, and works very well with the motetus voice for the rest of the piece. For these reasons and because of the congruity of subject matter between the triplum and the motetus, one could well omit the French quadruplum voice and leave standing a Latin double Marian motet.

James H. Cook has provided a useful stemma for the transmission of these *Et gaudebit* motets that is included as Figure 1.1.[14] The conductus motet in Châlons-sur-Marne, which in the extant portion is not proved terminal[15] in any of its variants, is a possible archetype, that is to say, the first motet version to follow the clausula. Its text, *O quam sancta*, is the most widespread one.

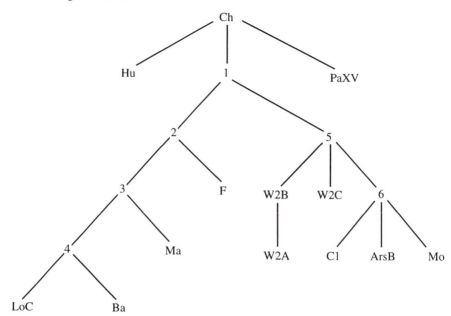

FIGURE 1.1   Stemma for *Et gaudebit* motets

Similarly, there are no variants to prevent the Las Huelgas two-voice motet and the *O quam sancta* text in PaXV from being directly derived from the archetype, so that is how they are represented. It would then have been a decision of the Huelgas scribe to omit the triplum.

Hypothetical intermediary 1 would have contained the first double motet version, which was then copied by hypothetical manuscripts 2, 3, 4, 5, and 6. The first double motet at hypothetical manuscript 1 was very likely the Latin double motet in F attributed to Philip the Chancellor, the texts contrasting good and bad priests. If this be so, then hypothetical manuscript 5 contained the first copy of the French text. If instead the vernacular motet was the first double motet (which I think is far less likely), hypothetical intermediary 2 contained the first copy of the Latin text. Regardless of whether the Latin or the French came first, the Latin motets in F, Madrid, Bamberg, and LoC form a family derived from hypothetical MS 2. LoC is a sibling of Ba that simply omitted the triplum. The motets that branch from hypothetical manuscript 5 are the principal French sources—W2C (the vernacular double motet, which is terminal because of its unique motetus text), Montpellier, and Clayette. These three all share the French pastourelle text, but their differing other texts make each of them terminal. Clayette, ArsB, and Montpellier all have the Marian motetus *O quam sancta*, but ArsB independently omitted the triplum and Clayette independently added a fourth part. Musical variants in the two-voice W2B and W2A indicate that both are reduced Latin contrafacts of the *O quam sancta* motetus in hypothetical manuscript 5. W2B is the result of independent action in this regard, but the variants in W2A, the Marian contrafact, indicate that it is derived from W2B, the hortatory two-voice motet. This is the only spot in the stemma in which one extant copy seems directly derived from another extant copy. This stemma is of course a hypothetical construct, but it is the simplest one that takes all the variants and their nature into account.[16]

There is, however, one striking group characteristic about all of these motet texts: None of them—not a single one—has anything directly to do with the idea of Ascension, either as a feast day in the church or as an event in the life of Christ. The text most frequently used, *O quam sancta, quam benigna*, does conclude with tropic references to the idea of rejoicing in the Lord, which reminds us that the tenor is *Et gaudebit*. But this in and of itself would not make clear that the Ascension is what is being celebrated. In point of fact, these motet texts simply ignore the Ascension.

If Perotin and Philip the Chancellor are jointly responsible for the Latin double motet *Ypocrite/Vellut stelle firmamente/Et gaudebit*, then that tells us one important thing about this motet complex: its avoidance of explicit mention of the feast at hand was sanctioned by the highest levels of authority at Notre-Dame. Furthermore, if the first text to be added to the clausula is indeed *O quam sancta, quam benigna*, then this motet was, from the beginning, a Marian motet on a non-Marian tenor. But whether it came first or not, this Marian text is undeniably the favorite text, both early and late, for this particular motetus voice.

In a paper given in May 1993 at the Kalamazoo medieval conference,[17] I asked the questions "Why were there Marian motets on non-Marian tenors in the early motet repertory? What function did they serve?" *O quam sancta*, a Marian motet on an Ascension chant, is in the company of some fifteen other motets in this special class, and one of the earliest is another one for Ascension, *Salve, mater, fons ortorum* (309) on the tenor *Captivitatem*, from the M23 *Alleluia Ascendens Christus*. I noted that in thirteenth-century iconography the Virgin is represented as being present with the Apostles at the Ascension as Christ's feet disappear into the clouds. That, however, is insufficient justification for performing a motet praising the Virgin as part of a liturgical organum whose text relates to the Ascension.

Ten years ago, when I first segregated this group of unusual Marian motets from the rest of the early sacred motets, I would have argued against the idea that they were ever incorporated into their parent organum composition and performed at its proper place in the liturgy. But today I do not hesitate to claim that these Marian motets were indeed intended for performance as part of non-Marian organa, for the following reason: a great deal of evidence indicates that the clergy of Notre-Dame viewed their role in life as making clear, as often as they could, with whatever means they could, the essential role of the Virgin Mary in salvation, and that there was no better place to encounter both the Virgin and salvation than in her cathedral church in Paris. The clergy asserted this primacy of the Virgin's role and the connection of their cathedral with the

Virgin in every way open to them.[18] One such way was the provision of Marian motets for important feasts between Christmas and the end of June, when Marian occasions in the calendar were few and far between. By assiduously asserting the role of the Virgin, the clerics who staffed the cathedral not incidentally asserted their own.

In the case of *O quam sancta/Et gaudebit*, we must admit that such an approach succeeded admirably. *Et gaudebit* began its career as a Perotinian clausula. Its first motet text was a Marian one that appears in eight different musical manuscripts, in the index of another manuscript no longer extant, as a text only in yet another source, and in citations by two theorists. This is surely a record among thirteenth-century motets. It is, in fact, part of a flood tide of Marian motets that surged ever higher in the later thirteenth century. Given the nearly ubiquitous presence of the polyphonic progeny of this clausula throughout the thirteenth century, perhaps it is not too far-fetched to say that the heart of *Et gaudebit* no. 2 would have rejoiced, also, to know how far and wide its offspring carried on.

NOTES

1. Friedrich Ludwig established the numbering for motets as well as the M (for Mass) and O (for Office) numbers for organa in his *Repertorium organorum recentioris et motetorum vetustissimi stili*, vol. 1, pt. 1 (Halle: Max Niemeyer, 1910; reprinted as Musicological Studies 7, Brooklyn: Institute of Mediaeval Music, 1964). The numbering system is continued in Friedrich Gennrich, *Bibliographie der ältesten französischen und lateinischen Motetten*, Summa musicae medii aevi 2 (Darmstadt: Author, 1958), a bibliographic catalogue of the thirteenth-century motet repertory in numerical order. More up-to-date in terms of recent manuscript discoveries is Hendrik van der Werf, *Integrated Directory of Organa, Clausulae, and Motets of the Thirteenth Century* (Rochester: Author, 1989); for the *Et gaudebit* complex, see p. 49.

2. Of the clausulae in this fascicle, it is no. 130 in Ludwig's count (*Repertorium*, 1/1:82); for a critical edition of the piece, see Rebecca A. Baltzer, ed., *The Two-Voice Clausulae in Fascicle 5 of Florence, Biblioteca Medicea-Laurenziana, Pluteus 29.1*, vol. 5 of *Le Magnus Liber Organi de Notre-Dame de Paris*, ed. Edward H. Roesner (Monaco: Editions de l'Oiseau-Lyre, 1995), where it is no. 129. The manuscript facsimile is by Luther Dittmer, *Firenze, Biblioteca Mediceo-Laurenziana, Pluteo 29, 1*, Publications of Mediaeval Musical Manuscripts 10–11 (Brooklyn: Institute of Mediaeval Music, 1966–67).

3. Facsimile in *The Music in the St. Victor Manuscript, Paris lat. 15139*, Introduction and Facsimiles by Ethel Thurston, Studies and Texts 5 (Toronto: Pontifical Institute of Mediaeval Studies, 1959). A transcription according to this source is in Jürg Stenzl, *Die vierzig Clausulae der Handschrift Paris Bibliothèque Nationale Latin 15139*, Publikationen der Schweizerischen Musikforschenden Gesellschaft, Serie II, vol. 22 (Bern: Verlag Paul Haupt, 1970), 199–200.

4. Published facsimiles and modern editions/transcriptions are cited as part of the list of manuscripts in Van der Werf, *Integrated Directory*, 147–58. The manuscripts ArsB, Bes, Ch, and PaXV have not been published in facsimile.

5. For quotation and translation of the two passages from treatises, see Gordon Athol Anderson, *The Latin Compositions in Fascicules VII and VIII of the Notre Dame*

Manuscript Wolfenbüttel Helmstadt 1099 (1206) (Brooklyn: Institute of Mediaeval Music, 1972), pt.1, pp. 354–55.

6. Text and the following translation are from *The Montpellier Codex, Part IV: Texts and Translations*, by Susan Stakel and Joel C. Relihan, Recent Researches in the Music of the Middle Ages and Early Renaissance, 8 (Madison: A-R Editions, 1985), 13.

7. Ernest H. Sanders, "The Question of Perotin's Oeuvre and Dates," *Festschrift für Walter Wiora zum 30. Dezember 1966*, ed. Ludwig Finscher and Christoph-Hellmut Mahling (Kassel: Bärenreiter Verlag, 1967), 241–49, esp. 247.

8. This attribution was first presented at the April 1985 Wolfenbüttel conference, "Das Ereignis 'Notre Dame'," and subsequently published in Peter Dronke, "The Lyrical Compositions of Philip the Chancellor," *Studi Medievali*, 3rd ser., 27/2 (1987): 563–92; see 586–87 and 592 on this text. The Latin text with English translation can be found in Anderson, *The Latin Compositions*, 1:346–48, and in *Medieval Music*, ed. W. Thomas Marrocco and Nicholas Sandon, Oxford Anthology of Music (London and New York: Oxford University Press, 1977), 96–99.

9. Thomas B. Payne, "Poetry, Politics, and Polyphony: Philip the Chancellor's Contribution to the Music of the Notre Dame School" (Ph.D. diss., University of Chicago, 1991), 2:342 ff.; edition, 4:919 ff.

10. This Latin double motet from the Florence manuscript is the only version to have been commercially recorded; it uses the edition in the Oxford Anthology mentioned in n. 8 above. The LP recording is *Medieval Music: Ars Antiqua Polyphony*, by the Pro Cantione Antiqua, Edgar Fleet, director (Peters International/Oxford University Press, PLE 115, 1978).

11. The sixth-mode triplum, first-mode motetus, and fifth-mode tenor are clearly differentiated by the amount of rhythmic activity in each voice; thus the triplum text is considerably longer than that of the motetus. See Ernest Sanders' comments about this motet in "The Medieval Motet," in *Gattungen der Musik in Einzeldarstellungen: Gedenkschrift Leo Schrade*, ed. Wulf Arlt et al. (Bern: Francke Verlag, 1973), 524, and in "Polyphony and Secular Monophony: Ninth Century—c. 1300," in *Music from the Middle Ages to the Renaissance*, ed. Frederick W. Sternfeld (New York: Praeger, 1973), 121–24 (with partial transcription and translation).

12. Anderson, *The Latin Compositions*, 1:345.

13. On Mary typifying the Church in medieval exegesis, see Adolf Katzenellenbogen, *The Sculptural Programs of Chartres Cathedral: Christ, Mary, Ecclesia* (Baltimore: Johns Hopkins Press, 1959), 59–61, and Margot Fassler, *Gothic Song: Victorine Sequences and Augustinian Reform in Twelfth-Century Paris* (Cambridge: Cambridge University Press, 1993), 330–33.

14. Taken with permission from James H. Cook, "Manuscript Transmission of Thirteenth-Century Motets" (Ph.D. diss., University of Texas at Austin, 1978), 1:212.

15. That is, at the end of a line of development or branch on the stemma, with no offshoots.

16. Cook's discussion of this stemma, to which I am indebted, is in "Manuscript Transmission," 1:208–17; the variants leading to the stemma are collated in 2:703–26. This dissertation provides similar treatment for each motet in the La Clayette manuscript that contains one or more Latin texts.

17. Baltzer, "Why Marian Motets on Non-Marian Tenors? An Answer" (publication forthcoming).

18. Other ways in which this idea was manifest at Notre-Dame together represent a phenomenon too large to cover in the context of this chapter. I shall have considerably more to say about it elsewhere.

Beyond Glossing

The Old Made New in *Mout me fu grief/Robin m'aime/Portare*

Discussions of the thirteenth-century motet have emphasized the presence of preexistent materials, most notably a chant segment in the tenor, and refrains, both textual and musical, in the upper voices. With few exceptions, the discussions stop short of explaining how these preexistent materials interact with newly composed ones. One is usually left with an impression that the chant is an immutable guiding foundation above which other voices are added, and that preexistent refrains tend to be merely incorporated within or grafted onto otherwise new material.[1] With regard to the first point, I have recently presented findings that tenor pitch organization usually, but not always, guides a motet's overall pitch organization: interactions among the three voices can create new tonal emphases.[2] Ardis Butterfield has begun a reevaluation of the second point, suggesting that motet composers engaged in a fluid process of combining and recombining musical refrain units to the point where a distinction between preexistent and original cannot always be maintained. She views this as a kind of creative play on the part of the composer.[3]

Against the backdrop of these recent studies, *Mout me fu grief/Robin m'aime/Portare* (Mo 7, 265)[4] offers a rich opportunity for futher investigation of how preexistent materials function in a late-thirteenth-century motet. Scholars such as Ludwig, Rokseth, and, most recently, Jeremy Yudkin, have noted that the rondeau *Robin m'aime* from Adam de la Halle's play *Le Jeu de Robin et Marion* appears as its motetus;[5] in addition, its tenor contains the chant segment *Portare*, and the triplum presents several fragments evidently drawn from another motet.[6] Pierre Aubry, who had also remarked on this combination of preexistent materials, further commented on the "imprecise tonality" of the work, apparently in a pejorative sense.[7] As I will show, the "imprecise tonality" to which Aubry referred can be viewed as a deliberate manipulation on the part of the motet composer: the borrowed rondeau directs the overall tonal plan, and even brings about several changes in the chant itself, as well as in the borrowed triplum materials. Thus, the three-part motet can be interpreted as a rich interaction of various strains, new and old, to create a distinctly integrated sounding complex. This integration also extends to the motet texts, where one finds a simultaneous presentation of several sacred and secular text traditions involving the Cross, Mary, and courtly and pastoral love. The latter part of this study will explore the various verbal interpretations that result from this textual intersection.

EXAMPLE 2.1 PRESENTS THE CHANT segment as it appears in an early thirteenth-century Notre-Dame missal, Paris, B.N. lat. 1112, where the word *portare* instead reads *sustinere*. It will become apparent later in the study that doubts remain as to whether this substitution has significance for interpreting the verbal meaning of the motet. In any case, the final of the entire chant verse is *g*, on which the *sustinere* melisma also ends. In this phrase and throughout the chant, the pitch *c'* is emphasized through reiteration, a common occurrence in mode 8 chants.[8] *g* and *c'* are distributed in *sustinere* so that *c'* dominates the first half, and then *g* emerges both through neighbor motion around it and as the goal of a descent. Yet *c'*, already in our aural memory, returns as the point of departure for that descent. Thus, this melisma creates a seesaw effect between its two tonal poles.

An examination of the motet (Example 2.2, with reduction in Example 2.3) suggests that the composer altered the chant in response to the preexistent rondeau melody that became the motetus. In that middle voice, the melodic units A and B unfold as a refrain with a distinctive pitch structure. The A phrase clearly focuses on *c'*, with neighbor motion to the semitone below, while the B phrase unfolds a descent through the pitches *g'–e'–c'*. The only contradiction to the *c'* profile is the raised tone *f♯'*, which momentarily emphasizes *g'*. To fit the tonal requirements of this preexistent motetus, the preexistent tenor was altered by raising its *f* in measure 3 and by appending a final *c'* in measure 5 (after the final chant note *g*) to provide an accompaniment to the *c'* ending of the motetus. The integration of the two voices also extends to the shape of the tenor as a whole, for, atypically, the repetitive structure of the tenor follows that of the rondeau: its first half repeats with each statement of A, its second half with each statement of B.[9]

Significantly, the integration of these two voices has created for the first two phrases a pitch emphasis slightly altered from what is found in the borrowed chant: the overall tonal thrust has been shifted to C, instead of G. Yet the momentary *f♯'–g'* inflection in the motetus is significant, since, as will become apparent, that particular semitone gesture becomes the catalyst for a continued play

EXAMPLE 2.1   *Sustinere* from *Alleluia Dulce lignum* (Paris, B.N. lat. 1112), fol. 169ᵛ

Sus - ti - ne   re

EXAMPLE 2.2 *Mout me fu grief/Robin m'aime/Portare* (Mo 7, 265)

EXAMPLE 2.2   (*continued*)

EXAMPLE 2.3   Melodic and harmonic reduction for selected measures of Mo 7, 265

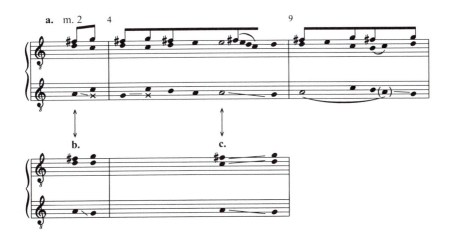

on *g'* in the triplum. This, coupled with harmonic progression towards G, ultimately revives the inherent two axes within the chant itself, thereby contributing to the tonal ambiguity of the motet's ending.

Before proceeding further with my analysis of *Mout me fu grief*, I want to state that my reading is based upon "hearable" features in its pitch organization, that is, features that I, as a twentieth-century listener, can detect, such as tension, resolution, movement, and stability. If one can judge by the lean pronouncements of contemporary theorists, these could also have been the concerns of a thirteenth-century listener. The theorists classify intervals as consonant and dissonant, insist on ending a piece on a consonance, and allow that a relatively more dissonant sonority itself becomes consonant by preceding a consonant interval. They thus suggest that dyads of a particular tension have a tendency to move toward a more stable goal (using stepwise motion, according to their examples). Certainly the concept of resolution is implied in these remarks, even if it is not explicitly stated. Given the theoretical evidence, one can reasonably argue that tonal tension and resolution may in turn have been relevant issues for motet composers and hearable features for their listeners. [10]

On the other hand, the theoretical evidence does not specifically inform us about attitudes toward tonal unity in an entire piece. As a twentieth-century listener with a background of common-practice music, I seek such unity—a sense of closure that comes from returning to something heard earlier or at least a sense that what I have heard "holds together" in some way. For someone in the thirteenth century with chant as a background listening experience, the issue of tonal unity may have been less dominant. But close examination of numerous motet examples reveals that there were composers exploring ways to make a piece cohesive in terms of pitch. For others it was apparently not an issue of concern. What I want to suggest here is that qualitative differences in this regard do exist, whether or not listeners were seeking such unity. This fact becomes apparent in the following remarks about other *Portare* motets.

An overview of the tonal designs of 16 other thirteenth-century motets based upon the *Portare* chant segment (see Table 2.1) suggests that at least one reason for the chant segment's popularity was the variety of tonal treatment it permitted. In Montpellier 5, 91 (see Example 2.4, m. 17), C is most often the tonal focus, appearing as the highest pitch of the motet, in some cases preceded by a leading motion over a tenor G. The motet ends on G (see Example 2.4, m. 23) where the third *a–c'* expands to the fifth *g–d'* and the sixth *a–f'* expands to the octave *g–g'*. The expression "directed progressions" has been applied in cases such as these where relatively unstable, imperfect or dissonant, intervals progress to stable perfect ones by stepwise motion—these are the resolution-seeking dyads of thirteenth-century theorists mentioned above. [11] Yet despite the directed progressions here, the earlier emphasis on C and relative lack of attention to G make this ending seem inconclusive and disconnected, not cohesively linked to what comes before.

In Montpellier 5, 142, on the other hand (see Example 2.5), the motet composer underplays C, giving it only occasional prominence—in measure 13, for example, one finds an unstable sixth above it. But G is regularly prepared

TABLE 2.1 Thirteenth-century motets based on the chant segment *Portare* or *Sustinere*

		Sources*		
Mo	Ba	Cl	Others	
5,81 *portare*	68 *portare*	53 *portare*		
5,91 *portare*	51 *portare*	16 *sustinere*		
5,96 *portare*				
5,142 *portare*				
5,148 *portare*			Bes	text incipit
5,159 *portare*				
6,233 *portare*			N 77	*portare*
7,257 *portare*			Tu 16	*portare*
7,259 *portare*	56 *portare*		Bes	text incipit
7,265 *portare*	81 *portare*		Bes	text incipit
7,296 *portare*				
8,305 *portare*				
8,335 *portare*				
3,41 *sustinere*	19 *portare*	18 *sustinere*	MüB 15	no tenor
			LoC 13	*sustinere*
			Bes	text incipit
6,188 *sustine*			W2 257	*sustinere*
			N 37	*portare*
			R 20	*portare*
		41 *portare*		

*The item numbers for Montpellier follow those of Hans Tischler's edition, *The Montpellier Codex*. Numbers for other manuscripts refer to item numbers within the manuscript according to *Manuscripts of Polyphonic Music. 11th–Early 14th Century*, ed. Gilbert Reaney, *Répertoire International des Sources Musicales* B IV[1] (Munich-Duisburg: G. Henle Verlag, 1966).

Ba	Bamberg, Staatliche Bibliothek, MS Lit.115 (olim Ed.IV.6)
Bes	Besançon, Bibliothèque Municipale, MS I, 716
Cl	Paris, Bibliothèque Nationale, MS nouv. acq. fr. 13521 (La Clayette)
LoC	London, British Library, Add. MS 30091
Mo	Montpellier, Bibliothèque Interuniversitaire, Section Médecine, MS H.196
MüB	Munich, Bayerische Staatsbibliothek, MS lat. 16444
N	Paris, Bibliothèque Nationale, MS fr. 12615 (Chansonnier de Noailles)
R	Paris, Bibliothèque Nationale, MS fr. 844 (Chansonnier du Roy)
Tu	Turin, Biblioteca Reale, Vari 42
W2	Wolfenbüttel, Herzog August Bibliothek, codex guelf. 1099 Helmstad. (Heinemann no. 1206)

by one or two directed progressions—see measures 11–12. Consequently, the final cadence on G strikes the ear as a natural unifying ending for the piece.

Another *Portare* motet, Montpellier 5, 159, gives equal attention to both pitches, C as highest pitch, and G regularly prepared with two directed progressions. Because of the alternating, equal treatment of the two pitches, either could be satisfying at the end. The piece seesaws, ending on G because the chant segment ends there, but without any inherent tension leading to that point.

In view of these three examples, *Mout me fu grief* (Example 2.2) reveals a

EXAMPLE 2.4   Excerpts from Mo 5, 91

EXAMPLE 2.5   Excerpt from Mo 5, 142

distinctively sophisticated tonal treatment of the chant segment *Portare*. [12] C is established as the primary tonal focus: In measures 1 and 2, the *c*'s of the tenor are placed consistently on strong beats, three out of four times carrying the simple sonority *c'–g'*. More significantly, the C sonority beginning measure 2 is approached by means of two directed progessions: a third to a unison and a seventh to a fifth. The other tenor *c'* in measure 2 receives a less standard preparation (see Example 2.3a, m. 2), [13] but the *c'–g'* sonority seems relatively stable because it has just been heard several times in more convincing contexts.

After the arrival of the second tenor *c'* of measure 2, neutral rather than directed progressions (fifths move to fifths and octaves to octaves) dominate from the end of measure 2 through the beginning of measure 4. Beginning in measure 3, the circled notes of the motetus refrain clearly ring through, leading to *c'* in measure 5. Yet melodic and harmonic complications in measure 4 prevent a simple hearing of the refrain; *g'*, as part of the gesture *f♯'–g'* in the triplum, is touched upon, then averted (leaving *f♯'* stranded), and directed progressions to G are set up but not fulfilled (see Example 2.3a, m. 4). [14] In the averting motion, there is a neat segue in measure 5 from the triplum *d'* into the motetus refrain.

The next two measures (mm. 6–7) set the first half of the rondeau refrain to new words over a partial tenor repetition. As the highest pitch in the motet, the high *c"* that introduces the section attracts attention in and of itself. But tonal context enhances its importance. It rings through with an open octave below, not only in the upbeat to measure 6, but also at the beginning of measures 7 and 8, and in the middle of measures 12 and 14.[15]

The triplum design is of particular interest in the next full tenor repetition in measures 8 through 12. In measure 8 *c"* moves quickly down to *g'*, which, with its semitone inflection to and from *f♯'*, remains the melodic focus throughout this stretch of music. This design contrasts with measure 4, where *f♯'* was stranded. Furthermore, the harmonic resolution missing earlier now takes place. As Example 2.3a, measure 9, shows, the major sixth *a–f♯'* does not immediately resolve outward to *g–g'*, yet that octave does occur within several beats; even though the second *f♯'* sounds over a *b*, the aural memory of the tendency-ridden sixth *a–f♯'* remains so that the *g–g'* octave is heard as a delayed resolution. This area then finally seems to realize the voice-leading shown in Example 2.3c.

With G solidly established as the focus of measure 9, measure 10 is all the more striking (see Example 2.2). Its counterpart, measure 3, presents a neutral and exposed setting of the gesture *f♯'–g'*. In measure 10, on the other hand, the motet composer enhances G by accompanying the gesture with a triplum that settles on *d'*.[16] In measures 11–12, the full *g–d'–g'* sonority remains prominent, although now without directed progressions. With the return of C in the middle of measure 12,[17] the highly concentrated emphasis on G has been dissipated.

The final tenor statement (mm. 13–17) presents an interesting conclusion to the interplay between C and G. Once again the triplum's *g'*s carry a C sonority underneath and a directed progression leads to the C sonority that begins measure 14. Yet even in the first measure of this statement, measure 13, the dissonant sonority *a–e'–f♯'* on beat 3 recalls G. By measure 15, the triplum has reached *g'*, which remains the melodic focus for the rest of the piece. Although in this case there has not been any harmonic preparation for G, the *f♯'–g'* gesture by now carries with it harmonic implications because of its intensive treatment earlier. So, the exposed duo in the upper two voices at the end of measure 15, which is exactly like the end of measure 10, creates a sense of returning to the G area.

Finally, in measure 17, the triplum sounds its last *g'* against the motetus *c'*. Despite the weakened harmonic progression to G in these measures,[18] the secure dominance of the melodic gesture *f♯'–g'* right up to the end, coupled with its harmonic "aural history," creates an expectation of a final G sonority. This is all the more so, given that the Montpellier version does not contain a final tenor note *c'*, and thereby the exposed upper duo recalls the end of measures 10 and 15, which were firmly grounded in G.

EXAMPLE 2.6   Four passages from Mo 3, 37

Passage 1
m. 1

Mout me fu gries li de-par - tir   de m'a-mi - e - te, la bele au cors

In   o - mni   fra - tre   tu - o   non

IN SECULUM

Passage 2
m. 8

si tres doz ris me fet fre - mir et   si oeil vair ri - ant lan-guir

plu - ri - bus   do-lum   a - cu - en - ti - bus

Passage 3   Passage 4
m. 24   m. 45

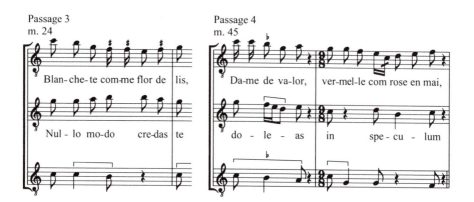

Blan- che- te com-me flor de | lis,   Da-me de va-lor,   ver-mel-le com rose en mai,

Nul - lo mo-do   cre-das | te   do - le - as   in   spe-cu - lum

36

Thus, the integration of the $f\sharp'-g'$ inflection from the preexistent refrain into the fabric of the motet as a whole has brought about the tonality described by Aubry as "imprecise." This close reading suggests that such a result was carefully calculated by the motet composer. This motet setting offers a clever realization of the dual tonal focus inherent within the chant fragment, even from the moment of choosing *Robin m'aime* for the motetus voice. The play upon the two tones goes beyond the seesawing observed in the chant itself and in a motet such as Mo 159: in *Mout me fu grief* both melody and harmony create tension between G and C, which becomes a primary goal in the cohesive tonal design of the entire piece.

Four melodic snippets within the triplum, apparently borrowed from an older motet, Mo 3, 37, support this tonal design.[19] Example 2.6 presents the four passages in Mo 37; the parallel passages in Mo 265 are indicated with open brackets in Example 2.2. The first instance, "Mout me fu grief li departir de m'amiete," appears in a C context in both. The second passage, "son tres douz ris mi fait fremir et si oell vair riant languir," supports an A tonality in Mo 37, while it is absorbed into the move from C to G in Mo 265. The third passage, "Blanchete comme flour de lis," appears in a predominantly C context in both cases. In the final instance, "Dame de valour, vermelle comme rose en mai," the passage supports a move to F in Mo 37, whereas it is incorporated into the C–G interplay of Mo 265.

For a moment one should consider how this information about the interaction of voices in Mo 265 affects our view of the chant segment as the foundation, the "authority" upon which the motet is based. This motet in particular, but other *Portare* motets as well, suggests that motet composers considered the chant as raw material that could be manipulated to different tonal ends, even to the point of altering some notes and adding others.[20] Certainly this is not the common modern musical view of how chant segments are treated in thirteenth-century motets. This very fluid process resembles the approach to medieval texts, as writers like Mary Carruthers have explained:

> No modern reader would think of adapting and adding to the work of someone else in the way that medieval readers freely did, sometimes indicating the difference by writing their own work in margins, but often not. . . . Rather than condemning them for this, we should understand that such wholesale private commentary is a form of compliment, a readerly contribution to the text's continuation, and a judgment that it is worthy to be a public source for *memoria*.[21]

In short, changing a text contributed to its authority. Given this tradition of textual glossing, our modern use of the expression "polyphonic glossing" needs revision. While in the past medieval scholars have viewed the tenor as the immutable foundation above which materials are added, there is a growing recognition that it was but one building block in a richly intertwined edifice.[22]

AN EXAMINATION OF THE TEXTS of Mo 265 reveals an interplay of textual traditions involving sacred and secular motives—the Crucifixion, Mary, and pasto-

ral and courtly love. Just as the tenor melody sounds new in light of the borrowed rondeau melody, these various texts enhance one another and radiate
additional meanings, both explicitly and implicitly, when combined:[23]

Triplum

Mout me fu grief li departir
de m'amiete,
la jolie au cler vis,
qui est blanche et vermellete
comme rose par desus lis,
ce m'est avis;
son tres douz ris mi fait fremir
et si oell vair riant languir.
Ha Diex, com mar la lessai!
Blanchete comme flour de lis,
quant vous verrai?
Dame de valour,
vermelle comme rose en mai,
pour vous sui en grant dolour.

(The departure of my dear sweetheart grieved me deeply, the pretty one with
the bright face, as white and vermillion as rose set against lily, or so it seems
to me; her ever so sweet laughter makes me tremble, and her gray-blue eyes,
languish. O God, woe that I left her! Little, white lily flower, when will I see
you? Worthy Lady, red as a rose in May, on your account I suffer great grief.)

Motetus

Robin m'aime, Robin m'a;
Robin m'a demandee, si m'avra.
Robin m'achata corroie
et aumonniere de soie,
pour quoi donc ne l'ameroie?
Aleuriva!
Robin [m'aime, Robin m'a;
Robin m'a demandee, si m'avra].

(Robin loves me, Robin has me; Robin asked for me, and he will have me.
Robin brought me a belt and a little purse of silk; why then would I not
love him? Robin loves me, Robin has me; Robin asked for me, and he will
have me.)

Tenor

Portare

My interpretation will begin with the tenor, where one immediately faces
a challenge in determining the significance of the tenor cue *Portare* in light of
our belief that the motet originates in Paris.[24] The chant segment *Portare* fits
the melody of the *Alleluia Dulce lignum*, used in Paris and elsewhere for two
celebrations of the Cross: its Invention on 3 May and its Exaltation on 14

September.[25] Yet Parisian chant sources use the word *sustinere* instead of *portare* in this Alleluia verse: "que sola fuisti digna *sustinere* regem celorum et Dominum."[26] But two other pieces of evidence are relevant. The use of *portare* in the *Alleluia Dulce lignum* in one non-Parisian chant source (Reims, B.M. 266), and in one source of clausulae probably from Sens (Paris, B.N. lat. 15139)[27] suggests there may have been a tendency to interchange the words *portare* and *sustinere*. This speculation is confirmed in the language of the Offices for the Exaltation and Invention of the Cross, where one repeatedly finds the expression "que sola fuisti digna *portare* . . ."[28] Given the liberal use of *portare* in the Offices, its substitution for *sustinere* in the Alleluia *Dulce lignum* in some motets may not have particular significance in determining the motet's origin.

But there is another fact to consider that does bear on interpretation and possibly origin as well. In a source connected with Rouen (Paris, B.N. lat. 904), the same chant segment with the word *portare* appears in an *Alleluia Dulcis virgo* for the Octave of the Assumption.[29] *Alleluia Dulcis virgo* also reappears in a list of nine Marian Alleluias, without feast associations, in Assisi 695, whose other contents suggest connections with Reims and Paris.[30] The two manuscript appearances of *Alleluia Dulcis virgo* are significant; they indicate that the chant segment for the motet under consideration and for other *Portare* motets could in fact relate to Mary. Furthermore, their evidence suggests a connection between the Cross and Mary, in the form of a contrafact Alleluia.[31] The texts for both Alleluias, where the sentiment of the Cross bearing the weight of Christ is changed to that of Mary carrying him, presumably both before birth and later as the Infant Jesus, are as follows:

Alleluia. *Dulce lignum, dulces claves*, dulcia ferens pondera, que sola fuisti digna *sustinere* regem celorum et Dominum.

(Alleluia. Sweet wood, sweet nails, bearing the sweet weight, you alone were worthy of bearing the Lord, king of heaven.)

Alleluia. *Dulcis virgo, dulcis mater*, dulcia ferens pondera, que sola fuisti digna *portare* regem celorum et Dominum.

(Alleluia. Sweet virgin, sweet mother, bearing the sweet weight, you alone were worthy of carrying the Lord, king of heaven.)

A fairly extensive group of Parisian chant sources does not list the *Alleluia Dulcis virgo* for the Assumption or Nativity of the Virgin.[32] It is also not found in connection with the Assumption or Nativity in any of the other chant sources associated with Rouen or Reims currently available to me,[33] or in another 21 northern French chant sources examined during this study.[34] On the other hand, a two-part organum in the eleventh fascicle of W1 (fol. 197[v,] old foliation) presents another Marian contrafact of the Alleluia whose verse begins "Salve virgo, dei mater," and where the word *sustinere* is replaced by *meruisti*.[35] Additional evidence indicates that this particular contrafact with the word *meruisti* was used as part of a Marian votive Mass in an early state of the Notre Dame cathedral liturgy, but was dropped in the middle of the thirteenth century.[36] Thus, the combined evidence of the manuscript study I have been able to accomplish to this point suggests that the Marian contrafact version *Alleluia Dulcis virgo* with *portare* is probably not Parisian, but that it was used in some northern French locale(s), possibly in connection with the Assumption or a Marian votive Mass.[37]

What I want to present now is liturgical and iconographic evidence suggesting that the concepts of Mary with Child and the Cross were linked in France in the late thirteenth century when *Mout me fu grief* was likely composed. Such a situation would increase the likelihood that the Cross chant was actually contrafacted into a Mary chant in more instances than the few I have discovered through a random sampling. Such linkage of the two concepts could also possibly lead a motet composer to reflect on Mary even if he knew the chant segment officially only in connection with the feasts of the Invention/ Exaltation of the Cross.

To begin with the liturgy, the Mary with Child/Cross connection reappears in the Second Nocturn of Matins, fourth lesson, for the Assumption:

> Hodie Eden novi Adam paradisum suscipit animatum, in quo soluta est condemnatio, in quo plantatum est *lignum vite*, in quo operta fuit nostra nuditas.
>
> (Today the Eden of the new Adam receives the living paradise in which our condemnation was dissolved, in which the *tree of life* was planted, in which our nakedness was clothed.)[38] (emphasis added)

Since medieval legend held that the Cross grew from the Tree of Life, this may be a loaded reference to Christ as the Crucified Lord, borne by the Virgin Mary.[39] Sylvia Huot has singled out two liturgical sequences, both possibly by Philip the Chancellor of Paris (d. 1236), that may be relevant. Regarding "Lignum vite querimus," she states:

> the Virgin and the Cross are presented as the two loci where the fruit of life must be sought, and hence as two manifestations of the tree of life. Each embodies a paradox that is part of the sacred mystery of the Incarnation and Redemption:
>
> > Hic virgo puerpera,
> > Hic crux salutifera,
> >   Ambe ligna mystica;
> > Haec hysopus humilis
> > Illa cedrus nobilis,
> >   Utraque vivifica.
>
> Here is the child-bearing virgin, here the salubrious cross, two mystical trees; this one a humble hyssop, that one a noble cedar, and both life-giving.

The second sequence, "Crux, de te volo conqueri," abounds with parallel images of the Cross and Mary "bearing the fruit of life."[40] It is also noteworthy that on Good Friday, most likely in a para-liturgical context, there sometimes appeared Lamentations of Mary or *planctus* at the foot of the Cross, where Mary recalls Christ's childhood and contrasts birth and death, happiness and sorrow. Although Good Friday does not enter into the liturgical associations of the chant under consideration here, the Lamentations of Mary offer another channel through which a thirteenth-century composer and his audience could have become familiar with the Mary with Child/Cross connection.[41]

The Mary with Child/Cross connection is supported by iconographic evidence: in a number of diptych paintings from thirteenth-century Italy Mary is depicted as mother with child, opposite Christ on the Cross. These dual images present a striking parallel to the two chant texts: in both cases, Mary, as well as the Cross, support Christ. Hans Belting believes that the diptychs come from the sphere of the mendicant orders whose written statements also emphasized these two images.[42]

With respect to France, a handful of surviving ivory diptychs suggests a French tradition of juxtaposing the two images in the late thirteenth century.[43] It is also of relevance that the dual images of Mary with Child and Cross seem to have originated in the Byzantine world.[44] As one scholar of Gothic ivories, Charles T. Little, has remarked, a relationship between early Gothic ivory diptychs and eastern icons would have been natural, considering the artistic exchanges that took place between the French and Byzantine worlds after the fall of Constantinople in 1204.[45] Apart from the direct interchange possible during the thirteenth century, one can also consider the fact that the mendicant orders, whom Belting associates with the dual image in Italy, were also active in France in the thirteenth century, and therefore may have brought the image north with them. Thus, there is ample reason to speculate that the dual image of Mary with Child/Cross was known in northern France at the time under consideration here, the late thirteenth century.[46]

The presence of both Mary and Christ in representations of the Tree of Jesse also seems significant, particularly since Mary is shown carrying the Infant Jesus in her arms in French examples as early as the twelfth century.[47] Although it is not the crucified Christ who usually appears on the Tree of Jesse,[48] the association of this tree with the Cross was made by a sermonizer as famous as Peter Damian in the eleventh century. In his sermon "De exaltatione Sancte Crucis," he wrote: "De virga Iesse devenimus ad virgam crucis, et principium redemptionis fine concludimus" (We come from the rod of Jesse to the Cross, and we bring the beginning of redemption to its end).[49] Both trees are linked to salvation, the Tree of Jesse a starting point, the Cross its culmination. Mary, who bears Christ in her arms on the Tree of Jesse, is by association linked to the Cross and its redemptive mission. Thus, the language of the liturgy, as well as various medieval artistic creations, support the notion that Mary, as bearer of Christ, was commonly associated with the Cross in late thirteenth-century France. As remarked earlier, this increases the likelihood that the Cross chant may have been contrafacted into the Mary with Child version, or that a motet composer who knew only the Cross version may have reflected on Mary as well.

For the sake of argument, I want to assume for the moment that the composers of *Portare* motets may have known both the Marian and Christological versions of the tenor text, where *sustinere* is most usually associated with the Cross and *portare* with the Mary version. This assumption allows us to question whether they might have intended to invoke one or the other image through the choice of the tenor cue word. A survey of all the thirteenth-century motets based on this chant segment (see Table 2.1) suggests that the answer is probably no, which is not surprising since we established earlier that the words were interchangeable within the Cross liturgy itself. But one motet, Mo 3, 41, complicates the answer somewhat. The upper-voice texts of all the other motets deal with love topics of various sorts.[50] In Mo 3,41 (also the Clayette version), the motetus voice treats the subject of Christ's Crucifixion.[51] In the version of Bamberg, both the motetus and triplum deal with this subject.[52] All the sources that include a tenor, except Bamberg, use the incipit *Sustinere*, thereby suggesting that motet composers chose this Crucifixion-related incipit when the subject matter of the upper voice(s) was the Cross.[53]

This complicated evidence of various sorts suggests that this chant segment could have brought to a composer's mind the Crucifixion, Mary with Child, or both, regardless of whether he used *Portare* or *Sustinere* as a tenor cue. Furthermore, given that different composers may have assigned different meanings to the chant segment in various motets, one can also assume that listeners with diverse prior experiences of motets may have "read" a given motet in diverse ways. Not incidentally, I am assuming that the motets' audiences included individuals belonging to an inner circle who may have been "cued" into potential dual meanings of a motet's texts through the composer himself or through their own intellectual game-playing.[54] In light of this background, the remainder of this study will offer three different interpretations of *Mout me fu grief*—one relating it solely to the Crucifixion, one solely to Mary, and one to the Cross and Mary; these readings suggest how a thirteenth-century composer and his various audiences may have heard this motet.

The text of the motetus expresses the simple love of the shepherdess Marion for the shepherd Robin; she gives of her love willingly and is happy for the gifts he brings. In the redaction of the poem found in the pastourelle from which the motetus text is taken, the gifts were a cloak of scarlet, a gown, and a sash.[55] In the motet redaction, the gifts instead are a belt and silk purse, perhaps intended to direct one's attention to the area below the waist, and hence bring sexuality to mind.[56] The triplum text offers a different rhetoric, that of the courtly lover who grieves for his departed lady. In contrast to the happy woman of the motetus text, one finds a distressed man.

Taken alone, the triplum's profane expressions of "pained love" and "languishing for love" could in a most general way lead to reflections on spiritual love; this sort of association follows in the tradition of the Song of Songs, where the expression "I languish for love" appears, taken to mean the soul longing for union with Christ. More specifically, the suffering lover could evoke in the manner of parody the Christological Man of Sorrows, who loved and suffered, rejected by his people.[57] But in view of the joyful motetus text, one also has to consider a tradition which viewed the Cross itself as paradoxically the site of suffering and joy—through Christ's mortification, man's spiritual redemption was made possible. In a few cases, the Cross is even identified in the language of the Song of Songs, as the nuptial bed, where Christ as bridegroom is united with the Church; as such, it becomes an amorous meeting place.[58] So, if the associations of the Cross as locus of joy and sorrow, of metaphorical union, were what came to the composer's mind with the segment *Portare*, then one can perhaps understand its appearance in a motet that deals with human love evoking joy and sorrow, physical union and separation. Human and earthly concerns are reflected upon side by side, as so often occurs in medieval art and literature.

In a Marian interpretation of the motet, the most direct level of reflection on Mary would lie in the triplum's list of attributes: the coveted woman is described as "blanche et vermellete comme rose par desus lis" (white and vermillion as rose set against lily), "blanchete comme flour de lis" (white as a lily), "Dame de valour" (worthy lady). The lily as a symbol of purity and chastity is traditionally considered the flower of the Virgin; her Immaculate Conception was specifically symbolized by the lily among thorns. She is also called a "rose without thorns," because of the tradition that she was exempt from the consequences of original sin. The specific wording of the triplum, "Blanche et vermellete comme rose par desus lis," may be a twist on these established images.

Furthermore, this text overall may represent an affectionately playful allusion to the Virgin who figured as a real person so prominently in the daily existence of the French in the twelfth and thirteenth centuries.[59] In a more serious vein, by casting the coveted lady in language reminiscent of the Virgin (including the reference to her worthiness), the motet composer may also intend to elevate the lady and dignify the love.[60] Another suggestive detail of the triplum text is the male lover's mentioning the departure of his sweetheart, which grieved him deeply. If the possible liturgical connection with the Assumption is considered, the departure could be interpreted as signifying Mary's assumption into heaven. Similarly, the appearance of "Marion" in the motetus text may be another playful reference to Mary.[61] Certainly the language and some of the intentions singled out here may be standard in courtly love poetry, but the possible Marian connection of the tenor justifies and intensifies such a reading.

Finally, if the chant summoned both the idea of Mary with Child and of Christ's Crucifixion, the composer may have intended to bring into focus two emotions experienced by Mary, one joyful and life-giving, the other sorrowing. Mary was, after all, a central figure at the Crucifixion. Similarly, if the composer had in mind the feasts of the Cross and of the Assumption, two opposing emotions of Mary would again come into play, her sorrowing posture at Christ's Crucifixion and her rejoicing reunion with the King of Heaven.[62] These paired emotions of Mary seem significant in view of the upper-voice texts which contrast joy and pain, fulfillment and loss, in both cases with the woman in a central role.

IN CONCLUSION, THIS INVESTIGATION of Mo 265 and of other *Portare* motets suggests that we need to continue broadening our understanding of the sophisticated ways in which thirteenth-century motet composers worked. In a case such as Mo 265 the composer was not merely layering a preexisting rondeau melody onto a well-known chant segment, but cleverly integrating into the chant structural and tonal features of the borrowed melody,[63] carrying this integration into the triplum voice as well. In the free treatment of the chant segment, one sees at work the same sort of creative rewriting of authority that is apparent in medieval textual practice. As to the upper-voice texts chosen, it seems certain that the motet composer intended to present the two sides of the medieval secular love world, courtly and pastoral. By bringing these texts into play with the *Portare* chant segment, the composer may have intended a more complex reflection as well: that the joy and suffering of earthly love are another manifestation of what Christ and Mary experienced in their redemptive mission.

NOTES

1. See, for instance, Richard Hoppin, *Medieval Music* (New York: Norton, 1978), 338; and Andrew Hughes, *Style and Symbol: Medieval Music, 800–1453* (Ottawa, Canada: Institute of Mediaeval Music, 1989), 239, 255, and 343.

2. See Pesce, "A Case for Coherent Pitch Organization in the Thirteenth-Century Motet," *Music Analysis* 9/3 (1990): 287–318.

3. Ardis Butterfield, "Repetition and Variation in the Thirteenth-Century Refrain," *Journal of the Royal Music Association* 116/1 (1991): 1–23.

4. The motet appears in Example 2.2 in my edition based on the version of Montpellier 7, 265, hereafter referred to as Mo 265. As shown here in Table 2.1, Mo 265 has a concordance in Bamberg.

5. Specifically, they note that the song's refrain appears intact, but that the *additamenta* have been changed. Yvonne Rokseth, *Polyphonies du XIIIᵉ siècle: Le manuscrit H 196 de la Faculté de Médecine de Montpellier*, 4 vols. (Paris: Editions de l'Oiseau Lyre, 1935–39), 4:289; Friedrich Ludwig, *Repertorium organorum recentioris et motetorum vetustissimi stili*, vol. 1, pt. 2, Musicological Studies 26, (n.p.: Institute of Mediaeval Music, 1978), 432; and Jeremy Yudkin, *Music in Medieval Europe* (Englewood Cliffs, N.J.: Prentice Hall, 1989), 402.

6. Yvonne Rokseth noted the triplum materials in common between Mo 265 and Mo 37, which are discussed further in this chapter; see *Polyphonies du XIIIᵉ siècle*, 4:289.

7. Pierre Aubry, *Cent motets du XIIIᵉ siècle, publiés d'après le manuscrit Ed. IV.6 de Bamberg*, 3 vols. (Paris: A. Rouart, Lerolle, 1908), 3:102.

8. For further discussion of the tonal emphases within chants, see Andrew Hughes, *Style and Symbol*, 121–23.

9. Mark Everist, in "The Rondeau Motet: Paris and Artois in the Thirteenth Century," *Music and Letters* 69 (1988): 20, states that *Mout me fu grief* is the only example of a rondeau motet "outside the Artesian repertory of a piece with a tenor structure which exactly mirrors that of its motetus." The article deals with the 13 rondeau motets apparently composed in Artois. See also Everist, *French Motets in the Thirteenth Century: Music, Poetry and Genre*, Cambridge Studies in Medieval and Renaissance Music (Cambridge: Cambridge University Press, 1994), chap. 5.

In Example 2.2, the phrases of the motetus are marked to show the rondeau structure.

10. See my article "A Case for Coherent Pitch Organization," 290–91, for reference to theorists' remarks.

11. I have adopted the expression "directed progression" in my article "A Case for Coherent Pitch Organization." It is also used by Sarah Fuller in her discussions of fourteenth-century music: "On Sonority in Fourteenth-Century Polyphony: Some Preliminary Reflections," *Journal of Music Theory* 30/1 (1986): 35–70; "Line, *Contrapunctus*, and Structure in a Machaut Song," *Music Analysis* 6/1–2 (1987): 37–58; and "Tendencies and Resolutions: The Directed Progression in *Ars Nova* Music," *Journal of Music Theory* 36/2 (1992): 229–58.

12. By the way, acknowledging that application of *ficta* could have varied, this study adopts one possible reading that consistently applies F♯.

13. Example 2.3a summarizes what happens, while 2.3b, immediately below, shows the more expected voice-leading in which the sixth moves outward to the octave *g–g′*.

14. Against the preeminent *e′* of measure 4, the triplum voice highlights the tone *f♯′*. The *f♯′* moves once to *g′* in imitation of the motetus's gesture from the previous measure, but then remains stranded as the triplum flows into *d′* in measure 5.

The harmonic movement too offers support for G, although again not fully realized. Specifically, as Example 2.3a, measure 4, shows, the first *f♯′* of measure 4 is the upper tone of a dissonant major seventh *g–f♯′* which calls for resolution to the *g–g′* octave. This does not occur, and one next hears *f♯′* as part of a *b–d′–f♯′* sonority which moves with one directed progression to *a–e′*, whereupon *a* then immediately supports a dissonant sonority *a–e′–f♯′*. At this point, the voice-leading relates to Example 2.3c where two directed progressions over *a* should expand to the *g–d′–g′* sonority. But in the motet, although the tenor does move to *g* and the third expands to the fifth, the complementary expansion of the sixth *a–f♯′* to the octave *g–g′* is thwarted.

15. Although the triplum's pickup descent to the first *g′* of measure 6 could give importance to that tone as a point of arrival, the imitative entry of the tenor on *c′* (see circled motive) once again reinforces C instead.

16. Also, on beats 2 and 4 of measure 10, *g′* and *f♯′* appear with open octaves below, a sound previously associated only with C.

17. Within the neutral progressions of measures 11–12, an imitative play between triplum and motetus on a four-note motive (see dotted brackets) leads back to C in the middle of measure 12.

18. When, in measure 16, the triplum picks up an undulating motion between *f♯′* and *g′* analogous to what occurred in measure 4, the motet composer avoids a harmonic tendency towards G by rejecting the *f♯′* over the tenor *a* he had used in measure 4.

19. Given that Mo 37 is found in fascicle 3, part of the Old Corpus of Montpellier, while Mo 265 appears in the presumably later fascicle 7, it seems reasonable to assume that the composer of 265 adopted these four snippets into his own creation, recognizing their potential for enhancing the C–G interplay that underlies it. Not incidentally, Mo 37 is based upon a different chant segment than Mo 265.

20. In *Mo 265*, the change within the tenor of *f* to *f♯* and the addition of a *c′* that doubles the motetus pitch and is thus perhaps disguised admittedly constitute minimal alterations to the chant, perhaps suggesting that the composer tried to retain its integrity as much as possible even while responding to the borrowed rondeau melody.

Mo 296, *Boine amours mi fait chanter liement/Uns maus savereus et dous/Portare*, is also of interest. This motetus also incorporates F♯s, contributing to a G tonal focus initially. But a remarkable switch occurs in the second half where the motet settles satisfyingly on F—the composer truncates the chant and manipulates the other two voices as well to make this possible. Once again, *Portare* yields tonal variety.

21. Mary Carruthers, *The Book of Memory: A Study of Memory in Medieval Culture* (Cambridge: Cambridge University Press, 1990), 214.

22. Certainly Renaissance scholars recognize this facet of cantus-firmus composition. Sarah Fuller has moved toward such an understanding of Machaut's motets in her recent article, "Modal Tenors and Tonal Orientation in Motets of Guillaume de Machaut," in *Studies in Medieval Music: Festschrift for Ernest H. Sanders*, ed. Peter M. Lefferts and Brian Seirup = *Current Musicology* 45–47, (1990): 199–245. Though Fuller does not have Machaut's tenor chant sources to work with, she argues that he apparently chose tenors that harbored particular tonal traits and that these tenors were then exploited to fulfill the composer's broader tonal plans. What I suggest here is that the tendency to view the tenor as raw material was already in place among thirteenth-century composers.

23. With the permission of A-R Editions, Inc., the translations are reprinted with modification from *The Montpellier Codex*, ed. Hans Tischler, trans. Susan Stakel and Joel C. Relihan, Recent Researches in the Music of the Middle Ages and Early Renaissance 8 (Madison: A-R Editions, 1985), pt. 4, 87.

24. The conjecture rests on the fact that the *Portare* motets are found with only one exception in the Montpellier and/or Bamberg codices, thought to be products of Paris. See Table 2.1. These as well as other thirteenth-century motet sources are discussed by Mark Everist in *Polyphonic Music in Thirteenth-Century France: Aspects of Sources and Distribution* (New York: Garland, 1989), particularly chaps. 3 and 4.

25. In Paris at least it was adopted as well for the Reception of the Cross on the first Sunday in August.

26. I want to thank Rebecca Baltzer and Nancy Lorimer for their assistance in reaching this conclusion, based on examination of a number of Parisian chant sources. See n. 32.

27. The information on this latter manuscript is taken from Jürg Stenzl, *Die vierzig Clausulae der Handschrift Paris Bibliothèque Nationale Latin 15139*, Publikationen der Schweizerischen Musikforschenden Gesellschaft, Serie II vol. 22 (Bern: Verlag Paul Haupt, 1970), 80–81.

28. In the modern breviary, for the feasts of the Exaltation and Invention, First Vespers, the Magnificat antiphon reads "O crux, splendidior cunctis astris . . . que sola fuisti digna *portare* talentum mundi, dulce lignum, dulces clavos, dulcia ferens pondera." In Matins, Third Nocturn, for both feasts one finds a form of both *portare* and *sustinere* in the responsory: "Dulce lignum, dulces clavos, dulce pondus *sustinuit:* Que sola digna fuit *portare* pretium hujus seculi." For the feast of the Exaltation only, Second Vespers uses as its Magnificat antiphon: "O Crux benedicta, que sola fuisti digna *portare* Regem celorum et Dominum, alleluja!"—the latter phrase exactly like the Alleluia verse.

For both feasts, at Matins, First Nocturn, one finds only a form of *sustinere* in this phrase of the responsory *Crux fidelis*: "Dulce lignum, dulces clavos, dulce pondus *sustinuit*"; likewise, for both feasts at Lauds one finds "Dulce ferrum, dulce lignum, dulce pondus *sustinent*" as part of the hymn *Crux fidelis*.

With the exception of the hymn, I have been able to verify all the language for the feast of the Exaltation in a thirteenth/fourteenth-century Parisian noted breviary, Paris, B.N. lat. 15182, fols. 354–360^v. With the exception of the hymn, I have also verified the language for the feast of the Invention in a thirteenth-century source from St-Vaast, Arras: Arras, Bibliothèque Municipale, MS 465 (893), fols. 383–385^v.

29. This source's contents date from around the beginning of the thirteenth century and it was probably written around mid-century. I am indebted to Nancy Lorimer for her help in verifying various facts about this manuscript and others.

30. This manuscript was kindly brought to my attention by Rebecca Baltzer. The ways in which its anthology of sequences reveals connections with Paris are explained by Margot Fassler, *Gothic Song: Victorine Sequences and Augustinian Reform in Twelfth-Century Paris* (Cambridge: Cambridge University Press, 1993), 155–56, 170, 256, 323.

31. Given that the chant melody appears most typically in connection with Feasts of the Cross, we can assume that the Marian text *Dulcis virgo* is a contrafact. See nn. 32, 33, and 34 for sources examined in reaching this conclusion.

32. The sources examined are those for the churches of Notre-Dame (Paris, B.N. lat. 1112 and Paris, Arsenal 110); St. Victor (Paris, Arsenal 197 and Paris, B.N. lat. 14452); St. Geneviève (Bibl. Ste. Geneviève 1259); St. Germain-des-Prés (Paris, B.N. lat. 14248); St. Magloire (Paris, B.N. lat. 13252); Trinitaires (Paris, B.N. lat. 1022); St. Maur-des-Fossés (Paris, B.N. lat. 12054 and Paris, B.N. lat. 13255); Dominicans (London, B.L. Add. 23935); and St. Denis (Paris, B.N. lat. 1107).

The Assumption and Nativity are the two Marian feasts for which the sentiment expressed in this Alleluia text would be most appropriate.

33. Reims sources examined are Reims, B.M. 224, 264, 265, and 266; the other Rouen source examined is Paris, B.N. n.a.l. 541.

34. These additional sources are connected with locations such as Arras, Compiègne, Châlons-sur-Marne, Dijon, Chartres, Bec, and Auxerre.

35. W1 (Wolfenbüttel, Herzog-August-Bibliothek Helmsdt. 628) is a source of Notre-Dame polyphony apparently copied in St. Andrews in the 1230s. See Mark Everist, "From Paris to St. Andrews: The Origins of W1," *Journal of the American Musicological Society* 43/1 (1990): 1–42.

For the Notre Dame two-part organa and clausulae related to the Cross version of the chant, *Alleluia Dulce lignum*, see Ludwig, *Repertorium organorum*, vol. 2, Musicological Studies 17, (Brooklyn: Institute of Mediaeval Music 1972), 37–41. Ludwig designates the *Alleluia Dulce lignum* M22 in his catalogue. See also Hendrik van der Werf, *Integrated Directory of Organa, Clausulae, and Motets of the Thirteenth Century* (Rochester, N.Y.: Published by the author, 1989), 44–45.

36. A Paris missal, British Library, Add. 38723, has this contrafact version (text only) as one of the Alleluias for the Marian votive Mass; this source, probably copied before the mid-thirteenth century, represents a very early state of the Notre Dame cathedral liturgy since its sanctorale contains no feast after 1200. The Marian votive Masses in the later manuscripts, Paris, B.N. lat. 1112 and lat. 15615, do not contain this Alleluia, suggesting that it had been dropped by mid-century.

That this particular contrafact version of the Alleluia played some role in the Parisian liturgy at an earlier time is also supported by its appearance in the Bari Gradual (Bari, San Nicola 85) (text and music) for Feria 5 of the Octave of the Assumption. Rebecca Baltzer has communicated to me that she suspects the Bari Gradual represents a twelfth-century state of the Paris liturgy that was altered at the cathedral of Notre Dame in the thirteenth century, but remained current with the royal family who were the patrons responsible for this volume.

37. Information on this contrafact at a later date appears in Alejandro Enrique Planchart, "Guillaume Du Fay's Benefices and His Relationship to the Court of Burgundy," *Early Music History* 8 (1988), 153–57. Planchart finds the *Alleluia Dulcis mater* within the polyphonic propers of Trent 88; it is transmitted with two sequences for the Virgin, *Verbum bonum* and *Mittit ad virginem*. Planchart states that these three pieces were commonly used in votive Masses for the Virgin. I have not been able to determine when this practice of using the *Alleluia Dulcis mater* for a Marian votive Mass was established, nor how widespread the usage was.

The *Alleluia Dulcis mater* in Trent 88 reveals a variant wording of what appears in the earlier French chant sources: "Dulcis mater dulcinato prebens ubera que sola fuisti digna *generare* regem celorum et Dominum." See *Auctorum anonymorum missarum propria XVI*, ed. Laurence Feininger, Monumenta polyphoniae liturgicae Sanctae Ecclesiae Romanae, ser. 2, no. 1 (Rome: Societas Universalis Sanctae Ceciliae, 1947), 192–93.

38. This passage is taken from a modern edition of the *Breviarium Romanum*. Its source is John Damascene's "Oratio in dormitionem B.M.V. secunda." The passage itself does not appear in the liturgy of late thirteenth-century Paris. The earliest known Latin translation of the sermon is found in the manuscript Karlsruhe, Bad. Landesbibliothek, cod. Aug. perg. 80, fols. 91ᵛ–106ᵛ; this manuscript dates from the tenth century, providing a *terminus ante quem* for the Latin translation, with a *terminus post quem* set at the first half of the eighth century when the sermon was conceived. It appears that the sermon did not circulate in Latin translation in Paris or other areas of northern France before or during the thirteenth century. See Bonifatius Kotter, O.S.B., ed., *Die Schriften des Johannes von Damaskos, 5: Opera homiletica et hagiographica* (Berlin: Walter de Gruyter, 1988), 56–57, 469–70; A. P. Orban, "Die lateinische Übersetzung von zwei Predigten des Joannes Damaskenos auf die Koimesis Mariä: Einführung, Ausgabe und Amerkungen," *Byzantion* 60 (1990): 232–91 (the passage appears in this edition on p. 268, lines 140–42); Albert Siegmund, O.S.B., *Die Überlieferung der griechischen christlichen Literatur in der lateinischen Kirche bis zum zwölften Jahrhundert* (Munich-Pasing: Filser Verlag, 1949), 177ff. I have not been able to find a related passage in *De fide orthodoxa*, Damascene's sole treatise that was really influential in the West throughout the Middle Ages; it was widely quoted by, among others, Thomas Aquinas. See Saint John Damascene, *De fide orthodoxa. Versions of Burgundio and Cerbanus*, ed. Eligius M. Buytaert, Franciscan Institute Publications, text series no. 8 (St. Bonaventure, N.Y.: The Franciscan Institute, 1995). I want to thank Dr. Robert Volk, who has succeeded Bonifatius Kotter as editor of the Greek works of John Damascene, and Dr. Irena Backus of the Institut d' Histoire de la Réformation at the University of Geneva, for their assistance in addressing this question.

39. See the entry on *Baum* in *Lexikon der christlichen Ikonographie*, ed. Engelbert Kirschbaum, S.J. (Rome: Herder, 1970), 2:260–61, where the author states that the Tree of Life became associated with three ideas: of Paradise according to Genesis 2–3, of the end of time, and of the martyrdom of Christ. The last developed into a medieval legend that the Cross was made from the wood of the Tree of Life or of the Tree of Knowledge of Good and Evil.

40. Sylvia Huot, *Allegorical Play in the Old French Motet: The Sacred and the Profane in Thirteenth-Century Polyphony* (Stanford University Press, 1997). The attributions to Philip the Chancellor are summarized in Thomas B. Payne, "Poetry, Politics, and Polyphony: Philip the Chancellor's Contribution to the Music of the Notre Dame School" (Ph.D. diss., University of Chicago, 1991), 3:574, 577.

41. The Lamentations of Mary were not adopted into the liturgy, but were probably attached to the ceremony of the Adoration of the Cross. Mary *planctus* were written in Paris as early as the twelfth century. See Karl Young, *The Drama of the Medieval Church* (Oxford: Clarendon Press, 1933), 1:496. Solange Corbin comments that the *planctus* appeared in the twelfth century and spread throughout all Christian countries, though Italy was the favored locale. See *La Déposition liturgique du Christ au vendredi saint; sa place dans l'histoire des rites et du théâtre religieux* (Paris: Société d'Editions, Les Belles Lettres, 1960), 210.

Finally, the language of Mary "bearing" Christ—although not explicitly linked to the Crucifixion—was very common in medieval French sermonizing as one way of characterizing her motherly attributes. See Hervé Martin, *Le Métier de prédicateur en France septentrionale à la fin du moyen âge (1350–1520)* (Paris: Editions de Cerf, 1988), 310–11; and Larissa Taylor, *Soldiers of Christ: Preaching in Late Medieval and Reformation France* (New York: Oxford University Press, 1992), 112.

42. Hans Belting, *The Image and Its Public in the Middle Ages: Form and Function of Early Paintings of the Passion*, trans. Mark Bartusis and Raymond Meyer (New Rochelle, NY: Aristide D. Caratzas, 1990), 133–38.

43. Whereas surviving examples in significant numbers date only from the fourteenth century, it seems evident that there was a preceding experimental stage leading to such developed artifacts with their standardized iconography. See *Masterpieces of Ivory from the Walters Art Gallery* by Richard H. Randall Jr. with texts by Diana Buitron, Jeanny Vorys Canby, William R. Johnston, Andrew Oliver Jr., and Christian Theuerkauff (New York: Hudson Hills Press, 1985), 182. One finds tantalizing examples of half of a diptych, some of Mary and Child, some of the Cross, possibly from the thirteenth century. This information has been conveyed to me by several art historians, among them Charles T. Little of the Metropolitan Museum of Art and Adelaide Bennett of the Index of Christian Art at Princeton University. One such case where the wings have been matched (the Crucifixion is found at the Toldeo Museum of Art and the Virgin with Child in the Louvre) is dated differently by two scholars: Richard H. Randall Jr. in *The Golden Age of Ivory: Gothic Carvings in North American Collections* (New York: Hudson Hills Press, 1993), 63–64, argues for early fourteenth century, while Danielle Gaborit-Chopin in *Nouvelles acquisitions du départment des objets d'art, 1985–1989* (Musée du Louvre, Paris, 1990), no. 20, pp. 52–55, insists that it is late thirteenth century. Also, a group of north French triptychs include the Crucifixion and the Virgin with Child in the central panel, one above the other. Raymond Koechlin gives three such examples dated to the late thirteenth century, in *Les Ivoires gothiques français* (Paris, 1924; repr. Paris: F. de Nobele, 1968), 2:22–26. The three examples are found in vol. 3, pls. 19 and 20, nos. 45, 47, and 60. Richard H. Randall Jr. adds another with the dating 1250–70 in *The Golden Age of Ivory*, 53, item no. 36. Unfortunately, Koechlin's dates are not considered universally sound by many scholars today.

On the issue of French diptych paintings, art historians consider the earliest examples bearing these images to date from the second half of the fourteenth century. Various studies are cited in Wolfgang Kermer, "Studien zum Diptychon in der sakralen Malerei" (Ph.D. diss., Eberhard-Karls-Universität zu Tübingen, 1967), 120, 263.

44. See Belting, *The Image and its Public in the Middle Ages*, particularly chap. 5.

45. Charles T. Little, "Ivoires et art gothique," *Revue de l'Art* 46 (1979): 64.

46. One other piece of suggestive iconographic evidence is mentioned by Wolfgang Kermer, in "Studien zum Diptychon," 121–22. He remarks upon a French diptych (possibly from Toulouse) which carries an inscription in the last decade of the thirteenth century (the so-called Diptych of Rabastens). On the left panel are depicted the scourging of Christ and his Crucifixion and on the right panel are depicted Mary's death and Thomas receiving Mary's girdle as she ascends into heaven. Here we find a juxtaposition of the Crucifixion and Mary's Assumption, the other Mary connection mentioned at the outset of this discussion.

47. Arthur Watson, *The Early Iconography of the Tree of Jesse* (London: Humphrey Milford, 1934), 79.

48. I have not found evidence that Christ is usually so depicted on the Tree of Jesse. On the other hand, George Ferguson, in *Signs and Symbols in Christian Art* (New York: Oxford University Press, 1954), 51, states: "The presence of the Crucified

Christ in the Tree of Jesse is based on a medieval tradition that the dead tree of life may only become green again if the Crucified Christ is grafted upon it and revives it with His blood." The entry *Wurzel Jesse* in *Lexikon der christlichen Ikonographie*, 4:551, mentions a representation in which a Cross-tree grows through Mary carrying a crucifix in its branches.

49. Cited in Watson, *The Early Iconography of the Tree of Jesse*, 52–53.

50. The two most common types of love lyric, courtly and pastourelle, predominate in this grouping. The grieving courtly lover appears most frequently, sometimes claiming to assuage his thwarted love through song, and occasionally mentioning his slanderers. In three motets pastourelle characters appear, engaged in typical merry-making in two of them (Mo 265, under discussion here, and Mo 259). The third, Mo 3, 41, is discussed further in the text.

A third sort of love poem, the *chanson de mal mariée*, is found in Mo 142, 148, 233, where one or several women speak of having and enjoying a lover or of wanting one.

51. Sylvia Huot discusses Mo 3, 41 in some detail in *Allegorical Play*. The triplum is distinctive as a pastourelle text in which the shepherdess grieves for her lost lover, rather than rejoicing in present merry-making.

52. LoC transmits a two-part version, whose triplum text is the same one found in Bamberg.

53. As Table 2.1 shows, Bamberg *always* uses the word *portare* in these motets, whereas Montpellier and Clayette include both words. One can reasonably assume that Bamberg, despite its use of *portare* in Ba 19, intends to invoke the Cross as the principal image in this particular motet.

The other appearances of *sustinere* in Table 2.1 are more paradoxical and further the notion that *portare* and *sustinere* were used interchangeably. MO 6, 188 (also the W2 version) uses *sustinere*, though the upper-voice texts are not related to the Crucifixion, but instead use the language of the suffering lover, as do many of the other motets that choose *portare*. Similarly, Cl 16 uses *sustinere* in a motet where the upper-voice texts speak of pained sleep and of the pained lover in general; concordant sources use *portare* here.

54. See Christopher Page, *Discarding Images: Reflections on Music and Culture in Medieval France* (Oxford: Clarendon Press, 1993), chap. 3, particularly 82–84, for a discussion of who would have been included in a motet's audience according to the theorist Johannes de Grocheio. Page argues for a rather wide-ranging group that includes clerics and anyone who pursued "learning" at different levels and in various disciplines. I hold that the nuances of verbal meaning suggested in the present study may have been available to only a select part of this vast audience.

55. In the pastourelle, the words are "Robins m'acata cotele / D'escarlate bonne et bele, Souskanie et chainturele." See Friedrich Gennrich, *Adam de la Halle: Le Jeu de Robin et de Marion, Li Rondel Adam*, Musikwissenschaftliche Studienbibliothek 20 (Langen: [author], 1962), 9.

56. I am grateful to Professors Norris Lacy and Samuel Rosenberg for engaging in a discussion with me about the language of this poem.

57. See Isaiah 52–53, in particular 52:3: "He was spurned and avoided by men, a man of suffering . . ."

58. Sylvia Huot, *Allegorical Play*, gives an example from a sequence by Philip the Chancellor.

59. As remarked by Henry Adams in *Mont-Saint-Michel and Chartres* (Princeton: Princeton University Press, 1905), 251, "The Virgin filled so enormous a space in the

life and thought of the time that one stands now helpless before the mass of testimony to her direct action and constant presence in every moment and form of the illusion which men thought they thought their existence."

60. Or perhaps in the manner of parody to belittle it.

61. Another suggestive reference in the motetus text is to the gift of a "belt." In connection with the Assumption, one finds the legend of the holy girdle where the Virgin, as she is transported upward by angels, throws down a girdle to the doubting apostle Thomas to prove that she had ascended into heaven. See Anna Jameson, *Legends of the Madonna as Represented in the Fine Arts* (London: Longmans, Green, 1890; repr. Detroit: Omnigraphics, 1990), 19–20. In the motet, the image is reversed in that the man gives the belt to the woman, a change of the sort that cultural anthropologists now call "inversion."

62. In the First Vespers antiphon for the Assumption, one reads "Maria Virgo assumpta est ad aethereum thalamum, in quo Rex regum stellato sedet solio" (The Virgin Mary has been taken up into the heavenly bridal chamber, where the King of Kings is sitting on a starry throne). For the Assumption the Offices thus adopted language that included the image of Mary united with Christ upon her arrival in heaven. Her reunion with Christ is cast in the language of the Song of Songs through the allusion to a bridal chamber. I have verified this language in the thirteenth/fourteenth-century Parisian noted breviary, Paris, B.N. lat. 15182, fols. 304–11.

63. Anne Robertson has suggested to me that the effect of the tenor combined with the very audible rondeau melody is that of a "polyphonic tenor."

Which Vitry?

The Witness of the Trinity Motet from the *Roman de Fauvel*

I f Philippe de Vitry stands in the shadow of his contemporary Guillaume de Machaut, it is only due to the haphazard survival of documents, for the acclaim he received during and after his lifetime bespeaks a career of nearly unparalleled proportions. Hailed by such personages as Jehan des Murs and Petrarch, he was celebrated equally as purveyor of musical innovations that we call the *Ars nova* and for his poetic, philosophical, historical, and mathematical writings. A politician and cleric of considerable skill, Vitry served kings and nobles and rose high in ecclesiastical circles. But whereas the poetic and musical works of Machaut are well known to us due to his penchant for gathering them into deluxe manuscripts, scarcely a note of music and only four poems can be attributed to Vitry with any confidence. Likewise, his biography is thinner than the one we can construct for Machaut.[1] Faced with this deficit, musicologists have recently looked for clues to Vitry's extraordinary career in some less familiar, but promising, places.[2]

A potentially fruitful if untried approach is to attempt to strengthen the musical attributions of Vitry's isorhythmic motets through a study of their tenor melodies. A number of his presumed works are cited in the *Ars nova* complex of theory treatises, formerly attributed to the composer but now viewed as a product of a teaching tradition that centered around him. This new assessment of the treatises, recently put forward by Sarah Fuller,[3] does not remove the pieces named therein from Vitry's canon, and there is no reason to discount his authorship on this account. One of these motets, *Firmissime fidem/Adesto sancta trinitas/Alleluia Benedictus es*, is preserved in Chaillou de Pesstain's musical additions to the *Roman de Fauvel* (F:Pn, fr. 146, fol. 43) and in the rotulus manuscript B:Br 19606 (no. 4).[4] Looking at this work afresh—literally from the bottom up—suggests a surer attribution to Vitry, a new focus for his biography, and some revisions in our view of the transmission of the motet in the late thirteenth and early fourteenth centuries.

The Trinity Motet from the *Roman de Fauvel*

Firmissime fidem/*Adesto sancta trinitas*/*Alleluia Benedictus es* is a praise to the Holy Trinity. The piece is constructed in two sections, defined by two statements of the tenor *color*, and the reiteration of the tenor in the second section is an early example of diminution. The *Ars nova* treatises that cite the work emphasize its duple modus and tempus,[5] and a recent analysis suggests that these and other binary features are a deliberate contradiction of the expected emphasis on the Trinity.[6] The number 3 does nonetheless figure prominently in the motet. Indeed, not only is "3" important here, but also the concept of "3 in 1." On one level this trinitarian allusion plays out in an interaction of binary and ternary elements, focusing on the number 4, which is the sum of 3 + 1. Both poems contain numbers of lines divisible by 4, and this permits organization of the texts into what are almost 3:1 proportions (see Table 3.1). The motetus, a trope of the popular hymn for the Trinity *Adesto sancta trinitas* (textual additions shown in italics in Table 3.1),[7] has eight lines. The composer assigns six lines to the first section of the piece and two lines to the second section, beginning with the final syllable of line 6. This arrangement produces a 6:2, or 3:1, relationship, barring the holdover syllable at the beginning of line 7. We would likewise expect the 20-line triplum to divide after line 15 in order to create the same 15:5, or 3:1 proportion. This is not quite the case, however, because of the rests at the beginning of the piece. The triplum can squeeze only 14 lines of text into the first section, leaving six lines for the second section (Example 3.1).

Aside from these textual features, the music of the motet displays an even more precise trinitarian orientation (Example 3.1). The organization of rhythm is a case in point.[8] Whereas the modus and tempus are imperfect—and many binary relationships in the piece stem from this fact—the tenor is set in perfect maximodus in the first section through the alternation of longs and maximas. This arrangement gives the effect of the old rhythmic mode 2. At the other end of the rhythmic spectrum, the various combinations of semibreves produce what sounds like perfect prolation in places where the groups of three semibreves are rendered, according to one of the recommendations for *tempus imperfectum*, as *semibrevis recta, semibrevis minor, minima* (♪♫).[9] As a result, the semibreve is effectively subdivided into three minims. These two perfect rhythms, the maximodus on the one hand and the triple subdivision of the semibreves on the other, frame the imperfect modus and tempus. In Section 2, the quickening of the tenor is due to the rewriting of all tenor longs and maximas in Section 1 as breves. Now the tenor *talea*, which extended over three perfect maximodus units in Section 1, is stated within the time of one unit, and this change once again illustrates the "3 in 1" concept. Although the second section seems to abandon the maximodus, the overriding triple impression remains, with one "foot" of Section 1 (♩ ○ ♩ ○ ♩ ‑) written here as five equal breves, followed by a breve rest (♩ ♩ ♩ ♩ ♩ ꞉) .

Even the numbers of notes promote the theme of "3 in 1." Table 3.2 shows that the tenor and motetus include 192 breves, all told. The triplum has

TABLE 3.1   Text of *Firmissime fidem/Adesto sancta trinitas/Alleluia Benedictus es*

Triplum (20 lines)
Section 1 (1st statement of color) has 14 lines of text

Firmissime fidem teneamus	Let us hold the faith of the Trinity
trinitatis patrem diligamus	most firmly. Let us love the Father
qui nos tanto amore dilexit,	who loved us with so much love
morti datos ad vitam erexit,	that he raised to life those given to death,
ut proprio nato non parceret,	that he did not spare his only Son,
sed pro nobis hunc morti traderet.	but handed him over to death for us.
Diligamus eiusdem filium,	Let us love his Son,
nobis natus, nobis propicium,	born for us, gracious to us,
Qui in forma dei cum fuisset	Who while in the form of God
atque formam servi accepisset.	also took on the form of a servant.
Hic factus est patri obediens	This he did, obedient to the Father;
et in cruce fixus ac moriens.	he was placed on the cross and died.
Diligamus sanctum paraclitum,	Let us love the Holy Spirit,
patris summi natique spiritum	spirit of the highest Father and Son,

Section 2 (2nd statement of color) has 6 lines of text

cuius sumus gracia renati,	through whose grace we are reborn,
unctione cuius et signati.	and with whose unction we are marked.
Nunc igitur sanctam trinitatem	Now therefore let us worship the Holy Trinity
veneremur atque unitatem	and let us praise its unity,
exoremus, ut eius gracia	so that we might be strong in its grace
valeamus perfrui gloria.	and enjoy its glory.

Motetus (8 lines)
Section 1 (1st statement of color) has 6 lines of text, less one syllable

Adesto sancta trinitas	Be near, Holy Trinity,
musice modulantibus,	while we sing [you] our music.
par splendor una deitas	Equal splendor, one deity,
simplex in personis tribus,	three persons in one,
Qui extas rerum omnium,	who stands above all things.
tua omnipotenci-	By your omnipotence,

Section 2 (2nd statement of color) has 2 lines of text, plus one syllable

-a sine fine principium	beginning without end,
duc nos ad celi gaudia.	lead us to the joys of Heaven.

EXAMPLE 3.1 *Firmissime fidem/Adesto sancta trinitas/Alleluia Benedictus es,* opening

TABLE 3.2   Breve count in *Firmissime fidem**

Section 1	Section 2
6 long (= 12 breve) rests + 132 breves in triplum	48 breves in triplum
144 breves in motetus	48 breves in motetus
144 breves in tenor	48 breves in tenor

144 : 48

3 : 1

*Longs and breves are imperfect throughout the motet.

a total of 180 breves, plus 12 breve rests at the beginning. All of these numbers are divisible by 3. Section 1 contains 144 breves, and Section 2 has 48 breves, demonstrating once again that the first section is exactly three times longer than the second.[10] The trinitarian symbolism likewise extends to the very folio of the *Roman de Fauvel* on which the motet occurs (F:Pn, fr. 146, fol. 43). Here an illumination shows three persons, and the poem mentions the Trinity outright and offers a trio of adjectives to describe God: "Sire diex pere esperitable/Tout pouissant, sage, immutable/Qui mainz en sainte trinité/En une mesme deïté."

Textual and musical focus on the Trinity in a work of medieval sacred music was certainly common, and Philippe de Vitry was no exception in placing numerology at the service of theology. But it is interesting that we find elsewhere in Vitry's oeuvre quite explicit mention not only of the Trinity, but also of the "3 in 1" concept. His poem *Le Chapel des trois Fleurs de Lis* is replete with this symbolism.[11] Written in the 1330s to promote an aborted crusade of Philip VI of Valois, the poem describes the three fleurs de lis— knowledge, faith, and chivalry—which, acting in concert, will defeat the infidel in the Holy Land. Further references appear from time to time in the poem, for example, in the invocation of the blessed triumvirate of the nation, the apostle to Gaul Saint Denis and his two companions Rusticus and Eleutherius. And twice in the brief work, Vitry actually enunciates the "3 in 1" concept: "Diex qui est treble en unité" (ll. 25, 1029), just as he incorporates it in the triplum ("trinitatem veneremus atque unitatem exoremus") and in one of the lines he added to the motetus: "simplex in personis tribus" (Table 3.1). While the Trinity motet cannot readily be associated with *Le Chapel*, written some two decades later, it is clear that Vitry's idea of an appropriate symbolism for the Trinity in his artistic creations embraced both the number 3 and the idea of "3 in 1." Surely we would press the case too far to suggest that his focus on both parts of the symbol in *Le Chapel des trois Fleurs de Lis* strengthens the attribution of *Firmissime fidem* to him. But certain it is that the ternary number, and more particularly the visible reduction of 3 into 1, is deeply imbedded in both the motet and the *dit*.

In light of this, we might ask why the tenor *color* has 40 notes, rather than 39 or 42, both numbers being divisible by 3. Is this a result of the binary features of the work that stand alongside the ternary elements? Or is there another reason for this number? Hardly stymied by the inconvenience, the composer converts the 40-note tenor to a melody divisible by 3 through his use of rests. We have already seen that the *talea* consists of five notes, arranged in a mode 2 pattern. In setting the tenor in this mode, Vitry puts rests at the end of each *talea*, and this arrangement yields nine longs (that is, *longa, maxima, longa, maxima, longa, maxima* rest) in each segment. There are thus 72 longs in the first section (nine longs in each of eight *taleae*), and this is contrasted in the diminution section by the presence of 48 breves, resulting in numbers that are both binary and ternary.[12]

The rests that segment the tenor likewise emphasize the modality of the piece. The division of the melody after every fifth note yields eight subgroups, five of which end on the final *f*, and three on *a*.[13] The second statement of the *color* preserves the rests that defined the ends of each five-note group in the first section, and thereby reiterates both the overall triple effect of the tenor melody and the modal center on *f*.

The Origin of the Motet Tenor, *Alleluia Benedictus es*

Our 40-note tenor thus pays homage to the ternary number through use of rests. To return then to the questions posed near the end of the previous section: Where did the composer get the melody of the *Alleluia Benedictus es* that appears in the tenor? Did he alter it in some way? Or is he simply recording faithfully a version he knew? Certainly composers often modify the chants they choose as tenors,[14] but they are not obliged to do so. In the case of *Firmissime fidem*, there are reasons to believe alteration has not occurred.

First, we have already noted that had the composer changed the number of pitches only slightly, he could easily have made the *color* divisible by 3. Second, the fourteenth-century theorists who discuss the composition of iso-rhythmic motets do not mention changing the notes of the chant used in the tenor. Egidius de Murino and Johannes Boen say simply that the composer should "select a tenor" and then "order and color it."[15] An anonymous theorist of the late fourteenth century states: "the tenors ought to follow the nature of ecclesiastical song; nevertheless they can begin differently as long as they end similarly."[16] What he means here is not that the beginning of the tenor should be purposely recomposed, but rather that tenors drawn from internal melismas, instead of from the opening of a chant, will not always begin with the characteristic gesture of a given mode. Since the theorists seem neutral on the question of melodic alteration, we should explore the possibility that the *Alleluia Benedictus es* has not been modified at all and ask if our tenor represents a particular local usage.

From the time of the appearance of *Le Graduel romain* of the monks of Solesmes, we have known that different versions of plainchant existed in virtually every city and town in Europe prior to the Council of Trent.[17] The usefulness of these readings to the medieval and Renaissance scholar as an aid in localizing examples of cantus-firmus-based polyphony is clear from a number of recent studies.[18] What has emerged from this work, among other things, is that the identity of the place in or for which a piece is written may be embodied in part in the very pitches of the cantus firmus. Normally, however, the comparisons made between cantus firmus and local reading have been used as corroboratory rather than primary evidence. That is, they have sometimes helped confirm the presumed origin of a piece, sometimes helped deny it, and sometimes helped point to another locale altogether. Common to most of these essays is some a priori notion of the general area from which a piece might come, based on knowledge of a composer's whereabouts and of the liturgical traditions (the saints venerated, the special offices) with which he was familiar.

The case of the motet *Firmissime fidem*, on the other hand, is unique. Here the concept of "local usage" is clearly incomplete, for we have no direct evidence other than the existence of the *Alleluia Benedictus es* as the tenor of the motet. That is, we are unsure of the composer of the piece, and the main source for the work, the *Roman de Fauvel*, is a secular manuscript with no connection to a church and whose beginnings, although undoubtedly in Paris, are nebulous at best. In leaning exceptionally heavily on the witness of the reading of the alleluia in the tenor, therefore, we must weigh our conclusions with particular care.

In fact, the precise nature of the correlation between local chant readings and late medieval polyphony has not been fully explained. A thorough examination would require detailed study of the link between written evidence and oral production in late medieval chant,[19] an inquiry that would differ from but probably complement the work done by Leo Treitler and others on the earliest notated sources. While it is beyond the scope of this essay to conduct such a study here, a few remarks are appropriate.

We know that medieval composers often select the tenors of their polyphonic compositions from the plainchants of particular houses. Common sense tells us that a musician who grew up in a certain tradition learned the music of his church.[20] His musical experience would have differed had he been raised elsewhere, and indeed, if his later wanderings took him to another establishment, he familiarized himself with the music of that place. Scholars have long recognized parochialisms in the plainchant repertories of the large geographical regions of Europe: the Celtic tradition differs from the Mozarabic one, and both are distinguishable from the Milanese rite, and so forth. What we do not command to any significant degree, however, is the phenomenon that exists at the micro-level of the medieval city, the individual town, the isolated church.

Here, too, ecclesiastical melodies were place-specific, and so oftentimes were the tenors that were drawn more or less precisely from these local tunes. The large number of similar forms that the tenor of the Trinity motet could have taken, therefore, is quite astonishing, even discounting entirely the possibility of deliberate melodic alteration by the composer. This melodic diversity is only hinted at in the different versions of the *Alleluia Benedictus es* found in Example 3.2.

What is noteworthy here is that to a medieval musician, the alleluia was a specific melody, born of a specific place. This specificity was realized in at least two ways. First, in the teaching and singing of the alleluia on an almost daily basis within the oral tradition, we must assume that mistakes in performance could be noted and corrected with reference to the prototypical version of the alleluia used by a particular church. And second, when a medieval musician encountered a version of the tune from another place, that tune would sound either "less correct" or "different," just as the errant versions produced in daily practice sounded less correct or different from the local prototype. The art of memory in the Middle Ages held in reverence both verbatim memory (*memoria ad verba*) and approximate or "gist" memory (*memoria ad res*).[21] The training that a church musician received certainly aimed at *memoria ad verba* in terms of the music of the institution that was his host, though this was probably rarely achieved due to fluctuations that resulted from the reproduction of chants through techniques of oral composition. This desideratum is evident in descriptions of singers' duties, which invariably call for attention to the music of the church in question.

Our privileged view as music historians, on the other hand, is somewhat skewed, for we are unavoidably swayed by the standardized melodies that were propagated beginning with the Council of Trent and the rise of the print culture. Hence our prototype of this same *Alleluia Benedictus es* is formed more through *memoria ad res*. That is, we might hear this chant as a sort of amalgam of readings, something akin to the version in the *Liber usualis*.[22] We lack that inculcated sense of the local melody—the sense that there is *a* local prototype for a tune—which would allow us to judge potential versions of the melody as correct or incorrect, the same or different. We acquire that sense artifically by singing or looking at a number of versions of the tune.[23]

In addition to studying comparative readings, how can we bridge the gap? Since the element of geography is inherent in the problem, we might examine folk song repertories for some models. For the ethnomusicologist, distinctive regional variants in folk songs are remarkably persistent and tend to define a style, even when that style is transplanted to another region. Some variants may be only vaguely characteristic of a region, while others are what a scholar of Scottish folk music has called "thumbprints," or "brief but unmistakable melodic turns."[24] We do have some sense of the "thumbprints" that distinguish the large historical groupings of western chant—the triadic gestures presumed to be indicators of Gallican chant, for instance.[25] But these sorts of bold, telltale signs do not differentiate the readings of a single chant in numerous locales. Here the variants are minor, not major, and hence we need a finer-toothed comb to retrieve them.

In this sense, the multiple, yet very similar forms of a given chant in the later Middle Ages are somewhat akin to the ethnomusicologists' concept of the "tune family," as first forged by Samuel Bayard and later refined by James Cowdery in their studies of British and Irish traditions.[26] Bayard defines the "tune family" as "a group of melodies showing basic interrelation by means of constant melodic correspondences and presumably owing their mutual likeness to descent from a single air that has assumed multiple forms through processes of variation, imitation, and assimilation." Cowdery enhances this idea to ac-

EXAMPLE 3.2   Tenor of *Firmissime fidem*, compared with French readings of *Alleluia Benedictus es*

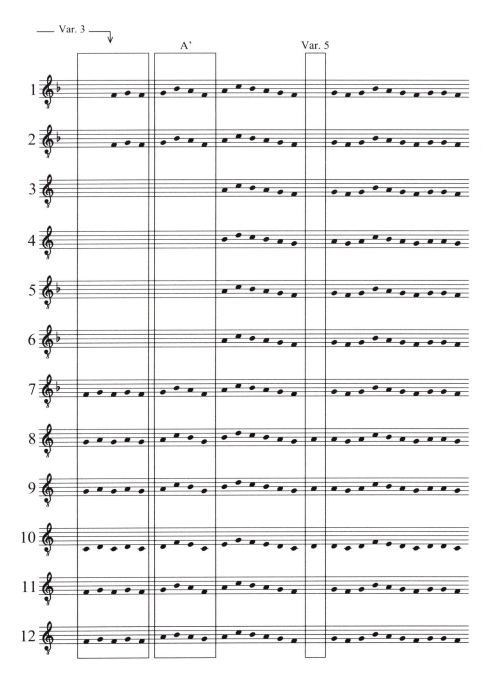

EXAMPLE 3.2 *(continued)*

61

count for similarities of formula as well as contour. This work shows that the study of variant forms tells much more about classification of this or that version of a melody, indeed about oral transmission itself, than about the "original" tune.[27] If there ever was an *Urmelodie* for a given folk tune, we shall never recover it, and it is irrelevant to try to do so.

The methodology for establishing a tune family, then, may be a promising line of investigation in the study of late medieval chant, for "this or that version of the melody" is exactly what we are after. In order to suggest the connection of the *Alleluia Benedictus es* with a specific place, we need to hear not the one *Liber usualis* version of the alleluia, but rather the many local readings preserved in late medieval sources. This we can do best through study of the individual melodies. And if it appears from such comparisons that the alleluia found in the tenor of *Firmissime fidem* was not altered, we may have a trustworthy line of evidence that could enable us to say something about its origin and perhaps that of the motet as well. This is the situation that presents itself in the case of the Trinity motet.

The *Alleluia Benedictus es* is an especially apt vehicle for comparison. Because it comes from the older layer,[28] this alleluia occurs in almost every manuscript that contains music either for the feast or the votive Mass of Trinity. Quite often the alleluia appears in both formularies within one and the same source. And since exemplars for music of the Mass have survived in greater numbers than those of the Office, it is possible to construct a compelling list of readings of this chant from northeastern France. The present study uses 70 different versions of the alleluia, taken from the thirteenth- and fourteenth-century manuscripts listed in Table 3.3.[29]

Example 3.2 shows an array of differences in the first section of the alleluia. The readings are clearly linked, however, through Cowdery's "conjoining" principle, according to which the nearly identical second halves of the tunes are joined with the first parts, which vary considerably after the opening gesture.[30] The chant is written on three different finals (*f*, *g*, *c*; see also Table 3.3) and displays other variants at the level of detail.[31] Since the *Roman de Fauvel* was put together in Paris, our first inclination is to seize on one of the Parisian readings as the model for the motet tenor. Apparently relying on the Parisian Dominican reading in GB:Lbm, Add. 23935 (Example 3.2, line 4), Daniel Leech-Wilkinson writes: "the original G-mode chant which provided the *color* for *Firmissime/Adesto* is transposed by de Vitry to *f*."[32] His assumption that transposition has occurred is premature, however, for Example 3.2 and Table 3.3 show that the Parisian versions of the *Alleluia Benedictus es* include both *f*- and *g*-mode readings. Indeed the version on *f* appears in sources not only from Notre Dame but also from the Left-Bank churches of Saint-Germain-des-Prés and Saint-Victor. The *g*-mode reading is found in books from the abbeys of Sainte-Geneviève and Saint-Denis, and in the Dominican reading in GB:Lbm, Add. 23935. And so, although we must bear in mind the fluidity of these notated witnesses, it seems that the selection and possible manipulation of our tenor might not have involved transposition at all, for the reading on *f* is both available in Paris and prevalent in the rest of northern France.

TABLE 3.3 Manuscript sources consulted for *Alleluia Benedictus es*

Manuscript	Genre	Date	Use	Chant Final
B:Br II 3824	gradual	13, mid	Dijon, St-Bénigne, f. 136–136ᵛ	f
3824	gradual	13, mid	Dijon, St-Bénigne, f. 137	f
19389	missal	13	St-Martin de Quesnat, Brabant	g
F:AB 7	missal	13/14	Noyon	g
F:AS 437	gradual	13	Arras, St-Vaast	f
444	missal	13, end	Arras, St-Vaast	f
F:DOU 113	gradual	14–15	Marchiennes (NE France)	f
F:LG 2 (17)	gradual	14	?Fontevrault (near Tours)	g
F:Lille 26	cantatorium/antiphoner	14	Lille, St-Pierre	c
F:LM 437	missal	14/1	Le Mans	g
F:Pa 110	gradual	14	Paris	f
135	missal	13/2	London or Canterbury, f. 118	f
135	missal	13/2	London or Canterbury, f. 224	f
197	gradual	13, end	Paris, St-Victor	f
279	breviary/polyphony	13	Bayeux, use of St-Sépulchre, Caen	f
595	missal/breviary	13–14	Châlons-sur-Marne	f
F:Pm 405	missal	13/1	Meaux, St-Faron	f
411 (241)	missal	ca. 1380	Paris, Notre-Dame	f
F:Pn, lat. 830	missal	13/2	Paris, St-Germain l'Auxerrois, f. 161	f
830	missal	13/2	Paris, St-Germain l'Auxerrois, f. 162	f
842	missal	1325	Châlons-sur-Marne	f
845	missal	14/2	Châlons-sur-Marne	f
861	missal	14/1	Paris	f
906	gradual	15	Amiens	f
907	gradual	16	Le Mans	f
1105	missal	1265–72	Bec, f. 109	f
1105	missal	1265–72	Bec, f. 208	f

(continued)

TABLE 3.3 (*continued*)

Manuscript	Genre	Date	Use	Chant Final
F:Pn, lat. (continued)				
1107	missal	1259–75	Paris, St-Denis	g
1112	missal	ca. 1225	Paris	f
1337	gradual	13–14	Paris	f
10502	missal	13	Sens	g
10503	gradual	14	Franciscan	g
10505	missal	14	Paris, St-Denis	g
13255	gradual	13, end	Paris, Cluniac	f
14452	gradual	13	Paris, St-Victor, f. 62ᵛ	f
14452	gradual	13	Paris, St-Victor, f. 63ᵛ	f
16823	missal	13	Compiègne, St-Corneille, f. 103ᵛ	g
16823	missal	13	Compiègne, St-Corneille, f. 104ᵛ	g
16828	gradual	14	Compiègne, St-Corneille	g
17310	missal	13–14	Chartres	f
17311	missal	14/1	Cambrai	f
17312	missal	13/1	Auxerre	c
17329	gradual	13	Compiègne, St-Corneille	c
F:Pn, n.a.l. 1413	gradual	1244	Chiaravalle, Lombardy	g
1773	missal	13	Evreux	f
F:Provins 11	missal	13	Sens	g
F:Psg 93	missal	13/1	Paris	f
99	missal/gradual	?13/?14	Senlis	f
1259	missal	13/1	Paris, Ste-Geneviève, f. 134	f
1259	missal	13/1	Paris, Ste-Geneviève, f. 250–250ᵛ	f

F:R(m) 250 (A. 233)	gradual	Jumièges	14	g
277 (Y. 50)	missal	Rouen, cathedral	ca. 1245	c
F:RSc 221	missal	Reims	12	g
224	missal	Reims, cathedral	14/2	g
264	gradual	Reims, St-Thierry	13	g
266	gradual	Reims, St-Denis	15	g
F:Sens 16	gradual	Sens	13–14	g
F:Vendôme 221 bis	gradual	Vendôme, Trinité	14, early	c
F:VN 98	missal	Verdun	14, early	g
759	missal	Verdun, St-Vanne	13/1	c
GB:Cfm 369	missal/breviary	Lewes	13	g
GB:Lbm 2.B.IV.	gradual	St Albans?	13	f
Add. 16905	missal	Paris, Notre-Dame	14	f
Add. 23935	Dominican liturgy	Paris, Dominican	ca. 1260	g
Eger. 3759	gradual	Crowland Abbey, Lincolnshire	13	f
GB:Mr 24	missal	Exeter, Sarum use	13/2	f
GB:Ob lat. lit. b. 5	gradual	York	15	g
I:Fl Plu.29.1	polyphony	Paris	1240s	f
I:Rvat, Reg. lat. 2049	missal	Franciscan	13	g
US:BAw 302	gradual	Paris	1415–20	f

If the motet tenor was not transposed, did the composer alter the *Alleluia Benedictus es* from which he derived it? Certainly he did if he modeled the tenor on a Parisian exemplar. Sources from Paris preserve almost exactly the same melody (ll. 4–7), the most common difference here being the presence or absence of the repeated segment A', along with the auxiliary figure (Var. 3) that precedes it. Two manuscripts from Paris contain the second A' (l. 7), five do not (ll. 4–6). In virtually all other respects the Parisian readings agree among themselves. Exact repetition of material, then, seems not to be as important in distinguishing between churches as other kinds of melodic difference. Reasons for this are easy to conjure up: certainly the most common error in written sources is the tendency of scribes to skip over short, repeated motives. More significant are variants that modify the melody in other ways.

Examples of small yet consequential melodic differences not due to repetition are evident in the manuscripts from Saint-Denis and Saint-Corneille-de-Compiègne (ll. 8–10), which vary mildly from the other Parisian sources (ll. 4–7). Not only do the readings from Saint-Denis and Saint-Corneille write the melody on *g* or *c*, but the missing note at Variant 4 and the added pitch at Variant 5 are consistent in both houses. The importance of these variants increases when we realize that they are preserved in several books over time: six manuscripts dating from the thirteenth and fourteenth centuries. On the one hand, these deviations establish the distinctiveness of the music of Saint-Denis and Saint-Corneille compared with Parisian sources, and on the other they bespeak the ties that existed between Saint-Denis and Saint-Corneille.[33] In sum, it should come as no surprise that the place to look for matching readings of the *Alleluia Benedictus es* is within the sources of a single church or in books of demonstrably linked churches.

To return to the Parisian versions (ll. 4–8): if the choice of an *f*-mode reading for the motet tenor is not at odds with the standard Parisian reading, the actual pitches are. Variant 1 shows a single *g* in the motet tenor, whereas Parisian (and virtually all other) sources have two *g*s at this spot. At Variant 2, the *g* that fills in the drop of a third from *a* down to *f* is omitted from the tenor, whereas most manuscripts fill in the third. While Variant 2 is minor, Variant 1 is significant, since none of the 70 sources surveyed, with the exception of those in lines 2 and 3 (to be discussed shortly), preserve the reading of the tenor.

The discrepancies that remain are even more telling. Variant 3, as noted, is a repeated *f*–*g* auxiliary figure of differing lengths that appears in practically all readings, but which is significantly shorter in the motet tenor. "Motive" A is a descending fourth that occurs in none of the Parisian books. Only with the arrival of the aforementioned segment A', an incompletely filled-in descending fourth, does Paris begin to agree with the motet tenor, but even here the differences in the length of the auxiliary figure (Var. 3) stand out. Variant 3 and "Motive" A thus determine the fluctuations in contour as well as length of the various readings of the *Alleluia Benedictus es*, and for this reason, the motet tenor, to one who was familiar with the Parisian dialect of this melody, probably sounded unusual.

In view of these differences, did the composer modify a Parisian melody to arrive at the version found in the motet? Previous studies of other motets of Vitry argue against this, for where a plausible source for the tenor exists, the "alterations" to the original chant involve the omission of only one or two notes, usually repeated or passing pitches.[34] No instances of wholesale composition, such as the insertion of segment A into a Parisian reading to create our motet tenor, have been found in Vitry's other works. Indeed, such extensive remodeling is rare in the tenors of thirteenth- and fourteenth-century polyphony. That is, normally the tenor is either quite close to a putative model, or it is paraphrased to the point that it bears little resemblance at all to the chant. The inescapable conclusion is that we need to seek a different source for our motet tenor. As it happens, the twists and turns that must be performed to make this melody conform to a Parisian reading are entirely unnecessary.

The *Alleluia Benedictus es* in Arras and Cambrai

The reason, of course, is that there is a perfect match for the motet tenor in the manuscripts from Arras (Example 3.2, l. 2). What is more, not one, but two chants from the city corroborate the motet tenor, and the independent reading from nearby Cambrai (l. 3) confirms most of the details. The similarities between the versions from Arras and Cambrai and the contrast with readings from other places demonstrate that the unique aspects of the tenor of *Firmissime fidem* were particular to this region of northern France.

The Cambrai reading illustrates particularly well the difference between essential and nonessential variants. Cambrai agrees with the motet tenor at Variants 1 and 2, and it differs only slightly at Variant 3 (the extra *g–f* prior to segment A) and in the omission of the second A'. While this latter discrepancy would appear to loom large, it is probably negligible, for reasons mentioned above in the description of the presence or absence of this very repetition in the seven manuscripts from Notre Dame of Paris. Since the Arras and Cambrai readings align so closely, we will postpone for the moment deciding which of these two places may prove to be the origin of our tenor. Other factors will cause us to prefer one city over the other.

It is understandable that the readings from Arras and Cambrai should be similar. The ecclesiastical relationship between the two cities dates from earliest times, and musical and liturgical connections between them abound.[35] A single bishop residing in Cambrai ruled both dioceses until the end of the eleventh century. David Hiley has shown that the two cities hold a large percentage of items of the ordinary of the Mass in common,[36] and the monks of Solesmes point to some common links between Arras and Cambrai in the oldest, neumatically notated layer of the gradual.[37]

The best explanation for the origin of the tenor of the Trinity motet so far, then, is that it came from Artois or the Cambrésis. But there is one other factor that bears on the question: the readings that match the motet tenor exactly (Example 3.2, l. 2) are from the Abbey of Saint-Vaast. No musical source from the cathedral of Arras has come down to us, and this lacuna prevents us from assuring ourselves that the reading from Saint-Vaast would have agreed with that from the cathedral. It does not, however, hinder the discovery that the *Alleluia Benedictus es* was in fact used there. Five unnotated missals from the cathedral from the thirteenth to fifteenth centuries all confirm its presence in the liturgy of Trinity Sunday.[38] And since the monastery of Saint-Vaast was named for and held the relics of the first bishop of Arras, it is reasonable to believe that a musical reading from the monastery would resemble a missing one from the cathedral. Moreover there exists the very similar reading from Cambrai, which had a close liturgical affiliation with Arras cathedral. The weight of the evidence thus strongly suggests that the melody for the *Alleluia Benedictus es* that is recorded elsewhere in the city at Saint-Vaast, and in neighboring Cambrai, is a reliable witness of the tune that was sung in the cathedral. In any case, we will see further on that the Abbey of Saint-Vaast plays a significant role in this nexus of Arras–Cambrai associations with our tenor.

Since the tenor hails from one of these two cities, the next question is what the connection with the motet itself might be. There seem to be two possibilities here: either the work was originally written for an institution in Arras or Cambrai and then was reused in the *Roman de Fauvel*, or it was composed expressly for *Fauvel*, drawing on a tenor from one of these northern towns. For now we will explore the former possibility. What immediately comes to mind is the intriguing notion that the city of Cambrai does in fact provide a famous venue for a work for the Trinity. The axial chapel of Notre Dame cathedral, which enjoyed a distinguished history in the fifteenth century, was dedicated to the Trinity. Here it was that the *petits vicaires* and choirboys sang a daily Mass after Matins. And, following the addition of a portrait of Notre Dame de Grâce to this oratory, Guillaume Dufay's Marian Masses and motets were sung around the altar on a routine basis.[39]

This record of musical performances in the Trinity chapel in the fifteenth century raises our curiosity about the level of activity there at the time of the composition of the Trinity motet in the early fourteenth century. Through Barbara Haggh's research into the endowments for this altar, we learn that Michel, canon and archdeacon of Hainaut, founded two chaplaincies and arranged for his burial there in 1240. Around 1280, archdeacon of Brabant Gerard de Pes added a third chaplaincy along with a weekly Mass. The fifth chaplaincy was also founded in the thirteenth century. More important, perhaps, was the establishment of nine *petites prébendes* in this chapel at the end of the thirteenth century.[40] These foundations, although not specific about the performance of music at the turn of the century, at least suggest a level of interest that might have inspired the composition of a motet and provided for its execution here, perhaps through an endowment.

The Trinity chapel in Cambrai cathedral thus offers a plausible site for the performance of the motet. But as close as the Cambrai reading of the *Alleluia Benedictus es* is to that of our tenor, the version from Arras is an exact match. And, as it happens, similar circumstantial possibilities for the use of the work existed at Arras as well. The original cathedral of Arras, once located in the *cité*, was destroyed during the French Revolution. As in Cambrai, the axial chapel in the chevet at Arras was dedicated to the Trinity.[41] The few documents remaining from the church point to the same type of foundations at the votive altars as are found in many other churches.[42] The liturgy and architecture of the cathedral of Arras itself, then, may provide a rationale for the composition of a motet dedicated to the Trinity and based on a chant from the repertory of this church.

But what are we to make of this? Arras was an important musical center in the Middle Ages, its renown in the thirteenth and fourteenth centuries stemming mostly from the cultivation of secular music, in particular that of one of its famous citizens, Adam de la Halle.[43] The Confrèrie des Jongleurs et des Bourgeois d'Arras arose in the thirteenth century in response to a miracle said to have occurred in the cathedral, and the list of its members includes Adam, along with a number of other trouvère poets and composers.[44] The roster does not name Philippe de Vitry, however. If the Trinity motet was his creation, did he in fact write it for the cathedral? Or does the use of a tenor from Arras suggest something else?

In view of the almost total loss of records, we will probably never know what the connection of the work with the cathedral might have been. But the identity of the motet tenor with the reading of the *Alleluia Benedictus es* from Arras is compelling, and so we must press the issue of what the use of the Arras tune means. There is a possible answer here. Recent research has shown that Vitry was resident in Paris in the second decade of the fourteenth century, at the time F:Pn, fr. 146 (*Fauvel*), the earliest source for the motet, was put together.[45] Might the Arras reading of the motet tenor suggest not his whereabouts at the time of composition of the work, but rather an erstwhile connection with that city? The likelihood of this explanation increases dramatically when we realize that a town called "Vitry" lies only a few kilometers to the east of Arras.

The Town of Vitry-en-Artois, near Arras

As fortunate as we are to know the precise date of Philippe de Vitry's birth (31 October 1291),[46] we have surprisingly little to go on concerning where he was born. The reason is simple: there are some fourteen towns named "Vitry" in France, and all but one of them existed in the fourteenth century (Table 3.4). Both contemporaries and later writers disagree on his *ville natale*. Poet Eustache Deschamps (ca. 1346–ca. 1406) lists Vitry among the illustrious musicians from the region of Champagne, no doubt believing that he hailed from Vitry-en-Perthois near Reims, now known as Vitry-le-François.[47] Fétis, on the other hand, points to the region around Arras, suggesting that "the name of Philippe de Vitry was given to him because of his birthplace, for *Vitriacum* is the Latin name of the little city of Vitry, in the department of the Pas-de-Calais."[48]

Fétis notwithstanding, a study of the various Latin and French renditions of "Vitry" (*Victoriacum*, *Vitriacum*, *Vittri*, etc.) yields little, since almost all

TABLE 3.4   Medieval towns named Vitry in France

Town	Department	Archdiocese
Vitry-en-Artois	Pas-de-Calais	Reims
Vitry-en-Charollais	Saône-et-Loire	Sens
Vitry-lès-Cluny	Saône-et-Loire	Sens
Vitry-le-Croisé	Saône-et-Loire	Sens
Vitry-Laché	Nièvre	Bourges
Vitry-aux-Loges	Loiret	Sens
Vitry-sur-Loire	Saône-et-Loire	Sens
Vitry-en-Montagne	Haute Marne	Lyon
Vitry-lès-Nogent	Haute Marne	Lyon
Vitry-sur-Orne	Moselle	Trèves
Vitry-en-Perthois	Marne	Reims
Vitry-sur-Seine	Val de Marne	Sens
Vitry-la-Ville	Marne	Reims

SOURCE: Compiled from Ernest Nègre, *Typonymie générale de la France*, 3 vols., Publications romanes et françaises 193 (Geneva: Droz, 1990), 594–95, 1688.

the towns with this name preserve the same spellings, which likewise appear in contemporaneous documents that record the composer's name (most often Philippus de Vitriaco). Nor can the prominence of a given town be a factor. Of the 13 medieval towns named Vitry, the most important were the aforementioned Vitry-en-Artois near Arras, Vitry-en-Perthois near Reims and Châlons-sur-Marne, and Vitry-sur-Seine on the southeastern edge of Paris. But the remaining 10 towns cannot be discounted simply because they were smaller than these three; hence, we must find other ways to narrow the list.

If Philippe de Vitry's whereabouts in his early years are difficult to pinpoint, his peregrinations from about age 30 on are somewhat easier to follow. Although best known as bishop of Meaux, Vitry assumed this post only in 1351, toward the end of this life. Prior to this, he held numerous other positions, ecclesiastical as well as secular. The former are documented beginning in 1323: while in possession of a canonry at Notre Dame of Clermont in the diocese of Beauvais, Vitry was notified of his future accession to prebends at Verdun, Soissons, and Saint Géry in Cambrai. By 1332, he had added to these posts other benefices at Saint-Pierre-en-Aire, Soissons, Verdun, Saint-Quentin, Clermont, and Vertus.[49] Notably, what these places have in common is their location in the archdiocese of Reims (see Table 3.4), with the exception of Verdun, which lies in the archdiocese of Trèves. This suggests that Vitry's career, like that of so many fifteenth-century composers, centered around a birthplace in the ecclesiastical province of Reims.[50] Of our 13 towns named Vitry, only Vitry-en-Artois, Vitry-en-Perthois and Vitry-la-Ville lay within these boundaries. And we can eliminate Vitry-la-Ville because its Latin spelling, unlike that of all the other Vitrys, includes the word "villa" (*Vitriacum Villa, Vitreivilla*, etc.).[51] This leaves us to examine the two cities that are therefore the likeliest prospects for Vitry's birthplace: Vitry-en-Artois in the diocese of Arras, and Vitry-en-Perthois in the diocese of Châlons-sur-Marne.[52]

Clearly the musical evidence strongly favors Vitry-en-Artois over Vitry-en-Perthois (Example 3.2, ll. 2, 11, 12). The Châlons version of the alleluia resembles the one from Paris, and it contains none of the variants that distinguish the Arras/Cambrai reading. In Arras, and only there, do these variants find a match in sources from a plausible birthplace for our composer, Vitry-en-Artois.

To summarize, the Vitry near Arras in the Pas-de-Calais is very possibly Philippe's birthplace (1) because of its proximity to Vitry's later ecclesiastical holdings in Cambrai and Saint-Pierre-en-Aire, and (2) because it is the place of origin of the tenor of the motet *Firmissime fidem/Adesto sancta trinitas/ Alleluia Benedictus es.* And yet, we still cannot entirely rule out the Vitry near Châlons. Two factors point to this town: (1) Deschamps claimed that Vitry was from this area, as we have just seen, and (2) Vitry's benefice in Vertus lies in what could be his home diocese of Châlons. There is reason to doubt Deschamps's opinion, however, for he may have been misled by the one mention Vitry makes of the Champagne region in *Le Chapel des trois Fleurs de Lis:* "Les beaulx lis, couches champenoises / Les bons vins et les froides caves."[53] Surely the vineyards of the Champagne region were known to persons not born there. Perhaps more telling, Deschamps was a *champenois* himself, and he may well have tried to make a partisan claim to Vitry, as he does to another musician, Guillaume de Machaut, who did come from this region. If Deschamps was mistaken, it would hardly be the first time the identity or place of birth of a famous person was incorrectly reported in the Middle Ages.[54]

The composer's use of the Arras version of the *Alleluia Benedictus es* takes on added significance, moreover, when we realize that the motet *Firmissime fidem* is early in his output, having been composed probably no later than 1316. Vitry, who would have been only 25 years old at this time, would have used either a Parisian tune or one that he had learned early in his life, before coming to Paris. We now know that the melody is not Parisian. And so, whereas the choice of a chant from Arras makes sense if Vitry was raised in this city, it is difficult to explain how a composer from Châlons in the Champagne region would have known this tune prior to holding any benefices in the area of Arras or Cambrai. In fact, one is tempted to say that if the Vitry in Champagne proves to be Vitry's birthplace, then the attribution of the motet— or at least of the tenor—to him is severely weakened. Arras, then, is a stronger contender than Châlons, both for reasons given so far and for others that follow.

Evangelized in the fourth century by Saint Martin, Vitry-en-Artois grew up around a church that was dedicated to this saint. The town lay within the jurisdiction of the bishop of neighboring Arras,[55] and the few documents that remain from Notre Dame of Arras show extensive interaction of citizens of Vitry with the mother church. One "Hugo de Viteriaco" signs a number of acts of the cathedral chapter between 1209 and 1219,[56] and others from Vitry are involved with the chapter in similar capacities throughout the thirteenth and fourteenth centuries. While it is impossible to know if one of these persons might have been related to Philippe, it is clear that the lines of communication between Vitry and Arras were open around the time of his birth at the end of the thirteenth century.

If Philippe de Vitry originated in Vitry-en-Artois, his association with the Cathedral of Arras or with the Abbey of Saint-Vaast would, moreover, have provided him with a means of coming to Paris shortly after 1300. Like several other cities in France, Arras promoted some of its youth through the foundation of a school in Paris in the early years of the fourteenth century. Such *collèges* in the Middle Ages were residence halls for poor students; they were not actively used for teaching until the fifteenth century.[57] The Collège de bons enfans d'Arras à Paris was supported in part through the sale or purchase of land and commodities,[58] including transactions with persons not only from Arras but also from surrounding cities, including Vitry, which actively subsidized the school.[59] Originally located in Paris in the clos Bruno, the Collège d'Arras was transferred in the fourteenth century to the rue Saint-Victor across from the Séminaire des Bons-Enfants.[60] Here each student had 25 écus, a room, a bed, and a chair. A monk from Saint-Vaast, a secular priest, and sometimes even a lay person named by the abbot ran the house. The *collège* lasted until 1764, when it merged with the Collège Louis-le-Grand. Significantly, when the school was established, Philippe de Vitry was in his teens.

Virtually no records from the *collège* have survived,[61] and thus we cannot know whether or not Vitry found his way to Paris under the auspices of this school. But the tenor of the Trinity motet now looms larger than ever, for it could certainly reflect Vitry's early training in his native Artois. More importantly perhaps, if he was a student at the Collège d'Arras, he may have remained in contact with the liturgy of his native city if the services in the school were carried out according to the use of Saint-Vaast.[62] And herein may lie the most direct explanation for the origin of the motet tenor.

Once in Paris, Vitry probably completed his education.[63] His genius seems to have been recognized at an early date, for although only in his mid-20s, he gained entrance to the circles that collaborated on Chaillou de Pesstain's edition of the *Roman de Fauvel* (F:Pn, fr. 146). Of the pieces in this manuscript attributed to Vitry, only the Trinity motet and one other have non-Parisian tenors. We will explore why this may have been the case in the final section.

The Attribution of the Motet and the Arras Connection

Having offered this explanation for the origin of the tenor of *Firmissime fidem*, let us return to the question of the authorship of the motet. Is the traditional attribution to Vitry strengthened by the discovery of the origin of the tenor? As we noted earlier, the ascription to the composer rests on the citation of the piece in the *Ars nova* treatises, writings that are somehow connected with Vitry and his circle but were not actually produced by him. The piece is one of the most advanced motets in the *Roman de Fauvel*, and it includes, as we have

shown, a very early example of diminution. The consensus on the work therefore has been: who else but Vitry could have composed a piece of this sophistication in the middle of the second decade of the fourteenth century? The lack
of anything firmer to go on explains the tentativeness of this reasoning.

We should now be able to put the question on surer footing. The hypothesis would go something like this: the Trinity motet, one of the most advanced
works in the *Roman de Fauvel*, is cited in the *Ars nova* treatises as an example
of new rhythmic practices. The tenor of the piece is based on an alleluia for
the Trinity, and the distinctive variants in this alleluia are found in manuscripts
from the city of Arras. The connection of the piece both with the *Ars nova*
treatises and with Arras suggests that Philippe de Vitry wrote it for two reasons:
(1) he was intimately involved with the new notational developments that are
both discussed in these treatises and illustrated in the motet, and (2) one of the
two towns named "Vitry" that might have been his birthplace is located next
to Arras.

The new connection between the motet and Arras coincides with what is
known about music in this city and its environs. In 1350 Vitry made two
supplications to Pope Clement VI, no doubt profiting from his rise in political
and ecclesiastical circles. For his brother Adam, a canon at Saint Donatian in
Bruges, Philippe requested benefices at two churches in the diocese of Cambrai
(Saint Géry and Lobbes).[64] The second petition was on behalf of one Lambertus Pander, a cleric in the diocese of Thérouanne.[65] The fact that both of
these persons held or sought posts in the region of Arras suggests that Philippe's
influence was strong in this area.

Manuscripts containing Vitry's motets likewise support the thesis. The
polyphonic source F:CA 1328 is a miscellany of works, including ordinary
settings, chansons, and motets from the fourteenth century. Among its contents
are several motets attributed to Philippe de Vitry (although not *Firmissime fidem*),
alongside works by Adam de la Halle. Irmgard Lerch has recently assigned this
source to Cambrai cathedral.[66] If her ascription is correct, we have yet another
possible witness to the connection of Philippe de Vitry with this part of France,
as well as further evidence of the musical affinities between Arras and Cambrai.
In like fashion, three other sources of Vitry's early motets, the rotulus manuscripts B:Br 19606 (which includes *Firmissime fidem*), F:Pn, coll. Picardie 67
(*Pic*), and PL:WRu Ak 1955/KN 195 (k. 1 & 2) likewise come from Artois or Pi-
cardy.[67] Ernest Sanders notes that the Brussels and Cambrai sources "preserve
more works of which [Vitry] is very probably the composer than does any other
manuscript."[68] Did the proliferation of his works in this area of northern France
occur in part because of the locals' pride in their favorite son?[69]

And finally, one of the so-called musicians' motets, *Musicalis scientie/*
Sciencie laudabilis/Tenor, contains a list of fourteenth-century musicians in the
generation following Vitry. A number of these composers come from the area
of Arras (Guisard de Cambrai, Jacques d'Arras, Reginald de Bailleul, Thomas
de Douai, Volquier de Valenciennes), and theorist Egidius de Murino likewise
originated in nearby Thérouanne. Leech-Wilkinson theorizes that the musicians were actual followers of Vitry,[70] and Richard Hoppin postulates the exis-

tence of a musical center in this corner of northern France.[71] In light of the findings presented here, perhaps they were also linked to Vitry by their place of origin. The thrust of all these suggestions is that the historical landscape of the motet of the thirteenth and early fourteenth centuries may need to be modified, with new emphasis given to the Arras–Cambrai–Amiens axis, and less to that of Paris–Reims.[72] The great flowering of polyphonic music along the Paris–Reims line was yet to come, in the oeuvre of Guillaume de Machaut.

A few other questions remain. If the Trinity motet was written for the *Roman de Fauvel* (F:Pn, fr. 146), why did the composer use a non-Parisian tenor? That is, if the *Roman de Fauvel* was put together in Paris, why is the tenor of *Firmissime fidem* so unlike the *Alleluia Benedictus es* from any institution in the city? There are at least two responses, as we noted earlier, and it may ultimately prove impossible to choose between them. The motet may have been composed for the Trinity chapel in Arras cathedral and then simply re-used in *Fauvel*. Although the piece certainly corresponds to the Trinitarian iconography in *Fauvel*, its texts, after all, are unrelated to the actual story; indeed, they are devotional and even possibly liturgical. The endowments for the Trinity chapel have not survived, however, and thus we cannot corroborate this interpretation.

A more speculative explanation suggests that the motet was composed expressly for *Fauvel*. The use of plainchant and of tenors based on chant in this manuscript is in fact quite special. It has long been known that the book contains both "real" and "made-up" plainsong, and Susan Rankin has recently shown that the newly composed melodies follow the typical contours of bona fide plainchants quite faithfully.[73] Not only is this the case, but there even seems to be a plan in the choice of the local versions of chants and motet tenors (including that of *Firmissime fidem*) for *Fauvel*. Either the readings are strictly Parisian, or they deviate markedly from Parisian models, and this dichotomy parallels the music given to earthly and heavenly characters, respectively, in the story.[74] The Trinity motet in this manuscript accompanies a text that serves as "a passing moment of triumph over the forces of evil"[75] and hence is provided with a non-Parisian tenor. For this reason, the motet might have been intended specifically for F:Pn, fr. 146, rather than having been imported from another venue.

With this possibility in mind, then, we can propose that the young Vitry who arrived in Paris in the first or early second decade of the fourteenth century was probably a student at the Collège d'Arras, where he may have continued to sing the plainchant of Saint-Vaast of Arras, all the while familiarizing himself with the Parisian versions of these melodies through his work elsewhere in the city. When his subsequent involvement with *Fauvel* called for a motet based on a non-Parisian tenor, he easily reverted to the only other melody he knew, the one from Arras.

CLEARLY THE COMPOSER COULD HEAR the melody he used for the tenor of this motet, but can we? The tenor of *Firmissime fidem*, like other cantus firmi, serves three important purposes: it gives thematic propriety to the motet, it establishes a modal framework that is then elaborated in the upper lines, and it reveals something about its own origin. This last function is enhanced through the tenor isorhythm, and thus "hearing the tenor" is in fact an important key to this piece. The tenor pitches are quite audible in their slow motion throughout the first section, and the diminution in the second section is likewise perceptible due to the absence of jarring counterrhythms in the upper lines.[76] The beginning of the triplum, moreover, imitates the opening of the tenor (Example 3.1), emphasizing once again the distinctive Arras dialect (cf. Example 3.2, Var. 1). Certainly a trained musician of the fourteenth century would recognize this tenor as the *Alleluia Benedictus es*, and a musician schooled in the liturgy of Paris might even notice that this was not the version of the melody that he knew.

The connection of the tenor with readings from Arras on the one hand and its palpable distance from Parisian traditions on the other are all the more apparent when one realizes that an older polyphonic setting from Paris exists. The work is Leoninus's two-voice organum on the *Alleluia Benedictus es*, written for the cathedral of Notre Dame and preserved in his *Magnus Liber Organi* of the twelfth century.[77] This piece hints at its Parisian heritage in the very opening tenor notes *f–f–g–g–a* (cf. Example 3.2, ll. 4–7). In the same way, the tenor of *Firmissime fidem*, with its different pitches *f–f–g–a* (l. 1), preserves another version of the alleluia. As we continue to study these local idiosyncrasies, where they are discernible in medieval polyphony, we will comprehend more fully the subtleties of this repertory.

One final observation is in order. What we know about the biography of Philippe de Vitry suggests that he was not only a person greatly admired but also one possessed of a keen sense of his own worth. With a certain panache, he penned the date of his birth in one of his books: "In this year [1291], on the vigil of All Saints, that is the last day of October, I Philip de [Vitry] was born."[78] In the tenor of his Trinity motet, it seems, he preserved the music of his place of birth as well.

NOTES

I am grateful to Margaret Bent, Philip Bohlman, Sarah Fuller, Barbara Haggh, Daniel Leech-Wilkinson, Nancy Lorimer, Monique Meunier of the Bibliothèque Municipale of Arras, Pamela Starr, Andrew Wathey, Craig Wright, and Lawrence Zbikowski for their generous help with this article. Manuscript abbreviations used herein follow the system set forth in *The New Grove Dictionary of Music and Musicians* (London, 1980).

1. The standard biography of Vitry is Alfred Coville, "Philippe de Vitri: Notes biographiques," *Romania* 59 (1933):520–47. For some new additions, see Craig Wright, *Music and Ceremony at Notre Dame of Paris, 500–1500*, Cambridge Studies in Music (Cambridge: Cambridge University Press, 1989), 300–1; Andrew Wathey, "Musicology, Archives and Historiography," in *Musicology and Archival Research: Proceedings of the Colloquium Held at the Algemeen Rijksarchief, Brussels, 22–23 April 1993*, ed. Barbara Haggh, Frank Daelemans, and André Vanrie, Archief- en Bibliotheekwezen in België, Extranummer 46 (Brussels: Archives Générales du Royaume, 1994), 3–26; and idem, "European Politics and Musical Culture at the Court of Cyprus," in *The Cypriot-French*

Repertory of the Manuscript, Torino J. II. 9, International Musicological Congress, 20–25 March 1991 (Heidelberg, forthcoming). Daniel Leech-Wilkinson reexamines the attributions to Vitry in "The Emergence of *Ars Nova*," *Journal of Musicology* 13 (1995):285–317.

2. Andrew Wathey, for instance, has explored the widespread circulation of the motet texts traditionally attributed to Vitry in collections devoted to Petrarch's new literary movement; "The Motets of Philippe Vitry and the Fourteenth-Century Renaissance," *Early Music History* 12 (1993):119–50.

3. "A Phantom Treatise of the Fourteenth Century? The *Ars Nova*," *Journal of Musicology* 4 (1985–86):23–50.

4. On the attribution of the motet to Vitry, see the new edition of F:Pn, fr. 146 in Edward Roesner, François Avril, and Nancy Freeman Regalado, *Le Roman de Fauvel in the Edition of Mesire Chaillou de Pesstain: A Reproduction in Facsimile of the Complete Manuscript, Paris, Bibliothèque Nationale, fonds français 146* (New York: Broude Brothers, 1990), 40. The criteria commonly applied in assigning works to Vitry is explained on p. 39. The Brussels rotulus is published in facsimile edition in *Rotulus: One Conductus and Nine Motets, Early 14th Century (Brussels, Koninklijke Bibliotheek, Ms. 19606)* (Peer, Belgium: Koninklijke Bibliotheek Albert I and Alamire, 1990). There are two additional sources for the motet: the text of the triplum is preserved in D:DS 521, fol. 228, and an intabluation of the piece exists in GB:Lbm, Add. 28550.

5. See Gilbert Reaney, André Gilles, and Jean Maillard, eds., *Philippi de Vitriaco Ars Nova*, Corpus Scriptorum de Musica 8 (Rome: American Institute of Musicology, 1964), 26, 67–68. The manuscripts that name the motet are I:Rvat, Barberini 307 and F:Pn, lat. 7378A. See the commentary on these sources in Fuller, "A Phantom Treatise," 24, 26–27.

6. See Eddie Vetter, "Philippe de Vitry and the Holy Trinity: An Early Manifesto of the Ars Nova," in *Liber Amicorum Chris Maas: Essays in Musicology in Honour of Chris Maas on His 65th Anniversary*, ed. Rob Wegman and Eddie Vetter (Amsterdam: Institute of Musicology, University of Amsterdam, 1987), 4–14. His conclusion that the work "is *governed* by binary divisions" (p. 8, my emphasis) seems forced in light of the triple aspects of the work that are present.

7. *Analecta Hymnica*, ed. C. Blume (Leipzig: O. R. Reisland, 1908), 51:102–3.

8. Only the beginning of the motet is given in Example 3.1. The entire piece is edited in Leo Schrade, *Polyphonic Music of the Fourteenth Century*, 1 (Monaco: L'Oiseau-Lyre, 1956), 60–63; and in Vetter, "Philippe de Vitry," 10–14.

9. As Roesner explains, this is the standard interpretation of groups of three semibreves when the first has a downward tail; *Le Roman de Fauvel*, 33–34.

10. Coincidentally, this is even evident in Schrade's edition of the piece (see n. 8), where the first section occupies three printed pages and the second section one.

11. Edited in Arthur Piaget, "*Le Chapel des Fleurs de Lis* par Philippe de Vitri," *Romania* 27 (1898): 55–92.

12. I thank Sarah Fuller for her close reading and comments on this discussion of the numerical elements of the motet.

13. Leech-Wilkinson notes Vitry's preference for tenors written on *f* in his *Compositional Techniques in the Four-Part Isorhythmic Motets of Philippe de Vitry and His Contemporaries*, 2 vols., Outstanding Dissertations in Music from British Universities (New York and London: Garland, 1989), 1:36.

14. See the chapters by Margaret Bent and Dolores Pesce in this volume.

15. Egidius's treatise is edited in Leech-Wilkinson, *Compositional Procedures*, 1:18–20: "Primo accipe tenorem . . . et ordinabis et colorabis." See also Johannes

Boen, *Ars [Musicae]*, ed. Alberto Gallo, Corpus Scriptorum de Musica 19 (Rome: American Institute of Musicology, 1972), 29.

16. ". . . eciam tenores sequi debere naturam cantuum ecclesiasticorum; tamen aliter incipi possunt, hii quam illi similiter et finiri;" Oliver B. Ellsworth, ed., *The Berkeley Manuscript*, Greek and Latin Music Theory (Lincoln: University of Nebraska, 1984), 75, lines 11–13.

17. *Le Graduel romain, édition critique*, 2 vols. (Solesmes: Abbaye Saint-Pierre de Solesmes, 1957). For an overview of the question of the use of local traditions, including local chants, in musicological scholarship of the last 40-odd years, see Mary Jennifer Bloxam, "A Survey of Late Medieval Service Books from the Low Countries: Implications for Sacred Polyphony, 1460–1520" (Ph.D. diss., Yale University, 1987), 1–7.

18. The list would include David Hiley, "Further Observations on W1: The Ordinary of Mass Chants and the Sequences," *Journal of the Plainsong and Mediaeval Music Society* 4 (1981); Wright, *Music and Ceremony at Notre Dame*, 81–96, 243–67, and passim; Bloxam, "In Praise of Spurious Saints: The *Missae Floruit Egregiis* by Pipelare and La Rue," *Journal of the American Musicological Society* 44 (1991): 163–220; ead., "A Survey of Late Medieval Service Books"; Glenn Pierr Johnson, "Aspects of Late Medieval Music at the Cathedral of Amiens" (Ph.D. diss., Yale University, 1991), chaps. 5 and 6; and in the volume *Plainsong in the Age of Polyphony*, ed. Thomas Forrest Kelly, Cambridge Studies in Performance Practice 2 (Cambridge: Cambridge University Press, 1991): Bloxam, "Sacred Polyphony and Local Traditions of Liturgy and Plainsong: Reflections on Music by Jacob Obrecht," 140–77; and my article, "The Mass of Guillaume de Machaut in the Cathedral of Reims," 100–39.

19. For an attempt within the Benedicamus Domino repertory, see my *"Benedicamus Domino: The Unwritten Tradition,"* *Journal of the American Musicological Society* 40 (1988): 1–62.

20. Examples of this process are to be found in almost every medieval customary and ordinary. For a few indications, see Bloxam, "Sacred Polyphony," 142, nn. 7, 8.

21. See Mary J. Carruthers, *The Book of Memory: A Study of Memory in Medieval Culture* (Cambridge: Cambridge University Press, 1990), 86–89.

22. Page 911. This reading closely resembles the ones from Paris found in Example 3.2 (ll. 4–7).

23. For a discussion of the concepts of categorization and prototype and their effects on music cognition, see Lawrence Michael Zbikowski, "Large-Scale Rhythm and Systems of Grouping" (Ph.D. diss., Yale University, 1991), 70–89.

24. Francis Collinson, *Traditional and National Music of Scotland* (London: Routledge and Kegan Paul, 1966), 23–24; cited in Anne Dhu Shapiro, "Regional Song Styles: The Scottish Connection," in *Music and Context: Essays for John M. Ward*, ed. Anne Dhu Shapiro (Cambridge, Mass.: Harvard University Press, 1985), 404–17.

25. See Michel Huglo, "Gallican rite, music of the," *The New Grove Dictionary of Music and Musicians* 20 vols., ed. Stanley Sadie (London: Macmillan, 1980), 7:117.

26. Bayard, "Aspects of Melodic Kinship and Variation in British-American Folk Tunes," *Papers Read at the International Congress of Musicology, 1939*, ed. Arthur Mendel, Gustave Reese, and Gilbert Chase, (New York: Music Educators National Conference for the American Musicological Society, 1944), 122–30; Cowdery, "A Fresh Look at the Concept of Tune Family," *Ethnomusicology* 28 (1984): 495–504.

27. See Anne Dhu Shapiro, "Black Sacred Song and the Tune-Family Concept," in *New Perspectives on Music: Essays in Honor of Eileen Southern*, ed. Josephine Wright with Samuel A. Floyd Jr., Detroit Monographs in Musicology, Studies in Music 11 (Detroit: Harmonie Park Press, 1992), 101–2.

28. See Karl-Heinz Schlager, *Thematischer Katalog der ältesten Alleluia-Melodien aus Handschriften des 10. und 11. Jahrhunderts, ausgenommen das ambrosianische, alt-römische und alt-spanische Repertoire*, Erlanger Arbeiten zur Musikwissenschaft 2 (Munich: W. Ricke, 1965), 208–9 (melody no. 302). Schlager's source for the alleluia, a Cluniac gradual from the early twelfth century (B:Br II 3823, fol. 90), writes the tune on *g*, but he notes that the melody also exists on *f*.

29. In the interests of space it was impossible to present all 70 readings in Example 3.2, and I have limited the numbers to those discussed in this article, that is, the versions from Arras, Cambrai, Paris, Saint-Denis, Saint-Corneille, and Châlons-sur-Marne. Identical readings are combined where possible, so that 19 melodies are represented. This type of comparative work will undoubtedly be aided as more volumes of the very useful CANTUS-Index series are released.

30. "A Fresh Look," 497–98.

31. In F:RSc 264 (fol. 23ᵛ, manuscript listed in the Table 3.3) the alleluia seems to be written on *e*, but this is clearly a clef error. The melody should be read on *g*.

32. *Compositional Techniques*, 1:36 (n. 42). He does not cite GB:Lbm, Add. 23935 in this spot, but rather on the previous page.

33. Not surprisingly, the identity of the readings from Saint-Denis and Saint-Corneille is explained by the fact that the abbey of Saint-Corneille drew its entire liturgy from Saint-Denis in the twelfth century. On the liturgical affinities between these two houses, see my study *The Service-Books of the Royal Abbey of Saint-Denis: Images of Ritual and Music in the Middle Ages*, Oxford Monographs on Music (Oxford: Clarendon Press, 1991), 48, 104, 105, and passim; and article "The Transmission of Music and Liturgy from Saint-Denis to Saint-Corneille of Compiègne," in *Trasmissione e recezione delle forme di cultura musicale*, Atti del XIV Congresso della Società Internazionale di Musicologia (Turin: Edizioni di Torino, 1990), 505–14.

34. See Leech-Wilkinson, *Compositional Techniques*, 1:35, 70–71.

35. *Gallia Christiana in provincias ecclesiasticas distributa*, 16 vols. (Paris: Victor Palmé, 1715–1865), vol. 3, cols. 320–23; P. Fanien, *Histoire du chapitre d'Arras* (Arras: Rousseau-Leroy, 1868), 18–20; Henry Gruy, *Histoire d'Arras* (Arras: Dessaint, Doullens, 1967), 34, 52; M. Rouche, "Topographie historique de Cambrai durant le haut moyen âge (Vᵉ–Xᵉ siècles)," *Revue du nord* 78 (1976): 342, 354; M. Rouche, H. Platelle, L. Trenard, R. Vandenbussche, J. Thiébaut, F. Machelart, R. Faille, *Histoire de Cambrai sous la direction de Louis Trenard*, Histoire des villes du Nord–Pas-de-Calais 2 (Lille: Presses Universitaires de Lille, 1982), 15. The devastating bombardment of Arras during World War I has severely hampered the study of the various aspects of the cathedral, since virtually all documents relating to it were destroyed. Scholars thus have to rely heavily on works written prior to 1915, among which Fanien's book, along with *Gallia Christiana*, Cardevacque and Terninck's study of the abbey of Saint-Vaast (see n. 59), and the printed cartularies (see notes 42 and 56) are important.

36. "Ordinary of the Mass Chants in English, North French and Sicilian Manuscripts," *Journal of the Plainsong and Medieval Music Society* 9/1 (1986): 12, 15–16.

37. *Le Graduel romain*, 4/1:396; 4/2:35.

38. F:AS 271 (929), fol. 72ᵛ; F:AS 309 (959), fol. 16ᵛ; F:AS 638 (966), fol. 19ᵛ; F:AS 886 (985), fol. 32; F:AS 391 (996), fol. 150.

39. Wright, "Dufay at Cambrai: Discoveries and Revisions," *Journal of the American Musicological Society* 28 (1975):199.

40. Private communication from Barbara Haggh, fall 1993.

41. Pierre Héliot, *Les Anciennes Cathédrales d'Arras*, Bulletin de la Commission Royale des Monuments et des Sites 5 (Brussels: Ministère de l'Instruction Publique,

1953), 41–2; and E. Fournier, "L'Ancienne Cathédrale d'Arras et ses chapelles," *Bulletin de la commission des monuments historiques* (Arras, 1929), 11.

42. For example, in 1299 a Mass for the Holy Spirit was established by Count Robert of Artois, and this Mass was converted to a Requiem sung weekly after his death; F:Pn, lat. 17737 (thirteenth-century cartulary with additions from the fourteenth and fifteenth centuries), fols. 126ᵛ–127. A similar foundation exists for the year 1320; ibid., fols. 130–130ᵛ. An analysis of this cartulary is found in Auguste de Loisne, *Le Cartulaire des chappellenies d'Arras, manuscrit de 1282 avec additions des XIVe et XVe siècles* (Arras: F. Guyot, 1907).

43. Indeed, according to Mark Everist, the rondeau-motets preserved in the Noailles chansonnier (F:Pn, fr. 12615) and in the *Chansonnier du roi* (F:Pn, fr. 844) are probably Artesian, with the former manuscript probably hailing from Arras itself; see his article "The Rondeau Motet: Paris and Artois in the Thirteenth Century," *Music and Letters* 69 (1988): 1–22; id., *Polyphonic Music in Thirteenth-Century France: Aspects of Sources and Distribution*, Garland Outstanding Dissertations in Music from British Universities (New York: Garland, 1989), 176–86; and id., *French Motets in the Thirteenth Century: Music, Poetry and Genre*, Cambridge Studies in Medieval and Renaissance Music (Cambridge: Cambridge University Press, 1994), 104.

44. On the confraternity, see A. Guesnon, *La Confrèrie des jongleurs d'Arras et le tombeau de l'évêque Lambert* (Arras: Répessé, Cassel, 1913); and Roger Berger, *Le Nécrologe de la confrèrie des jongleurs et des bourgeois d'Arras* (Arras: Commission Départementale des Monuments Historiques du Pas-de-Calais, 1963–70). The statutes of the confraternity are found in F:Pn, fr. 8541, fol. 46, and a French version of the miracle exists in F:Pn, fr. 17229, fol. 352v.

45. Andrew Wathey, "The *Roman de Fauvel* and the Crisis of 1316–17," paper read at the 59th Annual Meeting of the American Musicological Society in Montréal in 1993.

46. Given in I:Rvat, Reg. lat. 544, fol. 361, and reported by Léopold Delisle in "Notice sur vingt manuscrits du Vatican," *Bibliothèque de l'école des chartes* 37 (1876): 510 (also see n. 79).

47. "Le Mangeur, qui par tres grant cure / Voult Escolastique traictier, / Saincte More Ovide esclairier, / Vittry, Machault de haulte emprise, / Poetes que musique ot chier"; from his ballade *Des meurs et condicions des champaynois*, in Eustache Deschamps, *Oeuvres complètes de Eustache Deschamps publiées d'après le manuscrit de la Bibliothèque Nationale*, ed. Gaston Raynaud, Société des Anciens Textes Françaises (Paris: Firmin Didot, 1892), 8:178. Vitry-le-François is not listed in Table 3.4 because it was founded in honor of Francis I in 1544, after Vitry-en-Perthois had burned. No town of this name existed in medieval times.

48. "Vraisemblablement le nom de *Philippe de Vitry* lui avait été donné à cause du lieu de sa naissance, car *Vitriacum* est le nom latin de la petite ville de *Vitry*, dans le département du Pas-de-Calais," *Biographie universelle des musiciens et bibliographie générale de la musique*, 2d ed. (Paris: Firmin Didot, 1883), 7:32.

49. Vitry's benefices were brought to light by Antoine Thomas in "Extraits des archives du Vatican pour servir à l'histoire littéraire," *Romania* 11 (1882): 177–79.

50. For numerous examples of musicians for whom this is the case, see Pamela F. Starr, "Music and Music Patronage at the Papal Court, 1447–1464" (Ph.D. diss., Yale University, 1987), 198–204, and especially 211–14.

51. Cf. Latin spellings of the other Vitrys above.

52. The almost contemporaneous career of Guillaume de Machaut may be taken as another example of the practice of collecting benefices in one's native archdiocese.

There seems to have been only one town named Machaut in France, and thus we can be fairly certain that the composer was born in the Champagne region. His subsequent career, in terms of the benefices he held, revolved around acquisitions largely in the archdiocese of Reims (Reims, Saint-Quentin, Houdain, Amiens, Soissons, Arras).

53. Piaget, "*Le Chapel*," 90 (ll. 1006–7).

54. Examples of this type of confusion abound; for another possible case of mistaken identity, see Margot Fassler, "Who Was Adam of St. Victor? The Evidence of the Sequence Manuscripts," *Journal of the American Musicological Society* 37 (1984): 268–69.

55. See Adolphe de Cardevacque, *Dictionnaire historique et archéologique du département du Pas-de-Calais—Arrondissement d'Arras* (Arras: Seuer-Charruey, 1874), 2:323–32.

56. Auguste de Loisne, *Cartulaire du chapitre d'Arras* (Arras: Rohard Courtin, 1897), 77–103.

57. Astrik L. Gabriel, "Paris, University of," and "Universities," in *Dictionary of the Middle Ages*, 13 vols. (New York: Scribner 1982–89), 9:408–10 and 12:291.

58. Adolphe de Cardevacque and Auguste Terninck, *L'Abbaye de Saint-Vaast: Monographie historique, archéologique et littéraire de ce monastère*, 3 vols. (Arras: A. Brissy, 1865–68), 3:12–18.

59. A fourteenth-century document records (emphasis mine): "Rentes des Boins Enfans d'Arras estudians à Paris, et sont séans a Arras et *Viteri* [= Vitry] et à Estrées en la Caucie et à Paris. . . . A Arras: IV l[ivres] par[isis] sur le manoir de Pierrot de Berles et XX s[ous] par[isis] sur une maison sise entre le maison signeur Gillon Louchart et le maison Hachin Saverel et sient en le rue qui est dite Sur Haugré; en le rue des Sarrasins, à *Vitry:* 8 mencauds; à Estrées-Cauchy: cinq quartiers de blé; trois maisons à Pis"; F:Pn, lat. 17737, fol. 133.

60. The color map entitled *Paris vers la fin du XIVe siècle*, published in 1975 by the C.N.R.S., shows the Collège d'Arras in the lower center portion, near the Abbey of Saint-Victor.

61. Paris, Archives Nationales, M.79 is an eighteenth-century copy of a document from 1327 dealing with the Collège d'Arras, and there are a handful of others from later periods. In document nos. 6 and 12 from the collection, we learn that Abbot of Saint-Vaast Nicholas le Caudrelier founded the school in 1302. Cardevacque and Terninck give the year 1308 (*L'Abbaye de Saint-Vaast*, 3:13–14).

62. Whereas the *collèges* did not offer much in the way of formal instruction, there is evidence that the divine office was heard within their walls. See Ursmer Berlière's discussion of the successful petition by the Collège de Cluny in Paris to celebrate the office, "Les Collèges bénédictins aux universités du moyen âge," *Revue bénédictine* 10 (1893): 151. Whether or not usages indigenous to the inhabitants of the *collège* in question would have been employed is a topic that seems not to have been explored.

63. The oft-repeated assertion that Vitry "studied at the Sorbonne, where he became *magister artium*" (see Ernest Sanders, "Vitry, Philippe de," *New Grove Dictionary*, 20:22) is based on no evidence I have seen. Sarah Fuller's revisionist look at Vitry's presumed career as a teacher calls in question such statements; "A Phantom Treatise," 45–46. Whereas he may never have played a major role as a teacher, there is no reason to doubt that he received some education in Paris in the first decade of the fourteenth century.

64. "Supp. vester capellanus commensalis Philippus de Vitriaco, quat. dilecto fratri suo germany, Ade Humbelini de Vitriaco, de can. et preb. ecclesie S. Donatiani de Brugis . . . non obst. quod in S. Gaugerici Cameracen., et in de Lobia, Cameracen.

dioc., ecclesiis canonicatus et prebendas obtinere noscatur"; Berlière, ed., *Suppliques de Clément VI (1342–1352): Textes et Analyses*, Analecta Vaticano-Belgica 1 (Rome: Institut Historique Belge, 1906), 532, no. 2042. I am grateful to Andrew Wathey for drawing my attention to the documents mentioned in this and the following footnote.

65. Ibid., no. 2043.

66. *Fragmente aus Cambrai: Ein Beitrag zur Rekonstruktion einer Handschrift mit spätmittelalterlicher Polyphonie*, Göttinger Musikwissenschaftliche Arbeiten 11 (Kassel: Bärenreiter, 1987), 158.

67. *Fragmente aus Cambrai*, 154–56, citing François Avril. On PL:WRu Ak 1955/KN 195 (k. 1 & 2), see Charles E. Brewer, "A Fourteenth-Century Polyphonic Manuscript Rediscovered," *Studia Musicologica Academiae Scientiarum Hungaricae* 24 (1982): 5–19.

68. "The Early Motets of Philippe de Vitry," *Journal of the American Musicological Society* 28 (1975): 31, n. 20.

69. Yet another motet source from Cambrai from the late thirteenth century, F:CA A 410, does not include works of Vitry. By coincidence, however, the book was once owned by a person named Jacques de Vitry (*Jacobi de Vitriaco, curati de Wasiers*); see Reaney, ed., *Manuscripts of Polyphonic Music: 11th–Early 14th Century*, RISM B/IV/1 (Munich: G. Henle, 1964), 261–63. Craig Wright kindly alerted me to the existence of this manuscript.

70. "Related Motets" from Fourteenth-Century France," *Proceedings of the Royal Musical Association* 109 (1982–83): 20–21.

71. "Some Remarks a propos of *Pic*," *Revue belge de musicologie* 10 (1956): 110–11.

72. On Amiens, see Johnson, "Aspects of Late Medieval Music at the Cathedral of Amiens," chaps. 4–6; and Everist, *Polyphonic Music*, 205–21.

73. Susan Rankin, "The Divine Truth of Scripture: Chant in the *Roman de Fauvel*," *Journal of the American Musicological Society* 47 (1994): 203–43.

74. I elaborate on this in a forthcoming article, "Local Chant Readings and the *Roman de Fauvel*," in *Fauvel Studies*, ed. Margaret Bent and Andrew Wathey (Oxford: Clarendon Press, forthcoming).

75. Rankin, "The Divine Truth of Scripture," 238.

76. In his analysis of several of Vitry's works, Leech-Wilkinson stresses the audibility of the isorhythmic structure that highlights the crucial role of the lower-voice *talea*; *Compositional Techniques*, 1:37.

77. The organum is contained in the Florence manuscript (I:Fl Plu.29.1), edited in Luther Dittmer, *Facsimile Reproduction of the Manuscript Florence, Bibliotheca Mediceo-Laurenziana, Pluteo 29.1*, Publications of Mediaeval Musical Manuscripts 10–11 (Brooklyn: Institute of Mediaeval Music, 1966), fol. 142[v].

78. Hoc anno [1291], in vigilia Omnium Sanctorum, id est ultima die Octobris, natus sum ego Philippus de etc."; Delisle, "Notice sur vingt manuscrits," 510. The manuscript is the first redaction of the chronicle of Guillaume de Nangis. Coincidentally, the final entry directly concerns Arras: it records the defeat of the inhabitants of Douai by the citizens of Arras in 1303 (fol. 371[v]).

Polyphony of Texts and Music in the Fourteenth-Century Motet

Tribum que non abhorruit/Quoniam secta latronum/Merito hec patimur and Its "Quotations"

The late-medieval motet has been criticized as an art form for the incomprehensibility of its simultaneous texts. It is true that such texts cannot be understood at an unprepared hearing, but neither can heterogeneous texts in an operatic ensemble, or certain kinds of musical art that address the mind and eye as much as the ear. Fourteenth-century motet texts were composed and coordinated at least as artfully as the music to which they are wedded, thus magnifying the "hearing" problem. We can only "hear" these compositions adequately if we also do some "listening" outside the real time of actual performance. Although we have no external evidence that our medieval counterparts practiced anything resembling modern analysis on this music, it is my belief that intelligent contemporary appreciation of motets must have depended on some reflection beyond performance, and that whatever form such reflection took, it must have been less visually determined than ours, conditioned as we are to reading scores. Many aspects of the sounds they heard are now wholly inaccessible to us. Analysis can, however, recover—albeit partially—some of the ingredients of informed listening. It is with such recoverable aspects that the present paper will be concerned, and it is in that sense that it addresses "hearing" the motet.[1] It is true that errors in the words as well as the music in the manuscripts that have come down to us give a clear indication that understanding was never complete or that it rapidly decayed, but although the texts may be corrupt, they are not always incorrigible, and the kind of observation and analysis to be exemplified in this paper may take on the status of tools for textual criticism and point to solutions that can inspire some confidence.

The fourteenth-century theorist Egidius made the recommendation, often cited, that the tenor should be chosen from "some antiphon or responsory or another chant from the Antiphonal, and [that] the words should concord with the matter of which you wish to make the motet." The derivation of a motet tenor from chant provides a richer opportunity for intertextual play than Egidius spells out (and this is not the only way in which his comments fall far short of the detail and insight we would have liked him or some other contemporary to give).[2] The opportunity to make the text and the choice of tenor correspond is often grasped by fourteenth-century composers, in specific as well as general ways. In many well-known examples, incipits testify to deliberate intent. There may be a counterpoint of sense, as between sacred and worldly love, or a counterpoint of sound, as in the alliterative openings between voices of some English motets. When the tenor has been identified, or re-identified, and attached to its words, it may provide a context that reinforces the message of the texts in the upper parts, or it may even provide a contrary or ironical comment upon them.

Even if the portion of chant adopted for a motet tenor lacks text in the manuscripts that have come to us, for the composer who selected it, it would have been inseparable from its words. It is particularly relevant to remember that the biblical or liturgical text from which a tenor is drawn invites us to invoke further levels of unstated, or at least of understated, context. Indeed, the full verbal context of a chant must often have prompted its choice, as cases of clear symbolic or intertextual significance attest. It is often likely, then, that the composer had the immediate context in mind, both with reference to the entire chant from which he took the tenor, and to the biblical context, if any, of the chant words.[3]

Another possible kind of context may be provided when several motets share a common tenor or structure their tenor in similar ways.[4] The fourteenth-century English repertory includes several motet pairs on the same tenor, examples that are all the more compelling when the tenor is unusual or otherwise unknown (such as the two English motets on *Marionnette douche*) than when it is a well-known chant (such as *Alma redemptoris*). Members of a connected network of motets may build upon each other. Particularly extensive intertextual play occurs between members of the related group of fourteenth-century motets celebrating and naming contemporary musicians, starting with *Apollinis eclipsatur/Zodiacum signis*.[5] Motets that are related in any of these ways must clearly be studied together since each will throw light on the others.

In the present chapter, one motet will be examined in light of these assumptions. The inquiry builds on our knowledge that its texts are clearly related to a given political situation involving the fall from power of a corrupt minister in early fourteenth-century France and his subsequent execution. Having noted that each of the texts for the upper voices ends with a quotation in the form of a couplet of quantitative verse commenting proverbially on the "tragic fall," I then observe that the tenor is drawn from the opening of a chant melody for a passage in Genesis relating to the story of Joseph, which makes a not too oblique comment on the contemporary political situation. It is then shown that (1) the freely composed remaining texts for the upper voices in the motet (in rhymed syllabic verse) are built up from certain key words and sound patterns in their final "quotations," and (2) that the two apparently independent texts are ingeniously related by the fact that three of the same words or their roots are placed in a pattern controlled by proportions. It is further shown (3) that the melodies of the upper voices both use elements of the tenor chant melody (the tenor being limited, significantly, to the first three words of that chant), and (4) that they are so composed that the duplum and triplum reflect and enhance the patterns found in the text considered independently and contrive "consonances" between related words and sounds in the texts. Having identified some significant features of its musical construction and the status of its preexistent material, I shall demonstrate textual-musical references between the motets *Tribum/Quoniam/Merito* and *Garrit Gallus/In nova fert*.

Tribum/Quoniam: Texts

Tribum/Quoniam survives in two main sources, the interpolated *Roman de Fauvel* in Paris, F:Pn, fr. 146, and the Brussels rotulus B:Br 19606, six of whose nine motets are in fr. 146 or in some way related to its repertory. A further version was in Strasbourg MS Sm222.[6] Two further versions of later date will not be considered here.[7] In fr. 146 it shares a page with the famous Fountain of Youth miniature, around whose triangulated top music and text are arranged.[8] The remaining text and music on the page are closely coordinated with the image, which presents a black baptism in which the progeny of Fauvel, shown as old men, are rejuvenated in filth and vice; the motet can be read as a further gloss on the same theme. It has long been recognized that this motet is one of a group alluding to events and people prominent in the crises that afflicted the French royal house and the series of accessions to the monarchy in the second decade of the fourteenth century. Philip IV (the Fair) died on 29 November 1314, and his discredited counselor Enguerran de Marigny was hanged on 30 March 1315. Philip was succeeded by his sons Louis X and Philip V, but this group of motets (*Garrit Gallus/In nova fert, Tribum/ Quoniam, Aman novi/Heu Fortuna*) refers only to Philip IV, as a blind lion whose reign is first present, then past, and to Marigny and his fall from favor.[9]

The last couplet of the duplum of *Tribum que non abhorruit/Quoniam secta latronum/Merito hec patimur* "quotes" an elegiac couplet from one of the letters Ovid wrote in exile, *Epistulae ex Ponto* IV. 3, lines 35–36, a work that arises out of his own fall and banishment. The tenor is the beginning of the Matins responsory for the third Sunday in Lent, *Merito hec patimur quia peccavimus in fratrem nostrum,* V. *Dixit Ruben fratribus suis.* Its biblical source is Genesis 42:21, which concerns Joseph's meeting with his brothers in Egypt. Both Ovid and Genesis deal with exile; both provide significant context for the newly written motet texts, underscoring the immediate and contemporary message and the calamitous events to which they refer. Ovid's letter was written from exile to an unnamed (and unidentified) faithless friend. The subject and unstated context of the tenor text from Genesis is the remorse of Joseph's brothers after deceiving their father Jacob about their abuse of Joseph, which led to his exile in Egypt. The Ovid couplet is introduced by the words "que dolum acuunt." The author "sharpens the deceit (or evil)" by counterpointing Ovid's exile to the exile of the Israelites in Egypt reported in Genesis as well as drawing both into service to lament the woes of France in a motet written for the amplified and politically pointed version of the *Roman de Fauvel* in F:Pn, fr. 146.[10]

Fortuna is an important figure in the *Roman* and in Ovid's letter. Lines 7 and 29 of the letter name Fortuna, who occupies a central position in the interpolated version of the *Roman de Fauvel* for which the motet was written, and in whose triplum Fortuna is also central. Fortuna is described in the lines preceding those used in the motet (italics mine):

> 7   nunc, quia contraxit vultum *Fortuna* recedis
>   . . .
>   quid facis, a! demens? Cur, si *Fortuna* recedat
> 30   naufragio lacrimas eripis ipse tuo?
>   Haec dea non stabili, quam sit levis, orbe fatetur,
>   quae summum dubio sub pede semper habet.
>   quolibet est folio, quavis incertior aura:
>   par illi levitas, improbe, sola tua est.
> 35   *Omnia sunt hominum tenui pendentia filo*
>   *et subito casu quae valuere, ruunt.*

(Now that Fortune has frowned, you draw back . . . Ah, what are you doing, madman? Why, if Fortune draws back, do you yourself thus refuse your ship-wreck its tears? This goddess declares by her unsteady wheel that she is fickle; she always has its top under her faltering foot. She is more uncertain than any leaf, than any breeze; the only thing that matches her inconstancy, repro-bate, is yours. All human affairs hang by a slender thread, and things that were strong collapse in a sudden fall.)[11]

We shall now consider the texts of the motet in themselves before ad-dressing the music. Here they are as edited and translated by David Howlett:[12]

Tribum que non abhorruit/Quoniam secta latronum/Merito hec patimur

> **Tribum** que non abhor<u>ruit</u>
> indecenter ascend<u>ere</u>
> furibunda non met<u>uit</u>
> Fortuna cito vert<u>ere,</u>
> 5   dum duci prefate **tribus**
> in sempiternum spec<u>ulum</u>
> parare palam omn<u>ibus</u>
> non pepercit patib<u>ulum.</u>
> Populus ergo vent<u>urus</u>
> 10   si trans metam | ascend<u>erit,</u>
> quidam forsitan *cas<u>urus,</u>*
> cum tanta **tribus ru<u>erit,</u>**
> sciat eciam quis fr<u>uctus</u>
> delabi sit in prof<u>undum.</u>
> 15   *Post zephyros plus ledit hyems, post gaudia l<u>uctus</u>;*
> *unde nichil melius quam nil habuisse sec<u>undum.</u>*

(Furious Fortune has not feared to bring down swiftly the tribe which did not shrink from ascending indecently, while for the leader of the foresaid tribe she has not refrained from preparing the gallows as an eternal mirror in the sight of everyone. Therefore if the people to come should ascend across the limit, let a certain man who might, perhaps, fall, since such a tribe has collapsed, know also what an outcome it would be to fall into the depth. Winter harms more after gentle west winds, griefs [harm more] after joys; whence nothing is better than to have had nothing for the second time [*that is*, better nothing at all than to have enjoyed good fortune in the past].)

> Quoniam secta lat<u>ronum</u>
> spelunca vispili<u>onum</u>
> vulpes que Gallos rod<u>erat</u>
> tempore quo regnav<u>erat</u>
> 5   leo cecatus *sub<u>ito</u>*
> suo **ruere merito**
> in mortem privatam b<u>onis</u>:
> concinat Gallus Nas<u>onis</u>
> dicta que dolum ac<u>uunt</u>:
> 10   *omnia sunt hominum tenui pendencia filo*
> *et* subito casu *que valuere* **r<u>uunt</u>**.

(Since the gang of thieves from a cave of reprobates (and) the fox which had gnawed the cocks in the time in which the blinded lion had ruled have fallen suddenly by their own deserts into a death deprived of good things, let the cock shout Ovid's words which intensify the deceit: "All human affairs are hanging by a slender thread, and with a sudden fall things which were strong crash.")

> **Merito** hec patimur.

(Justly we suffer these things.)

A network of verbal repetitions (distinguished in boldface above) underpins and gives structure to the two texts. The first word of the triplum, as "tribus" or "tribum," occurs three times in the triplum. The third "tribus" directly precedes "ruerit," which (as "ruunt") is the last word of the duplum and hence of the Ovid couplet. This verb (as "ruunt" and "ruere") occurs twice in the duplum, with "ruere" directly preceding "merito," which in turn is the first of the three tenor words. The first word of the triplum and the last word of the duplum are thus linked in a pattern that is structurally fundamental to the motet and exists independently of verbal sense although it is used to reinforce that sense. The lattice is further reinforced by—though by no means dependent upon—the proportioned positions of the words within their own texts. "Tribus/m" recurs at words 16 and 38, that is, at or immediately adjacent to the major and minor parts of the golden section (GS) of its text by word count (62).[13] "Ruunt" to "ruere" span the major part of the GS counting words from the end of the duplum: "ruere merito" are the 25th and 24th words from the end of a total of 41 words.

The triplum's fourteen octosyllabic lines are followed by a hexameter couplet, a self-contained proverb without literary context.[14] The couplet, despite its own innocence of rhyme and its longer lines, is integrated into the overall rhyme scheme ABAB CDCD EFEF GHGH. Thus, of the triplum's eight di-

syllabic rhymes, the last two are made to rhyme with these preexistent hexameters. The duplum has nine octosyllabic lines rhymed in pairs, followed by an
elegiac couplet. The last (odd, uncoupled) line of its syllabic verse (*dicta que
dolum acuunt*) is made to rhyme (-*uunt*) with the—likewise preexistent—pentameter; it also shares -*u* -*u* assonance (or what I shall call vowel rhyme) with
the triplum "fructus," tying together the eight double -*u* -*u* vowel rhymes of
the triplum with the rhymed pair in the duplum, "acuunt" introducing the
Ovid couplet and "ruunt" ending it. This insistence on the same vowel is all
the more striking because both the final rhymes are full rhymes ("fructus, luc-
tus; profundum, secundum"), that is, showing identity from the stressed syllable to the end; the musical setting, however, suggests French end-stressing.
(The first six pairs would be considered "imperfect" in vernacular verse of this
period, because the identity is limited to the two unstressed syllables.) There is
confirmation that this insistence on the one vowel is deliberate: the final two
vowels of the last word in the last line in the duplum, "ruunt," which rhymes
with "acuunt" in the antepenultimate (and last rhythmic) line, also have the
repeated *u u* vowels, something that can take on an important dimension in
musical performance. On the assumption that everything is constructed backward from the Ovidian quotation at the end of the duplum, this insistence on
u–u may be a way of reinforcing the idea of "collapse" or "downfall" in the
verb "ruunt." The intentions of this densely crafted writing are confirmed and
underscored by their musical setting. "Fructus" closes a line (triplum 13) in
which triplum and duplum coincide musically in identical rhythm (at L[ongs]
51–55); this immediately follows the triplum's crucial "tribus ruerit," suitably
set to a striking descending scale in semibreves in L50–51.[15] The Ovid couplet
is integrated into both texts. Triplum (see Example 4.1) "profund*um*" and
duplum "homin*um*" arrive together on L61: the internal -*um* of the duplum
hexameter is thus brought into rhyming and musical alignment with the
triplum word that is in turn arranged to rhyme with the last word of *its* preexistent hexameter couplet. Although not used as rhyme words or line ends in
their respective couplets, triplum "gaud*ia*" and duplum "penden*cia*" arrive together on L67, and thus similarly connect the separate texts by "imperfect"
rhyme. The vowels and two of the consonants of the first duplum word "Quoniam" are those of the first word of the Ovid couplet "omnia" (and the vowels
are reversed at the end of the same line, "-a filo"). In addition the motet concludes with musically aligned vowel rhyme between the ends of both borrowed couplets:

Tr   meli-*us qu*am nil *ha-bu*is-se se-*cundum*
Du   ca- *su que*   *va-lu-* *e-re ruunt* (u q a u e e u u).

Such vowel rhyme was contrived to be a conspicuous feature of these texts.
The treatment of individual syllables, and their adjacent and simultaneous
combination, mark them as words carefully calculated for musical treatment.
Many are easily audible from outside, though some would remain privy to
participating performers. To someone already familiar with the motet, the

triplum's "abhorruit" can then be heard (in a solo opening, uncomplicated by other voices) as relating to "ruit", further underscored by the palindrome of the opening vowels *i-u, u-i*: tri*bum*–hor*ruit*. The 62 words of the triplum divide in half between "metam" and "ascenderit" (31 + 31). The words "trans metam ascende-|rit" take us "over the boundary" to the second *color*, set to a melodic palindrome that hinges around the structural center of the motet. The two *-tam* syllables in triplum and duplum coincide: "trans me*tam*" and "mortem priva*tam*" (the middle word of the duplum, 21st of 41), hooking the parts firmly together at the *color* join, to words that mean "across the limit." Puns with words of measure are quite common in fourteenth-century motets at such positions of structural or proportional importance in text or music.

Words denoting "fall" abound in both texts ("vertere, delabi, profundum"), ending with the fundamental "ruunt." Ovid alludes in the letter to his exile ("insultare iacenti te mihi") [you insult me in my fall], lines 27–28). "Casu" and "ruunt" in the pentameter of the Ovid duplum couplet are echoed by "casurus–ruerit" in the triplum. Both *color* statements are introduced with the word "ascendere" or "ascenderit" at verse line ends, and with the same notes A G F E F. Their reversals,"vertere, profundum, patibulum," also occur at line ends, as do the three recapitulated words, two of which mean "fall:" "subito, casurus, ruunt." "Patibulum" and "patimur" also create a pun.

Ovid wrote "sum tamen haec passus" (I however have suffered this [line 55 of the letter]). The motet tenor's three words, "merito hec patimur," use the same deponent verb also in the first person. Only the three words "Merito hec patimur" are provided, and only their music is used. This leads us to another very significant connection (in lines 25–26 of the letter):

> si mihi rebus opem nullam factisque ferebas,
>> venisset verbis charta notata tribus

> (If you brought me no aid in facts, in deeds, you might have sent me three words on a sheet of paper.)

Puns on three are central to the motet, starting with the triplum's "tribum/ tribus." "Tribum" of course means tribe, not three, but as the opening word of the triplum, it is unquestionably used with punning intent; the word "tribum" or "tribus" occurs three times in the triplum text. As we have seen, three words from Ovid's pentameter line, "subito, casu, ruunt," are all picked up in the new motet texts, emphasized by repetition, and given significant positions. "Subito" in the duplum follows "leo cecatus" and ends the line immediately preceding "ruere merito." "Casurus" ends the triplum line immediately preceding "tribus ruerit." "Ruere/ruunt" have already been shown to be fundamental and are specially placed. But even more telling is the choice of tenor, just the three words, "Merito hec patimur," linked in various ways to the texts of the motet and determining its musical form and substance. The portion of chant selected corresponds to those three words and no more.

A final observation on the Ovid letter becomes persuasive only when one is aware of the considerable importance given to the golden section in motet construction: the couplet lies at the GS of the total couplets in Ovid's original;

or, to put it another way, the pentameter line that ends with the foundation word "ruunt" is line 36 of the 58 lines of Ovid's letter, that is, the GS line. This position gains in significance as the same proportion can be seen to have governed the placement of the crucial words in the new texts.[16]

Cumulatively, the evidence which has just been presented makes it certain that the newly written rhythmical parts of the two texts were composed very carefully, on the foundations of the quotations, in conjunction with each other, and in conjunction with the intended musical setting.[17] The Ovid couplet has yielded the sense and the verbal units that govern the composition of both texts; it is as fundamental to the verbal composition as is the choice of plainsong for the musical construction, a choice strongly governed in turn by the words. Indeed, these words underpin the verbal structure in the same way that the notes of a derived tenor underpin the musical structure. It is even likely that the chant tenor was chosen to fit Ovid rather than Ovid to fit the tenor, a significant reversal of how motets have been thought to be written. A normal assumption would be that the notes of the chant tenor were the first compositional constraint to be adopted once the subject of the texts had been decided. I think it can be proposed instead that the Ovid couplet was primary to those texts, and must have been chosen at least as early as, or before, the Genesis source of the motet tenor. These twin pillars of text and music are intimately linked and provide a striking marriage of pagan and Christian elements.[18] The status of "pre-compositional" material must therefore be accorded in equal measure to the Ovid couplet and to the choice of tenor. The one is no more a quotation than the other; both are starting points and building material for the texts and music. Egidius already implied that the words might exist before a tenor was chosen to go with them. Here we have internal evidence that they must have done so, and this gives a central role in the creation of this motet to the composition and disposition of the words.

Tribum/Quoniam: Music

We turn now to an analysis of the music (see Example 4.1), having already noted some features of the texts that were so planned that they would be heard simultaneously.

The particular preoccupation with "Tribus/m" seems to have affected all the main proportions of the motet, textual and musical. The motet is 78 imperfect longs (= 78L) in duration, arranged in perfect maximodus (with longs grouped in threes). The triplum enters alone, for three longs, followed by the duplum, for three longs, then the tenor. Each of the two equal *color* statements occupies 12 × 3 longs:

$$3 + 3 + (color \text{ I}) \, 12 \times 3 + (color \text{ II}) \, 12 \times 3 = 78L$$

Without the 6L (12B) introduction, the motet is 72L = 144B (breves) in length. For purposes of these calculations, the final long is considered to be extended to its official full length of three longs, corresponding to the rests that complete *color* I.

As we have seen, the tenor is the beginning of the Matins responsory for

EXAMPLE 4.1 *Tribum que non abhorruit/Quoniam secta latronum/Merito hec patimur*

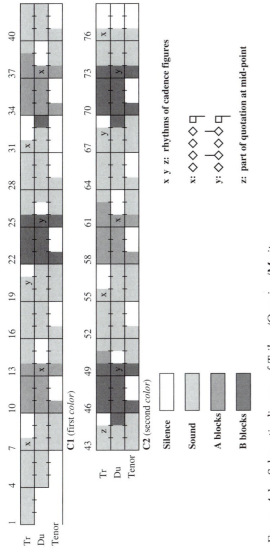

C1 (first color)

C2 (second color)

x y z: rhythms of cadence figures

z: part of quotation at mid-point

Silence

Sound

A blocks

B blocks

FIGURE 4.1   Schematic diagram of *Tribum/Quoniam/Merito*

EXAMPLE 4.2   *Merito hec patimur*

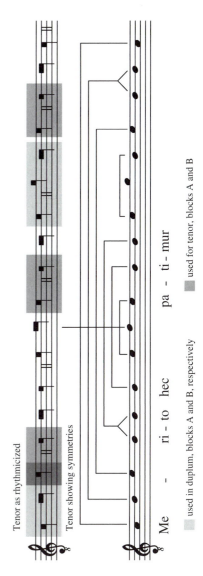

Tenor as rhythmicized

Tenor showing symmetries

Me - ri - to hec pa - ti - mur

used in duplum, blocks A and B, respectively

used for tenor, blocks A and B

91

the third Sunday in Lent, *Merito hec patimur quia peccavimus in fratrem nostrum.* The chant is transposed up a fifth from F to C. *Antiphonale Sarisburiense* 174 had presented the hitherto closest available version of the melody, differing in only one note from the motet tenor, but Anne Walters Robertson has now found a perfect match in the Parisian source Pn 12044, fol. 80.[19] This removes any need to assume that the chant was even slightly manipulated by the composer in order to achieve a tidy structure of 6 × 3 *talea* groups which then yield three identical three-note groups (A G G transposed, for the motet, to E D D) within each of the two *colores.*[20] The composer contrived that the recurring pattern "E–rest–D" from this group should provide six equidistant and identical bases on which two alternating sets of three identical blocks of music are erected (A B A B A B).

Figure 4.1 shows the musical plan schematically. While the tenor has the same rhythmic pattern in both *color* statements, the patterns of sound and silence in the upper parts differ slightly, corresponding to the alternating cadential patterns (*x* and *y*) that link the blocks to "non-block" music, and give a special place to the phrase marked at "*z*," whose significance will become clear later.

Each trio (three of A, three of B) of 4L blocks is identical not only in pitch but in rhythm. With thrice two blocks of music arranged over twice three identical places in the tenor, the composition becomes a grand hemiola of threefold form arranged over a twice-stated tenor *color.* An analysis commited to isorhythmic primacy, and particularly to demonstrating the primacy of the lower parts, will give only subsidiary attention to the amazing interlocked tripartite structure, with its own internal identities, that is counterpointed against the two identical tenor *color* statements, and to the ternary pattern set up by the three pairs of A + B that cut across those two statements. While the tenor can at the most basic level be described as isorhythmic, with six short *taleae* or *ordines* in each *color*, the upper parts might be said to superimpose an overlapping, tight, but counter-isorhythmic structure upon it.

A few previous analysts have noted the outlines of this structure, though their significance and extent has largely been passed over.[21] It has not yet been proposed that Schrade's transcription be emended to match these observations; the blocks can easily be made much more closely identical than they there appear. Our understanding of musical language at this period is still so fragile that we timidly fail to recognize as nonsense some manuscript readings that demand to be corrected in accordance with musical sense. Analysis can provide a text-critical tool to refine the edition where deviations from a pattern of identity or parallelism are apparently casual. In this case, the new readings are corroborated by an analysis that treats the motet as an equal and interrelated partnership of text and music.[22]

Is isorhythm or any other kind of recurrent pattern a conscious background model from which purposeful deviation is intended to be recognized as such, or is it simply a means of filling in neutral space between primary formal events? Can it be both? I think it can; and the balance differs in different pieces. Textual and musical events often cut across or dislocate hitherto accepted measurements of the tidiness or maturity of a motet. When analysis upholds the purposefulness of such "deviations" they cannot be dismissed as manifestations of untidiness or early date. Such analysis may demonstrate that more than one formal pattern is at work in the music, just as there may be deliberate ambiguity in the text when a biblical and a secular sense, or two different stories, are superimposed.

A common weakness of judgments about orderliness of structure, or of analytical bases for determining chronology, is that only a single criterion, or criteria that are too limited, are taken into account. Ernest Sanders demonstrated the extent and importance of regular periodicity of phrases between rests in the upper parts of motets, even where there is no regular isorhythm between those phrases.[23] Ursula Günther's study of the fourteenth-century motet invoked the amount and extent of isorhythm as a measure of chronology.[24] Neither of them takes closely into account either the text-music relationship of individual parts (examined by some scholars, including Georg Reichert) or[25] networks of relationships between texts and musical lines, within and between pieces, which are just one aspect of the compositional possibilities. In short, each motet is different, unique, and can only in the most limited and approximate senses be measured by conventional standards of isorhythm. Several of the motets on Heinrich Besseler's list of isorhythmic motets are not in a strict or primary sense isorhythmic; they may use mensural transformation rather than simple proportioned restatement (as in Vitry's motet V*os quid*/*Gratissima*), or they may balance a variety of constructional resources much more complex than simple tenor replication (as in *Tribum*/*Quoniam*).[26]

The portion of melody used for the tenor has several palindromic features: the beginning and end, CDE–EDC, resemble the *Neuma quinti toni* of *Garrit Gallus*, which starts and ends with ut re mi, mi re ut.[27] A conjunct palindrome from notes 5 to 11, D D E F E D D, abuts the only melodically disjunct group E G D (notes 12–14), and at the same time contributes to a melodic sequence with the opening four notes. Discounting repeated notes, the whole melody can be seen as a conjunct palindrome into which the disjunct group is inserted; this is the way the composer must have treated it in fashioning the upper parts (see Example 4.2).

Each of the six blocks (ABABAB, see Ex. 4.1) starts on an octave A in triplum and duplum flanking the tenor E, and each is always preceded by triplum rests and followed by duplum rests. Each block begins a new triplum text line and contains only that line (lines 3, 6, 8, 11, 14, 16); the longer last hexameter line, 16, extends beyond the block to the final cadence. The identity is sometimes extended into adjacent groups. The middle A block, and the second and third B blocks are preceded by duplum semibreves B D C B, and the central A and B blocks followed by triplum semibreves D D C B.

Each block presents three prominent notes of the chant in its duplum (see Example 4.3). Block A has C D E, the opening of the chant. In the central A block indeed these words occur on the duplum word "merito," underscoring both in its musical placing and in its notes the significance of this word in the verbal lattice.[28] The only disjunct group of notes in the tenor, E G D, is

EXAMPLE 4.3   Three notes of the chant as used in the duplum of each block

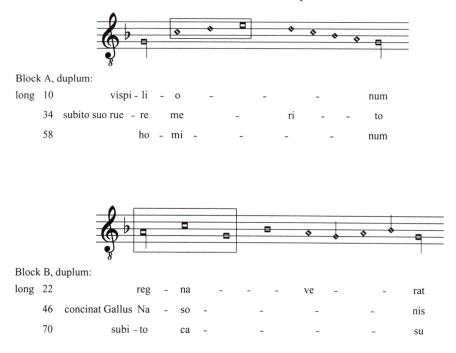

Block A, duplum:

long	10		vispi - li	-	o	-		-		-		num
	34	subito suo rue	- re		me		-		ri	-	- to	
	58		ho	-	mi -		-		-		-	num

Block B, duplum:

long	22		reg	-	na	-		-		-	ve	-		-	rat
	46	concinat Gallus Na	-		so	-		-		-		-	nis
	70		subi - to		ca	-		-		-		-	su

transposed to A C G (its original pitch) in the duplum of each of the B blocks, for the words—all significant—"*regna*verat, N*asonis, subito casu*." The chant is freely paraphrased in the triplum on F (an octave above its original pitch and a fourth above the tenor). The first phrase of *Tribum* paraphrases the entire chant segment except for the three-note disjunct cell A C G (see Example 4.4). The omission of these three notes at this stage leaves a perfectly palindromic phrase (the final four notes of the chant are given in parentheses). The triplum then proceeds to paraphrase the disjunct cell in its next phrase (L10), avoiding any further F cadences until the new *color* at L43 and the final cadence. This paraphrase of the disjunct cell forms the triplum of the A block and combines with the duplum presentation of the first three notes of the chant (at tenor pitch). Many other hints of chant paraphrase result from general parallelism.

In F:Pn, fr. 146, the triplum presents three text lines, nine words, before the critical word "Fortuna," which in that manuscript is made to stand at the top of the recto page; the thrice three words preceding it are at the foot of the preceding verso.[29] Fortuna is of course central to to Ovid's letter, to Fauvel, to the observations on the career of Marigny, developed covertly here but more overtly in the other Marigny motet, *Aman novi/Heu Fortuna*. The three voices of the motet enter in succession, at intervals of three longs, triplum, duplum, tenor, that is, first one, then two, then all three parts sound. The verbal repetition pattern involves three triplum words, two duplum words and one tenor

EXAMPLE 4.4   *Tribum* showing chant paraphrase

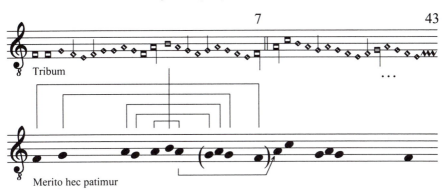

word. The beginning and end of the tenor melody are on scale degrees 1, 2, and 3. There are twice three blocks of identical material in all three parts. The tenor has two *color* statements, each of six three-note *ordines* separated by rests. The maximodus is perfect, three longs to the maxima. The total number of lines (27) is 3 cubed.[30]

This motet is one of very few in which the tenor is not the lowest in range but the middle voice of the texture. It mostly sounds fifths between the triplum–duplum octaves.[31] The duplum is the contrapuntal foundation, and is always a fifth below the tenor on downbeats of the large modus groups, except at L67, where exceptionally an octave is used, for an exceptional position (accommodating a triplum–duplum imitation that links the two borrowed texts). The duplum here twice makes its own insistence on the distinctive A C G motive, at L64–67, and then in the final B block from L70, independently of its adhesion to the tenor. The duplum deceptively usurps the tenor's role as the true foundation of the piece—perhaps a further mirror of a series of deceptions in the Genesis story (recalled by the tenor), since Jacob had previously cheated his brother Esau out of his birthright before himself being deceived by his own sons about the fate of Joseph.

Tribum and *Garrit Gallus*

We have seen how the last couplet of the duplum of *Tribum que non abhorruit/ Quoniam secta latronum/Merito hec patimur* uses an elegiac couplet from one of the letters written by Ovid in exile. *Tribum* can be linked to at least two other motets that are rich in contemporary historical allusions. Of these, *Garrit Gallus/In nova fert* is placed at the culmination of the expanded and interpolated version of *Fauvel* in F:Pn, fr. 146. It embodies a range of animals that stand for the human subjects of this grand *admonitio* and could be said to be a motet about bestial transformation. It is therefore particularly appropriate that the first line of its duplum "quotes," or rather, presents, the first line of Ovid's *Metamorphoses*: "In nova fert animus mutatas dicere formas"

(The mind inclines to speak of forms changed into strange things). This is the literary work, widely known and quoted then as now, which above all others deals with and stands for transformations between gods, humans, and animals. The protagonist of the *Roman de Fauvel* is a horse unnaturally transformed to human estate and kingly status. *In nova fert* on the last full folio of the *Roman* thus comes full circle from the first folio in which Fortuna raised Fauvel from stable to palace. In addition, the novelty and strangeness of the events portrayed is signaled not only by Ovid's words but by the earliest use of red notation to signify mensural, indeed temporal, metamorphosis of perfect to imperfect time. As in the case of *Tribum*, it can likewise be argued for *Garrit Gallus* that its Ovidian line is not so much a quotation as a foundation.

The second half of *Tribum/Quoniam*, at the second *color* statement, starts with a clearly audible musical quotation of the beginning of *Garrit Gallus/In nova fert*. It is a quotation that involves all three parts, changing their roles and applying light camouflage. Recognition of the full resonances of the quotation depends on taking text and music combinations together. The quotation directly follows the central words of the triplum *trans metam*—a kind of "meta"morphosis—and is followed by the words "concinat Gallus Nasonis." "Concinat" is the verb used by Philippe de Vitry to indicate his authorship in the motet *Cum statua/Hugo Hugo* as "hec concino Philippus publice." Then comes the word "Gallus," which clearly has multiple meanings in this context. Most obviously, "gallus" is both a rooster/cockerel and a Frenchman. Gallus was also Petrarch's name for Vitry, whose identity as the Gallus of the fourth eclogue of Petrarch's *Bucolicum carmen* has recently been reaffirmed,[32] and Gallus is the opening gambit, perhaps authorial, of *Garrit Gallus*. Gallus was also the name of an earlier Latin poet regarded as one of Ovid's important models and predecessors, but of whose work almost nothing survives. Gallus may gain further significance from the so-called "cock" king, as Philip V is represented, particularly in *Un songe*, one of the French dits in F:Pn, fr. 146.[33] Philip IV is now dead (*Quoniam*, duplum line 4, past tense: "tempore quo regnaverat leo cecatus"). Ovid named himself (Naso) in line 10 of the letter: "quisquis sit, audito nomine, Naso, rogas." Naso is named in line 8 of the motet duplum as the author of the couplet from the letter. Naso is Ovid's signature name: the author aligns himself with Ovid by announcing the *Tribum* couplet from *Epistulae ex Ponto* from both authorial mouths ("concinat gallus nasonis dicta"). At the same time, he alludes to the opening of *Garrit Gallus/In nova fert* which presents the declaiming *Gallus* simultaneously with *In nova fert*, the first line of Ovid's *Metamorphoses*. Example 4.5 shows how the musical material of the tenor of *Garrit Gallus* appears in the duplum (here unusually the lowest voice) of *Tribum*; its triplum outlines the *Tribum* tenor *Merito*. The Ovidian duplum *In nova fert* which (unusually) lies above the triplum *Garrit Gallus* corresponds to the triplum of *Tribum*. In addition, *Garrit Gallus* receives a free musical recapitulation within that motet at the words "gallorum garritus."

The multiple quotation cements the authorial link between the Gallus "singing out" (*concinat*) in *Tribum/Quoniam/Merito*, "prating" (*garrit*) in *Gar-*

EXAMPLE 4.5   Musical relations between *Garrit Gallus/In nova fert* and *Tribum/Quoniam*

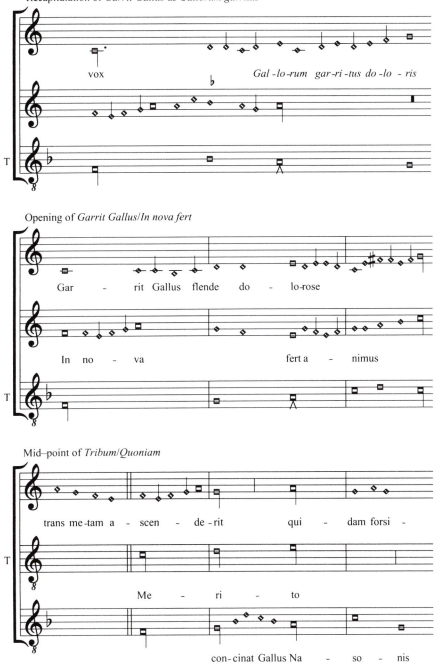

Recapitulation of *Garrit Gallus* as *Gallorum garritus*

Opening of *Garrit Gallus/In nova fert*

Mid–point of *Tribum/Quoniam*

rit Gallus/In nova fert, and the Ovid whose words are present in and fundamental to both motets. *[Con-]-cinat Gallus* is set to a prominent four-note
motive (B D C B) that precedes three of the blocks, and recurs in conjunction
with words whose special significance we have already observed. It introduces
the second (central) A block at L33 ("ruere" before "merito"), the central B
block at L45 (*Gallus Nasonis*) and the final B block with the Ovid couplet at
L69 ("subito/casu."). This placing of duplum "casu" reflects the triplum "casurus" in the middle B block.

The quotation is located as prominently as it could be. The middle of the
central B block in *Tribum que/Quoniam* falls on "Nasonis." This is the GS
word of the duplum (25 of 41); it spans the GS of all the music (which falls at
96.4 of 156 breves); it stands between the beginning of *color* II and the GS of
the music measured by *colores* (i.e., excluding the introduction), which falls in
L51 (44.4 + 6 = 50.4) between the triplum words "tribus" and "ruerit." The
minor part of the musical GS falls at 27.4 + 6 = 33.4, on "ruere." Thus the
same words and music are emphasized by repetition and quotation and by
positions that are proportioned in relation to each other as well as internally.
We now see that the central interruption to the pattern of musical rhyme (*z* in
Figure 4.1) is made precisely for the sake of the centrally placed quotation from
Garrit Gallus. There are at least four significant coincidences at the junction
to *color* II: the GS of triplum and duplum lines (the 10th and 7th respectively);
the middle words of both parts, which occur in those lines; a palindrome in
triplum and duplum melodies; and a repetition of "ascendere/-it" that introduces *color* II with a coincidence of music and words.

Tribum/Quoniam and *Garrit Gallus/In nova fert* share the same beasts:
"gallus, vulpes, pullis," and "leo." *Garrit Gallus* twice has in the tenor (at B92
and 129) the notes B♭ A at the duplum's "leo," the second of these at its
musical GS (see example 4.6). The two triplum lions fall at the midpoint of
each color (B36 and 111), the latter at the GS of the duplum text. In *Tribum/
Quoniam* the blinded lion, "leo cecatus" (duplum line 5), is placed at the GS
of the first half of the music, thus at the minor part of the GS of all the music
(L29.7). The *Garrit Gallus* tenor notes B♭ A at "leo" become the long and
deliberate Bb A for "leo" in the duplum of *Tribum/Quoniam* at L27–28. These
notes sound, as they do in the tenor of *Garrit Gallus*, as the lowest notes of
the texture, and are written at the same pitch in both motets. They are preceded, in the first B block, by the emphatic past tense verb "regnaverat," also
set to long notes, as if to suggest that he (Philip IV) reigned too long.

Measured music has unique power to give precise temporal positions to
words. Polyphonic music has power to place texts and their component words,
indeed syllables, in precisely determined temporal relationship to each other.
The semantic, structural, and sonic counterpoint can become very complex,
especially when different verbal texts sound simultaneously. But precisely because of the mutual corroboration of its simultaneous structures, music can
provide concrete authority for certain ways of reading not only musical but also
verbal ingredients. When the texts and their relationships make active counter-
points in sense, sound, and form to each other and to the musical organiza-

Garrit Gallus B92

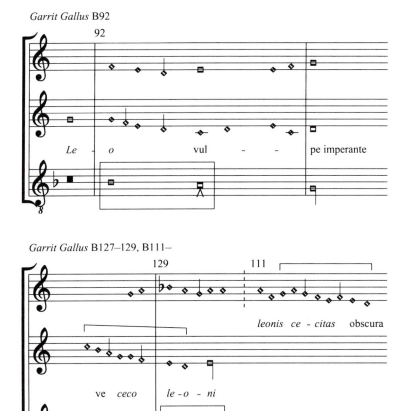

Garrit Gallus B127–129, B111–

Tribum/Quoniam L27–28

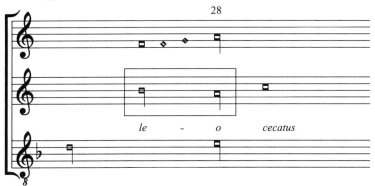

tion, and are not merely parasitic attachments to the music, the possibilities for multiple counterpointing are greatly increased, exercising and displaying the composer's verbal and musical craft to a high degree.

NOTES

A summary of this chapter appears in "The Vitry Motet *Tribum que non abhorruit/ Quoniam secta latronum/Merito hec patimur* and Its 'Quotations'," *Actas del XV Congresso de la Sociedad Internacional de Musicologia: culturas musicales de Mediterraneo y sus ramificaciones, Madrid/3–10/IV/1992,* vol. 3 (Madrid: La Sociedad, 1993), in ser. *Revista de Musicologia* 16, 542–47.

1. The "audience" for motets is discussed by Christopher Page in *Discarding Images: Reflections on Music and Culture in Medieval France* (Oxford: Clarendon Press, 1993), and addressed in my review "Reflections on Christopher Page's *Reflections, Early Music* 21 (1993): 625–33. His "A Reply to Margaret Bent" (*Early Music* 22 [1994]: 127–32) misrepresents the sense and formulations of that review, while seeming to defend some of the colleagues and their positions that I sought to defend against his criticisms. Our understandings of "Audience" are different, if both valid: he is there concerned mainly with casual or untrained hearers, I with informed and prepared listening, whether by creators and performers or by those who listen with attention but without participation.

2. For Egidius, see Wulf Arlt, "Der Tractatus figurarum: Ein Beitrag zur Musiklehre der 'ars subtilior'," *Schweizer Beiträge zur Musikwissenschaft* 1 (1972): 35–53. For a conveniently accessible text and translation, see Daniel Leech-Wilkinson, *Compositional Techniques in the Four-Part Isorhythmic Motets of Philippe de Vitry and His Contemporaries* (New York: Garland, 1989), 18–23.

3. See Margaret Bent (with David Howlett), "*Subtiliter alternare:* The Yoxford Motet *O amicus/Percursoris,*" in *Studies in Medieval Music: Festschrift for Ernest H. Sanders,* ed. Peter M. Lefferts and Brian Seirup = *Current Musicology* 45–47 (1990): 43–84; Kevin Brownlee, "Machaut's Motet 15 and the *Roman de la Rose,*" *Early Music History* 10 (1991): 1–14; Margaret Bent," Deception, Exegesis and Sounding Number in Machaut's Motet 15 *Amours qui a le pouoir/Faus samblant/Vidi dominum,*" ibid., 15–27.

4. See Daniel Leech-Wilkinson, "Related Motets from Fourteenth-Century France," *Proceedings of the Royal Musical Association* 109 (1982–83): 1–22.

5. Reprinted from volumes 5 and 15 in the series Polyphonic Music of the Fourteenth Century as *Musicorum Collegio: Fourteenth-Century Musicians' Motets* (Monaco: Editions de l'Oiseau-Lyre, 1986). Study in progress with David Howlett.

6. For manuscript abbreviations see *The New Grove Dictionary.* F:Pn, fr. 146 has been published in facsimile with magisterial commentary as *Le Roman de Fauvel in the Edition of Mesire Chaillou de Pesstain: A Reproduction in Facsimile of the Complete Manuscript Paris, Bibliothèque Nationale, Fonds Français 146.* Introduction by Edward H. Roesner, François Avril, and Nancy Freeman Regalado (New York: Broude Brothers, 1990). B:Br 19606 is published in facsimile by Brussels, Koninklijke Bibliotheek Albert I and Alamire (1990). The Strasbourg version (lost through fire) survives in a copy by Edmond de Coussemaker. See Le Manuscrit Musical M 222 C 22 de la Bibliothèque de Strasbourg. [Ed. Albert Vander Linden. Facsimile edition of portions of Coussemaker's descriptive notes, now in Brussels, Bibliothèque du Conservatoire Royal de Musique, MS 56286.] Thesaurus Musicus II. Brussels [n.d., 1977], fo. 71v, no. 115, pp. 110–111.

7. One of these is an ornamented keyboard adaptation of (mainly) triplum and

duplum in the Robertsbridge manuscript, GB:Lbl 28550, transposed up a tone and with a partial version of the triplum text. A facsimile of this source is in H. E. Wooldridge, *Early English Harmony*, 1 (London: Plainsong and Mediaeval Music Society, 1897), pls. 42–45. The other is a small single leaf in D:Mbs 29775 (= Clm 29775/10), pre-serving a curiously notated and textually corrupt version of the triplum alone, transposed down a seventh (to the G an octave below the keyboard version), and with a page turn. Up-stemmed, flagged, and down-stemmed minims are used, with no obvious relation-ship to the rhythms of the motet. Martin Staehelin dates it early fifteenth century, but the down-stems might suggest an even later date, despite their appearance in some early German organ tablatures, which this is not. See Martin Staehelin, "Münchner Frag-mente mit mehrstimmiger Musik des späten Mittelalters," *Nachrichten der Akademie der Wissenschaften in Göttingen*, 1, Philologisch-historische Klasse, Jahrgang 1988, no. 6, 167–90; see pp. 176–7 and pl. 5 (facsimile).

8. The composition is published in Philippe de Vitry, *Complete Works*, ed. Leo Schrade, Polyphonic Music of the Fourteenth Century 1 (Monaco: Editions de l'Oiseau-Lyre, 1956), 54–56. A musical omission in the duplum of the fr. 146 copy renders it unperformable without emendation. Both sources have other slight blemishes in words and music that do not hobble the total effect even if they diminish the subtle-ties that the scribes could pass on to us.

9. See the exposition and review of earlier bibliography in Ernest H. Sanders, "The Early Motets of Philippe de Vitry," *Journal of the American Musicological Society* 28 (1975): 24–45. While this chapter was in press, Andrew Wathey made an exciting discovery (see "Myth and Mythography in the Motets of Philippe de Vitry," *Musica e Storia* 6 [1998], 81–106), namely, that the final hexameter couplet of the triplum *Tri-bum que non abhorruit* (see note 14), is not an independent proverb but derives from Joseph of Exeter's *De bello troiano*, VI.804–5, in the context of the reversal of King Priam's fortunes and his murder. In turn, the sentiment, but not the wording, derives from Lucretius, *De rerum natura*. (David Howlett had earlier identified the last triplum line of *Garrit Gallus* in *De bello troiano*, I.386.) Even more strikingly, Vitry used this same couplet to annotate a passage in his own copy of the *Chronicon of Guillaume de Nangis*, which recounts Parthian defeat (38 B.C.) and subsequent tragedies, in moral and historical conditions parallel to those of the motet, where, too, it was better to have nothing than to suffer a calamitous loss. This discovery offers further support for Vitry's authorship of the motet, as well as for his direct involvement in the Fauvel project.

10. Exile and eclipse are central themes of F:Pn, fr. 146, particularly in the *dits* of Geffroy de Paris. One of his French poems uses an eclipse of the sun and the moon to stand for the vacant papacy in 1314–16 and also for the uncertainties of the French royal succession and the eclipse of its dignity at the same period (*De la Comète et de l'Eclipse de la Lune et du Soulail*); another deals with the exile of the papacy from Rome to Avignon (*La Desputoison de l'Eglise de Romme et de l'Eglise de France pour le Siège du Pape*). See Walter Storer and Charles Rochedieu, eds., *Six Historical Poems of Geoffroi de Paris* (Chapel Hill: University of North Carolina Press, 1950). The Latin poem *Natus ego* also treats of this topic, but applies the theme of Babylonian captivity more generally (and traditionally) to the sins and sufferings of the Church. See Leofranc Holford-Strevens, "The Latin *Dits* of Geffroy de Paris: An *Editio Princeps*," in *Fauvel Studies: Allegory, Chronicle, Music and Image in Paris, Bibliothèque nationale de France, MS français 146*, ed. Margaret Bent and Andrew Wathey (Oxford: Clarendon Press, 1998, 246–274).

11. This passage is a vivid choice to evoke the theme of Marigny, whose hanging is more graphically presented in another Fauvel motet, *Aman novi/Heu Fortuna*. The text is here quoted and the translation adapted from the Loeb Classical Library edition

by A. L. Wheeler (Cambridge, Mass.: Harvard University Press, 1924). For the group of three Marigny motets, see Margaret Bent, "Fauvel and Marigny: Which Came First?," *Fauvel Studies*, 35–52.

12. I acknowledge the great pleasure and stimulus of continuing collaborative work with David Howlett on this repertory. Many of the analytical approaches I have applied here were jointly discovered and are hereby so acknowledged. The texts as printed here can also be found, with others, in the booklet published with the Orlando Consort recording, *Philippe de Vitry and the Ars Nova*, CD-SAR 49. Italics and underscoring are added.

13. The special properties of this proportion were known to classical antiquity and the Middle Ages, more usually in geometric form, or approximated in the whole-number series known by the name of Fibonacci (the mathematician Leonard of Pisa). It is also—and more appropriately—known as the proportion of extreme and mean ratio. Its special quality is that the proportion of the greater part of the division to the whole is the same as that of the smaller part to the greater. For its application to the counting of text elements, see D. R. Howlett, "New Criteria for Editing *Beowulf*," in *The Editing of Old English*, ed. D. S. Brewer (Cambridge: Boydell and Brewer, 1994), 69–84.

The GS can be derived arithmetically by multiplying the total number—in this case of words—by .618, repeating the process to reproduce the proportion successively. In the triplum, $62 \times .618 = 38.316 \times .618 = 23.679 \times .618 = 14.6$. These numbers can be rounded (38, 24, 15), or the GS can be considered to fall in the next word (39, 24, 15). In the duplum, $41 \times .618 = 25.338 \times .628 = 15.658 \times .618 = 9.677$. These numbers can be rounded (25, 16, 19), or the GS can be considered to fall in the next word (26, 16, 10). Counting must sometimes be done from the end and internally as well as from the beginning. There may be for these reasons (that is, direction, and rounding of fractions) two candidates for the position of the word at or nearest the GS position, hence the admission of adjacent words.

14. H. Walther, *Proverbia sententiaeque latinitatis medii aevi: Lateinische Sprichwörter und Sentenzen des Mittelalters*, 5 vols., Carmina Medii Aevi Posterioris Latina 2 (Göttingen: Vandnhoeck and Ruprecht, 1963–7), no. 22073 (*Carminum proverbialium, loci communes . . .*). See note 9 above.

15. Musical references are given by longs (L) as numbered in the accompanying score, or the values referred to as breves (B), semibreves (S). The GS of the structured music (that is, discounting the introductory 6L) falls halfway through L51 on "ru|- erit" (triplum) and "dicta" (duplum).

16. "Fortuna recedis/-at" occurs in lines 7 and 19. The 23 lines that they span are the minor part of the GS of the total lines in the Ovid letter, 58–35.

17. I am grateful to Professor Patrick Boyde for alerting me to an interesting case of strategic quotation (probably before 1340) in the Petrarch *canzone*, *Lasso me, ch'i' non so in qual parte pieghi* (no. 70 in the *Canzoniere*). It has five stanzas of 10 lines each. The last line of each stanza is the first line of an existing *canzone* by a noted poet, respectively by Arnaut Daniel (so Petrarch believed), Cavalcanti, Dante, Cino, and finally Petrarch's own *Nel dolce tempo de la prima etade* (no. 23, his first *canzone*, on the theme of metamorphosis). In each case the penultimate line of the stanza forms a rhyming couplet with the final imported line.

18. It is tempting to see in this some support for Vitry's authorship. It would not be surprising that Vitry, a friend and respected associate of Petrarch, should pioneer such boldly clerical-humanistic juxtapositions. This is entirely in line with the further pointers to Vitry's humanist identity that result from Andrew Wathey's discovery of some of his motet texts in humanist poetry manuscripts. See "The Motets of Philippe de Vitry and the Fourteenth-Century Renaissance," *Early Music History* 12 (1993): 119–50.

19. "Local Chant Readings and the *Roman de Fauvel*," *Fauvel Studies*, 495–524.

20. There is an extra minim in the triplum at the end of L12. The other corrections in the present edition that bring out this identity are based on alternative manuscript readings, and supported by musical sense (parallel readings, and avoidance of harmonic fourths).

21. They seem to have been published only by Sarah Fuller, albeit noted in less detail; see *European Musical Heritage 800–1750* (New York: Knopf, 1987), 99–103. The translation is improved by Howlett's reading, Schrade's musical transcription (reproduced by Fuller) by the present version. Sanders partly makes this observation ("The Early Motets," 27) when he says that the *taleae* could be treated as 3 × 4 instead of 2 × 6, reflecting isomelic correspondences, and notes with approval the periodicity of the upper parts. Wulf Arlt kindly showed me his own similar unpublished version when I discussed the present one with him.

22. My transcription differs from Schrade's at 34 (as Br; fr. 146 omits 35–39), 47 (as Br), 66 (as fr.146, rescuing the imitation by descent from D), 71 (Br and Pn are wrong, but this and 47, 66 are confirmed by Sm 222 and by the intabulation in Lbl 28550); L74 is possibly a further candidate for emendation, but without support from the manuscripts. Also, the identities are better seen if the plicas are left unrealized in the transcriptions. There are no plicas in Sm 222, which confirms all details of the identical passages.

23. Ernest H. Sanders, "The Medieval Motet," in *Gattungen der Musik in Einzeldarstellungen: Gedenkschrift Leo Schrade*, ed. W. Arlt et al. (Bern: Francke, 1973), 497–573.

24. Ursula Günther, "The 14th-Century Motet and its Development," *Musica Disciplina* 12 (1958): 27–58.

25. Georg Reichert, "Das Verhältnis zwischen musikalischer und textlicher Struktur in den Motetten Machauts," *Archiv für Musikwissenschaft* 13 (1956): 197–216.

26. Heinrich Besseler, "Studien zur Musik des Mittelalters II: Die Motette von Franko von Köln bis Philipp von Vitry," *Archiv für Musikwissenschaft* 8 (1926–27): 137–258, esp. 222–24.

27. This neuma is also used for Vitry's *Douce playsance/Garison* and for the motet *Floret/Florens* that Sanders—not entirely persuasively—would also attribute to him; see Sanders, "The Early Motets."

28. The other two occurrences of this musical phrase fall on "vispilionum" and "hominum," thus drawing attention to the first "rhyme" of the duplum ("latronum–vispilionum") with the caesural "hominum" of the Ovid hexameter.

29. It was not necessary to space the piece in this way. It could have been accommodated on the recto, starting at the top of the page, without displacing any other material, by the simple expedient of writing a single statement of the tenor. The tenor is notated once only in B:Br 19606, twice (unnecessarily) in F:Pn, fr. 146.

30. There are 27 words in the duplum of the neighboring *Adesto/Firmissime*, a strongly trinitarian piece studied in this volume by Anne Walters Robertson (see Chap. 3).

31. The piece is set up in such a way as to encourage parallel part-writing, especially if viewed in the long term rather that in a contrapuntally local way. Parallel octaves and fifths occur between triplum and duplum, parallels with the tenor only at 20, 44, and 55.

32. Nicholas Mann, "In margine alla quarta egloga: piccoli problemi di esegesi petrarchesca," *Studi Petrarcheschi*, NS 4 (1987): 17–32. For further references see the article by Andrew Wathey cited above, n. 18.

33. Storer and Rochedieu, *Six Historical Poems*.

Du Fay and the Cultures
of Renaissance Florence

As with other Italian cities during the Quattrocento, the fortunes of polyphonic music in Florence tended to wax and wane with the circumstances of patronage, the changing interests of the political and intellectual elites. Although the palimpsest manuscript Archivio Capitolare di San Lorenzo 2211, compiled ca. 1418–21, testifies to continued Florentine traditions of song and motet, by the following decade these traditions, as nearly as we can determine, had become moribund.[1] The musical life of Renaissance Florence took a decided turn in June 1434 with the arrival of Pope Eugenius IV and the entire papal Curia, seeking refuge from the unsafe precincts of Rome. The papal chapel was dominated by a group of singers from France and the regions of Burgundy, especially Liège and Cambrai, a circumstance that could not but attract the attention of the newly installed Medici party in Florence.

Still, the most visible effect of the papal stay came only a year later, in June 1435, when the renowned musician Guillaume Du Fay rejoined the papal chapel of Eugenius IV. The apparent fruits of Du Fay's ten months in Florence comprise the motets *Nuper rosarum flores*, *Salve flos tusce gentis florentia salve/Vos nunc etrusce iubar salvete puelle*, and *Mirandas parit hec urbs florentina puellas*, all of which celebrate the city in no uncertain terms.[2] As David Fallows exclaims, "Three more radically different works are difficult to imagine. All three are masterpieces of the utmost perfection; they are as clear an embodiment of the Renaissance as Brunelleschi's dome."[3]

Another motet that likely belongs to Du Fay's period in the papal chapel—Rome, October 1428 to August 1433, and Florence, June 1435 to 18 April 1436—is the prayer motet *Gaude virgo mater christi*.[4] The work appears in the third and latest layer of the manuscript Bologna, Civico Museo Bibliografico Musicale, Q 15, the most important source for the polyphonic Mass and motet of the early Quattrocento, and must have been written by ca. 1436.[5] Its entry in Bologna Q 15 postdates that of Du Fay's *Supremum est mortalibus* (fols.

190ᵛ–191ʳ), performed in Rome, May 1433. The circumstance is significant in that the Bologna Q 15 scribe had access to virtually all of Du Fay's motets and Mass music of the 1420s and early 1430s. *Gaude virgo mater christi* appears in Bologna Q 15 alongside a motet with similar text, *Gaude tu baptista christi*, by Benedictus Sirede, *dictus* Benoit, a composer first known from documents entered in Florence, November 1436 to February 1437; their simultaneous inscription may indicate that the two motets circulated together.[6] Regardless of the place of composition, it seems certain that *Gaude virgo mater christi*, as a sacred work by the first singer of the papal chapel, belonged to the repertory of the chapel while it remained in Florence.[7]

Of the three secure motets Du Fay composed during his Florentine sojourn, *Mirandas parit* makes an illuminating contrast to *Gaude virgo mater christi*, for while they both utilize the same basic style, what I have called "the equal-discantus motet style," they realize that style in markedly different ways.[8] *Mirandas parit*, the latest datable equal-discantus motet in Italy, in many ways sums up the tradition that developed from the Italian Trecento motet, as described by Margaret Bent, following the Council of Pisa in 1409.[9] The contrasting musical characteristics of *Mirandas parit* and *Gaude virgo mater christi* are attributable not only to the absolute differences between their texts, but to the divergent cultural milieux those texts represent. By tracing the connections that relate culture, text, and music to one another in a continuous process, one ultimately can make inferences concerning the diverse audiences for whom the motets were intended. *Mirandas parit* and *Gaude virgo mater christi*, I believe, emerge from two of the prominent cultural currents of the fifteenth century in Italy: the secular wave of humanism, and the devotional experience of lay piety.

The humanist conception of *Mirandas parit* may best be seen in comparison with another of Du Fay's Florentine motets, *Salve flos tusce gentis* (Cantus II):[10]

Mirandas parit

Mirandas parit hec urbs florentina puellas
In quibus est species et summo forma nitore.
Quale helenam decus olim nos habuisse putamus
Virginibus patriis talis florescit ymago.
Ad te precipuam genuit clarissima virgo
Nam reliquas superas et luce et corpore nimphas,
Ut socias splendore suas dea pulchra diana
Vincit et integrior quacumque in parte videtur.

(This Florentine city brings forth wonderful girls,
Among whom there is splendor and beauty of the highest luster.
Such loveliness we believe Helen once to have had:
In the homelands so fine a likeness began to blossom among the virgins.
To you, special one, the most renowned Virgin gave birth,
But now you surpass the rest of the Nymphs in both light and body.
As you unite her maidens in splendor, the sweet goddess Diana
Prevails and is seen to be fuller on every side.)

Salve flos tusce gentis, **Cantus II**

Vos nunc etrus[c]e iubar salvete puelle
    Sic sedet hoc animo nec sine amore moror.
Stant foribus nimphis similes stant naiades utque
    Aut [ut] am[a]zonides aut proc[i]dives venus.
Fervet in amplexus atque oscula dulcia quisque;
    Si semel has viderit captus amore cadet
Ista dee mundi vester per secula cuncta
    Guillermus cecini natus [et] ipse fay.

(Now you Etruscan girls, hail! The radiance
Thus lingers within this heart, nor without love do I delay.
They stand at the doors like Nymphs, they stand like Naiads;
Or like Amazons, or prostrate Venus.
Each one burns in embraces and sweet kisses;
If once one sees these, he will fall, captured by love.
This song, O goddesses of the world, through all the ages
I, your Guillaume, born and called "Fay," have sung.)[11]

The two motets assume the guise of the contemporary humanist panegyric, in which the deliberate classical patterning of meter, language, and figure are meant to dignify both subject and poet.[12] *Mirandas parit* makes use of strict dactylic hexameters, organized in syntactic couplets, while the texts of *Salve flos tusce gentis* are composed in elegiac couplets, or distichs.[13] The choice of elegiac verse may be attributable to the occasional nature of the poetry, in imitation of classical models.[14] Both works are replete with classical vocabulary and allusions, of a kind that would have been familiar to educated listeners.

Moreover, both *Mirandas parit* and *Salve flos tusce gentis* praise the young women of Florence, the latter in the second discantus. This in itself is remarkable, for occasional motets of the Quattrocento rarely address themselves toward women.[15] The rhetoric implies that their audience included mixed groups in terms of gender and generation, normal for the elaborate *feste* of the Florentine elite. Indeed, the first discantus of *Salve flos tusce gentis* delivers a more typical encomium upon the virtues of the city. Neither motet so much as mentions Church or pope, although *Salve flos tusce gentis* acclaims the "religione viros" native to Florence. One line of *Mirandas parit*—"Ad te precipuam genuit clarissima virgo"—suggests a special relationship between the Virgin Mary and the city, but I view this as a rhetorical gesture typical for the occasional motet. The text of *Mirandas parit*, seen in its relation to *Salve flos tusce gentis*, demonstrates a strongly secular orientation, characteristic of Florentine humanist culture in the 1430s.[16]

Gaude virgo mater christi belongs to another world altogether. The text, often described as a "sequence" in liturgical books, originated in the thirteenth century:[17]

1. Gaude virgo mater christi
    Que per aurem concepisti
    Gabriele nuncio.

2. Gaude que a deo plena
    Peperisti sine pena
    Con pudoris lilio.

3. Gaude quia tui nati
    Quem dolebas mortem pati
    Fulget resurexio.

4. Gaude christo ascendente
    Et in celum te vidente
    Fertur motu proprio.

5. Gaude que post ipsum scandis
    Et est honor tibi grandis
    In celi palacio.

6. Ubi fructus ventris tui
    Per te detur nobis frui
    In perhenni gaudio. Amen.

(Rejoice, Virgin, mother of Christ
Who conceived through the ear
At Gabriel's announcement.

Rejoice, you who, pregnant by God,
Gave birth without blame;
With the lily of modesty.

Rejoice, because the one born of you,
Whose death you sorrowed to experience,
Shines in resurrection.

Rejoice in Christ who ascends,
And who, seeing you in heaven,
Is moved of His own accord.

Rejoice, you who ascend after Him;
And there is great honor to you
In the palace of heaven,

Where the fruit of your womb
May be given to us, through you, to delight
In eternal rejoicing. Amen.

By the fifteenth century it had broken loose from its liturgical moorings, and become one of the best known of all rhymed prayers.[18] It is the prayer most frequently appended to Books of Hours, especially in French sources, and even appears in some *laudari*, vernacular collections of the Italian *lauda*, or song of praise.[19] Transmitted in multiple versions, ranging from six to 24 stanzas, *Gaude virgo mater christi* commemorates the Joys of the Blessed Virgin.[20] It was set not only by Du Fay, but by the northerner Heinrich Battre, and in the late fifteenth century by Josquin des Prez.[21] The widespread popularity of the text, together with its lack of a specific location in the liturgical year, suggests that the motet was composed for lay audiences, to whom a polyphonic setting would be at once familiar and powerful.

Mirandas parit, addressed to the young ladies of Florence, presents an uncomplicated Latin syntax appropriate to its theme. Each line is self-contained, forming an independent or dependent clause; enjambment occurs only between the last two verses. The organization into syntactic couplets means that two couplets appear in each half of the motet. The poem builds a proportional structure based on addition by pairs: two lines, two couplets, two halves. In the second half of the poem, the form of address changes from description to apostrophe. The halves are balanced topomorphically, by the reiteration of similar images between lines in corresponding position (lines 1 and 5, 2 and 6, and so on):[22]

> parit / genuit
> forma nitore / luce et corpore
> helenam / diana
> florescit ymago / integrior . . . videtur

The opposition of "helenam" and "diana" situates the two main, classical comparisons of the poem in relation to one another. A chiastic device bridges the midway point, the placement of the word "Virginibus" at the start of line 4, and "virgo" at the end of line 5. The two lines also share a partial end-rhyme, "ymago" / "virgo." A symmetrical but elegant structure and straightforward syntax contribute to the insouciant, polished tone of *Mirandas parit*. Its poetic devices, as well as its meter and style, reflect the ambience of fifteenth-century humanism.

Du Fay's setting fully realizes and accentuates the formal qualities of the text. *Mirandas parit* divides into two sections by mensuration: *tempus perfectum diminutum* (∅, unmarked) for the first four lines, *tempus imperfectum diminutum* (¢) for the second four lines. Du Fay balances the motet almost equally, with 225 semibreves in the first section versus 216 semibreves in the second, a 25 : 24 ratio.[23] The change in mensuration coincides with the change in voice from impersonal to direct address.

Du Fay's musical setting creates its own formal processes, interacting with but not dependent upon the poetry. All voices, including the tenor, are free, in marked contrast to the four-part texture of *Salve flos tusce gentis*, which operates with *color* in the tenors, and *talea* in all voices.[24] *Color, talea,* and *diminutio* may be classified as external structural devices, a priori manipulations of the form, especially of the cantus firmus. Equal-discantus motets like *Mirandas parit*, on the other hand, rely on a variety of internal devices to create formal cohesion. Cadences assume a high importance under such circumstances, acting as anchors to the luxuriantly curved melodic lines in diminished tempus. They lend a sense of tonal direction and control with respect to the final, F. Furthermore, cadences punctuate the text at the end of each poetic verse.[25] Verses 2, 4, 6, and 8 possess internal cadences; all but the last divide at the caesura, extending the length of each unrhymed couplet.

Du Fay employs imitation, sustained harmonies, and voice reduction for textural contrast and formal effect. Since the tenor proceeds at a leisurely, but flexible, pace, unlike the interlocking, repetitive tenors of *Salve flos tusce gentis*, the texture gains a greater variety of harmonic color and rhythm. Verses 1, 2, 3, 4, and 7 begin with an imitative gesture, as do the phrases that set the second parts of verses 4 and 8 (mm. 33–37 and 84–91). Verses 1, 3, and 4, in fact, employ the same imitative melodic idea, in different guises. In contrast, verses 5, 6, and 8 begin with relatively sustained textures, lacking decided rhythmic motion. Phrase beginnings thereby enhance the line-by-line correspondence between musical and poetic syntax, and underscore the parallels between the first and second halves of the text.

The importance of formal devices, in the absence of a structural cantus firmus, can also be seen in Du Fay's treatment of the introductory and closing passages. *Mirandas parit* begins with a short imitative *introitus*, in which cantus I sings alone for two longs, then continues in accompaniment to the same idea in cantus II. The tenor joins in at measure 5, where another, stronger melodic surge points toward the cadence in measure 9. The reiteration of solo statements emphasizes the motet's opening verse, which announces its main subject. Du Fay gives *Mirandas parit* a strong sense of completion by means of a dense imitative passage on the word "videtur" (mm. 84–89). Cantus II and the tenor begin a *fuga* at the fifth below, one semibreve apart. The composer constructs the melody in two repeated rhythmic cells, enabling cantus I to follow in rhythmic imitation on the third semibreve; the technique harks back to the motets of Johannes Ciconia. Both the *introitus* and closing passage, used as framing devices, are typical features of the equal-discantus motet style.

Mirandas parit exemplifies the texture of the equal-discantus motet, opposing two discantus voices in the same range, with melodic, rhythmic, and verbal activity divided quite equally between them. Du Fay captures the essence of the style in his exploitation of continuously shifting harmonic and rhythmic relations between the discantus voices. Fleeting parallel thirds and fourths abound between the upper parts, thirds and tenths between the discantus voices and the tenor (Example 5.1). Brilliance of sound, together with carefully placed dissonance, accentuates the poetic distance created by the elevated, polished suface of the poem. The motet is highly consonant, with a harmonic clarity that lets the words penetrate distinctly. As denoted by the conflicting B-flat signature, the tenor range lies one fifth lower than the cantus voices; it crosses cantus II only twice in the course of the work. The upper voices, singing the same words, cross freely, but not so often as to mitigate their independence of line. We hear a contrapuntal clarity admirably suited to the poetic tone and theme.

Textural lucidity allows the competing melodic lines to be heard to their fullest. In stark contrast to the continuous texture and mellifluous but meandering contours of *Salve flos tusce gentis*, the melodic structures of *Mirandas parit* are strongly shaped and directed—a prime reason why such motets have in the past been called, though with small historical justification, "cantilenae." In general, the higher of the two discantus voices tends to predominate at any one moment, a main reason for the limited degree of voice-crossing. The lines proceed in shorter subphrases that arrive at weak, elided cadences, headed to-

EXAMPLE 5.1 Du Fay, *Mirandas parit* (*Opera omnia*, ed. Besseler, 1:12–14), mm. 54–66: treatment of parallel intervals. Reprinted by permission of the American Institute of Musicology

ward a stronger cadential goal—an additive method that dates back to motets of the early Quattrocento (Example 5.2). Within subphrases, the melodic lines maintain direct contours, disguised or delayed by momentary reversals of direction (cantus I, m. 25). Frequent leaps of a third or fourth lend the melodic profiles a degree of distinction. Rhythmic treatment also varies beween the mensurations of the two parts: the second, in ₵, employs a higher degree of syncopation, in contrast to the more flexible rhythms of ø.

Du Fay controls the pace of *Mirandas parit*, the perception of forward momentum and retardation, partly through textural means. Two passages that seem deliberately to slow down the pace help illustrate the point. Verse 4 be-

EXAMPLE 5.2   Du Fay, *Mirandas parit* (*Opera omnia*, ed. Besseler, 1:12–14), mm. 17–26: length and construction of phrases. Reprinted by permission of the American Institute of Musicology

gins with a phrase in double subject imitation (mm. 27–33). The tenor carries a simple melodic idea against the more prominent, untexted figuration of cantus I, which derives from the *introitus*. In equal-discantus motets, tenor texting, as occurs here, is normally restricted to moments when the tenor assumes greater musical importance. The tenor idea is repeated at the unison by cantus I against the second subject in cantus II, then by cantus II against free counterpoint in the other voices. The passage serves as a respite before the intense drive to cadence at the end of the motet's first half (mm. 33–37).

The corresponding passage in the motet's second half, verse 8 (mm. 74–83), similarly slows down the pace just before the closing passage. The phrase begins with three longs in reduced texture, without the tenor. Shortly after the tenor reenters, cantus I splits into two parts (mm. 80–81), with the additional, higher part indicated by coloration. This creates a momentary four-part imperfect consonance, $d'-b-f\sharp'-b'$, with cantus II on the bottom. The phrase then resumes movement toward the perfect cadence in measure 83, on $c'-g'-c''$. As already shown, the closing section operates in dense, three-part rhythmic imitation. In sum, *Mirandas parit* displays a subtle, urbane treatment of structure, texture, and pacing, interacting with the inherent proportionality of the poetic text.

Gaude virgo mater christi sets a very different kind of text from *Mirandas parit*, although the musical contrasts between the motets are not attributable solely to the qualitative differences between the poems. Each of the first five stanzas begins with the word "Gaude," and describes one of the important events in the life of the Virgin Mary in her relationship to Christ: the Annunciation, Nativity, Resurrection, Ascension, and Assumption. Since the text functions as a prayer, each of these topoi leads the listener to a different place, or set of mental images associated with the event—the brevity of the strophes should not disguise the devotional connotations of the five stages, or stations, within the poem. The sixth, final, stanza contains an appeal to the Virgin, ending with the word "gaudio," which rounds off the rhetorical schema. The three-line stanzas are organized with the rhyme pattern AAX BBX and so on. A steady, trochaic meter, 8 + 8 + 7 syllables per stanza, contrasts with the unaccented hexameters and variable syllable count of *Mirandas parit*. Such a contrast between accented and quantitative meters is characteristic of the divide between sacred and secular Latin poetry of the fifteenth century.[26] Each strophe works as a single, self-contained unit: within the strophe, the first two lines set up the topic or narration, while the last line resolves the chain of thought, emphasized metrically by an accented syllable and double rhyme at the end of the third line.

The subtle, flexible formal control that Du Fay exerts in *Mirandas parit* finds scant counterpart in *Gaude virgo mater christi*. Just as the text originates in a different cultural realm, so too does the polyphonic setting. Du Fay creates a deliberately static structure to delineate the stanzaic divisions of the "sequence" text. Strong cadences at the end of each stanza, lasting one long apiece, repeatedly emphasize D, and the final, G.[27] The size of the sections shrinks as the motet progresses, from 16 to 13, 13, 11, 11, and 13.5 longs. In other words, the treatment of each strophe becomes more compact, with an extension in the last stanza for the "Amen" (mm. 73–77). Compared with *Mirandas parit*, the overall pacing turns unidirectional, with a final intense flourish at the end. The musical setting can be heard as a series of stages, parallel to the text, and progressing toward the same goal. Du Fay further emphasizes the strophic setting by starting stanzas 1 and 2 with the same melodic idea, in cantus II and cantus I, respectively; the same idea returns in shortened form at the beginning of stanza 6.

Strophic construction is heightened by the likelihood that the tenor should be underlaid throughout. In the Bologna Q 15 redaction, the tenor has one

EXAMPLE 5.3 Du Fay, comparative voice ranges and finals in (a) *Nuper rosarum flores* (1436); (b) *Salve flos tusce gentis* (1436); (c) *Gaude virgo mater christi* (1428–33 or 1435–36); (d) *Mirandas parit* (1435–36) [T = tenor, T2 = second tenor, C2 = second cantus, C1 = first cantus]

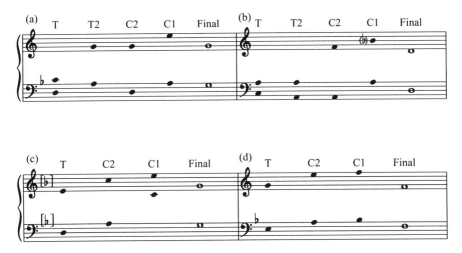

note or ligature for every syllable of text, with the exception of a single ligature that must be broken (m. 68). Within strophes, text underlay is often staggered between parts, but the cantus voices uniformly arrive with the tenor at the last cadence. The untexted contratenor, on the other hand, is demonstrably inauthentic, in part because it interferes with normal cadential patterns.[28] The similar verbal sound at each cadence, caused by the rhymed ending of the third line, helps to consolidate the point of arrival, just as the opening word, "Gaude," articulates each new beginning. Full tenor texting also creates a heavier acoustical effect, and suggests a different performance space than does *Mirandas parit*, possibly within the more resonant ambience of a cathedral or chapel, as opposed to a large hall or outside pavilion: by and large, fully texted motets, such as Hugo de Lantins's *Ave verum corpus*, are restricted to works with sacred texts.[29]

Another aspect of musical organization that distinguishes *Gaude virgo mater christi* from *Mirandas parit* is the distribution of voice ranges. Whereas the latter typifies the usual texture of the equal-discantus motet, the second discantus in *Gaude virgo mater christi* has a range and clef one third lower than the first discantus. Despite the difference in range, the two upper voices maintain their equality in all other respects. *Supremum est mortalibus*, written in May 1433, is Du Fay's first datable motet to employ a lower voice range for the second discantus, which in effect acts like a texted contratenor, covering the same range as the tenor: tenor *d–g'*, cantus II *d–g'*, cantus I *d'–e"*. A similar pattern of voice ranges occurs in *Nuper rosarum flores*, *Salve flos tusce gentis*, and later works, but not for *Mirandas parit* (Example 5.3).[30] The differ-

EXAMPLE 5.4   Du Fay, *Gaude virgo mater christi*, mm. 30–35: dissonance treatment

entiation of vocal ranges associates *Gaude virgo mater christi* with Du Fay's motets of the 1430s, and supports its dating to 1428–33 or 1435–36.

The discantus melodies in *Gaude virgo mater christi* lend the motet a warmth and intimacy that contrast with the highly polished, but cooler, melodic and textural surfaces of *Mirandas parit*. The swirling melodic lines appear unpredictably, and dissolve just as quickly. Du Fay pays a price for his freedom of melodic treatment, however, in the lesser degree of control he exerts over the counterpoint. The texture sustains a comparatively higher level of dissonance as the discantus voices rub against each other in passing, or conflict momentarily with the tenor (see the dissonances marked with an *x* in Example 5.4). *Gaude virgo mater christi* makes a virtue of this circumstance by using it to add piquancy to the melodic surfaces—in passing tones, escape notes, suspensions, and cadential appoggiaturas—and to cut against some of the overall sweetness of tone. In general, the motet operates on a series of shifting spotlights within each strophe, as attention swivels from one discantus voice to the other. Particularly interesting is the technique, heard in the first five measures, of isolating the second discantus in the middle against sustained harmony in the first discantus and tenor. Since the second discantus has a range one third lower than the first, they tend to maintain those relative positions when singing extended passages in semibreves and minims. The latter circumstance may explain why this motet shows no more voice-crossing than does *Mirandas parit*.

The solid formal structure of *Gaude virgo mater christi* provides a frame for its intricate melodic lines and sudden changes of pace. In tonal terms, Du Fay places special emphasis on the corresponding melodic fifths from *d″* to *g′*, in the soft hexachord, and from *a′* to *d′*, in the natural hexachord, which outline the plagal ambitus from *d″* to *d′*. Exploitation of modal elements, already seen in the large-scale cadential structure, contrasts with the freer, and more typical, use of tonal resources in *Mirandas parit*. The melodic writing itself works in two ways: with insistent, descending motion in breves and semibreves, set off by upward leaps of a fourth, fifth, sixth, or even an octave (m. 25), and with curved, conjunct motion in minims. The two styles flow into each other within strophes and within individual voices, creating plasticity and contrast.

Such writing is reminiscent of two Du Fay motets from the early 1420s, *Flos florum* and *Vergene bella*. The comparison is instructive: both are Marian, they are written in the newly accessible motet styles of the early Quattrocento, with an attendant emphasis on the melodic line in *tempus perfectum diminutum*, and they demonstrate the kind of melismatic, curvilinear motion in semibreves and minims that characterizes *Gaude virgo mater christi*.[31] *Vergene bella*, of course, sets the first strophe of Francesco Petrarca's *canzone* in praise of the Virgin Mary, a poem that, like *Gaude virgo mater christi*, counts among the most widely distributed texts of the fifteenth century. The poem, 366th and last in Petrarca's *Canzoniere*, appears in numerous *laudari*, and even Du Fay's polyphonic setting, which incorporates the qualities of both motet and *lauda*, survives in three different manuscripts.[32]

Du Fay, in choosing these texts, or having them assigned to him on commission, appealed to a wider audience, that of the religious laity who wished to have access to the power and solace offered by ecclesiastical ceremony. The composer could not but be aware that motets with familiar or, in the case of *Flos florum*, evocative Marian texts would carry his name and music far beyond the bounds of his present patron and employment. In the fifteenth century, lay spirituality took several forms, which varied from region to region. In Florence, piety manifested itself through membership in religious confraternities, the construction of family chapels in Florentine churches, such as San Lorenzo (collegiate) or Santa Maria Novella (Dominican), in the possession and private use of Books of Hours or *laudari*, and through the endowment of commemorative Masses said or sung for the souls of oneself and one's family.[33]

In the fifteenth century, Florence could boast of over thirty religious confraternities.[34] Prominent among these were the *laudesi* companies, who, until at least 1430, gathered each weeknight to sing or hear *laude*, and who held shortened services at their chapels within the city's churches.[35] By the fifteenth century, many *laudesi* companies hired professional singers, usually Florentine tradesmen, but at times including outsiders, such as the composer Benoit in 1436.[36] Confraternal organizations were open to a cross-section of society, including artisans and all but the lowest class of workers, and in this respect overlapped with the elite social world of the merchants and bankers.[37]

One contemporaneous equal-discantus motet, *Missus est Gabriel angelus*, attributed to Petrus Rubeus (Pietro Rosso) in Bologna Q 15, likely was performed in a confraternal environment. It combines two responsories and their verses to create a polyphonic, texturally elaborate paraphrase of Luke I:26–32, the scene of the Annunciation. Treviso, where Rosso was active from 1417 through 1446, had a well-established *festa* of the Annunciation that involved an elaborate procession from the cathedral to Santa Maria Maggiore and back, followed by a *sacre rappresentazione* in the cathedral.[38] The entire event was sponsored and paid for by the confraternity of Santa Marie dei Battuti, and presented in conjunction with the cathedral chapter. A document from 1443 states that "Master Pietro Rosso, priest, made the song [that] is sung at the crossroads: Missus est angelus Gabriel" ("messer pre' Piero Rosso fé el canto [che] se canta in + di via/ missus est angelus Gabriel"). The original records show that Rosso's motet was performed every year between 1443 and 1447, if not earlier, with the confraternal and ecclesiastical authorities of Treviso all in attendance.

Gaude virgo mater christi, in its particular text–music relations, appeals to the lay audience in a number of ways. Its melodic style recalls the Trecento song tradition and the closely associated polyphonic *lauda*; the song motet *Vergene bella* draws on the same traditions. In its intensity of expression, carried out within a well-defined but largely static framework, *Gaude virgo mater christi* contrasts with the transparent textures and perfect balance of vertical and horizontal elements that characterize *Mirandas parit*. The polyphonic setting amplifies the five Joys of the Virgin described by the text, presenting them to the listener and drawing him or her along in the act of prayer. The sixth strophe offers a request to the Virgin, portrayed as crowned in Paradise, on behalf of all.

In contrast, the strong humanist bent of *Salve flos tusce gentis* and *Mirandas parit* makes it likely that they were commissioned by the Florentine merchant class associated with the Medici.[39] Cosimo de' Medici himself was renowned as a patron of humanists, and the Florentine government possessed a long tradition of employing humanist writers, notably the Chancellor, Leonardo Bruni.[40] In *Salve flos tusce gentis*, Du Fay makes reference to the commission itself, in a witty play upon the traditional employment motet:

> Nunc cecini et grate voces placuere canore
> Premia mercedes nec pe[t]iere simul.
>
> (Now I have sung the tones, and willingly, to please with song;
> And not to seek gifts and salary together.)

The passage can be read as a comment on Du Fay's dual role as papal singer ("mercedes") and as composer to the city ("premia"). The text gives further information concerning its audience: it praises the "honorable arts" ("artis honeste"), those great in council and in loyalty ("magnos consilio atque fide"), as well as men of "genius" and "eloquence" ("ingenii" and "eloquii"), all ideal characteristics of the merchant class and professional humanists who ran the government and business enterprises of the Florentine republic. The same social group was responsible for the commission of *Mirandas parit*. The selection of women as addressees in the latter motet suggests a familial ambience, rather than public ceremony or ambassadorial display.[41] A less complex work than *Salve flos tusce gentis*, *Mirandas parit* is at once brilliant and subtle. It creates a flexible musical design that sharpens and accentuates the humanist praises of the ladies of Florence.

Polyphonic motets could only flourish in the presence of a competent choir, as was the case in Florence during Eugenius IV's first stay in the city. Papal singers, individually or together, undoubtedly sang in Florence cathedral and other churches. It was in Eugenius IV's interest, and their own, that his musicians generate goodwill in their host city. As a papal singer, administrator, and composer, Du Fay had multiple obligations, which included the fulfillment of outside commissions. The audience for *Gaude virgo mater christi* and other Du Fay works such as *Ave virgo que de celis* overlaps in social composition with the audience for *Salve flos tusce gentis* and *Mirandas parit*, but represents a different aspect of the same society.[42] Such intertwined relations characterize the dense social organization of fifteenth-century Florence. *Mirandas parit* and *Gaude virgo mater christi* were thus heard in very different ways and contexts. The motets represent two different ideals, two different cultures of the Florentine Renaissance, coexisting and at times overlapping, sometimes within the same creative mind.

NOTES

1. John Nádas, "The Lucca Codex and San Lorenzo 2211: Native and Foreign Songs in Early Quattrocento Florence," paper read at the American Musicological Society Annual Meeting, Austin, Texas, October 1989.

2. See Guillaume Dufay, *Opera omnia*, 6 vols., ed. Heinrich Besseler (Rome: American Institute of Musicology, 1951–66), 1; id., *Opera omnia*, 4 vols., ed. Guillaume de Van (Rome: American Institute of Musicology, 1947–49), 1–2. All measure numbers cited herein refer to the Besseler edition. *Nuper rosarum flores* was composed for the dedication of the cathedral of Santa Maria del Fiore on 25 March 1436. Although the matter is too complex to be considered here, *Salve flos tusce gentis* may be dated between 25 March and 5 April 1436, that is, between Passion Sunday and Maundy Thursday. *Mirandas parit* is only datable to the period of Du Fay's residence in Florence, June 1435 to 18 April 1436.

3. *Dufay* (London: J. M. Dent, 1982), 47. Alejandro Enrique Planchart, "The Early Career of Guillaume Du Fay," *Journal of the American Musicological Society* 46 (1993): 351, n. 45, suggests that the texts of *Nuper rosarum flores*, *Salve flos tusce gentis*, and *Mirandas parit* number among those that may be attributed to Du Fay himself.

4. *Opera omnia*, ed. Besseler, 5:1–4; and Robert Michael Nosow, "The Florid and Equal-Discantus Motet Styles of Fifteenth-Century Italy" (Ph.D. diss., University of North Carolina at Chapel Hill, 1992), 369–75. On Du Fay's career in the papal chapel and Savoy, see Fallows, *Dufay*, 32–51.

5. Margaret Bent, "A Contemporary Perception of Early Fifteenth-Century Style: Bologna Q 15 as a Document of Scribal Editorial Initiative," *Musica Disciplina* 41 (1987): 185–87, 198. The other source for *Gaude virgo mater christi*, Munich, Bayerische Staatsbibliothek, MS 14274, belongs to the years 1438–44. On the dating of this source, see Ian Rumbold, "The Compilation and Ownership of the 'St. Emmeram' Codex (Munich, Bayerische Staatsbibliothek, Clm 14274)," *Early Music History* 2 (1982): 195–200, 206–7.

6. Blake Wilson, *Music and Merchants: The Laudesi Companies of Republican Florence* (Oxford: Clarendon Press, 1992), 84–85. The identification of Benoit with Benedictus Sirede is made in Pamela F. Starr, "The 'Ferrara Connection': A Case Study of Musical Recruitment in the Renaissance," *Studi musicali* 18 (1989): 8–9. In light of Benoit's Florentine employment, it is worth pointing out that *Gaude tu baptista christi* addresses John the Baptist, the patron saint of Florence.

7. Fallows, *Dufay*, 43, shows that Du Fay became first singer in October 1435.

8. Nosow, "The Florid and Equal-Discantus Motet Styles," chaps. 3 and 4, 38–151; id., "The Equal-Discantus Motet Style after Ciconia," *Musica Disciplina* 45 (1991). The analysis of *Mirandas parit* herein addresses the salient style features of the equal-discantus motet.

9. Ibid., chap. 3, 38–107. On the Italian motet, see Margaret Bent, "The Fourteenth-Century Italian Motet," *L'ars nova italiana del Trecento: Certaldo VI*, ed. Giulio Cattin (Certaldo: Edizioni Polis, 1984), 85–125; on the motet in the Veneto, Julie Emelyn Cumming, "Concord out of Discord: Occasional Motets of the Early Quattrocento" (Ph.D. diss., University of California, Berkeley, 1987), chaps. 7–9, 213–336. The fourteenth-century Italian motet was first briefly described in Heinrich Besseler, "Studien zur Musik des Mittelalters," *Archiv für Musikwissenschaft* 17 (1925): 235.

10. The unique source for *Mirandas parit* and *Salve flos tusce gentis* is Modena, Biblioteca Estense, MS α.X.1.11, fols. 62ᵛ–63ʳ and 64ᵛ-65ʳ, respectively. The music of *Mirandas parit* also exists as a contrafact, *Imperatrix angelorum*, in Trent, Castello del Buon Consiglio, Monumenti e collezioni provinciali, MS 88, fols. 24ᵛ–26ʳ.

11. Translation after Peter James, notes to *Dufay: Missa 'L'homme armè'*, *Motets*, Hilliard Ensemble, CD sound recording (London: EMI, 1987), 27–29. The text of both cantus I and cantus II is corrupt, as at the word "proc[i]dives"; the emendations are those of Richard Kienast in Dufay, *Opera omnia*, ed. Besseler, 1:12–13. I also employ one translation of the last verse given by David Fallows, *Dufay*, 9.

12. Thomas Christian Schmidt, " 'Carmina gratulatoria'—Humanistische Dichtung in der Staatsmotette des 15. Jahrhunderts," *Archiv für Musikwissenschaft* 51 (1994): 87–89.

13. Dactylic hexameter consists of six metrical feet, of which the first five are dactyls, that is, a long syllable followed by two short syllables, or spondees, that is, two longs. The sixth foot is always a spondee. In classical Latin, long syllables have twice the spoken length as short ones, hence the term "quantitative meter." Elegiac couplets consist of one verse of dactylic hexameter followed by one of dactylic pentameter. The pentameter divides symmetrically into 2½ + 2½ feet, and is therefore closely related to hexameter. Schmidt, " 'Carmina gratulatoria'," 96, points out that "Dufays metrische Texte hingegen sind fast völlig einwandfrei."

14. Du Fay also employs elegiac couplets for the occasional motet *Magnanime gentis laudes paciare minerva/Nexus amicicie musa m[o]dulante camenam* written for a peace treaty signed in Basel, May 1438. On the date, see Fallows, *Dufay*, 49–50.

15. In Florence, there had been a vigorous Trecento tradition whereby composers dedicated their songs to specific women, using the literary device of the *senhal*. In the

motet repertory, an exceptional example is Antonio da Cividale's *Strenua quem duxit/ Gaudeat et tanti*, edited by Gilbert Reaney in *Early Fifteenth-Century Music*, 7 vols. to date, Corpus Mensurabilis Musicae 11 (Neuhausen-Stuttgart: American Institute of Musicology, 1955–), 5:36–39. Reaney, p. xviii, finds that the motet addresses Giorgio Ordelaffi in cantus I, and his wife Lucrezia in cantus II, probably upon the celebration of their marriage in Forlì, 3 July 1412. On the disputed occasion and date of this motet, see Hans Schoop, "Antonius de Civitate Austrie," in *The New Grove Dictionary of Music and Musicians*, 20 vols., ed. Stanley Sadie (London: Macmillan, 1980), 1:494, and Nosow, "The Florid and Equal-Discantus Motet Styles", 71–72.

16. Paul Oskar Kristeller, "Humanism and Scholasticism in the Italian Renaissance," in *Studies in Renaissance Thought and Letters* (1956; repr. Rome: Edizioni di Storia e Letteratura, 1984), 559–60, comments on the utility of humanist literature: "A modern classical scholar is not supposed to write a Latin poem in praise of his city, to welcome a distinguished foreign visitor with a Latin speech, or to write a political manifesto for his government. . . . The humanists were not classical scholars who for personal reasons had a craving for eloquence, but vice versa, they were professional rhetoricians, heirs and successors of the medieval rhetoricians, who developed the belief, then new and modern, that the best way to study eloquence was to imitate classical models, and who thus were driven to study the classics and to found classical philology."

17. Alejandro Enrique Planchart, " 'What's in a Name?': Reflections on Some Works of Guillaume Du Fay," *Early Music* 16 (1988): 171.

18. Ibid., 171–72.

19. Roger S. Wieck, "Accessory Texts," in *Time Sanctified: The Book of Hours in Medieval Art and Life*, ed. Roger S. Wieck (London: Sotheby's Publications, 1988), 103.

20. Planchart, " 'What's in a Name?' " 171–72.

21. Battre's setting appears in Trent, Castello del Buon Consiglio, Monumenti e collezioni provinciali, MS 87, fols. 262^v–264^v. The two earliest sources for the Josquin setting are Brussels, Bibliothèque Royale, MS 9126, fols. 178^v–180^r, and Ottaviano Petrucci, *Motetti libro quarto* (Venice, 1505), RISM 1505^2.

22. Roy Eriksen, "God Enthroned: Expansion and Continuity in Ariosto, Tasso, and Milton," in *Milton in Italy: Contexts, Images, Contradictions* (Binghamton, N.Y.: Medieval and Renaissance Texts and Studies, 1991), 405, n. 4, states that "A topomorphical approach to a text involves studying the distribution of topoi and themes, or textual segments devoted to specific topoi, with particular reference to their structure and the interrelationships they form."

23. The total number of semibreves, 441, equals 21 squared. The count includes final longs in both sections, and assumes minim and semibreve equality between ø and ₵.

24. The fourth and final section of *Salve flos tusce gentis* employs *talea* in the tenor and contratenor alone. Jon Michael Allsen, "Style and Intertextuality in the Isorhythmic Motet, 1400–1440" (Ph.D. diss., University of Wisconsin-Madison, 1992), 119, 468, 475–76, demonstrates that the motet's proportional and numerical structure corresponds to that of *Nuper rosarum flores*.

25. In the first section, strong cadences fall on C (m. 9), F (17), C (21), A (26), F (33), and F (37), emphasizing the tenor final and confinal. In the second section, they fall on G (47), D (53), A (66), F (73), C (83), and F (91), thereby circling away from the final until the end of verse 7 (73).

26. Schmidt, "'Carmina gratulatoria',", 93, points out that sacred motets of the period employ exclusively accentual meter or rhymed verse in Leonine hexameters.

27. Cadences at the end of strophes fall on G (m. 16), G (29), D (42), D (53), G (64), G (77).

28. On the original state of the musical text with respect to mensuration, signatures, and the *contratenor bassus*, see Nosow, "The Florid and Equal-Discantus Motet Styles," 123–24.

29. Edited in Nosow, ibid., 349–56.

30. Example 5.3(c) omits the low *b* of cantus I of *Gaude virgo mater christi*, which occurs incidentally at two ornamented cadences, measures 34 and 69. On ranges, see Fallows, *Dufay*, 115.

31. At least one scholar, Julie E. Cumming, "Genre and Subgenre in the Early Renaissance Motet," paper delivered at the American Musicological Society Annual Meeting, Oakland, California, November 1990, considers motets that begin with *tempus perfectum diminutum* to constitute a distinct stylistic category.

32. Bologna Q 15, fols. 208ᵛ–209; Oxford, Bodleian Library, MS Canonici misc. 213, fols. 133ᵛ–134; Bologna, Biblioteca Universitaria, MS 2216, pp. 70–71. The music is published in *Opera omnia*, ed. Besseler, 6:7–9. On the work's classification as a motet, see Planchart, " 'What's in a Name?' " 165–170. *Flos florum* is edited in the *Opera omnia*, ed. Besseler, 1:6–7; *Opera omnia*, ed. de Van, 1; and Nosow, "The Florid and Equal-Discantus Motet Styles," 363–68.

33. Richard A. Goldthwaite, *The Building of Renaissance Florence: An Economic and Social History* (Baltimore: Johns Hopkins University Press, 1980), 9–13, 98–102, offers a brief overview of private patronage in chapel construction. On testamentary endowments of chapels, art, and commemorative Masses, see Samuel K. Cohn, *The Cult of Remembrance and the Black Death: Six Renaissance Cities in Central Italy* (Baltimore: Johns Hopkins University Press, 1992). Virginia Reinburg discusses the Book of Hours as an instrument of lay piety in "Popular Prayers in Late Medieval and Reformation France" (Ph.D. diss., Princeton University, 1985), 25–172; ead., "Prayer and the Book of Hours," in *Time Sanctified*, ed. Wieck, 39–44. Studies of the *laudario* include Cyrilla Barr, *The Monophonic Lauda and the Lay Religious Confraternities of Tuscany and Umbria of the Late Middle Ages* (Kalamazoo: Medieval Institute Publications, Western Michigan University, 1988); Francesco Luisi, *Laudario giustinianeo*, 2 vols. (Venice: Fondazione Levi, 1983); Vincent Moleta, "The Illuminated *Laudari* Mgl¹ and Mgl²," *Scriptorium* 32 (1978): 29–50; Wilson, *Music and Merchants*, 63–64, 103–4, 133, 154–59, 165–68, 244.

34. John Henderson, *Piety and Charity in Late Medieval Florence* (Oxford: Clarendon Press, 1994), 120, 441–74. See also Ronald F. E. Weissman, *Ritual Brotherhood in Renaissance Florence* (New York: Academic Press, 1982), and the bibliography cited p. 44 n. 1.

35. Wilson, *Music and Merchants*, 149–50, 164–65, finds that ferial services in the *laudesi* companies were gradually discontinued during the years 1430–48.

36. Ibid., 78–139, especially tables 3, 4, 6, 8, and 10. Benoit is identifiable with the "Benotto cantore" cited in the important *lauda* manuscript Biblioteca Apostolica Vaticana, MS Chigi L.VII.266, fol. 28ʳ. Rubrics to the Latin hymn *Ava maris stella* state that it should be sung to the melody written by Benoit, or associated with him: "In sul modo di Benotto cantore." The identification is made more secure by the *Te Deum* immediately following, fol. 28ʳ, which bears the rubric "nel modo di Piero di Mariano laudese," thereby drawing a distinction between the status of the two musicians.

37. Weissman, *Ritual Brotherhood*, 67–77, analyzes the relative social and geographic composition of the *laudesi* and *disciplinati* (flagellant) companies; the latter tended to enlist a higher percentage of the city's economic and cultural elite. Giuliano

Di Bacco, "Alcune nuove osservazioni sul codice di Londra (British Library, MS Additional 29987)," *Studi musicali* 20 (1991): 198, points out that the madrigal-motet *Cantano gli angiol lieti/Sanctus* (fols. 133ᵛ–34ʳ), represents a fusion of high-art or ecclesiastical form (the troped Sanctus) with a vocal style closer to common (oral) practice; the language is also a mixture of Latin and Italian. Such a fusion takes on added significance in a manuscript from the very early fifteenth century that includes clerical composers like Gherardello da Firenze, as well as artisans like Bonaiuto di Corsino, a painter of wedding chests with well-documented ties to the *laudesi* Company of San Zanobi (ibid., 200–203). *Cantano gli angiol lieti/Sanctus* would seem to be a logical candidate for the kind of music performed at the festal services of religious confraternities.

38. On the biography of Pietro Rosso, see Luigi Pesce, *Ludovico Barbo, vescovo di Treviso (1437–1443)*, 2 vols. (Padua: Antenore, 1969), vols. 9–10 of *Italia sacra*, 53 vols. to date, 1:94–95. Information on the *festa* of the Annunciation (25 March) derives from id., *La chiesa di Treviso nel primo Quattrocento,* 3 vols. (Rome: Herder, 1987), vols. 37–39 of *Italia sacra*, 1:74–77, 2:470–75, 2:596–98, and the confraternal records.

39. Du Fay's later ties to the Medici are well known: on this subject, see Fallows, *Dufay*, 71, 76–77, and the reassessment offered in *id.*, "Polyphonic Song in the Florence of Lorenzo's Youth *ossia* The Provenance of the Manuscript *Berlin 78.C.28*: Naples or Florence?," in *La musica a Firenze al tempo di Lorenzo il Magnifico*, ed. Piero Gargiulo (Florence: Olschki, 1993), 47–61.

40. James Hankins, "Cosimo de' Medici as a Patron of Humanistic Literature," in *Cosimo "il Vecchio" de' Medici, 1389–1464*, ed. Francis Ames-Lewis (Oxford: Clarendon Press, 1992), 69–94. A translation of the fourth part of Bruni's "Laudatio" (1405), the oration in praise of Florence, appears in *The Humanism of Leonardo Bruni*, trans. Gordon Griffiths et al. (Binghamton, N.Y.: Medieval and Renaissance Texts and Studies, 1987), 116–21.

41. For one such public ceremony, see Timothy McGee, " 'Alla battaglia': Music and Ceremony in Fifteenth-Century Florence," *Journal of the American Musicological Society* 36 (1983): 287–302.

42. Planchart, " 'What's in a Name?' " 172–73, discusses the textual relationships between *Gaude virgo mater christi* and *Ave virgo que de celis*. The latter is published in *Opera omnia*, ed. Besseler, 1:8–10; *Opera omnia*, ed. de Van, 1:19–22.

For Whom the Bell Tolls

Reading and Hearing Busnoys's *Anthoni usque limina*

Postmodernism is said to celebrate the multiplicity of meanings in musical works. What is meant by this, principally, is this: since every composition admits a variety of possible interpretations (depending on who is performing or listening), no preferred interpretation can be claimed to be objectively true, that is, immanent in the music itself. If others hear or perform the same work as we do, it cannot be the *work* that compels us to prefer our interpretation over theirs. The reasons for our preference must lie rather in what makes us different from others: the particular beliefs, values, interests, and paradigms that are constitutive of our musical interpretation. Rather than expecting music to be aloof from this human diversity, we should celebrate its capacity to embrace it.

However, it has often been objected that the positive valuation of multiplicity may lead to extreme relativism, to a point where there might be as many valid interpretations as there are human beings. How can scholarship be expected to maintain agreement under such a philosophy? The answer comes from the reinstatement of a concept that was central to medieval society: *community*, or, more specifically: interpretive community. Paradoxically, in our "age of the individual," reading and listening begin to be understood again as activities having an essential communal dimension: the times of direct aesthetic communion with the composer are past.[1]

Community means principally *shared* beliefs, values, interests, and paradigms. This has always been true of the scholarly community, of course: interpretations or readings are advanced there as hypotheses, and shared methodological standards guarantee that the multiplicity of hypotheses is always limited to those that can compete on the same, agreed terms. Yet those very standards and terms may separate us from other interpretive communities: performers and listeners, for instance, but also the communities whose music we study (see below). Here, the concept of multiplicity expresses the historical truth that different interpretive communities may perceive music as meaningful in different ways, and (as the history of scholarship shows) that accepted interpretations can change quickly even within a single community. There may not be a uniquely "true" meaning hovering above this historical and cultural diversity, and even if there is, it may not be our privilege to know it.

Yet how can our scholarly standards separate us even from the communities whose music we study (as observed above), when those very standards dictate that our interpretations be historically accurate? I will answer this question by turning from the concept of "multiplicity" to that of "meaning." The idea that music has *meaning*, that it *signifies*, is a typical postmodern belief, which has become influential largely because of the ascendancy of literary criticism (and has been fueled, in addition, by the reaction against the modernist credo of musical autonomy). Music, today, is perceived principally as text, and texts must signify.

For medievals this was quite different. Although they would have agreed that texts can be scrutinized for meanings (as their traditions of biblical exegesis confirm), they would not immediately have thought of music as signifying in this way. This is mainly because music was perceived in essence not as an object, but as physical *motion* in air, produced by action upon objects.[2] Since motion always has a cause and an effect, the question was not what music means (as if it were a sign), but rather what it *does*, what its effects are. This explains, for instance, why a theorist like Johannes Tinctoris remained completely silent on the meaning of music, yet devoted a whole treatise to its effects.[3] It is true that music could become a physical object by virtue of being written down *(res facta)*. Yet insofar as notational symbols could be seen as signifiers (and theorists did indeed describe them as *signa* which can *significare*), they signified the measured sounds that constitute music, and which do not exist except as motion caused by human action.[4]

We no longer share this aesthetic today: if we were still concerned about the beneficial effects once attributed to late medieval music, we would perform it more often, and write less about it (since this is to produce texts, not musical effects). Even so, we have every reason to perceive late medieval compositions, anachronistically, as texts. It allows us to see them as full of "signifiers" that demand interpretation and criticism: cantus firmi, structural ground plans, formal layouts, borrowings, allusions, stylistic devices, and so on. Interpretation of those elements may help us to arrive at historical understanding, yet for this it is necessary, in addition, to expand the range of perceived signifiers to contextual evidence outside the work itself. (For instance, the knowledge that medievals valued music principally for its effects may be vital to the historical interpretation of individual works, but the latter do not actually provide that knowledge.) This extension of the range of signifiers beyond the work turns *history* into text: a fabric of signifiers in which the musical work is fully interwoven. (Whence the New Historicist concern with "the historicity of the text and the textuality of history.")

The perception of music as text distinguishes our scholarly community from the medieval interpretive communities whose music we study. *We* wish to "read" their music in its historical context: *they* wished to have it performed for a variety of social and religious purposes. Consequently, we cannot justify the musical meaning perceived by us as in any way "authentic": the meaning we perceive is relevant to our interpretive community, which posits the notion of musical meaning to begin with. Medievals themselves did not look for musical meaning in this way, yet our approach is not invalidated by this, for the very fact that they did not can itself be taken as a signifier, adding to the meaning of their music.

Antoine Busnoy's *Anthoni usque limina* provides a beautiful illustration of this. As I will argue in the present chapter, the motet was meant to produce concrete effects, in Heaven as well as on earth. Among the musical effects itemized by Tinctoris, the following in particular are relevant: music increases the delight of saints (third effect), prepares for the receiving of God's blessing (fifth), chases away the Devil (ninth), cures those who are ill (fourteenth), and blesses the souls of believers (nineteenth).[5] Since we belong to a different interpretive community, however, we would not expect the motet to have any of these effects today. Yet the knowledge that Busnoys and his contemporaries did expect this is part of what *we* might perceive to be its meaning. And that knowledge is only one of many contextual signifiers pertinent to Busnoy's setting. One of the truly remarkable features of *Anthoni usque limina* is that the fabric of signifiers in which it is interwoven extends far beyond musical beliefs alone: ultimately, as I hope to show, it covers all the essentials of the medieval outlook on life and the world. Few works, therefore, seem better suited to illustrate "the historicity of text and the textuality of history" than *Anthoni usque limina*.

The essay is structured in three sections. In the first, I will address the question of the liturgical function of *Anthoni usque limina*, for which it will be necessary to trace the sources for several of its textual elements. Although a tentative answer to the question can be formulated, the isolation of textual elements leaves the impression of a random patchwork of imagery. In the second part, therefore, I will attempt to pull together the various strands of meaning, in order to arrive at a coherent and historically plausible reading. In the third part, finally, that reading will be considered in the context of Busnoys's life.

Before proceeding, it may be worthwhile to summarize what is known about *Anthoni usque limina*.[6] The motet is dedicated to St. Anthony Abbot, the composer's name saint. It survives uniquely in the Burgundian choirbook Brussels, Bibliothèque Royale, MS 5557, where it was almost certainly copied by Busnoys himself.[7] Three vocal parts are written out; a verbal canon gives instructions for a fourth (in tenor position): a bell is to be struck at regular intervals in both sections.[8] The verbal canon is incorporated in a drawing which shows a T-shaped cross (tau) with pendant bell: both are attributes of St. Anthony.[9] Busnoys "camouflaged" his first and last names at the beginning and end of the Latin text: the syllables corresponding to his name are written in red ink in the manuscript (italics in the transcription below), and a second verbal canon also alerts the reader to the wordplay.[10] The text of the motet, to which reference will be made throughout this essay, is as follows:

1	*Anthoni, us*que limina	Anthony, who, as far as the edges
	Orbis terrarumque maris,	of the earth and the sea,
	Et ultra, qui vocitaris	and even beyond, art invoked
	Providencia divina,	through divine providence,
5	Quia demonum agmina	because thou hast manfully overcome
	Superasti viriliter:	the hosts of demons:
	Audi cetum nunc omina	hear the gathering now
	Psalentem tua dulciter.	sweetly singing thy miracles.
	Et ne post hoc exilium	And, lest after this exile
10	Nos igneus urat Pluto,	fiery Pluto burn us,
	Hunc ab orci chorum luto	bear assistance, delivering this choir
	Eruens, fer auxilium:	from the mire of the underworld:
	Porrigat refrigerium	let the water of grace
	Artubus gracie moys,	offer refreshment to the limbs,
15	Ut per verbi misterium	so that the Spirit, through the mystery
	Fiat in omni*bus noys.*	of the Word, may be in all.

I

The first question to be addressed is that of the liturgical status of *Anthoni usque limina:* Was it meant to fit into the liturgy of St. Anthony, and if so, where? Formally, the motet is a prayer: it is addressed to the saint directly, and contains several verbal resonances with known prayers from his liturgy. In particular, the phrase "let the water of grace offer refreshment to the limbs" (13–14) was a standard clause in collects from the liturgy of St. Anthony.[11] It refers to the extremely painful disease of gangrenous ergotism, known in the Middle Ages as the holy fire *(ignis sacer)* or St. Anthony's fire. The powerful Antonian Order (based in Saint-Athoine-de-Vienne) was dedicated to its cure, and held the monopoly on the blessing and administration of the healing holy water of St. Anthony. Although the disease occurred only sporadically after the twelfth century, the order continued to collect offerings of the faithful in return for indulgences, to support its vast network of over 350 monasteries, *commanderies,* and hospitals in western Europe.[12]

By the late Middle Ages, St. Anthony's fire was reinterpreted in many liturgical texts as a metaphor for the flames of hell and purgatory, and even for the "fires" of sin. Although the saint continued to be invoked for aid in epidemic diseases, particularly the plague,[13] he came to be regarded more broadly as a powerful helper against temptation and against the pains of purgatory. The latter idea was developed most fully in collects—among the more flexible items in the liturgy—although incidental allusions can also be found in chants (see below). Busnoys's supplication for deliverance "from the mire of the underworld" (11) parallels this trend, and confirms the debt to collects from the liturgy of St. Anthony, as the following examples illustrate:[14]

> God, who grantest, on account of the perseverance of St. Anthony, that the morbid fire be extinguished and *that refreshment be offered to the infected limbs, deliver us benevolently, on account of his merits and prayers, from the*

flames of hell, that we be presented joyfully, and whole of spirit and body, before Thee in Glory. Through Christ our Lord. Amen.

O almighty and eternal God, who on account of the prayer and the merits of the holy father and abbot Saint Anthony alleviates the diseases of the fire and *offers refreshment to the infected limbs*, we pray that we, on account of his prayer and his merits, be delivered from the fires of pride, avarice, impurity, rage, hate, and envy, and from all sins. And that we be *protected from the pains of hell and released from the pains of purgatory*, so that we may blissfully attain to the glory of Thy Resurrection . . .

It is not possible, however, to consider *Anthoni usque limina* as a possible polyphonic replacement for a collect: formal liturgical prayers are by definition addressed to God, and refer to saints only in the third person. As the above examples illustrate, they are typically cast in the form "*Deus, qui . . .* [invocation of the saint's miracles and intercession], *concede . . .* [one or more specific supplications]. *Per Christum Dominum nostrum . . .* [doxology]. *Amen.*" Busnoys, on the other hand, addresses his supplications to St. Anthony directly. Such direct prayers to saints tend to be found not in collects, but rather in chants, whose texts are not subject to rigid textual constraints. Although *Anthoni usque limina* is written as prayer, and plainly borrows some of its imagery from prayers in the Antonian liturgy, it was almost certainly not written to replace one.

Is it then possible to regard Busnoys's motet as a musical replacement for a chant for St. Anthony? The vital piece of evidence for this hypothesis is missing: *Anthoni usque limina* does not use a chant as its cantus firmus (whose liturgical position it might then have assumed, despite the resultant polytextuality), but is based rather on the sound of a bell, struck at regular intervals in the course of both sections. Still, there is at least the suggestion that the motet was embedded in a context in which liturgical chants were sung. Its first section ends with the supplication "hear the gathering now sweetly singing thy miracles" (7–8). Although chant texts frequently include praises and prayers to saints, they tend to be mostly devoted to narratives of their glorious deeds, often quoted verbatim from their *vitae*. St. Anthony was no exception:[15] the miracle most often referred to in his liturgy (and depicted in very many altarpieces) was the temptation by the demons, and it seems at least plausible that lines 7–8 of *Anthoni usque limina* were meant to draw attention to this surrounding liturgical context. I quote the famous episode from St. Anthony's life here in full, as recounted by Jacobus de Voragine in the Golden Legend (italics mine):[16]

Another time, when he was living hidden away in a tomb, a *crowd of demons* tore at him so savagely that his servant thought he was dead and carried him out on his shoulders. Then all who had come together mourned him as dead, but he suddenly regained consciousness and had his servant carry him back to the aforementioned tomb. There, lying prostrated by the pain of his wounds, in the strength of his spirit he challenged the demons to renew the combat. They appeared in the forms of various wild beasts and tore at his flesh cruelly with their teeth, horns, and claws. Then of a sudden a wonderful light shone in the place and drove all the demons away, and Anthony's hurts were cured. Realizing that Christ was there, he said: "Where were you, O good Jesus, where were you? Why did you not come sooner to help me and heal my wounds?" The Lord answered: "Anthony, I was here, but I waited to see how you would fight. *Now, because you fought manfully, I shall make your name known all over the earth."*

The verbal resonances in Busnoys's motet are obvious: "because thou hast manfully overcome the hosts of demons" (5–6), and "as far as the edges of the earth and the sea, and even beyond" (1–3) are clearly based on narratives of the saint's life. The same episode is alluded to in several chants for St. Anthony, including *Alleluia Vox de celo,* the offertory *Inclito Anthonio,* and the antiphon *Vox de celo.*[17] It seems plausible that Busnoys's supplication "hear the gathering now sweetly singing thy miracles" (7–8) referred to such and other chants as much as to lines 1–6 of the motet itself.[18]

If the first part of the motet recalls the typical content of chants for St. Anthony, and may allude directly to their performance in a liturgical framework, the second part seems incompatible with their nature. It is not just that lines 13–14 are inspired by collects, but the explicit reference to hell and purgatory in lines 9–12 is highly untypical of chants,[19] and goes far beyond even the imagery employed in prayers. In chants for St. Anthony allusions of this kind tend to remain sporadic and oblique. Closest to the content of collects is the Magnificat antiphon *O lampas ardens in virtute*—like Busnoys's motet a prayer to St. Anthony rather than to God: it ends with the supplication "that through thy merits we may be worthy to escape all dangers, and the conflagrations of the fire of Hell."[20] The alleluia *Felix corpus* is likewise cast as a prayer to St. Antony, yet the allusion to hell is less direct: "the conqueror of the demon presently chokes the flames of the fire and the conflagrations of the underworld *(orcus)."*[21]

In the latter passage we may find a possible source for Busnoys's use of the word "orcus," for underworld (11), yet his motet develops the imagery of the hereafter much further than either chants or prayers. "Lutum," for mire (11), must be derived from the Psalms, where it is associated with the Hebrew image of the underworld as a pit (Ps. 40:2). There is, in fact, a direct verbal resonance between lines 11–12 of Busnoys's motet ("hunc ab orci chorum luto eruens") and Psalm 69:14:

> *Erue me de luto* ut non infigar: libera me ab his qui oderunt me et de profundis aquis.
>
> (Deliver me out of the mire, and let me not sink: let me be delivered from them that hate me, and out of the deep waters.)

It seems consistent with our earlier observations that Busnoys attributes the power to release tormented souls in the underworld to St. Anthony rather than to God. Strictly speaking only the saint's intercession could be effective: the supreme judge was Christ himself. Noteworthy is the felicitous rhyme between the Old Testament image of mire and the classical image of Pluto, the lord of the underworld ("Pluto/luto," 11. 10–11). Clearly, in developing the association between the punishments of the afterlife and the intercession of St. Anthony, Busnoys achieved a conflation of poetic imagery that went far beyond any models he could have found in the liturgy of the saint. We must return to a closer reading of these crucial passages below.

Surveying lines 1–14 as a whole, one is struck by the sheer range of ideas and images associated with St. Anthony: universal veneration (1–4), the temptation by the demons (5–6), the veneration of the saint (7–8), the burning of souls by Pluto (9–10), the mire of the underworld (11–12), and refreshment to the limbs (13–14). We have traced the textual sources for several of these ideas and images in order to establish the liturgical status of the motet, yet the evidence remained ambiguous. Some elements are closer to chants, others more to collects, but in the end *Anthoni usque limina* cannot be classified as either: unlike chants, the motet develops unusually elaborate infernal imagery, and unlike collects, it is addressed to St. Anthony rather than to God.

The final two lines (15–16) remove us even further from the typical content of chants and prayers, and indeed from all imagery associated with St. Anthony. Whereas collects from the saint's liturgy typically link the deliverance from purgatory with the hope eventually to behold the glory of God at the Second Coming (see above), Busnoys's poem ends on a very different note: "so that the Spirit, through the mystery of the Word, may be in all" (15–16). Significantly, his ending expresses a pentecostal concern for inspiration by the Holy Spirit, in the here and now, rather than an eschatological concern for eternal life, at the end of time. Unlike in the liturgy of Pentecost, however, the Holy Spirit is not addressed directly. Rather, its inspiration is to be effected through "the mystery of the Word," that is, the mystery of Christ's incarnation. Busnoys refers, of course, to the opening of St. John's Gospel (1:1 and 14): "In the beginning was the Word, and the Word was with God, and the Word was God . . . And the Word was made flesh." Such imagery seems strangely incongruous in a prayer to a saint: how can Anthony's "assistance" (12) be expected to enable that mystery to have its beneficial effect, and how can the final lines of the motet anticipate this happening in the here and now?

The solution probably lies in a eucharistic interpretation of these lines: the incongruity evaporates if we assume that *Anthoni usque limina* was written for a votive Mass for St. Anthony.[22] Although the celebration of Mass is principally a reenactment of Christ's sacrifice, as an event in history, the mystery of transubstantiation brought his flesh and blood in direct physical presence of the faithful, in the here and now: this turned the ceremony simultaneously into a celebration of his victory over death. The mysteries of incarnation and transubstantiation were seen as intimately connected. Then, as now, the opening of St. John's Gospel, to which Busnoys alludes, was read at the end of every Mass, and special spiritual benefits were attributed to hearing it at that point.[23] But the primary benefits in attending Mass, of course, came from gazing on the Host: to behold it at the Elevation was to receive grace, to be blessed. (The host was not normally received in communion except at Easter.)

The actual moment of Elevation was frequently made to coincide with the Benedictus.[24] According to one of the most influential sources for the eucharistic theory of the late fifteenth century, Gabriel Biel's *Canonis Misse Expositio* (1487–88), the Sanctus had a bipartite structure: Sanctus–Pleni represented the angelic choirs ("vox angelica"), whereas Osanna–Benedictus–Osanna represented the voice of the faithful ("vox humana"). The latter part in turn was divisible into prayer (Osanna, preceding the Elevation), and the giving of thanks (Benedictus). The Benedictus, marking the actual moment of transubstantiation, was not only an expression of the gratitude of the faithful, however, but also an acknowledgment of the mystery of incarnation ("confessio mysterii incarnationis Christi"). Precisely at the most sacred point of the Mass, then, the two mysteries were consciously thought of as connected. It was nothing less than the Word that became flesh in the host.[25]

Anthoni usque limina, as a prayer on behalf of the faithful ("gathering," 1. 7), and anticipating the Christian mystery (15–16), seems to parallel the preparatory function that Biel associates with the Osanna—irrespective of whether it was meant to replace that particular item or not. As such the motet would have coincided with a liturgical action that was in fact structurally incorporated in the music. Just before the Elevation in every Mass a bell was rung to warn worshippers absorbed in their own prayers to look up, because the moment of consecration was near: the peal of the bell announced the arrival of the Saviour.[26] Small sacring-bells were kept with every altar in every church: particularly in larger churches with many side chapels, several Mass celebrations could be going on at the same time, and nothing but the pealing of bells could alert the faithful to yet another opportunity to behold the living Christ in the consecrated host.

It seems attractive to consider *Anthoni usque limina* as a pre-Elevation prayer in a Mass for St. Anthony, surrounded by—but not replacing—Mass proper chants ("sweetly singing thy miracles"), and imploring the saint to make possible full spiritual or actual communion with the Saviour. It is true, as already said, that the bell is also an attribute of St. Anthony:[27] Busnoys's verbal canon in the Brussels manuscript is incorporated in a drawing in which the saint's bell is combined with another of his attributes, the T-shaped or tau cross. Yet perhaps we might regard the double significance of the bell in *Anthoni usque limina* as yet another conflation of meaning, this time not textual but musical.[28] Certainly if the motet was to be sung before an altar devoted to the saint, any available Anthony's bell that was not merely an artistic ornament but could be expected to compete with a dozen or so singers would have been the sacring-bell, since its sound could normally carry across the entire interior of a church.[29] That the verbal canon specifies its pitch as *nete synemmenon* (corresponding to the note *d* la sol re, or *d'*) is no objection either: since there was no absolute pitch standard, any bell that approximated a pitch in mid-range could be used to anchor the notation, defining *d* la sol re for the particular performance.

A eucharistic reading of *Anthoni usque limina* may also enable us to interpret the phrase "let the water of grace offer refreshment to the limbs" (13–14) as more than an apparently random borrowing from prayers associated with St. Anthony. Masses celebrated with special solemnity began with an elaborate ceremony in which salt and water were exorcised, blessed, and mixed: not only the altar but also the congregation was sprinkled with holy water, which was thought to banish demons, to ensure blessing, and to effect real spiritual and physical healing.[30] By linking, in one sentence (13–16), the "refreshment" of the "water of grace" with the imminently desired inspiration of the Holy Spirit, Busnoys evidently prayed for a spiritual cleansing that would make the benefits of communion available "to all."

Yet this interpretation answers only some of the many questions raised by Busnoys's motet. In collects, as we have seen, the fear of hell and purgatory is logically connected with the hope for the beatific vision in heaven. Yet this eschatological element is played down in *Anthoni usque limina*, even though the infernal imagery, curiously, is intensified. It is true, of course, that the celebration of Masses was the principal means by which the living could hasten the release of souls from purgatory—provided they included special prayers for the dead.[31] Yet Busnoys's prayer is clearly not concerned with the dead, but rather with "the gathering" (7), more specifically "this choir" (11), and perhaps even more specifically "Anthonius Busnoys" himself (1 and 16).

It is also true that the Mass itself represents Christ's promise of salvation and eternal life. Yet Busnoys stresses not this aspect, but rather—if my interpretation is correct—the immediately expected benefits of grace through the sacrament of the eucharist. For this it would have been far more natural to pray to Christ directly (as in Elevation prayers),[32] since he, after all, was to become physically present in the consecrated host. When it came to the punishment of hell and purgatory, on the other hand, Christ was to be an impartial judge, and here it would have been more natural to secure St. Anthony's help as advocate, pleading for a lenient sentence against the prosecutor, "fiery Pluto"— yet Busnoys avoids calling on the saint for this.[33] Several apparent incongruities thus seem to remain, and this only adds to the sense that the text, for all its sophisticated concentration of imagery, lacks coherence. Can the seemingly disparate strands of meaning be tied together to yield a more coherent message?

II

If *Anthoni usque limina* develops any theme consistently, it is that of the Christian believer beleaguered by hostile troops of demons seeking the destruction of body and soul; St. Anthony is his example, guide, and friend. The text elaborates this theme on three different levels: this life, the hour of death, and the afterlife. However, there is no essential distinction between these levels, and Busnoys's text admits simultaneous readings on more than one: all three are stages in the pilgrimage of human life, a pilgrimage whose destination is not reached until the Last Day.

In late medieval thought the Devil and his fallen angels were held to be the source of all evils that afflicted humanity: natural disasters, wars, enmity, disease, and sin. Any believer who had patiently endured these ordeals during his life, and had dutifully discharged the debts of penance incurred by his sins, could still expect a severe onslaught of demons at the hour of death: this was the Devil's last chance to tempt him into eternal damnation, and hence the most steadfast belief was required spiritually to survive that final battle.[34] Once the soul had parted from the body, nothing could be done to change the balance between evil and good, and the Devil waited as anxiously for the verdict as the soul. A provisional judgment was made immediately in the court of St. Michael: heaven (in practice only saints), purgatory (most Christian believers), or hell (infidels and unrepentant sinners). Only in case of the latter verdict was the soul definitively in the Devil's possession: whoever was sentenced to purgatory was in principle saved, although he still needed to have sins purged away in order to complete his penance, and to be worthy of salvation at the second, final judgment, at the end of time. Souls in purgatory thus awaited with certainty the glory to come, but were meanwhile subjected to purgation at the hands of demons.

Whatever the stage in this pilgrimage, the believer was expected to undergo the temptations and tribulations of the demons patiently, not losing faith and hope: impatience was itself a temptation of the Devil.[35] St. Anthony, in this respect, provided a realistic and human model to follow. Unlike St. Michael, whose army had inflicted a crushing defeat on the Devil and his angels by casting them out of Heaven (Rev. 12:7–9; a feat no human being could hope to emulate), Anthony had physically endured their tortures and temptations alone. Indeed he was a virtual specialist in resisting the temptations of the Devil: "he bore countless trials inflicted by the demons," Jacobus de Voragine commented in the Golden Legend, proceeding to recount several such incidents.[36] Busnoys seems to underscore the suffering humanity of the saint in *Anthoni usque limina.* All liturgical texts quote the phrase "dimicasti viriliter" literally from the *vita* of St. Anthony, implying active battle ("thou hast fought manfully"). In the motet, however, this has been changed into "superasti viriliter," implying patient endurance ("thou hast overcome").

The miracle alluded to by Busnoys emphasizes the physical pain inflicted on St. Anthony—other miracles show him resisting such temptations as lust, greed, and loss of faith. The aspect of disease recurs elsewhere in the motet. On a literal reading, "refreshment to the limbs" (13–14) means relief from the pains of Anthony's fire and, by the fifteenth century, of other epidemic diseases as well. It seems only appropriate, therefore, that *Anthoni usque limina* should contain a verbal allusion to Ps. 69, which can be read in places as indicating sickness and proximity to death (vv. 2–3, 14–17, 20, 29).

Just as in that psalm, however, such a reading should not be pursued to the exclusion of others: the powerful metaphors in the psalm are general enough to cover any great physical or spiritual distress, and the same is true of *Antoni usque limina.* By the late Middle Ages, St. Anthony's association with the "holy fire" had become metaphorically extended to a range of other afflictions. As we have seen, one fifteenth-century prayer for the liturgy of the saint speaks of the "fires" of sin, and proceeds to enumerate such deadly sins as pride, avarice, impurity, rage, hate, and envy. This ties in with an observation made earlier, that in solemnly celebrated Masses the "water of grace" (14) was administered to chase away all demons who sought to tempt the flesh ("limbs") with such fires, allowing (as Busnoys's motet anticipates) divine grace to nurture the truly penitent (15–16).

Yet not even this metaphorical extension exhausts all the possible readings of lines 13–14. With allusions to hell and purgatory close by (9–12), it is difficult not to sense the additional awareness that it is the limbs, in particular, that will be subject to the punitive and purgative flames of hell and purgatory (the soul was thought to retain a corporeal quality that made it sensitive to pain). This, however, is not so much an alternative reading as an amplified reading, for there was no essential difference between sickness and tribulation patiently borne in this life and the physical torments of purgatory: both went towards discharging the same debt of penance, and both were thought to be administered by demons.[37] The only real difference was one of quantity: penance in purgatory was universally known to be far more severe than in this life.

In this amplified reading, "refreshment" (13) may additionally refer to mitigation of infernal punishment, to be received either because of the suffrages of the living (alms, fasting, Masses, and prayers), or, in this case, because of the intercession of St. Anthony, whose "assistance" (12) is called for in the motet.[38] This reading is strengthened by the fact that the word "refrigerium" had a long-standing association with the afterlife, going back to the earliest centuries of Christianity (when it in fact denoted the repose of the dead).[39] From a very early date onward, however, as the notion of infernal punishment became more developed, "refrigerium" was increasingly regarded as relief from, or mitigation of, the torments of purgatory.[40] Thus the late ninth-century Vision of Charles the Fat described how, thanks to the intercession of St. Peter and St. Rémi, a tormented soul is placed every other day in a basin of cool water.[41] It seems possible that lines 13–14 of Busnoys's motet call on St. Anthony to intercede for similar relief from purgatorial pains.

The text of *Anthoni usque limina* is thus unified by four closely interrelated themes:

1. Sin and punishment, both seen as "fires" inflicted by demons. As far as punishment is concerned, this can take the form of either physical illness in this life (14), or purgation in the hereafter (9–10).
2. St. Anthony's example, providing the Christian believer with a realistic model to follow (5–6), and, thanks to his merits, his powers of intercession, which can be called upon universally (1–4), are specifically entreated here (7–8, 12), and may effect mitigation of punishment, whether in this life or after (13–14).
3. The Devil and his demons, who visited St. Anthony (5–7), seek to tempt the suppliants into sin (14), drag them down into disease and death (11–14), and hope ultimately to burn them in hell (9–10).
4. The mediation of the church, providing the faithful with powerful weapons against the demons, principally the sacrament of the eucharist (15–16), but also objects and actions with known apotropaic powers, such as holy water (14), the bell, the cross (the tau in the drawing), and indeed the mere invocation of the Word (16).

Busnoys's motet thus embodies a remarkably unified vision of the precarious life of the Christian believer, torn between the tribulations of demons, on the one hand, and the promise of redemption, on the other, and pinning his hopes on St. Anthony as friend and intercessor, to guide and help him in all stages of his pilgrimage, now and in the hereafter. This was the general vision of human life in the late Middle Ages, of course, yet it seems unlikely that it would have received such elaborate emphasis in a votive motet unless there were specific circumstances in which St. Anthony's "assistance" was urgently needed. Somehow "the gathering," "this choir," or "Anthonius Busnoys" himself must have reached a particularly anxious point in the pilgrimage of human life, a moment of great physical or spiritual distress: "hear *now* . . . bear assistance."

As far as the interpretation of *Anthoni usque limina* is concerned, perhaps it is enough to have arrived at just that conclusion. It would not actually increase our understanding of the motet if we proceeded now to speculate about possible dates and places of composition. On the contrary: this might cause us to limit the range of possible readings allowed by the motet to those that seemed pertinent only to the putative historical occasion. The crucial point is surely this: whatever the particular circumstances in which Busnoys and "the gathering" had found themselves—disease, danger, or proximity of death—in *Anthoni usque limina* they were situated and interpreted in a far wider cosmological framework. The least we can say is that the motet must have been written in the years around 1470: in the Brussels manuscript it was a later addition, entered on adjacent blank pages belonging to two layers dated ca. 1464–65 and 1468,[42] and there is a remarkable similarity of style with *Missa O crux lignum* (ca. 1467–75), with which the motet moreover shares a direct musical resemblance.[43]

III

Still, it is not difficult to sense something of the significance that this motet must have had for Busnoys personally, a significance to which his cleverly incorporated "signature" in the text may bear witness. I am referring to an incident of which documentation was only recently discovered in the Vatican by Pamela Starr: sometime in 1460 or early 1461 the composer had beaten up an unnamed priest in the cloisters of Tours cathedral (where he was a cleric), and arranged to have him beaten up five times by others, crimes for which he incurred the sentence of excommunication.[44]

Excommunication was an extremely severe verdict: it meant expulsion from the sacraments of the church (and in addition total ostracism by the rest of the community), and Busnoys in fact aggravated his crime by continuing, unwittingly, to attend Mass and other services. Spiritually, the composer was in grave peril: since he was barred from the sacraments of absolution, penance, and extreme unction, death without repentance and confession would cast him certainly and immediately into eternal damnation. And even if he were to repent and confess *in extremis*, his outstanding debt of penance, at best, would still have

to be repaid in purgatory—with no hope of mitigation, since a last-minute reha-
bilitation would have left him no time to secure the help of a powerful intercessor
(such as St. Anthony) or to make provisions for suffrages that might reduce his
debt in this world (Masses, prayers, alms-giving, and fasting).

Whether to escape this fate—which admittedly might not have seemed
immediately threatening to a young man—or to end his expulsion from the
established social order (which effectively terminated his career as a professional
musician), urgent action was needed. After the priest had fully recovered, and
after Busnoys must have duly repented and confessed, the composer submitted
a formal supplication to the Cardinal Penitentiary at Rome. In it, he requested
absolution from the crime of bloodshed, and dispensation of the irregularity
of attending and celebrating Mass while excommunicated.[45] His petition was
approved by the cardinal on 28 February 1461.

While the sacrament of absolution thus effaced the guilt of Busnoy's
crime, its necessary punishment still required satisfaction through the sacrament of penance—lest far more severe punishments would be administered to
him in purgatory.[46] Busnoys, being a clerk at the bottom rung of minor orders,
probably a vicar-singer, would hardly have had the means to pay for lavish acts
of charity and worship. We may take it that he spent much of the early 1460s
accumulating indulgences by personal acts of piety: prayer, fasting, and (most
lucrative) pilgrimage to famous shrines.[47] In particular, it would have been
important for him to develop a personal bond with a specific saint through
particular devotions, and St. Anthony would have been an obvious choice—if
only because he was the composer's name saint.[48] Moreover, the hermit's
shrine in Vienne was the nearest major pilgrimage center: from Tours, Busnoys
would have needed to travel about 400 kilometers, mainly upstream along the
Loire. While it would be speculative to suggest that he would have undertaken
a pilgrimage to Saint-Antoine-de-Vienne (it was not necessarily a more likely
destination than, say, Rome, Compostela, or Jerusalem) the possibility is
hardly farfetched. In 1479, as is well known, the Milanese singer Joschino de
Picardia received a travel pass for a 3-month votive pilgrimage to Vienne.[49]

Yet even without such speculations it is possible to read *Anthoni usque
limina* as a document that must have had a deeply personal significance for
Busnoys. To begin with, the composer had committed the deadly sin of anger
("ira"), and his very calculation in arranging five beatings shows that, unlike
St. Anthony (5–6), he had offered not the slightest resistance to temptations
attributable to the Devil and his demons. The sentence of excommunication
had made the prospect of hell a certainty for Busnoys (9–10), and barred him
from the saving grace of the holy sacrament (15–16). Yet the composer had
received absolution, and this made him worthy once again to partake in the
sacrament of penance: at least he could now work actively toward reducing his
debt of penance in this life, a debt he would otherwise have to repay more
dearly in the hereafter. St. Anthony was Busnoys's name saint, and he had
experienced the kinds of temptations to which the composer had succumbed
(5–6). Yet prayer and worship (7–8) could persuade him to bear assistance
(12), enabling Busnoys once again to receive the full spiritual benefits from

the sacrament of the eucharist (15–16). On this personal level, then, as the incorporation of the composer's name confirms, *Anthoni usque limina* is itself a votive offering, strengthening a personal bond between sinner and saint which may have been established originally by means of pilgrimage and other devotions. While such pious acts would have given Busnoys the necessary indulgences to discharge his debt of penance, *Anthoni usque limina* shows that the composer was interested in more than mere "accountancy" of sin.[50] The saint's help continued to be needed in order to avoid the temptation of sin in the future and to bear the tribulations of this life patiently (13–14), to be protected from death (11–12), and to negotiate between sinner and Saviour (15–16). In a very real sense, Busnoys seems to have sought St. Anthony's friendship.[51]

How is all this to be reconciled with the fact that *Anthoni usque limina* is also a prayer on behalf of "the gathering" and "this choir"? The contradiction is only apparent: here, as elsewhere, there is a conflation of meaning that does not spring from any particular ingenuity on Busnoys's part, but rather from the remarkably integrated worldview of the late Middle Ages. It is quite possible that by the early 1470s, when the composer was permanently in Burgundian service,[52] he did possess the financial wealth to establish a votive service for St. Anthony—of which the motet might then have been a part.[53] Yet no matter how personal the reasons or circumstances for such a private benefaction, every liturgical celebration was principally a communal event, with spiritual benefits accruing to whomever celebrated and attended.[54] (A direct parallel is provided by Josquin's *Illibata Dei virgo nutrix*, whose text is a prayer to the Virgin on behalf of the *la-mi-la canentes*, yet also incorporates the composer's name as an acrostic.)

How are we to envision that community? Who were "the gathering" and "this choir"? Several years ago I proposed that *Anthoni usque limina* was written for the Order of Saint-Antoine-en-Barbefosse, a wealthy devotional confraternity with aristocratic and bourgeois membership, founded originally as an order of chivalry by the counts of Hainaut.[55] The main evidence for this hypothesis came from the tau with pendant bell depicted in the Brussels manuscript, which, in this particular combination, constituted the emblem of the order.[56] My speculation that the motet might have been written for Busnoys's induction into the confraternity now appears to me implausible, if only because the inaugural ceremony did not involve the celebration of Mass (although one might well have followed).[57] Moreover, there are grounds for caution about necessarily connecting the motet with Barbefosse in particular, since the tau and bell seem to have been incorporated in the emblems of other confraternities as well, both within and outside the Antonian Order.[58]

Still, it would be difficult to explain the drawing in BrusBR 5557 as anything other than the emblem of a confraternity (whether in Barbefosse or elsewhere). While the bell is plainly needed to specify the "me" in the verbal canon who is to be "countersounding" (*anthipsilens*) in tenor position (see n. 8), the tau is musically superfluous, and the combination of the two attributes—having been used by several confraternities—could hardly have been coincidental. Moreover, one of the main purposes of confraternities was the service for the dead: members were assured of funeral services after their deaths (for which they were required to leave a fee in their wills), prayers and Masses in their memory (if they made financial provisions for them), and, in many cases, burial.[59] It is not at all implausible that Busnoys, whose peripatetic existence as Burgundian court singer has been amply documented by Paula Higgins,[60] would have been concerned to establish a "home base," a place he could return to whenever he felt his death approaching, and where he could be assured of a local community that cared for him in his final moments and beyond. *Anthoni usque limina*, in this regard, could be seen as expressing a communal sensibility about disease, death, and dying, as much as an individual sensibility about sin, judgment, and penance: the personal and the communal are fully conflated. Being sung, perhaps, in the chapel of a confraternity, and incorporating its sacring-bell, the motet could have been a fitting prayer and votive offering to the saint at any time of danger and distress—and might conceivably even have guaranteed perpetual remembrance of "Anthonius Busnoys" in endowed Masses after his death.

WITH THIS WE HAVE returned once again to the concept of community: *shared* beliefs, values, interests, paradigms. *Anthoni usque limina* presupposes an interpretive community, yet it also shapes it, gives it a voice, to express shared anxieties, aspirations, hopes, and beliefs. Beyond that, the motet could itself be taken as a metaphor of the medieval community—each voice having its assigned place in a hierarchical structure, unfolding freely, yet firmly guided by the straight melodic path set out, with perfect metric regularity, by the saint's attribute, the bell. This seems like an image of the way medievals sought to give saints a place in their midst—beacons of stability around whose worship their every movement, private and communal, was organized: *sine me non.* But at the end comes the final cadence, terminating the life of this brief motet, its last reverberations quickly dying out. What remains is the hope, of Busnoys as well as his "gathering," that the saints might one day give them a place in their midst, in the community of heaven.

NOTES

The writing of this article was made possible through a British Academy Postdoctoral Research Fellowship. I am grateful to Bonnie Blackburn, Paula Higgins, Leofranc Holford-Strevens, Craig Monson, and Dolores Pesce for reading and commenting upon an earlier version of the text.

1. For the concept of interpretive community, see Stanley Fish, "Interpreting the *Variorum*," in *Modern Criticism and Theory: A Reader*, ed. David Lodge (London: Longman Group, 1988), 310–29. The current turning away from the ideal of direct aesthetic communion with the composer is linked with the postmodern reluctance to locate interpretive authority exclusively in the author (rather than in the "reader-response" of a community of which the author might have been a part); see Roland Barthes, "The Death of the Author," and Michel Foucault, "What Is an Author?" ibid., 166–72 and 196–210.

2. The distinction is Aristotelian. Cf. Boethius's definition of sound in terms of motion (a definition that was universally known in the Middle Ages): "sound is not produced without some pulsation and percussion [cause]; and pulsation and percussion cannot exist by any means unless motion precedes them [prior cause]. . . . For this reason, sound is defined as a percussion [action] of air [passive object, or patient] remaining undissolved all the way to the hearing [from where it may go on to produce an effect]." See Anicius Manlius Severinus Boethius, *Fundamentals of Music*, trans. Calvin M. Bower, ed. Claude V. Palisca (New Haven: Yale University Press, 1989), 11.

3. *Complexus effectuum musices*; see Tinctoris, *Opera theoretica*, ed. Albert Seay, Corpus Scriptorum de Musica 22 (n.p.: American Institute of Musicology, 1975), 2:159–77.

4. It is true that music-as-written possessed intelligible qualities in which symbolic meaning could be perceived, for instance numbers of notes or units of length. However, such forms of musical symbolism represent only a small part of the multiplicity of meanings that is nowadays postulated for music—a multiplicity that really reflects the diversity and historical dynamism of the interpretive communities through which music passes. In fact, these forms of symbolism tend to appeal mainly to communities that place great emphasis on authorial intention and intellectual apprehension (e.g., modern scholarship), and hardly at all to communities concerned primarily with music as entertainment or pleasurable activity.

5. Tinctoris, *Opera theoretica*, 2:159–77.

6. For literature, see Wolfgang Stephan, *Die burgundisch-niederländische Motette zur Zeit Ockeghems* (Kassel: Bärenreiter, 1937), 22; C. L. Walther Boer, *Het Anthonius-motet van Anthonius Busnoys* (Amsterdam: H. J. Paris, 1940); Charles Van den Borren, *Etudes sur le XVe siècle musical* (Antwerp: N. V. de Nederlandsche Boekhandel, 1941), 238–44; Edgar H. Sparks, "The Motets of Antoine Busnoys," *Journal of the American Musicological Society* 6 (1953): 225–26; Edgar H. Sparks, *Cantus Firmus in Mass and Motet 1420–1520* (Berkeley: University of California Press, 1963), 217 and 227–29; Flynn Warmington, "A Busnois–Fétis Collaboration: The Motet " 'Anthoni usque limina'," paper read at the meeting of the American Musicological Society, 6–9 November 1986; Rob C. Wegman, "Busnoys' 'Anthoni usque limina' and the Order of Saint-Antoine-en-Barbefosse in Hainaut," *Studi musicali* 17 (1988): 15–31; Antoine Busnoys, *Collected Works, Part 2: The Latin-Texted Works*, ed. Richard Taruskin, Masters and Monuments of the Renaissance 5/2–3 (New York: Broude Trust, 1990), 3:64–69.

7. Hereafter BrusBR 5557 (fols. 48^v–50^r).

8. *Monostempus silens/Modi sine me non/Sit tot anthipsilens/Nethesinemenon* (BrusBR 5557, fol. 48^v); see n. 29.

9. See the illustrations in Walther Boer, *Het Anthonius-motet*, following p. 16, and *The New Grove Dictionary of Music and Musicians*, 20 vols., ed. Stanley Sadie, (London: Macmillan, 1980), 3:506.

10. *Alpha et o cephasque deutheri/cum pos decet penulti[mum] queri/actoris qui nomen vult habere* (BrusBR 5557, fol. 49^v).

11. See Wegman, "Busnoys's 'Anthoni usque limina'," 25–27, and below. "Water" is written by Busnoys as "moys" (14; a Latin transliteration of the Coptic word for water), to make it rhyme with the Greek-derived "noys" (16), for "spirit." See Noel Swerdlow, "Musica Dicitur a Moys, Quod Est Aqua," *Journal of the American Musicological Society* 20 (1967): 3–9.

12. P. Noordeloos, "Antoniana," *Archief voor de geschiedenis van de katholieke kerk in Nederland* 1 (1959): 27–107, particularly 72–74.

13. For example in Ghent, 1489, see Paul Trio, *Volksreligie als spiegel van een*

stedelijke samenleving: De broederschappen te Gent in de late middeleeuwen (Louvain: Universitaire Pers Leuven, 1993), 278 and n. 13 (foundation of a confraternity in honor of St. Anthony and St. Roch, described as "marshals and averters of unforeseen death and the plague and disease of pestilence").

14. Wegman, "Busnoys's 'Anthoni usque limina'," 26–27.

15. See the office of St. Anthony, edited after several fifteenth-century Dutch sources by Hélène Wagenaar-Nolthenius and Joseph Smits van Waesberghe, in *Het officie van Antonius Eremita*, Scripta Musicologica Ultrajectina 5 (Utrecht: Instituut voor Muziekwetenschap der Rijksuniversiteit, 1975): the office borrows extensively from the famous *vita* of St. Anthony written by St. Athanasius. (I am grateful to Marcel Zijlstra for procuring me a copy of this edition.)

16. Jacobus de Voragine, *The Golden Legend*, trans. William Granger Ryan (Princeton: Princeton University Press, 1993), 1:93–94.

17. Cf. Trent, Castello del Buon Consiglio, Museo Provinciale d'Arte, MS 1376 (*olim* 89), fols. 64^v–65^r and 68^v–69^r, and Wagenaar-Nolthenius and Smits van Waesberghe, *Het officie van Antonius Eremita*, 16.

18. Since the actual verb used is "psallere" (8), it may be significant that Busnoys labels the bass of his motet "barripsaltes" and describes the bell as "anthipsilens." "Chorus" (11) need not necessarily mean a polyphonic choir: see, for instance, the phrase "quem chorus exultat" in the Nunc Dimittis antiphon *Da patris Anthonii meritis* (Wagenaar-Nolthenius and Smits van Waesberghe, *Het officie van Antonius Eremita*, 6).

19. Jacques Le Goff, *The Birth of Purgatory* (Aldershot: Scolar Press, 1984), 122–24 and 233.

20. "ut per tua merita valeamus cuncta evadere pericula et gehenne ignis incendia"; see Wagenaar-Nolthenius and Smits van Waesberghe, *Het officie van Antonius Eremita*, 22.

21. "Flammas igni et orci incendia mox suffocat victor demonii"; cf. Trent *MS* 1375 (*olim* 88), fols. 179^v–180^r.

22. See Eamon Duffy, *The Stripping of the Altars: Traditional Religion in England c.1400–c.1580* (New Haven: Yale University Press, 1992), 373, for the resolution of the distinction "between the essential sacrifice which constituted the Mass, on one hand, and which was efficacious for all the quick and the dead who share the divine life of charity, and the particular prayers which formed the proper of each Mass, on the other, which, like any other prayers, could be directed to specific purposes or persons."

23. Ibid., 124 and 214–15; *Liber usualis* (Tournai: Desclée & Socii, 1962), 7. The opening of St. John's Gospel was believed to have special protective power; see Keith Thomas, *Religion and the Decline of Magic: Studies in Popular Beliefs in Sixteenth- and Seventeenth-Century England* (London: Penguin, 1973), 34 and 39.

24. For what follows, see Michael Long, "Symbol and Ritual in Josquin's *Missa Di Dadi*," *Journal of the American Musicological Society* 42 (1989): 1–22, at 4–7.

25. Cf. John Quidort's (d. 1306) discussion of the eucharist, in which the nature of the consecrated bread is assumed to be coextensive with the Word, rather than annihilated by full transubstantiation; Miri Rubin, *Corpus Christi: The Eucharist in Late Medieval Culture* (Cambridge: Cambridge University Press, 1991), 31.

26. Rubin, *Corpus Christi*, 58–60 and 152; Duffy, *The Stripping of the Altars*, 97–98.

27. Cf. Busnoys, *Collected Works*, 3:66.

28. In addition, the pealing of bells was thought to chase away demons, for instance when they caused storms or natural disasters. For an example in Ghent, 1473,

see Rob C. Wegman, *Born for the Muses: The Life and Masses of Jacob Obrecht* (Oxford: Clarendon Press, 1994), 51.

29. On reflection, Flynn Warmington's resolution of the bell canon ("A Busnoys–Fétis Collaboration"; adopted with modifications by Richard Taruskin in Busnoys, *Collected Works*, 2:138–48) no longer appears entirely plausible to me. Since the bass enters after nine *tempora* under O in the first section, and after the (notationally equivalent) period of 18 tempora under O2 in the second, Warmington reasonably assumes that a single resolution of the verbal canon (Busnoys writes "canon ubi supra" at the beginning of the second section) made sure that the first peal of the bell would have coincided with the entry of the bass in both sections. For this it is necessary to assume that "monostempus silens" must refer to a breve rest in 9:1 augmentation. However, no such proportion is specified in the canon, and in the absence of any directions it is natural to assume that "monostempus" refers to whatever the tempus happens to be in O or O2. Moreover, in Warmington's resolution the augmentation would lead to hypothetical durations of the bell sound which, as she points out, far exceed its normal decay (cf. *Collected Works*, 3:69). More importantly, it is difficult to assume an initial period of silence which, to judge from recent recordings of the motet, would have lasted about 25–35 seconds in performance. The unaccompanied introductory trios/duos could very easily have resulted in changes of pitch level, leading to an extremely awkward sound when the bell entered (cf. David Fallows, *Dufay* [London, 1982], 118–19). An example in one of the recordings, after an equal period of silence, can be heard in measure 28 (1'23") of the performance by the New London Chamber Choir ("The Brightest Heaven of Invention," Amon Ra Records, CD-SAR 56, 1992). Plainly, regular pealing would have been necessary from the very beginnings of the two sections to avoid such moments, and Busnoys's canon clearly calls for this: "Being silent for one tempus [whether in O or O2], let so many modi [as remain] not be without me, countersounding *nete synemmenon*."

30. Duffy, *The Stripping of the Altars*, 124 and 281–82. For the protective powers attributed to holy water, see also Thomas, *Religion and the Decline of Magic*, 32–33, 211, and 236.

31. Le Goff, *The Birth of Purgatory*, 81–82, 146–47, 175, 275–76, 308; Philippe Ariès, *The Hour of Our Death* (New York: Oxford University Press, 1991), 154–61.

32. Rubin, *Corpus Christi*, 155–63.

33. It was considered vital to secure the help of saints during his life, since souls might otherwise find themselves without any advocate to plead against the accuser, Satan, in St. Michael's court, at which provisional judgments were made in anticipation of Christ's final judgment. This predicament was described in the widely known treatise *Le pèlerinage de l'âme*, by Guillaume de Deguileville (of which Guillaume Dufay, incidentally, possessed a copy): after Satan had delivered his damning accusation before the court, "I heard [my guardian angel] speak of an advocate, [and] I began to think whether I had ever served any saint who might take up my cause in this distress. . . . But I realized that I would have nothing to give my adviser or advocate, nor had I served, during my life, any particular saint to whom, after the advice of Job, I might turn myself in prayer to take up my quarrel [with the devil]." After Rosemarie Potz McGerr, ed., *The Pilgrimage of the Soul: A Critical Edition of the Middle English Dream Vision* (New York: Garland, 1990), 15–16. The poor soul was sentenced to purgatory (ibid., 53–54).

34. For the "dramatization" of the hour of death, see Ariès, *The Hour of Our Death*, 107–10; Le Goff, *The Birth of Purgatory*, 230 and 292–93; Duffy, *The Stripping of the Altars*, 313–27.

35. In the *ars moriendi* impatience was itemized as one of the five temptations in the hour of death; Duffy, *The Stripping of the Altars*, 315–16. See also Jacobus de Voragine, *The Golden Legend*, 2:282: "It is, however, believable that the good angels frequently visit and console their brothers and fellow citizens in purgatory and exhort them to suffer patiently."

36. *The Golden Legend*, 1:93.

37. Although there had been considerable debate as to whether purgatory (as an intermediate place between heaven and hell) was operated by devils or angels, the late Middle Ages veered toward an infernal rather than pre-paradisical image of this place of penance; see Duffy, *The Stripping of the Altars*, 343–46; Le Goff, *The Birth of Purgatory*, 252 and 322.

38. On the other hand, it seems inconsistent that such "refreshment" would then be expected to come from water, since Busnoys also evokes the fear of sinking into "the mire of the underworld" (1.11). In Ps. 69, from which the latter image was borrowed, the Hebrew underworld (*sheol*) is represented as a bottomless pit of water (vv. 1–2): "Save me, O God; for the waters are come in unto my soul. I sink in deep mire, where there is no standing: I am come into deep waters, where the floods overthrow me." Jacques Le Goff intriguingly notes (*The Birth of Purgatory*, 26–27): "There is a close connection . . . between *sheol* and the symbolism of chaos, sometimes embodied in the desert, sometimes in the ocean. Closer attention should perhaps be paid to the possible links between the medieval Purgatory and certain saints or anchorites who [like St. Anthony] wander the oceans or live in solitude in the forest or desert."

39. Ariès, *The Hour of Our Death*, 25–26; Le Goff, *The Birth of Purgatory*, 46–48. Busnoys and his contemporaries could still have been aware of this through the Wisdom of Solomon 4:7: "Justus, si morte preoccupatus fuerit, in refrigerio erit" (The righteous man, if he was mindful of death, will be in paradise).

40. The third-century Apocalypse of Paul (which was to become a highly influential document for medieval beliefs about purgatory) describes in a vision how, "when the souls of the damned see one saved soul pass by, wafted by the archangel Michael to Paradise, they beg him to intercede on their behalf with the Lord. The archangel invites the damned, along with Paul and the angels who accompany him, to beg God in tears for a modicum of 'refreshment' (*refrigerium*). This sets off a tremendous concert of tears, which causes the Son of God to descend from heaven to remind the sinners of his passion and their sins. Swayed by the prayers of Michael and Paul, Christ grants respite (*requies*) from Saturday night to Monday morning" (Le Goff, *The Birth of Purgatory*, 37).

41. Ibid., 197–98. See also the phrase "Consolator optime, dulcis hospes anime, dulce refrigerium" in the Pentecost sequence *Veni creator Spiritus* (*Liber usualis*, 880–81). (I am grateful to Bonnie Blackburn for pointing out this reference to me.)

42. Rob C. Wegman, "New Data Concerning the Origins and Chronology of Brussels, Koninklijke Bibliotheek, Manuscript 5557," *Tijdschrift van de Vereniging voor Nederlandse Muziekgeschiedenis* 36 (1986), 5–25.

43. Rob C. Wegman, "Petrus de Domarto's *Missa Spiritus almus* and the Early History of the Four-Voice Mass in the Fifteenth Century," *Early Music History* 10 (1991): 235–303, at 262–64; id., *Born for the Muses*, 97, n. 7.

44. For this and what follows, see Pamela F. Starr, "Rome as the Centre of the Universe: Papal Grace and Music Patronage," *Early Music History* 11 (1992), 223–62, at 249–56 and 260.

45. Irregularity was an impediment to receiving orders, for which dispensation was required; it could be either *ex defectu* (e.g., bodily defect or illegitimacy) or *ex delicto*

(e.g., unlawful exercise of orders, as in Busnoys's case). See W. Nolet and P. C. Boeren, *Kerkelijke instellingen in de middeleeuwen* (Amsterdam: Urbi et Orbi, 1951), 90–91, and Starr, "Rome as the Centre of the Universe," 247. Busnoys petitioned for dispensation of the irregularity in order to qualify for tonsure again.

46. For the distinction, see Duffy, *The Stripping of the Altars*, 288, and Le Goff, *The Birth of Purgatory*, 213–20.

47. It may be no coincidence that the next document to mention Busnoys, more than four years after he had received absolution and dispensation (7 and 13 April 1465), sees him skipping several lower orders to the rank of acolyte and, a week later, to the holy order of subdeacon: evidently there had been considerable delay in his ecclesiastical career. See Paula Higgins, "*In hydraulis* Revisited: New Light on the Career of Antoine Busnois," *Journal of the American Musicological Society* 39 (1986): 36–86, at 70–71.

48. Duffy, *The Stripping of the Altars*, 160–62. See also n. 33 for the importance of particular devotions to saints who might eventually act as advocate at the court of St. Michael.

49. Helmuth Osthoff, *Josquin Desprez* (Tutzing: Hans Schneider, 1962–65), 1:16 (Vienne was approximately 340 kilometers from Milan).

50. For the concepts of accountancy and bookkeeping, see Le Goff, *The Birth of Purgatory*, 229 and 292.

51. On the perception of saints as friends, see Duffy, *The Stripping of the Altars*, 160–63.

52. Higgins, "*In hydraulis* Revisited," 43.

53. For the possibility for private benefactors to exercise control over prayers in votive Masses, see Duffy, *The Stripping of the Altars*, 114.

54. See ibid., 121–26 and 139–41 for "the extent to which late medieval Christians identified individual spiritual welfare with that of the community as a whole, an identification in which personal initiative and corporate action in pursuit of salvation could converge without any sign of incongruity or tension" (141).

55. Wegman, "Busnoys' 'Anthoni usque limina'."

56. Ibid., 19 and 23.

57. Noordeloos, "Antoniana," 101–3.

58. See ibid., 61, for a description of the emblem of the (non-Antonian) brotherhood of St. Anthony at Antwerp: a tau, crowned by a bundle of flames, and surrounded by a corona of flames (note the prominence of fire symbolism), as well as a bell, all enclosed within two laurel branches. Closer to the emblem of Barbefosse is the insignia of the (Antonian) Order of St. Anthony at the convent of Issenheim, south of Colmar, now in the Unterlinden Museum; see Christian Heck, *Grünewald and the Issenheim Altar* (Colmar: Delta, 1987), 59 (I am indebted to Andrew Kirkman for drawing this publication to my attention). See also P. Noordeloos, "Enige gegevens over broederschappen van S. Antonius," *Publications de la Société historique et archéologique dans le Limbourg* 85 (1949): 477–99, at 490 (Maastricht and Bailleul).

59. For the link between confraternities and death and burial, see Le Goff, *The Birth of Purgatory*, 327–28, Duffy, *The Stripping of the Altars*, 143–44, and Ariès, *The Hour of Our Death*, 183–88, especially 185: "Of all the works of mercy, the service for the dead became the main purpose of the confraternities. Their patron saints were often chosen from among the saints known as protectors against the plague and epidemics: Saint Sebastian, Saint Roch, and Saint Gond." For the fifteenth-century association of St. Anthony with plague and other epidemic diseases in the Ghent confraternity of St. Anthony and St. Roch, see n. 13.

60. "*In hydraulis* Revisited."

Love and Death in the Fifteenth-Century Motet

A Reading of Busnoys's *Anima mea liquefacta est/Stirps Jesse*

Recent critical interpretations of late fifteenth-century works continue to offer stunning examples of how the ostensibly devotional music of Josquin, Obrecht, and their contemporaries conceals a "signifying universe,"[1] a network of symbols, which, once unraveled, often yields latent clues about the extraliturgical circumstances motivating the musical creation. Hitherto unimaginable hermeneutic horizons for late medieval music have unfolded in the wake of Reinhard Strohm's demonstration that an array of seemingly unrelated cantus firmi in Obrecht's St. Donatian Mass illustrates specific details of the life of the Bruges merchant Donaes de Moor, whose widow endowed the Mass;[2] Michael Long's exegesis of Josquin's *Missa Di Dadi* as a metaphorical medieval dice game;[3] Jennifer Bloxam's revelation that the cantus firmi of the *Missae Floruit egregiis* by Pipelare and La Rue narrate the lives and careers of their composers;[4] and Patrick Macey's reading of Josquin's motet *Misericordias Domini* as a musical therapeutic for a dying monarch.[5] Alerting us to the meaning-laden potential of seemingly conventional liturgical texts and cantus firmi, these studies encourage us to develop a similarly sensitive eye even when the work itself fails specifically to hint at a meaningful context.[6]

Scholars have long recognized *Anima mea liquefacta est/Stirps Jesse*[7] as an anomaly among Antoine Busnoys's Latin-texted works. Some 40 years ago, Edgar Sparks earmarked the piece as Busnoys's most "primitive" motet, citing its polytextuality, three-voice texture, tenor as lowest-sounding voice, octave-leap cadences, contratenor moving both above and below the tenor, tentative use of sequence and imitation, and above all its "contrapuntal and harmonic procedures definitely related to those of the first half of the century."[8] Concurring with Sparks's assessment, Richard Taruskin recently called it "a very old-fashioned composition and very likely Busnoys' earliest surviving motet."[9]

Neither Sparks nor Taruskin hazarded a guess as to precisely how "early" Busnoys's "earliest" motet might be—and one can hardly fault them for failing to do so. We still have no concrete evidence for Busnoys's birthdate, and consequently no truly sound basis for dating his "earliest" music. The two extant sources for the motet, Cappella Sistina 15 and Brussels 5557, dating from the 1460s to the 1500s, are of little help in pinpointing the motet's possible date of composition. Even if it can be demonstrated, as I believe it can, that many aspects of *Anima mea*'s style are technically less accomplished than, say, *In hydraulis*, dating from ca. 1466 and the only firmly datable work in Busnoys's output, what do we really know about the evolution of a composer's style in this period? Precisely how much time would have elapsed—months, years, decades?—between the writing of a Busnoys piece that we consider "early" and one we regard as a more "mature" style?

While acknowledging the relatively archaic musical features of *Anima mea*, Mary Natvig assigned it to the period around August 1468, coinciding with the festivities surrounding the marriage of Margaret of York and Charles the Bold. She connects the motet to the newly wed duchess of Burgundy on the basis of several compelling observations: the traditional exegesis of Song of Songs texts as epithalamia; the seasonal coincidence of Margaret's August itinerary with the liturgical feasts of the Assumption and Nativity of the Virgin associated with the two chants used in the motet; the predominance of Song of Songs antiphons in Margaret's native Sarum rite; and finally, the concern with procreation suggested by the use of the chant *Stirps Jesse*.[10] Natvig views the motet's unusual stylistic features as a matter of choosing a "more reserved manner appropriate for a noble patron," rather than as a function of an earlier date of composition.

Natvig's solution, while neatly sidestepping the biographical problems posed by an "early" date for the motet, essentially asks us to accept the notion that a composer possessed of the considerable musical gifts evident in a piece like *In hydraulis* would set out to alter his approach to compositional process merely for the sake of writing a single work. To my mind *Anima mea* is not merely "more reserved" than *In hydraulis* and the *L'Homme armé Mass*; it manifests an approach to composition entirely at odds with these better known and decidedly more skillful works. Since I shall develop the full musical argument at length elsewhere, I shall restrict myself here to the following cursory observations.[11] Busnoys's use of the *Stirps Jesse* tenor as the lowest part of *Anima mea*'s three-voice texture is wholly uncharacteristic of works from the 1460s, but entirely typical of earlier fifteenth-century practice. *Anima mea*'s cantus-firmus treatment, though quite literal, is fully incorporated rhythmically into the texture of the other two voices, decidedly unlike the rigid tenors that serve as the inner scaffolding of both his Masses and some of his motets that have been more firmly dated to the 1460s. The motet's fairly unusual clef combination of C3, F3, F3 is unique among all of Busnoys's attributed works, and the only other instances of exactly the same combination I have located thus far occur in pieces attributed to Dunstable, Dufay, and Binchois.[12] The scoring for three nearly equal male voices in the tenor-baritone range is similarly unmatched in Busnoys's other Latin-texted works, and the only secular pieces in roughly comparable ranges are the rondeaux *Joye me fuit* and *Bel acueil*, the latter of which I shall return to later. Were it not for the presence of a number of unmistakably Busnoysian fingerprints in this motet, one might be inclined to dismiss it from his canon altogether.

Contextualized with respect to earlier Song settings,[13] Busnoys's *Anima mea* is equally unusual in employing a cantus firmus, a double text, and a freely contrapuntal and largely non-declamatory style. Although, like many Song settings, *Anima mea* does paraphrase a chant in the upper voice at several strategic structural points, the tune is not that of the Mode 7 antiphon *Anima mea* that some composers, including Dufay, used, but rather that of the Mode 2 responsory *Stirps Jesse*, set to the text of *Anima mea*, recalling Dunstable's setting of the sequence *Veni sancte spiritus* to the music of the hymn *Veni creator spiritus*. Somewhat surprisingly, Busnoys's *Anima* bears a stronger generic resemblance to the Song settings of his insular rather than his Continental antecedents. Morphologically, Busnoys's motet is similar to Power's *Quam pulchra es* and his late three-voice *Anima mea*, and to the three *Anima mea* settings of the mysterious "Forest," whose Song settings manifest a proto-Busnoysian penchant for melodic sequence and imitation, and one of whose *Anima* settings specifically shares with Busnoys's setting duos on identical portions of the *Anima* text, triple-meter setting of the line "Filiae Jerusalem," and multiple shifts in mensuration in the final segment of the text.[14] Moreover, Forest's three-voice motet *Alma redemptoris/Anima mea* is the only other Song text besides Busnoys's that simultaneously employs polytextuality, a plainchant residing in the tenor as lowest-sounding voice, and two texts liturgically appropriate to the Feast of the Assumption.[15]

Any attempt to reckon with a potential dating of *Anima mea* must seriously interrogate its unequivocal stylistic relationship to works of the first half of the fifteenth century—a task not only hitherto unexplored but indeed virtually uncontemplated in Busnoys studies to date and one that takes us well beyond the scope of this article.[16] Nevertheless, by acknowledging both the possibility of an early dating for the piece and at least the plausibility of the hypothetical historical context for Busnoys's earlier career in the late 1440s or early 1450s that I have already outlined elsewhere,[17] I was led to a somewhat provocative reading of *Anima mea/Stirps Jesse* that would link it with dramatic historical events that took place at the French royal court in 1445–46. This reading, drawing on medieval traditions of literary and biblical exegesis and their convergence in Busnoys's motet (as well as in an intertextually related song), neither excludes other readings of *Anima mea/Stirps Jesse* nor rules out the likelihood of its appropriation for use in a number of other liturgical or paraliturgical settings. And while I recognize that as yet unknown and possibly unknowable empirical facts about Busnoys's career and about the actual date of piece will ultimately validate or negate the legitimacy of this interpretation, I am less concerned in this chapter with the ultimate truth value of my speculation than with the emergent historical framework for which it has provided the hermeneutic catalyst. My primary goal is rather a case study in contextual reading, for which I ask the reader to accept a necessary working hypothesis, one which happens incidentally to corroborate an early date for the motet suggested by

Sparks and Taruskin and thereby reconciles some of the biographical, stylistic, and chronological problems posed by Natvig's 1468 dating.

BUSNOYS'S *Anima mea/Stirps Jesse* arguably presents a most unlikely candidate for hermeneutic exploration because its appropriation of not only one but two liturgical texts unequivocally associated with high Marian feasts would seem to obliterate any doubt as to its purely liturgical function, especially since Jennifer Bloxam has recently noted the contiguous placement of the two chants at First Vespers on the Feast of the Assumption in the rite of Paris.[18] On the other hand, as Bloxam has shown us in her own insightful work on multi-texted Masses and motets, composers often use polytextuality to create a network of textual and musical associations within a piece, and often choose the texts "primarily for their content, and only secondarily for their liturgical associations."[19]

Indeed, Busnoys's choices with regard to both liturgical texts employed in the motet seem highly distinctive and unusual. Although English composers like Power, Dunstable, Forest, and Plummer wrote numerous polyphonic settings of Song texts in the first half of the fifteenth century, Song texts do not seem to have exercised the musical imaginations of Continental composers of the same or immediately succeeding generations, with the notable exceptions of Hugo de Lantins and Johannes de Limburgia. Dufay's *Anima mea*, his only Song text, dates from before 1426[20] and hence corresponds with the English phenomenon. Binchois, despite a large production of functional liturgical music, much of which uses chants of the Sarum rite, eschewed Song texts entirely, as did, apparently, Ockeghem,[21] Regis, Obrecht, and Compère.[22] In fact, with the exception of two anonymous settings of *Anima* in the Trent codices and Weerbeke's *Anima* written for Milan, Busnoys's *Anima mea* appears to be the only setting of the text by a composer working in French or Burgundian territories from the 1430s through at least the 1480s,[23] and it is, moreover, the only work by a French composer of the fifteenth century to use both the entire text and the music of the festal prolix reponsory *Stirps Jesse* as a cantus firmus.[24]

Anima mea's ostensibly impeccable liturgical credentials notwithstanding, the unique marriage of these two texts, together with the motet's anomalous musical features, lead me to suspect that it may conceal deeper levels of meaning that may yield clues about its original composition. It seems unlikely that Busnoys, a man possessed of exceptional clerical erudition, would have been unaware of the long history of allegorical exegesis of the Song triggered by the perception that its interpretation *ad litteram* posed "no small difficulty and danger" to the unwary reader. Origen, whose massive third-century commentary spearheaded nine centuries of exegetical tradition that interpreted the Song's literal carnality as a veil for hidden spiritual meanings, regarded the Song as "so lushly erotic that it endangers the carnally minded reader who approaches it and is seemingly incited to fleshly lust by sacred Scripture itself."[25] It is almost unthinkable that a composer like Busnoys, who manifests virtually unrivaled sensitivity to the ludic aspects of medieval textuality, would have turned a blind eye to the powerfully sensual texts of the Song that made it the most controversial and most heavily glossed book of the Bible in the Middle Ages; that the same composer who exchanged obscene double-entendres with the poet Jean Molinet,[26] would have blithely ignored the Song's scarcely veiled sexual metaphors and its richly symbolic language; or that the author of the verses "I can't live like this any longer unless I have some comfort for my pain, just one hour, or less or more," describing a classic case of late medieval lovesickness,[27] would have entirely overlooked their indebtedness to the verse "quia amore langueo" that closes the *Anima mea* text.

Modern critics have labeled the segment from which *Anima mea* derives the "erotic dream sequence" or the "sexual fantasy" of the Song (5:2–6) and not without good reason:[28]

2   I slept, but my mind was alert.
Hark, my love knocks.
Open to me, my sister,
My darling, my dove, my perfect one!
For my head is drenched with dew,
My locks with the night mist.
3   I have removed my tunic;
How shall I put it on?
I have washed my feet;
how shall I soil them?
4   My love thrust his "hand" into the hole,
And my inwards seethed for him.
5   I rose to open for my love,
And my hands dripped myrrh,
My fingers liquid myrrh,
On the handles of the bolt.
6   I opened to my love,
But my love had turned and gone.

The dream rapidly takes on aspects of phantasmagoria, as the Beloved opens the door to her Lover, only to find that he has vanished. Against this narrative background directly follows the *Anima mea* "story," here given as Busnoys's complete motet text *Anima mea/Stirps Jesse:*

Anima mea liquefacta est
ut dilectus locutus est.
Quesivi illum et non inveni,
vocavi, et non respondit michi.
Invenerunt me custodes murorum*
Percusserunt me,
et vulneraverunt me.
Tulerunt pallium meum
custodes murorum.
Filie Jherusalem,
nuntiate dilecto
quia amore langueo.

My soul melted
as he spoke.
I sought him but did not find him.
I called him but he did not answer me.
The watchmen of the walls found me,
they beat me,
and they wounded me.
They took away my cloak,
the watchmen of the walls.
O daughters of Jerusalem,
tell my beloved
that I am sick with love.

*Vulgate: civitatis

Tenor

Stirps Jesse virgam produxit	The stem of Jesse brought forth a shoot,
virgaque florem; et super hunc	and the shoot a flower; and on this
florem requiescit spiritus almus.	flower rested the Spirit of life.

The female speaker describes how her soul melts when her lover speaks. She seeks, but cannot find him; she calls to him, but he does not answer. She rushes into the streets to search for him, only to be apprehended and beaten by certain "watchmen" of the walls, who also strip her clothes off. She then begs the "daughters of Jerusalem" to announce to her lover that she is "sick with love." This nightmarish scenario culminating in physical violence against the Beloved leads me to ask why Busnoys would have chosen this particular text, rather than any other of the far more appropriate and far less ambiguous Song texts, to celebrate the presumably joyous postnuptial ceremonial entries of a recently married duchess.

The tragic life of another Margaret, however, who also hailed from the British Isles, resonates with uncanny similarities to the text of *Anima mea*: the Scottish princess, Margaret of Scotland, or Marguerite d'Ecosse, about whom I have already written at length elsewhere in connection with the creation of Busnoys's Hacqueville songs.[29] Let me briefly review the details of Margaret's life most relevant to my purpose at hand. In 1436, the 12-year-old daughter of King James I of Scotland went to France to wed the future Louis XI in extravagant nuptial festivities held at Tours. Nine years later, at the age of 21, this "melancholy *dauphine*" as Champion dubbed her, whispered her dying words: "To hell with the life of this world; don't talk to me about it any longer."[30] The "it" to which she alluded concerned the forgiveness of one Jamet de Tillay in the interest of sparing the eternal damnation of her soul. Jamet de Tillay, *bailli de Vermandois*, was Louis's courtier and alleged spy accused of spreading mendacious rumors about Margaret to the dauphin and to the court at large. Although doctors officially attributed the dauphine's untimely death on 16 August 1445 to pneumonia, rumors at court suggested that her fatal illness had been triggered by the insinuations of infidelity perpetrated by the courtier Jamet de Tillay.[31]

The serious nature of the allegations against Tillay prompted Charles VII to order two legal inquests into the matter, conducted in October 1445 and in June 1446, during which sworn depositions were taken from many ladies-in-waiting and gentlemen of the court. A number of witnesses explicitly attributed the rapid decline in the dauphine's physical condition to her deep chagrin about Tillay's defamatory statements.[32] Several days after the dauphine had fallen ill, she told her lady-in-waiting, Jeanne de Tasse (Appendix I, at 1a), that "she had good reason to be melancholy and to make herself sick for the words that had been said about her, which were wrong and without basis." To Marguerite de Hacqueville (Appendix I, at 3), another of her ladies, she confided that "Jamet de Tillay had been going to considerable trouble every day to disgrace her in the eyes of her husband the dauphin, and that she had already had and continued to have a great deal of trouble from him; and that one could never say worse things about a woman than [Tillay] had said of her." Three days before the dauphine's death, two of her ladies described her as crying out from her sickbed: "Ah Jamet! Jamet! you have succeeded in your intention; if I die, it is because of you and the fine words that you said about me without cause or reason" (Appendix I, at 1c and 4b).

One incident that furnished abundant grist for Tillay's rumor mill occurred late one night when Tillay suggested to the dauphine's *maître d'hôtel* Regnault de Dressay: "Allons voir les dames!" (Let's go see the ladies). Proceeding toward the dauphine's quarters, they discovered that the torches had yet to be lit in her chambers; peering into the room brightened only by the light of the burning fireplace, they saw the dauphine reclining on her divan, surrounded by her ladies and two gentlemen, one of whom was leaning against the divan in a somewhat compromising position (Appendix II, no. 1).[33] Scandalized, Tillay proceeded to broadcast the "great lewdness" of the situation and on other occasions was said to have decried the dauphine's behavior as "more fitting of a whore than of a great lady" (Appendix II, nos. 8 and 10).

Tillay himself repeatedly denied any wrongdoing throughout the inquests, and when confronted with the contradictory testimony of others, he artfully twisted their words or suffered attacks of selective amnesia.[34] He blamed the dauphine's illness on a chronic lack of sleep resulting from her habit of writing rondeaux and ballades into the wee hours of the morning:

> And the king asked him what caused her illness; and [Tillay] said that it came from a lack of sleep, as the doctors had said, and that she frequently stayed up so much that it was often dawn before she went to bed; and sometimes my lord the dauphin had been asleep for some time before she joined him, and often she was so busy writing rondeaux that she sometimes wrote a dozen in a day, which was not good for her. And when the king asked if that could give her headaches, my lord the treasurer, Maistre Jehan Bureau who was present, said, "Yes, if she does it too much; but these [i.e. writing poetry] are pleasurable things. (Appendix II, no. 6)

Earlier in the same testimony he had explicitly named three of her ladies-in-waiting[35] as aiding and abetting the dauphine in her nocturnal literary pursuits:

> The said Nicole asked him [Jamet de Tillay] what was wrong with her, and what caused her illness and [Jamet] answered that the doctors said she had much rancor in her heart, which was harmful to her and exacerbated by lack of sleep; and then the said Nicole replied that the doctors had told him the same thing, and also added: "If only she had not had that woman [in her service]!" "Who?" said [Tillay]. Nicole answered, "Marguerite de Salignac." And Tillay retorted: "Nor Prégente, nor Jeanne Filloque [*sic*: Filleul]!" Asked why he said such things, he answered that he had heard that they were the ones who kept her up too late writing rondeaux and ballades. (Appendix II, no. 4)

In Tillay's eyes, writing poetry was not only detaining the dauphine from the conjugal bed, it was contributing to her moral depravity, and worst of all, it "was not good for her"—it was making her sick. Indeed, more than one witness quoted Tillay as saying that the dauphine's illness was caused by "Amours" (see Appendix II, nos. 2, 3, 5, 9), that is, she was "lovesick," implying that the object of her love was presumably a man other than the dauphin, her husband. Tillay's suspicions were perhaps excessively heightened not only by the highly charged sexual climate of the French royal court, where Charles VII was alleged to have routinely availed himself of the ladies-in-waiting of both the dauphine and the queen (who, incidentally, included his most celebrated mistress, Agnes Sorel),[36] but also because writing poetry seems to have been a recognized medical remedy for curing lovesickness, as Mary Wack's recent work has shown.[37]

Much has been written about Louis's reluctance to marry the Scottish princess, chosen for him by his father Charles VII as part of a politically strategic alliance with James I of Scotland. The reasons for Louis's evidently intense dislike of her are not clear, since contemporary chroniclers described the princess as "beautiful, well-formed, and endowed with every positive attribute that a noble and high-born lady could have."[38] Despite its powerful hold on the historiography of Louis and Margaret, there is no documentary basis for the often repeated and somewhat misogynous sixteenth-century testimony that her poor hygiene and bad breath drove him away.[39] Whatever Louis's genuine feelings toward Margaret, it seems clear that he spent as little time as possible with her, that he failed to visit her sickbed in the last days of her life, and that he left town the day after she died.[40]

Turning now to the opening lines of *Anima mea:* "My soul melted when my beloved spoke / I looked for him but found him not / I called him but he did not answer me" describe not only Margaret's daily life with her absentee consort, but also Louis's particularly distressing silence with regard to Tillay's insinuations; these, in turn, seem almost eerily evocative of the next lines of *Anima mea:* "The watchmen of the walls found me, / they beat me, and they wounded me." It is hard to imagine a more appropriate human embodiment of *Anima*'s sinister "watchmen of the walls" than Tillay and his cohorts who, as Louis's agents, surreptitiously monitored Margaret's nocturnal behavior. Perhaps they did not literally "beat" her, but they certainly inflicted serious psychological trauma upon the dauphine, as the sworn testimony amply documents. And although they did not "take away her cloak / the watchmen of the walls," they shamed her and stripped her of her dignity by saying "the worst things about her that could be said of a woman."

Why do the watchmen beat, wound, and strip the Beloved? Undoubtedly because she was wandering around in the streets at night, in a fashion unthinkable for a respectable lady, and they mistook her for a prostitute.[41] Modern exegetes have noticed the resemblance of her behavior to that of the adulteress in Proverbs 7:5–21 who goes out into the night to look for a young man and tells him "I came out to meet you; I looked for you and have found you . . . I have perfumed my bed with myrrh aloes and cinnamon."[42] Others have emphasized a similarly striking intertextuality between Song 5:7–9 and Hosea 2 with its explicit concern with the adultery of Hosea's wife Gomer, and its condoning of violent means to prevent her from going to her lover:[43]

2 . . . Let her remove the adulterous look from her face . . . 3 Otherwise *I will strip her* naked and make her as bare as on the day she was born; . . . 6

I will block her path with thornbushes; *I will wall her in* so that she cannot find her way. *She will chase after her lovers but not catch them; she will look for them but not find them* . . . 10 *so now I will expose her lewdness* before the eyes of her lovers; no one will take her out of my hands . . .

Neither reference is likely to have been overlooked by an astute medieval biblical exegete. It is clear, as Michael Fox notes, "that the Shulammite was breaching the walls of expected behavior and as a result suffered the mockery and brutality of the representatives of the social order, 'those who watch the walls'."[44] Legal testimony about Tillay's personal opinion of the dauphine's nocturnal escapades, his alleged insinuations of adultery, and especially his explicit comment, aired throughout the court, that her behavior was "more befitting of a whore than of a great lady," reverberate with echoes of both medieval and contemporary exegeses of the text of Song 5:6–8.

During the last days of her life, the dauphine swore repeated oaths to several different ladies that "she had never done the things of which she was accused, much less thought about it." Two ladies heard her swear on the damnation of her soul that she had never wronged the dauphin (Appendix I, at 1b and 4b), and one of them graphically described Margaret pounding her hand on her chest, crying out "I swear to God on my soul and on the waters of my Baptism, or else let me die, that I never disrespected or wronged my lord" (Appendix I, at 1d). Margaret's repeated professions of innocence to her ladies-in-waiting, who seem to have been omnipresent during her final hours, and the striking consistency of their testimony with regard to the deathbed scene as recounted in their depositions, invites a parallel with the Song's "daughters of Jerusalem" who are instructed to "Tell my beloved / that I am sick with love." Even more astonishingly, the lines "quia amore langueo" echo Tillay's gossip that the dauphine's sickness, and hence her impending death, was caused "by Love, or a Love Affair"—in other words, that she was quite literally, at least in Tillay's eyes, "sick with love."

Now, a central preoccupation of Tillay's gossip was the dauphine's infertility, which the doctors variously attributed to a lack of sleep, to drinking too much vinegar, eating sour apples, and wearing her belts too tight (Appendix II, no. 7). Whatever its etiology, the dauphine's sterility would have had more sinister implications for Tillay and his courtly scandalmongers who suspected that such bizarre practices were methods of birth control (Appendix II, no. 11). The virtually palpable anxiety about the state of the royal sucession permeated the entire court, reaching King Charles VII himself, who had even asked Tillay if the dauphine was sick because she was "pregnant" (*impédumée*) (Appendix II, no. 6). There is absolutely no doubt that the dauphine's failure to produce an heir after nine years of marriage represented a central preoccupation for everyone at court. Contextualized in this way, Busnoys's choice of the tenor "Stirps Jesse," with its literal and metaphorical concerns with procreation and the perpetuation of a lineage (see the preceding text and translation), seems suddenly to make rich historical sense. Moreover, the "flos" (flower) upon which the "spiritus almus" (spirit of life) rested could aptly describe a woman whose name in French was also that of a flower (Marguerite = daisy). By setting long stretches of the *Stirps Jesse* chant at three strategic points in the upper voice of the motet to the text of *Anima mea*, Busnoys thus overlays a kind of musical metatext concerned with "procreation anxiety" onto the *Anima mea* "story" itself. Such a reading would represent a music historical analog to the literary anxiety about the queen's adulterous body that gets played out in numerous medieval romances, an anxiety that centered "on the inexpressed fear of production of illegitimate offspring and the implicit threat it posed to 'proper dynastic succession'."[45]

In my proposed reading, then, the combination of the two texts *Anima mea* and *Stirps Jesse* creates a web of fascinating intertextual allusions to the historical circumstances surrounding the death of the dauphine of France, Margaret of Scotland, to the concerns about her inability to ensure the perpetuation of the royal line, and to the unfounded and damaging rumors about her alleged adultery. Even the larger context of the Song of Songs is not without parallel to the dauphine's situation. Like the Shulamite, the dauphine was an "Other"—a strange princess, with peculiar customs from a faraway land. Louis's alleged animosity toward Margaret would seem to explode the analogy, although one does need to ask why Louis would have had his agents spy on her unless he was jealous, which seems unlikely, or, more probably, motivated by a fear that an adulterous queen-to-be might threaten dynastic succession by producing illegitimate offspring. So, whether out of genuine love or sheer self-interest, Louis's base desire to keep tabs on Margaret was fueled by a kind of "jealousy," precisely the subject of Song's "climax" (8:6ii): "love is strong as death; jealousy is cruel as the grave."

Barbara Haggh has shown that obit foundations in the fifteenth century frequently designated a combination of Marian texts with those alluding to the "Holy Spirit." Based on Haggh's information, Rob Wegman postulated that Domarto's *Missa Spiritus almus*, whose cantus firmus is based on the final phrase of *Stirps Jesse*, may have been written for a funeral context; significantly, in the same article, Wegman demonstrated several interesting musical connections between Busnoys's *Anima mea* and Domarto's Mass.[46] Moreover, recent biblical scholarship has connected the Song of Songs with ancient Near Eastern funeral rituals that were love feasts celebrated with wine, women, and song.[47] Coincidentally, Margaret of Scotland died on 16 August 1445, a day after the Feast of the Assumption, appropriate to both *Anima mea* and *Stirps Jesse* in the Paris rite, and well within the three-week period from the Assumption to the Nativity of the Virgin proper to the Sarum and some other rites.[48] After the dauphine's death, a commemorative service was celebrated every day for the first twelve months, and thereafter every year on the anniversary of her death, occasions that might conceivably have called for suitably devotional music.[49]

The idea that Busnoys's reading of *Anima mea* conceals a reference to a specific historical woman would be perhaps no more incongruous than Leonel Power's appropriation of Binchois's courtly love song *De plus en plus* in his two-voice *Anima mea*,[50] or Josquin's use of the cantus firmus *Comme femme desconfortée* in his motet *Stabat mater*.[51] In fact, my own reading of these

FIGURE 7.1   Jean Fouquet, Diptych of Melun (right panel). Antwerp, Koninklijke Museum voor Schone Kunsten (Inv. 132). Used by permission.

ostensibly Marian texts in light of the historical Margaret of Scotland invites a direct parallel with a pictorial representation originating at the French royal court around exactly the same time: the right panel of Jean Fouquet's *Diptych of Melun,* which features Charles VII's celebrated mistress, Agnes Sorel (a lady-in-waiting to Queen Marie d'Anjou), as the bare-breasted Virgin Mary (see Figure 7.1). Fouquet's work had been commissioned by royal counselor Etienne Chevalier, one of the three executors of her will, shortly after Sorel's death in 1450 in an effort to rehabilitate her tarnished reputation through association with a woman of less dubious moral credentials.[52]

This blending of the secular and sacred dimensions has long been recognized as a fundamental characteristic of late medieval culture, one which happens also to be reflected in the shifting modes of interpretation of the Song. From the late eleventh century onward, the long tradition of allegorical exegesis of the Song initiated by Origen in the third century began to be supplanted by the tropological mode of interpretation practiced by a new breed of biblical exegetes working in Paris, particularly the Victorines, who manifested renewed interest in literal and historical interpretations. This tropological, as opposed to allegorical, mode of exegesis sought to convey a more powerful spiritual message by encouraging readers to identify with the bride of the Song and draw parallels between their individual life experiences and hers.[53] The works of Hugh of St. Victor, one of the first writers to depart from the purely allegorical mode of earlier exegetes, explicate tropology as "the reader's response to the rhetorical appeal of the text, rightly understood: the meeting point of life and letter. . . . It consists in each reader's heartfelt, personal discovery of what he or she ought to do in order to realize the moral implications of the event recorded."[54] As the recent work of Ann Astell has shown, while biblical scholars have acknowledged the importance of the shift toward a reliteralization of the Song, they have insufficiently understood its rhetorical implications: "the more 'historical' the letter of the text is perceived to be—with respect to actual events and literal reference—the more immediately applicable it becomes to the lives of its auditors."[55] For example, the twelfth-century commentaries of Rupert of Deutz and others clearly reflect intensifying interest in mariological interpretation of the Song—literally relating its story to the life of the Virgin; an anonymous late eleventh-century French paraliturgical lyric *Quant li solleiz converset en Leon* compares a young woman weeping for reunion with her lover to the longing of Mary to join her celestial bridegroom.[56] One twelfth-century vernacular commentary from northern France translates the Song into a secular form and function: it is dedicated to a lady and written in the form of a *roman* in which the interlocutors are referred to as "Damoiselle" or "Bel sire."[57]

Precisely because its graphic descriptions of human love and unabashedly carnal themes were unparalleled in biblical literature, the Song of Songs exerted a profound influence both on secular Latin verse and even on vernacular courtly love poetry throughout the late Middle Ages.[58] This incontestable influence, as others have noted, extended to the famous *Roman de la Rose*, with which it shares a number of superficial thematic similarities: both feature enclosed gardens, walls, towers, and flowers symbolizing the beloved.[59] One thirteenth-century French paraphrase of the Song makes specific allusion to the *Roman de la Rose*, characterizing its discussion of love as "less honest" than its own.[60] An even more direct link exists between chapter 5:2–8 of the Song, the source of *Anima mea*, and the *Roman de la Rose*: both are "erotic dreams," involving a search, laden with obstacles, for a beloved. It is in the context of an erotic dream that the Beloved seeks her Lover, and within the context of an erotic dream that the Amant begins his quest for the "Rose." In the Song, it is the "watchmen of the walls" who impede the Beloved's quest for her Lover; in the *Roman* it is the negative personifications Dangier, Malebouche, Faulx Semblant, and their cohorts. The Beloved in the Song languishes for her Lover, just as the Lover of the *Roman* becomes lovesick and consumed with uncontrollable desire for the Rose.

Busnoys's *Bel acueil*, one of a handful of songs he set alluding to characters from the *Roman de la Rose*,[61] has the same unusual scoring for low voices in

nearly equal ranges as *Anima mea*. The allegorical character in question, Bel
Acueil or Fair Welcome, represents "the young girl's accessibility, that part of
her which her lover most directly encounters and which most directly encounters him";[62] in other words, a positive personification, one of the few, in fact,
peopling the *Roman*. As Walter Kemp noted, "*Bel acueil*, in general courtesy,
was the art of welcome, the ideal friendliness 'based on the recognition of the
essential connaturality of all men'. In the narrower amatory system it represented a 'fair welcome', in which the lady opened herself to pleasant conversation."[63]

Busnoys's *Bel acueil* happens to open the Mellon Chansonnier, dedicated
to Beatrice of Aragon, and by virtue of its identification with the largely positive
allegorical persona in the *Roman*, has come to be regarded as a conventional
courtly love song.[64] But this is no "courtly love" text in the traditional sense,
nor, incidentally, does the rather sinister character portrayed here correspond
even remotely to the Bel Acueil of the *Rose*:[65]

Bel acueil le sergent d'Amours	Fair Welcome, Love's constable
Qui bien sait faire ses *esploitz*	Who knows well how to serve his writs,
M'a ja *cité* par plusieurs fois	Has already summoned me several
D'aler à l'une de ses *cours*.	times,
	To go to one of his courts.
Et m'a promis qu'à tous les jours	And has promised me that he will make
Mectra *default* se je n'y vois.	my days
	Full of confusion if I do not go there.
Bel acueil . . . ses esploys.	Fair Welcome . . . writs.
Et que se bref je n'y accours	And that if quickly I do not speed there
O mes consulz secretz et cois,	With my privy and covert counsels,
M'en *bannira* de toutes vois	He will banish me on the spot,
Et plus ne m'y fera secours.	And nevermore come to my aid.
Bel acueil . . . ses cours.	Fair Welcome . . . courts.

Busnoys's Bel Acueil involves himself in secret intrigues and wields a kind
of dangerous power; and the speaker of the poem obviously fears his retribu-
tion.[66] Moreover, Bel Acueil is not the "sergent d'Amours," and is never described as such in the *Roman de la Rose*; that designation more properly belongs to the character Dangier, who is responsible for keeping the Amant away
from the Rose. Widely used "as an allegory of outside interference with a romance,"[67] Dangier, in C. S. Lewis's classic formulation, is "the real enemy
who cannot be flattered or overcome, who must be kept asleep because, if he
wakes, your only course is to take to your heels, the ever-present dread of lovers
and the stoutest defence of virgins."[68] That Dangier, and not Bel Acueil, was
understood by medieval readers to be the "sergent d'Amours" of the *Rose* is
clear from the texts of a number of anonymous songs in the Dijon chansonnier, one of which specifically names him as such.[69]

What then would account for this seemingly deliberate misreading of Bel
Acueil in Busnoys's text and why then did Busnoys not use the name "Dangier"

(*a*)   B E L   A C U E I L   L E   S E R G E N T   D' A M O U R S

=

M A R G U E R I T E   D' E C O S S E

Leaves the following letters unused: B, A, L (×3), U/V, E, N

(*b*) B E L   A C U E I L   L E   S E R G E N T   D' A M O U R S

=

L E   B A I L L I   D E   V E R M A N D O I S
(i.e., Jamet de Tillay)

Reuses letters I (×2) and D
Leaves the following letters unused: G, U, R, T, E (×2), C, S

(*c*)   B E L   A C U E I L

=

B A I L L (I) + V E   O F   V E R M A N D O I S   A N D   E C   O F   E C O S S E

FIGURE 7.2   Anagrams on the incipit of Busnoys's *Bel acueil*

as he did in other of his *Roman* texts?[72] Possibly because the name "Bel Acueil" was more useful to his program of incorporating anagrams into the incipit of the text, namely, those of the two characters in today's story: "Marguerite d'Ecosse" and "Le Bailli de Vermandois" (see Fig. 7.2, *a* and *b*).[71] Interestingly enough, the nine-letter name "Bel Acueil" happens to contain five of the six letters in Jamet's official title "bailli," and the four remaining unused letters supply the first two letters of both Vermandois (VE) and "Ecosse" (EC)[72] (see Fig. 7.2,*c*). What seems most remarkable about the two anagrams embedded in the incipit of *Bel acueil* is that after spelling out each name, the remaining letters are, without exception, precisely those necessary to effect the spelling of the other. There is at least one respect in which the identification of Bel Acueil with the repellent Jamet de Tillay is not at all incongruous. Just as Bel Acueil of the *Roman* symbolizes access to the Rose, Tillay represents Louis's conduit to privy information about the imaginary amorous encounters of Margaret of Scotland, whose name, as mentioned, is also that of a flower (albeit a daisy, rather than a rose). In this sense, Tillay was indeed Louis's "sergent d'Amours."

Further evidence suggestive of an association of *Bel acueil* with Jamet de Tillay involves an intriguing intertextual play on the words "bailli," Jamet's title, the "sergent" of *Bel acueil*, and the "custodes" of *Anima mea*, each of which clearly designates a kind of surrogate authority, a subordinate individual wielding power on behalf of a more highly placed entity. "Bailli," which literally means "bailiff," by the twelfth century generically designated an officer of the king's court,[73] so Jamet the "bailli" was also a "sergent" as well; and the

Latin word "custodes" or "watchman" of *Anima mea* seems quite literally descriptive of his more ignoble duties at court.

Also intriguing is the poem's rhetorical and musical emphasis on medieval
legal terminology such as "esploitz," "citer," "cours," "default," and "banir,"
highlighted above. "Exploitz" refers to a legal document, or a subpoena, signed
by a court officer requiring one to appear before a tribunal;[74] "cité," the action
of having been "summoned" to appear in court;[75] "cours," the tribunal or
venue for the legal proceedings;[76] "default," the judicial repercussions for failing to show up;[77] and "banir," referring to banishment, or the legal ousting of
an individual from a city or a court.[78] None of these words makes any sense
within the actual *Roman de la Rose* story. But they do fit nicely within the
context of my earlier discussion of the legal inquests surrounding Margaret's
death. Worth interjecting here are a few words about the aftermath of the
sordid affair. Despite the rather incriminating evidence that emerged about
Tillay's behavior, no punitive action was ever taken against him, either by
Charles VII or Louis dauphin, nor does he appear to have lost his position at
court. According to Duclos, the early eighteenth-century historian who first
published the inquest documents, several male courtiers who had testified
against Tillay were incensed that he had received no formal censure. Charles
VII was compelled to stifle the affair by banishing from the court several individuals whose posthumous championing of the dauphine's honor had become
too vocal.[79] In this connection it is worth speculating as to whether Busnoys's
Bel acueil might conceivably be construed as a sarcastic and censorious commentary, duly concealed behind seemingly innocuous allegory, about Tillay's
reprehensible behavior and the power he continued to wield at court.

In the absence of my extensive earlier work on Margaret's literary circle
and its possible connection with Busnoys's Hacqueville songs,[80] the plausibility
of the scenario I have constructed here with regard to the creation of *Anima
mea liquefacta est* and *Bel acueil,* and their possible connection with events
surrounding the death of Margaret of Scotland, would seem dubious at best.
My earlier arguments focused on the striking literary interests of the dauphine
and her ladies-in-waiting, whose poetry is preserved in the poetry collection
F-Pn 9223 that transmits a rondeau attributed to Busnoys[81]; the intertextuality
of one of the ladies-in-waiting's poems with the text of an anonymous song
possibly related to Busnoys's Hacqueville songs; and finally the uncovery of
anagrams in the incipits of certain song texts. The circumstantial evidence
pointing to a musical and literary interaction between Busnoys and the poets
in F-Pn 9223, many of whose texts were set to music in the Dijon chansonnier
and elsewhere, is outlined in Tables 7.1–3, which show: the poets in the
manuscript F-Pn 9223 and their connection with Margaret (Table 7.1); the
poems in the manuscript set to music by Busnoys and others, including four
anonymous unica in Dijon 517 (Table 7.2); and a short list of poems from the
same manuscript quoted in Busnoys songs (Table 7.3). Since Dijon 517 contains such a large number of known Busnoys works, the probability is high that
several of these anonymous settings are his as well. Our knowledge that Busnoys did write music to several texts by poets in Margaret's literary circle con-

TABLE 7.1   Poets in F-Pn 9223 linked with Margaret of Scotland

Poet*	Connection with Margaret
Blosseville (29)	lament on Margaret's death; rondeau playing on the 'M' of Margaret's name
Tanneguy du Chastel (3)	exchange with Jamette de Nesson
Jean d'Estouteville (2)	cited by Tillay as one of the two men seen in Margaret's chamber
Antoine de Cuise (12)	brother of Annette and Jeanne de Cuise, ladies-in-waiting to Margaret
Jeanne Filleul (1)	lady-in-waiting to Margaret
Busnoys (1)	poetic exchange with Jacqueline de Hacqueville, lady-in-waiting to Margaret

* Total numbers of poems in MS given in parentheses.

siderably enhances the likelihood that *Anima mea/Stirps Jesse* and *Bel acueil* might have originated in the same milieu.

In the final analysis, the speculative reading I have offered here should not be construed as the only one possible for the motet; indeed, the very commonality of the texts Busnoys chose would admit a multiplicity of appropriate liturgical and paraliturgical contexts for the use and performance of the piece. Rather, I have offered a case study in how historically informed hypothesis about the possible origins of a musical work enables a range of new observa-

TABLE 7.2   Poems in F-Pn 9223 set to music

Poem in F-Pn 9223	Author	Musical Setting*
Les douleurs dont me sens tel somme	Antoine de Cuise	Dufay (Dij and Niv)
Nul ne me doibt de ce blasmer	Monsieur d'Orvilier	Anon. (Dij)
C'est par vous que tant for soupire	Meschinot	Anon. (Dij)
A ceste foiz je me voy	C. Blosset	Anon. (Dij)
J'en ay le dueil et vous la joye	Blosseville	Anon. (Dij)
Quant jamais aultre	Le Roussellet	Anon. (Pav)
Malleureux cueur que veulx tu faire	Le Roussellet	Dufay (Lab and Wolf)
En tous les lieux ou j'ay esté	Monsieur Jacques	Busnoys (Dij and Niv)
Qu'elle n'y a je le maintien	Antoine de Cuise	Anon. (Dij)

* Lab = Washington, D.C., Library of Congress, Music Division, MS M2.1.L25 Case ("Laborde Chansonnier")
Niv = Paris, Bibliothèque Nationale, Département de la Musique, Rés. Vmc. 57 ("Chansonnier Nivelle de la Chaussée")
Pav = Pavia, Biblioteca Universitaria, MS Aldini 362
Wolf = Wolfenbüttel, Herzog August Bibliothek, MS Guelf. 287 extrav. ("Wolfenbüttel Chansonnier")

TABLE 7.3   Portions of poems in F-Pn 9223 quoted in Busnoys songs

Poetic Source	Musical Setting
R. le Senechal, "De ma joye n'est plus nouvelle," line 4	Incipit of *En soustenant vostre querelle*
Monsieur d'Orvilier, "Nul ne me doibt de ce blasmer," incipit	Last line of *Enfermé suis je en la tour**
Antoine de Cuise, "Joye me fuit, Douleurs m'assault," first line	First line (paraphrased) of *Joye me fuyt et douleur me quert seure*

* Attributed to Busnoys on stylistic grounds by Perkins, *The Mellon Chansonnier*, 2:349, and by Vivian Ramalingam ("A *Hymenaeus* for Beatrice," paper read at the Fiftieth Annual Meeting of the American Musicological Society, Philadelphia, 1984).

tions about it, a new way of looking at the piece—in this case, a rich web of intertextuality, an exploration of medieval traditions of literary and biblical exegesis, and their confluence in Busnoys's *Anima mea* and *Bel acueil*—that would otherwise have proved impossible without having risked the hypothesis as an initial point of departure. In weaving together historical, literary, and exegetical strands of evidence that might initially be seen as random, conventional, and unworthy of closer scrutiny, the contextual reading offered here enables the motet to make richer historical sense and to resonate with greater significance than before.

To conclude this investigation of multiple layers of meaning and intertextuality in a Busnoys motet, it seemed appropriate to invoke the testimony of a medieval witness whose thoughts on an entirely unrelated subject seem nevertheless to capture the spirit of my reading: Lady Reason from the *Roman de la Rose*. The lines I have chosen derive from her famous discourse on "coilles" (testicles), certainly the most memorable in the story and one that seems unlikely to have escaped the notice of even the dullest of medieval readers:

> In our schools indeed they say many things in parables that are very beautiful to hear; however, one should not take whatever one hears according to the letter. In my speech there is another sense, at least when I was speaking of testicles, which I wanted to speak of briefly here, than that which you want to give to the word. He who understood the letter would see in the writing the sense which clarifies the obscure fable. The truth hidden within would be clear if it were explained. You will understand it well if you review the integuments on the poets. There you will see a large part of the secrets of philosophy. There you will want to take your great delight, and you will thus be able to profit a great deal. You will profit in delight and delight in profit, for in the playful fables of the poets lie very profitable delights beneath which they cover their thoughts when they clothe the truth in fables. If you want to understand my saying well, you would have to stretch your mind in this direction.[82]

APPENDIX I

Extracts from "Information faite . . . sur certaines paroles dites et proférées par Jamet de Tillay, de très haute et puissante princesse, feue madame la dauphine, dont Dieu ait l'ame."[83]

1. [Deposition of Jeanne de Tasse, dame de St-Michel, 11 October 1445]
   (a) . . . environ deux ou trois jours après que madite dame fut malade, comme il lui semble, madite dame étant sur une couche toute pensive, et elle qui parle lui demanda ce qu'elle avoit, et pourquoi elle ne faisoit meilleure chiere, et qu'elle ne se devoit pas ainsi merencolier, et madite dame lui répondit qu'*elle se devoit bien merencolier et donner mal pour les paroles qu'on avoit dites d'elle, qui étoient à tort et sans cause* (b) et *prenoit sur le damnement de son ame que onc elle n'avoit fait le cas qu'on lui mettoit sus, non pas seulement l'avoir pensé* (c) . . . [le] mercredi avant son trépas, que madite dame étant sur sa petite couche, dit telles paroles ou semblables: *Ah Jamet! Jamet! vous êtes venu à votre intention; si je meurs, c'est pour vous et vos bonnes paroles que vous avez dites de moi sans cause ne sans raison.* d) Et adonc madite dame leva le bras, férant de sa main à sa poitrine, et disant ces paroles: *Et je prens sur Dieu et sur mon ame, et sur le baptême que j'apportai des fonts, ou je puisse mourir, que je ne l'ai déservi onc, ne ne tins tort à monseigneur . . .* (28–32)
2. [Deposition of Marguerite de Villequier, 12 October 1445]
   . . . Dit et dépose par son serment que deux ans a ou environ, autrement du temps ne se recorde, elle qui parle, a, par plusieurs fois, ouï dire à madite dame la dauphine, ainsi qu'on parloit aucune fois de malveillances, *qu'elle n'étoit point tenue à Jamet de Tillay, et qu'elle le hayoit plus que tous les hommes du monde, et qu'il avoit mis peine de la mettre mal de monseigneur le dauphin . . .* (32-33)
3. [Deposition of Marguerite de Hacqueville, 12 October 1445]
   . . . Dit et dépose, par son serment, que huit jours avant que la reine partit de Nancy, elle qui parle ouït dire à madite dame [Margaret of Scotland], ainsi comme l'on parloit de gens qui parloient légièrement, que il y en avoit un qui parloit bien légièrement, et qu'elle le devoit bien haïr; et, elle qui parle, lui demanda qu'il étoit; *et madite dame lui répondit que c'étoit Jamet de Tillay, et qu'il avoit mis et mettoit peine de jour en jour de la faire être en la malgrace de monseigneur le dauphin, et qu'elle avoit eu et encore avoit beaucoup de maux par lui, et qu'on ne pourroit jamais dire plus mauvaises paroles de femme qu'il avoit dit d'elle.* (33–34)
4. [Deposition of Marguerite de Vaux, 14 October 1445]
   (a) . . . Dit et dépose, par son serment, que le roi étant à Sarry, et madame la dauphine, ainsi que l'on parloit de plusieurs choses au com-

mencement de la maladie de madite dame, dit à elle qui parle, *qu'elle n'étoit point tenue à Jamet de Tillay, et elle qui parle lui demanda pourquoi c'étoit. Madite dame lui répondit que ledit Jamet avoit dit des paroles d'elle que onc en sa vie n'avoit faites ne pensées* . . . (b) et peu de temps après, madite dame fut amenée à Chaalons toute malade, et deux ou trois jours avant sa mort, comme il semble à elle qui parle, madite dame étant sur son lit, sans ce qu'on lui parlât d'aucune chose, et elle qui parle étant auprès d'elle, dit ces paroles: Ah! ah! *Jamet, vous êtes venu à votre intention; après lesquelles paroles madite dame prit sur le damnement de son ame qu'il n'étoit rien de tout ce que l'on lui avoit mis sus, ne onc ne le fit ne le pensa.* Et semble, à elle qui parle, que madite dame disoit de grand courage, dolente et courroucée, lesdites paroles . . . (35–36)

APPENDIX II

Extracts from the Interrogations of Jamet de Tillay, bailli de Vermandois, 1 June and 23 August 1446[84]

Interrogation of 1 June 1446

L'an mil quatre cent quarante-six, le premier jour de juin, noble homme Jamet de Tillay, écuyer, bailli de Vermandois, âgé de quarante-six ans ou environ, juré, examiné par nous Jean Tudert et Robert Thiboust, conseillers du roi notre seigneur, sur les paroles que l'on dit par lui avoir été dites de la personne de feue madame la dauphine, et autres choses contenues ès informations à nous baillées par monseigneur le chancelier,

1. dit qu'environ Noel, l'an 1444, un soir environ neuf heures de nuit, autrement du jour ne du temps ne se recorde, le roi étant à Nancy en Lorraine, lui qui parle [Jamet de Tillay] et Messire Regnault de Dresnay, chevalier, allèrent en la chambre de ladite dame, laquelle étoit lors couchée sur sa couche, et plusieurs de ses femmes étoient autour d'elle; aussi y étoit Messire Jean d'Estouteville, seigneur de Blainville, appuyé sur la couche de ladite dame, et un autre qu'il ne connoît; et pour ce que ladite dame étoit en sadite chambre sans ce que les torches fussent allumées, il qui parle dit audit messire Regnault, maître d'hôtel de ladite Dame, que c'étoit grande paillardie à lui et autres officiers de ladite dame, de ce que lesdites torches étoient encore à allumer, et dit qu'il dit lesdites paroles pour le bien et honneur de ladite dame et de sa maison . . . (40–41)

2. Interrogé s'il dit point audit Nicole Chambre que ladite dame fût malade seulement d'amour:

   Dit par son serment que de ce il n'est pas de présent recors . . . (42–43)

3. Interrogé s'il dit point à Marie de Lespine, durant la maladie, que ladite feue dame fût malade d'amour:

> Dit que de ce onc ne parla à ladite Marie . . . (44)

Interrogation of 23 August 1446

4. . . . ledit Nicole lui demanda ce qu'elle avoit, et d'où procédoit cette maladie, et il qui parle [Jamet de Tillay] lui répondit que les médecins disoient qu'elle avoit un courroux sur le coeur, qui lui faisoit grand dommage, et aussi que faute de repos lui nuisoit beaucoup; et lors ledit Nicole dit que lesdits médecins lui en avoient autant dit, et aussi dit: Plût à Dieu qu'elle n'eût jamais eu telle femme à elle! Et quelle dit il qui parle? Et lors ledit Nicole lui répondit: Marguerite de Salignac. Et il qui parle, lui dit: Plût à Dieu, ne aussi Prégente, ne Jeanne Filloque [*sic*: Filleul]! Requis pourquoi il dit lesdites paroles, dit pour ce qu'il avoit ouï dire que c'étoient celles qui la faisoient trop veiller à faire rondeaux et balades. (50)

5. Interrogé s'il lui dit point qu'elle étoit malade d'amour:

> Dit, il qui parle, qu'il n'en a point souvenance . . . (50)

6. . . . Et lors *le roi lui demanda si elle étoit impédumée*; et il qui parle répondit que non, comme disoient les médecins. Et le roi lui demanda d'où procède cette maladie, et il qui parle lui dit qu'il venoit de faute de repos, comme disoient les médecins, et qu'elle veilloit tant, aucunefois plus, aucunefois moins, que aucunefois il étoit presque soleil levant avant qu'elle s'allât coucher, et que aucunefois monseigneur le Dauphin avoit dormi un somme ou deux avant qu'elle s'allât coucher, et aucunefois s'occupoit à faire rondeaux, tellement qu'elle en faisoit aucunefois douze pour un jour, qui lui étoit chose bien contraire. Et lors le roi demanda si cela faisoit mal à la tête, et monsieur le trésorier maître Jean Bureau, là présent, dit: Oui, qui s'y abuse trop; mais ce sont choses de plaisance . . . (50–51)

7. . . . ainsi qu'ils parloient de madite dame, *ledit M. de Charny dit qu'il avoit entendu qu'elle n'étoit point habile à porter enfans, et si ainsi étoit qu'elle allât de vie à trespassement, il faudra marier monseigneur le Dauphin à une autre qui fût encline à porter enfans*; et lors il qui parle [Jamet de Tillay] dit qu'il avoit ouï dire à madame Dubois Menart qu'elle avoit autrefois dit à madite dame *qu'elle mangeoit trop de pommes aigres et de vinaigre, et se ceignoit aucunefois trop serrée, aucunefois trop lâche, qui étoit chose qui empêchoit bien à avoir enfans* . . . (51–52)

8. Interrogé s'il a point dit ces paroles ou semblables en substance, en parlant de madite dame: Avez-vous point vû cette dame-là? *elle a mieux manière d'une paillarde que d'une grande maîtresse.*

> Dit que non, et s'il y a avoit homme qui le voulsist maintenir, il offre à le défendre par son corps devant le roi, et ne vit onc dame ne

damoiselle qui eût mieux manière de gentille femme ne de grande maîtresse . . . (52)

9. . . . Et depuis le vingt-sixième jour, eussent comparu par-devant nous ledit Jamet et Nicole Chambre; et, quand ils furent confrontés, ledit Nicole Chambre dit qu'après plusieurs paroles qu'eurent ensemble ledit Jamet et lui de la maladie de madame la dauphine et de ses veilleries qu'elle faisoit, ledit Nicole demanda: que peut-elle avoir? elle a quelque chose sur le cueur. Et ledit Jamet lui répondit: Que sçait-on? *Et icelui Nicole lui demanda que c'étoit; et, il qui parle, lui répondit: Ce sont amours* . . . (55)

10. . . . ledit Jamet a dit et répondu audit messire Regnault, en la présence de nous dessusdits, que bien avoit dit que madame avoit eu honte; mais *il ne dit onc qu'elle tint mieux manière de paillarde que de grande maîtresse*, en persévérant et continuant en sa confession par lui premièrement faite. A quoi ledit messire Regnault a répondu qu'il veut maintenir que ledit Jamet a dit et proféré, de madite dame la dauphine, les paroles telles que déposées les a en sa première confession . . . (55)

11. . . . Et ce fait, a été interrogé sur ce qu'il avoit dit à monsieur de Charny, présens monsieur le maréchal et maître Jean Bureau, *que madame avoit mangé du vinaigre en santé, pour eschiver de porter enfans:*

    Dit et affirme sur sa conscience, qu'il ne cuide avoir rien dit audit monsieur de Charny, *sinon qu'il avoit ouï dire qu'autrefois madite dame, durant sa santé, avoit mangé du vinaig*re *et des pommes crües qui lui pussent avoir empêché*, si elle ne s'en fût pris garde. . .(56)

NOTES

I wish to thank Rob C. Wegman for a deeply insightful and stimulating commentary on an earlier draft of this essay.

1. Thomas M. Greene, *The Light in Troy: Imitation and Discovery in Renaissance Poetry* (New Haven: Yale University Press, 1982), 20.

2. Reinhard Strohm, *Music in Late Medieval Bruges* (Oxford: Clarendon Press, 1985), 146–47.

3. Michael Long, "Symbol and Ritual in Josquin's *Missa Di dadi*," *Journal of the American Musicological Society* 42 (1989): 1–22.

4. M. Jennifer Bloxam, "In Praise of Spurious Saints: The *Missae Floruit egregiis* of Pipelare and La Rue," *Journal of the American Musicological Society* 44 (1991): 163–220.

5. Patrick Macey, "Josquin's *Misericordias Domini* and Louis XI," *Early Music* 19 (1991): 163–77.

6. Given what we know of Busnoys's profound influence on composers like Josquin and Obrecht, it is not at all surprising that equally provocative readings of several of his Latin-texted works have recently begun to emerge as well. Jaap van Benthem has hypothesized that numerical proportions corresponding to the letter values of Johannes Ockeghem's name are embedded in the structure of *In hydraulis*; see his "Text, Tone,

and Symbol: Regarding Busnoys's Conception of *In hydraulis* and Its Presumed Relationship to Ockeghem's *Ut heremita solus*," in Paula Higgins, ed., *Antoine Busnoys: Method, Meaning, and Context in Late Medieval Music* (Oxford: Clarendon Press, forthcoming); and Mary Natvig has proposed a reading of *Anima mea liquefacta est/ Stirps Jesse* as a postnuptial devotional piece for Margaret of York, discussed in her dissertation, "The Latin-Texted Works of Antoine Busnois" (Ph.D. diss., Eastman School of Music, 1991), 279–301.

7. Edited in *Antoine Busnoys: The Latin-Texted Works*, ed. Richard Taruskin, Masters and Monuments of the Renaissance 5, Parts 2–3 (New York: Broude Trust, 1990), 2:132–37.

8. Edgar Sparks, *Cantus Firmus in Mass and Motet, 1420-1520* (Berkeley: University of California Press, 1963), 223.

9. *Antoine Busnoys: The Latin-Texted Works*, 3:62.

10. Natvig, "The Latin-Texted Works of Antoine Busnois," 279.

11. See my forthcoming book *Parents and Preceptors: Authority, Lineage, and the Conception of the Composer in Early Modern Europe* (Oxford: Clarendon Press).

12. Other pieces with the same cleffing include: Dunstable: *Gloria*, in *John Dunstable Complete Works*, ed. Manfred Bukofzer; second rev. ed. by Margaret Bent, Ian Bent, and Brian Trowell, Musica Britannica 8 (London: Stainer and Bell, 1970), no. 2; *O crux gloriosa*, ibid., no. 53; *Beata Dei Genitrix*, ibid., no. 41 (only the Bologna Q15 version has C3, F3, F3 cleffing); Binchois: *Magnificat Secundi Toni*, in *The Sacred Music of Gilles Binchois*, ed. Philip Kaye (Oxford: Oxford University Press, 1992), no. 23; *Amoreux suy*, in *Die Chansons von Gilles Binchois (1400–1460)*, ed. Wolfgang Rehm, Musikalische Denkmäler 2 (Mainz: B. Schott's Söhne, 1953), no. 6; *Esclave puist yl*, ibid., no. 15; Dufay: *Dona gentile*, in *Chansonnier de Jean de Montchenu*, ed. Geneviève Thibault and David Fallows (Paris: Société Française de Musicologie, 1991), no. 3; Anonymous, *Quant du dire adieu*, ibid., no. 41. Fallows describes the last piece as one of the oldest compositions in the Chansonnier Cordiforme, probably dating from the 1430s, and remarks that its musical style is similar to Binchois's. Ibid., p. cxxii.

13. Most Song of Songs settings are short, devotional antiphons featuring largely declamatory style, setting one text in all voices, eschewing the quotation of a tenor cantus firmus, and occasionally paraphrasing a chant in the top voice. See Shai Burstyn, "Early 15th-Century Settings of Song of Songs Antiphons," *Acta musicologica* 49 (1977): 200–27, as well as the dissertation by the same author, "Fifteenth-Century Polyphonic Settings of Verses from the Song of Songs" (Ph.D. diss., Columbia University, 1972) (UMI 75-9320).

14. For Power's motet see *Leonel Power: Complete Works*, ed. Charles Hamm, 2 vols., Corpus Mensurabilis Musicae 50 ([Rome]: American Institute of Musicology, 1969), 1:57 and 59. The Forest *Anima mea* is in *Der Kodex des Magister Nicolas Leopold: Staatsbibliothek München Mus. ms. 3154*, ed. Thomas L. Noblitt, 2 vols., Das Erbe deutscher Musik 80 (Kassel: Bärenreiter, 1987), 1:3. Virtually nothing is known about the composer Forest; the strongest candidate is thought to be the Englishman John Forest who lived from ca. 1365–70 to 1446. See Margaret Bent, "Forest," *The New Grove Dictionary of Music and Musicians*, 20 vols., ed. Stanley Sadie (London: MacMillan, 1980) 6:705. Alejandro Planchart has recently located an archival reference attesting to the presence of "the composer John Forest" at the Council of Constance in 1417 in the company of the bishop of Lichfield. See "The Early Career of Guillaume Du Fay," *Journal of the American Musicological Society* 46 (1993): 354. Lichfield was one of the places where the Englishman mentioned above was known to have held prebends.

15. On Forest's three-voice *Alma redemptoris/Anima mea* see Burstyn, "Fifteenth-Century Polyphonic Settings," 178–82 (commentary) and 296–99 (edition).

16. Rob Wegman has independently drawn attention to explicit features of Busnoys's mensural practice that link him to insular practices of the first half of the fifteenth century, particularly via the influence of English practice on the music of the Low Countries. See his "Mensural Intertextuality in the Sacred Music of Antoine Busnoys," in Higgins, ed., *Antoine Busnoys: Method, Meaning, and Context in Late Medieval Music*.

17. See Paula Higgins, "Parisian Nobles, A Scottish Princess, and the Woman's Voice in Late Medieval Song," *Early Music History* 10 (1991): 145–200.

18. *Anima mea* appeared as the fifth and final psalm antiphon at First Vespers on the Feast of the Assumption, followed immediately by the festal prolix responsory *Stirps Jesse*. See M. Jennifer Bloxam, "On the Origins, Contexts, and Implications of Busnoys's Plainsong Cantus Firmi: Some Preliminary Remarks," in Higgins, ed. *Antoine Busnoys: Method, Meaning, and Context in Late Medieval Music*.

19. Ibid.

20. David Fallows, *Dufay* (London: Dent, 1982), 28.

21. Unless he is the author of *Permanent Vierge*, a polytextual song-motet with the cantus firmus *Pulchra es et decora*. For an edition of the piece, see *Johannes Ockeghem: Collected Works*, 3, ed. Richard Wexler with Dragan Plamenac (Boston: E. C. Schirmer, 1992), 96–97. Wexler published the work among Ockeghem's *opera dubia*.

22. Compère used the text of *Anima mea* in the lowest voice of his song-motet *Plaine d'ennuy/Anima mea*, in *Loyset Compère: Opera Omnia*, ed. Ludwig Finscher, 5 vols. ([Rome]: American Institute of Musicology, 1972), 5:6.

23. In the later fifteenth and early sixteenth century, Isaac, Ghiselin, La Rue, Mouton, Févin, Brumel, Barbireau, and Bauldeweyn all demonstrated renewed interest in the Song, although Josquin himself, who was otherwise deeply attracted to texts from the Hebrew Bible, set only two from the Song of Songs. The musical trend of setting Song texts intensified into the sixteenth century with settings by Gombert, Clemens non Papa, Festa, Arcadelt, Rore, Willaert, Jachet, de Silva, J. Lupi, Lhéritier, and Verdelot, culminating in Palestrina's collection discussed by Jessie Ann Owens in the present volume, ch. 14.

24. Petrus de Domarto based his *Missa Spiritus almus* on the final "Spiritus almus" melisma from *Stirps Jesse*, as Rob Wegman has shown; see "Petrus de Domarto's *Missa Spiritus almus* and the Early History of the Four-Voice Mass in the Fifteenth Century," *Early Music History* 10 (1991): 235–303.

25. Ann W. Astell, *The Song of Songs in the Middle Ages* (Ithaca: Cornell University Press, 1990), 1.

26. The Molinet–Busnoys exchange is edited in Jean Molinet, *Les Faictz et dictz de Jean Molinet*, 3 vols., ed. Noel Dupire (Paris: Société des Anciens Textes Français, 1936–39), 2:795–801.

27. See the text of Busnoys's *Je ne puis vivre ainsi*, in *The Mellon Chansonnier*, 2 vols., ed. Leeman L. Perkins and Howard W. Garey (New Haven: Yale University Press, 1979), 1:231–32. The song is one of four whose texts allude in acrostics or puns to "Jacqueline d'Hacqueville"; Busnoys is presumed to have written the texts as well as the music of all four. For a fuller discussion of the Hacqueville poems and their possible historical context see Higgins, "Parisian Nobles." On lovesickness in the Middle Ages, particularly with regard to the striking correspondence between accounts of the "disease" in medical treatises and medieval literary manifestations of the phenomenon, see Mary F. Wack, *Lovesickness in the Middle Ages: The Viaticum and Its Commentaries* (Philadelphia: University of Pennsylvania Press, 1990).

28. The translation is from *Song of Songs*, trans. Marvin H. Pope, Anchor Bible Series, 7C (Garden City, NY: Doubleday, 1977), 7–8. Among the numerous critical studies of the Song of Songs in the Middle Ages, see especially Peter Dronke, "The Song of Songs and Medieval Love Lyric," in *The Bible and Medieval Culture*, ed. W. Lourdaux and D. Verhelst (Leuven: Leuven University Press, 1979), 236–62; Astell, *The Song of Songs*; E. Ann Matter, *The Voice of My Beloved: The Song of Songs in Western Medieval Christianity* (Philadelphia: University of Pennsylvania Press, 1990); Athalya Brenner, *The Song of Songs* (Sheffield: Sheffield Academic Press, 1989); ead., *A Feminist Companion to the Song of Songs* (Sheffield: Sheffield Academic Press, 1993).

29. Higgins, "Parisian Nobles." Since one "Jacqueline de Hacqueville" was a lady-in-waiting to the dauphine in 1445, I suggested that she, rather than the Parisian no-blewoman of the 1460s, might be the one alluded to in four of Busnoys's songs. This hypothesis raises the intriguing possibility that Busnoys was already active as a composer in the late 1440s and early 1450s, which would in turn seriously challenge received opinion about the presumed dates and chronology of Busnoys's works.

30. Pierre Champion, *La Dauphine mélancolique* (Paris, 1925). For further information on Margaret of Scotland, see L. A. Barbé, *Margaret of Scotland and the Dauphin Louis* (London, 1917), 114-49; Robert S. Rait, *Five Stuart Princesses* (Westminster: A. Constable, 1902), 3–46; Gaston Louis Emmanuel du Fresne, marquis de Beaucourt, *Histoire de Charles VII*, 6 vols. (Paris: Librairie de la Société Bibliographique, 1881–91), 4:89–111; Charles Pinot Duclos, *Oeuvres complètes de Duclos*, 20 vols. (Paris, 1820), 5; Auguste Vallet de Viriville, *Histoire de Charles VII*, 3 vols. (Paris, 1863–65), 3:81–90; Le Roux de Lincy, *Les Femmes célèbres de l'ancienne France* (Paris, 1848), 1:451–53; Marcel Thibault, *La Jeunesse de Louis XI, 1423–1445* (Paris: Perrin, 1907), 503–51; Henri Menu, "Charles VII et la Dauphine Marguerite d'Ecosse à Châlons-sur-Marne (4 mai–18 août 1445)," *Annuaire administratif, statistique, historique et commercial de la Marne* (1895), 555–64; D. B. Wyndham Lewis, *King Spider: Some Aspects of Louis XI of France and His Companions* (New York: Coward-McCann, 1929), 162–94.

31. Beaucourt, *Histoire de Charles VII*, 4:109–10.

32. The depositions from the two inquests are published in Charles Pinot Duclos, *Histoire de Louis XI* (Paris, 1745–46), which exists in numerous editions. The edition I have used for the present study is Duclos, *Oeuvres complètes*, 5:27–56.

33. In his second interrogation of 23 August 1446, Tillay told the same story in slightly different words. It is in this version that he adds the phrase, "Allons voir les dames." *Oeuvres de Duclos*, 5:54.

34. See, for example, Appendix II, excerpts 2, 3, 5, 8 and 10, as well as numerous other citations in the interrogations published in *Oeuvres de Duclos*.

35. The three in question were Jeanne Filleul (misnamed in Tillay's testimony as "Filloque") and Marguerite de Salignac, both *damoiselles d'honneur* of Marguerite d'Ecosse, and Prégente de Melun, *damoiselle d'honneur* of Marie d'Anjou, Charles VII's queen. See Beaucourt, *Histoire de Charles VII*, 4:90, n. 4. A bergerette ascribed to Jeanne Filleul survives in the poetry collection Paris, Bibliothèque Nationale, fonds français 9223 (hereafter: F-Pn 9223): "Helas mon amy sur mon ame," fol. 46, ed. Gaston Raynaud, *Rondeaux et autres poésies du XVe siècle* (Paris: Firmin Didot, 1889), 76. The poem is also published and discussed in Higgins, "Parisian Nobles," 182–85. F:Pn 9223 transmits 34 poems by three male courtiers in the dauphine's circle: Blosseville (29), Tanneguy du Chastel (3), and Jean d'Estouteville, seigneur de Torcy et Blainville (2). For the most recent biographical information on these poets see Barbara L. S. Inglis, *Le Manuscrit B. N. Nouv. Acq. Fr. 15771* (Paris: Champion, 1985), 19–24 (Blosseville), 35–36 (Tanneguy du Chastel), and 58–60 (Seigneur de Torcy). This

manuscript preserves dozens of poems by other of the dauphine's courtiers (see Table 7.1), no fewer than nine texts of which were set to music (see Table 7.2). For a fuller discussion of the dauphine and the literary activities of her circle, see Higgins, "Parisian Nobles."

36. See F. F. Steenackers, *Agnès Sorel et Charles VII: Essai sur l'état politique et moral de la France au XVe siècle* (Paris, 1868), 250–59.

37. Wack, *Lovesickness in the Middle Ages*, 41 and 46.

38. "belle et bien formée, pourvue et ornée de toutes bonnes conditions que noble et haute dame pouvoit avoir," and "excellentement belle et prudente dame"; Beaucourt, *Histoire de Charles VII*, 4:89.

39. "the lady Margaret maryed to the Dolphin, was of such nasty complexion and evill savored breath, that he abhorred her company as a cleane creature doth a caryon." Beaucourt, *Histoire de Charles VII*, 4:90, n.1, citing *Chronicle at large and meere history of the affayres of Englande*, etc. (London, 1809), 1:612.

40. Thibault, *La Jeunesse*, 546.

41. Michael V. Fox, *The Song of Songs and the Ancient Egyptian Love Songs* (Madison: University of Wisconsin Press, 1985), 142.

42. Ibid.

43. Fokkelien van Dijk-Hemmes, "The Imagination of Power and the Power of Imagination," in Brenner, ed., *A Feminist Companion to the Song of Songs*, 163–64.

44. Ibid.

45. See Peggy McCracken, "The Body Politic and the Queen's Adulterous Body in French Romance," in Linda Lomperis and Sarah Stanbury, eds., *Feminist Approaches to the Body in Medieval Literature* (Philadelphia: University of Pennsylvania Press, 1993), 38–64.

46. Wegman, "Petrus de Domarto's *Missa Spiritus almus*," 241, n. 16. For a discussion of the relationship between Domarto's Mass and Busnoys's *Anima mea*, see pp. 241–44.

47. *Song of Songs*, trans. Pope, 210–29.

48. It is worth remembering that the Feast of the Assumption commemorates the physical death of the Virgin and the subsequent assumption of her body and soul into heaven. Popular wisdom about the circumstances surrounding the death, funeral, and burial of the Virgin is richly detailed in Jacobus Voragine, *The Golden Legend: Readings on the Saints*, 2 vols. trans. William Granger Ryan (Princeton: Princeton University Press, 1993), 2:77–97. The Golden Legend's account of the Assumption includes numerous striking intertextual references to the Song of Songs, as well as to the *Stirps Jesse* text, which were kindly drawn to my attention by my colleague Alexander Blachly.

49. Thibault, *La Jeunesse de Louis XI*, 547.

50. Shai Burstyn, "Power's *Anima mea* and Binchois' *De plus en plus*: A Study in Musical Relationships," *Musica Disciplina* 30 (1976): 55–72.

51. Long, "Symbol and Ritual," 1–2.

52. Klaus G. Perls, *Jean Fouquet* (London: Hyperion, 1940), 19. The right panel of the diptych, featuring the Virgin and child, is now in Antwerp, Koninklijke Museum voor Schone Kunsten (Inv. 132). The left wing, representing Etienne Chevalier with St. Stephen, is in Berlin, Deutsches Museum, no. 1617. Until 1793 both paintings were housed in the vestry of Notre-Dame at Melun. The identification with Agnes Sorel has been accepted by art historians on the basis of the similarity to an early sixteenth-century drawing (see Perls, *Fouquet*, pl. 43) based on a Fouquet portrait of her. Interestingly enough, several art historians have interpreted the extreme pallor of the Virgin's skin color as the "idea of death" and the "apotheosis" of Agnes Sorel. See

Jean Fouquet, ed. Nicole Reynaud, *Les dossiers du département des peintures* 22 (Paris: La Réunion des Musées Nationaux, 1981), 21.

53. Astell, *The Song of Songs,* 16. For more on the increased dignity accorded to historical sense in the work of Hugh of St. Victor, see the classic study of medieval biblical exegesis by Beryl Smalley, *The Study of the Bible in the Middle Ages* (Oxford: Blackwell, 1952; repr. Notre Dame: University of Notre Dame Press, 1964), 83–105.

54. Astell, *The Song of Songs,* 20–21.

55. Ibid., 22.

56. Matter, *The Voice of My Beloved,* 189.

57. Ibid., 190.

58. Dronke, "The Song of Songs and Medieval Love Lyric"; Matter, *The Voice of My Beloved,* 187–93.

59. Burstyn, "Fifteenth-Century Polyphonic Settings," 44–56.

60. Matter, *The Voice of My Beloved,* 190.

61. *En voyant sa dame, Laissez Dangier faire tous ses effors, Faulx mesdisans.*

62. Maxwell Luria, *A Reader's Guide to the Roman de la Rose* (Hamden, Conn.: Archon Books, 1982), 45.

63. Walter Kemp, *Burgundian Court Song in the Time of Binchois: The Anonymous Chansons of El Escorial, MS V.III.24* (Oxford: Clarendon Press, 1990), 92.

64. See Perkins and Garey, *The Mellon Chansonnier,* 1:31; 2:187–90; and the edition on 1:39

65. The text is taken from the setting in Dijon, Bibliothèque Publique, MS 517, fols. 22ᵛ–23.

66. Bel Acueil, who critics agree is the most peculiar personage in the *Rose,* is a male personification of accessibility to the Rose, which is in turn an allegory for the woman's virginity, which the Lover wishes to conquer. By the end of the *Roman,* Bel Acueil has been transmogrified into the 'Rose' itself, that is, the character that started out as a male personification ends up being identified with the female character. As one critic has noted, "the incongruity of this male personification leads to bizarre complications of gender . . . and makes the Lover's association with him (her?) oddly bisexual, halfway between that of lovers and that of male companions." Luria, *A Reader's Guide,* 45.

67. Planchart, "The Early Career of Guillaume Du Fay," 366, quoting Frédéric Godefroy, *Lexique de l'ancien français,* ed. J. Bonnard and A. Salmon (Paris: Champion, 1968), s.v. "Dangier." According to Godefroy's definition, Dangier signifies "en matière d'amour, toute personne fâcheuse qui s'oppose aux désirs d'un amoureux."

68. C. S. Lewis, *The Allegory of Love: A Study in Medieval Tradition* (London: Oxford University Press, 1936; repr. 1976), 123.

69. Dijon 517, fols. 145ᵛ–146. "De la montaigne ou je souloie / Mener esbatement et joie / *Amours par son sergent Dangier* / m'a banny et fait eslongnier / Dont tout le cueur en plours me noie . . ."

70. *En voyant sa dame* and *Laissez Dangier.* For sources, see Paula Higgins, "Antoine Busnois and Musical Culture in Late Medieval France and Burgundy" (Ph.D. diss., Princeton, 1987), 317 and 324.

71. In Higgins, "Parisian Nobles," 178–79, I drew attention to the existence of another, imperfect, anagram in the Mellon Chansonnier's version of *Bel acueil:* "Beatrice d'Aragon," the dedicatee of the manuscript. I suggested that Mellon's variant spelling of "sergant" vs. Dijon's "sergent" may have arisen from the need for an extra letter "a" to effect the anagram on the name "Beatrice d'Aragon." The obvious chronological problems posed by the datings of the two sources of *Bel acueil* had always trou-

bled me; since Dijon is clearly the earlier of the two versions, *Bel acueil* could not have been originally conceived for Beatrice of Aragon, despite the correspondence of the initials of her first name with those of the allegorical character Bel Acueil of the *Rose*. Nevertheless, the possibility that the Mellon version did represent an attempt to create an anagram on the name of the recipient of that manuscript suggested to me the possibility that anagrams may have already been embedded in the Dijon version of the poem, which explains how my present readings of the two names "Marguerite d'Ecosse" and "Le bailli de Vermandois" came about. Although there is some disagreement about the dating of Dijon (some would place it in the 1470s, as opposed to the 1460s, as I have argued elsewhere), a musical variant between the two versions—a rewriting and correction of a contrapuntally flawed passage in measures 5–7 of the Dijon version—removes any doubt that the Mellon version is the later of the two. For an edition of the Dijon version of the piece, see Eugénie Droz, Geneviève Thibault, and Yvonne Rokseth, eds., *Trois chansonniers français du XVe siècle* (Paris, 1927; repr. New York: Da Capo, 1978), no. 19; for an edition of the Mellon version see Perkins and Garey, *The Mellon Chansonnier*, 1, no. 1.

72. Remarkably, the name "Jamet de Tillay" is also found the incipit, but its 13-letter name requires the reuse of two letters.

73. *Lexique historique du Moyen Age*, ed. René Fédou (Paris: Armand Colin, 1980), 21.

74. Randle Cotgrave, A *Dictionarie of the French and English Tongues, 1611* (Menston, England: Scolar Press, 1968), s.v. *Exploict: . . . de sergent*. The Warrant which hee hath for, also, the report, or returne he makes of, an Adiournment, Arrest, Execution, or seisure of person or goods, ordered by the court."

75. Ibid., s. v. *cité*: "cited, summoned, adiourned, warned, to appeare."

76. Ibid., s.v. *cours*: "A Court of Law or Iustice; any Session or Assemblie of Iudges; or the place wherein they use to assemble."

77. Ibid., s.v. *Défault, ou defaut*: "A default, fault, offence, defect; want of appearance before a Iudge."

78. Ibid., s.v. *bannir*: "To banish, exile, expulse; outlaw, proscribe; seize, confiscate, by publicke act, a proclamation."

79. Lewis, *King Spider*, 193.

80. Higgins, "Parisian Nobles."

81. Raynaud, ed., *Rondeaux et autres poésies*, 153.

82. Guillaume de Lorris and Jean de Meun, *The Romance of the Rose*, trans. Charles Dahlberg (Princeton: Princeton University Press, 1971), 136, lines 7153–81.

83. Duclos, *Oeuvres complètes*, 5:27–56. Numbers in parentheses after each excerpt refer to its page number in Duclos.

84. Ibid., 40–45 and 48–56. Numbers in parentheses at the end of each excerpt refer to its page number in Duclos.

Obrecht as Exegete

Reading *Factor orbis* as a Christmas Sermon

As its title suggests, this study dwells on analogies: analogies between composers and theologians, between composing and preaching, between the medieval motet and the medieval sermon. Such comparisons are slippery things, sometimes obfuscating more than they illuminate. Why do we persist in drawing analogies? Sigmund Freud once wrote: "Analogies decide nothing, that is true, but they can make one feel more at home."[1] Freud's observation captures the essence of this author's motivation in attempting an analysis by analogy: the construction of analogies relating various expressions of medieval sensibilities (a kind of contextualization) is just one way in which we moderns seek to mediate the "alterity" of the medieval world—the essential otherness of the medieval mentality that precludes our ever experiencing the remnants of that culture as did its original audience.[2] If we can detect a sympathetic resonance between a particularly abstruse medieval motet and ways of thinking and communicating peculiar to medieval people, then perhaps we can approach a step closer to "feeling at home" with this distant music.

Figure 8.1 reproduces a page from one of the most widely used books of the Middle Ages, the *Glossa ordinaria*, the standard source of biblical exegesis throughout the later Middle Ages. Compiled in the early twelfth century under the direction of Anselm of Laon, the *Glossa ordinaria* is a huge collection of glosses elucidating individual words and phrases of the Bible, drawing principally upon the writings of the Fathers and Doctors of the Church. This enormous book served as the standard reference on which doctrinal instruction in the *schola*, the *studium generale*, and the university was based; it was copied again and again, and printed innumerable times.[3] Adolph Rusch published the edition from which this illustration derives in Strassburg no later than 1480, and this page reveals the typical page layout of the glossed Bible: a short section of the biblical text is placed at the center of the page in large black type with an eye-catching red initial, while the commentaries on that bit of text appear

FIGURE 8.1   *Glossa ordinaria*, printed in Strassburg, by Adolph Rusch, not after 1480. Chapin Library of Rare Books, Williams College. Reproduced by permission.

as interlinear and marginal glosses in smaller type. The phrase discussed on this page is "Canite tuba in Sion" (Blow the trumpet in Sion), which opens the second chapter in the Old Testament Book of Joel.

Figure 8.2 displays the opening of the motet *Factor orbis*, an ambitious five-voice piece by the late-fifteenth-century Flemish composer Jacob Obrecht on which this study will focus. Shown here is the earliest manuscript source

FIGURE 8.2   MS Cappella Sistina 42, fols. 36ᵛ–37ʳ. Vatican City, Biblioteca Apostolica Vaticana. Reproduced by permission.

for the motet, the choirbook Cappella Sistina 42, copied in the first decade of the sixteenth century for the use of the Sistine Chapel.[4] A striking visual parallel to the biblical gloss is immediately apparent, a resemblance that effectively distills the conceptual similarity between this motet and the *Glossa ordinaria*. At the heart of the motet lies the tenor part, placed in the middle of the page. The importance of this tenor part is asserted visually even before a note sounds: its few large (that is, long) black notes immediately command attention. Their appearance reminds the viewer of plainsong notation, and indeed this tenor is quoting a chant melody, the compositional equivalent of quoting Scripture. Lauds on the fourth Sunday of Advent furnished the source of this plainsong, which is none other than "Canite tuba in Sion."

Around this tenor part the scribe arrays four other voice parts, and they are both visually and musically quite distinct from the tenor. As the glosses to the scriptural text are set in smaller type, so do these musical lines around the tenor use smaller note values; as the glosses comment with copious and contrasting text, so do these vocal lines offer a musically florid and textually different commentary to the tenor cantus firmus. In short, the comparison of these two documents, one literary, one musical, reveals a kinship between the medieval theologian's approach to biblical exegesis and Obrecht's approach to composing this motet. For both, an authoritative "text" (in one case Scripture, in the other case plainsong) furnishes the basis for the creation of a more complex construction intended to amplify or interpret that authoritative text. The medieval literary concepts of *auctor* and *auctoritas* apply to both the scriptural and the chant quotation: the term *auctor* denoted a writer (and, by extension, a composer) possessing *auctoritas*, an authority commanding respect and belief; in the specific sense, an auctoritas was a quotation from a revered auctor.[5] To medieval writers and composers, readers and listeners, both Scripture and plainsong were of divine authorship, thus possessing the ultimate auctoritas.[6]

Congruent roles for the scriptural text in exegesis and the tenor in polyphonic music are apparent also in certain efforts at definition made by medieval theologians and musical theorists. The hermeneutic method of biblical exegesis, in which the literal sense of Scripture formed the basis for elaborate allegorical and moral interpretations, was described by Gregory the Great (d. 604) using an architectural metaphor that remained current well into the fifteenth century: "First we lay the foundations [of scriptural exegesis] in history; then by following a symbolical sense, we erect an intellectual edifice to be a stronghold of faith; and lastly, by the grace of moral instruction, we as it were paint the edifice in fair colors."[7]

In his early fourteenth-century treatise *De musica*, Johannes de Grocheio employed a similar metaphor to define the tenor: "The tenor is that part on which all the others are founded, just as the parts of a house or of a building are placed on their foundation. And it regulates them and gives them their quantity."[8]

Biblical exegesis—its aims and methods—can thus serve as a useful, if general, analogy for the fifteenth-century tenor motet as exemplified by *Factor orbis*. Indeed, the idea of glossing an authoritative text has been invoked for repertories extending from troped plainsong through cantus-firmus-based compositions of the sixteenth century,[9] and Andrew Hughes has gone so far as to declare that "glossing . . . is the conceptual framework within which most if not all the written music of the Middle Ages can be brought together."[10]

But another promising parallel between the medieval study of Scripture and medieval music invites exploration, an analogy that follows logically from the generalized "conceptual framework" of glossing observed by Hughes. For Obrecht is more than a musical exegete, crafting a gloss (a musical and textual addition) to an authoritative text (a plainsong cantus firmus). He is a musical preacher, delivering a sermon in sound to a listening assembly. Indeed, the methods, structures and goals of medieval preaching furnish a compelling analytic context for hearing and reading the motet *Factor orbis*.[11] Before proceeding with this analysis, however, a foray into the context, materials, and means of medieval sermonizing and homiletic theory is needed.[12]

In the doctrinal and educational framework of the Middle Ages, the exegesis of the sacred text fulfilled only half of the Christian theologian's mission. To complete this mission and do full justice to the message of Scripture, it was essential to teach—to communicate to others—that learned through the rigorous analysis of the sacred texts. And just as a sophisticated hermeneutic theory developed around biblical exegesis, as philosophers sought to penetrate the several layers of meaning that could be discerned in Scripture, so did a complex theory evolve concerning how best to present the understanding gained through exegesis. Thus, to quote St. Augustine, "There are two things necessary to the treatment of the Scriptures: a way of discovering those things which are to be understood, and a way of teaching what we have learned."[13]

These words began the first chapter of St. Augustine's treatise *De Doctrina Christiana*, finished in A.D. 426. In the first three books of this profoundly influential work, Augustine formulates the basic hermeneutic theory of biblical analysis that was to shape the intellectual life of the next millennium; in the fourth and final book he provides what is in essence the first manual of homiletics, that is, instruction on the art of preaching. Augustine's advice for the effective delivery of the message of Scripture to the faithful rests on the fundamentals of Ciceronian rhetoric adapted for the first time to the needs of the Christian orator.[14]

The interest in homiletic theory sparked by Augustine's treatise in the fifth century took about 800 years to ignite, but the production of manuals of preaching instruction exploded from the thirteenth through the fifteenth century, as did the creation of aids to preaching, including collections of model sermons, biblical concordances, and collections of fables and other morally instructive stories called *exempla*.[15] These manuals on preaching and the various aids to preaching were produced primarily by scholastic theologians on university faculties, both for the training of their students and for the education of clergy outside the university setting. Over 300 *Artes praedicandi* were written during the late Middle Ages, many of which exist in numerous manuscript copies and some of which were published many times over.[16] In Europe as a whole, over 5,000 volumes of sermons and related preaching aids appeared in print between 1460 and 1500.[17] The sheer volume of this production testifies eloquently to the widespread popularity of these materials.[18]

The type of sermon whose method and structure dominated the pulpit from the thirteenth century well into the sixteenth and whose theory was expounded in the preaching manuals was the so-called university or thematic sermon. Although the structure of the thematic sermon, which will be examined shortly, has its roots in ancient rhetorical theory, the genre grew to maturity and was fostered and disseminated from the medieval universities, most notably from Paris and Oxford. Scholasticism, that medieval mode of thinking stressing the art of dialectical argument, provided the intellectual framework within which the university sermon grew and flourished. Most successful public preachers were mendicants holding the degree Master of Theology, but every educated man, particularly the university-educated man, was intimately familiar with the analytic method and structure of the thematic sermon. This is an important point insofar as Obrecht had earned the master's degree by 1480, while still in his early 20s.[19]

What, then, would Obrecht have known about exegetical methods and about homiletic theory in particular? Where he studied is not known (a university in the Empire and or in Italy appears most likely[20]), but the substance of his education would have revolved around the two basic types of pedagogical exercises common to all medieval faculties, namely the *lectio* and the *disputatio*. In lecture, the teacher read the official texts of the discipline (whether arts, law, medicine, or theology), along with the accepted commentaries, thereby giving the student command of the authorities in that discipline; as a master's candidate, Obrecht would have both attended and given lectures on a daily basis for several years.[21] The disputation was an oral debate in which a given thesis was defended or refuted by means of constant reference to these authorities, following the rules of Aristotelian syllogistics; as a student, Obrecht would have both observed and participated in regular disputations. Thus training in reasoned argumentation, in which a text was dissected into its smallest parts and subjected to exhaustive analytic commentary (a process called *divisio*) founded on the citation of authority (auctoritas), comprised the gist of Obrecht's formal education.[22]

Delivering sermons to the academic community was the capstone educational experience reserved for masters on the faculty of theology. A man had to be at least 30 years old to receive the master's degree in theology; Obrecht, who earned his master's degree while in his early 20s, would therefore not have preached at university.[23] As a student, however, he was expected to attend not only the daily Mass but also the daily university sermon. Thus Obrecht, experienced in reading and disputing, would also have heard literally hundreds of sermons crafted according to the guidelines codified in the manuals of preaching.

Following his experience at university, Obrecht sought appointment as choirmaster at a succession of churches in Bergen op Zoom, Cambrai, Bruges, and Antwerp. His exposure to preaching and homiletic theory would have continued, as every urban center in the late Middle Ages attracted hundreds of itinerant preachers,[24] and every church library counted among its tomes various *Artes praedicandi* and other aids for preaching to assist its clergy in educating the local congregation.[25] Obrecht may even have owned such books, as did Dufay and many other secular canons in northern centers.[26]

What exactly was the thematic sermon style known so well by Obrecht? And how might its rhetorical techniques and formal structure inform our hearing of *Factor orbis?* With the broad context for an analysis of both sermon and motet now established, a detailed exploration of the relationship between the medieval homily and *Factor orbis* can be undertaken.

The general outlines and materials of *Factor orbis* are shown in Example 8.1, a and b. The motet falls into two large sections, each closing on the modal final D. Obrecht has chosen a wide array of texts primarily from the Advent liturgy, twenty in all; he draws not only upon Office antiphons, but also upon Matins responsories and plainsongs for the Mass. In most cases only the liturgical text is employed, but six times Obrecht joins the text to its plainsong melody; twice these quotations are treated as slow-moving, unadorned tenor cantus firmi (labeled **C** and **J**, in Example 8.1a and b), and at other times the chant melody is sculpted into an animated melodic line (labeled **b**, **h**, **i**, and **r**, in the examples). Only once does the composer reach outside the liturgy for a text: the opening plea (labeled a), "Factor orbis," appears to be newly created for this motet. Every text is in Latin save the joyful French exclamation "noe."

Contrast of texting procedure and texture create this motet's most effective features. Reduced textures—duets and trios as well as quartets in which only the tenor is silent—serve to deliver single units of text (that is, all singing parts use the same text); imitation and homophony prevail in such contexts. Four times, however, all five voices engage in an intensely polytextual nonimitative counterpoint in which as many as five texts are delivered simultaneously. These dense passages occur near or at the beginning and end of both *partes*.

Two notable large-scale repetitions bind this sprawling structure together. The melody serving as the main cantus firmus of the *prima pars* (labeled **C** in Example 8.1a), associated there with the text *Canite tuba in Sion*, reappears only slightly altered as the tenor cantus firmus in the *secunda pars* (labeled **J** in Example 8.1b) with the text *Erunt prava in directa*. This is no arbitrary text substitution: as shown in Example 8.2, the antiphons *Canite tuba* and *Erunt prava* belong to the same melodic family, and Obrecht simply accentuates the similarities in the two plainsongs when he recasts them as tenor cantus firmi.

Noteworthy also is the wholesale repetition of the ending of the *prima pars* (mm. 74–87) at the conclusion of the *secunda pars* (mm. 174–213) (see Example 8.3). But only the music is repeated: upon repetition, five new texts replace those heard at the end of the *prima pars*. Textual congruence is maintained, however, in the tenor part: *Canite tuba* concludes with the phrase "Ecce veniet ad salvandum nos" (Behold, he is coming to save us, labeled **C3** in Example 8.1a), which sentiment is echoed by the final phrase of *Erunt prava*, "Veni Domine et noli tardare" (Come, Lord, and do not delay, labeled **J3** in Example 8.1b).

Most texts selected by the composer treat the theme of the joyful anticipation of the birth of Christ. But two striking anomalies command attention: a text from the liturgy of Epiphany concerning the judgment of the poor (text g in Example 8.1a), and a Lenten text evoking the image of death (text h in Example 8.1a). Also noteworthy is the emphasis on texts extoling the Virgin Mother at the culmination of the piece (texts q, r, and s in Example 8.1b).

These structural complexities and textual incongruities of *Factor orbis* defy explanation within the general analogy of biblical glossing, but virtually every textual and musical feature of *Factor orbis* finds an analog in the thematic sermon, from the macro to the micro level. Several general congruencies deserve first mention.

Both the thematic sermon and the polytextual motet as exemplified by *Factor orbis* deliver their message in sound; both, however, possess a complexity of structure and meaning appreciable only by the educated reader able to consider the sermon or the motet at leisure, outside its performance in time.

Both sermon and motet are based on the multiple quotation of authorita-

EXAMPLE 8.1a   Obrecht, *Factor orbis*, Prima Pars. Summary of texts with textual and textural graph

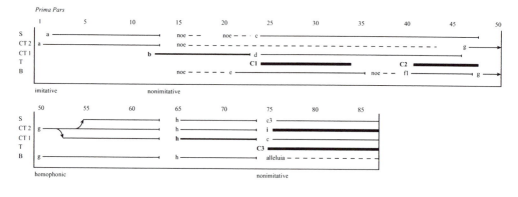

Text	Translation	Liturgical Function	Biblical Source
a) Factor orbis, Deus, nos famulos exaudi clamantes ad te tuos, et nostra crimina laxa die ista lucifera.	a) Maker of the earth, Lord, listen to us your servants crying to you, and relieve our sins this bright day.	—	—
b) Veni, Domine, et noli tardare, relaxa facinora plebis tuae Israel.	b) Come, Lord, and do not delay, loosen the bonds of your people's sins.	Advent Week I or III, feria vi, Lauds, ant. 3	Hab. 2:3
C) 1. Canite tuba in Sion, 2. quia prope est dies Domini, 3. ecce veniet ad salvandum nos.	C) 1. Blow the trumpet in Sion, 2. for the day of the Lord is near, 3. behold he is coming to save us.	Advent Dom. IV, Lauds, ant. 1	Joel 2:1
d) Ad te, Domine, levavi animam meam, Deus meus, in te confido, non erubescam.	d) To you, Lord, I lift up my soul, my God, in you I confide without shame.	Advent Dom. I, Introit	Ps. 25:1–2
e) Ecce Dominus veniet, noli timere. Alleluia.	e) Behold the Lord shall come, do not fear. Alleluia.	?	—
f) 1. Crastina die erit vobis salus, 2. dicit Dominus exercituum.	f) 1. Tomorrow salvation shall be yours, 2. says the Lord of Hosts.	Christmas vigil, Lauds, ant. 5	2 Chron. 20:17
g) Deus, qui sedes super thronos et iudicas aequitatem, esto refugium pauperum in tribulatione, quia tu solus laborem et dolorem consideras.	g) God, you who sit upon thrones and judge fairly of the poor, because you alone consider their work and sorrow.	Dom. II after Epiphany, Matins, resp. 2	Ps. 9:5, 10

Text	Translation	Liturgical Function	Biblical Source
h) Media vita in morte sumus, quem quaerimus adjutorem, nisi te, Domine.	**h)** In the middle of life we are in death, to whom do we turn but you, Lord.	Lent Dom. I, III, or IV, Compline, ant.	—
i) O clavis David et sceptrum domus Israel, qui aperis, et nemo claudit, claudis, et nemo aperit; veni, et educ vinctum de domo carceris, sedentem in tenebris et umbra mortis.	**i)** O key of David and scepter of the house of Israel, you open and no man closes, you close and no man opens; come and deliver him from the chains of prison who sits in darkness and the shadow of death.	"O" ant., Advent Week IV, feria, Mag. ant.	Rev. 3:7 Isa. 42:7

tive "texts" (auctoritas), be they the words of Scripture or the texts and melodies of liturgical chant. Understanding thus depends in both cases on the listeners' familiarity with material drawn from the Christian experience of worship.

Even the preservation of sermon and motet in written notation bears comparison. Model sermons were usually transmitted only in outline form, supplying merely the essential citations and sketching the main interpretive points to be made, thereby leaving much for the person crafting a sermon from the outline to surmise.[27] Likewise, the musical notation of the period provides only the essentials of pitch, rhythm, and text, leaving matters of text underlay, tempo, timbre, dynamics, articulation, etc. to the performer's discretion. Recreation of either a sermon or a motet from the written page thus demanded that the medieval reader/performer participate as co-creator, effectively merging the roles of author and reader.[28]

Most telling, however, are parallels in the actual structure and method of the medieval sermon and Obrecht's *Factor orbis*. Prescriptions for the thematic sermon contained in the *artes praedicandi* manuals, when considered in tandem with the musical and textual details of *Factor orbis* summarized above, proffer an analytic framework within which key textual and musical strategies of the motet can be understood. Because the thematic sermon quickly became a highly standardized genre, the manuals treating it share much the same substance. Four representative manuals spanning the period during which the thematic sermon flourished thus serve to supply the background for this investigation: the early-thirteenth-century *Summa de arte praedicandi* by Thomas Chabham, an Englishman active at Paris and Salisbury; the *Forma praedicandi* (1322) of Robert of Basevorn, a shadowy figure familiar with the curricula at both Paris and Oxford; the late-fourteenth-century German *Tractatus de Arte Praedicandi* by one Henry of Hesse; and the so-called Aquinas-Tract by an unknown fifteenth-century Dominican.[29] Henry's treatise and the Aquinas-Tract were among the first homiletic treatises to appear in print; both survive in German editions published before 1500.[30]

EXAMPLE 8.1b   Obrecht, *Factor orbis*, Secunda Pars. Summary of texts with textual and textural graph

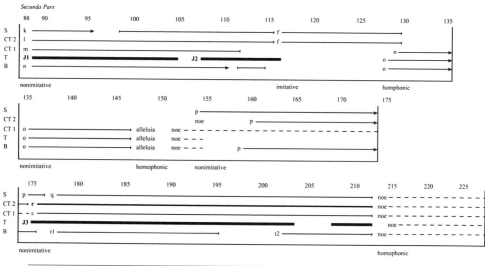

Text	Translation	Liturgical Function	Biblical Source
J) 1. Erunt prava in directa, et aspera 2. in vias planas 3. veni, Domine, et noli tardare. Alleluia.	J) 1. The rough land shall be made a plain, and the rough country 2. a broad valley, 3. come, Lord, and do not delay.	Advent Dom. IV, Lauds ant. 3	Isa. 40:4
k) Spiritus Domini super me, evangelizare pauperibus misit me.	k) The spirit of the Lord is upon me, to bring good news to the poor he has sent me.	Advent Week III, feria iv, Lauds ant. 2 or 3	Luke 4:18
l) Veniet fortior me, cuius non sum dignus solvere corigiam calciamentorum eius.	l) After me is coming one mightier than I, the straps of whose sandals I am not worthy to loose.	Advent Week I, feria iv, Vesp. II, Mag. ant.	Luke 3:16
m) Hodie scietis, quia veniet Dominus, et mane videbitis gloriam eius.	m) Today you shall know that the Lord is coming, and tomorrow you shall see his glory.	Christmas vigil, Lauds, ant. 2	Exod. 16:6–7
n) Bethlehem, civitas Dei summi, ex te exiet dominator Israel.	n) Bethlehem, city of the highest God, from you went forth the ruler of Israel.	Advent Dom. III, Matins, resp. 2	Mic. 5:2
o) Crastina die delebitur iniquitas terrae, et regnabit super nos salvator mundi.	o) Tomorrow the iniquity of the earth will be blotted out, and the savior of the world will rule over us.	Christmas vigil, Lauds, ant. 3	4 Esd. 16:53
p) De caelo veniet Dominus dominator et in manu eius honor et imperium.	p) From heaven comes the Lord and ruler and in his hand are honor and dominion.	Advent Week II, feria ii, Lauds, Ben. ant.	Dan. 7:13–14

178

Text	Translation	Liturgical Function	Biblical Source
q) Ave Maria, gratia plena, Dominus tecum, benedicta tu in mulieribus, et benedictus fructus ventris tui.	q) Hail Mary, full of grace, the Lord is with you, blessed are you among women, and blessed is the fruit of your womb.	Advent Dom. IV, Offertory	Luke 1:18
r) O virgo virginum, quomodo fiet istud, quia nec primam similem visa est, nec habere sequentem; filiae Hierusalem, quid me admiramini? Divinum est misterium hoc quod cernitis.	r) O virgin of virgins, how can this be, since she did not appear to be like the foremost of women, having no husband; daughters of Jerusalem, why are you astonished at me? Divine is this mystery that you see.	"O" ant., Advent Week IV, feria, Mag. ant.	—
s) Beata es, Maria, quae credidisti, quae perficientur in te, quae dicta sunt tibi.	s) Blessed are you, Mary, because you believed the things which the Lord told you would be fulfilled in you.	Advent Dom. II or III, Vesp. II, Mag. ant.	Luke 1:45
t) 1. Ecce Dominus veniet et omnes sancti eius cum eo, 2. et erit in die illa lux magna. Alleluia.	t) 1. Behold the Lord shall come and all his saints with him, 2. and there shall be a great light that day. Alleluia.	Advent Dom. I, Lauds, ant.	Zech. 14:5–7

EXAMPLE 8.2   Comparison of the cantus firmi *Canite tuba* and *Erunt prava* with their plainsong models

* *Processionale Insignis Cathedralis Ecclesiae Antverpiensis B. Mariae* (Antwerp: Christopher Plantin, 1574); only extant copy in Antwerp, Museum Plantin–Moretus, A363.

The basic outline of the thematic sermon that emerges from these treatises comprises five parts, called theme, protheme, division, subdivision, and conclusion, of which the theme and division were considered essential. First the preacher simply stated his chosen *thema*, the scriptural passage upon which the sermon was to be based. Certain criteria were essential for the thema: Robert of Basevorn offers a typical list of requirements when he declares that the thema must concur with the feast, have a fully perceived meaning, employ a biblical text that is not changed or corrupted, and contain not more than three statements or a statement convertible to three.[31]

Obrecht's thema is, of course, his main cantus firmus, *Canite tuba in Sion*. This cantus firmus, "Blow the trumpet in Sion, for the day of the Lord

EXAMPLE 8.3　Obrecht, *Factor orbis* (a) from conclusion of Prima Pars; (b) from conclusion of Secunda Pars

EXAMPLE 8.3 *(continued)*

181

is near, behold he is coming to save us," derives from the first antiphon of Lauds for the fourth Sunday of Advent and uses a text from the Old Testament Book of Joel (Joel 2:1). Robert's requirements for a good thema clearly apply. Obviously appropriate to the Christmas vigil both in its musical and textual content, this cantus firmus is complete in its textual sense as well as musically (an entire antiphon melody furnishes the melodic material). The chant tune presents itself unchanged and uncorrupted, and both text and melody divide neatly into three statements (see Example 8.1a).

Next the preacher had the option of providing an introduction to the main body of the sermon; this might include offering a prayer, and introducing a *prothema*, designed, according to Thomas of Chabham, to "lay out a sort of brief theme before the main one, thus helping to make the audience attentive, docile, and well disposed."[32] The prothema, according to Henry of Hesse, "should be composed of authorities drawn from the Bible and from theologians," and "should generally . . . correspond to the sense of the thema."[33]

Obrecht commences his motet with an introductory section comparable to a sermon's prayer and prothema (see Example 8.4). The opening imitative superius/contratenor II duet can be heard as a prayer: it is freely composed, and features an apparently original text that appeals to the Creator of the Earth for forgiveness using the first person plural ("listen to us your servants . . ."). Following this initial duet, the contratenor I introduces a subsidiary cantus firmus using the text and tune of another Lauds antiphon, *Veni Domine et noli tardare*, for Friday in the third week of Advent. This text also comes from the Old Testament (Hab. 2:3), and its sense ("Come Lord and do not delay, loosen the bonds of your people of Israel") intersects with that of the principal cantus firmus. Here, then, is the musical equivalent of the prothema. The surrounding voices (with the exception of the still-silent tenor) begin to exclaim "noe" as this musical prothema proceeds; as a vernacular response to the Latin sermon, it conjures up the preacher's audience, responding to the sermon much as the African American congregation today exhorts the minister during his sermon.

With the first emphatic cadence of the piece in measure 23, Obrecht ends his musical prothema, and now the main body of the sermon can begin. Homiletic manuals call this essential section *divisio*: the preacher is instructed to divide his theme into its component phrases (three being the preferred number) and to amplify the meaning of these divisions in turn through various rhetorical devices. Chief among the means of amplification was the citation of biblical or patristic authorities in order to prove the component parts of the thema.[34] This is precisely how Obrecht now proceeds (see Example 8.1a). The principal cantus firmus, *Canite tuba*, is broken into its three textual/musical phrases, each cadentially articulated, while the surrounding voices offer commentary based on textual and sometimes musical material drawn from the liturgy of Advent and ultimately, in most cases, from the Bible. Those lines heard simultaneously with the divisions of the cantus firmus all "prove" the cantus firmus with complementary text and music; for example, as the tenor delivers the first and second divisions of the cantus firmus, "Blow the trumpet in Sion, for the day

EXAMPLE 8.4 Obrecht, *Factor orbis*, beginning of Prima Pars

EXAMPLE 8.4 (*continued*)

EXAMPLE 8.4   (*continued*)

of the Lord is near," the bassus sings "Behold, the Lord shall come, do not fear" (letter e, Example 8.1a), followed by "Tomorrow salvation shall be yours" (letter f, Example 8.1a), while the contratenor I states "To you Lord I lift up my soul, in you I confide without shame" (letter d, Example 8.1a). Moreover, the three black breves that announce the entrance of the cantus firmus in the tenor constitute an aural as well as a visual "trumpet call" that is both sounded and seen in the superius, contratenor I, and bassus parts (see Figure 8.2).[35]

This intense polyphony of text and counterpoint is then interrupted by an extended section (mm. 48–74) that is both monotextual and largely homophonic, and in which the tenor is silent. Here are heard the two anomalous texts drawn from outside the Advent liturgy, the first from Epiphany focused on the merciful judgment of the poor (letter g, Example 8.1a), and the second from Lent that raises the specter of death (labeled **h,** Example 8.1a). In homiletic theory, such a passage corresponds to the technique described by Robert of Basevorn as "Digression, which is equivalent to Transition. It occurs when one proceeds artistically from one part to another . . ." and ". . . consists of a certain skillful connecting of two principal statements, by verbal and real concordance."[36] Obrecht's juxtaposition of glad tidings with dreadful anticipation of the Final Judgment parallels a device common to Advent sermons, in which the First Coming serves as an allegory for the Second Coming.[37] In effect, the composer here exercises a method of homiletic expansion founded in biblical hermeneutics, that is, analysis based upon the multiple interpretation of Scripture.[38]

Obrecht's calculated collage of texts and tunes resumes at the third division of his musical thema, when the tenor enters with the final phrase of the cantus firmus (m. 74) (see Example 8.3a). Against the tenor's slow intonation of the final phrase of *Canite tuba,* "Behold he is coming to save us," the composer sets the complementary text and melody of the "O" antiphon *O clavis David* (labeled **i,** Example 8.1a), an Advent chant invoking the metaphor of Christ as the key to salvation, able to unlock the prison chains of darkness and death. Simultaneously, the contratenor I restates the entire text of the musical thema, *Canite tuba.* Homiletic theory provides an explanation for this wholesale repetition. Restatement of the thema of a sermon was allowed, according to the Aquinas-Tract, when the various divisions of the theme had been set forth, "so that if the hearers have not attended to the beginning, they may know on what the sermon is effectively based."[39] This concludes the *prima pars.*

Just as the sermon could conceivably conclude at this point, with the third and final division of the thema and its proof, so could the motet *Factor orbis* end here, with the strong cadence on the modal final and the emphatically conclusive exclamations of "alleluia" that bring the *prima pars* to a close. But a preacher might choose to develop or subdivide his theme, and so Obrecht continues with the further explication of his chosen cantus firmus. The *secunda pars* thus invites comparison with another method of amplification termed *subdivisio,* which Robert of Basevorn says "consists of adding a division . . . immediately after the verification of parts of the theme once the theme has been divided and the parts stated."[40]

Obrecht makes it clear that the *secunda pars* functions as further commentary on his musical thema by selecting a cantus firmus, *Erunt prava,* whose melody, as mentioned above, closely resembles that of the main cantus firmus *Canite tuba.* As shown in Example 8.1b, *Erunt prava,* like the cantus firmus *Canite tuba,* falls into three phrases or divisions, which are subjected to still more textual and musical commentary. Obrecht's method is here analogous to that recommended by Robert of Basevorn concerning the technique of subdivisio: "Preachers using this method should make sure that when they divide themes they make a general description of the first division; thus in the subdivision descend as it were from genus to species or from some whole to its parts."[41] By retaining the basic melody as a cantus firmus in the *secunda pars,* Obrecht in effect "makes a general description of the first divisions," thereby facilitating further commentary upon them.

The text of *Erunt prava* (labeled **J,** Example 8.1b) derives from the Old Testament Book of Isaiah (Isa. 40:4), and prophesies the coming of Christ through geographical allegory. Obrecht thus focuses the first part of this musical *subdivisio* on the prophets' forecast of the birth of Christ, citing various authorities heard during the liturgy of the Advent season. The superius text comes from the Gospel of St. Luke, from a passage in which Christ is reading from the Book of Isaiah: "The spirit of the Lord is upon me, to bring good news to the poor he has sent me" (letter k, Example 8.1b). Luke also furnishes the text carried by the contratenor II, but here the speaker is John the Baptist: "After me is coming one mightier than I, the straps of whose sandals I am not worthy to loose" (letter l, Example 8.1b). The bassus text derives from the minor Old Testament prophet Micah, who identifies Bethlehem as the place from which the Savior will come (letter n, Example 8.1b). And contratenor I pronounces the prophetic words of Moses to the people of Israel as told in the book of Exodus (16:6–7): "Today you shall know that the Lord is coming, and tomorrow you shall see his glory" (letter m, Example 8.1b).

Like the *prima pars*, the *secunda pars* devotes its middle section to reduced textures that deliver one text at a time in a blend of transparent counterpoint or pure homophony, and the response of the audience is once again evoked with cries of "noe" and "alleluia." But unlike the corresponding section of the first part, all three texts here introduced belong to the Advent liturgy and serve simply to compound the authorities proving the thema.

The final important structural event of the motet transpires at measure 174 with the wholesale reiteration of the music from the closing measures of the *prima pars*; each voice however, is supplied with new text (see Example 8.3b). In homiletic terms, this section functions as the sermon's *conclusio*. It is probably no accident that the final phrase of the tenor cantus firmus *Erunt prava* (labeled **J3,** Example 8.1b) employs the same text, "Come, Lord, and do not delay," heard as the musical equivalent of the prothema in the introduction of the motet (labeled **b,** Example 8.1a); this neat link back to the beginning of the piece resonates with Robert of Basevorn's remarks concerning the sermon's conclusion: "Just as nature, if bent from its natural path by violence, always returns to its original state, so the sermon must end as it began. The more the end is like the beginning, so much the more elegantly does it end."[42]

There remains only to address the sudden Marian focus of the three upper voices at the conclusion of *Factor orbis* (see Example 8.1b, letters q, **r,** and s). Theological, liturgical, musical, and homiletic justifications coalesce to explain this attention to the Blessed Virgin. The conglomeration of texts in *Factor orbis* suggests that this motet was probably destined specifically for the vigil of Christmas, whose Gospel reading (Matt. 1:18–21) dwells on the spotless conception of the Savior.[43] All three Marian texts introduced at the end of the motet focus on this centerpiece of the Christmas mystery, and indeed the liturgy of Advent unfolds as a story culminating with the Angel Gabriel's annunciation to the Blessed Virgin. Thus *Factor orbis*, with its initial concentration on Old Testament prophecies of the coming of Christ and its subsequent emphasis on the miracle of His conception, effects a musical distillation of the message of Advent.

A musical transformation to Marian plainsong is also facilitated by the melody on which contratenor II is based: because all the "O" antiphons of Advent employ the same second mode tune, the text of O *clavis David* heard with this melody at the end of the *prima pars* is easily replaced by the text O *virgo virginum*.[44] And finally, manuals of preaching often recommend reciting the *Ave Maria* (Example 8.1b, letter q), albeit as an internal articulation at the end of the introduction rather than as a final invocation.[45]

With the sesquialtera acceleration for the crowd's concluding homophonic cries of "noe", this musical sermon on the theme of Christ's imminent birth comes to a dramatic close. Was Obrecht conscious of the parallels in structure and method between this motet and the myriad homilies he heard throughout his life? The question, while intriguing, is moot. Obrecht did not need to search for analogies to help him understand his music. But for us today, longing to bridge the unbridgeable gulf between our time and Obrecht's, the analogy here drawn between sermon and motet may open our ears and our minds to another way of seeing, of reading, and of hearing the medieval motet, a way that, recalling Freud's words, might help us to feel more at home with this music.

NOTES

Research for this study was assisted by a fellowship from the Oakley Center for the Humanities and Social Sciences at Williams College. For his insightful comments and suggestions, the author is indebted to Professor Craig Wright.

1. Sigmund Freud, *New Introductory Lectures on Psycho-Analysis* (1933), in *The Standard Edition of the Complete Psychological Works of Sigmund Freud*, trans. James Strachey, Anna Freud, Alix Strachey, and Alan Tyson, 24 vols. (London: Hogarth Press for the Institute of Psychoanalysis, 1966–74), 22:72.

2. On the idea of "alterity"—a term familiar to literary theorists but clearly relevant to the study of all aspects of medieval culture—see H. R. Jauss, "The Alterity and Modernity of Medieval Literature," *New Literary History* 10 (1979–80): 181–229.

3. A fine general history of the *Glossa ordinaria* is C. F. R. de Hamel, *Glossed Books of the Bible and the Origins of the Paris Booktrade* (Woodbridge, Suffolk: D. S. Brewer, 1984). For the only modern edition, see *Patrologiae cursus completa: Series latina*, ed. J.P. Migne, 221 vols. (Paris: J. P. Migne, 1844–64), 113–14, which is much abridged and should be used with caution. A facsimile of the fifteenth-century edition consulted for this study is *Biblia Latina cum Glossa Ordinaria: Facsimile Reprint of the Editio Princeps Adolph Rusch of Strassburg 1480/81*, intro. Karlfried Froelich and Margaret T. Gibson, 4 vols. (Turnhout: Brepols, 1992). See also the invaluable guide to sources of medieval biblical exegesis, Friedrich Stegmüller, *Repertorium Biblicum Medii Aevi*, 12 vols. (Madrid: Consejo Superior, 1950–80), esp. the book-by-book analysis of the *Glossa Ordinaria* in 9:465–567.

4. For the dating, see Richard J. Sherr, *Papal Music and Papal Music Manuscripts in the Late Fifteenth and Early Sixteenth Centuries*, Renaissance Manuscript Studies 5 (Neuhausen-Stuttgart: American Institute of Musicology), in preparation.

5. On the medieval concepts of "auctor" and "auctoritas," see A. J. Minnis, *Medieval Theory of Authorship: Scholastic Literary Attitudes in the Later Middle Ages*, 2d ed. (Philadelphia: University of Pennsylvania Press, 1988), 10–12.

6. Despite the reverence accorded the great *auctores* in literature of the medieval period, certain literary theorists have argued that the fluid merging of author and audience that results from the process of glossing—and the concomitant textual instability generated by such commentary—allows an indeterminacy of meaning in medieval literature that essentially undermines any claim of authorial intention. Although they lie beyond the scope of this study, such proposed intersections between aspects of medieval textual exegesis and the postmodern emphasis on the indeterminacy of literary meaning have obvious repercussions for the analysis of medieval music. A fine overview of the applicability of the postmodern concept of indeterminacy of meaning to medieval studies is Robert S. Sturges, *Medieval Interpretation: Models of Reading in Literary Narrative, 1100–1500* (Carbondale: Southern Illinois University Press, 1991), esp. 1–20.

7. "Nam primum quidem fundamenta historiae ponimus; deinde per significationem typicam in arcem fidei fabricam mentis erigimus; ad extremum quoque per moralitatis gratiam, quasi superducto aedificium colore uestimus." *S. Gregorii Magni Opera: Moralia in Iob, Libri I–X*, ed. Marci Adriaen, Corpus Christianorum Series Latina 143 (Turnholt: Brepols, 1979), Epistola 3:110–14 (dedication of his lecture on the Book of Job, the *Magna Moralia*, to Leander of Seville). The passage is discussed in Harry Caplan, "The Four Senses of Scriptural Interpretation and the Mediaeval Theory of Preaching," *Speculum* 4 (1929), 282–90, reprinted in *Of Eloquence: Studies in Ancient and Mediaeval Rhetoric*, ed. Anne King and Helen North (Ithaca: Cornell University Press, 1970), 93–104; and in Beryl Smalley, *The Study of the Bible in the Middle Ages* (Oxford: Clarendon Press, 1941), 18–21.

8. "Tenor autem est illa pars, supra quam omnes aliae fundantur, quemadmodum partes domus vel aedificii super suum fundamentum. Et eas regulat et eis dat quantitatem." *Die Quellenhandschriften zum Musiktraktat des Johannes de Grocheio*, facsimile, ed. Ernst Rohloff (Leipzig: Deutscher Verlag für Musik, 1972), 146. Translated by Albert Seay in Johannes de Grocheio, *Concerning Music (De Musica)*, Colorado College Music Press Translations 1 (Colorado Springs: Colorado College Music Press, 1967), 26.

9. For an ambitious and elegant demonstration of this general analogy as it pertains to the sequence repertory, see Margot Fassler, *Gothic Song: Victorine Sequences and Augustinian Reform in Twelfth-Century Paris* (Cambridge: Cambridge University Press, 1993), esp. 1–82; Howard Mayer Brown invoked the comparison in "Emulation, Competition, and Homage: Imitation and Theories of Imitation in the Renaissance," *Journal of the American Musicological Society* 35 (1982): 47–48.

10. Andrew Hughes, *Style and Symbol: Medieval Music, 800–1453*, Musicological Studies 51 (Ottawa: Institute of Mediaeval Music, 1989), 10; his extensive and thoughtful consideration of the general relevance of the ideas of glossing and exegesis to music is contained in 33–39.

11. Two exemplary studies have already demonstrated composers' attention to the content of specific medieval sermons: see Patrick Macey, "Savonarola and the Sixteenth-Century Motet," *Journal of the American Musicological Society* 36 (1983): 422–52, wherein the influence of the Dominican martyr Savonarola's sermons is traced in a variety of Renaissance motets, including Josquin's *Miserere mei Deus*; and Craig Wright, "Dufay's *Nuper rosarum flores*, King Solomon's Temple, and the Veneration of the Virgin," *Journal of the American Musicological Society* 47 (1994): 411–12, in which a sermon by Bede for the Dedication of the Church proves to have influenced the poetry of Dufay's famous motet.

12. The literature on the medieval commentary tradition and on the art of preaching in particular is vast; see the immensely useful bibliographic guide by R. E. Kaske,

Arthur Groos, and Michael W. Twomey, *Medieval Christian Literary Imagery: A Guide to Interpretation*, Toronto Medieval Bibliographies 11 (Toronto: University of Toronto Press, 1988), esp. 3–52 and 80–90, and James J. Murphy, *Medieval Rhetoric: A Select Bibliography*, Toronto Medieval Bibliographies 3, 2d ed. (Toronto: University of Toronto Press, 1988), esp. 136–56. The following studies have proven most useful for the general background sketched here: Smalley, *The Study of the Bible*; Th. M. Charland, O.P., *Artes Praedicandi: Contribution à l'histoire de la rhétorique au moyen âge*, Publications de l'Institut d'Etudes Médiévales d'Ottawa 7 (Paris: Vrin; Institute d'Etudes Médiévales, 1936); Jean Longère, *La Prédication médiévale* (Paris: Etudes Augustiniennes, 1983); James J. Murphy, *Rhetoric in the Middle Ages: A History of Rhetorical Theory from St. Augustine to the Renaissance* (Berkeley: University of California Press, 1974), esp. 269–355; and Johann Baptist Schneyer, *Geschichte der katholischen Predigt* (Freiburg im Breisgau: B. Seelsorge Verlag, 1969). For studies devoted to sermons and preaching in France, see Marie Magdeleine Davy, *Les Sermons universitaires parisiens de 1230–31: Contribution à l'histoire de la prédication médiévale*, Etudes de philosophie médiévale 15 (Paris: Vrin, 1931); Hervé Martin, *Le Métier de prédicateur en France septentrionale à la fin du moyen âge (1350–1520)* (Paris: Editions du Cerf, 1988); and Larissa Taylor, *Soldiers of Christ: Preaching in Late Medieval and Reformation France* (Oxford: Oxford University Press, 1992).

13. "Duae sunt res, quibus nititur omnis tractatio scripturarum, modus inueniendi, quae intellegenda sunt, et modus proferendi, quae intellecta sunt." See St. Augustine, *De Doctrina Christiana/De Vera Religione*, Corpus Christianorum Series Latina 32: *Aurelii Augustini Opera*, Pars IV, I (Turnholt: Brepols, 1962), 6. Translation by D. W. Robertson Jr. from St. Augustine, *On Christian Doctrine* (New York: Liberal Arts Press, 1958), 7.

14. On St. Augustine's seminal role in Christian rhetorical theory, see Murphy, *Rhetoric in the Middle Ages*, 43–64 and 284–92.

15. For an introduction to these sermon aids and a discussion of one particular work, see Richard H. Rouse and Mary A. Rouse, *Preachers, Florilegia and Sermons: Studies on the* Manipulus Florum *of Thomas of Ireland* (Toronto: Pontifical Institute of Mediaeval Studies, 1979).

16. See Harry Caplan, *Mediaeval Artes Praedicandi: A Hand-List*, Cornell Studies in Classical Philology 24 (Ithaca: Cornell University Press, 1934); id., *Mediaeval Artes Praedicandi: A Supplementary Handlist*, Cornell Studies in Classical Philology 25 (Ithaca: Cornell University Press, 1936); on printed editions of preaching manuals, see Susan Gallick, "*Artes praedicandi*: Early Printed Editions," *Mediaeval Studies* 39 (1977): 477–89.

17. Taylor, *Soldiers of Christ*, 5.

18. Janet Coleman argues that the increased demand for these written aids coincides with the decline of the art of memory in medieval society; see *Medieval Readers and Writers, 1350–1400* (New York: Columbia University Press, 1981), 157–231.

19. Regarding Obrecht's education, see Rob C. Wegman, *Born for the Muses: The Life and Masses of Jacob Obrecht* (Oxford: Clarendon Press, 1994), 70–76. While the documents are never explicit as to what university faculty awarded Obrecht's degree (the arts, law, or theology), the fact that he received the degree while in his early twenties strongly suggests that his was a master's degree in either the arts or law, as the master of theology was conferred only upon a man at least thirty years of age. See Monika Asztalos, "The Faculty of Theology," chap. 13 in *A History of the University in Europe*, 1: *Universities in the Middle Ages*, ed. Hilde de Ridder-Symoens (Cambridge: Cambridge University Press, 1992), 419.

20. Wegman, *Born for the Muses*, 72–73.

21. Students at university made use of a note-taking system for lectures that duplicates the appearance and method of the *Glossa ordinaria:* the main text upon which the lecture was based was copied in large letters on the page, with the commentary in small and much-abbreviated script surrounding. For a facsimile of representative student notes from a lecture on Aristotle's *De anima* given at the University of Uppsala in 1482, see Anders Piltz, *The World of Medieval Learning*, trans. David Jones (Oxford: Blackwell, 1981), 114–15.

22. Regarding the general course of studies followed by medieval faculties of the arts, see Gordon Leff, "The Faculty of Arts," chap. 10 in *A History of the University in Europe*, 1: *Universities in the Middle Ages*, ed. Ridder-Symoens, 325–33. See also the detailed overview of medieval university curricula by Hastings Rashdall, *The Universities of Europe in the Middle Ages*, 3 vols. (Oxford: Clarendon Press, 1895), esp. vol. 1, wherein the course of studies at Bologna and Paris is explored. A useful general summary of medieval teaching techniques is Arthur O. Norton, *Readings in the History of Education: Mediaeval Universities* (Cambridge, Mass.: Harvard University Press, 1909), 107–40.

23. See n. 19.

24. Regarding the mileau of preachers in the late Middle Ages, see Martin, *Le Métier de prédicateur*, 73–102, and Taylor, *Soldiers of Christ*, 15–51.

25. Regarding the contents of church libraries in northern Europe, see R. De Keyser, "Het Boekenbezit en het Boekengebruik in de Seculiere Kapittels van de Zuidelijke Nederlanden tijdens de Middeleeuwen," in *Archives et bibliothèques de Belgique. Numero spécial 11: Contributions à l'histoire des bibliothèques et de la lecture aux Pays-Bas avant 1600* 11 (Brussels: Bibliothèque Royale, 1974), 52–68.

26. On Dufay's personal library, which included two volumes of sermons and a *Florilegium*, see Craig Wright, "Dufay at Cambrai: Discoveries and Revisions," *Journal of the American Musicological Society* 28 (1975): 214–18. The private libraries of many northern secular canons are surveyed in De Keyser, "Het Boekenbezit," 13–52; Barbara Haggh summarizes the book collections of several clerics of Brussels in "Music, Liturgy and Ceremony in Brussels, 1350–1500" (Ph.D. diss., University of Illinois, 1988), 479–81.

27. The conventional transmission of model sermons in outline form is discussed in David L. D'Avray, *The Preaching of the Friars: Sermons Diffused from Paris before 1300* (Oxford: Clarendon Press, 1985), 96–104.

28. Such a merging of the roles of author/composer with reader/performer in medieval sermons and motets invites analysis from a postmodernist perspective; the literary theorist Sturges notes that "For medieval as for postmodern writers, the author, text, and reader can easily seem less distinct from one another than we have been trained to conceive of them, and indeed they might be regarded less as separable entities than as three literary functions that continuously interact in various combinations." See *Medieval Interpretation*, 3.

29. On Thomas Chabham and his manual, see Murphy, *Rhetoric in the Middle Ages*, 317–26. For the Latin text of Robert of Basevorn's treatise, see Charland, *Artes praedicandi*, 233–323; for a full translation, see Leopold Krul, O.S.B., "Robert Basevorn: *The Form of Preaching* (1322 A.D.)," in *Three Medieval Rhetorical Arts*, ed. James J. Murphy (Berkeley: University of California Press, 1971), 109–215; a somewhat truncated translation is also supplied by Murphy in *Rhetoric in the Middle Ages*, 344–55. Harry Caplan provides a translation of Henry of Hesse's manual in "'Henry of Hesse' on the Art of Preaching," *Proceedings of the Modern Language Association* 48 (1933):

340–61, and of the Aquinas-Tract in "A Late Mediaeval Tractate on Preaching," *Studies in Rhetoric and Public Speaking in Honor of James Albert Winans*, ed. A. M. Drummond (New York: Century, 1925), 61–90; both articles are reprinted in Caplan, *Of Eloquence* (Ithaca: Cornell University Press, 1970).

30. For a summary of early printed preaching manuals, see Gallick, "*Artes Praedicandi*: Early Printed Editions," 477–89.

31. Murphy, *Rhetoric in the Middle Ages*, 348.

32. Ibid., 323.

33. Caplan, " 'Henry of Hesse'," 147.

34. Robert of Basevorn calls this "Proof of Parts," saying "This is done in various ways. The Parisians supply an authority for each part which is divisible into three. . . . Other methods aim at producing verbal correspondences between the divisions of the authorities and the divisions of the theme or its parts"; Murphy, *Rhetoric in the Middle Ages*, 352.

35. For the idea of the aural and visual "trumpet call," the author is indebted to Dr. Bonnie Blackburn.

36. Murphy, *Rhetoric in the Middle Ages*, 353.

37. Taylor, *Soldiers of Christ*, 17–18. For a study devoted to typology—that exegetical approach interpreting Old Testament characters and events as foreshadowing those of the New Testament—see Jean Daniélou, *Sacramentum futuri: Etudes sur les origines de la typologie biblique* (Paris: Beauchesne, 1950); trans. Wulstan Hibberd as *From Shadows to Reality: Studies in the Biblical Typology of the Fathers* (London: Burns and Oates, 1960).

38. Virtually all *artes praedicandi* manuals recommend expounding on the four senses of Scripture (the literal or historical, the tropological or moral, the allegorical, and the anagogical or mystical); see Robert of Basevorn (Murphy, *Rhetoric in the Middle Ages*, 353), Henry of Hesse (Caplan, " 'Henry of Hesse'," 143–45), and the Aquinas-Tract (Caplan, "A Late Mediaeval Tractate," 64–66).

39. Caplan, "A Late Mediaeval Tractate," 78.

40. Murphy, *Rhetoric in the Middle Ages*, 353.

41. Ibid.

42. Ibid., 354.

43. That *Factor orbis* was probably meant for the Christmas vigil is implicit in certain texts included therein; see Example 8.1a, letters a and f, and Example 8.1b, letters m and o. Moreover, a motet as ambitious and joyful as this properly belongs not to the penitential Advent season but rather to the Christmas celebration itself, as the celebratory "noe" refrain confirms. The Vespers services of the vigil or the evening Marian devotion known as the *lof* were likely occasions for such a motet, judging from accounts of practices in two venues known to Obrecht, Bruges and Antwerp; see Reinhard Strohm, *Music in Late Medieval Bruges*, rev. ed (Oxford: Clarendon Press, 1990), esp. 13–59; and Kristine K. Forney, "Music, Ritual and Patronage at the Church of Our Lady, Antwerp," *Early Music History* 7 (1987): 1–57.

44. Only the two manuscript sources of *Factor orbis*, Cappella Sistina 42 and Florence, Biblioteca Nazionale Centrale, MS II.I.232, provide the text of *O virgo virginum* at the conclusion of the motet; Petrucci's print (RISM 1508[1]) is lacking the *contratenor secundus* partbook that would include this text. Albert Smijers mistakenly supplied the text of *Canite tuba* instead of *O virgo virginum* at the end of the *secunda pars* in his edition of the motet (*Jacob Obrecht: Opera omnia, editio altera* (Amsterdam, 1953–64), 2/2: *Motetti*, 54–56).

45. Caplan, "A Late Mediaeval Tractate," 59.

Conflicting Levels of Meaning and Understanding in Josquin's *O admirabile commercium* Motet Cycle

As Willem Elders has pointed out in an article on the use of chant in Josquin's motets, Josquin's settings of five antiphon texts used at Lauds, Vespers, and other canonical hours of the Feast of the Circumcision (1 January)—"O admirabile commercium," "Quando natus es," a Rubum quem viderat," "Germinavit radix Jesse," and "Ecce Maria genuit"—"form a cycle unique in the works of Josquin in that their liturgical function is clear."[1] This implies that something concrete is known about these motets and the context in which they would have been performed (that is, how they were "heard") and presents them as a good subject for discussion in a conference devoted to "hearing the motet."

The sources of the motets (they are always transmitted as a group) are as follows.[2]

Cambridge, Magdalene College, Pepys MS 1760 [CambriP 1760], fols. 7^v–15^r (Josquin des Prez)[3]

Florence, Biblioteca Nazionale Centrale, MS II.I.232 [FlorBN II.I.232], fols. 35^v–40^r (Josquin)[4]

Florence, Biblioteca Mediceo-Laurenziana, MS Acquisti e Doni 666 [FlorL 666], fols. 14^v–22^r (Josquin)[5]

Paris, Bibliothèque Nationale, Fonds du Conservatoire, MS Rés. F. 41 [ParisBNC 41] (Jusquin)[6]

Vatican City, Biblioteca Apostolica Vaticana, Fondo Cappella Sistina 46 [VatS 46], fols. 50^v–55^r (Anonymous)[7]

Motetti libro primo (Venice: Antico, 1521) [1521^3] (Josquinus)

Secundus tomus novi operis musici (Nuremberg: Grapheus, 1538) [1538^3] (Josquini)

Because of the evidence of the sources and what I believe to be the high quality of the music, it can be confidently asserted that Josquin wrote the motets (this is no small claim these days); the source situation also suggests that they are fairly late works, possibly written after Josquin had returned from Italy to the north, in 1504.

It is also possible to identify at least one of the audiences for the motets. Although the date and place of composition have not been determined, three of the main sources of the motets indicate that the pieces were known in the Rome of Leo X (r. 1513–21): the motets are present in the Cappella Sistina manuscript VatS 46 (compiled during Leo's reign), in a manuscript most likely originally intended for Leo's private use, the so-called Medici Codex of 1518, FlorL 666, and in Antico's *Motetti libro primo* (1521[3]), first published in Rome in 1518.[8] That is, at least one of the audiences that heard these pieces probably consisted of the sophisticated clerical papal court.

We also can access to some degree the religious and musical background that such an audience would have brought to their hearing of the music. We can assume that they (like us) understood the texts (in fact may have known them by heart), that they (like us) could recognize the imagery used in the texts, that they (like us) had some experience of the normal chant melodies that set the texts, and that they (like us) could respond to obvious events in the foreground of the polyphony (imitation, cadences, when there were and were not duets, possibly recognizing when the first and last notes were the same, etc.). Therefore, we can, by investigating how we might hear the motets, learn something about the way the contemporary audience might have heard them.

So how would the motets have been heard? If they functioned liturgically as Elders suggests (that is, as antiphons), then they would have been presented as single pieces, each performed twice (before and after the chanting of entire psalms) in the course of the canonical hours for the Feast of the Circumcision. At Lauds, for instance, the performance presumably would be as follows: Motet 1, psalm, Motet 1; Motet 2, psalm, Motet 2; Motet 3, psalm, Motet 3; Motet 4, psalm, Motet 4; Motet 5, psalm, Motet 5. Motet 1 stands alone, followed by the progression 1 + 2, 2 + 3, 3 + 4, 4 + 5, with 5 then standing alone. All five motets would never be heard in a row, but perhaps the listeners would gain a better chance of remembering what went on in each individual work because of the repetition built into the liturgical function.

There is even something to suggest that the works were considered in this way. The five settings follow each other in the correct liturgical order in the sources and some of these (including the presumed earliest source, the French court MS CambriP 1760 [ca. 1509], as well as the Antico print) restate Josquin's name at the head of every setting, implying that these are separate pieces (indeed, Smijers gave the motets separate numbers).[9] The problem is that the occasions in which one would presumably hear the settings functioning as true antiphons were not ones in which antiphons to psalms were generally sung polyphonically; Lauds was not an Hour ever singled out for polyphony as far as I know, and even at Vespers, polyphony seems in fact to have been reserved for the Magnificat (and possibly the Magnificat antiphon) and the hymn. It is easy to see, then, why most scholars have assumed that the works comprise a five-part motet, a single piece in five movements; and indeed this is the way the settings are presented in other sources where Josquin's name is given only once at the head of *O admirabile* (the Italian MSS FlorL 666 and FlorBN II.I 232). There is some further corroborative evidence for that point of view also in the setting by Piéton (the only other setting of all five texts known to me), which is clearly labeled as a five-part motet (*prima pars, secunda pars*, etc.) in the print in which it appears.[10] In this view, the five settings would have been heard one after the other without interruption.

The liturgical function (if indeed it could be called that) of such a motet cycle was quite different from that of an antiphon, at least it was in the one place for which we can actually posit a performance of an *O admirabile* cycle, the papal court. Here, motets were used in the Mass as a kind of "filler" after the Offertory and the choice of motet was entirely arbitrary; the text did not have to be directly connected to the feast being celebrated.[11] Furthermore, there was an old tradition of the papal singers singing motets for the pope during the lunch that was held after Mass on important feast days; here the motet seems to reflect the monastic idea of readings during meals, but in any case, motets sung in this context were clearly extraliturgical and much more like "concert music." In fact, the Roman sources reflect both usages: one (VatS 46) is a manuscript prepared for the papal singers, while the other (FlorL 666) would have been intended for Leo's private singers, who could well have performed motets for the pope's private enjoyment. So knowing the liturgical function of the texts in fact tells little about how and where the music might have been heard.

But the amiguity of performance context, particularly of liturgical "suitability," does work very well with a theory of why Josquin chose these texts out of all liturgical texts available. Such a theory would state that he chose these texts for setting as an extended motet: (1) because the texts themselves are uniquely suited for presentation as a musical cycle; and (2) because the texts contain ambiguities and even conflicts of meaning that would be recognized by those hearing the motets, especially if they were highlighted by a composer who was supersensitive to texts and the listeners were not constrained to hear the motets in one particular liturgical context. In other words, the theory posits that Josquin set the texts precisely because he knew that the resultant polyphony would *not* be restricted to the Feast of the Circumcision. In fact, the actual texts were not originally intended for the Feast of the Circumcision, a feast which probably did not exist when the antiphons entered the Western liturgy, probably as translations of Byzantine originals, sometime in the sixth or seventh century and were attached to Christmas and then translated to the Octave of Christmas (which later became the Circumcision).[12]

Although it is true that by Josquin's time the liturgical connection of the antiphons with the Circumcision was clear (in VatS 46, for instance, the motets are placed in the liturgical order of the manuscript precisely at the point of the Circumcision, between Christmas and Epiphany), and it cannot be expected that many would have been cognizant of the historical circumstances of their entry into the liturgy, the texts did exist in another liturgical context. Jaquelyn Mattfeld, for instance, listed the settings among Josquin's Marian motets because she realized that they were also used as antiphons in the Saturday Commemorative Office of the Virgin to be said or sung between the Octave of Epiphany (13 January) and Purification (2 February).[13] Included in innumerable books of hours intended for private devotion, they had in this form a transmission that far exceeded that of breviaries or antiphonals. Indeed, the texts lend themselves to this double use. Although they do concern themselves with the Nativity and by extension with the doctrine of the Incarnation, a major theme of the Feast of the Circumcision, the Circumcision proper is never mentioned, and the emphasis of most of the texts seems clearly on Mary and her Virginity rather than on Christ. One sees a similar intrusion of Mary into the Circumcision in the iconographical record, where the Mother of God is often shown present and participating in a ceremony that, according to Jewish custom, she probably would not have attended. Andrea Mantegna even goes so far as to conflate the Circumcision with the Presentation at the Temple, the true Marian Feast of the Purification.[14]

A closer examination of the texts shows how they could be thought to form a cycle and how they create the double emphasis on Mary and on Christ.[15] The first indication of a text cycle is in the first and last words. The set of texts begins with the vocative "O" (used only once at the beginning) and ends with the standard concluding word "alleluia" (used only once as the last word). That tends to tie the texts together. They also can be divided in a 1 + 3 + 1 pattern: three closely connected texts surrounded by a "prelude" and a "postlude."

> 1. O admirabile commercium
>   Creator generis humani
>   animatum corpus sumens
>   de virgine nasci dignatus est.
>
> (O wondrous exchange! the Creator of man, having assumed a living body, deigned to be born of a Virgin, and having become man without man's aid, enriched us with His divinity.)[16]

This text enunciates one of the important themes of the Nativity and the Circumcision: the mystery of God actually *becoming* man through the Virgin birth, the Incarnation, demonstrated in the Nativity and proved by the act of circumcision, because only a real baby boy could shed blood. This was a matter of some importance, particularly in the time period under discussion. As Leo Steinberg has shown, representations of the Christ child in the late Middle Ages and Renaissance demonstrate a kind of fixation on that part of the male anatomy involved in the Circumcision because its very existence demonstrated that the Incarnation had taken place.[17]

> 2. Quando natus es ineffabiliter ex Virgine
>   tunc impletae sunt Scripturae
>   sicut pluvia in vellus descendisti
>   ut salvum faceres genus humanum
>   te laudamus Deus noster.

(By Your ineffable birth of a Virgin the Scriptures were fulfilled. Like rain upon the fleece You descended to save mankind. <u>Our God, we praise You.</u>)

The first of the central texts is addressed to Christ and announces what is going to be their main concern: the Virgin birth as a fulfillment of Scripture. In fact, what follows is a quotation from Scripture (the first in the antiphon cycle). The next phrase, "Like the rain upon the fleece You descended," is drawn directly from verse 6 of Psalm 71 ["Deus iudicium tuum regi da"]: the only thing that is changed is the verb. The psalm verse reads: "Descendet sicut pluvia in vellus: et sicut stillicidia stillantia super terram." (He shall descend like rain on the fleece: and like showers that drop upon the earth).

Curiously, the reference to rain on a fleece seems to make no sense in the context of this psalm verse, as the parallelism between raining on a fleece and showering the earth is not clear; in fact, "vellus" (fleece) seems to be a mistranslation by the Vulgate of the Hebrew word for grass or mown grass, as evidenced by the King James Version (where this is Ps. 72) which translates the verse as: "He shall come down like rain upon the mown grass; as showers that water the earth." However, the mistranslation turns out to have been a happy one for the purposes of the writer of the antiphon text, for it allows a reference to the Fleece of Gideon that was and was not watered by dew, and was one of the standard symbols of Mary's intact virginity (she remained a virgin after the birth of Christ).[18] So the fulfillment of Scripture is somehow more, or at least as much, Mary's virginity than it is the birth of Christ.

3. Rubum quem viderat Moyses incombustum
  conservatum agnovimus tuam laudabilem virginitatem
  Dei Genetrix intercede pro nobis.

(We recognize in the bush that Moses saw burning and yet not burnt, your virginity gloriously preserved. <u>Mother of God, intercede for us</u>).

The force of Scripture is carried forth in the next antiphon and at the same time the Virgin becomes central. It begins not with a quotation but with a reference to the burning bush,[19] another symbol of intact virginity, and ends with a direct invocation of the Virgin herself and plea for intercession (the only such plea in the text cycle).

4. Germinavit radix Jesse
  Orta est stella ex Jacob
  Virgo peperit Salvatorem
  Te laudamus Deus noster.

(The root of Jesse has blossomed; the star of Jacob has risen; a Virgin has brought forth the Savior. <u>Our God we praise you.</u>)

The density of scriptural references is greatest in the fourth antiphon, with at least two and possibly three direct references presented in a row: the root of Jesse from Isaiah,[20] the star of Jacob from the prophecy of Balaam (in Numbers),[21] and the birth of Christ from the annunciation of Gabriel to Mary in the New Testament (Luke).[22] The imagery now brings together Mother and Son. Mary is the rod ("virga") that grows from the root of Jesse and flowers (the flower being Christ),[23] she (according to Bernard of Clairvaux, at least) is also the star of Jacob, an image more often associated with Christ,[24] she receives the Annunciation, and she gives birth.

5. Ecce Maria genuit nobis Salvatorem
   quem Joannes videns exclamavit dicens
   Ecce Agnus Dei
   Ecce qui tollit peccata mundi
   Alleluia.

(Behold, Mary has given birth to our Savior. When John saw Him, he exclaimed: "Behold the Lamb of God; behold Him who takes away the sins of the world." Alleluia).

After all this emphasis on the Mother, in the concluding antiphon Christ finally appears; we actually "see" the result of the prophecies (and it is only here that a direct unaltered quotation from the Bible is used).[25] And with the word of rejoicing, the texts end.

Thus the texts can be read as an enunciation of the mystery of the Incarnation through virgin birth, followed by a progression of biblical symbols of Mary's virginity and prophecies of her unique role in the Incarnation (David, Gideon, Moses, Isaiah, Balaam; fleece, burning bush, root of Jesse, star of Jacob), followed by the specific prediction of the mystery (the Annunciation of Gabriel), followed by the actual physical manifestation of the mystery (what John the Baptist saw). In this sense the texts are "end-oriented" toward the birth of Christ and the concomitant doctrine of the Incarnation. Yet the symbolism of the texts leads in a different direction, toward Mary, reinforced by textual symmetry pointing toward the middle antiphon: the repetitions of "te laudamus deus noster" in the second and fourth antiphon (underlined in the translation). In a chiastic reading this would place the structural emphasis on the one antiphon of the cycle containing the direct invocation to the Virgin (underlined in the translation). Here, she becomes the most important figure in the text cycle. The point is that both readings are possible, something the early liturgists clearly recognized when they assigned the texts to Christological and Marian liturgies.

It would of course be too much to suggest that the chant composer or composers who set these texts would respond to the elaborate structure described above. Nonetheless, there seems to have been a recognition on the part of a surprising number of chant editors or notators of the symmetrical structure of antiphons 2 to 4. They reflect this by creating musical rhyme in the two musical settings of "te laudamus deus noster" in antiphons 2 and 4. This is evident in the very earliest sources and, in fact, the desire for musical rhyme was so strong that in many cases it overpowered the not insignificant fact that the two antiphons in question are supposed to be in different modes ("Quando natus es" in mode 3 on E, "Germinavit" in mode 2 on D). For instance, Example 9.1 shows the chant of these antiphons as it appears in a fourteenth-century manuscript from Saint-Martin of Tours (Tours, Bibliothèque Municipale, MS 149). The settings of "te laudamus" in this manuscript are identical,

EXAMPLE 9.1   (a) "Quando natus est" from Tours, Bibliothèque Municipale, 149 (a 14th-century winter breviary of Saint-Martin of Tours); (b) "Germinavit radix Jesse" from Tours, Bibliothèque Municipale, 149

meaning that the final of "Quando natus est" has become D, thus effectively changing the mode of the antiphon to the mode of "Germinavit" (indeed, they both have the same *seculorum amen*). German/Dutch sources take another tack: they change the mode of "Germinavit" instead by repeating the "te laudamus" of "Quando natus est" that ends on E (see Example 9.2). This point is worth making first because it is an interesting indication of the reaction to the texts and also because Josquin completely ignores this rather obvious cue for musical repetition in his setting; in fact he seems to go out of his way to negate it (see following discussion).

A full discussion of the antiphon chants and Josquin's use of them in the motets must be postponed to another time.[26] A preliminary study based on a number of chant sources of the antiphons produces results that are not heartening to anyone who wants to find the exact chants that Josquin utilized.[27] For instance, the manuscript of the usage of Saint-Martin of Tours represented by

EXAMPLE 9.2   "Te laudamus deus noster": (a) from "Quando natus est" in Utrecht, Bibliotheek der Rijksuniversiteit, 404 (a 15th-century antiphoner from the collegiate church of St. Mary, Utrecht); (b) from "Germinavit radix Jesse" in Utrecht 404

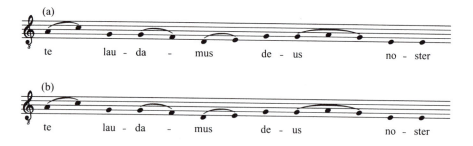

Example 9.1 would seem to be just perfect as a source for Josquin's chants, given what is surmised about his relationships to the French court.[28] And indeed, the chant that can be extrapolated from Josquin's polyphony is very close to the readings in Tours 149 until the last antiphon, "Ecce Maria." Here the Tours manuscript and all French manuscripts consulted by me (and a printed source from Cambrai) have a chant in the fifth mode, totally different from the one Josquin uses (which is in the second mode).[29] A search for a chant source of Josquin's "Ecce Maria" turns up a prototype in German sources and a closer version in Spanish sources (and the *Liber usualis*), but also in Rome in a Cappella Sistina manuscript copied around 1510 and therefore very close to Josquin's own sojourn in that city.[30] This last would seem to be especially significant, given Josquin's known association with the papal chapel, were it not that the other chants of the antiphons in this manuscript contain radical differences from the chants Josquin seems to have used.

In fact, preliminary research suggests the uncomfortable conclusion that looking for specific chant traditions in these motets will lead to a dead end, not the least because the paraphrase technique Josquin uses obscures the details of the chant. Furthermore, it could be posited that the settings do not represent any one chant source or tradition and may represent a purposeful conflation of traditions.[31] As an example, consider the setting of the word "descendisti" in *Quando natus es*, where such a conflation of chant versions seems to have taken place, a conflation that further led Josquin's musical imagination in a strange direction. Example 9.3 gives the polyphonic setting.

There seem to have been two chant traditions of setting these words; one sets them as *a–g–b–a* (see Example 9.1a); another tradition sets them as *a–g–c′–a*. Example 9.4a and b gives the two chant versions adopting Josquin's transposition down a step, followed by the chant that can be extrapolated from Josquin's setting (Example 9.4c), which appears to incorporate both versions. This seems to have given him an idea by reminding him of another use he had made of very similar material, represented as Example 9.4d. This, of course, is the famous "Hercules dux Ferrariae" cantus firmus. The clue that this hypothesis might indeed represent Josquin's thought process at this point is that the

Example 9.4   (a) Chant version 1 of "descendisti"; (b) chant version 2 of "descendisti"; (c) chant version apparently used by Josquin; (d) the "Hercules dux Ferrariae" motive

EXAMPLE 9.5　Josquin, *Missa Hercules Dux Ferrariae*, Gloria, mm. 19–25

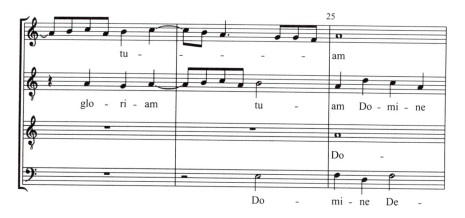

polyphonic setting of "descendisti" is almost a direct quote from a passage in the Gloria of the *Missa Hercules dux Ferrariae* (Gloria, mm. 19–25—see Example 9.5). There seems to be no motivation for creating this relationship other than the purely musical one just outlined.

Returning to the main question regarding text cycles and ambiguities of meaning, it seems demonstrable that Josquin's large-scale response to the texts as texts is indeed a musical reflection of their cyclic construction.[32] For instance, consideration of the first notes of the antiphons shows that Josquin has, by manipulating chant transpositions and imitation, arranged it so that the three central antiphons all begin on the same note (D), something not reflected in the chant settings but a good way of tying the polyphonic settings together. The last notes of the antiphons (the root of the final chords) produce the sequence Bb, D, A, G, G where the chant had F, E, E, D, D. Here, Bb and G enclose the three central antiphons that are tied together by fifth relationships: the D of antiphon 2 is fifth-related to the G of antiphon 4, while the A of antiphon 3 is fifth-related to the end of antiphon 2 (D), and to the beginning of antiphon 4 (which ends on G but begins on D). This tends to emphasize the outline of a triad (G minor) in the finals of all the antiphons save one. Josquin used a similar technique of manipulating chant transposition in another cycle based on different chants, the *Missa de Beata Virgine* (where a C major triad is outlined: the Kyrie and Gloria end on G, the Sanctus and Agnus end on C, and the Credo ends on E).[33] The analogy does not quite work because in *O admirabile* the third antiphon ends on a final unrelated to the triad being outlined. But in context, that only serves to highlight musically that antiphon's centrality and importance to the basic dichotomy of reference in the texts; the antiphon with the anomalous A final is the one exactly in the middle, the one that speaks directly to the Virgin.

The choice of finals would appear to argue that Josquin is trying to demonstrate structurally the centrality of the Virgin suggested by the structure of the texts. Yet a structure created by final chords is not really something that would be immediately audible. Much more audible are strong indications that Josquin wished more to concentrate on the forward motion of the texts' meaning, and that his musical setting is "end-oriented." This can be seen in his resistance to the chance to reinforce through musical rhyme the symmetry that the chant notators noticed in the repetitions of the text "te laudamus deus noster" in antiphons 2 and 4. Josquin ignores this completely; not only are the two polyphonic settings not identical, they are not even equivalent. In setting the "te laudamus" of antiphon 2, Josquin abandons the antiphon chant entirely, thereby making sure that not even a residual resemblance will remain with the setting in antiphon 4, which does quote the chant. But that does not mean that Josquin thereby ignores the emphasis that the texts give to Mary. Arguably the most surprising thing that happens in the cycle is the sudden shift in antiphon 3, the central one, from the expected D-Phrygian final to its dominant A at the point of the invocation of the Virgin, an invocation in which the antiphon chant has been abandoned for a chant-like prayer for intercession possibly made even more striking by the sharp that indeed could have been added to the A triad that ends the motet. This puts the spotlight on Mary in a clearly audible way that musical rhyme does not and also pushes the listener to expect the beginning of the next, and I would argue, most dramatic and problematic of the motets, *Germinavit radix Jesse*, the only one to be discussed in detail in this study.

First the chant setting (see Example 9.1b). The progress of the chant can easily be described: Each phrase is clearly demarcated and the musical setting reinforces the coherent reading of the text in the following way: "Germinavit radix Jesse; orta est stella ex Jacob. Virgo peperit Salvatorem. Te laudamus deus noster." "Germinavit radix Jesse" is a phrase rising gently from the final to the fifth (on "radix") then descending for an inconclusive close on the subfinal *c* (thereby encompassing the entire range of the antiphon) but leading naturally to "Orta est stella ex Jacob," which uses the subfinal to leap a fourth, rising more quickly than the first phrase to the fifth, possibly in reaction to the meaning of the text, but making a cadence on the reciting tone of the second mode, F, on "Jacob." "Virgo peperit Salvatorem" takes off from the reciting tone (actually repeats the music for "ex Jacob"), rises to the fifth, and gently descends back down to the final. "Te laudamus deus noster" rises from the final to the fifth in the quickest motion so far, then descends to the subfinal, rising again and coming to rest on the final.

The correct way to set this text would be obvious to any composer with sense. As an example, consider Piéton's setting, based on a chant very like the one in Example 9.1b (see Example 9.6).[34] Piéton responds to the text and the chant exactly the way he is supposed to: the chant is clearly present, the points of imitation correspond to the beginings of the text phrases, the first two phrases are run together in the polyphony, but there is a clear, unambiguous (one might say ponderous) cadence on "Jacob," after which the piece picks up again with a cadence on the final at "salvatorem" and concludes with a "te laudamus deus noster" (not shown in the example) that is repeated exactly for emphasis. There is little difference between Piéton's reading and a chant singer's reading of this antiphon as regards its meaning and syntax.

Compared to this, Josquin's setting is positively perverse.[35] It starts out innocently enough with the first Old Testament prophecy, "Germinavit radix Jesse," presented in fairly standard interlocking duets presenting the chant at pitch (D) in the bassus and altus and transposed (G) in the tenor and superius.[36] Only the superius and altus, however, follow the chant by closing on the subfinal (*f* in the motet, *c* in the chant—see Example 9.1b) in measure 19, that cadence on F interlocking in measures 18–19 with the beginning of the next prophecy, "Orta est stella ex Jacob." The main thing about the setting of this line of text is the way the music lifts the listener to the stars (indeed it is the word "stella" that stands out here), starting in the bassus, adding the successive voices, increasing the tension with two close cadences on B-flat in the bassus in measures 22 and 27 (the first time all four voices sing at once) as the setting moves toward the end of the text: "ex Jacob." Those cadences indicate that the goal of motion at "Jacob" is precisely what the chant dictates, the third of the mode (see Example 9.1b). But at the cadence on B-flat between the superius and tenor on "Jacob" (in m. 31—which is, by the way, as with the equivalent cadence in the Piéton setting, about halfway through the motet), the whole thing is negated by the continuing counterpoint in the altus and bassus arising out of a typical "evasion" of the cadence as the bassus moves from *f* in measure 30 (which supports the cadence on B-flat) to *g* in measure 31, making it impossible to hear the cadence between superius and tenor as strong (see Example 9.7). That might be disturbing; what follows is worse.

In measures 32–40 (see Example 9.7) the motet appears to approach the strongest cadence yet, on B-flat, the clear goal of motion of this entire section, reached in measure 40, made the result of a strong expectation through close imitation and repetition, first in three voices, then in four, of an unmistakable cadential phrase (mm. 32–36 in the tenor are repeated as mm. 37–40 in the superius), a kind of reinforcing closure that is very audible (in fact it has a chanson-like quality to it).

But there is a problem here. It is true that the B-flat cadence is duly made between the superius and tenor in measure 40. Yet the altus does not really participate in the cadence (having reached its note a measure before), and the

EXAMPLE 9.6   Piéton's setting of *Germinavit radix Jesse*, mm. 24–40, transcribed from 1532[10]

EXAMPLE 9.7 Josquin's setting of *Germinavit radix Jesse*, mm. 31–50, transcribed from CambriP 1760, fols. 12ᵛ–13ʳ. Bracketed text in the tenor follows VatS 46, fol. 53ᵛ

EXAMPLE 9.7   (*continued*)

bassus, which could have reinforced the cadence with an *f–B♭* move, suddenly drops out while the superius is given no chance to pause, moving immediately into a duet with the bassus. Then there is a curious ambiguity regarding the text placement. The cadence would appear to be on the word "peperit." But while the sources seem to agree that the word at the cadence for superius, altus, and bassus is "peperit," they disagree as to the word to be sung by the tenor. At least two of the most authoritative sources (CambriP 1760 and FlorI 666, sources that, according to Cummings, are unrelated)[37] have the tenor singing "salvatorem" here while at least one (VatS 46) continues "peperit" in the tenor (see Example 9.7).[38] The point is that to make a cadence on "salvatorem" is clearly correct, but to make a cadence on "peperit" is clearly a misreading of the text; the text phrase is not "Virgo peperit," it is "Virgo peperit salvatorem." We will, of course, never know what Josquin's true "intentions" were regarding this passage, but the disposition of the sources suggests strongly that the original exemplar introduced an ambiguity at "Virgo peperit salvatorem" (as Piéton's almost certainly did not); either it had "salvatorem" in the tenor and "peperit" in the other voices and was followed by some scribes, or it did not indicate "salvatorem" in the tenor and scribes in certain venues felt obligated to have the tenor (the "official" carrier of the cantus firmus) continue the text phrase in the correct way and added "salvatorem." This is anything but strightforward and it might be worthwhile to consider its implications.

What would happen in a performance of this passage following any of the extant sources? It seems entirely likely that the force of the surrounding voices singing a different word would effectively obscure the tenor's word, leading the listeners to hear "peperit" as the true (but not overwhelming) goal of motion, something that would, of course, be clearer if the tenor did not sing "salvatorem." But either way, it could be argued that Josquin's setting deliberately and uncomfortably misreads the text in a way that emphasizes, not the child, but the mother; strongly if all voices sing "peperit," bringing the two together if the tenor sings "salvatorem" (the child ["salvatorem"] then is, after all, literally "within" the mother who gives birth ["peperit"]). One might argue that the force of this is to stress musically that it is what the mother does that is important; it is the mother's achievement that is the climax of the Old Testament prophecies. The child—"salvatorem"—finally appears in all voices as a curious yet insistent afterthought; the texture suddenly dissolves into five short imitative duets that seem to "float," balancing through insistence the previous emphasis on "peperit."[39]

So the sense of the motet as a reading of the text up to this point is: "Germinavit radix Jesse; orta est STELLA (ex Jacob); Virgo peperit(!)" "Salvatorem" (salvatorem, salvatorem, salvatorem, salvatorem). But before "salvatorem" is finished, another misreading is thrust upon us. In measure 47, a clear chant quotation begins (easily recognizable in its long notes, easily heard because it enters at the top of the tenor range as the highest notes at that point—see Example 9.7). The words are "Te laudamus" and the listeners all would have known that the text really is "te laudamus deus noster." But because Josquin is not finished with "salvatorem" in the other voices (there is no text-setting problem here, and in any case the word would have been ringing in their ears because of all the repetitions) they actually would have heard another grammatical construction not envisioned by the writer of the antiphon text: "Te Salvatorem laudamus." Since the text then goes on, the following reading would be heard: "Te (salvatorem) laudamus . . . deus noster."

Christ ("Salvatorem") and God ("deus") have become one through music. The Mother has given birth; the Savior is the birth; the Savior is God; the Incarnation has taken place. We praise You, our God. The doctrine of the Incarnation is thus made musically evident. At the same time the double emphasis of the whole cycle of texts on Mary and Christ has also been presented in musical terms that would be especially relevant to hearers who knew the texts intimately. Thus, the motet could be heard as a dramatic (mis)reading of the antiphon text, with the climax of all the ambiguities and multiple readings inherent in the previous texts reached at measures 40ff., the stretched out "te laudamus deus noster" acting as a kind of denouement, a relaxation after extreme tension (bearing in mind of course the scale of the pieces and the musical forces employed). Of course, such a "hearing" of the piece would probably require almost a full stop on the cadence in measure 40, probably after an accellerando in the previous measures. I have consulted two recordings of the antiphon cycle. In both of them, the performers strive to negate Josquin's misreading (realizing it for the misreading it is) by getting off the cadence in measure 40 as quickly as possible.[40] It might be interesting if someone tried it the other way.

Now, in spite of what has been said about the motets as a cycle, what if it were heard, not as a cycle, but "liturgically" (that is, as separate pieces)? The large structure might be lost, but the force of the individual close readings would not be. Thus, it could be argued that the liturgical and interpretive ambiguities posed by the texts are in fact addressed by the polyphony: the motets could work as well as antiphons as they do as the continuous cycle in which they were originally composed; the chant references could be considered to reflect different chant traditions while, more important, the musical settings of the texts as a whole and in particular show enormous sensitivity to the imagery that makes these texts perfectly appropriate for two entirely different types of celebrations. In short, it would appear that Josquin has composed a work that would exist comfortably in all the different places that its circulation would take it (and since these seem to be late works, Josquin would have known that there would be a wide circulation).

The publisher George Thomson once grumpily remarked in reference to Beethoven's settings of Irish and Scottish songs, which were too difficult for the amateurs for whom Thomson intended them, that Beethoven "composes for posterity."[41] That, perhaps, is too much to expect of a Renaissance composer, but we still might posit that Josquin composed *O admirabile commercium* with all it multifarious readings and hearings for an audience wider than his immediate colleagues, an audience that stretched across Europe from Condé to the court of France to the court of the Pope and (unbeknownst to him) across the centuries to us.

APPENDIX

Chant Sources Consulted

Arras. Bibliothèque Municipale, 465 (893).

Bamberg. Staatsbliothek, Lit. Hs. 25 (Ed.IV.11).

Benevento. Biblioteca Capitolare, IV-19.

Cambrai. Bibliothèque Municipale, Impre. XVI C4.

Cambridge. University Library, Mm.2.9 (Sarum Antiphoner)

Huesca. Archivo de la Catedral, 2.

Huesca. Archivo de la Catedral, 7.

Karlsruhe. Badische Landesbibliothek, Aug. LX

Karlsruhe. Badische Landesbibliothek, Cod. St. Georgen 6

Lucca. Biblioteca Capitolare Feliniana, 601.

Lucca. Biblioteca Capitolare Feliniana, 602.

Lucca. Biblioteca Capitolare Feliniana, 603.

Metz. Bibliothèque Municipale, 461.

Paris. Bibliothèque de l'Arsenal, 279.

Paris. Bibliothèque Nationale, lat. 12584.

St. Gall. Stiftsbibliothek, 390–91 (Codex Hartker)

Tours. Bibliothèque Municipale, 149.

Troyes. Bibliothèque Municipale, 571.

Troyes. Bibliothèque Municipale, 720.

Turin. Biblioteca Nazionale, F.IV.4.

Vorau. Stiftsbibliothek, 287 (29).

Vatican City. Biblioteca Apostolica Vaticana, fondo Cappella Sistina 27.

Utrecht. Bibliotheek der Rijksuniversiteit, 404.

NOTES

1. Willem Elders, "Plainchant in the Motets, Hymns, and Magnificat of Josquin des Prez," in *Proceedings of the International Josquin Festival-Conference*, ed. Edward E. Lowinsky (London: Oxford University Press, 1976), 523–42, esp. 536.

2. For a discussion of the sources and their relationships to one another, see Anthony M. Cummings, "The Transmission of Some Josquin Motets," *Journal of the Royal Musical Association* 115 (1990): 1–21.

3. Facsimile edition in the series Renaissance Manuscripts in Facsimile 2 (New York: Garland, 1988).

4. See Anthony M. Cummings, "A Florentine Sacred Repertory from the Medici Restoration (Manuscript II.I.232 of the Biblioteca Nazionale Centrale, Firenze)" (Ph.D. diss., Princeton University, 1980).

5. See Edward E. Lowinsky, ed., *The Medici Codex of 1518*, Monuments of Renaissance Music 3–5 (Chicago: University of Chicago Press, 1968).

6. The motets are manuscript additions to a print of the Masses of Carpentras (Avignon, 1532), RISM G1571.

7. Facsimile edition in Renaissance Music in Facsimile 21 (New York: Garland, 1986).

8. On VatS 46, see the introduction by Jeffrey Dean to the facsimile edition; the literature on the Medici Codex is too vast to reproduce here; on the Antico print, see Martin Picker, ed., *The Motet Books of Andrea Antico*, Monuments of Renaissance Music 8 (Chicago: University of Chicago Press, 1987), 3; and Picker, "The Motet Anthologies of Andrea Antico," in *A Musical Offering: Essays in Honor of Martin Bernstein*, ed. Edward H. Clinkscale and Claire Brook (New York: Pendragon Press, 1977), 211–38.

9. See *Werken van Josquin des Prés*, ed. Albert Smijers (Amsterdam: G. Alsbach, 1926–64), Motets nos. 5–9.

10.. *Primus liber cum quatuor vocibus. Motteti del fiore* (Lyons: Moderne, 1532), 1532[10].

11. See Anthony M. Cummings, "Toward an Interpretation of the Sixteenth-Century Motet," *Journal of the American Musicological Society* 34 (1981): 43–59.

12. See D. O. Rousseau, "Les Antiennes de la Circoncision," *Revue Liturgique et Monastique* 10 (1924–25): 55–61; A. Hodüm, "O admirabile commercium," *Collationes Brugenses* 32 (1932): 394–409; Anton Baumstark, "Byzantinisches in den Weinachtstexten des römischen Antiphonarius Officii," *Oriens Christianus*, 3d ser., 9 (1936): 163–87; Hieronimus Frank, "Das Alter des römischen Laudes- und Vesperantiphonen der Weihnachtsoktav und ihrer griechischen Originale," *Oriens Christianus*, 3d ser., 14 (1939–41): 14–18; Wulf Arlt, *Ein Festoffizium des Mittelalters aus Beauvais in seiner liturgischen und musikalischen Bedeutung*, 2 vols. (Cologne: Arno Volk Verlag, 1970).

13. Jacquelyn A. Mattfeld, "Some Relationships between Texts and Cantus Firmi in the Liturgical Motets of Josquin des Prés," *Journal of the American Musicological Society* 14 (1961): 159–83. Indeed, as Arlt (*Ein Festoffizium*, 1:39) has pointed out, the Octave of Christmas, the first feast to which these texts were translated, was originally celebrated as a Marian feast.

14. See Jack M. Greenstein, *Mantegna and Painting as Historical Narrative* (Chicago: University of Chicago Press, 1992), 143–80.

15. Here I build on the published studies of the texts mentioned in n. 12.

16. Translations adapted from Lowinsky, *The Medici Codex*, 3:130.

17. Leo Steinberg, *The Sexuality of Christ in Renaissance Art and in Modern Oblivion* (New York: Pantheon, 1983).

18. Cf. Judges 6:36–40.

19. Exod. 3:1–3.

20. Isa. 11:1 "Et egredietur virga de radice Jesse et flos de radice eius ascendet."

21. Num. 24:17: "Orietur stella ex Jacob."

22. Luke 1:31: "Ecce concipies et paries Filium èt vocabis nomen ejus Jesum."

23. See Louis Réau, *Iconographie de l'art chrétien* (Paris: Presses Universitaires de France, 1955–59), 2:2, 129–40.

24. See *Magnificat, Homilies in Praise of the Blessed Virgin Mary by Bernard of Clairvaux and Amadeus of Lausanne*, trans. Marie-Bernard Saïd and Grace Perico (Kalamazoo: Cistercian Publications, 1979), 30, Homily II of Bernard: "She is indeed that noble star risen out of Jacob."

25. John 1:29: "Altera die vidit Ioannes Iesum venientem ad se et ait: Ecce agnus Dei, ecce qui tollit peccata mundi."

26. I hope to consider all the motets in more detail in a future study.

27. A list of chant sources consulted for this study (derived from the CANTUS database at the Catholic University of America) is appended to this article. I am extremely grateful to Ruth Steiner and two graduate students at the Catholic University of America, Charles Downey and Keith Glaeske, who went way beyond the call of duty in responding to what I thought was a simple question about chant sources of the antiphons. See also Ruth Steiner, "Antiphons for Lauds on The Octave of Christmas," in *Laborare fratres in unum: Festschrift László Dobzay zum 60. Geburtstag*, Spolia Berolinensia, vol. 7, ed. Janka Szendrei; and David Hiley (Hildesheim: Weidmann, 1995), 307–15.

28. See Patrick Macey, "Josquin's *Misericordias Domini* and Louis XI," *Early Music* 19 (1991): 163–77.

29. In fact, the French source of the polyphonic O *admirabile* cycle (CambriP 1760) also contains a setting of *Ecce Maria* by the French court composer Mouton that uses the "French" chant.

30. VatS 27.

31. I do not make this claim about all of Josquin's chant-based music, of course, although it might be recalled here that in the course of his career Josquin worked in a number of centers and was thereby exposed to different chant traditions.

32. For reasons of space, the motets cannot be presented here. The most accessible edition is in Lowinsky, ed., *The Medici Codex*, 4:33–47.

33. That this was not originally composed as a cycle is irrelevant to the present argument.

34. For reasons of space, the entire motet cannot be presented here (it was sung in its entirety by the Hilliard Ensemble during the conference). Piéton's O *admirabile* motets will eventually be published in vol. 9 of my series Sixteenth-Century Motet (New York: Garland, 1987–).

35. See Lowinsky, *The Medici Codex*, 4:41–44. Lowinsky discusses the use of chant in this motet in his Commentary, 3:130.

36. I ignore here the problem of conflicting signatures.

37. Cummings, "The Transmission of Some Josquin Motets."

38. Of course, I am speaking here only of the *general* sense of the text, not the exact placement of the syllables (which is not specified). I have been unable to consult every source of the motets.

39. They do so even more because Josquin has emended the chant again, this time I think on his own. The chant approaches to the final on "salvatorem" are always from the fourth (*g–d* in Example 9.1b). Yet Josquin, in his tenor, seems to have elevated the fourth to a fifth (*d–g*), thereby strengthening the move to the final G that is the musical goal of this phrase.

40. *Missus est Gabriel angelus: Motetten van Mouton, Josquin, Obrecht*, Cappella Pratensis, Rebecca Stewart, dir. Jubal CD ZV 91133–2 (1991); *O Magnum Mysterium: Christmas Motets from Renaissance Europe*, Fortuna, Patricia Petersen, dir. Titanic Ti-211 (1992). I am grateful to Peter Urquhart for directing me to these recordings.

41. Joel Sachs, "Hummel and George Thomson of Edinburgh," *Musical Quarterly* 56 (1970): 270–87, at. 271, n. 3.

Josquin, Good King René,
and O *bone et dulcissime Jesu*

S tudents of Josquin's music must wrestle with a series of difficult problems,
not the least of which is the construction of a chronology for his works. The
lack of securely datable sources, indeed of hardly any sources datable before
approximately 1490, when Josquin had already reached middle age, makes the
task especially daunting. As well, there are still gaps in Josquin's biography, so
that his activities and patrons remain shrouded in mystery for important parts
of his career. We have no records concerning Josquin's early years or his training—presumably as a choirboy in northern France at the collegiate church of
St-Quentin, if a French seventeenth-century source is accurate.[1] The main
centers of Josquin's activity seem to have been in Italy, but recently new evidence indicates that he also worked in France, and this will have a direct
bearing on material presented in this study.

As a brief reminder of what we do know about his career, a certain "Judo-
cho de frantia" turns up in Milan as a "biscantor" in 1459 and remains in the
cathedral choir for some 14 years.[2] If this singer is indeed Josquin des Prez,
then in 1473 he transfers to the court chapel of Duke Galeazzo Maria Sforza,
where he receives handsome remuneration.[3] His good fortune is short-lived,
however, for just three years later, in December of 1476, the duke is assassi-
nated. By April 1477 Josquin is in southern France at Aix-en-Provence, the
court of the art-loving René d'Anjou, also known as Good King René; somewhat later, in 1478, he is in line to receive a benefice from René.[4] René
inherited many illustrious titles from his Angevin ancestors, including the hon-
orary title of King of Jerusalem and the real title of King of Sicily (including
Naples); further details about his patronage will emerge below. In addition to
contact with René, Josquin must have maintained ties with Milan as well, for
in 1479 he received a travel pass to leave Milan and visit the shrine of St-
Antoine-de-Vienne, to the southeast of Lyon.

For the next stage of his career I believe Josquin had ties with the court of

King Louis XI of France at some point between 1480 and 1483, although no primary documents survive that would place him securely in France during these years. But the text of Josquin's *Misericordias domini* held special importance for Louis XI in the years just prior to that monarch's death in 1483, and this circumstantial evidence will be briefly reviewed below.

The next certain date for Josquin's whereabouts is 1483; a document discovered by Herbert Kellman notes his arrival sometime between January 6 and March 30 in Condé-sur-l'Escaut, a small town in the Imperial County of Hainaut. Today the town lies in France, close to the Belgian border. The document states that this is "Josquin's first return after the French wars," thus indicating previous visits to Condé.[5]

A recent study by Peter Király cites evidence that Josquin served at the court of King Matthias Corvinus in Hungary sometime in the 1480s, perhaps after leaving Condé-sur-l'Escaut, and certainly before the death of Corvinus in 1490.[6] In 1476 the Hungarian king had married Beatrice of Aragon, a former pupil of Tinctoris in Naples, and she had proceeded to import many Italian musicians to her court in Hungary, including Pietrobono, the famous lutenist from Ferrara. It would come as no surprise to learn that Josquin too sojourned at such an illustrious court.

Josquin subsequently sang in the papal chapel in Rome from approximately 1489 until at least 1494,[7] then spent a year as *maestro di cappella* to the aged Duke Ercole I d'Este of Ferrara in 1503–4, before finally retiring to Condé in 1504, where he lived until his death in 1521.

It is apparent from this brief overview of Josquin's career that significant periods remain incompletely documented, including 1480–82, 1483–89, and 1495–1502. Faced with this rather moth-eaten biographical record, as well as a lack of early sources for Josquin's music, our next resort is to turn to the music itself—in this case, the motets. Here we can focus on two aspects: the provenance of the motet texts, and musical style. Style can be deceptive in an attempt to construct a chronology of works, because experienced composers from this period had at their fingertips a number of different styles from which to choose, depending on the type of text to be set, the occasion, and the patron's own particular tastes. Nevertheless, scholars such as Ludwig Finscher and Joshua Rifkin have led the way in developing a consensus about the kind of music Josquin composed in Milan, based in part on the presence of similar traits in the music of Loyset Compère and Gaspar van Weerbeke, who were Josquin's colleagues in the chapel of Galeazzo Maria Sforza in the 1470s.[8]

But I would like to defer discussion of musical style for a moment, and focus first on a few of the texts for Josquin's motets, particularly nonliturgical texts that might be associated with individual patrons. These hold an advantage over liturgical texts like the Marian antiphons *Salve regina* or *Alma redemptoris mater*, because the common occurrence of the latter texts in the polyphonic repertory generally precludes the possibility of relating them to any particular patron. On the other hand, two unique texts that were set to music by Josquin can be associated with individual patrons, and these are *Misericordias domini* and *O bone et dulcissime Jesu*.

First, with regard to *Misericordias domini*, the text is a unique compilation from various psalms (only two lines do not appear to derive from biblical sources, including line 2 and "O quam bonus dominus, o quam dulcis" in the *secunda pars*).[9]

prima pars

Misericordias domini in aeternum cantabo.
Misericordia domini cuncta creata sunt.
Misericordia domini plena est terra.
Misericordia domini quia non sumus consumpti.

secunda pars

Quoniam est dominus suavis, et mitis, et patiens,
et multum misericors, et multae misericordiae
omnibus invocantibus eum.
O quam bonus dominus, o quam dulcis,
o quam suavis est dominus universis
et miserationes ejus super omnia opera ejus.

tertia pars

Miserere nostri, domine, miserere nostri.
Fiat misericordia tua, domine, super nos,
quemadmodum speravimus in te.
In te, domine, speravi,
non confundar in aeternum. Amen.

(I will sing the mercies of the Lord forever.
By the mercy of the Lord all things are created.
With the mercy of the Lord the earth is filled.
Through the mercy of the Lord we are not destroyed.

For the Lord is gentle, and mild, and patient,
and plenteous in mercy, and plenteous in mercies
to all who call upon him.
O how good is the Lord, O how sweet,
O how pleasant is the Lord to all,
and his mercies are over all his works.

Have mercy on us, O Lord, have mercy on us.
Let thy mercy, O Lord, be upon us,
because we have hoped in thee.
In thee, Lord, I have hoped,
let me not be condemned for eternity. Amen.)

The first line of this text held special meaning for Louis XI of France. In 1481 he had it painted in gold and azure on no fewer than 50 scrolls by his court artist, Jean Bourdichon, and he then proceeded to have the scrolls displayed in various locations at his chateau of Plessis-les-Tours. On his deathbed in 1483, Louis's final words were "In te domine speravi, non confundar in aeternum,"

EXAMPLE 10.1   Josquin, *Misericordias domini*, superius, mm. 1–10

EXAMPLE 10.2   *Misericordias domini*, mm. 10–14

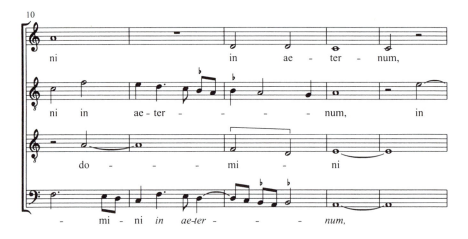

followed by "misericordias domini in aeternum cantabo," the closing and opening phrases of the motet, respectively. Given the importance of these texts to the king, the possibility arises that Josquin composed his work at the dying monarch's behest so that he could hear it sung in his chapel and at his sickbed. Subsequently the motet could have served as a monument to his memory, as well as a reminder to the Lord of the king's good works, which included lavish endowments for collegiate chapels to sing Masses for his soul. Louis did indeed plan to have the mercies of the Lord sung forever!

Having established a probable context and time (ca. 1480–83) for the composition of *Misericordias domini*, a brief look at Josquin's musical setting is in order; some striking parallels with *O bone et dulcissime Jesu* will emerge later. Josquin employs various musical strategies to emphasize the regular occurrences of the word "domini" as the motet reiterates over and over its plea for the Lord's mercy. The paired imitative entries at the opening feature an unadorned subject with repeated notes and an ascending leap of a fifth; the superius (shown in Example 10.1) proceeds up to the seventh degree to the peak note c″ at "domini." After a deceptive cadence in measure 10, the lower voices continue on to a Phrygian cadence in measure 13 (Example 10.2); the superius rests for a measure, but then reenters at "in aeternum" to fill out the cadential third. Near the end of the motet, the superius repeats this rather curious entry; I will return to this detail below.[10]

Josquin further emphasizes "domini" in the fourth phrase of text in the *prima pars* in a series of strictly canonic entries, again with leaps up to *a'* as at the opening, followed by scalewise descents, and finally an ascent to the peak *d"* in bar 79 on "domini" (Example 10.3). This descending scalar motion calls to mind a cascade because it resembles a slow-motion waterfall in sound; it plays an important role in *Misericordias*, for Josquin uses it to create key climactic events in the *secunda* and *tertia partes*, as we shall see.

In the *secunda pars*, the principle of *varietas* is apparent as Josquin presents a series of exquisitely crafted paired duets on "O quam bonus dominus, o quam dulcis," that contrast with the preceding full-voiced section. The music evolves effortlessly from these duos to a forceful passage at the words "o quam suavis est dominus," where the full complement of voices brings back the cascade figure from the *prima pars*, but now in condensed form. The voices enter canonically, each leaping two fourths in succession (outlining a minor seventh) in a striking ascent to the peak on "dominus" before cascading back down the scale (Example 10.4).

A further variation on the cascade appears at the end of the *tertia pars* where Josquin reverses the figure's direction so that now the voices ascend the scale, again outlining a minor seventh (Example 10.5). Here Josquin extends the figure by linking together three distinct ascending passages; this powerful conclusion makes an unforgettable impression on the listener.

Several aspects of the musical style of *Misericordias domini* add up to support a dating for the work around 1480. First, there are prominent features that recall Milanese motets of the 1470s, including the use of the cascade figure.[11] In particular, the principle of *varietas* is evident, as almost every phrase of the motet features some new textural or mensural approach. Other contrapuntal procedures recall Milanese works by Weerbeke and Compère, such as the device in which one voice in strict imitation drops out soon after the entry of the next imitative voice. All of these stylistic factors jibe with the evidence afforded by the text of the motet, which itself provided the initial clue for dating the piece around 1480.

Turning to the next motet, *O bone et dulcissime Jesu*, again our initial focus falls on the provenance of the text, which is a prayer found in just a few Books of Hours from the fifteenth century. Josquin's version of the text is as follows:

1. O bone et dulcissime Jesu,
   per tuam misericordiam esto mihi Jesus.
2. Quid est Jesus nisi plasmator,
   nisi redemptor, nisi salvator?
3. Ergo, bone et dulcissime Jesu,
   qui me plasmasti tua benignitate,
   rogo te, ne pereat opus tuum mea iniquitate.
4. Ergo quaeso anhelo suspiro,
   ne perdas quod tua fecit omnipotens divinitas.

EXAMPLE 10.3 *Misericordias domini*, mm. 68–82

EXAMPLE 10.4   *Misericordias domini,* mm. 175–81

175

O   quam   su - a - vis   est   do - mi - nus

5. Recognosce quod tuum est
   et ne respicias quod meum est.
6. Noli cogitare malum meum,
   ut obliviscaris bonum meum.

secunda pars

7. Si ego commisi per quod dannare me debes,
   tu non amisisti, unde salvare me potes.
8. Et si secundum iustitiam tuam dannare me vis,
   ad tuam piissimam et ineffabilem misericordiam appello.
9. Ergo quaeso: miserere mei
   secundum magnam misericordiam et pietatem tuam. Amen.

(1. O good and most sweet Jesus,
    through your mercy you shall be Jesus to me.
2. What is Jesus if not a shaper,
   if not a redeemer, if not a savior?
3. Therefore, good and most sweet Jesus,
   who have shaped me through your goodness,
   I ask that you not let your handiwork perish through my iniquity.
4. Therefore I beseech you, I draw heavy breath, I sigh,
   so that you may not destroy what your omnipotent divinity has made.
5. Recognize what is yours,
   and do not consider my deeds.
6. Do not reflect on my evil,
   so that you do not forget my good.

7. If I have committed that for which you ought to damn me,
   you have nevertheless not sent me away, so that you might save me.
8. And if according to your justice you wish to damn me,
   I entreat your most compassionate and ineffable mercy.
9. Thus I beseech you: have mercy on me
   according to your great and compassionate mercy. Amen.)

After examining several hundred Books of Hours during the course of the past decade, I have been able to locate only three manuscript sources for this prayer, all dating from the fifteenth century: Brussels MS 11051, and Paris MS lat. 13290 and MS lat. 1346.[12] The rubric attached to the prayer in Brussels 11051 states that in 1330 Pope John XXII instituted large indulgences for any penitent who recited it: "Pope John XXII granted to all true penitents for each time they will say this prayer which follows, three thousand days of indulgence

EXAMPLE 10.5 *Misericordias domini*, mm. 258–76

EXAMPLE 10.5   *(continued)*

for mortal sins, and for venial sins one thousand years. And this was issued and made public by the said Pope in Avignon on Holy Thursday 1330."[13] Such generous indulgences, which reduced the time that the penitent's soul would be required to languish in purgatory, must have held special appeal for elderly persons who were preparing to meet their Maker.

For comparison with Josquin's text, here is the complete text of the prayer as it occurs in Paris 13290; the italicized portions correspond to Josquin's version, while words in brackets are present only in Josquin's setting.

1. O *bone* [et dulcissime] *ihesu*
   per tuam misericordiam esto michi ihesus.
2. *Et quid est Jesus nisi plasmator,*
   nisi redemptor, nisi salvator?
   Ergo bone ihesu per te plasmatus sum.
3. O *bone* [et dulcissime] *ihesu*
   qui me plasmasti tua benignitate,
   rogo te, ne pereat opus tuum mea iniquitate.
4. *Ergo queso anhelo suspiro,*
   ne perdas quod tua fecit omnipotens divinitas.
5. O bone ihesu, *recognosce quod tuum est*
   et ne respicias quod meum est.
6. O bone ihesu *noli cogitare malum meum,*
   ut obliviscaris bonum tuum.
7. O bone ihesu *si ego* miser peccator
   commisi per quod me dampnare debes,
   tu misericordissime domine *non amisisti,*
   unde salvare me potes.
8. *Et si secundum iustitiam tuam dannare me vis,*
   ad tuam piissimam [et ineffabilem] *misericordiam*
   bone ihesu *appello* que super exaltat iudicium.
9. *Ergo queso: miserere mei* bone et dulcissime ihesu
   secundum magnam misericordiam [et pietatem] *tuam. Amen.*

The text of the prayer corresponds very closely with Josquin's, except for several interpolations at the beginnings and in the middle of phrases, especially the words "o bone ihesu."

The prayer occurs in one other fifteenth-century source, the *Thesauro spirituale* (Milan, 1494), an early printed book compiled by the Franciscan friar Bernardinus de Bustis. The heading—"Sanctus Anselmus ponit in suis meditationibus neminem fore damnandum qui quolibet die flexis genibus sequentem orationem devote dixerit"—indicates that the prayer occurs in the meditations of the eleventh-century Archbishop of Canterbury, St. Anselm, and that whoever says it on bended knee will not suffer damnation (that is, should they happen to die on that day, any mortal sins will be absolved and they will not be condemned to hell). The complete passage from the second meditation of St. Anselm is given in Appendix I. Only De Bustis's book specifically identifies an author for the prayer.

A longer prayer appears in many Books of Hours from the fifteenth century, with a similar text that begins "O bone Jesu, o dulcissime Jesu"; the text appears to be a greatly amplified version of the one that Josquin set to music. Appendix II gives this version of the text, referred to here as Text A, and this version of the prayer seems to be most common in Books of Hours originating in France.[14] If a rubric is present, it usually states simply "Oratio de nomine iesu" or "Devota oratio ad iesum."

A closely related form of this long version of the prayer, referred to here as Text B, also occurs frequently in Books of Hours; the full text is provided in Appendix III. The opening and conclusion are somewhat different from Text A, but the interior verses correspond almost exactly in their derivation from St. Anselm's meditation. This version of the prayer occurs most commonly in Books of Hours from England, the Low Countries, and Germany.[15]

By now it is clear that all of the versions of the prayer under discussion here—the short version as set to music by Josquin as well as the two long versions designated as Texts A and B—derive from the conclusion of the second meditation of St. Anselm of Canterbury. While St. Anselm was not widely venerated in the fifteenth century, nor even declared a doctor of the church until the eighteenth century, there was on the other hand a much more recent and popular saint with whom the long form of the prayer (Text B) became regularly associated in Books of Hours.[16] This is the Franciscan friar Bernardino of Siena, who died in 1444 and was swiftly canonized in 1450; as one of the extremely few saints created during the fifteenth century, he naturally became the focus of widespread veneration.[17] Already in the closing decades of the fifteenth century rubrics began to be attached to Text B, indicating that it was a prayer of St. Bernardino. For example, the rubric found at the beginning of the prayer in a Book of Hours from England in the 1470s states: "Sequitur oratio sancti bernardini confessoris ordinis minorum" (Appendix III). Another source, a *Hortulus animae* printed in Strasbourg by Sebastian Brant in 1503, further asserts that St. Bernardino said the prayer daily: "Oratio quam sanctus bernardinus confessor ordinis minorum quottidie [*sic*] dicitur orasse" (sig. y.iii).

This version of the prayer was displayed on a tablet near the high altar in St. Peter's in Rome, according to a Latin rubric in a Book of Hours from the late fifteenth century.[18] A translation of this rubric appears in a Book of Hours printed for the English market in Antwerp in 1525; here it indicates that the prayer would provide general absolution from mortal sin:

> Oratio sancti bernardini de senis ordinis minorum. This most devout prayer said the holy father saint Bernardine daily kneeling in the worship of the most holy name Jesus. And it is well to believe that through the invocation of that most excellent name of Jesu, saint Bernard[ine] obtained a singular reward of perpetual consolation of our Lord Jesu Christ. And this prayer is written on a tablet that hangs at Rome in Saint Peter's church near to the high altar. There our holy father the pope alone is wont to say the office of the mass, and whoever devoutly with a contrite heart daily says this oraison [i.e., prayer], if he be that day in the state of eternal damnation, then this eternal pain shall be changed into temporal pain of purgatory; and if he has deserved the pain of purgatory, then it shall be forgotten and forgiven through the infinite mercy of God.[19] [spelling modernized]

The version of the prayer associated with St. Bernardino (Text B) was set to music by Ninot le Petit, and appropriately so, for he was a singer in the papal chapel in Rome in the 1490s, and he must often have seen the prayer in St. Peter's.[20] The text continued to appear in devotional books during the sixteenth century, and there were settings of Text B by composers active in Bavaria, such as Lassus and his pupil Ivo de Vento.[21] Philippe de Monte, on the other hand, composed a setting of Text A, and this corresponds with the version that appeared in the reformed office of the Blessed Virgin issued in 1571 by Pope Pius V.[22] Other greatly abbreviated versions of the prayer were set to music by Continental composers such as Cornelius Canis,[23] Petit Jean de Latre,[24] and Palestrina.[25]

In England and Scotland three settings of the text have come down to us. A somewhat abbreviated form of Text A was composed as a motet by Robert Fayrfax, but only the Medius part survives.[26] Robert Carver also based a massive setting for 19 voices on Text A.[27] The choice of this version of the text may be due to its presence in royal Books of Hours, such as the hours of King Henry VII (see n. 14). Text B proved particularly popular in the 1530s and 1540s with editors of English primers, where it was given both in Latin and English; it continued to appear in the Marian primer of 1555, as well as in Elizabethan prayerbooks from 1559, 1560, and 1578.[28] An abbreviated form of Text B was set to music for four men's voices by an anonymous English composer, probably dating from 1553–58, the reign of the Catholic Queen Mary.[29]

As an explanation for the association of St. Anselm's meditation with St. Bernardino of Siena, it should be noted that the latter achieved much of his fame through a campaign to promote devotion to the name of Jesus. He felt that Christians had directed too much attention to veneration of the saints and the Blessed Virgin, and that more devotion should be focused on the name of Jesus. Many paintings from the late fifteenth century depict St. Bernardino

FIGURE 10.1   St. Bernardino of Siena, by Sano di Pietro (1406–81). New York, Metropolitan Museum of Art, Robert Lehmann Collection, 1975.1.45. Reproduced by permission.

with the symbol of the name, YHS (= yhesu), enclosed in a sunburst (Figure 10.1). He would commonly hold this symbol aloft on a tablet during open-air sermons that he preached to the crowds gathered to hear him. (It thus comes as no surprise that Bernardino is the patron saint of Madison Avenue; advertisers too must have their advocate in heaven!)

Direct personal contacts between St. Bernardino of Siena and Good King René (1409–80) raise some intriguing possibilities regarding the text of the prayer O *bone et dulcissime Jesu*. René d'Anjou (Figure 10.2), brother-in-law of King Charles VII and uncle of Louis XI, pursued a distinguished career as a cultivated patron of the arts; as a leader of military campaigns, on the other hand, he was less effective.[30] As a young man his claim to the duchy of Lorraine was contested by the duke of Burgundy, who captured René in battle and imprisoned him for a large ransom in Dijon for several years in the 1430s. Released in 1437, the following year René led an army down the Italian peninsula to make good his claim to the throne of Naples, which had been bequeathed to him by Queen Joan of Aragon. There he ruled briefly, until 1442, when he was defeated by Alfonso of Aragon and forced into retirement in Provence, where he lived out the remainder of his days. At his death on 10 July 1480 he left the titles of duke of Anjou, count of Provence, and king of

FIGURE 10.2   René d'Anjou. Paris, Bibliothèque Nationale, MS lat. 1156a, fol. 81ᵛ.
Reproduced by permission.

Sicily to his nephew Louis XI, while the duchy of Lorraine passed to his grand-
son, René II.[31]

During his sojourn in Naples, René had taken Bernardino as his personal
confessor, and he was later instrumental in obtaining the friar's speedy canon-
ization in 1450.[32] René's last testament stipulated that his body should be in-
terred in Angers cathedral, but his heart was to be encased in an urn and
placed in the chapel of St. Bernardino that he had constructed during the
1450s in the observant Franciscan convent in Angers—strong evidence indeed
of René's devotion to the saint. René also ordered that a daily low Mass should
be celebrated for his soul in the chapel, and each year on the anniversary of
his death a polyphonic Mass ("une messe à notte") was to be sung.[33]

While the text that Josquin set to music in his motet *O bone et dulcissime
Jesu* does not correspond exactly with the longer one associated with St. Bernardino of Siena, both prayers do derive from St. Anselm's meditation, and I

TABLE 10.1　Sources for *O bone et dulcissime Jesu*

	Attribution	Date
Manuscripts in Chronological Order		
Vatican, Cappella Sistina, MS 45	Josquin	1511–12
Bologna, San Petronio, MS 29	anon.	1512–27
St. Gall, Stiftsbibliothek, MS 463, Discantus and Altus only	Iosquinus Pratensis	ca.1540
Munich, Bayerische Staatsbibliothek, MS 41, arrangement for 6 voices	anon.	ca.1550
Leiden, Gemeente-Archief, MS 1442	anon.	1559
Print		
Motetti et carmina gallica [RISMc.1521[7]; recte 1524], Altus partbook only	anon.	1524

would suggest that Josquin's version could also have been associated with Bernardino in the later decades of the fifteenth century. Thus Bernardino's devotion to the name of Jesus could have caused this shortened form of the prayer to be linked with him as well. Given René's devotion to St. Bernardino, and the large indulgences associated with the prayer in Books of Hours such as Brussels 11051, Josquin's motet seems especially suitable for René as a patron who was nearing the end of his life. As we recall, Josquin arrived at René's court in Aix-en-Provence in 1477 and he was in line for a benefice there in 1478; the possibility thus seems good that he composed *O bone et dulcissime Jesu* for René sometime between 1477 and the king's death in 1480.[34] Keeping in mind René's stipulation that a polyphonic Mass should be performed in perpetuity on the anniversary of his death, Josquin's motet would provide an appropriate supplement to this annual observance.

In pursuing this hypothesis, we can examine the sources for the motet as well as its musical style. Unfortunately, the sources all date from after 1500, and thus offer little help in determining a more specific date of composition. The five manuscripts and one print are listed in Table 10.1; the earliest, Vatican, Cappella Sistina 45, is one of only two sources that include an attribution to Josquin. The other works in CS 45 bear reliable attributions to such well-known composers as La Rue (five), Févin (one), Mouton (one), de Silva (one), Brumel (one), Isaac (one), Prioris (one), and Josquin (four). The manuscript, which contains ten Masses, two Credos, and four motets, includes several famous works by Josquin: the *Missa de Beata Virgine*, *Missa Hercules dux Ferrariae*, and *Huc me sydereo*.

The only other source that attributes *O bone et dulcissime Jesu* to Josquin is St. Gall 463, a set of two surviving partbooks (discantus and altus) compiled around 1540 that belonged to Aegidius Tschudi, a student of Glarean. In his study of the partbooks, Donald Loach states that some one dozen of the pieces, including *O bone et dulcissime Jesu*, were drawn from the print *Motetti et carmina gallica* [RISM c.1521[7]], of which only the Altus partbook survives. There are no attributions in this single partbook, but the tenor of the original set may have contained a table of contents with composer ascriptions.[35]

Munich 41, a manuscript choirbook copied ca. 1550, manifestly preserves the best readings for *O bone et dulcissime Jesu* despite two mitigating factors: it dates from thirty years after Josquin's death,[36] and it presents the motet in an arrangement for six voices, with two voices added to fill out the transparent texture of the four-voice original. (The added voices in fact merely thicken the counterpoint with rather graceless lines that do nothing to enhance the quality of the work.) The Munich choirbook contains 18 motets, mostly without attribution, but the majority of the works can be attributed based on concordant sources. The composers are Mouton (four motets), Ludwig Senfl (one), Clemens non Papa or Crecquillon (one), Stephan Mahu (one), Iacobus Vaet (one), Johannes Lupi (one), Ja. Blanchus (one), Ludwig Daser (one), Mathieu Gascongne (one), Josquin (two), and anonymous (four). The only specific attributions are to Blanchus and Daser. The first ten motets are scored for eight voices followed by one for seven, while the final seven motets are all for six voices. This closing group consists of what were originally four-voice works, to which two new voices have been added, including Mouton's *Spiritus domini replevit*, *Illuminare Iherusalem*, and *In illo tempore Maria magdalena*, as well as Josquin's *Ave Maria. . . virgo serena*[37] and *O bone et dulcissime Jesu*.

The musical style of *O bone et dulcissime Jesu* does not contradict a dating between the years 1477 and 1480, for it features many elements common to the Milanese repertory of the mid-1470s. These include variety of texture, such as four-voice passages in imitation or homorhythm contrasting with brief paired imitative duos that are exchanged quickly among the voices.[38] Moreover, *O bone et dulcissime Jesu* constitutes in several ways a stylistic twin of *Misericordias domini*. First, the opening subject features an ascending leap of a fifth from d' to a', then up to c'', as at the outset of *Misericordias domini* (compare Example 10.1 with Example 10.6). Next, the cadence in measures 23–25 features the unexpected entry of the superius and altus to fill out the sonority on "Jesu" (Example 10.7). Similar cadences occurred in *Misericordias domini* (Example 10.2). Finally, there are several appearances of the cascade figure in *O bone et dulcissime Jesu* that are almost identical to passages in *Misericordias domini*. In the passage immediately following the filled-out cadence at measures 23–25 in *O bone et dulcissime Jesu* (Example 10.8), the voices enter in stretto, and the ascent by thirds outlines a minor seventh. Compared with Josquin's setting of the words "In te domine speravi" at the end of *Misericordias domini* (Example 10.5), the entries are nearly identical. *O bone et dulcissime Jesu*, however, states only the first ascent of the cascade before cadencing in measure 39, but later, at the words "mea iniquitate" (Example 10.9), it picks up the last limb of the triple cascade from *Misericordias* ("non confundar in aeternum"; see Example 10.5, mm. 269–73).

Up to this point in *O bone et dulcissime Jesu*, the middle limb of the triple

EXAMPLE 10.6 Josquin, *O bone et dulcissime Jesu*, superius, mm. 1–11

EXAMPLE 10.7 *O bone et dulcissime Jesu*, mm. 20–25

EXAMPLE 10.8 *O bone et dulcissime Jesu*, mm. 26–33

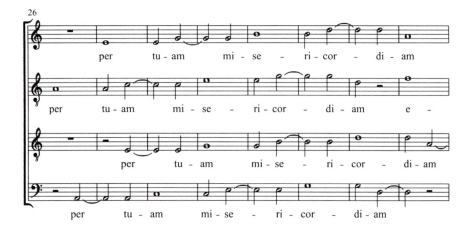

EXAMPLE 10.9   *O bone et dulcissime Jesu,* mm. 82–87

EXAMPLE 10.10   *O bone et dulcissime Jesu,* mm. 171–75

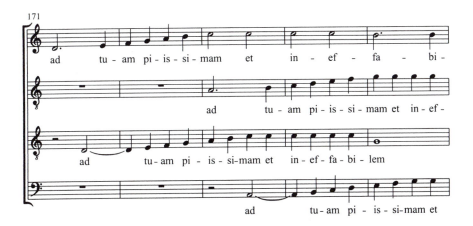

ascent from *Misericordias domini* has not been heard, but it finally appears near the end, at "ad tuam piissimam" (Example 10.10), where the entries on D in the superius and tenor continue up the scale a minor seventh to C, as in *Misericordias domini* (Example 10.5, mm. 265ff.). *O bone et dulcissime Jesu* features a slight difference in the order of the paired entries, so that now the altus and bassus enter after the superius and tenor.

In accounting for the similarity of the cascade passages in the two motets, it would be helpful to clarify the order in which I believe Josquin composed them. Circumstantial evidence suggests that *O bone et dulcissime Jesu* came first as a work for Good King René, sometime between 1477 and 1480. Josquin then composed *Misericordias domini* for Louis XI shortly thereafter, between

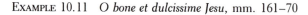

Example 10.11   *O bone et dulcissime Jesu,* mm. 161–70

1480 and 1483. He thus initially created three separate ascending cascades for
O bone et dulcissime Jesu, placing them near the beginning, middle, and end
of the motet at measures 26, 82, and 171. Then when he came to compose
Misericordias domini, in a flash of inspiration he apparently decided to connect
the three cascades in a continuous series, reordering them in the process to
create a powerful setting for the final words of Louis XI, "In te, domine, speravi, non confundar in aeternum." This juxtaposition of the individual cascades
from *O bone et dulcissime Jesu* could explain the parallel octaves between altus
and tenor in *Misericordias domini* (Example 10.5, mm. 267–68, D–E–F).
The strict canonic construction in stretto and the continuous sounding of all
four voices in each of the three successive cascades could have induced Josquin
to tolerate the unexposed parallel octaves in the two inner voices. By contrast,
it was easy to avoid parallels in *O bone et dulcissime Jesu,* because the entry of
the altus and bassus could be adjusted to occur a few beats later.[39]

EXAMPLE 10.12   *Josquin,* Ave Maria . . . virgo serena, *mm. 94–99*

Further stylistic aspects of *O bone et dulcissime Jesu* help to locate its creation in the late 1470s, for they recall yet another motet of Josquin's, his famous *Ave Maria. . . virgo serena,* which itself can be dated to his Milanese
period in the 1470s, because it was copied into the manuscript Munich 3154
by 1476.[40] First, the shift from duple to triple mensuration in the *secunda pars*
of *O bone et dulcissime Jesu* (Example 10.11) features the superius, altus, and
bassus in chordal harmony against a quasi-canonic entry in the tenor at the
lower fifth. The canon, at the distance of a half-note (semibreve in the original), dissolves after measure 164. At the hemiola in measures 167–68 an unusual B♭ and E♭ are introduced, leading to a plagal cadence on B-flat in a
work that centers on E! With this drooping harmony, Josquin vividly creates
the dejection of the sinner at the words "dannare me vis" (you wish to damn
me). The structure, but not the harmony, of this passage closely resembles a
similar one in triple mensuration from *Ave Maria* (Example 10.12), where
again the superius, altus, and bassus are homorhythmic against a canonic tenor
that enters at the lower fifth and at the distance of a semibreve, as in *O bone
et dulcissime Jesu.* One other passage in triple mensuration in the *prima pars*
of *O bone et dulcissime Jesu* features a similar canonic entry of the tenor against
chordal harmony in the superius, altus, and bassus (Example 10.13). The static
repeated notes suggest the exhausted sighs of the sinner ("Ergo quaeso, anhelo,
suspiro"), and while the texture is comparable to the above two passages, here
there is an effect of choral recitative that is quite distinct from the more lyric
contours of the other two.[41]

Still further passages call to mind *Ave Maria.* These consist of a subject in
canon in which the voices ascend stepwise using the vertical intervals 5–6–5–
6–5. Josquin employs this figure to create the first climactic section of *Ave
Maria,* at the words "coelestia, terrestria, nova replet laetitia" (Example 10.14),
where the superius and tenor, in a canonic stretto, trace a powerful sequential
ascent of stepwise fourths (from G to C, A to D, etc. in the superius), until
the superius reaches the peak *f″* of the piece; throughout the passage the bassus

EXAMPLE 10.13   *O bone et dulcissime Jesu*, mm. 88–94

supports the superius in parallel tenths. Josquin employs this technique in *O bone et dulcissime Jesu* (Example 10.15), but now the 5–6 motion occurs in paired duos, followed by a third statement in which the bassus and superius move in parallel tenths as in *Ave Maria*. The effect is less climactic than in *Ave Maria*, but the passage does lead to a strong cadence for the first section of the motet, and it immediately reminds the listener of the analogous one in *Ave Maria*.

Finally, *O bone et dulcissime Jesu* and *Ave Maria* share one other technique with motets written by Compère and Weerbeke in Milan in the 1470s. This is a shortened form of canonic imitation in which each subject drops out after only a few bars, referred to by Ludwig Finscher as "verkümmerte Kanontechnik," or truncated canon.[42] Although this is not a particularly common device in the motets of Josquin, *Ave Maria* does feature it prominently in its opening points of imitation, and it occurs again at the end of *O bone et dulcissime Jesu* for the words "ergo quaeso" (see mm. 182–87 of the score in the *Werken*). *Misericordias domini* features the device as well, at measures 49–57 and 133–43.

Another scholar of Josquin's music, Helmuth Osthoff, in fact perceived the clear similarity of style between *Ave Maria* and *O bone et dulcissime Jesu*, and he drew a direct comparison between the two motets:

> Closely related to the *Ave Maria* in style, and of hardly lesser quality, is *O bone et dulcissime Jesu*. . . . The stylistic resemblance in the combination of Netherlandish and Italian traits is so pronounced, that one can forgo a more detailed description. The related styles do not mean in this case, however, expressive similarity. As Glarean aptly remarks, the praise of Mary produces through every means of its art an impression of loveliness ("jucundissime"), while *O bone et dulcissime Jesu*, with its theme of guilt and the forgiveness of sins, produces the image of an individual in a state of spiritual distress who wrings the prayer out of himself.[43]

EXAMPLE 10.14   *Ave Maria . . . virgo serena*, mm. 44–48.

EXAMPLE 10.15   *O bone et dulcissime Jesu*, mm. 45–56

It should be recalled that *Ave Maria* and *O bone et dulcissime Jesu* had also been singled out for six-voice arrangements in Munich 41. Could this be another recognition, on the part of a sixteenth-century arranger, of the stylistic similarity of these two motets?

In recapping the arguments presented so far, a word on method seems in order. The starting point for this study was the provenance of the text of *O bone et dulcissime Jesu*, which initially suggested the possibility of a connection with René d'Anjou; similarly, the text of *Misericordias domini* turned out to have a unique association with Louis XI. Without these extra-musical cues, it would have been difficult to make a case regarding the composition date of these two motets solely on the grounds of musical style. The reconstruction of contexts for these works subsequently allowed the striking and previously unnoticed musical parallels between them to emerge into high relief. Further musical similarities between *O bone et dulcissime Jesu* and *Ave Maria* had been noticed by Osthoff, and now these can be supported by an extra-musical clue, the secure dating of the earliest source for *Ave Maria* to 1476 or before. The factors of patronage, sources (when available), and musical style all turned out to be mutually reinforcing, but the primary impetus for constructing a probable chronology for these motets arose from extra-musical evidence regarding their texts, while aspects of musical style entered the picture only at a secondary stage. Of course final documentation is lacking: we have not yet uncovered, and perhaps never will uncover, archival records that preserve specific orders from particular patrons for the composition of motets like these, nor do we have the written testimony of any contemporary witnesses. Circumstantial evidence such as that provided in this study may well represent the best that we can do in coming to understand the creation of these works.

Before concluding, I would draw the reader's attention to a famous motet that Josquin composed for another patron who was nearing the end of his life. This is the setting of Ps. 50, *Miserere mei, deus*, created by Josquin at the request of Duke Ercole d'Este of Ferrara, probably in 1503, more than 20 years after the apparent composition of *Misericordias domini* and *O bone et dulcissime Jesu*. Just as in *Misericordias domini*, the plea for the Lord's mercy is highlighted in *Miserere mei, deus*, but now emphasized by no fewer than twenty-one statements of an ostinato that appears after each verse of the psalm as a refrain. And of course *O bone et dulcissime Jesu* closes with a varied statement of the first verse of the same Psalm: "Miserere mei, deus, secundum magnam misericordiam tuam." I would thus speculate that these three motets, *O bone et dulcissime Jesu*, *Misericordias domini*, and *Miserere mei, deus* are musical testaments that aptly express the sentiments of three of Josquin's patrons as they approached the end of their days.[44] Each of these patrons must have recognized Josquin's ability when they selected him over many other accomplished and available composers to create their final musical monuments. And there can be no doubt that the late fifteenth century witnessed competition on an unprecedented scale for musical talent, as evidenced by the attempts of patrons such as Ercole d'Este, Galeazzo Maria Sforza, and King Ferrante of

Naples to attract musicians and retain them at their courts.[45] As Ercole's agent wrote to him in recommending Josquin for the post of *maestro di cappella* in 1502: "My Lord, I believe that there is neither lord nor king who will now have a better chapel than yours if Your Lordship sends for Josquin. . . . by having Josquin in our chapel I want to place a crown upon this chapel of ours."[46] Indeed, what better means could these patrons have found to prepare for eternity than through commissioning Josquin to compose powerful petitions for mercy that could be sung in their respective musical chapels? How could the Lord turn a deaf ear to such eloquent supplications?

APPENDIX I

From second meditation of St. Anselm of Canterbury
Sancti Anselmi liber meditationum et orationum, in J.-P. Migne, *Patrologiae cursus completus,* 158 (Paris, 1864), cols. 724–25.

Asterisks indicate corresponding phrases in Appendix II and III.

Meditatio II: De terrore judicii, ad excitandum in se timorem

Jesu, Jesu, propter hoc nomen tuum,
   fac mihi secundum hoc nomen
     tuum.
Jesu, Jesu, obliviscere superbum provo-
   cantem,
   respice miserum invocantem
   *nomen dulce, nomen delectabile,
   nomen confortans peccatorem,
     et beatae spei.
   *Quid est enim Jesus, nisi Salvator?
Ergo Jesu, propter temetipsum esto mihi
   Jesus,
   qui me plasmasti, ne peream;
   qui me redemisti, ne condemnes;
   qui me creasti tua bonitate,
   ne pereat opus tuum mea iniquitate.
*Rogo, piissime, ne perdat mea iniquitas
   quod fecit tua omnipotens bonitas.
*Recognosce, benignissime, quod tuum
   est;
   et absterge quod alienum est.

*Jesu, Jesu, miserere, dum tempus est
   miserendi,
   ne damnes in tempore judicandi.
*Quae namque tibi utilitas in sanguine
   meo,
   si descendero in aeternam corrup-
     tionem?
*Neque enim mortui laudabunt te,
   domine,
   neque omnes qui descendunt in in-
     fernum (Ps. 113:17).
Si me admiseris intra latissimum
   tuae misericordiae sinum,
   non eris angustior propter me,
   domine.
*Admitte ergo, o desideratissime Jesu,
   admitte me intra numerum electorum
   tuorum,
   ut cum illis te laudem, te perfruar, et
   gloriar
   in te inter omnes qui diligunt nomen
     tuum.
Qui cum Patre et Spiritu sancto gloriaris
   per interminata saecula. Amen.

APPENDIX II

Prayer Text A
Hours of Louis de Laval, Paris, Bibliothèque Nationale, MS lat. 920 (ca. 1480), fol. 294.

Numbered lines in italics correspond to lines from Josquin's motet. Asterisks refer to concordant lines from the meditation of St. Anselm in Appendix I.

[1.] O *bone* ihesu, o *dulcissime ihesu*, o
   pie ihesu,
   o fili marie, plenus misericordia et
   pietate,
   o dulcis ihesu, secundum magnam
   misericordiam tuam
   miserere mei.
O clementissime ihesu, te deprecor
   per illum sanguinem preciosum,
   quem pro peccatoribus effundere vo-
   luisti,
   ut abluas omnes iniquitates meas,
   et in me respicias humiliter petentem,
   et hoc nomen sanctum tuum invocantem,
   *nomen ihesu, nomen delectabile,
   ihesu nomen confortans.
*[2.] *Quid est ihesus nisi salvator?*
O ihesu, propter nomen sanctum tuum
   salva me ne peream.
*[3.] Et *qui plasmasti me* et redemisti
   me,
   ne permittas dampnari quem tu ex
   nichilo creasti.
*[5.] O ihesu, *recognosce quod tuum est
   et absterge quod alienum est.*
*[4.] O bone ihesu, *ne perdat* iniquitas
   mea,
   quem fecit omnipotens bonitas tua.

*O ihesu benignissime, miserere mei
   dum tempus est miserendi,
   ne dampnes me in tempore iudicandi.
*Que utilitas in sanguine meo
   dum descendo in eternam corruptionem?
*Neque mortui laudabunt te, domine
   ihesu,
   neque omnes qui descendunt in
   infernum (Ps. 113:17).
O amantissime ihesu, o mitissime ihesu,
   o ihesu, ihesu, ihesu,
   *admicte me inter numerum elec-
   torum tuorum.
O ihesu, salus in te sperancium,
   o ihesu, salus in te credencium,
   o ihesu, solacium ad te confugien-
   cium,
   o ihesu, dulcis remissio omnium
   peccatorum,
   o ihesu, fili marie virginis,
   infunde in me graciam sanctam,
   fidem, sapienciam, spem,
   caritatem, humilitatem et castitatem,
   *ut te possim perfecte diligere, et in te
   gloriari,
   et omnes qui invocant hoc nomen
   sanctum tuum, quod est ihesus.
   Amen.

APPENDIX III

Prayer Text B
Hours, Sarum use; New York, Pierpont Morgan Library,
M. 24 (ca. 1470), fol. 69.

Sequitur oratio sancti bernardini confessoris ordinis minorum

O bone ihesu, o dulcis ihesu,
   o ihesu fili virginis marie
   plenus misericordia et veritate.
O dulcis ihesu miserere mei
   secundum magnam misericordiam
      tuam.
O benigne ihesu te deprecor
   per illum sanguinem preciosum
   quem pro nobis miseris peccatoribus
   effundere dignatus es in ara crucis
   ut abicias omnes iniquitates meas
   et ne despicias humiliter te petentem
   et hoc nomen tuum sanctissimum
   ihesus invocantem.
*Hoc nomen ihesus nomen dulce,
   *hoc nomen ihesus nomen salutare.
*Quid enim est ihesus nisi salvator?
O bone ihesu qui me creasti
   et redemisti tuo precioso sanguine
   ne permittas me damnari
   quem ex nichilo creasti.
*O bone ihesu ne perdat me iniquitas
      mea
   quem fecit omnipotens bonitas tua.
*O bone ihesu recognosce quod est
      tuum in me
   et absterge quod alienum est a me.
*O bone ihesu miserere mei dum
      tempus est miserendi
   ne perdas me in tempore tui tremendi
   iudicii.

O bone ihesu si merui miser peccator
   de vera tua iusticia penam eternam
   pro peccatis meis gravissimis
   adhuc appello confisus de tua iusticia
      vera
   ad tuam misericordiam ineffabilem
   utique misereberis mei ut pius pater
   et misericors dominus.
*O bone ihesu que enim utilitas in san-
      guine meo
   dum descendero in corruptionem eter-
      nam.
*Non enim mortui laudabunt te
   neque omnes qui descendunt in
   infernum (Ps. 113:17).
O misericordissime ihesu miserere mei,
   o dulcissime ihesu libera me,
   o piissime ihesu propitius esto michi
      peccatori,
   *o ihesu admitte me miserum pecca-
      torem
   inter numerum electorum tuorum.
O ihesu salus in te sperancium,
   o ihesu salus in te credencium
   miserere mei,
   o ihesu dulcis remissio omnium
   peccatorum meorum,
   o ihesu fili virginis marie infunde in
   me gratiam tuam
   sapientiam, caritatem, castitatem et
   humilitatem,
   ac etiam in omnibus adversitatibus
   meis patientiam sanctam
   ut possim te perfecte diligere
   et in te gloriari ac delectari
   in saecula saeculorum. Amen.

NOTES

   1. Gustave Reese and Jeremy Noble, "Josquin Desprez," in *The New Grove High Renaissance Masters* (London: Macmillan, 1984), 3.

2. Claudio Sartori, "Josquin des Prés cantore del duomo di Milano," *Annales musicologiques* 4 (1956): 55–83.

3. Edward E. Lowinsky, "Ascanio Sforza's Life: A Key to Josquin's Biography and an Aid to the Chronology of His Works," in *Josquin des Prez: Proceedings of the International Josquin Festival-Conference*, ed. Edward E. Lowinsky in collaboration with Bonnie J. Blackburn (London: Oxford University Press, 1976), 31–75. For more recent documentation concerning Josquin's presence in the chapel of Galeazzo Maria Sforza, see Evelyn S. Welch, "Sight, Sound and Ceremony in the Chapel of Galeazzo Maria Sforza," *Early Music History* 12 (1993): 151–90, and Lora Matthews and Paul A. Merkley, "Josquin Desprez and his Milanese Patrons," *Journal of Musicology* 12 (1994): 434–63.

4. Yves Esquieu, "La Musique à la cour provençale du roi René," *Provence historique* 31 (1981): 299–312; Françoise Robin, "Josquin des Prés au service de René d'Anjou?" *Revue de musicologie* 71 (1985): 180–81.

5. See Reese and Noble, "Josquin Desprez," 6.

6. Peter Király, "Un séjour de Josquin des Prés à la cour de Hongrie?" *Revue de musicologie* 78 (1992): 145–50.

7. Formerly it was thought that Josquin joined the papal chapel in 1486, but Pamela Starr has demonstrated that the correct date is 1489; see "Josquin, Rome, and a Case of Mistaken Identity," *Journal of Musicology* 15 (1997): 43–65.

8. Ludwig Finscher, "Zum Verhältnis von Imitationstechnik und Textbehandlung im Zeitalter Josquins," in *Renaissance-Studien: Helmuth Osthoff zum 80. Geburtstag*, ed. Ludwig Finscher (Tutzing: Hans Schneider, 1979), 57–72; Joshua Rifkin, "Josquin in Context: Toward a Chronology of the Motets," unpublished paper read at the National Meeting of the American Musicological Society, Minneapolis, 1978. I would like to thank Joshua Rifkin for making a copy of his paper available to me.

9. The *Tertia pars* quotes a portion of the *Te Deum*. For a more extended discussion of the context for this motet, see Patrick Macey, "Josquin's *Misericordias domini* and Louis XI," *Early Music* 19 (1991): 163–77.

10. See the full score of *Misericordias domini* in the *Werken van Josquin Des Prés*, ed. Albert Smijers et al. (Amsterdam: G. Alsbach, 1921–69), motet no. 43, mm. 244–45.

11. See, for example, the motet *Ora pro nobis* at the words "rectis corde" from Josquin's cycle of *motetti missales* for Milan titled *Vultum tuum deprecabuntur*, in *Werken*, motet no. 24.

12. Brussels, Bibliothèque Royale, MS 11051, fols. 230–32; the manuscript dates from the first half of the fifteenth century. See Isabelle Hottois, *L'Iconographie musicale dans les manuscrits de la Bibliothèque royale Albert 1er* (Brussels: Bibliothèque Royale Albert 1er, 1982), 95. Paris, Bibliothèque Nationale, MS lat. 1346, a Book of Hours according to the usage of Poitiers, dates from the fifteenth century; the prayer occurs on fol. 98^v^. Paris, Bibliothèque Nationale, MS lat. 13290 follows the usage of Paris, and it dates from the second half of the fifteenth century; the prayer can be found on fol. 150 with the rubric "Oraison dévote." For information on dating and a summary list of contents of the latter two Books of Hours, see Vincent Leroquais, *Les Livres d'heures manuscrits de la Bibliothèque nationale*, 3 vols. (Paris: [Macon: Protat], 1927), 1:153–54, 2:109–11. Bonnie J. Blackburn has kindly notified me of another source for the prayer, the Saluces Hours, British Library, Add. MS 27697, fol. 28 (no rubric); the manuscript was copied in Savoy in the third quarter of the fifteenth century.

13. Brussels 11051, fol. 230: "Le pape Jehan XXIIe a concedé et ottroyé a tous vrais penitens pour chacune fois quils diroit ceste orison qui s'ensuive trois mil iours de

indulgence des pechies crimineulx et des pechies venieulx mil ans. Et fu donnée et publiée ceste orison par le dit pape en avignon le ioidi saint l'an mil iiii[c] et trente. O bone ihesu per tuam misericordiam esto michi ihesus" [etc.]. The rubric indicates that the text was instituted in Avignon on Holy Thursday in 1430, but this must be an error for 1330, because Pope John XXII (Jacques Duèse) reigned in Avignon from 1316 to 1334.

14. Text A occurs consistently in Books of Hours that follow the usage of Rome. Among countless other books, it is found in Books of Hours that belonged to Duke Philip the Good of Burgundy (Brussels, Bibliothèque Royale, MS 76.F.2, fol. 167), where it has the rubric "Devotissima oratio ad Ihesum." King Henry VII of England also had the prayer in his Hours, which were copied in France in the 1470s; the book is now in New York, Pierpont Morgan Library, M. 815, fol. 28v.

15. For a brief overview, see Hope Emily Allen, *Writings Ascribed to Richard Rolle, Hermit of Hampole* (London: Oxford University Press, 1927), 314–17.

16. See *De Sancti Bernardini Senensis Operibus, Ratio criticae editionis*, ed. P. Dionysius Pacetti (Florence: Ad claras aquas [Quaracchi], 1947), 101–2. There are a few exceptions dating from the sixteenth century in which Text A is also associated with St. Bernardino: Vatican, Reg. Lat. MS 156, fol. 12, and Brussels, Bibliothèque Royale, MS 3063, fol. 184[v].

17. See A. G. F. Howell, *St. Bernardino of Siena* (London: Methuen, 1913).

18. See P. A. López and P. L. M. Nuñez, "Descriptio codicum Franciscalium Bibliothecae Ecclesiae Primatialis Toletanae," *Archivo Ibero-Americano* 12 (1919), 398. The fifteenth-century Book of Hours is in Toledo, Biblioteca Ecclesiae Toletanae, cod. 34–28, fol. 150: "Orationem in honorem nominis Jesu. Hanc orationem devotissimam cotidie oravit flexis genibus Sanctus Bernardinus, ad reverentiam illius sanctissimi nominis Ihesu. Et est pie credendum quod per invocationem ipsius nominis Ihesu singulare premium eterne consolationes apud eumdem Dominum Ihesum Christum obtinuit fideliter. Et sciendum quod hec oratio scripta in tabula pendet Rome in ecclesia Sancti Petri, iuxta summum altare, ubi solus sanctissimus Pontifex officiari solet. . . . O bone ihesu, o dulcis ihesu" [etc.].

19. *Hore beate Marie virginis ad usum Sarum* (Antwerp: Byrckman, 1525), fol. 89[v] (*Short Title Catalogue of English Books in the British Library*, no. 15939).

20. Ninot Le Petit, *Opera omnia*, ed. Barton Hudson ([n.p.]: American Institute of Musicology, 1979), 66ff. The motet survives in only one source, Petrucci's *Motetti libro quarto* (Venice: Petrucci, 1505).

21. Orlando di Lasso, *Sämtliche Werke*, ed. F. X. Haberl and A. Sandberger, 1 (Leipzig: Breitkopf & Härtel, 1894), 69ff. Probably a late work, Lassus's setting was first published in 1582 in *Lectiones sacrae novem ex libris Hiob*. For Ivo de Vento's motet there is no modern edition, but it was published in *Liber motettorum* (Nuremberg, 1571).

22. *Officium B. Mariae Virginis, nuper reformatum, et Pii* V. *Pont. Max. iussu editum* (Rome, 1571). For Monte's motet, see Philippe de Monte, *Opera omnia*, ed. George van Doorslaer, 2 (Düsseldorf: L. Schwann, 1927), 1ff; the motet was first published in RISM 1596^{2}.

23. No modern edition; see RISM 1542^{7} and 1556^{9}.

24. No modern edition; see RISM 1564^{5}.

25. Four settings of O *bone Jesu* are attributed to Palestrina, but only one of them, a brief work for four voices that is an *opus dubium*, actually sets the complete opening sentence of Text A; see Pierluigi da Palestrina, *Gesammtausgabe*, ed. Franz Xavier Haberl, 32 (Leipzig, 1892), 131. The other three motets are settings of a different text.

26. The Medius part is in London, British Library, Harley 1709 (datable before 1509); see Robert Fayrfax, *Collected Works*, ed. Edwin B. Warren, 2 ([n.p.]: American Institute of Musicology, 1964), 22. For Fayrfax's parody Mass on his own motet, see *Collected Works*, 1 ([Rome:] American Institute of Musicology, 1959), 1ff.

27. Robert Carver, *Collected Works*, ed. Denis Stevens ([n.p.]: American Institute of Musicology, 1959), 1ff. The setting exists in only one manuscript in the National Library of Scotland, Adv. MS 5.1.15, with inscriptions as early as 1513 and as late as 1546; see Kenneth Elliott, "The Carver Choir-Book," *Music and Letters* 41 (1960): 349–57.

28. See Helen C. White, *The Tudor Books of Private Devotion* (Madison: University of Wisconsin Press, 1951), 62, 99, 116, 199–201.

29. *O Bone Jesu, Motet for Four Men's Voices by an Anonymous (English) Composer of the 16th Century (British Museum Add. Mss. 17802–5)*, ed. H. B. Collins (London: J. and W. Chester, Ltd., 1936). See Roger W. Bray, "British Museum Add. Mss. 17802–5 (The Gyffard Part-books): An Index and Commentary," *Royal Musical Association Research Chronicle* 7 (1969): 31–50. *O bone Jesu* is the last item in the partbooks (no. 94).

30. The standard biography is Albert Lecoy de La Marche, *Le Roi René*, 2 vols. (Paris: Firmin-Didot, 1875; repr. Geneva, 1969).

31. The crown of Naples was in fact never successfully regained by the French, though King Charles VIII invaded Italy in 1494 with that end in view, thereby inaugurating a series of invasions by his successors, Louis XII and Francis I, that had disastrous consequences for Italy.

32. See M. Le Comte de Quatrebarbes, *Oeuvres complètes du Roi René* (Angers: Imprimerie de Cosnier et Lachèse, 1845), p. cxxi: "Il avait obtenu la canonisation de son saint confesseur, le bienheureux Bernardin, et lui avait fait élever aux Cordeliers, d'Angers, une magnifique chapelle." The original testament reads: "In honore et reverentia D.N.J.-C. et pro singulari affectione quam habuimus et habemus ad sanctum, gloriosissimum beatum Bernardinum. . ."

33. Ibid., 1:85. "Item, ledict seigneur veult et ordonne que son cueur soit pourté, le lendemain de son obit, a l'eglize des freres minneurs dudict lieu d'Angiers pour estre inhumé et sepulturé en la chappelle de Sainct-Bernardin, qu'il a faict eriger, ediffier, parer et fournir contigue à l'eglize des dictz freres minneurs. Item, ledict seigneur veult et ordonne que en la dicte chapelle de Sainct-Bernardin soit dicte et celebrée chascun jour de l'an a tousjours mais perpetuellement une basse messe et chascun an, à tel jour qu'il trespassera, une messe *à notte* et le jour devant vigilles des trespassez solempnelles, pour le remede et salut de son ame et de ses predecesseurs, parens et amys trespassez." The tomb and the decorations of the chapel no longer exist, but for a description and illustrations, see Christian de Mérindol, *Le Roi René et la seconde maison d'Anjou* (Paris: Leopard d'Or, 1987), 68–70, and pl. 41.

34. The possible connection between Josquin's setting of *O bone et dulcissime Jesu* and René would be strengthened if the prayer were contained in any of René's several Books of Hours, but having searched for it in several of these books, I have not been successful in locating it. One of the books, in Aix-en-Provence, Bibliothèque Méjanes, Res. MS 1, does include a prayer addressed to St. Bernardino on p. 421 ("Beati famuli tui Bernardini nobis quesumus . . ."), but it does not include a prayer that begins "O bone et dulcissime Jesu." See Christian de Mérindol, *Le Roi René (1409–1480): Décoration de ses chapelles et demeures* (Paris: Éditions de la Réunion des musées nationaux, 1981), 36. Two other Books of Hours that belonged to René are Paris, Bibliothèque Nationale, MS 1156A, and London, British Library, Egerton MS 1070. See John Har-

than, *The Book of Hours* (New York: Crowell, 1977), 86–93. Both manuscripts appear to have been copied in the early fifteenth century, before Bernardino had established a reputation, and neither of them includes the friar in their calendars, nor do they contain the prayer. One other Book of Hours connected with René is preserved in the Bibliothèque d'Angers, but I have not yet been able to see it. See Quatrebarbes, *Oeuvres complètes,* 1, p. cxliii.

35. Donald Loach, "Aegidius Tschudi's Songbook (St. Gall Ms 463): A Humanistic Document from the Circle of Heinrich Glarean" (Ph.D. diss., University of California, Berkeley, 1969), 200. On p. 77 Loach provides a complete table of contents for *Motetti et carmina gallica,* showing concordances with St. Gall 463.

36. It should be remembered, however, that a more recent source is not therefore necessarily less reliable: "recentiores non deteriores."

37. The six-voice version is edited in Josquin's *Werken,* motet no. 1a.

38. See the full score of the motet in Josquin's *Werken,* motet no. 96.

39. There are other imitative passages in the two motets that are remarkably similar, and these can readily be detected by the reader who wishes to pursue them.

40. See Thomas L. Noblitt, "Die Datierung der Handschrift Mus. ms. 3154 der Staatsbibliothek München," *Die Musikforschung* 27 (1974): 36–56. See also Ludwig Finscher, "Imitationstechnik," 69–72, for an illuminating discussion of Milanese style traits in *Ave Maria.*

41. Both of the passages in triple mensuration in *O bone et dulcissime Jesu* gave rise to divergent readings in the sources, but the readings in Munich 41 correspond better with Josquin's style. In Munich 41 the tenor shifts in bar 161 to triple mensuration at the same time as the other voices, instead of maintaining an awkward duple mensuration until measure 164 against the triple mensuration of the other parts. For the earlier passage in triple mensuration at measure 88, most of the sources show the tenor entering at the same time as the other three parts, thus creating a "dead spot" in measure 91, where all the voices simply hold on to a C-major triad. The subsequent passage in the other sources is patently incorrect: instead of paired duos (S–A and T–B, mm. 92–94) on "ne perdas," as in Munich 41, they feature a trio (S–A–T) on "ne perdas" answered by the solo bassus. This unbalanced distribution of the voices contradicts the immediately following texture of paired duos (S–A echoed by T–B) at "quod tua fecit" (mm. 94–97), and it departs from the norm for Josquin's other motets.

42. Finscher, "Imitationstechnik," 63–64.

43. Helmuth Osthoff, *Josquin Desprez,* 2 vols. (Tutzing: Hans Schneider, 1962–65), 2:88–89.

44. In a related case, Galeazzo Maria Sforza issued an order just a few days before his assassination in 1476 that his singers should perform the verset "Maria mater gratiae, mater misericordiae" at daily Mass. This invocation for mercy, addressed here to the Blessed Virgin, appears in sets of *motetti missales* composed for Galeazzo by Josquin, Compère, and Weerbeke; see Macey, "Galeazzo Maria Sforza and Musical Patronage in Milan: Compère, Weerbeke, and Josquin," *Early Music History* 15 (1996): 147–212.

45. For an account of the diplomatic discord that arose when Galeazzo Maria Sforza hired the tenor Jean Cordier away from Ferrante of Naples, see Allan W. Atlas, *Music at the Aragonese Court of Naples* (Cambridge: Cambridge University Press, 1985), 41; Guglielmo Barblan, "Vita musicale alla corte sforzesca," in *Storia di Milano,* 9 (Milan: Fondazione Trecanni degli Alfieri per la Storia di Milano, 1961), 843–46; and Richard Walsh, "Music and Quattrocento Diplomacy: The Singer Jean Cordier between Milan, Naples, and Burgundy in 1475," *Archiv für Kulturgeschichte* 60 (1978): 439–42. Regarding the intense cultivation of music and musicians by Ercole d'Este,

see Lewis Lockwood, *Music in Renaissance Ferrara 1400–1505* (Cambridge, Mass.: Harvard University Press, 1984), esp. 130–34 and 199–208; and Rob C. Wegman, *Born for the Muses: The Life and Masses of Jacob Obrecht* (Oxford: Clarendon Press, 1994), 346–49.

46. Lewis Lockwood, "Josquin at Ferrara: New Documents and Letters," in *Proceedings of the Josquin Festival-Conference*, ed. Lowinsky, 131.

Miracles, Motivicity, and Mannerism

Adrian Willaert's *Videns Dominus flentes sorores Lazari* and Some Aspects of Motet Composition in the 1520s

As with his colleague and predecessor as Ferdinand Schevill Distinguished Service Professor at the University of Chicago, Edward E. Lowinsky, I had my share of differences with Howard Mayer Brown. In recent years, however, as he edged past his 50s and I edged toward mine, I began to find more of his work to my taste and, at the same time, to develop a sneaking personal fondness for him. Back-to-back conferences at Wolfenbüttel and Cremona in the autumn of 1992 brought a chance for some enjoyable, if brief, conversations; and on a Tuesday in mid-February 1993, I found myself pleased to discover Howard "lurking with intent," as he put it, in the hallway outside a rehearsal room at the Schola Cantorum Basiliensis. Although we had both spent the last several weeks in Basel—he teaching at the university, I preparing a production of Monteverdi's *L'Orfeo* at the Schola—we had not seen one another. He had just a couple of days left in town, he now said, and hoped to have dinner with me before his departure. We met that evening and had a long, wide-ranging conversation over an excellent meal—for which he picked up the tab. In the course of our talk, it turned out that his strongest recent interest intersected with an equally strong interest of mine: his hobbyhorse, which he liked to call "varied repetition," nestled snugly into something that I like to call "motivicity."

Two and a half weeks later, a series of accidents brought me to Florence and, on a Thursday morning, to the Brancacci chapel. Viewing the frescoes without a guidebook and trying to work out their content, I chanced to think about the raising of Lazarus; and thinking of Lazarus brought to mind Adrian Willaert's four-voice motet *Videns Dominus flentes sorores Lazari*, long a favorite piece of mine. *Videns Dominus* contains what I have always regarded as an absolutely stunning example of varied repetition, and I thought that I must drop Howard a note suggesting he take a look at it.

That very evening, I met Karol Berger and Anna Maria Busse Berger for a dinner also attended by Bonnie Blackburn and Leofranc Holford-Strevens. Hardly had we sat down to eat than Karol told me of Howard's death four days after I had seen him. Needless to say, the news shook me deeply; and the next day, it occurred to me that I might pursue my ideas on Willaert and—as I do now—offer them up in Howard's memory.

I

Before turning to *Videns Dominus* itself, I might say a word or two about motivicity.[1] I have used this term to describe a compositional phenomenon that becomes increasingly prominent in the later fifteenth and early sixteenth centuries, above all in the music of Josquin des Prez and those younger composers—most notably Willaert's teacher, Jean Mouton—who appear to have absorbed many of his innovations. We might define motivicity informally as the maximum permeation of a polyphonic complex by a single linear denominator or set of denominators. By "linear denominator," I understand a unit of music characterized not just diastemmatically but rhythmically as well. This would seem to coincide—and in fact often does coincide—with what we conventionally call "motive"; hence my terminological bow to familiar coinage. Nevertheless, I must distinguish what I have in mind here from our common conceptions of motive and motivic treatment as we inherit them from the analysis of eighteenth- and nineteenth-century music.[2] For one thing, the units to which I refer do not—or not, for the most part, in any structurally meaningful sense—undergo the kind of evolution and transformation that we consider part and parcel of tonal composition since the Classic era. On the contrary, in the earlier stages of Renaissance motivicity at least, they remain essentially fixed, altering their shape in detail only as local contrapuntal exigency demands. Moreover, these units do not invariably partake of certain characteristics that we associate with motives: they do not necessarily have a distinctive profile, nor, even more important, do they necessarily initiate events or otherwise function as incises—they can occur without any articulative individuation within the middle of a longer melodic span. In this respect, we may better liken them to modules, or to "segments" in twelve-tone theory. But in regard to this last comparison, I must make two significant distinctions: as already emphasized, the denominators of my motivicity include rhythm as well as pitch; and they do not presuppose the embracing context of the larger set.

Given all these qualifications and restrictions, the reader may well ask how one identifies the operative units of motivicity in the first place. In practice, this proves disarmingly simple: something—almost anything, under this construct—becomes a motive in the sense used here through repetition, whether within a single voice or projected among several voices.[3] Projecting a motive among several voices, of course, commonly produces what we understand as imitation; and indeed, imitation represents the most obvious and, in the course of the sixteenth century, the increasingly dominant manifestation of motivicity. Nevertheless, we cannot equate motivicity with imitation alone. I would see it revealed just as much in Josquin's pervasive ostinatos, for instance, or in his play with different motives set against one another. Moreover, our normal understanding of imitation, like our traditional understanding of motive, proceeds from incises. But as we shall see in *Videns Dominus* itself, the music in question does not always operate in this fashion.

If the "motives" of Renaissance motivicity achieve their identity through repetition, this leads all but inevitably to Brown's "varied repetition": a variation not so much of the motives themselves, I hasten to reiterate, as of the polyphony in which they appear. For right from the start, the practice of motivicity seems to have implied the exploitation of multiple combinative possibilities: multiple in terms not just of what—the motive combined with itself, with another motive, or deployed against a fixed line such as a preexisting cantus firmus—but also how: at what level of transposition and at what temporal distance. To take the simplest example, the same motive might undergo imitation at the fifth in one instance, the octave in another, or—whether or not the transposition level changes—once at the distance of a breve, then at two breves. In some situations, the result of such operations corresponds to what we call multiple, or invertible, counterpoint. Yet multiple counterpoint, as traditionally defined, does not comprehend all the possibilities of varied repetition: it typically refers to longer, nonimitative linear units and does not explicitly deal with time-shifting; nor does it really address such procedures as the ostinato-like deployment of motivic fragments against a fixed cantus firmus—a device especially important with Josquin if less so in Willaert and his contemporaries.[4]

As my various subexamples reveal, the concept of motivicity in fact embraces a series of smaller phenomena, some of them by no means unknown, but few of them studied intensively to date, and none, to the best of my awareness, previously brought together with the others under a single theoretical roof. The individual procedures, too, may by now appear simple enough to us; but I believe, and have argued elsewhere, that they in fact represent a momentous intellectual leap in the practice of composition.[5] And in any event, what composers like Josquin or, as we shall now see, Willaert could make of them certainly merits any description but "simple."

II

I would guess that Willaert composed *Videns Dominus* in the years immediately preceding his departure from Ferrara for Venice in 1527. The music strikes me as more evolved in style than that of the relatively few Willaert motets transmitted before 1520, while the earliest source, an incomplete set of partbooks housed at the Royal College of Music in London under the call number MS 2037, clearly comes from Ferrara and would seem to date from no later than 1530.[6] Of the seven further sources listed in Table 11.1, two also date from 1535 or earlier: the so-called Massimo partbooks, a collection of motets copied at Rome between 1532 and 1534, and the eleventh in the great series of motet publications issued by Pierre Attaingnant at Paris in the years 1534–35.[7] In all these appearances, as well in the two most significant later ones, *Videns Dominus* explicitly bears Willaert's name; its occurrence in the

TABLE 11.1   Sources of *Videns Dominus flentes sorores Lazari*

Leipzig, Universitätsbibliothek, MS 49/50, fols. 291ᵛ–292ʳ, anon.

London, Royal College of Music, MS 2037, fols. 12ᵛ–13ʳ, "Adrianus vvillaert"

Rome, Palazzo Massimo, VI.C.6.23–24, fols. 8ʳ–9ʳ, "Adrian"

Treviso, Biblioteca Capitolare, MS 7, fols. 83ᵛ–84ʳ, "Iachet" (crossed out and replaced by a later hand on the facing page with "Magni Adriani")

Lib. vndecimus .xxvj.musicales habet modulos quatuor | et quinque vocibus . . . (Paris: Pierre Attaingnant, 1535; RISM 1535³), fol. xiiiᵛ, "Vvillart"

SYMPHONIAE IV-|CVNDAE ATQVE ADEO BREVES | QVATVOR VOCVM, AB OPTIMIS QVIBVSQVE MVSICIS COMPO|sitae . . . (Wittenberg: Georg Rhau, 1538; RISM 1538⁸), No. XXIX, "Verdelot"

FAMOSISSIMI ADRIANI | VVILAERT . . . | *Musica* QVATVOR VOCVM, (*quæ uulgo* MOTECTA *nuncupa-|tur*) . . . | LIBER PRIMVS (Venice: Girolamo Scotto, 1539), No. II

ADRIANI VVILAERT | . . . MVSICA QVATVOR VOCVM | (MOTECTA *uulgo appellant*) . . . | LIBER PRIMVS (Venice: Antonio Gardane, 1545), No. XIX

Wittenberg printer Georg Rhau's *Symphoniae jucundae* of 1538 under the name Verdelot, therefore, must surely count as an error.[8] In 1539, Girolamo Scotto of Venice included *Videns Dominus* in the first of the two volumes devoted to Willaert's four-voice motets that he issued that year; and in 1545, Scotto's colleague and rival Antonio Gardano published it once more in his revised—and by all indications authoritative—edition of the same repertory.[9] With this, the story of its transmission essentially ends. An anonymous copy in Leipzig 49/50, a manuscript written at Leipzig about 1550, clearly depends on Rhau, while the north Italian manuscript Treviso 7, from the third quarter of the sixteenth century, just as clearly derives from Scotto—although the relationship did not keep the scribe from encumbering the motet with another misattribution, this time to Jachet.[10] In modern times, Hermann Zenck transcribed *Videns Dominus* both in the abortive complete edition of Willaert's music that he launched in 1937 and in the second, more successful, attempt begun in 1950.[11] Further transcriptions have appeared in modern reeditions of Attaingnant's motet books and Rhau's *Symphoniae jucundae*, as well as in Anne-Marie Bragard's dissertation on Verdelot; to all these, I add yet another in the Appendix.[12] Bragard, who did not know of the attributions to Willaert, also offers a brief descriptive account of the piece; the only other discussion that I know occurs in an excerpt from Zenck's *Habilitationsschrift* of 1929 that Walter Gerstenberg published 30 years later in a posthumous collection of Zenck's writings under the title "Über Willaerts Motetten."[13]

Videns Dominus sets the text of the Communion for Friday after the fourth Sunday in Lent, a free compilation of material from John 11:33, 35, and 43–44:[14]

Videns Dominus flentes sorores Lazari ad monumentum, lachrimatus est coram Judeis, et clamabat:	The Lord saw the sisters of Lazarus weeping at the tomb, and wept before the Jews, and cried out:

Lazare veni foras:	Lazarus, come forth;
et prodiit ligatis manibus et pedibus,	And he that had been dead four days
qui fuerat quatriduanus mortuus.	came forward bound hand and foot.

As I've chosen the layout above to reflect, the music falls into three sections, the outer two both considerably longer than the middle one. The outer sections in fact have almost exactly the same length: the first reaches its final note 33 breves—each a measure of the modern transcription—after its start, and the motet ends 34 breves after the initial entry of the phrase "et prodiit ligatis manibus et pedibus." The motet as a whole exhibits, in refreshingly unproblematic fashion, the characteristics typical of pieces assigned by more than a few sixteenth-century theorists and printers to the eighth mode: the music starts and ends on G; tenor and superius project the plagal octaves d–g–d' and d'–g'–d'', respectively; and the bassus and altus complement the other two voices with the authentic octaves G–d–g and g–d–g'.[15]

With these preliminaries out of the way, we can zero in for a closer look at the music. *Videns Dominus* begins with the traditional gambit of an imitative duo answered by a second imitative pair built on the same subject. Several details of Willaert's treatment, however, would seem worthy of mention. As Willaert inherited this scheme from the generation of Josquin and Mouton, it contained a high degree of inbuilt clarity and symmetry: for the most part, the duos overlapped only minimally; apart, perhaps, from the modally induced fifth–fourth exchange at the start, they typically maintained exact imitative precision within themselves; and the second duo normally presented a literal reiteration of the first. On all these counts, Willaert departs significantly from his predecessors. Most obviously, he keeps the voices of the opening duo in play after the second pair enters.[16] The second pair, moreover, no longer corresponds exactly to the first: in place of imitation at the octave at a distance of two breves, we now have imitation at the lower fifth at a distance of two and a half breves.[17] This alerts us to a further bending of the norm: both here and in the first duo, the two voices do not imitate each other with absolute precision. Altus and superius differ by one note in setting the word "flentes" in measures 3–6, while the late entry of the bassus in measure 11 stretches the final note of "Dominus" in the tenor. Contrapuntal necessity obviously dictated the reading of the altus in measure 4; but in principle, at least, Willaert could have had the bassus enter directly with the tenor's g in measure 10. Whatever his reasons for not doing so in this specific instance, the sum total of these small irregularities produces a subtly diffracted picture: not only do the two duos fail to show the expected correspondence, but of the four statements of the theme, only two—those of the superius and the bassus—match each other precisely.

The rest of the first section, while maintaining a full texture throughout, also unfolds around an armature of linear reiteration—paradoxically, one generally more precise than the opening exposition but at the same time more covert in its presentation. As the superius and tenor bring the opening clause to a cadence in measures 16–18, the altus presents an eight-note figure on the words "lachrimatus est" that the bassus repeats a sixth below starting in the last quarter of measure 18. The two statements together form a bridge between the cadence and the entry of the tenor in measure 20—which we can easily recognize as a rhythmically and decoratively plainer version of the subject in the altus and bassus; indeed, we might even harbor the suspicion that Willaert initially conceived the subject as it stands here and only then worked backwards to the statements that now precede it. In any event, the tenor clearly plays the dominant role in shaping the continuation of the music. The final note of its "lachrimatus est"—the *d* at the start of measure 23—simultaneously sets in motion a new linear connection: the three measures from here to the end of measure 25 recur literally in the superius from measure 25 to the end of measure 27, thus girding the entire polyphonic span up to the cadence in measures 28–29.

This brings us, after a brief link on the words "et clamabat," to the middle section—and to the passage that I wanted to share with Howard Brown. Despite its modest length, this forms the core of the motet—in more ways than one.[18] In formal terms, both musically and textually, the greater dimensions of the outer sections press this central portion into sharp relief. In narrative content, too, everything focuses on Jesus' words, the three words that work the miracle of bringing the dead Lazarus back to life. Plainly, Willaert recognized a challenge here: to come up with something miraculous of his own.

Described superficially, what he did looks simple enough: the voices sing "Lazare veni foras" and then, as rhetorical emphasis demands, sing it again, to the same music. If we went no further, this could sound like a passage in, say, Josquin or Mouton. But two things set Willaert's "Lazare veni foras" apart. First, while the earlier composers typically cast such repeated phrases in a homophonic style, Willaert adopts a loosely imitative polyphonic texture. More important, while the individual voices repeat exactly—I consider the minor declamatory variant in the tenor at measure 34 wholly insignificant, the curtailment of the same voice at the second half of measure 39 hardly less so—the complex as a whole does not.[19] Granted, the superius and tenor maintain the same relationship to one another in both statements; we may note, too, that the first statement of the altus combines with the second statement of the bassus to reproduce the same polyphony as superius and tenor a fourth below. But these qualifications hardly lessen the kaleidoscopic variety of the relationships among the voices as a whole, nor the virtuosity of Willaert's accomplishment as both contrapuntist and textual exegete.

Rather than examine the entire concluding section of *Videns Dominus*, I should like simply to focus on a single aspect of its first clause: Willaert's handling of the subject to which he sets the words "et prodiit ligatis manibus et pedibus." This subject appears five times in all, rising from its initial entry in the bassus at measure 40 through variously transposed statements in tenor, altus, and superius, then returning at its original pitch level to the bassus in measure 50. On tonal and rhythmic grounds, we could perhaps read these statements as two pairs—bassus–tenor, then superius–bassus—separated and mediated by the statement of the altus beginning in measure 43. The pairs follow a symmetrical transposition scheme, C–G–G–C; within each pair, the answering voice substitutes an offbeat minim for the semibreve opening of the *dux* but otherwise maintains rhythmic identity with its predecessor until the last word, "pedibus"; and the second pair differs from the first through its altered rhythmicization of "prodiit ligatis." Between these two blocks of relative stability, the altus acts as both a differentiating and a binding force. It alone stands at a different pitch level, D; and its rhythmic shape—the syncopated opening and the unbroken minim setting of "(pro)diit ligatis"—partakes of elements from all the other statements of the subject.

Whether or not Willaert in fact worked out this passage on such a systematic basis, however, its effect certainly does not make any of these refined symmetries evident, if only because the temporal distances seem to link the first four statements into a continuous chain but set the final statement substantially apart from the rest. For all their careful balance, moreover, the various alterations of rhythmic detail add up to a basically unstable whole: in no two statements does the subject assume quite the same shape—those which share a common reading of "prodiit ligatis" differ in their opening gesture, and vice versa. As with the opening and middle sections, therefore, this music treats the elements of formal cohesion—repetition, symmetry, articulation—in a decidedly equivocal fashion, retaining them as a structural foundation yet obscuring and distorting them in their surface presentation. As my occasional references to Josquin and Mouton may already have suggested, we may read this approach not just analytically, but historically as well; and I should now like to address this dimension more directly.

III

The art of motivicity as embodied in the music of Josquin and Mouton quite obviously served as the starting point for Willaert's own compositional practice. But in every detail, Willaert drives his inherited techniques down paths not traveled by his models. Josquin already varied the repetition of some multivoice configurations by shifting one of their constituent elements in pitch, temporal position, or both.[20] Yet neither he nor Mouton ever came even close to shaking up an entire texture so thoroughly as Willaert does with "Lazare veni foras." Nor, as already intimated, do Josquin or Mouton go anywhere so far as Willaert in altering the relationships even between repeated pairs of voices, especially at the beginning of a work or section. The freedom, too, with which Willaert bends his imitative subjects has no direct precedent. However much Josquin in particular may shuffle relationships among motives, he seems clearly at pains to preserve the exact identity of the motives themselves unless compelled to do so by local contrapuntal demands. But Willaert, as we have seen, would appear to alter his motivic shapes almost as a matter of principle. In *Videns Dominus*, at least, he retains them strictly only where they do not form part of a conventional imitative field: in the hidden duos of measures 17–27, and for all of "Lazare veni foras." Perhaps we may infer a sort of dialectic here: the more complex or unusual the handling of the subject, the more strictly the subject retains its identity; conversely, the more the externals of the handling conform to regular precedent—balanced pairs, for example—the more readily the subject itself undergoes transformation. Whether or not this holds throughout Willaert's output, we shall see it borne out in another instance shortly.

The first of the duos that underlie measures 17–27—that between the altus and the bassus—draws attention to yet another development. With the exception of sequential passages or "trick" canons, composers of the generation before Willaert hardly ever employ any interval of transposition—whether for individual lines or for entire polyphonic complexes—other than those inherent in the hexachordal system itself, the fourth, fifth, and octave; the relationship between this restriction and the tonal transparency so characteristic of Josquin and his immediate successors hardly requires elaboration.[21] Now, however, what we might call "imperfect transposition"—transposition at the second, third, sixth, or seventh—becomes a significant option. Admittedly, *Videns Dominus* takes a somewhat conservative stance in this regard; beyond measures 17–21, it contains no more than a hint of further imperfect transposition: the entry of the bassus in measure 67, which suggests a transposition at the second of the subject initially exposed in the same voice at measure 58, quickly veers from its implied continuation. But to get a better idea of what Willaert can do with this new possibility, we might do well to take a sideways glance at another motet first transmitted in the 1520s, *Congratulamini mihi omnes.*[22]

Like *Videns Dominus*, *Congratulamini* focuses on a miracle—in this instance, Jesus' own resurrection from the dead. In accordance with the text, a responsory for Easter Monday, both *partes* end with the same music; and our interest will center on a portion of this repeated material, the setting of the final words, "vidi Dominum meum."[23] The passage, which I reproduce here in Example 11.1, begins with what looks like a traditional gesture. At measures 56–57, Willaert reduces the texture to an imitative duo at the fifth between altus and superius. Under normal circumstances, we might anticipate a repetition of this music in the lower voices—a convention particularly frequent near the close of a work or section, and one that Willaert himself observes at corresponding places in other motets.[24] But the response both confounds and surpasses expectation: not only does Willaert have the tenor enter at measure 59 on the hexachordally remote level of E, but he answers it at the lower sixth, then trumps this immediately with a further entry at the seventh. At measure 63, moreover, he goes even this one better, repeating the entire three-voice complex originally formed by tenor, bassus, and superius a tone lower in the tenor, bassus, and altus, with an additional entry in the superius doubling the bassus in tenths. This last entry, already implicit in the altus at measures 60–61, adds a new element of motivic play as well. As the passage begins, the rhythmic shape of the superius would seem to mark it as simply an amplificatory derivative of the bassus, whose primary status would appear self-evident both from its own rhythm and from its prior role in measures 59–62. Yet in measure 65, the roles switch: the bassus swerves off its expected course, while the superius carries the subject through to completion at the start of measure 66.

Even within this passage, of course, the hexachordal levels of transposition inevitably retain their privileged position: despite the spellbinding array of en-

EXAMPLE 11.1   Willaert, *Congratulamini mihi omnes,* mm. 56–67

tries on no fewer than five different pitches, statements on G or D clearly anchor each polyphonic complex into the larger seventh-mode structure.[25] The strict retention of the subject, too, affords a stable point of reference. Nevertheless, the ultimate effect plainly deemphasizes such elements of balance and stability, relegating them at best to the middle distance: the foreground emphasizes not only the expanded transpositional palette but also a swirling rhythmic activity of a sort essentially foreign to Willaert's predecessors. Josquin certainly wrote imitative lines separated by a semibreve and moving largely in minims. But he and Mouton typically reserve this sort of thing for duos; rarely if ever does it occupy an entire four-voice texture—or if it does, the individual lines will consist largely of note repetitions, thus effectively moving in semibreves.[26] Willaert's precipitate cascade of voices, entering from almost every possible location in the tonal space and moving in constant harmonic flux, takes us into a new world of turbulent activity, one that evokes perhaps nothing so much as the dense stacking of serpentine figures with which painters of the 1520s replaced the airy symmetries and gracefully poised forms of Raphael's classic example.

IV

With this last remark, the interdisciplinary cat named in the third *M* of my title takes its first step out of the bag; for my invocation of post-Raphaelite painting unmistakably raises the specter of mannerism. Mannerism notoriously has at least as many definitions as we have writers on it—not for nothing did John Shearman begin his useful and influential traversal of the subject with the remark, "This book will have at least one feature in common with all those already published on Mannerism; it will appear to describe something quite different from what all the rest describe."[27] In regard to music, a proliferating debate on mannerism some 20 to 30 years ago all but imploded under its own multiform weight, and the subject has remained largely silent since then.

In reviving it now, I wish less to reheat old controversies than to pluck forth and develop further a single strand of the discussion. I take as my point of departure some remarks in James Haar's splendid article "Classicism and Mannerism in 16th-Century Music," a work itself indebted more than a little to the study of Shearman just cited.[28] According to Haar, "Those who speak of mannerism as an epoch in music history may be said to follow the art historians in that they see musical equivalents to the visual mannerism of Roman and Florentine painting, sculpture, and architecture after 1520—an art mannered in comparison to the classicism of the High Renaissance that preceded it." This leads the music historian "to discuss musical mannerism as a phenomenon following in time, and dependent upon, a generally recognized classical norm, the polyphonic style of Josquin Des Prez and some of his contemporaries in the first two decades of the 16th century."[29]

Even under this assumption, however, musical mannerism continues to present a shifting target. Shearman, for example, suggests, "There may . . . be some justification for extending the term Mannerism to the luxuriant, beautiful and often unintelligible polyphonic Masses and motets of the post-classical sixteenth century before the restraining influence of the Counter-Reformation; but better still is its application to an offshoot of that style, the madrigal."[30] Yet Shearman's focus on the madrigal seems motivated chiefly by criteria not primarily rooted in its musical language: by the propinquity of the madrigal to "the main centres of Mannerism around 1530," Florence and Rome; its connection to the literary movement known as *Bembismo*; and above all its artificiality "in style and as an idea."[31] These criteria do not really jibe with Shearman's own emphasis elsewhere on the internal technical features of mannerism in the visual arts. Nor does the musical language of the early madrigal seem particularly manneristic under any definition; Haar captures its essence nicely when he writes of "the placid flow of imitative and chordal polyphony used to set Petrarchan and Petrarchistic verse."[32] Mannerism in painting, moreover, hardly remained restricted to, or even concentrated on, a single genre. If it did have a particular locus, then this lay in the area that had always functioned as the proving-ground of the most ambitious artistic enterprise, large-scale sacred painting.

This consideration, therefore, could well turn our emphasis back to those "luxuriant, beautiful and often unintelligible . . . Masses and motets"—and to the motets above all. For despite the continued liturgical precedence of the Mass, the motet had without question become the central and most prestigious realm of creative activity for composers after Josquin: not for nothing do motets significantly outnumber Masses in the outputs of Josquin himself, Mouton, Willaert, and virtually every other major composer before Palestrina. Some remarks of Haar's, while not explicitly directed toward sacred repertories, seem to me especially pertinent to the question of mannerism and the motet. Noting that most musicologists writing on mannerism "have stressed the new interdependence of text and music," Haar raises the possibility of "a more purely musical mannerism, a technical, 'painterly' rather than a literary mannerism." In the music "of the . . . generation . . . active between 1520 and 1550," he writes,

> there is an observable thickening of texture, even in music written for the classical medium of four voices. Imitative entries are more frequent, and more closely spaced; the paired voices disappear in favor of fuller contrapuntal texture; and the number of well-marked cadences, or points of articulation, in the music is deliberately lessened by use of a technique called by mid-century theorists the art of "fuggir la cadenza". . . . The style is . . . a musical *maniera*, characteristic of a number of composers in a greater or lesser degree, but particularly noticeable in the work of Nicholas Gombert. . . . Whether we call it manneristic or not, this is music showing a *maniera* based on elements of a recognized *ars perfecta*. . . . The comparison with the self-conscious elegance, deliberate distortions, and artifice of painters like Pontormo and Parmigianino seems to me rather a close one.[33]

Haar does not pursue this line further; but I shall obviously want to do so. The catalog of technical traits that he offers quite clearly dovetails with my own observations about Willaert's motets.[34] More precisely, we might say that our concentration on the details of motivicity—the varied repetition, irregular transposition, and so forth—draws us into the interior of the edifice whose outward features Haar describes so well. As important, our analyses reinforce his understanding of the way the newer style revalues and self-consciously seeks to trump the precedents it has absorbed from its canonized models.

Haar, of course, differs from me in associating the kind of mannerism he describes here chiefly with Gombert; in this he follows a familiar musicological trope that goes back ultimately to the German theorist Hermann Finck.[35] Thanks to the early reception of Finck by such historians as August Wilhelm Ambros, Gombert has come to dominate the discussion of post-Josquin music in a way that might not accurately reflect his position in his own time; without necessarily wishing to question his artistic stature, we must note that in Italy, at least, his music does not appear to have enjoyed very wide circulation before the late 1530s.[36] Especially in regard to mannerism, I think that we might well place greater weight on a figure such as Willaert, who so plainly occupied a dominant position in the land of mannerism's origin, and whose development of the kind of musical *maniera* under discussion appears to have preceded Gombert's, if only by a narrow margin.

Of course, we needn't lose ourselves in quibbles. Analogs of time and place never work with complete precision; and given the fact that even in Italy the most significant musicians continued to come from north of the Alps, we can never establish musical mannerism as a fundamentally Italian phenomenon fully akin to mannerism in the visual arts. Chronologically, too, we must accept a measure of leeway—and not just within the musical realm. Consider, for example, Shearman's description of Michelangelo's cartoon for *The Battle of Cascina*, a work whose self-conscious virtuosity Shearman sees as a significant harbinger of mannerism: "The cartoon . . . demonstrated . . . comprehensively that Michelangelo's art enjoyed absolute sovereignty over the human figure; its message, to the sixteenth century, was that there were now no limitations in the complexity of postures and the variety of aspects in which the body might be re-created and seen."[37] Substitute "musical figure" for "human figure," and "motive" for "body," and you have a perfect characterization of Willaert's art. But Michelangelo's cartoon dates from the years 1504–5; and despite the awesome technical accomplishments of Josquin's music from around that very time, I seriously doubt that anyone would describe it in terms of "no limitations in the complexity of postures."[38] Nor can we simply dispose of the chronological discrepancy with an appeal to the old adage about time lags between music and the visual arts.

So I shall not wish to push the notion of Willaert's music as mannerist too far. But it remains to me an inescapable fact that the traits conventionally described as typical of post-Raphaelite mannerist art—the compacting of structure, distortion of symmetry, distention of figures, and softening of outlines—find a perfect analog in compositions like *Videns Dominus*. Eventually, of course, Willaert's post-, even anticlassical, art became the foundation of a new classicism, defined and codified by his pupil Zarlino. In our day, writing on Willaert has, it seems to me, too readily followed the agenda that Zarlino set toward the end of Willaert's life. But looking at the music of the younger Willaert, we see something other than the stern and austere figure of the history books, the grizzled old man all too familiar from the frontispiece to *Musica nova*: we see a vibrant, energetic artist eagerly displaying his virtuosity, transforming the heritage of his biographical and spiritual teachers into a new kind of art—an art that, by all accounts, took Italy by storm. Properly heard, it can still do the same to us.

NOTES

I wrote most of this paper during an academic quarter spent at the Ohio State University, where I benefited greatly from the observations of my students and colleagues; particular thanks for their insights, challenges, and generally delightful conversation go to Charles Atkinson and Margarita Mazo. I owe a special debt to David Schulenberg, of the University of North Carolina, for prodding me to formulate the definition of "motivicity" offered in Section I.

1. Readers of this article may want also to consult my earlier study "Motivik – Konstruktion – Humanismus: Zur Motette *Huc me sydereo* von Josquin des Prez," in *Die Motette: Beiträge zu ihrer Gattungsgeschichte*, ed. Herbert Schneider, Neue Studien zur Musikwissenschaft 5 (Mainz: Schott, 1992), 105–34, to which it forms something of a pendant. Although I have invoked the notion of motivicity in papers read at various public forums since the mid-1980s, I have not previously used the word itself in print: the editors of the article just cited balked at the neologism "Motivizität" and insisted on substituting the more traditional German "Motivik." David Schulenberg has used the term independently of me in his article "Composition as Variation: Inquiries into the Compositional Procedures of the Bach Circle of Composers," *Current Musicology* 33 (1982): 77, although not with the same meaning; for its further dissemination, see Cristle Collins Judd, "Modal Types and *Ut, Re, Mi* Tonalities: Tonal Coherence in Sacred Vocal Polyphony from about 1500," *Journal of the American Musicological Society* 45 (1992): 446.

2. Joseph Kerman, " 'Write All These Down': Notes on a Song by Byrd," in *Byrd Studies*, ed. Alan Brown and Richard Turber (Cambridge: Cambridge University Press, 1992), 112–28, repr. in id., *Write All These Down: Essays on Music* (Berkeley: University of California Press, 1994), 106–24, conflates the two notions of motive that I attempt to separate here, at the cost of some confusion in an otherwise admirably sensitive analysis.

3. I add the hedging "almost" to allow, say, the disqualification of such things as stereotypical cadential patterns whose repetition may have no real motivic significance in the sense foreseen here.

4. See, for example, Klaus-Jürgen Sachs, "Counterpoint," §11: "16th-Century Double Counterpoint," *The New Grove Dictionary of Music and Musicians*, ed. Stanley Sadie (London: Macmillan, 1980), 4:842–43; or "Invertible Counterpoint," *The New Harvard Dictionary of Music*, ed. Don Michael Randel (Cambridge, Mass.: Harvard University Press, 1986), 404–6.

5. See "Motivik – Konstruktion – Humanismus."

6. Concerning London 2037, see principally *Census-Catalogue of Manuscript Sources of Polyphonic Music 1400–1500*, Renaissance Manuscript Studies 1 (Neuhausen–Stuttgart: American Institute of Musicology–Hänssler-Verlag, 1979–88), 2:

121–22, as well as Edward E. Lowinsky, *The Medici Codex of 1518: A Choirbook of Motets Presented to Lorenzo de' Medici, Duke of Urbino. Historical Introduction and Commentary*, Monuments of Renaissance Music 3 (Chicago: University of Chicago Press, 1968), 116–17, and my review of Albert Dunning, *Die Staatsmotette 1480–1555* (Utrecht: A. Oosthoek's Uitgeversmaatschappij, 1970), in *Notes* 28 (1971–72): 426. I know of 11 motets by Willaert, all but one for four voices, that appear in sources predating 1520: seven in the so-called Medici Codex of 1518, Florence, Biblioteca Medicea-Laurenziana, MS Acquisti e doni 666 (*Beatus Joannes Apostolus, Christi Virgo dilectissima, Intercessio quesumus Domine, Regina celi, Saluto te sancta Virgo Maria, Veni Sancte Spiritus,* and *Virgo gloriosa Christi*); three in Bologna, Civico Museo Bibliografico Musicale, MS Q 19 (*Dominus regit me, O gemma clarissima Catherina,* and *Quia devotis laudibus*); and one in Petrucci's *Motetti de la corona libro quarto* of 1519 (*Verbum bonum et suave*, 6vv).

7. On the provenance and date of the Massimo partbooks, cf. Friedrich Lippmann, "Musikhandschriften und -Drucke in der Bibliothek Massimo," *Studien zur italienisch-deutschen Musikgeschichte* 11, Analecta musicologica 17 (Cologne: Arno Volk Verlag, 1976), 267, or *Census-Catalogue* 3:114–15.

8. Cf. Norbert Böker-Heil, *Die Motetten von Philippe Verdelot* (Frankfurt am Main: author, 1967), 55–56. The otherwise complete list of sources for *Videns Dominus* in Mary S. Lewis, *Antonio Gardano, Venetian Music Printer 1538–1569: A Descriptive Bibliography and Historical Study*, 1 (New York: Garland, 1988), 492, omits Rhau 1538[8], no doubt through a mechanical error, as the listing for the volume in the index of sources (604) includes a reference to *Videns Dominus*.

9. On the Scotto and Gardano publications and the question of their relationship to each other, see particularly Lewis Lockwood, "A Sample Problem of *Musica Ficta*: Willaert's *Pater Noster*," in *Studies in Music History: Essays for Oliver Strunk*, ed. Harold Powers (Princeton: Princeton University Press, 1968), 174–75; Mary S. Lewis, "Antonio Gardane's Early Connections with the Willaert Circle," in *Music in Medieval and Early Modern Europe: Patronage, Sources and Texts*, ed. Iain Fenlon (Cambridge: Cambridge University Press, 1981), 224–25; and Anne Smith, "Ordering Willaert's Motets à la Mode," *Basler Jahrbuch für historische Musikpraxis* 16 (1992): 117–18. As Lewis notes, Gardano's readings often stand particularly close to those of London 2037, which would appear to lend them special credibility; *Videns Dominus* reinforces this observation, as the two sources correspond in every musical particular, and in several details of text placement as well.

10. For Leipzig 49/50, see the variants recorded in *Adrian Willaert: Sämtliche Werke*, ed. Hermann Zenck, 1, Publikationen älterer Musik 9 (Leipzig: Breitkopf and Härtel, 1937; repr. Hildesheim: Georg Olms, 1968), xvi. Treviso 7, which Zenck does not log, corrects one error present in Scotto (tenor, m. 34) but otherwise reproduces all its musical readings, including further errors (altus, m. 46; tenor, m. 38); the sources correspond in virtually every detail of wording and text placement as well. An unknown hand subsequently corrected the ascription to Jachet; cf. Table 11.1 and *Census-Catalogue* 3:238.

11. See *Sämtliche Werke* 1:62–63, and *Adriani Willaert Opera Omnia*, ed. Hermann Zenck, Walter Gerstenberg, and Helga Meier, Corpus Mensurabilis Musicae 3 (Rome: American Institute of Musicology, 1950–), 1:71–73.

12. See *Treize livres de motets parus chez Pierre Attaingnant en 1534 et 1535*, ed. Albert Smijers and A. Tillman Merritt (Monaco: Editions de l'Oiseau-lyre, 1934–64), 11:158–61; *Georg Rhau: Musikdrucke aus den Jahren 1538 bis 1545 in praktischer Ausgabe*, vol. 3, ed. Hans Albrecht (Kassel: Bärenreiter, 1954), 98–101; and Anne-Marie

Bragard, *Étude bio-bibliographique sur Philippe Verdelot, musicien français de la Renaissance*, Académie Royale de Belgique, Classe des beaux-arts: Mémoires, ser. 2, vol. 11, fasc. 1 (Brussels: Académie Royale de Belgique, 1964), 141–44. My own transcription, like Zenck's, depends on Gardano; cf. n. 9.

13. See Bragard, *Verdelot*, 71, and Hermann Zenck, "Über Willaerts Motetten," in id., *Numerus et Affectus: Studien zur Musikgeschichte*, ed. Walter Gerstenberg, Musikwissenschaftliche Arbeiten 16 (Kassel: Bärenreiter, 1959), 55–66, esp. 61–62, as well as 86.

14. Cf. *Sämtliche Werke* 1:xvi, and Zenck, "Über Willaerts Motetten," 61, neither of them, however, wholly accurate. As Zenck notes, Willaert does not make any reference to the melody associated with *Videns Dominus* in both the modern Gradual and most early chant books; I have not had the opportunity to consult the other melodies cited by Michel Huglo, *Les Tonaires: Inventaire, analyse, comparaison*, Publications de la Société Française de Musicologie, ser. 3, vol. 2 (Paris: Société Française de Musicologie, 1971), 153. Readers should bear in mind that the liturgical assignment of the chant need not specifically define the performance context of Willaert's motet; cf., among other sources, Anthony M. Cummings, "Toward an Interpretation of the Sixteenth-Century Motet," *Journal of the American Musicological Society* 34 (1981): 43–59.

15. As many will recognize, my formulation seeks to dodge the most heated questions on modality in sixteenth-century music. In the present context, those eager for more information might consult Harold S. Powers, "Tonal Types and Modal Categories in Renaissance Polyphony," *Journal of the American Musicological Society* 34 (1981): 428–70; and Smith, "Ordering Willaert's Motets à la Mode."

16. Norbert Böker-Heil has already drawn attention to this procedure as characteristic in Willaert, Verdelot, and their contemporaries; see *Die Motetten von Philippe Verdelot*, 130.

17. The imitative disposition thus created—upper three voices at the octave or unison, lowest voice a fifth apart—in fact reverts to a layout common among the earliest layer of compositions with imitative openings. Many of the motets in Rome, Biblioteca Apostolica Vaticana, MS Cappella Sistina 15, an important repertory copied in the 1490s, illustrate this type, as does Josquin's *Missa Gaudeamus*; cf. *Werken van Josquin des Prés*, ed. Albert Smijers, Miroslaw Antonowycz, and Willem Elders (Amsterdam: G. Alsbach, 1921–66), Missen, no. 3. By the 1520s, however, this kind of opening had long since given way to matched pairs—octave–octave or fifth–fifth.

18. Zenck, "Über Willaerts Motetten," 61, also recognizes this passage as "the spiritual center of the piece," although he does not share any of the musical observations that follow.

19. Attaingnant in fact provides the declamatorily correct reading of two minims in measure 34; cf. the edition cited in n. 12. Although the modern edition of Rhau cited in the same note also shows this reading, the original has the semibreve found in the majority of sources. I have not had occasion to check the Massimo partbooks, the only other independent source to include the tenor.

20. An especially notable example occurs in the five-voice *Salve regina* near the end of the *prima pars*, where a recurring cadential figure intersects with statements of the ostinato in constantly different configurations; see *Werken van Josquin des Prés*, Motetten, no. 48. The otherwise comprehensive analysis of the motet in Cristle Collins Judd, "Josquin des Prez: *Salve regina* (à 5)," in *Models of Musical Analysis: Music before 1600*, ed. Mark Everist (Oxford: Blackwell, 1992), 114–44, does not call attention to this aspect of the passage in question, although Judd's Ex. 6.6 (122) shows her awareness of it.

21. See also "Motivik – Konstruktion – Humanismus," 117.

22. For editions, see *Sämtliche Werke* 1:29–32, and *Opera omnia* 1:26–30, as well as H. Colin Slim, *A Gift of Madrigals and Motets* (Chicago: University of Chicago Press, 1972), 1:72–81, and *Treize livres de motets parus chez Pierre Attaingnant*, 2:32–41. The earliest source, the so-called Newberry-Oscott partbooks edited by Slim, originated at a still disputed time between 1525 and 1529. Cf. Slim, *A Gift*, 1:16–37 and 105–16; id., *Ten Altus Parts at Oscott College, Sutton Coldfield* (n.p., n.d.), 6–7; and Iain Fenlon, "La Diffusion de la chanson continentale dans les manuscrits anglais entre 1509–1570," in *La Chanson à la Renaissance: Actes du XXᵉ Colloque d'Etudes humanistes du Centre d'Etudes Supérieures de la Renaissance de l'Université de Tours. Juillet 1977*, ed. Jean-Michel Vaccaro (Tours: Editions Van de Velde, 1981), 178–80. Readers should not confuse the *Congratulamini mihi omnes* discussed here with the different *Congratulamini*, with the *secunda pars* "Beatam me dicent," published in *Sämtliche Werke* 1:101–5 and *Opera omnia* 2:18–23.

23. For details of the text source, see *Sämtliche Werke* 1:xiv, and Slim, *A Gift of Madrigals and Motets*, 1:220.

24. See, for example, *Benedicta es celorum regina* (*Sämtliche Werke* 1:67–70; *Opera omnia* 1:78–82), mm. 70–73, or *Pater noster* (*Sämtliche Werke* 1:97–101; *Opera omnia* 2:11–17), mm. 168–72.

25. For further insights into the issue touched on here, readers might consult Smith, "Ordering Willaert's Motets à la Mode," esp. 126–27, and its companion study, "Willaert's Use of Mode in *Mirabile mysterium* and *Ave regina coelorum*," *Basler Jahrbuch für historische Musikpraxis* 16 (1992): 141–65.

26. See, for example, Josquin's *Memor esto verbi tu*, in *Werken van Josquin des Prés*, Motetten, no. 31.

27. John Shearman, *Mannerism* (Harmondsworth: Penguin, 1967), 15; quoted also by Haar (see the following note), 56.

28. James Haar, "Classicism and Mannerism in 16th-Century Music," *International Review of Music Aesthetics and Sociology* 1 (1970): 55–67.

29. Ibid., 57.

30. Shearman, *Mannerism*, 98–99.

31. Ibid., 99.

32. Haar, "Classicism and Mannerism," 66.

33. Ibid., 61–62.

34. I might take this opportunity to add yet another element to the picture: the heightened level of dissonance. Barely a measure of Willaert's music goes by without an extracadential suspension between at least one pair of voices. But to pursue this further would take another article.

35. Cf. Haar, "Classicism and Mannerism," 62, n. 16, with reference to Hermann Finck, *Practica musica* (Wittenberg: n.publ., 1556; facs. Hildesheim: Georg Olms, 1971), sig. Aijʳ.

36. On its very first page of text, the particularly influential third volume of Ambros's *Geschichte der Musik* states that Netherlandish composers of the period 1450–1550—which "in the history of music quite properly deserves the name Century of the Netherlanders"—"could be divided into three epochs called, in accordance with their foremost representatives, the epochs of Ockeghem, Josquin, and Gombert"; see August Wilhelm Ambros, *Geschichte der Musik*, 3 (Breslau: F.E.C. Leuckart, 1868), 3. Works by Gombert figure regularly in French and German printed editions from 1529 onwards, and the publications with which Buglhat, Gardano, and Scotto spearheaded the revival of Italian music printing in 1538 and 1539 accord him considerable prominence

as well. But he remains largely absent from Italian manuscripts of the 1530s, with only two pieces—one of them misattributed (cf. Joshua Rifkin, "Hesdin, Nicolle des Celliers de," *New Grove* 8:530–31)—in Rome, Biblioteca Apostolica Vaticana, MS C.G. XII.4, and one each in the Massimo partbooks; Florence, Biblioteca Nazionale Centrale, MS Magl. XIX.125bis; Modena, Biblioteca Estense e Universitaria, MS α N.1.2; and Rome, Biblioteca Vallicelliana, MS S¹ 35–40. The initial spur to my thoughts on Gombert came from discussions held many years ago with Mary Lewis, whom I thank belatedly for the stimulus she provided me.

37. Shearman, *Mannerism*, 52.

38. See the analysis of *Huc me sydereo* in "Motivik – Konstruktion – Humanismus."

Willaert, *Videns Dominus*

261

Lasso as Historicist

The Cantus-Firmus Motets

During the course of the sixteenth century there was a perceptible growth of historical consciousness on the part of musicians and students of European musical culture. The music of classical antiquity was almost completely lost, but scholars of humanistic bent could and did make careful study of ancient writings about music.[1] As for the musical traditions of postclassical Europe, chant of course continued to be sung and to be regarded as canonical; but there is no evidence that its historical development was of interest to, or even conceptualized by, anyone. Polyphony, though denigrated by some humanists and by sixteenth-century musicians under the humanist spell, was praised by many writers and was recognized as having run a historical course. But no one attempted to sketch a history of polyphonic practice from early organum, or even Notre Dame polyphony, onwards, in the spirit of Vasari; the surviving musical evidence was scattered, multinational and probably undecipherable, and really old music—apart from chant—was sometimes physically saved, in a way an object of veneration, but was not studied as sounding art.

What did develop was, as Jessie Ann Owens has convincingly reminded us, a kind of short-term historical awareness, with writers on music commemorating the work of one or two generations before their own.[2] By the end of the sixteenth century this awareness stretched, increasingly thin at its early end, to the span of about a century. Theorists could cite their medieval predecessors, back to Guido d'Arezzo in the eleventh century; but no music of that remote period was available even had they wished to refer to it.

Historical reference is explicit, hence relatively easy to find, in the writings of music theorists. It can also be charted, with the same short-term bias, in the output of music publishers such as the Nuremberg printers of the music of Josquin and his contemporaries in the 1530s, the retrospective anthologies of Pierre Attaingnant and Nicolas du Chemin a decade later, and the issue of a volume of Josquin motets by the Parisian firm of Le Roy and Ballard in 1555.[3]

Publishers in the Netherlands contributed to this phenomenon by bringing out, in the 1540s and 1550s, collections of music by a generation of composers whose careers were over, or nearly so, by that time.[4] Printers were actively concerned with publishing new music, but they also cultivated a market for an older repertory.

How do composers fit into this picture? There was as yet no out-and-out historicizing movement encouraging them to write in genuinely archaizing fashion; in the 1550s everyone wrote 'new' music. Yet certain elements of an older tradition remained available to musicians. We do not yet, perhaps, recognize all of these. A passage in *fauxbourdon* may or may not have been intended as an archaism; open fifths and octaves are not necessarily references to musical antiquity; thematic allusions to older music may reflect only the survival of a particular musical gesture no longer known in its original context. One practice of composers active in the middle third of the sixteenth century does seem genuinely historicist in intent: the use of cantus firmi in Masses and motets, especially when in the latter genre these melodies have texts separate from that of the pieces as a whole. Motets of this type written by Orlando di Lasso are the subject of this chapter.

Lasso was certainly not an epigonal composer, even if by the end of his life he was no longer writing "a la nouvelle composition d'aucuns d'Italie," as his 'op. 1' of 1555 proclaimed.[5] His employment of separately texted cantus firmi in motets was not a reference to Busnoys or Ockeghem—though possibly if indirectly to Josquin—but imitation of a practice he had observed in the music of Willaert and Rore and of Franco-Netherlandish composers being published in Antwerp and Louvain at the same time as he was beginning his own career in print. To call Lasso's cantus-firmus motets historicist is thus to place him in the short-term framework described by Owens; nonetheless the tradition itself was an old one and was perhaps deliberately archaizing, in the case of ceremonial motets a use of musical regalia of suitably antique character. Though there are other aspects of Lasso's work that are attractive when viewed through a historicist lens—the stylistic features singled out by Bernhard Meier,[6] the use of motets by Josquin as the basis for parody Magnificats,[7] the existence of a Mass written entirely in sesquialtera proportion[8]—I chose to look at the cantus-firmus motets because of the tradition of which they are a part.

Lasso's motets using separately texted cantus firmi number 15 in all. They are listed in the Appendix and will be discussed in the order of their presentation there. These pieces, referred to singly in the Lasso literature, are treated as a group by Wolfgang Boetticher, whose discussion formed the basis for my investigation.[9]

Given the frequency with which cantus firmi appear in ceremonial motets,[10] one would expect to find that Lasso used this technique often when composing such occasional pieces, but this is not the case, or at least not certainly so. The first three motets in the list are settings of secular texts, two of them clearly of dedicatory nature. The rest are set to sacred texts, including psalms, liturgical and paraliturgical texts, and devotional works. One, the last on the list, appears to be a half-humorous teaching piece, setting the Guidonian hymn *Ut queant laxis*. Some use a part of the motet text for the cantus firmus, but most have separate texts, of varied origin, for that voice. These texts differ in length and nature but incline toward epigrammatic utterance. Few of these motets can be dated with any precision, but they appear as a whole to come from the first half of the composer's career. As will be seen, Lasso uses various techniques, for all of which there was plenty of precedent, in handling the cantus firmus; only canon, prominent in many earlier cantus-firmus motets, is neglected.

Two of these motets have clear ceremonial or dedicatory texts. Both are quite early works. No. 1, *Cernere virtutes*, though not printed until 1568,[11] suggests from its text that it was written for a state wedding in January of 1557, that of Philibert of Baden to Mechtilda of Bavaria, daughter of Wilhelm IV and sister of Lasso's employer Duke Albrecht V.[12] If this is true, the work must be among the earliest of Lasso's Munich compositions. In this motet the cantus firmus is placed in a high voice (cantus II, in G_2 clef), sounding above the other parts except in passages where the names of the bridal pair or of Bavaria occur. It is also distinct rhythmically, moving as it does largely in breves, from the prevailing minim motion of the other voices. The long melody, from which the opening of the first cantus part seems to be derived, is heard twice, repeated exactly except for one rhythmic alteration.[13] It seems to have been composed for the purpose, its rhythms fitting the text in suitably declamatory fashion and its melodic contour in accord with the mode (plagal on D, transposed up an octave) of the motet.

Si qua tibi (no. 2), which appears in Lasso's Antwerp motet book of 1556, is composed to an encomiastic text of humanistic character; the cantus firmus text acts as a sort of summary. The recipient of all the praise is unnamed. Haberl assumed it to be Antoine Perrenot de Granvelle, to whom the motet volume is dedicated; Boetticher thinks this hardly possible but does not say why.[14] Albert Dunning, following Edward Lowinsky, thinks the motet was meant for the Emperor Charles V.[15] This is conceivable but I can see no way to prove it; and it would have been aiming rather high on Lasso's part unless he had been commissioned to set the text.

The cantus firmus, shorter than that of *Cernere virtutes*, is heard six times, alternating entries on G and C; it fits the mode of the piece, is in a middle register, and though written in breves and semibreves does not stand out very much from the remaining five voices. The distance between entries at first appears to be simply irregular. On closer inspection it looks as if the composer may have chosen a scheme of separating entries by five breves of rest, then altered it to suit the demands of the piece as it was composed out. These would seem to have been primarily textual. The main text of the motet can be divided into six sections, to each of which a statement of the cantus firmus is attached. This would conform to traditional procedures for tenor motet composition; but the sections are not uniform in length of text or in musical setting. Lasso may have begun with the tenor cantus firmus, but the latter was then subordinated to the flow of the piece surrounding it. Here is a first example of Lasso conforming only partially to a venerable compositional framework he may not have completely understood and in any event did not feel obliged to honor.

There was of course ample precedent for Lasso as he set these ceremonial texts, and one does not have to go back to the fifteenth century to find it. Motets by Gombert (*Felix Austria domus*), Rore (*Quis tuos presul*), Jachet (*Ploremus omnes et lacrimemur*), Pieter Maessens (*Discessu dat*), and Willaert (*Inclite Dux salve victor*) are possible precedents. Particularly likely is Manchicourt's *Nil pace est melius*, given Manchicourt's presence in Antwerp and his connections with Perrenot de Granvelle.[16] All of these are ceremonial works, and all use separately texted cantus-firmus melodies, some of them as long as that of *Cernere virtutes*.

The next work on our list, no. 3, *Quod licet id libeat*, is a short (35–breve) piece setting a brief, rather enigmatic text. Its cantus firmus, *Si licet libet*, is derived from the motet text—or perhaps, in this case, the other way round. The tenor text sounds like a device or motto and was indeed used as such. Its source appears to be a passage in the fourth-century *Scriptores Historiae Augustae*, a composite history of later Roman emperors well known in the Renaissance.[17] The motet may celebrate, as a kind of musical emblem, a person, as yet unknown to me, who used the cantus-firmus text as motto. No publication of this work earlier than the posthumous *Magnus opus musicum* is known; the date of the work's composition is hard to guess at.

The melody, heard in two forms, is based on the solmization syllables *mi re*, "cavato dalle vocali" of its text.[18] It is thus our first example of Lasso drawing on a fifteenth-century tradition, the most famous example of which is Josquin's *Missa Hercules dux Ferrariae* (many sixteenth-century motets by the composers named above and others also draw upon this tradition). It is heard first in breves, then semibreves, with symmetrically tailored rests separating statements. The final repetition, in a mix of minims and semibreves, separated by a minim rest, is not quite symmetrical, offering another bit of evidence that Lasso adjusted his cantus firmi to fit the contrapuntal structure rather than relying on a rigid constructivist scheme.

All the remaining texts in this group of motets are sacred. Three have possible liturgical connections. The first of these, *Libera me Domine* (no. 4), has for its text the opening of the responsory at Absolution in the Burial Service.[19] The second tenor of this six-voice work uses a five-note cantus firmus on the text "Respice finem." An appropriate sentiment, certainly; but this seems not to be a biblical phrase, and though it is listed in many collections of proverbs and Latin quotations, its source is never specified. A possible ultimate source may be a phrase attributed to Solon.[20] Perhaps the most famous use of the term is in Shakespeare's *Comedy of Errors* (4.4), where it is part of an earthy punning passage. Shakespeare's source, and that of other Renaissance users of the term, may have been a Latin translation of Aesop's *Fables*, well known in the sixteenth century.[21]

The cantus firmus is a simple five-note scalar descent, appropriate to the sense of the text, heard first in the natural, soft, and hard hexachords where its last two notes are the *mi-re* of the text's vowels; but the fourth statement, C–F, breaks this pattern. The cantus firmus is heard four times in breves, each statement separated by rests of two breves; four statements in semibreves, punctuated by one breve's rest, follow, and a final semibreve statement on A–D rounds off the piece. The repetitions of the cantus firmus are independent of textual phrases in the other voices; this is (apart from the opening six-breve rest) one of the most consistently symmetrical patterns among these motets. As for its date, the work was first published in 1568 but was probably not new when it appeared in print.[22]

No. 5, *Multae tribulationes*, a brief (40-breve) six-voice motet published in 1577,[23] is confusingly over-specific textually. The main text is psalmodic (Ps. 38:20), used as the Introit for the feast of SS. John and Paul, fourth-century martyrs.[24] Tenor II has a separate text, a line from the Gospel of Luke that is found as the fifth antiphon at Vespers for feasts of Apostles and Evangelists.[25] How these two liturgical assignments may be reconciled I am not sure, unless the similarity of saints' names can account for it. The sentiments of the two texts do not seem to me particularly close to each other; something of the intended meaning is escaping me.

Lasso did not make obvious reference to the chant melody for the text *Multae tribulationes*. The cantus firmus, on the other hand, cites the chant antiphon *In patientia* note for note (transposed up a fifth). The melody is given in semibreves, then repeated exactly and in full, its somewhat plodding progress perhaps a reflection of the text. The quiet semibreve motion and smoothly stepwise melody of the cantus firmus make it all but disappear into the six-voice texture of the work. There may well have been specific reference, individual meaning here; but it would seem now to be irrecoverable.

A much different case is that of no. 6, *Fremuit spiritus Jesus*. For this work we know Lasso's immediate source, a six-voice motet on the same text and with the same cantus firmus by Clemens non Papa, published in 1554.[26] The second part of the motet text, *Videns Dominus*, from the final phrase of which the cantus firmus takes its words, was a popular one, with settings by Verdelot, Willaert, Phinot, and Wert.[27] There is a liturgical place for the motet; its *secunda pars*, including the final exhortation used for the cantus firmus, is the Communion on Friday after the fourth Sunday of Lent.[28] It is also said to be used in the liturgy for the feast of St. Lazarus, something I have as yet been unable to verify. The text is a combination of citation and paraphrase from the Gospel of John.[29] Its theme, that of Christ raising Lazarus from the dead, is one that must have had wide appeal.

Lasso clearly knew and imitated Clemens's motet; he retains its F mode, uses almost the same cleffing, places the cantus firmus in the same high voice (cantus II), and alludes to the older composer's opening melodic gesture, itself derived from the cantus firmus.[30] His cantus firmus is the same as that of Clemens, at least initially, and even the statement on Bb is found in Clemens's setting. Both composers alter the length of beginning and ending notes of the melody, as well as the distance between statements, but Lasso does not copy Clemens's pattern exactly. The most striking difference between them is Lasso's final statement on Eb, which rings out above the other voices; this effective use of cantus firmus for rhetorical power is typical of Lasso's setting, much more vivid and speech-like than Clemens's motet. The young Lasso evidently aimed at surpassing his model in affective power.

Several motets use psalm texts; they were presumably useful for a number of occasions. *Jubilate Deo omnis terra* (no. 7) sets Ps. 99, complete. This text was also set by Clemens, who did not employ a cantus firmus; the two pieces are not much alike, but Lasso appears to have drawn the opening of his cantus firmus from the first four notes of Clemens's beginning motive, and both pieces are set in an exultant G mode (Lasso uses a higher cleffing and ambitus).[31] The cantus-firmus text for Lasso's motet, "Si Deus nobiscum quis contra nos?", is drawn from a New Testament source, Paul's Epistle to the Romans.[32] This phrase enjoyed some popularity as a motto; one German use of it was for the Order of Philip the Magnanimous of Hesse (d. 1567).[33]

Lasso's six-voice setting places the cantus firmus in the middle of the texture (tenor II). It shows the strictest symmetry of any of the cantus-firmus motets. The tenor melody is heard six times, alternating entries on G and F, in each of the two *partes*, and each statement, including the first, is preceded by rests of three and one-half breves. Thus the two parts of the motet are exactly the same length even though the second part has three lines of text to the first's two. At some points the whole texture changes at the entrance or end of a cantus-firmus statement. It is clear that in this piece the cantus firmus has determined the structure and at least in part the character of the music. Whether by accident or by intention, Lasso here wrote a piece in something of the spirit of the old cantus-firmus motet.

No. 8, *Homo cum in honore esset*, is also based on a psalm text; it quotes Ps. 48:13 (repeated in 21).[34] Published in 1566,[35] this short (39-breve) work is another of Lasso's enigmatically compact motets, its doubtless specific original intent lost to us. This six-voice piece has as its second altus a cantus firmus with the text "Nosce teipsum." The words are a standard Latin translation of the famous inscription on the temple of Apollo at Delphi—γνῶθι σεαυτὸν (know thyself). Attributed as primary source to Thales, the saying was famous in antiquity, cited by Plutarch, included in a satire of Juvenal, and mentioned in translation by Latin writers, including Cicero; all of this and more is summarized in an adage of Erasmus.[36] The phrase was often used as a motto; whether there was someone who commissioned this motet because its sobering message had special meaning I do not know, although I strongly suspect that this was the case. The words of Edward Lowinsky on cantus firmi of this type deserve quoting here: "Often the idea of using a *cantus firmus* or an *ostinato* based on a separate text seems inspired less by considerations of construction than by the composer's desire to express a fundamental thought in relation to his main text."[37] To this I would add only that the thought may not have been the composer's but one given him by some patron.

The cantus firmus is a solmization-pun melody based on the vowels of the text. It is heard twice, once in the natural and once in the soft hexachord, in breves, with a two-breve rest between. Then come two statements in semibreves with a breve rest's separation; a pair of statements in inexact diminution (minims and semiminims) follows, and a final statement in semibreves and minims in the natural hexachord, ending on the dominant of the mode, concludes the piece. There is no observable coincidence with the main text in the other voices; the cantus firmus is a real but hidden message added to that of the motet.

Congregati sunt inimici (no. 9) is a five-voice setting of a text popular with sixteenth-century composers; among those who set it are Verdelot, Arcadelt, Janequin, Leonardo Barrè, Josquin Baston, and Crecquillon.[38] The motet text is a responsory for Matins on the first Sunday of October.[39] This is clearer in some other settings than it is in that of Lasso; Verdelot's motet, for example, is in two *partes*, the second beginning with "Disperge illos in virtute sua" and ending with a repetition of "ut cognoscant . . . Deus noster" (see Appendix, no. 9, for Lasso's text). Lasso would appear not to have intended his composition for liturgical use as a responsory.[40] This is evident from his choice of text for the cantus firmus; whereas Verdelot and Crecquillon use *Da pacem Domine*, from the same liturgical source as the motet text, Lasso uses a psalm verse, "Dissipa gentes quae bella volunt" (Ps. 67:31), appropriate in sentiment and set to a psalm-like melodic formula, but not liturgically relevant so far as I can determine.

The cantus firmus, placed in cantus I, is heard five times, descending from D to G and dipping under cantus II as it does so, perhaps in illustration of its textual meaning. Another five repetitions, in the same order and with the same note values, follow; but whereas the first series of statements are separated by three breves' rest, the second set has a regular succession of breve-plus-semibreve rests between each statement. Thus a quasi-symmetrical scheme, with diminution of rests but retention of original note values, results. This again may be intended to illustrate the meaning of the cantus-firmus text, which thus not only comments on the motet text but gives it specific application. The date of Lasso's motet, published posthumously, is unknown; but emulation of Crecquillon's version, here not involving any direct allusion, might be possible and thus indicate an early date of composition.[41]

A psalm-related text, the exact source of which I have not yet found, is set in no. 10, *Tu Domine benignus es*; the last phrase of its *secunda pars*, "quoniam inops et pauper sum ego," is the opening of Ps. 85, and other phrases are drawn from Ps. 24. The cantus-firmus text, "Clamantem ad te, exaudi me Domine," is also suggestive of the psalms but does not precisely duplicate any single psalm verse.[42] Further search may reveal a liturgical source for the motet text.

The motet, published in 1565,[43] places the cantus firmus in tenor II, buried in the middle of the five-voice texture. Its melody is a solmization-pun one, derived from the text, and heard successively in the soft and natural hexachords. In the *prima pars* the melody is given in semibreves enclosed by an opening and closing breve; then follow two statements in an inexact diminution, a mix of semibreves and minims. This brings the first part to rest on D, the dominant of the mode. In the *secunda pars* the same scheme is followed, though this time the diminution uses more minims; and at the end a fifth statement on D, still in diminution, is added to bring the cantus firmus to rest on the modal final G. Here Lasso is clearly subordinating the cantus firmus to the tonal and contrapuntal demands of the other voices.

Quid prodest stulto (no. 11) has a text drawn from the Book of Proverbs, similar to *Homo cum in honore* (no. 8) in its dismissal of worldly success; motets such as this may have been wanted when Lasso's employers or other well-placed patrons were in a penitential mood. The text ends, abruptly but appropriately, with the famous phrase "Vanitas vanitatum, et omnia vanitas" from Ecclesiastes.[44] These are also the words of the cantus firmus, set to an odd, quasi-palindromic melody, in semiminims and minims, of an almost flippant character, about as far removed from the cantus-firmus norm as possible. In this short (45-breve) piece the cantus firmus is heard eleven times, in a pattern of repetitions on C–E–A, C–E–A, D–G, C–E–A, separated by rests of varied lengths, suggesting, as in *Si qua tibi* (no. 2), a rhythmic pattern that was altered to fit the needs of the piece. By way of finishing off this odd little motet, Lasso brings the cantus firmus to rest on a pedal point around which the other four voices chatter in its rhythms without using its melodic outline (see Example 12.1).

No. 12, *Exsultet coelum mare*, so far remains something of a puzzle. The text appears to be a Nativity hymn or sequence,[45] and the cantus-firmus text, "Quis audivit talia dic mirabilia," sounds like the final line of that hymn; but as yet I have found no source for it.[46] Perhaps it enjoyed only local circulation. The cantus firmus, a rather insouciant tune declaimed in a steady pattern of

EXAMPLE 12.1   Lasso, ending of *Quid prodest stulto*

minims, is placed in tenor I, in the middle of the five-voice texture, alternating entries on C and F (the piece is in mode five on F). After its initial entrance in the seventh measure of the piece it is completely regular, notes and rests. Though it does not stand out in the contrapuntal texture the cantus firmus determines the structure of the piece, and its entries coincide with many though not all of the changes of text phrase in the other voices.

The next motet, *O peccator si Filium Dei* (no. 13), is composed to a naively charming devotional text addressed to Mary as Mother of God. Its source is again unknown to me. The cantus firmus, "Audi nos nam te Filius nihil negare honorat," adds a short supplementary prayer to that of the main text. The piece, published only in the *Magnus opus musicum*, cannot be dated exactly; Boetticher cautiously places it as a relatively early Munich work.[47]

The cantus firmus, divided into three phrases separated by breve rests, is another solmization-syllable melody, heard alternately in the hard and natural hexachords, ending on a C-fa of the hard hexachord. C is the final of the piece, which is in transposed F or G mode; it is not easy to say which. The work seems deliberately ambiguous tonally; it has an extraordinary exordium in which the opening motive is heard in five successive entrances on C (bassus), G (tenor II), D (cantus I), A (altus), and E (cantus II) before the cantus firmus comes in on C to restore a semblance of tonal order (see Example 12.2). The cantus firmus is heard twice in breves, then three times in exact diminution, rests as well as notes. Like that of no. 12, this cantus firmus could have been given in a single statement accompanied by a canonic inscription.

A special problem is posed by no. 14, *Confisus Domino tua pectora*. The text, of as yet unknown origin, is religious in a somewhat minatory way but is written in a humanistic Latin that is hard to construe and could scarcely have been clear in meaning to the motet's auditors. And it is frankly too long, especially the *secunda pars*, which even Lasso with all his powers of conciseness cannot get through in fewer than sixty breves, with almost no textual repetition. The motet is thus extremely wordy and in consequence highly declamatory, though Lasso does manage a few Rore-like melismas here and there.

The cantus firmus text is in contrast very short: "Confide et ama," almost suggesting a simple way for dealing with the complexities of the motet text. In deploying it Lasso uses the most complex scheme that any of these motets can show. In the *prima pars* the melody is heard twice in breves, once on F and once on D. Then statements on F and D are given in dotted semibreves, with the original two-breve rest of separation shortened to breve plus semibreve. After a breve's rest there is a statement in semibreves on F and then—puzzlingly—a semibreve rest and a statement in semibreves on A. It works contrapuntally, with the cantus firmus ending on C, the dominant of the mode (the final sonority of the *prima pars* is a C chord). But a promisingly symmetrical scheme has here been interrupted.

The *secunda pars* shows the cantus firmus entering, after an odd seven-measure rest, with the melody in augmentation, all in longs, on F. There follows the expected statement on D, but this is in dotted breves, so to speak before its turn. In partial keeping with the *prima pars* there are then statements on F, in breves, on D, in dotted semibreves, on F in semibreves, on A in

EXAMPLE 12.2   Lasso, beginning of *O peccator si Filium Dei*

semibreves. Then comes a disconcerting entry on E♭ in semibreves, followed by a final one on D, also in semibreves. Breve and semibreve rests separate these entrances. This can be seen only as the ruins of a grand scheme worthy of the fifteenth-century motet. It is of course absurd to take Lasso to task for this; the piece, though perhaps not one of his most felicitous creations, works perfectly well. But nothing could demonstrate more clearly where the composer's priorities lay: an effective *concentus* outweighed any considerations of historically correct constructivism.

With a certain sense of relief—the list has been a long one—we turn to the last motet of this group, *Ut queant laxis* (no. 15). This setting of the famous Guidonian hymn may belong here only by a kind of whimsical courtesy. The cantus firmus, in tenor I, consists of the isolated (breve) notes *ut–la* in the hard hexachord, followed by "Sancte Joannes" in a descending scale heard twice on A–D and twice on D–G. The other voices get the text minus the operative opening syllables; then all join in the final phrase. The whole piece is only twenty-two breves in length (for its opening see Example 12.3). Haberl considered this motet a "Scherz mit den Solmisationssilben," adding that it was for a piece "mit liturgischen Texte unpassend." Boetticher counters by saying that the work is "keineswegs" a joke.[48] Surely Haberl was right; this must be an example of Lasso in playful mood, an aspect of his personality well demonstrated in his extant letters.[49] What his publishers thought in issuing the work we cannot know, but let us hope their mood was not a solemn one.[50]

WHAT DO THESE MOTETS have to tell us about Lasso's career? Only a few of them were reprinted enough to suggest real popularity.[51] One or two of the earliest ones may have helped him in getting the appointment to the Bavarian court. For one (no. 1) we know the recipients and the nature of the commission, and we may suspect that at least some of the others have a specific commission behind them. Motets using cantus firmi were popular at the Habsburg court, always watched with half-friendly, half-suspicious interest by the Wittelsbachs in Munich. One such motet, Jacob Vaet's *Qui operatus es Petro*, with its puzzle-canon cantus firmus "Sancte Petre ora pro nobis," was printed in an

EXAMPLE 12.3   Lasso, beginning of *Ut queant laxis*

elaborate presentation form with its canon unresolved, then later included in a volume of Vaet's motets where its canon is resolved.[52] Patrick Macey has recently suggested that Josquin's *Missa Hercules dux Ferrariae*, known to us with its tenor cantus firmus fully written out in Petrucci's print, may have originally been presented in unresolved form accompanied by a verbal canon.[53] Several of Lasso's cantus-firmus motets (nos. 7, 9, 12, 13) could have been first seen in manuscript in such form; we know them only from prints and late Munich working manuscripts where the cantus firmus is given *ad longum*, that is, in resolution.

A number of possibly telling details about these works remain for us to "resolve." But I think we can see that Lasso was here responding to an old tradition, at times faithful to it in a literal sense, but more often using it as an appendage to his own style, thus proving himself at least something of a musical historicist.

APPENDIX

Lasso's Cantus-Firmus Motets: Texts and Cantus-Firmus Melodies

1. Cernere virtutes qui vult compagine in una,
       laudandum immensus quicquid et orbis habet:
   Marchio magnanimus de Baden idest Philibertus,
       Mechthildisque simul, quos modo junxit Hymen.
   Ille quidem numeros virtutum contines omnes,
       Bavariae haec laus est atque decoris honos.
   Quis te felicem non dixerit, inclite Princeps,
       qui, quae omnes optant, omnia solus habes.
   CF: Ista Hymenaee precor tibi sint connubia curae,
       grata ubi sunt stabilis vincula nexus erit.
   5v. *Date:* 1557; for the wedding of Philibert of Baden and Mechthilde of Bavaria. First published in RISM 1568b. *Sämmtliche Werke* [SW] 3:114.

2. Si qua tibi obtulerint culti nova carmina vates,
   ingenii voverant et monimenta sui,
   accipis haec placida legis haec et fronte serena,
   ornatusque tuis laudibus autor abit,
   ampla quidem merces laudes meruisse merentes,
   maxima laudari principis ore boni.
   CF: Aequabit laudes nulla camena tuas.
   6v. *Date:* published in 1556a; Munich, Mus. Ms. 20 (ca. 1560). *SW*
   11:118.

3. Quod licet id libeat, libeat quod suadet honestas,
   sic licet atque libet symbola clara fero.
   CF: Si licet libet. *Source: Scriptores Historiae Augustae*, Antoninus
   Caracallus 10. 2.
   5v. *Date:* uncertain. Published in *Magnum opus musicum. SW* 11:16.

4. Libera me Domine de morte aeterna in die illa tremenda: quando
   coeli movendi sunt et terra: dum veneris judicare saeculum per ignem.
   Source: Joel 3:16 (paraphrase); Responsory at Absolution in the Requiem liturgy.
   CF: Respice finem. *Source:* Aesop, *Fabulae* xxii, 5.
   6v. *Date:* published in 1568a. *SW* 15:109.

5. Multae tribulationes justorum, et his omnibus liberavit eos Dominus.
   Source: Ps. 38:20.
   Introit for Mass of SS. John and Paul, Martyrs

CF: In patientia vestra possidebitis animas vestras. *Source:* Luke 21:9.
Fifth antiphon at Vespers, Common of Apostles and Evangelists.
6v. *Date:* published in 1577e. SW 15:65.

In pati - en - ti-a   ve-stra   possidebitis a - ni-mas vestras   ij

6. Fremuit spiritus Jesus, et turbavit seipsum, et dixit Judaeis: Ubi posu-
isti Lazarum? Dicunt ei: Domine, veni et vide: et lacrymatus est Jesus.
2.p. Videns Dominus flentes sorores Lazari ad monumentum, lacrymatus est coram Judaeis, et clamabat: Lazare veni foras. *Source:* John
11:33, 34, 40. Communion on Friday after the fourth Sunday of Lent;
feast of St. Lazarus, 17 December.
CF: Lazare veni foras.
6v. *Date:* published in 1556a. SW 15:23.

Lazare veni foras ij   ij   ij   ij

ij   ij   ij   ij   ij   ij

Lazare,   Lazare...

7. Jubilate Deo omnis terra, servite Domine in laetitia. Introite in con-
spectu ejus in exsultatione: scitote quoniam ipse est Deus, ipse fecit
nos et non ipsi nos. *2.p.* Populus ejus et oves pascuae ejus introite
portas ejus in confessione, atria ejus in hymnis, confitemini illi: laudate nomen ejus quoniam suavis est Dominus, in aeternum misericordia ejus et usque in generatione et generationem veritas ejus. *Source:*
Ps. 99, entire.
CF: Si Deus nobiscum quis contra nos? *Source:* Rom. 8:31.
6v. *Date:* published in 1565a. SW 17:149.

Si Deus nobiscum quis contra nos ij   ij   ij   ij   ij

8. Homo cum in honore esset non intellexit: comparatus est jumentis insipientibus, et similis factus est illis. *Source:* Ps. 48:21.
CF: Nosce teipsum. *Source:* Oracle of Apollo at Delphi (see above and n. 36).
6v. *Date:* published in 1566e. SW 15:90.

Nosce te ipsom ij   ij   ij   ij   ij   ij   ij   ij

9. Congregati sunt inimici nostri, et gloriantur in virtute sua, contere fortitudinem illorum, Domine, et disperge illos ut cognoscant quia non est alius qui pugnet pro nobis nisi tu, Deus noster. Disperde illos in virtute tua et destrue eos, protector noster Domine. *Source:* in part from Eccles. 36:13, Hag. 2:23 and Ps. 58:12. Responsory 3 at Matins, first Sunday of October.
CF: Dissipa gentes quae bella volunt. *Source:* Ps. 67:31.
5v. *Date:* published in 1597[3]; in Munich, Mus. Ms. 15 (1577). SW 9:186.

Dissipa gentes quae bel-la vo - lunt ij   ij   ij   ij   ij   ij   ij

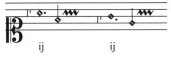

ij   ij

10. Tu Domine benignus es et clemens, et supra quam dici potest misericors in omnes, qui tuum implorant auxilium. *2.p.* Respice me, vide humilitatem meam et laborem meum, ede signum aliquod pristini favoris erga me tui, quoniam inops et pauper sum ego. *Source:* Ps. 24:16, 18; Ps. 85:1 (phrases of the *secunda pars*).
CF: Clamantem ad te, exaudi me Domine. *Source:* Ps. 140:1 (inexact)
5v. *Date:* published in 1568b. SW 5:87.

Clamantem ad te exaudi me Domine ij   ij   ij

2a

ij   ij   ij   ij   ij

11. Quid prodest stulto habere divitias, cum sapientiam emere non possit?
    Qui altam facit domum suam, quaerit ruinam et qui evitat discere
    incidit in malum: qui perversi cordis est, non invenit bonum. Vanitas
    vanitatum, et omnia vanitas. *Source:* Prov. 17:16, 20; Eccles. 1:2.
    CF: Vanitas vanitatum, et omnia vanitas. *Source:* Eccles. 1:2.
    5v. *Date:* published in 1564d. *SW* 7:41.

12. Exsultet coelum mare sol luna et sidera / Quia fulgens clare Deus per
    omnia / En jacet in cunabilis et pendet ad ubera / Concrepat vagitibus
    ipsa laetitia / Potentia fit impotens fit egens divitia / Et sitit atque esurit
    qui pascit omnia / Vexatur et algoribus qui vestit lilia / Immensus et
    innumerus fert infantilia.
    CF: Quis audivit talia dic mirabilia.
    5v. *Date:* published in 1571a; in Munich, Mus. ms. 24 (ca. 1565–
    80). *SW* 3:144.

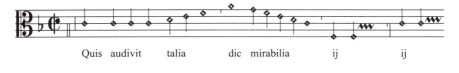

13. O peccator si Filium Dei non audes accedere, vade ad matrem pecca-
    torum, et ostende ei facinora tua, et ipsa ostendet pro te Filio pectus
    et ubera, et Filius ostendet Patri latus et vulnera: Pater non negabit
    Filio postulanti, et Filius non negabit Matri interpellanti, et Mater
    non negabit peccatori ploranti.
    CF: Audi nos nam te filius nihil negans honorat.
    6v. *Date:* unknown; first published in *Magnum opus musicum*. *SW*
    13:163.

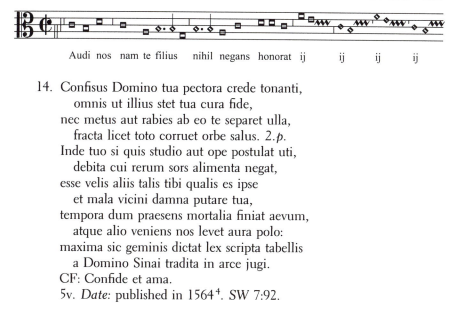

Audi nos nam te filius   nihil negans honorat ij   ij   ij   ij

14. Confisus Domino tua pectora crede tonanti,
    omnis ut illius stet tua cura fide,
    nec metus aut rabies ab eo te separet ulla,
    fracta licet toto corruet orbe salus. *2.p.*
    Inde tuo si quis studio aut ope postulat uti,
    debita cui rerum sors alimenta negat,
    esse velis aliis talis tibi qualis es ipse
    et mala vicini damna putare tua,
    tempora dum praesens mortalia finiat aevum,
    atque alio veniens nos levet aura polo:
    maxima sic geminis dictat lex scripta tabellis
    a Domino Sinai tradita in arce jugi.
    CF: Confide et ama.
    5v. *Date:* published in 1564⁴. SW 7:92.

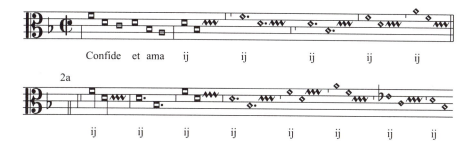

Confide   et ama   ij   ij   ij   ij   ij

2a

ij   ij   ij   ij   ij   ij   ij   ij

15. [Ut] queant laxis, [Re]sonare fibris,
    [Mi]ra gestorum, [Fa]muli tuorum,
    [Sol]ve polluti, [La]bii reatum,
    sancte Joannes.
    Source: hymn by Paul the Deacon, Nativity of St. John the Baptist,
    24 June (*LU* 1504).
    CF: Ut re mi fa sol la, sancte Joannes.
    5v. *Date:* published in 1582d. SW 5:152.

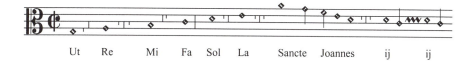

Ut   Re   Mi   Fa   Sol   La   Sancte   Joannes   ij   ij

NOTES

1. The best study of this subject is Claude Palisca, *Humanism in Italian Renaissance Musical Thought* (New Haven: Yale University Press, 1985). There is no equivalent work on Northern humanists' study of ancient music theory.

2. Jessie Ann Owens, "Music Historiography and the Definition of 'Renaissance,'" *Notes* 47 (1990): 305–30.

3. Among the Nuremberg prints there are two Mass collections (RISM 1539[1] and 1539[2]) and two of motets (1537[1], 1538[3]). French prints of retrospective bent include chanson collections by Attaingnant (1549[17], 1549[18]) and Du Chemin (1549[28]). A collection of Josquin chansons was issued by Attaingnant (RISM J681, 1549), one of motets by Le Roy and Ballard (J678, 1555).

4. For discussion of the Antwerp motet books published by Susato and Waelrant, and those of Phalèse in Louvain, see Edward E. Lowinsky, *Der Antwerpener Motettenbuch Orlando di Lasso's und seine Beziehungen zum Motettenschaffen der niederländischen Zeitgenossen* (The Hague: Nijhoff, 1937), republished in English translation as "Orlando di Lasso's Antwerp Motet Book and Its Relationship to the Contemporary Netherlandish Motet" in Lowinsky, *Music in the Culture of the Renaissance and Other Essays*, ed. Bonnie J. Blackburn, 2 vols. (Chicago: University of Chicago Press, 1989), 1:385–431, esp. 410ff.

5. This language is from the title page of Susato's *Le quatoirsiesme livre . . . par Rolando di Lassus* (Antwerp, 1555); see RISM L755 (Lasso 1555a).

6. Bernhard Meier, "Alter und neuer Stil in lateinisch textierten Werken von Orlando di Lasso," *Archiv für Musikwissenschaft* 15 (1958): 151–61.

7. See David Crook, *Orlando di Lasso's Imitation Magnificats for Counter-Reformation Munich* (Princeton: Princeton University Press, 1994), 175 ff.

8. For the four-voice *Missa sesquialtera* see Lassus, *Sämtliche Werke: Neue Reihe*, ed. Siegfried Hermelink et al. (Kassel: Bärenreiter, 1956–), 10:69.

9. Wolfgang Boetticher, *Orlando di Lasso und seine Zeit, 1532–1594* (Kassel: Bärenreiter, 1958), 239–45.

10. On ceremonial motets, see Albert Dunning, *Die Staatsmotette 1480–1555* (Utrecht: Oesthoek, 1970); id., *Staatsmotten für Erzherzog Karl II. von Innerösterreich*, Musik alter Meister 21–22 (Graz: Akademische Druck- und Verlagsanstalt, 1971).

11. It appears in RISM L816 (1568b), *Selectissime cantiones . . . partim omnino novae, partim nusquam in Germania excusae, quinque et quatuor vocibus compositae* (Nuremberg: Gerlach).

12. *Allgemeine Deutsche Biographie*, 43 vols. (Leipzig: Duncker and Huniblot, 1875–1912), 25:740; cf. Ignace Bossuyt, "Lasso's erste Jahre in München (1556–1559): Eine 'cosa non riuscita'?" in *Festschrift für Horst Leuchtmann zum 65. Geburtstag*, ed. S. Hörner and R. Schmid (Tutzing: Hans Schneider, 1993), 55–67, esp. 63–64.

13. The two semibreves at measure 18 of the work are replaced by two breves in the repetition of the cantus firmus (mm. 49–50).

14. For Granvelle, secretary-minister to Charles V and Philip II, see Bossuyt, "Lassos erste Jahre," 55–56, and the references there cited. Haberl's opinion is to be found in Lassus, *Sämmtliche Werke*, ed. F. X. Haberl and Adolf Sandberger, 21 vols. (Leipzig: Breitkopf und Härtel, 1894–1926), 11:xi; cf. Boetticher, *Orlando di Lasso*, 136n.

15. Dunning, *Die Staatsmotette*, 210; Lowinsky, "Orlando di Lasso's Antwerp Motet Book," 398, 427.

16. On Manchicourt and Granvelle, see Bossuyt, "Lassos erste Jahren," 56. For discussions of the motets cited, see Dunning, *Die Staatsmotette.*

17. The phrase occurs in the life of Caracalla (10. 2), in *Scriptores Historiae Augustae,* ed. Ernst Hohl, 2 vols. (Leipzig: Teubner, 1965), 1:191 .

18. The phrase is from Gioseffo Zarlino, *Le istitutioni harmoniche* (Venice: Franceschi, 1558), pt. 3, p. 267. See Adolf Thürlings, "Die soggetti cavati dalle vocali in Huldigungskompositionen und die Hercules-Messe des Lupus," *Bericht über den zweiten Kongress der internationalen Musikgesellschaft zu Basel,* 1906 (Leipzig: Breitkopf and Härtel, 1907), 83–94, the earliest and among the best of many brief discussions of this topic to be found in the scholarly literature.

19. See *Liber usualis,* 1767. The text quotes a few words from Joel 3:16. Lasso's music seems unrelated to the chant melody, though he keeps its mode.

20. Andrea Alciati, *Emblemata cum commentariis* (Padua: P. P. Tozzio, 1621), emblema 187, p. 785: "Respexisse Solon finem jubet."

21. The phrase is not identified in any of the otherwise formidably detailed Shakespeare commentary I have consulted. The Aesop phrase is "Si quid agas, prudenter agas, et respice finem" (*fable of the Fox and the Goat*); see T. B. Harbottle, *Dictionary of Quotations (Classical)* (London: Swan Sonnenschein, 1897), 254. It has been suggested to me that "respice finem" is a motto associated with St. Jerome, but I have been unable to confirm this.

22. The motet is printed in RISM L815 (1568a), *Selectissime cantiones . . . quatuor, quinque, sex et pluribus vocibus* (Nuremberg: Gerlach). Boetticher, *Orlando di Lasso,* 370, points out some similarities in Lasso's setting to Andrea Gabrieli's five-voice *Libera me Domine,* printed in the latter's *Sacrae cantiones* (Venice: Gardano, 1565). Gabrieli's motet, however, is based on a different text.

23. It is to be found in RISM L904 (1577e), *Moduli, quatuor, 5, 6, 7, 8 et novem vocum* (Paris: Le Roy and Ballard); see Boetticher, *Orlando di Lasso,* 239.

24. *Liber usualis,* 1507.

25. Ibid., 1112.

26. For Clemens's motet, first published in 1554, see Clemens non Papa, *Opera omnia,* ed. K. Ph. Bernet Kempers and Chris Maas, 21 vols. ([n.p.]: American Institute of Musicology, 1951–76), 14:32. The work is discussed by Lowinsky, "Orlando di Lasso's Antwerp Motet Book," 419–20. On pp. 427–29 Lowinsky describes Lasso's *Fremuit spiritus Jesus,* suggesting that it might have been composed to commemorate Clemens's death.

27. Boetticher, *Orlando di Lasso,* 128n.

28. *Graduale Romanum,* 137.

29. John 11:33–34, 43.

30. The cantus firmus is unrelated to the chant melody for its text.

31. Clemens set all but the last phrase of the psalm text. For his motet, see Clemens, *Opera,* 16:30. Lasso's motet was published in RISM L784 (1565a), *Modulorum . . . secundum volumen* (Paris: Le Roy and Ballard).

32. Rom. 8:31: "Si Deus pro nobis quis contra nos."

33. L. G. Pine, *Dictionary of Mottos* (London: Routledge and Kegan Paul, 1983), 212.

34. The motet text closes a psalm the general message of which is well summarized by the cantus-firmus text. This must surely have been part of the composer's plan.

35. RISM L796 (1566e), *Sacrae cantiones . . . sex et octo vocum* (Venice: Gardano).

36. For Thales see Diogenes Laertius, *Vitae philosophorum* (Oxford: Clarendon Press, 1964), 1. 1. 13. 40. The phrase occurs in Juvenal, *Satires*, 11. 27 (see A. *Persi Flacci et D. Iuni Iuvenalis Saturae* (Oxford: Clarendon Press, 1908); as "nosce te" it is found in Cicero's *Tusculan disputations*, ed. and transl. J. E. King (Cambridge, Mass.: Harvard University Press, 1971) 1. 22. 52. Alciati, *Emblemata*, 767, says of the Greek phrase that Plutarch attributed it to Aesop; Ovid, to Pythagoras; Plato, to Socrates as an Apollonian dictum; Diogenes, to Thales. Erasmus gives a very full account of the sources of the motto in his *Adages*, where "Nosce te ipsum" is found as no. 595 in the influential 1526 edition (*Adagiorum opus* [Basel: Frobenius]); Erasmus's work, first published in 1500, was very well known throughout the sixteenth century. For a modern edition of it see *Collected Works of Erasmus*, 22: *Adages*, trans. and ann. R. A. B. Mynors (Toronto: University of Toronto, 1989). I am grateful to Donna Cardamone Jackson for alerting me to Erasmus's volume.

37. Edward E. Lowinsky, "A Newly Discovered Sixteenth-Century Motet Manuscript at the Biblioteca Vallicelliana in Rome," *Journal of the American Musicological Society* 3 (1950): 173–232, at 175.

38. According to Barton Hudson, ed., *Thomasii Crequillonis Opera omnia*, 5 vols. ([n.p.]: American Institute of Musicology, 1974–1990), 5, p. xliv, there are "at least nine" extant motets on this text (not always with the same *secunda pars*; that of Crecquillon is completely different from Lasso's).

39. See Karl Marbach, *Carmina scripturarum* [1907] (Hildesheim: G. Olms, 1963), 295. The text makes some references to Eccles. 36:13.

40. This would appear to be true of other settings as well. Arcadelt sets only the first half of Lasso's text; see his *Opera omnia*, ed. Albert Seay, 10 vols. ([n.p.]: American Institute of Musicology, 1965–1970), 10:1. On Verdelot's setting, see Norbert Böker-Heil, *Die Motetten von Philippe Verdelot* (Köln-Sülz: A. Bothmann, 1967), 79–80. Crecquillon's setting is discussed in Lowinsky, "Orlando di Lasso's Antwerp Motet Book," 424–25.

41. Boetticher, *Orlando di Lasso*, 240, suggests "um 1565" as a date for Lasso's motet. Its presence in Munich, Mus. MS 15, dated 1577 and perhaps containing revised versions of earlier works, is at least oblique proof of fairly early compositional date. See *Bayerische Staatsbibliothek. Katalog der Musikhandschriften I: Chorbücher und Handschriften* (Munich: Henle Verlag, 1989), 82.

42. The closest would seem to be Ps. 140:1: "Domine clamavi ad te, exaudi me."

43. RISM L784 (1565a), *Modulorum . . . quaternis . . . denis vocibus . . . secundum volumen* (Paris: Le Roy and Ballard).

44. One wonders if Lasso thought of this apt juxtaposition himself. Certainly his music for the Preacher's famous phrase is highly individual.

45. Boetticher, *Orlando di Lasso*, 648, includes it among Lasso's hymns but does not identify it further.

46. Many hymns and sequences begin with "Exsultet coelum" but none, at least none in standard reference works such as *Analecta hymnica* and *Repertorium hymnologicum*, continue with the text used by Lasso.

47. *Orlando di Lasso*, 236, 240.

48. See Lasso, *Sämmtliche Werke*, 5, p. viii; Boetticher, *Orlando di Lasso*, 555. Hans T. David, "Themes from Words and Names," in *A Birthday Offering to Carl Engel*, ed. Gustave Reese (New York: Schirmer, 1943), 67–87, at 73, finds Lasso's "responsorial effect . . . most impressive."

49. See Horst Leuchtmann, *Orlando di Lasso*, 2 vols. (Wiesbaden: Breitkopf and Härtel, 1976–77), 2: *Briefe*.

50. The work was published in RISM L938 (1582d), *Sacrae cantiones quinque vocum . . . opus planè novum* (Munich: Adam Berg).

51. Boetticher, *Orlando di Lasso*, 240.

52. See Milton Steinhardt, "A Musical Offering to Emperor Maximilian II: A Political and Religious Document of the Renaissance," *Studien zur Musikwissenschaft: Beihefte der Denkmäler der Tonkunst in Österreich* 27 (1977), 19–27.

53. Patrick Macey, "Frescobaldi's Musical Tributes to Ferrara," in *The Organist as Scholar: Essays in Memory of Russell Saunders*, ed. Kerala Snyder (Stuyvesant, N.Y.: Pendragon, 1994), 197–231, at 218.

Tonal Compass in the Motets
of Orlando di Lasso

In the third volume of his *General History of Music,* the eighteenth-century music historian Charles Burney drew a striking distinction between the music of Cipriano de Rore and Orlando di Lasso on the one hand and Giovanni Pierluigi da Palestrina on the other. Rore and Lasso,

> by having spent the chief part of their time in the courts of princes, had acquired a lighter and more secular craft of melody than Palestrina, who residing constantly at Rome, and writing chiefly for the church, had a natural and characteristic *gravity* in all his productions. Indeed, the compositions *à Capella* of Cyprian Rore and Orlando Lasso are much inferior to those of Palestrina, in this particular; for by striving to be grave and solemn they only become heavy and dull; and what is unaffected dignity in the Roman, is little better than the strut of a dwarf upon stilts in the Netherlanders.

The primary significance of the music of Rore and Lasso, Burney concluded, lay in their "frequent attempts at *new harmonies* and *modulation.*" They were "great masters of harmony, and, out of the church, prepared the colors, and furnished the musician's pallet with many new tints of harmony and modulation, which were of great use to subsequent composers, particularly in dramatic painting."[1]

In support of his argument, Burney provided complete transcriptions of two motets: Rore's *Calami sonum ferentes* and Lasso's *Alma nemes,* both published by Tylman Susato in 1555.[2] He commented that *Alma nemes* provided the earliest example of an A♯ known to him and that *Calami sonum ferentes* contained "not only an A-sharp but an A-flat . . . and almost every accident usual in modern Music."[3] Burney nevertheless feared that "the laboured and equivocal modulation of these composers, though often learned and ingenious, sometimes borders so much on caprice and affectation as to fatigue the attention, and disgust the ear." He had included these two chromatic compositions in his discussion, he admitted, only out of his sense of the "duty of the historian" to point out innovation wherever it has been attempted.[4]

In *Tonality and Atonality in Sixteenth-Century Music,* Edward Lowinsky drew attention to another chromatic composition from the 1550s, Lasso's motet cycle *Prophetiae Sibyllarum.* Focusing on the first nine measures of *Carmina chromatico,* the prologue to the cycle, Lowinsky observed that Lasso "uses all twelve tones; he builds triads on ten different degrees, six of which result in harmonies foreign to the mode." Concluding that this phrase has no stable frame of tonal reference, Lowinsky characterized it as "triadic atonality" and speculated that in "rendering the Sibylline prophecies in chromatic style, the young genius probably implied that chromaticism was the music of the future."[5]

Both Burney and Lowinsky present an evolutionary model of tonality in which Lasso—whether a young genius or a dwarf on stilts—stands as an innovator on a path leading from antique modality to modern (i.e., major-minor) tonality and beyond. As Harold Powers has pointed out, such a model falsifies the relationship between modality and tonality by placing them on the same evolutionary plane.[6] In this particular instance, it also obscures the fact that Lasso's early chromatic essays seem to have been something of a dead end in the composer's own evolution. Lasso, having developed this musical language at the beginning of his career and having apparently gained a certain fame or notoriety for it, abandoned it and confined himself to a more restrictive collection or compass of available tones.[7] The nature of that tonal compass, the tonalities Lasso cultivated within it, and a possible reason why he chose to place such a restriction on his music form the subject of this study.

IN THE YEARS SINCE Lowinsky's discussion of *Carmina chromatico* appeared, Lasso's little piece has become his most analyzed motet and probably the most analyzed piece of Renaissance music by any composer in any genre.[8] More recent scholars have rejected Lowinsky's atonal view of the piece and have used a variety of analytical approaches to show how they perceive its tonal coherence. In addition, they have posed important questions about the nature of sixteenth-century tonal organization and appropriate modes of analysis. Significantly, these broader questions are today very much at issue for Lasso's motets as a whole and Renaissance music in general. How are we to comprehend the tonal organization of these pieces? How are we to analyze and discuss them? How are we to hear the sixteenth-century motet?

Sixteenth-century theorists, when they discussed the tonal structure of polyphonic music, invoked modal concepts and terminology derived from medieval chant theory, ancient Greek theory, or a combination of the two. Some modern scholars, most notably Bernhard Meier, have used those same terms and concepts to investigate Renaissance polyphony, and have regarded sixteenth-century modal theory sufficient to explain sixteenth-century tonal structure.[9] Other scholars have felt that we must go beyond the terminologies and conceptualizations of the period if we wish to explain the tonal structure of its music adequately.[10]

In a seminal study of late sixteenth-century tonalities published in 1960, for example, Siegfried Hermelink pointed out the discrepancy that exists between Renaissance modal theory—whether the eight-mode or twelve-mode variety—and the 20 distinct tonalities he observed in the music of Palestrina and his contemporaries.[11] Hermelink's 20 tonalities are minimally marked by three criteria: first, the selection of the *cantus durus* system with no flats (or sharps) in the signature or the *cantus mollis* system with a one-flat signature; second, the selection of one of two standard clef combinations, either the so-called *chiavette* or high-clef combination (g2, c2, c3, f3 or g2, c2, c3, c4) or the low-clef combination (c1, c3, c4, f4); and third, the final, that is, the pitch-class of the lowest note of the last sonority of the composition. In the shorthand tonal designations that follow, the symbols "♭" and "♮" represent *cantus mollis* and *cantus durus*, respectively. I signify the standard high-clef combination with the word "high," the standard low-clef combination with the word "low." The final is represented by a single capital letter.

   Tables 13.1 and 13.2 list the 516 motets contained in the *Magnum opus musicum*, the great posthumous *Gesamtausgabe* of Lasso's motets published by his sons in 1604.[12] Motets written in the *cantus durus* system appear in Table 13.1, those in *cantus mollis* in Table 13.2. Motets with the same final are grouped together: first those with the high-clef combination, then those with low cleffing, and finally those employing a nonstandard combination of clefs. Nonstandard clef combinations include (1) those that employ one or more clefs not included in either of the two standard combinations, for example, no. 354, ♮–E–c2c3c4f4f5, (2) those that mix members of the high combination with those of the low combination, for example, no. 210, ♮–D–g2c1c3c4f4, and (3) those that could be assigned to either of the two standard categories, for example, the two-voice motet no. 21, ♮–G–c1c4. Multisectional motets are categorized according to the final of their last section. Motet no. 199, *Alma parens, dilecta*, which comprises five sections and survives only in the *Magnum opus musicum*, is the only motet—if it is indeed a single unified motet—written partly in *cantus durus* and partly in *cantus mollis*. The first two sections (♭–G–low) are designated "199.1" in Table 13.2; sections three, four, and five, which have finals on G, D, and E respectively, are listed in the ♮–E–low category as "199.2" in Table 13.1.

   The distribution of motets among the various categories is highly irregular. The 81 ♭–G–low motets make up the largest group; other categories, such as ♮–A–low, are represented by a single composition. D-final pieces are common in *cantus durus* and extraordinarily rare in *cantus mollis*; E-final pieces are also common in *cantus durus* but completely nonexistent in *cantus mollis*. F-final pieces, on the other hand, were almost always composed in *cantus mollis*. In both systems, Lasso favored G finals above all others: taken together, pieces ending on G make up more than 45 percent of the motets in the *Magnum opus musicum*. In each of the two systems, Lasso used only six finals: in *cantus durus*, the notes of the natural hexachord (C, D, E, F, G, and A), in *cantus mollis*, the notes of the soft hexachord (F, G, A, B♭, C, and D).

   The strikingly uneven distribution of motets among the tonal categories outlined in Tables 13.1 and 13.2 raises a number of questions not directly related to the concept of tonal compass, which I wish to explore here, but

TABLE 13.1. *Cantus durus* motets in Lasso's *Magnum opus musicum* (1604)

Tonal Markers	Number in *Magnum opus musicum*	Total	
♮–A–high	102, 103, 104, 126, 178, 191, 207, 265, 282, 304, 324, 325, 395, 448, 450, 452, 476, 481, 496	19	24
♮–A–low	146	1	
♮–A–other	314, 456, 501, 514	4	
♮–C–high	120, 121, 141, 145, 161, 167, 174, 175, 176, 330, 341, 361, 370, 440, 441, 449, 455, 502	18	25
♮–C–low	396, 409, 485, 498	4	
♮–C–other	74, 77, 142	3	
♮–D–high	3, 4, 30, 42, 150, 157, 255, 292, 297, 356, 364, 369	12	54
♮–D–low	1, 2, 27, 36, 56, 63, 78, 82, 83, 84, 85, 147, 168, 183, 188, 195, 220, 221, 290, 294, 295, 362, 372, 380, 381, 382, 383, 384, 385, 386, 398, 399, 404, 421, 422, 423, 424	37	
♮–D–other	210, 319, 348, 453, 507	5	
♮–E–high	none	0	60
♮–E–low	19, 37, 38, 39, 57, 58, 64, 70, 71, 72, 105, 106, 107, 108, 109, 138, 171, 186, 198, 199.2, 215, 216, 226, 227, 228, 256, 257, 258, 260, 261, 262, 263, 264, 291, 306, 305, 307, 308, 367, 392, 403, 407, 408, 431, 432, 433, 434, 435, 436, 460, 470, 491, 500	53	
♮–E–other	259, 335, 354, 465, 475, 482, 489	7	
♮–F–high	none	0	3
♮–F–low	20, 229, 438	3	
♮–F–other	none	0	
♮–G–high	10, 29, 41, 122, 123, 143, 154, 162, 187, 203, 205, 231, 235, 281, 283, 284, 313, 317, 347, 374, 394, 416, 451, 454, 509, 511	26	98
♮–G–low	11, 12, 23, 24, 28, 40, 53, 67, 73, 75, 127, 128, 129, 130, 131, 132, 133, 134, 135, 136, 137, 153, 163, 164, 165, 181, 182, 189, 190, 204, 206, 285, 286, 287, 288, 289, 315, 331, 333, 334, 343, 344, 352, 357, 359, 366, 379, 397, 414, 415, 457, 458, 459, 461, 462, 471, 473, 486, 487, 499, 510, 512, 516	63	
♮–G–other	21, 22, 51, 61, 66, 342, 355, 468, 513	9	

warranting further investigation on their own terms. Why, for example, did Lasso compose 53 ♮–E–low motets and not a single ♮–E–high motet? Why did he write 37 ♮–D–low motets and avoid ♭–D–low altogether? Considerations of such questions will certainly need to take into account both aspects of Lasso's musical culture and characteristics of the individual categories. Traditional

TABLE 13.2.   *Cantus mollis* motets in Lasso's *Magnum opus musicum* (1604)

Tonal Markers	Number in *Magnum opus musicum*		Total	
♭–A–high	5, 232, 236, 311, 375, 463	6		
♭–A–low	6, 101, 271	3	12	
♭–A–other	35, 353, 484	3		
♭–B♭–other	44	1	1	
♭–C–high	33, 437	2		
♭–C–low	310	1	3	
♭–C–other	none	0		
♭–D–high	80, 148	2		
♭–D–low	none	0	3	
♭–D–other	400	1		
♭–E	none	0	0	
♭–F–high	7, 34, 69, 110, 111, 119, 124, 125, 144, 158, 179, 201, 202, 230, 234, 266, 267, 268, 269, 270, 309, 323, 338, 410, 439, 442, 474, 479, 490	29		
♭–F–low	8, 9, 25, 26, 31, 43, 46, 47, 54, 76, 112, 113, 114, 115, 116, 117, 118, 151, 152, 159, 160, 180, 192, 193, 194, 217, 233, 272, 273, 274, 275, 276, 277, 278, 279, 280, 312, 321, 322, 332, 340, 358, 360, 368, 373, 378, 393, 411, 412, 413, 443, 446, 447, 466, 467, 472, 477, 478, 483, 488, 506, 515	62	95	
♭–F–other	48, 172, 444, 445	4		
♭–G–high	13, 14, 15, 32, 55, 59, 60, 68, 86, 87, 88, 89, 90, 91, 92, 149, 155, 166, 169, 170, 184, 208, 209, 211, 212, 213, 214, 218, 219, 238, 239, 240, 241, 242, 243, 244, 293, 296, 298, 299, 318, 349, 387, 401, 417, 418, 419, 420, 492, 497	50		
♭–G–low	16, 17, 18, 49, 52, 62, 65, 79, 81, 93, 94, 95, 96, 97, 98, 99, 100, 139, 140, 156, 173, 185, 196, 197, 199.1, 200, 222, 223, 224, 225, 237, 245, 246, 247, 248, 249, 250, 251, 252, 253, 254, 300, 301, 302, 303, 316, 320, 326, 327, 328, 329, 336, 337, 339, 345, 350, 351, 363, 365, 371, 376, 377, 388, 389, 390, 391, 402, 405, 406, 425, 426, 427, 428, 429, 464, 480, 493, 495, 503, 504, 508	81	139	
♭–G–other	45, 50, 177, 346, 430, 469, 494, 505	8		

modal theory, for example, seems a plausible explanation for Lasso's apparent preference for the four traditional modal finals of D, E, F, and G. On the other hand, it seems just as likely that a purely musical characteristic of the ♭–E tonalities—the absence in the background diatonic of a perfect fifth above the final—contributed to his complete avoidance of them.

More recent scholars have extended Hermelink's approach in two directions; the one theoretical, the other analytical. In a series of articles exploring the relationships between the tonalities Hermelink identified and the traditional modal theory he rejected, Harold Powers has shown that while Hermelink's tonalities were not modes they were often used to *represent* modes.[13] In numerous anthologies and cycles of the late sixteenth century, composers and printers ordered compositions according to their tonalities—as represented by their combinations of system, final, and cleffing—in such a way as to represent the eight (or in some cases 12) modes. In such collections all three of Hermelink's markers function as crucial constituents of a system of polyphonic representation of modal categories.

The analytical potential of Hermelink's work has been pursued most rigorously by Horst-Willi Groß in a study of an aspect of Lasso's music that has received relatively little attention—its vertical sonorities.[14] Hermelink's own analyses of the cantus parts of selected compositions by Palestrina had shown how the tonalities he identified by system, final, and cleffing distinguish themselves from one another through contrasts of melodic contour and emphasis. Groß's essential contribution was the expansion of Hermelink's approach to include a consideration of chordal structure and chordal relationships. In his comprehensive study of Lasso's Masses and motets, Groß identified two kinds of consonant sonorities: 5/3/1 chords and 6/3/1 chords. The latter have none of the independence or self-sufficiency of the former: a composition never ends on a 6/3/1 sonority, for example. Such 6/3/1 chords function primarily as passing or linking sonorities between 5/3/1 chords. Groß also sought to expand the profiles of Hermelink's tonalities by enumerating the chords used and explaining the normative chord progressions in each tonality. For the seven most common categories, he provided diagrams showing the sonorities available and the ways those sonorities relate to one another.

Significantly, Groß found no differences between the sonorities in high-clef pieces and those in low-clef pieces having the same final and key signature. Consequently, he considered the two types of pieces together and thereby eliminated one of Hermelink's markers. The categories ♮–D–high and ♮–D–low, for example, he conflated in a single ♮–D or "untransposed Dorian" category, while ♭–G–high and ♭–G–low were both reckoned under ♭–G or "transposed Dorian."

Groß's abandonment of cleffing as a relevant criterion in the establishment of analytical tonal categories suggests that cleffing is a subordinate determinant of late sixteenth-century tonalities, that it may be important in some respects but not in others. (And here I define tonality simply as a hierarchy of pitches in which the constituent pitches assume varying degrees of importance based on their placement and frequency of appearance within a given composition or group of compositions.) That is not to say that clefs—or other factors, such as modal theory and sixteenth-century pedagogical traditions—are irrelevant to our understanding of Lasso's tonalities in particular or sixteenth-century tonalities in general. On the contrary, as Hermelink, Meier, and Powers have shown, differences in cleffing account for very real differences in melodic contour and

EXAMPLE 13.1   Lasso, *Carmina chromatico*, mm. 1–9

emphasis, and are, moreover, crucial to our understanding of sixteenth-century modal representation. My point is simply that cleffing operates within a context—a specific compass of available tones—established by system (*cantus durus* or *cantus mollis*) and final. In what follows I shall argue, moreover, that Hermelink's three criteria are hierarchical determinants of sixteenth-century tonalities, with system playing a primary role, final a secondary role, and cleffing a more subtle tertiary role.

ACCORDING TO HERMELINK'S three criteria, *Carmina chromatico* is a member of the tonality ♮–G–low. Its tonal character, however, differs dramatically from all other ♮–G–low motets. Indeed, as a comparison of Examples 13.1 and 13.2 reveals, the differences in tonal character between *Carmina chromatico* and a typical ♮–G–low motet such as *Domine in auxilium* are sufficient to call into question the value of regarding two such pieces as members of the same tonality.

The very real differences in sound between these two pieces are a matter of what I call tonal compass—the collection of all pitch positions used in a given composition or repertory. Pitch positions are letter note names (A, B♭, C♯, etc.) and differ from pitches in two respects. First, they are not tied to one specific pitch frequency. The pitch position A, for example, does not necessarily denote a pitch frequency of 440 cycles per second. Second, pitch positions do not recognize enharmonic equivalence. Whether or not they end up in practice possessing the same pitch frequency, D♯ and E♭, for example, remain distinct and separate pitch positions. It should be stressed, moreover, that the distinction between two such pitch positions turns not so much on differences in frequency due to tuning conventions as on the differences in function that the letter names themselves imply. Stated simply, the D♯ in measure 3 of *Carmina chromatico* functions as *mi*, the E♭ in measure 8 as *fa*.[15]

Example 13.2 Lasso, *Domine in auxilium*, mm. 1–9

The tonal compasses, and indeed the tonalities, of both typical and exceptional motets within Lasso's oeuvre are best understood as expansions of what Harold Powers has dubbed the Guidonian diatonic, the conceptual system of pitch relationships formed by the overlapping succession of natural, soft, and hard hexachords, which was attributed to Guido of Arezzo in the late Middle Ages and Renaissance.[16] Figure 13.1, from Adam Gumpelzhaimer's *Compendium musicae* of 1591, shows how one composer and music teacher in nearby Augsburg presented this system during Lasso's lifetime. A prolific composer, Gumpelzhaimer served as Kantor and Praeceptor of the school and church of St. Anna in Augsburg from 1581 until his death in 1625. His responsibilities included the musical instruction of the church school's students, and with the *Compendium*—which went through 13 editions between 1591 and 1681—he provided a well-ordered textbook on the rudiments of music. In the left-hand column of Figure 13.1, Gumpelzhaimer lists all the letter note names of the Guidonian gamut, or *scala musicalis* as he calls it, from G (Γ *ut*) to e″ (ee *la*). In the seven organ pipes to the right of the column he presents the overlapping hexachords. Natural, hard (♮ *duralis*), and soft (B *mollaris*) hexachord labels appear at the bottom of the diagram. The pitch positions B♭ (*fa* in the soft hexachord) and B♮ (*mi* in the hard hexachord) share a common location (b or bb) within the *scala musicalis* of the left-hand column.

The eight pitch positions contained in this Guidonian diatonic (C, D, E, F, G, A, B♭, and B♮) constitute the tonal system of the medieval plainchant repertory as well as the central core of pitches in the tonal systems employed in medieval and Renaissance polyphony. What has not been pointed out before is that although Lasso's motets expand the Guidonian diatonic by adding new pitch positions to it, all of his motets—with the exception of a small number of compositions like *Alma nemes* and the *Prophetiae Sibyllarum*—observe one of two manifestations of a single, normative tonal compass.[17] The primary determinant of

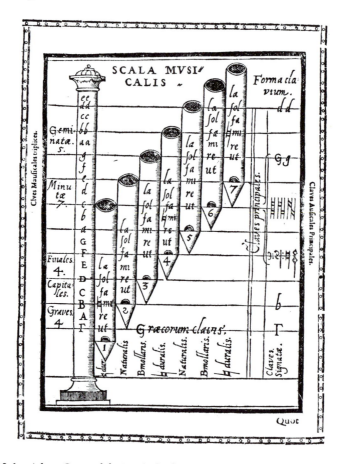

FIGURE 13.1   Adam Gumpelzhaimer's *Scala musicalis*. Reproduced with permission of the University of Michigan Music Library.

that compass, moreover, is the first of Hermelink's three criteria. All compositions set in *cantus durus*—regardless of cleffing, final, or any putative modal representation—use the first or untransposed manifestation, consisting of A, B, B♭, C, C♯, D, E, F, F♯, G, and G♯; all compositions in *cantus mollis* use the second or transposed version, consisting of A, B, B♭, C, C♯, D, E, E♭, F, F♯, and G. Figure 13.2 presents the eight pitch positions of the Guidonian diatonic as a (purely heuristic) string of ascending fifths from B♭ to B♮ and extends this central series in both directions, with chromatically raised positions on the right and chromatically lowered positions on the left.[18] The brackets entered below this series show the tonal compasses of the Guidonian diatonic, *Alma nemes, Carmina chromatico*, Rore's *Calami sonum ferentes*, and both the *cantus durus* and *cantus mollis* versions of Lasso's normative tonal compass.

Within Lasso's normative compass, the chromatic positions between members of the Guidonian diatonic are always spelled in only one way: chromatic

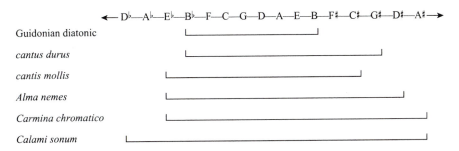

FIGURE 13.2   Tonal compass

pairs, such as the D♯/E♭ and A♯/B♭ pairs in *Carmina chromatico*, are entirely absent. Most striking, however, is the complete absence of a pitch position between two particular members of this background diatonic: in *cantus durus*, between D and E; in *cantus mollis*, between G and A. Example 13.3 shows Lasso's normative tonal compass as a pair of chromatically filled fourths separated by a missing half-step. The three pitch positions forming the two fourths are stable. In *cantus durus*, for example, A, D, and E are never inflected to A♭ or A♯, D♭ or D♯, or E♭ or E♯, respectively. The two pitch positions within each fourth, on the other hand, may be inflected. In *cantus durus*, for example, B♮ and B♭ are both members of the background diatonic, whereas C, F, and G can all be raised chromatically.

The boundaries of Lasso's normative tonal compass also set limits on the sonorities available to him. As Figure 13.3 shows, major 5/3/1 chords (designated "M") occur in *cantus durus* on all members of the Guidonian diatonic except B♮ and in *cantus mollis* on all members of the transposed Guidonian diatonic except E♮. Minor 5/3/1 chords (designated "m") also occur on G, D, A, E, and B in *cantus durus* and C, G, D, A, and E in *cantus mollis*. Minor 5/3/1 chords could also be constructed on F♯ and C♯ in *cantus durus* and B♮ and F♯ in *cantus mollis* without going beyond the limits of Lasso's normative tonal system, but he seems to have avoided 5/3/1 chords based on pitches outside the Guidonian diatonic.

EXAMPLE 13.3   Lasso's normative tonal compass as two disjunct chromatically filled fourths

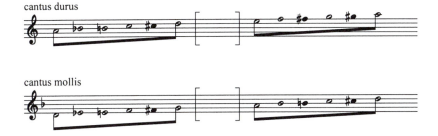

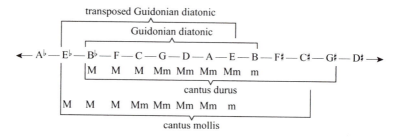

FIGURE 13.3   Sonorities available within Lasso's normative tonal compass

While system is the primary determinant of the tonal compass of a composition, Hermelink's second marker, the final, assumes a secondary function. In Lasso's motets, selection of a particular pitch position as final tends to limit, or in some cases eliminate altogether, inflections of the final itself and the pitch position a perfect fifth above. Table 13.3 illustrates this tendency by enumerating all the inflected pitch positions in a sample of 30 motets—in this case, all the motets contained in Lasso's *Cantiones sacrae* of 1594. (Inflections occurring simultaneously in two or more voice parts are counted as a single inflection.) A D final in either *cantus durus* or *cantus mollis* does not limit inflections since D and A are already stable in both systems (see Example 13.3). To put it another way, a D final cannot limit inflections since D♭, D♯, A♭, and A♯ already lie outside Lasso's normative *cantus durus* and *cantus mollis* systems. Selection of an E final restricts inflections of E and B. Since E♭, E♯, and B♯ already lie outside Lasso's *cantus durus* system, the only effect is to limit occurrences of B♭, as illustrated by the paucity of B♭s in the five ♮–E–low motets.

A G final limits no inflected pitch positions in *cantus mollis* (since G♭, G♯, D♭, and D♯ all lie outside that system's normative compass) and one inflected position (G♯) in the *cantus durus* tonalities ♮–G–low and ♮–G–high. Finals on C (in *cantus durus*) and F (in both systems) exert the greatest limiting power since a C final limits both C♯ and G♯ in *cantus durus* and an F final limits F♯ and C♯ in both systems. The number of occurrences of an inflected pitch position varies from one motet to another within a given tonality or final group, of course: the incidence of E♭ in the ♭–F–high and ♭–F–low tonalities provides the most dramatic example, where the number of E♭s varies from one (in motet no. 19) to nine (in motet no. 20). Inflections of the final and the pitch position a fifth above it, however, are consistently few in number.

The limiting force of finals within the normative compasses of Lasso's *cantus durus* and *cantus mollis* systems may be summarized as follows: in each system two finals limit none of the potentially inflectable pitch positions (the finals A and D in *cantus durus*, and D and G in *cantus mollis*); two limit one position (the finals E and G in *cantus durus*, and A and C in *cantus mollis*); and two limit two positions (the finals C and F in *cantus durus*, and B♭ and F in *cantus mollis*). These limitations imposed by finals have much to do with

TABLE 13.3   Inflected pitch positions in Lasso's *Cantiones sacrae* (Graz, 1594)

cantus durus	B♭	F♯	C♯	G♯	Other
♮–D–low					
4. *Deficiat in dolore vita mea*	16 (+2)	10 (+2)	8 (+3)	3 (+3)	0
5. *Qui timet Deum*	12 (+2)	9 (+4)	7 (+2)	4 (+3)	0
6. *Ego cognovi*	11 (+1)	14 (+3)	21 (+1)	6 (+3)	0
♮–E–low					
12. *Timor Domini principium*	1	8 (+3)	6	9 (+3)	0
13. *Ad Dominum cum tribularer*	3	12 (+4)	9	6 (+1)	0
14. *Vidi calumnias*	6	20 (+7)	23 (+6)	15 (+5)	0
15. *In dedicatione templi*	0	7 (+7)	9 (+3)	8 (+6)	0
27. *Diligam te, Domine*	4	11 (+6)	5	8 (+6)	0
♮–G–low					
23. *Genuit puerpera regem*	8	13 (+6)	3 (+3)	0	0
24. *Quam bonus Israel Deus*	15 (+1)	26 (+5)	5 (+3)	1	0
25. *Confitebor tibi Domine*	4	16 (+8)	6 (+3)	4	0
26. *Musica Dei donum*	7 (+2)	9 (+3)	2	2 (+1)	0
♮–G–high					
28. *Exaltabo te Domine*	6 (+3)	7 (+6)	3	0	0
♮–A–high					
21. *Cantabant canticum Moysi*	12 (+2)	15 (+2)	17 (+4)	5 (+2)	0
22. *Fratres nescitis*	2	8	10 (+1)	6	0
♮–C–high					
18. *Multifariam multisque*	5	5 (+1)	1	0	0

cantus mollis	E♭	B♮	F♯	C♯	Other
♭–G–high					
1. *Nectar et ambrosiam*	12	11 (+4)	18 (+2)	6 (+3)	0
2. *Prolongati sunt dies mei*	27 (+5)	18 (+9)	14 (+7)	8 (+9)	0
3. *Si coelum et coeli*	17 (+1)	10 (+2)	9 (+4)	3 (+2)	0
♭–G–low					
7. *Vere Dominus est*	13	7 (+1)	9 (+1)	4 (+1)	0
8. *Lauda anima mea*	6	16 (+2)	18 (+2)	7 (+1)	0
9. *Respicit Dominus*	11 (+2)	13 (+3)	9	1 (+2)	G♯ (m. 32)
10. *Vincenti dabo edere*	20 (+2)	9 (+4)	14 (+7)	3 (+3)	0
11. *Luxuriosa res vinum*	14	10 (+3)	5 (+1)	4 (+2)	0
♭–F–high					
16. *Beatus homo cui donatum*	4	6 (+3)	2 (+1)	2	A♭ (m. 24)
17. *Ad primum morsum*	5 (+2)	13 (+2)	4 (+1)	1	0
♭–F–low					
19. *Deus iniqui insurrexerunt*	1	9 (+1)	3 (+2)	0	0
20. *Heu quis armorum furor*	9	15 (+5)	3 (+2)	1	0
29. *Conserva me Domine*	3	6 (+2)	0	1	0
♭–D–low					
30. *Recordare Jesu pie*	12 (+5)	2 (+3)	11 (+3)	6 (+2)	0

Numbers in the left-hand column show the order of the motets in the print. Numbers in parentheses represent inflections that are not marked explicitly but would have been applied in performance to avoid melodic tritones and to form major-sixth-to-octave cadential progressions.

TABLE 13.4   Motets of the *Magnum opus musicum* using pitch positions outside Lasso's normative tonal compass

Tonal Markers	Motet Title	Measure*	Pitch Position	Text
♮–A–high	*Evehor invidia*	2:16	E♭	"praeciptare lacus"
♮–A–other	*Mira loquor*	21	E♭	"requiesco"
♮–D–high	*Concupiscendo concupiscit*	1:12	D♯	"(laudare) te (o Domine)"
		2:11	E♭	"et benedicam"
		2:20	D♯	"nomine tuo in saeculum"
♮–D–low	*Agimus tibi*	11	D♯	"(Rex omnipotens De-)us"
♮–E–low	*Alma nemes*	2	D♯	"Alma (nemes)"
		26	E♭	"serenas"
		39	D♯	"ergo tibi"
		51–52	D♯, A♯	"dulce novumque melos"
♮–E–low	*Memento peccati*	32	D♯	"ut timeas"
♮–E–low	*Sponsa quid* (=*Quid tamen*)	2:2	D♯	"(Non me) lascivae"
♮–E–other	*Unde revertimini* (=*Unde recens*)	37	E♭	"haeresibus"
♮–G–high	*Dominator Domine*	31, 35	E♭	"orationem"
♮–G–low	*Timor et tremor*	1:29–31	D♯	"miserere mei"
		2:4	E♭	"Deus"
		2:31	D♯	"non confundar"
♭–F–high	*Beatus homo cui donatum*	24	A♭	"(timor) Dei"
♭–F–low	*Heu quos dabimus*	1:53–54	A♭	"gemitus"
		2:23	G♯	"miseris"
♭–G–low	*Anna mihi* (=*Christe Dei*)	1:5	A♭	"veni"
		1:10	G♯	"nectareus"
		1:14	D♯	"liquor"
		1:15–16	G♯	"nympha"
		1:17–18	G♯, D♯	"nympha"
		1:28, 36	G♯	"charior"
		2:11	G♯	"mutuus"
		2:24, 30	G♯	"placere"
♭–G–low	*O bone Jesu*	3:64	G♯	"castitatem"
♭–G–low	*Respicit Dominus*	32	G♯	"multitudine stultitiae"

*Numbers before colons designate sections in multisectional motets.

the distinctive characteristics that distinguish one tonality from another. Tonalities with finals on A and D in *cantus durus* and D and G in *cantus mollis* are rich in inflections and often rich in cross-relations. Tonalities with finals on C and F in *cantus durus* and B♭ and F in *cantus mollis* have relatively few inflections and sound predominantly diatonic. E and G tonalities in *cantus durus* and A and C tonalities in *cantus mollis* form a middle ground between the diatonic and chromatic poles of the continuum.

As we have seen, individual motets occasionally fall short of Lasso's normative tonal compass when the stabilizing power of the final eliminates one of the normally employed inflections altogether. In the five ♮–E–low motets of the 1594 collection, for example, B♭ is extremely rare; in *In dedicatione templi* it disappears entirely. Six of the 1594 motets (nos. 15, 18, 19, 23, 28, and 29) lack one such inflection.

Far more rare are motets in which Lasso moves beyond his normative tonal compass. Of the 1,924 breve-measures contained in the 1594 motet collection, for example, only two measures contain pitch positions that breach Lasso's normative tonal compass. Such instances are, moreover, extraordinarily rare in Lasso's motets as a whole: *Alma nemes* and the *Prophetiae Sibyllarum* are, of course, the most famous instances; Table 13.4 lists all such occurrences in the 516 motets of the *Magnum opus musicum*. (Here, as in Table 13.3, inflections occurring simultaneously in two or more voice parts are counted as a single inflection.)

One of the compositions listed in Table 13.4 deserves special comment. *Anna mihi* (♭–G–low), which was first published in 1579, is the only motet after *Alma nemes* and the *Prophetiae* that exceeds the normative tonal compass as consistently and dramatically as they do. Here, as in the two earlier pieces, the impetus for such extravagant chromaticism apparently came from the unusual text Lasso set—in this case, profane love lyrics that combine overt carnality with classicizing elements such as a reference to Atropos, one of the three Roman goddesses of Destiny. The inclusion of this piece in a list of prohibited compositions drawn up for Munich's Jesuit college in 1591–92 shows that Lasso's contemporaries considered it scabrous.[19] And when his sons included it in the *Magnum opus musicum*, they substituted a new text that transforms the carnal love of the original into pious love for Christ. It is in that form—divorced from the racy lyrics that seem to have inspired it—that this remarkable chromatic essay appears in the modern *Sämtliche Werke*.[20]

If Lasso composed *Anna mihi* not long before it appeared in print in 1579, it serves as an important reminder that he did not abandon entirely the chromaticism of *Alma nemes* and the *Prophetiae* later in his career. Nevertheless, the small number of compositions contained in Table 13.4 is striking. Most of those motets, moreover, contain only a single pitch position that lies beyond the boundaries of Lasso's normative compass. These inflections stand out and call attention to themselves simply by virtue of their rarity. They are special events that I believe should be brought out in analysis and highlighted in performance. Indeed, in many cases, the words on which these inflections fall seem to prove that Lasso expected his listeners to hear them as meaningful excursions beyond the tonal pale. With these aberrant pitch positions Lasso intended to mirror or highlight the sense of the text being set. For example, the only deviation from the normative tonal compass in *Unde revertimini*—an eight-voice motet set in *cantus durus* with a mix of high and low clefs and a final on E—occurs in measure 37, where Lasso blasphemes his own tonal orthodoxy by introducing heretical E♭s on the word "haeresibus."[21] At the beginning of the *secunda pars* of his epithalamium *Sponsa quid*, Lasso deviates from the normal tonal compass of ♮–E–low when he sets the word "lascivious" ("lascivae") to a sonority containing a wanton D♯. And in measure 24 of *Beatus homo cui donatum*, he underscores the fear of God ("timor Dei") with an awesome chord built on A♭. A simultaneous thinning of the texture and slowing of the rhythm heighten the effect of this sonority.

Finally, it should be pointed out how masterfully Lasso was able to compose richly chromatic and affective passages within the confines of his normative tonal compass. Much of the fame and popularity of the motet *Timor et tremor* surely derives from what Jerome Roche has called its "amazing chromatic harmonies."[22] But in only three places (listed in Table 13.4) does Lasso's polyphony involve pitch positions beyond his normal boundaries. Elsewhere, he was able to craft stunning chromatic passages without exceeding his normal limit. As Example 13.4 illustrates, the startling chromatic alterations and cross-relations that express the "fear and trembling" with which the motet text begins remain entirely within the normative *cantus durus* compass.

IDENTIFICATION OF THE NORMATIVE tonal compass of Lasso's motets raises two broad questions. First, to what extent is the concept of normative tonal compass relevant to other genres and other composers? Can we, for example, establish a normative tonal compass for a late sixteenth-century madrigalist like Luca Marenzio? How useful—or appropriate—is the concept for the music of earlier composers like Adrian Willaert and Josquin des Prez? Obviously such broad questions cannot be answered here, but the several examples offered below suggest that the concept's validity does indeed extend beyond both Lasso and the motet. In 1594, the same year in which the Graz *Cantiones* appeared and the year of the composer's death, Lasso dedicated to Pope Clement VIII his *Lagrime di San Pietro*, a modally ordered cycle of 21 spiritual madrigals composed in seven tonalities—four in *cantus durus* and three in *cantus mollis*. In only two places (shown in Examples 13.5 and 13.6) in the entire cycle does Lasso breach the normative tonal compass. In measure 22 of the third madrigal, *Tre volte haveva*, E♭s appear in a *cantus durus* piece on the words "great mistake" ("gran fallo"). In measure 7 of the fourteenth madrigal, *E vago d'incontrar*, a G♯ appears in *cantus mollis* on the words "serious error" ("grave error"). Only a single pitch position outside the normative tonal compass occurs in the 30 madrigals contained in Palestrina's *Madrigali spirituali* of 1594. In measures 38–40 of the twenty-eighth madrigal (Example 13.7), on the words "changing state" ("mutando stato"), Palestrina writes E♭s in *cantus durus*.

EXAMPLE 13.4   Lasso, *Timor et tremor*, mm. 1–8

Ti - mor et tre - mor,   ti - mor et tre - mor

EXAMPLE 13.5 Lasso, *Tre volte haveva*, mm. 20–23

EXAMPLE 13.6 Lasso, *E vago d'incontrar*, mm. 6–8

EXAMPLE 13.7   Palestrina, *Regina de le Vergini*, mm. 35–42

A second question posed by the preceding discussion is why Lasso chose to restrict the tonal compass of his music so severely and consistently. The limits he set himself went well beyond a general disavowal of the paths opened up by *Alma nemes* and the *Prophetiae Sibyllarum*. In his *cantus durus* compositions, for example, Lasso might easily and fruitfully have employed D♯s to construct cadences on E, and he could have done so without pursuing any of the extravagant chromaticism of the pieces mentioned above. Why did he draw the boundaries where he did?

EXAMPLE 13.8   Cadences on the eight pitch positions of the Guidonian diatonic

Although a definitive answer to this question probably lies beyond our reach, an intriguing possibility presents itself. Perhaps by restricting the tonal compass of his music in this way Lasso was adhering to the Guidonian diatonic as closely as the contrapuntal exigencies of sixteenth-century polyphony permitted. Example 13.8 presents the eight pitch positions of the untransposed, *cantus durus* Guidonian diatonic in octaves, each preceded by a major sixth. Such a 6–8 progression, the backbone of cadence formation in Renaissance polyphony, was available in the background diatonic for all pitch positions except D and G. Lasso needed F♯ and C♯ for cadences on G and D respectively. Since both B♮ and B♭ already exist in the background diatonic, he also needed a major sixth above each for cadences to A. G♮ was already available; G♯, like F♯ and C♯, had to be acquired.

I wonder if Lasso's observance of this neo-Guidonian tonal compass presents another instance of the spirit of rediscovery and reaffirmation of past traditions that so strongly stamps the history of sixteenth-century arts and letters. By the second half of the sixteenth century, composers of polyphonic music must have felt a tremendous need to respond to the humanistic discourse surrounding them. The study of Greek and Roman art, science, and literature gave rise to enthusiastic imitation of ancient models by contemporary artists, poets, and music theorists. Composers, of course, had no ancient compositions to take as models, but that hardly made them immune to the humanist-inspired historicism of sixteenth-century thought. Sixteenth-century theorizing about mode, itself inspired in no small part by recovered ancient modal theory, surely provided the main impetus for the increasingly common modal ordering of sets of compositions in the sixteenth century. Lasso's participation in that particular compositional response has already been pointed out. Perhaps his normative tonal compass reflects the same historicist tendency. By embracing the Guidonian diatonic and accommodating it to modern practice, Lasso asserted the validity of the tonal system of the most ancient—and most unequivocally modal—musical repertory known to him.

If Lasso's normative tonal compass represents a kind of musical historicism, it also carries with it a certain irony, for the chromaticism it set aside was itself partially the product of humanist historicism. But that only tells us that Lasso's view of the past was not, say, Vicentino's. Rather than troubling us, such an apparent conflict should remind us of the generally dynamic and pluralistic nature of sixteenth-century musical thought. By the same token, the fact that Lasso's neo-Guidonian system was not purely Guidonian should not trouble us any more than the fact that Glarean's modes were not purely Aristoxenian, or that Erasmus's prose was not purely Ciceronian. Completely in the spirit of his own age, Lasso reaffirmed the authority of ancient tradition while asserting his own right to creative appropriation of it.

NOTES

I am grateful to Peter Bergquist, Lawrence Earp, James Haar, Brian Hyer, Dolores Pesce, and Harold Powers, all of whom read an earlier version of this study and offered valuable suggestions.

1. Charles Burney, *A General History of Music* (London, 1789), 3:314–15.

2. *Le quatoirsiesme livre contenant dixhuyct chansons italiennes, six chansons francoises, & six motetz faictz (a la nouvelle composition d'aucuns d'Italie) par Rolando di Lassus* (Antwerp, 1555). Rore's *Calami sonum ferentes*, the last item in the collection, is the only composition by a composer other than Lasso. A facsimile reprint of this publication appeared as vol. 15 of the Corpus of Early Music (Brussels: Editions Culture et Civilisation, 1972).

3. Burney, *A General History*, 315.

4. Ibid., 321.

5. Edward E. Lowinsky, *Tonality and Atonality in Sixteenth-Century Music* (Berkeley: University of California Press, 1961), 38–39.

6. Harold S. Powers, "Tonal Types and Modal Categories," *Journal of the American Musicological Society* 34 (1981): 467.

7. A letter addressed to Lasso by the Parisian printer Adrian Le Roy on 14 January 1574 indicates the kind of fascination and enthusiasm that the opening of the *Prophetiae Sibyllarum* continued to arouse nearly twenty years after Lasso composed it. Le Roy reports that King Charles IX of France, upon hearing the beginning of the Sibyls ("commencement de Cibiles") was so impressed that he commanded Le Roy to publish them lest they not be preserved for posterity. See Horst Leuchtmann, *Orlando di Lasso: Sein Leben* (Wiesbaden: Breitkopf and Härtel, 1976), 169, 311–12.

8. See especially William J. Mitchell, "The Prologue to Orlando di Lasso's Prophetiae Sibyllarum," *Music Forum* 2 (1970): 264–73; Klaus-K. Hübler, "Orlando di Lassos 'Prophetiae Sibyllarum' oder Über chromatische Komposition im 16. Jahrhundert," *Zeitschrift für Musiktheorie* 1 (1978): 29–34; Karol Berger, "Tonality and Atonality in the Prologue to Orlando di Lasso's *Prophetiae Sibyllarum*: Some Methodological Problems in Analysis of Sixteenth-Century Music," *Musical Quarterly* 66 (1980): 484–504; William E. Lake, "Orlando di Lasso's Prologue to *Prophetiae Sibyllarum*: A Comparison of Analytic Approaches," *In Theory Only* 11 (1991): 1–19. See also Reinhold Schlötterer's introduction to his edition of the cycle in Orlando di Lasso, *Prophetiae Sibyllarum, Sämtliche Werke*, neue Reihe, 21 (Kassel: Bärenreiter, 1990), pp. xvii–xx.

9. Bernhard Meier, *The Modes of Classical Vocal Polyphony*, trans. Ellen S. Beebe (New York: Broude, 1988).

10. Two recent studies address the relevance of historical music theories to our own analysis and criticism of historical repertories: Thomas Christensen, "Music Theory and Its Histories," in *Music Theory and the Exploration of the Past*, ed. Christopher Hatch and David W. Bernstein (Chicago: University of Chicago Press, 1993), 9–40; and Peter Schubert, "Authentic Analysis," *Journal of Musicology* 12 (1994): 3–18.

11. Siegfried Hermelink, *Dispositiones modorum: Die Tonarten in der Musik Palestrinas und seiner Zeitgenossen*, Münchner Veröffentlichungen zur Musikgeschichte 4 (Tutzing: Hans Schneider, 1960).

12. Franz Xaver Haberl's edition of the motets contained in the *Magnum opus musicum* appeared as the 11 odd-numbered volumes of Orlando di Lasso, *Sämtliche Werke*, 21 vols. (Leipzig: Breitkopf and Härtel, 1894–1926). These volumes and the original 1604 print lack the *Penitential Psalms*, the *Prophetiae Sibyllarum*, and a small

number of motets apparently unavailable to Lasso's sons in 1604. In his edition, Haberl followed the order of the *Magnum opus musicum* but provided the individual sections of multisectional motets with separate numbers. On the first page of each motet, his number is followed by the *Magnum opus musicum* number in parentheses.

13. Harold Powers, "Tonal Types and Modal Categories," 428–70; "Modal Representation in Polyphonic Offertories," *Early Music History* 2 (1982): 43–86; "Is Mode Real?: Pietro Aron, the Octenary System, and Polyphony," *Basler Jahrbuch für historische Musikpraxis* 16 (1992): 9–52.

14. Horst-Willi Groß, *Klangliche Struktur und Klangverhältnis in Messen und lateinischen Motetten Orlando di Lassos*, Frankfurter Beiträge zur Musikwissenschaft 7 (Tutzing: Hans Schneider, 1977). Horst Leuchtmann has outlined a second approach to the study of the chordal component of late sixteenth-century music in his preface to *Musik der bayerischen Hofkapelle zur Zeit Orlando di Lassos, 2. Auswahl, Sdegnosi Ardori*, Denkmäler der Tonkunst in Bayern, new series, 7 (Wiesbaden: Breitkopf and Härtel, 1989), pp. xix–xxi.

15. I favor the term "tonal compass" over expressions such as "pitch-class collection" precisely because pitch classes—at least as they are commonly defined in analyses of later, especially twentieth-century, repertories—comprise enharmonically equivalent pitches such as D♯ and E♭.

16. Harold Powers, "Is Mode Real?," 15. Eric Chafe has provided the most extensive demonstration of the value of analytical systems grounded in the hexachords of the Guidonian diatonic in *Monteverdi's Tonal Language* (New York: Schirmer, 1992).

17. This statement derives from an examination of the *Prophetiae* and the 516 motets contained in the *Magnum opus musicum* of 1604.

18. Although rather different in form and intent, my heuristic string of ascending fifths derives from the model presented by Reinhold Schlötterer in his insightful introduction to Orlando di Lasso, *Prophetiae Sibyllarum*, *Sämtliche Werke*, neue Reihe, 21, p. xvii.

19. This list of *Cantiones quo ad textum et notas prohibitae* appears along with a complementary list of *Cantiones probatae* in a manuscript set of rules and regulations compiled by the Jesuit Provincial, Ferdinand Alber. I reported on the portions of the manuscript dealing with music in a paper read in November 1993 at the fifty-ninth annual meeting of the American Musicological Society in Montreal, Quebec. An expanded version of that paper, provisionally titled "An Instance of Post-Tridentine Music Censorship," is forthcoming.

20. I am grateful to Peter Bergquist, who provided me with an edition of *Anna mihi* based on RISM 1579b.

21. Another version of this motet, with the text *Unde recens reditus*, apparently functioned as the introductory dialogue to a ballet that was performed during the Parisian festivities given by Catherine de' Medici between 14 and 28 September 1573 to celebrate the election of her youngest son Henry, Duke of Anjou, as King of Poland. Horst Leuchtmann, "Lassos Huldigungsmottete für Henri d'Anjou 1573," *Musikforschung* 23 (1970): 165–66, provides both texts. In *Unde recens reditus* the E♭s would occur at the only mention of Catherine's name, paying special tribute to the woman for whom the poem was written. *Unde revertimini* first appeared in print in the so-called *Viersprachendruck*, published in Munich by Adam Berg in 1573. Lasso's dedication of this print is dated 30 January. Leuchtmann suggests that the French version of the motet is the original and *Unde revertimini* a contrafact, but Peter Bergquist has argued that *Unde revertimini* preceded *Unde recens reditus* and has demonstrated that the surviving music accommodates the former far better than the latter. For a detailed discus-

sion of the evidence supporting the chronological precedence of *Unde revertimini* and an edition of both versions of the motet, see Orlando di Lasso, *The Four-Language Print for Four and Eight Voices* (Munich, 1573), ed. Peter Bergquist, Complete Motets 10 (Madison: A-R Editions, 1995). I thank Professor Bergquist for making his researches available to me prior to their publication.

22. Jerome Roche, *Lassus*, Oxford Studies of Composers 19 (London: Oxford University Press, 1982), 5.

Palestrina as Reader

Motets from the Song of Songs

Palestrina's fourth book of five-voice motets, *Motettorum quinque vocibus liber quartus* (Rome, 1584), was one of his most unusual and interesting publications. The little information that has survived about its genesis can be quickly recounted. The book must have been in production by the end of 1583 because two of the five partbooks (tenor and bassus) bear this date. The printing was complete by 27 April 1584, the date when Palestrina sent "un libbro nuovo de Mottetti della Cantica" to Duke Guglielmo Gonzaga in Mantua. The volume was printed in Rome by Alessandro Gardano, heir with his brother Angelo of the firm established in Venice by Antonio Gardano. Gardano may have been working on commission from two Roman bookmen, the printer Giacomo Tornieri and the bookseller Giacomo Berichia. On 13 April 1584 Tornieri and Berichia received a privilege (a form of copyright) from Pope Gregory XIII; from this document it is reasonable to infer that they financed the print.[1] Clearly it was a venture worth protecting: the *Liber quartus* achieved extraordinary popularity even by Palestrina's standards, being reprinted possibly as many as 15 times, in Milan, Venice, and Antwerp, as late as 1650.[2]

Even less is known about the circumstances that led Palestrina to compose the music in his *Liber quartus*. He dedicated the print to his patron and employer, Pope Gregory XIII.[3] Although there is no way of knowing if he had composed the music at the pope's behest, there was clearly a strong connection between Palestrina and his patron. Gregory had commissioned Palestrina and Zoilo in 1577 to revise the chant for the post-Tridentine liturgy.[4] For his part, Palestrina dedicated four of the five books that he published between 1581 and 1584 (one of Masses, one of spiritual madrigals, two of motets) either to Gregory or to his natural son, Giacomo Boncompagni. The story recounted by Palestrina's biographer and hagiographer Giuseppe Baini, supposedly drawn from a now lost manuscript of *memorie*, of Palestrina presenting a copy of the fourth book of motets to Gregory and receiving his blessing, should probably be regarded as fictitious.[5]

Palestrina's letter of dedication in the *Liber quartus* is an unusually interesting document that provides information crucial for understanding the musical contents:[6]

Sanctissimo D. N. Gregorio XIII. Pont. Max.

To our most holy lord, Gregory XIII, supreme pontiff

Extant nimis multa poetarum carmina, nullo alio, nisi amorum a Christiana professione, et nomine alienorum argumento: ea vera ipsa carmina hominum vere furore correptorum, ac iuventutis corruptorum magna musicorum pars, artificii, industriaequae suae materiam esse voluerunt, qui quantum ingenii laude floruerunt, tantum materiae vitio apud bonos, et graves viros offenderunt.

Exceedingly many songs of the poets are on no theme other than loves that are alien to the name and profession of Christian. These very songs, by men carried away by passion and corrupters of youth, the majority of musicians have chosen as material for their art and industry—[musicians] who, however much they have flourished from the renown of their genius, have as much offended among honest and serious men by the immorality of their material.

Ex eo numero aliquando fuisse me, et erubesco et doleo. Sed quando praeterita mutari non possum nec reddi infecta, quae facta iam sunt, consilium mutavi. Itaque et antea elaboravi in iis, quae de laudibus Domini nostri JESU CHRISTI, Sanctissimaeque eius matris, et Virginis MARIAE carminibus scripta erant, et hoc tempore ea delegi, quae divinum Christi, sponsaeque eius animae amorem continerent, Salamonis nimirum cantica. Usus sum genere aliquanto alacriore, quam in caeteris Ecclesiasticis cantibus uti soleo: Sic enim rem ipsam postulare intelligebam.

I blush and grieve to have been among their number. But since the past can never be changed, nor things already done rendered undone, I have changed my views. And therefore I have before this worked on those songs which had been written in praise of Our Lord JESUS CHRIST and his most holy mother the Virgin MARY. And at this time I have chosen the Songs of Solomon, which contain the divine love of Christ and his spouse, the soul. I have used a style somewhat more spirited than I am wont to use in other church compositions, for so I perceive the subject itself to require.

Volui autem hoc quiquid est operis offerre Sanctitati tuae, cui, si minus re ipsa, at certe voluntate et conatu, satisfactum iri non dubito. Sed si, quod utinam contingat, re etiam ipsa satisfecero, incitabor ad alia edenda, quae tuae Sanctitati grata fore exstimabo. Conservet nobis Deus quam diutissime GREGORIUM Pastorem vigilantissimum, suique gregis amantissimum, cumeletque omni felicitate.

I wanted, moreover, to offer this work, such as it is, to Your Holiness, who I do not doubt will be satisfied, surely by the intent and the effort, if less so by the thing itself. But if (would that it happen!) I give satisfaction with the thing itself, I will be encouraged to bring out others which I will hope may be pleasing to Your Holiness. May God preserve for us for as long as possible GREGORY, the most vigilant shepherd and the most loving of his flock, and may he bestow every happiness on him.

Humilis servus
Joannes Aloysius Preaenestinus

His humble servant
Giovanni Aloysio Palestrina

As the letter makes clear, the *Liber quartus* is unusual in a number of respects. Palestrina explains that he took all of the texts from a single source, the Song of Songs. In contrast, his other six motet prints are anthologies consisting of texts from many different sources. The *Liber quartus* stands apart from the rest because its contents form a unified whole (see Table 14.1). Its motets are similar in length and structure. And as we shall see, there is good reason to suspect that Palestrina composed the music at one time. In contrast, the other books combine pieces that employ a variety of musical structures or approaches, and sometimes even differing numbers of voices. While the chronology of Palestrina's music is still very much a matter of debate, it seems

TABLE 14.1 Contents of Palestrina's *Liber quartus* (1584)

No.	Incipit	System	Clefs	Final	Chapter: Verse	Measures	Words	Segments
1	Osculetur me	♭	g2c2c3c3F3	G	1:1–2	63	22	5
2	Trahe me post te	♭	g2c2c3c3F3	G	1:3	69	28	7
3	Nigra sum sed formosa	♭	g2c2c3c3F3	G	1:4–5	68	33	9
4	Vineam meam non	♭	g2c2c3c3F3	G	1:5e–6	55	23	5
5	Si ignoras te	♭	g2c2c3c3F3	G	1:7–8	68	30	8
6	Pulchrae sunt genae	♭	g2c2c3c3F3	G	1:9–11	66	27	10
7	Fasciculus myrrae	♭	g2c2c3c3F3	G	1:12–14	57	29	8
8	Ecce tu pulcher es	♭	g2c2c3c3F3	G	1:15–2:1	57	23	6
9	Tota pulchra es	♭	g2c2c3c3F3	G	4:7–8	58	35	7
10	Vulnerasti cor meum	♭	g2c2c3c3F3	G	4:9–10	68	39	9
11	Sicut lilium inter spinas	♮	g2c2c3c3c4	G	2:2–3	72	31	7
12	Introduxit me rex	♮	g2c2c3c3c4	G	2:4–5	57	19	3
13	Laeva eius	♮	g2c2c3c3c4	G	2:6–7	61	27	9
14	Vox dilecti mei	♮	g2c2c3c3F3	G	2:8–10	58	35	12
15	Surge propera amica	♮	g2c2c3c3c4	G	2:10b–13	62	42	11
16	Surge amica mea	♮	g2c2c3c3c4	G	2:13c–14	69	33	12
17	Dilectus meus mihi	♮	g2c2c3c3c4	G	2:16–3:1	63	42	14
18	Surgam et circuibo	♮	g2c2c3c4c4	G	3:2	55	18	5
19	Adiuro vos filiae	♮	c1c3c3c4F4	A	5:8–10	77	41	14
20	Caput eius	♮	c1c3c3c4F4	E	5:11–12	61	28	8
21	Dilectus meus descendit	♮	c1c3c3c4F4	E	6:1–2	64	28	7
22	Pulchra es	♮	c1c3c3c4F4	E	6:3–4	55	23	6
23	Quae est ista quae	♮	c1c1c3c4F4	E	6:9	61	19	5
24	Descendi in hortum	♮	c1c1c3c4F4	E	6:10	61	17	3
25	Quam pulchri sunt	♭	g2g2c2c3F3	F	7:1b–2	68	33	9
26	Duo ubera tua	♭	g2g2c2c3F3	F	7:3–5	74	47	14
27	Quam pulchra es et	♭	g2g2c2c3F3	F	7:6–8	69	40	10
28	Guttur tuum	♭	g2g2c2c3F3	F	7:9–10	68	24	4
29	Veni dilecte mi	♭	g2g2c2c3F3	F	7:11–12	67	30	8

likely that the other motet prints reflect work carried out over a longer period of time, perhaps a five- or ten-year period prior to publication.

The dedication is famous for Palestrina's repudiation of his earlier work as a madrigal composer and his statement that he had turned to religious or sacred themes. These remarks have occasioned comment from nearly every scholar who has written about Palestrina.[7] Some of them have questioned Palestrina's sincerity because two years later, in 1586, a year after Gregory's death, he published a second volume of four-voice secular madrigals. For example, Alfred Einstein wrote: "How else can one interpret this *Pater peccavi* but as a purely formal, rhetorical obeisance to the spirit of the Counter Reformation, in plain English, as pure hypocrisy? . . . Or did he intend, with his self-reproaches, to discourage the dubious worldly interpretation of his motets on the Song of Solomon?"[8]

At issue is whether Palestrina continued to *compose* secular music after 1584. Harold Powers, arguing that the apology was "no specious piety," explained the 1586 publication of the madrigals by interpreting a reference in the dedication to "frutti già maturi" to mean that the madrigals had actually been composed many years earlier.[9] The 1586 publication, which bears a dedication to Giulio Cesare Colonna, the prince of Palestrina, could then be viewed simply as a rather pragmatic decision to honor the ruling family of his native city, perhaps as a prelude to retirement.[10] Palestrina's numerous publications of sacred music in the final decade of his life (12 volumes of motets, hymns, lamentations, offertories, litanies, Magnificats, Masses, and spiritual madrigals) make the conversion toward the sacred seem genuine, but there is no way to be sure. After all, previously unpublished (newly composed?) madrigals by Palestrina continued to appear regularly in printed anthologies after 1584.[11]

Some readers find it difficult to reconcile Palestrina's condemnation of the secular with his setting of some of the most erotic love poetry ever written. The Song of Songs contains a series of highly charged dialogues between two lovers, sometimes identified as a bride and bridegroom, with occasional interjections by a chorus of young women. Its language, with its rich imagery of breasts and bodies, of sexual union, of searching, finding, and losing, is unique among books of the Bible.[12] The temptation is to interpret Palestrina's Song of Songs settings as madrigals that happened to be in Latin and to see in this choice of text a way to write madrigals in reform-minded Rome.

To be sure, there is one witness—the composer and theorist Lodovico Zacconi—who seems to acknowledge what Einstein referred to as "the dubious worldly interpretation" of the texts:

> I have always praised, in Palestrina, the fact that he spent little time writing madrigals; for God had created him for the purpose of adorning the Church by his sweet songs, as in fact he did. But if I had been near him and in a position to give him my view, I should have done all in my powers to dissuade him from composing his *cantica* motets; for today many singers like to sing as solos "Quam pulcra es, amica mea, quam pulchra es"; "Tota pulchra es, amica mea, formosa mea"; "Fulcite me floribus quia amore langueo," and

other things of like character, *which they sing with God only knows what intention.* [13]

Zacconi published this comment in 1622 at a time when *cantica* texts were extremely popular (though nearly 40 years after Palestrina's Song of Songs collection was published). His statement may in fact reflect the views of contemporary composers and singers, but it does not seem to characterize Palestrina's intentions, at least as he explained them in his letter of dedication.

The dedication makes clear that Palestrina viewed the book in allegorical terms. He described the texts as containing "the divine love of Christ and his spouse, the soul." This "reading" of the meaning of the text belongs to a long exegetical tradition associated with the Song of Songs. As Robert Kendrick has shown in an illuminating study of seventeenth-century Song of Songs settings, Palestrina and his contemporaries were far readier than we today to read the text on many different levels. [14] We are inclined toward a literal interpretation; for us, a kiss between a man and a woman means human sexual activity. They, as inheritors of traditions of medieval exegesis, viewed the book in allegorical terms: not so much the love between a bride and a bridegroom (i.e., a woman and a man) as between Christ and the soul or between Christ and the church or between Christ and the Virgin Mary, to list three of the most common interpretations. [15]

The richness of this allegorical thinking is revealed in numerous commentaries whose length and complexity are astonishing. For example, Michael Ghisleri's commentary, published in Rome a few decades after Palestrina's *Liber quartus*, occupies 1,057 pages in folio format, plus indices. [16] The entire text of the Song of Songs itself required only about four folio pages in the 1592 edition. [17] Ghisleri gave four parallel interpretations for *each* verse: (1) "according to the sound of the letters," that is, the literal sense of the words; (2) "concerning the first bride, which is the holy church"; (3) "concerning the second bride, which is the soul of the just man"; (4) "concerning the third bride, which is the Blessed Mary." An appendix offers readings collected from the Church Fathers. An index at the beginning lists 163 feasts of the church year in calendrical order; under the excerpts of the Gospel appointed for the day are references to specific verses and commentary. Each Gospel is explicated in some way by reference to the Song of Songs. For example, feast number 121 is for the apostles Peter and Paul. In the index we read: "Peter and Paul are like the two breasts of the church, giving forth milk." There is a reference to p. 598, col. 2, location b, the commentary on the line "Duo ubera tua." A marginal note reads: "holy prelates are like the breasts of the church" ("prelati sancti ubera ecclesia"). In effect, every line had relevance to some feast, to some portion of the church's teaching.

Palestrina was probably familiar with all of the contemporary interpretations, but he focused on the tropological, that is, the *sponsa* as the soul, the individual striving for a mystical spiritual union with Christ. Given Palestrina's own words, as well as the traditions of Song of Songs interpretations that surrounded him, and particularly the absence of any Catholic interpretations of it as a marriage text, it seems most unlikely that his purpose was to compose "madrigals" that would be acceptable to the Church.

Of course Palestrina was no stranger to Song of Songs settings. Like his contemporaries, he frequently set texts consisting of excerpts drawn from the Song of Songs that played an important role in the liturgy.[18] For example, his *Motecta festorum totius anni cum Comuni Sanctorum . . . liber primus* of 1563 includes his setting of *Quam pulchri sunt gressus tui*, identified as appropriate to the Feast of the Conception of the Virgin (see Table 14.2).[19] Like other texts drawn from the Song of Songs for use in the liturgy, the text of *Quam pulchri sunt gressus tui* is a free amalgamation of phrases, here taken from Song of Songs 7:1b–6. The setting is characteristic of Palestrina's early motets both in its prolixity (the motets in the early books are much longer than those published later) and in its undifferentiated polyphonic style. Palestrina, the master of counterpoint, never has a note out of place, but there is nothing special in his treatment of the text; the setting is indistinguishable from his settings of other liturgical texts.

In contrast, Palestrina explained in the dedication to his *Liber quartus* that he was responding to the text in a way that he considered unusual: he had "used a style of music somewhat more spirited ("alacriore") than I am wont to use in ecclesiastical melodies, for so I perceive the subject itself to require." In other words, though he had often set Song of Songs texts before, this time he was responding differently. In fact, both his choice of texts and the settings he provided for them invite our attention. By working first with the texts and then with his music we can see how Palestrina functioned as "reader": in choosing the texts, in organizing the settings as a collection and even as a cycle, and in setting—that is, interpreting or "reading"—the individual texts.[20]

In choosing the Song of Songs as his source, Palestrina avoided the many popular centonizations used for liturgical or paraliturgical purposes (*Nigra sum, Tota pulchra es*, etc.) and instead chose a series of excerpts drawn *verbatim* directly from the Bible.[21] His focus seems to have been on setting extended portions of the text as text. For example, he created three motets (Motets 25, 26, and the beginning of 27) from the portion of chapter 7 cited above (see Table 14.2). One indication of the special character of the particular excerpts he chose is that he did not set any of them a second time.[22] In contrast, he composed multiple settings of many clearly liturgical pieces like *Ave regina caelorum* or *Alma redemptoris mater*; he even composed two settings of *Quam pulchri sunt gressus tui*, the Marian antiphon mentioned above. Furthermore, few other composers chose these excerpts either, perhaps because they served no liturgical purpose.[23]

I assume that Palestrina's first task was to go from a book consisting of eight chapters to a shorter text that could in turn be divided into 29 individual pieces.[24] He obviously could not set the entire book, not just because of its length, but also because of its repetitiveness, its occasionally difficult and obscure language, and its contradictions: there is as much searching and losing in the text as there is searching and finding. He selected certain portions to set

TABLE 14.2   Song of Songs 7:1–6 and the motets based on it from the 1584 and 1563 prints

Song of Songs 7	1584	1563
(phrases in 1563 motet given in italic type)		
[7:1] Quid videbis in Sulamite, nisi choros castrorum? *Quam pulchri sunt gressus tui* in calceamentis, *filia principis!* Iuncturae femorum tuorum sicut monilia quae fabricata sunt manu artificis. [7:2] Umbilicus tuus crater tornatilis, numquam indigens poculis. Venter tuus sicut acervus tritici vallatus liliis.	**Motet 25** Quam pulchri sunt gressus tui in calceamentis, filia principis! Iuncturae femorum tuorum sicut monilia quae fabricata sunt manu artificis. Umbilicus tuus crater tornatilis, numquam indigens poculis. Venter tuus sicut acervus tritici vallatus liliis.	**Motet 28** (In festo conceptionis Beatae Mariae) Quam pulchri sunt gressus tui, filia principis. Collum tuum sicut turris eburnea, oculi tui divini et comae capitis tui sicut purpura regis. Quam pulchra es et quam decora carissima. Alleluia.
[7:3] Duo ubera tua sicut duo hinnuli gemelli capreae. [7:4] *Collum tuum sicut turris eburnea.* Oculi tui sicut piscinae in Hesebon, quae sunt in porta filiae multitudinis. Nasus tuus sicut turris Libani, quae respicit contra Damascum. [7:5] Caput tuum ut Carmelus: *et comae capitis tui sicut purpura regis* vincta canalibus.	**Motet 26** Duo ubera tua sicut duo hinnuli gemelli capreae. Collum tuum sicut turris eburnea. Oculi tui sicut piscinae in Hesebon, quae sunt in porta filiae multitudinis. Nasus tuus sicut turris Libani, quae respicit contra Damascum. Caput tuum ut carmelus: et comae capitis tui sicut purpura regis iuncta canalibus.	
[7:6] *Quam pulchra es, et quam decora charissima, in deliciis!* *	**Motet 27** (beginning) Quam pulchra es, et quam decora charissima, in deliciis!	

* Text from *Biblia sacra vulgatae editionis Sixti quinti* (Rome, 1592).

313

to music: all of chapters 1 and 2 and the first few verses of chapter 3; a small portion of chapters 4 and 5; a longer portion of chapter 6; most of chapter 7, but nothing from chapter 8 (see Table 14.1.)

In fact, the location of the material that Palestrina sets gives a valuable indication of the large-scale structure. He essentially used the material in the order in which it appeared in the Bible, but with one major exception. He placed the excerpts from chapter 4, motets 9–10, *after* the material from chapter 1 and *before* the material from chapter 2 (see Table 14.1). The presence of this material that is out of order defines a large opening section, consisting of 10 motets (eight from chapter 1, two from the bridegroom's long speech in chapter 4). Motet 1 and Motet 10 function as a frame for the unit. Motet 1 articulates the rich images found throughout this chapter: "Your breasts are better than wine, fragrant with the best ointments." Motet 10, with its text "Your breasts are fairer than wine, and the fragrance of your unguents above all spices," echoes the opening.[25]

There are three additional large sections, defined in part by where the material comes in the Song of Songs. The second section, like the first, consists of an almost completely continuous block, going from 2:2 through 3:2. Palestrina omitted a verse from chapter 2—"catch for us the foxes, the little foxes who destroy the vineyards"—presumably because it interrupted the otherwise idyllic scene. The third section, in contrast, consists of carefully selected and balanced portions of chapters 5 and 6. The fourth section once again presents continuous material, drawn from chapter 7.

Palestrina confirmed the large-scale structure of four sections by setting each to a particular tonality or tonal type (as defined by system, cleffing, and final): the first group (1–10) in *cantus mollis*, high clefs, G (♭ g2 G); the second (11–18) in *cantus durus*, high clefs, G (♮ g2 G); the third (19–24) in *cantus durus*, low clefs, A or E (♮ c1 A or E); and the fourth (25–29) in *cantus mollis*, high clefs, F (♭ g2 F).[26] It might be tempting to call this a modal collection and identify the groups as mode 1 transposed, mode 7, mode 3, and mode 5, but in his true modally ordered collections Palestrina used all eight modes in order.[27] Furthermore, it is not easy to label Motet 19 (♮ c1 A), written in a tonality that Palestrina did not use in any of his other modal collections.[28] The other pieces in this print are authentic in disposition (that is, the cantus and tenor have an ambitus of roughly an octave above the final); only this one is plagal. In terms of the text, Motet 19 forms a unit with Motet 20 (setting, respectively, 5:8–10 and 5:11–12), perhaps an indication that it should be thought of as the first part of a two-part motet ending on E.

It is hard to know what Palestrina intended with this choice of tonalities. Perhaps he was simply interested in exploring the four (or five) different sounds that we usually characterize as "Dorian" (♭G), "Mixolydian" (♮G), "Aeolian"/"Phrygian" (♮A/E), and "Lydian"="Ionian" (♭F), or that his contemporaries would likely have referred to as "re," "ut" (both "Mixolydian" and "Ionian"), and "mi" tonalities.[29] Perhaps he was even interested in the symmetry of pieces in *cantus mollis* framing pieces in *cantus durus*. There is no apparent large-

scale program to explain these four large divisions beyond the overarching narrative of the soul's spiritual journey.

It seems likely that Palestrina was on his own in choosing the texts,
though, of course, he could have worked with a collaborator. An important
factor for him seems to have been the opportunity to shape the text into units
by using connections of various kinds. We have seen that he used the material
from chapter 4 out of order to function like a refrain that frames the first large
unit. There are other instances where he selected sections from the larger text
because of the presence of useful structural elements and then used the elements to shape the texts into units. For example, in working with the text of
chapter 6, he left out four verses between the end of Motet 22 and the beginning of Motet 23. The result is the close juxtaposition of a section of text—
"terribilis ut castrorum acies ordinata"—that occurs in both motets; he emphasized the connections by using similar music.[30] Another example is the unit
consisting of Motets 15–18. He divided the bridegroom's speech (Motets 15–
16) into two unequal parts to set up textual and musical parallels: "Surge . . .
columba mea" (Motet 15) and "Surge . . . columba mea" (Motet 16). And he
brought out the parallels in the bride's response (Motets 17–18). "Quaesivi
quem diligit" becomes a kind of refrain (see Table 14.3). The presence of these
structures may have been a sufficient reason for Palestrina to end his second
large section with Motet 18, rather than continue with the rest of chapter 3.

In creating the texts of the individual motets, Palestrina was clearly working within certain limits, presumably of his own choosing. Most of the pieces
had between 22 and 40 words; just a few were shorter or longer (17 at the
shortest, 47 at the longest). They fit into strict conventions of length: most were
between 60 and 70 measures long (in modern transcription); just a few were
less than 60 (55 was the shortest) or more than 70 (77 the longest). Within
these norms, he made adjustments as necessary to fit the requirements of the
text. For example, Motet 26, *Duo ubera*, is one of the longest by every measure: number of words, measures, and musical segments. An explanation for
its unusual length is that Palestrina was setting an entire speech (sometimes
assigned to the chorus, sometimes to the bridegroom), consisting of five verses.
The logical point of division in this speech created unbalanced halves, one of
two verses (Motet 25), and a longer one (Motet 26) with three. Virtually all the
"anomalous" pieces can be explained in similar fashion, by examining the context and the choices he faced.

Palestrina frequently divided the text into sections corresponding to
speeches or portions of dialogue.[31] But a number of motets shift speaker midway.[32] In any case analyzing the texts in terms of the speaker is difficult because
the speaker cannot always be identified or is identified differently from edition
to edition.

A major factor that guided Palestrina in dividing the larger text into 29
motets was probably the possibilities he could see for setting each of the texts.
As "reader" he made decisions about how to segment each text into smaller
units, and how to shape these small units into larger units. He balanced the

TABLE 14.3   Musical and textual connections in motets 15–18

Motet 15

2:10b	1	Surge propera amica mea
	2	columba mea
	3	formosa mea
	4	et veni.
2:11	5	Iam hiems transiit
	6	imber abiit et recessit.
2:12	7	Flores apparuerunt in terra nostra
	8	tempus putationis advenit
	9	vox turturis audita est in terra nostra
2:13	10	ficus protulit grossos suos
	11	vinea florentes dederunt odorem suum.

Motet 16

2:13c	1	Surge amica mea
	2	speciosa mea
	3	et veni
2:14	4	columba mea
	5	in foraminibus petrae
	6	in caverna maceriae
	7	ostende mihi
	8	faciem tuam
	9	sonet vox tua
	10	in auribus meis
	11	vox enim tua dulcis
	12	et facies tua decora.

Motet 17

2:16	1	Dilectus meus mihi et ego illi
	2	qui pascitur inter lilia
2:17	3	donec aspiret dies
	4	et inclinentur umbrae.
	5	Revertere
	6	similis esto
	7	dilecte mi capreae
	8	hinnuloque cervorum
	9	super montes Bether.
3:1	10	In lectulo meo
	11	per noctes quaesivi
	12	quem diligit anima me.
	13	quaesivi illum
	14	et non inveni.

Motet 18

3:2	1	Surgam et circuibo civitatem;
	2	per vicos et plateas
	3	quaeram
	4	quem diligit anima mea.
	5a	Quaesivi illum
	5b	et non inveni.

Note: numbers on the left refer to biblical verses; numbers with text show my division
of the music into segments.

requirements of syntax and meaning; he brought out parallels and repetitions, just as he had when working at the larger level of the collection as a whole; and he focused on important words or ideas that could serve as the key to his interpretation.

The segments—by which I mean a textual unit that presents discrete musical material—are Palestrina's building blocks. Segments usually end with cadences, but some are very short and depend on the segments on either side for musical meaning. In many cases, a particular portion of text is repeated by some or all of the voices. The repetition helps to define the boundaries of a particular segment.[33]

Palestrina's decisions about segmentation depend on the text itself. As a rule, when the text is short, with few words, the segments tend to be fewer in number but longer. Longer texts tend to have more segments that are shorter in length. Somehow, even given this variety of approach, Palestrina generally works toward a motet with two, three, or four large sections, sometimes built from a number of small segments, sometimes not.

Decisions about segmentation reveal Palestrina as reader at the most profound level. *Quam pulchra es* (Motet 27) can serve as an example (see Appendix). The text consists of four large sections, each a syntactic unit:

1. An exclamation: "Quam pulchra es, et quam decora, charissima in deliciis!" (How fair you are and how beautiful, dearest in delights!)
2. A declamatory sentence describing the bride's attributes: "Statura tua assimilata est palmae et ubera tua botris" (Your stature is likened to a palm and your breasts to clusters of grapes).
3. A statement in the first person: "Dixi: Ascendam in palmam et apprehendam fructus eius" (I said I will go up into the palm and I will gather its fruit).
4. Another declamatory sentence, describing the bride's attributes: "Et erunt ubera tua sicut botri vineae et odor oris tui sicut odor malorum" (And your breasts will be like clusters of grapes of the vine and the fragrance of your mouth like the scent of apples).[34]

Palestrina did not take the obvious syntactic structure as his guide for creating a musical structure, though he did not violate it either (see Table 14.4). Instead he chose to bring out other aspects of the text's meaning and structure. The key phrase for him was "Ascendam in palmam." He created a large two-part structure, with its midpoint not before "Dixi" but before "et apprehendam." The climax is segment 5, "Ascendam in palmam," where the cantus reaches its highest note, g'', and all voices participate in a cadence on C.[35] The sharp change in texture at the beginning of segment 6, "et apprehendam," signals the beginning of the second half. This segmentation brings out the repetition: "*et* apprehendam," "*et* erunt," "*et* odor." Palestrina thus created two unbalanced halves, ending on C (open) and F (closed), that function like a first and second part of a motet.

Many commentators interpreted the palm tree as the cross, and Christ as the lover willing to ascend even to the cross.[36] Was Palestrina aware of this

TABLE 14.4   Segmentation of text and music in *Quam pulchra es*

Phrases of Text	Cadence	Measure	Comments
(1) Quam pulchra es et quam decora	F	6	cantus: A
	C	10	
	F	13	tenor: D
(2) carissima, in deliciis.	F	17	
	C	20	
	Ami	22	
(3) Statura tua assimilata est palmae	F	25	
	C	28	
	C	29	
	C	32	
(4) et ubera tua botris.	G	35	cantus: B♮
	D	38	
(5) Dixi: ascendam in palmam	F	44	
	C	46	
(6) et apprehendam fructus eius	F	50	cantus: A
(7) et erunt ubera tua	[A]	52	close
(8) sicut botri vineae	F	56	
	C	58	
(9) et odor oris tui	[D]	62	close
(10) sicut odor malorum.	F	66	

interpretation and did he let it influence his musical setting? Or was his reading simply a reflection of his own reading of the text? These are questions that cannot be answered at present.

Palestrina drew attention in the dedication to his unusual musical language, "a style somewhat more spirited ("alacriore") than I am wont to use in other church compositions, for so I perceive the subject itself to require." Just what did he mean by "alacriore"?[37]

In terms of its pitch collection, *Quam pulchra es* makes considerable use of "colored" notes. Palestrina used a leading-tone motive in the first segment on two levels (F G E F, within the *cantus mollis* system, and up a fifth, C D B♮ C, using a sharp to indicate Bmi). He introduced sharps on B, F, C for cadences on C, G, and D. He juxtaposed the "foreign" cadences on G and D ("et ubera tua botris") with those at "Dixi," firmly anchored in F. Another "colored" passage is a brief descent along the flat side of the circle of fifths (C F B♭ E♭) in segment 9 that works itself out to a fleeting close on D. While the tonal language is vivid, Palestrina "paints" the text primarily with melodic and rhythmic gestures (for example, the rising "Ascendam in palmam" and the climactic *g″* at the top of the palm tree) rather than with pitches.

Surely one of the defining characteristics of the motets in this collection is the quick shifts from phrase to phrase, not just of the pitch collection but also of texture and scoring, possibly what Zacconi calls "dispositione."[38] *Quam pulchra es* begins with an upper-voice duet answered by the lower voices, enriched by the addition of the fifth voice. The second section plays low off against high. The third has a stately point of imitation, from low to high, describing the woman's very stature (characterized not only by the majestic ascent through the voices, but by the theme itself, with its leap of a fifth, continuing right up to the octave). The fourth, juxtaposed in function to the second, reverses the disposition of voices, playing high against low. Section five, the heart of the piece, brings in all voices. Six, still full, is followed by seven and eight, both a series of duets. Nine and ten bring the piece to its conclusion. The setting reveals Palestrina's consummate control and his ability to juxtapose moments of greater and lesser intensity.

Palestrina's comments about his language for these motets invite comparisons with his other motets, and with other works, for example, the spiritual madrigals and the secular madrigals. It would be interesting to see how his use of such stylistic traits as tonal "color" and quickly shifting sonorities changes from genre to genre.[39] Other factors come into play as well, including the number of words relative to the length of the music, the length of individual musical segments, the responsiveness of music to the words, and the kinds of note values employed.[40] The task of understanding the style of the Song of Songs motets relative to other genres is made even more complicated because Palestrina's style changed during the course of his life, moving from prolixity to conciseness.

In the Song of Songs settings, we can observe Palestrina as reader. In contrast to his *Vergine* settings or to the late *madrigali spirituali*, he was working not with poetry but with prose, not with a set text but with one that he probably carved out for himself. But it is clear that he was striving to create a large-scale composition, a cycle of motets related to one another through a variety of techniques. The motets capture his vivid response to an extraordinary text.

NOTES

I read versions of this paper at the Eastman School of Music, New York University, and the III.° Convegno Internazionale di studi "Palestrina e l'Europa." I would like to thank Richard Caldwell and Thalia Farazzi, two students in my undergraduate seminar on Palestrina, whose papers contributed to my understanding of this collection, and Megumi Nagaoka, a graduate student, who helped with the research for this paper. I am also grateful to Professors Robert Kendrick, Patrick Macey, and John O'Malley for their comments.

1. Raffaele Casimiri, "Il Palestrina e il Marenzio in un privilegio di stampa del 1584," *Note d'Archivio* 16 (1939): 253–255. At the same time they requested and received a privilege for Palestrina's second book of four-voice motets, also published in 1584, and for Marenzio's first book of spiritual madrigals. (Palestrina's second book is often listed erroneously as dating from 1581, including in my worklist in *The New Grove Dictionary of Music and Musicians*, 20 vols., ed. Stanley Sadie [London: Mac-

millan, 1980]; since a privilege could only be issued for a newly published work, the 1584 edition must have been the first edition.) On Gardano, Tornieri, and Berichia, see Claudio Sartori, *Dizionario degli editori musicali italiani* (Florence: Olschki, 1958). I am grateful to Professor Jane Bernstein for this interpretation of the role of Tornieri and Berichia. See Jane Bernstein, "Financial Arrangements and the Role of Printer and Composer in Sixteenth-Century Italian Music Printing," *Acta musicologica* 66 (1991), and her forthcoming study, "The Publishing of Palestrina's Music in Sixteenth-Century Rome and Venice," III.° Convegno Internazionale di Studi "Palestrina e l'Europa."

2. To my knowledge, there has been no thorough study of the editions of this book. I arrive at the total of 15 by combining the editions listed in G. P. da Palestrina, *Werke*, ed. F. X. Haberl et al. (Leipzig, 1862–1907), 4, and in *Répertoire internationale des sources musicales*: 1583/1584 (Rome: Alessandro Gardano); 1584 (Venice: Angelo Gardano) [lost?]; 1587 (Venice: Angelo Gardano); 1587 (Milan: Francesco and eredi di Simon Tini); 1588 (Venice: Vincenti); 1593 (Milan: Eredi di Francesco and Simon Tini); 1596 (Venice: Erede di Girolamo Scotto); 1601 (Venice: Angelo Gardano); 1603 (Venice: Erede di Girolamo Scotto); 1605 (Antwerp: Pierre Phalèse); 1607 (Venice: Alessandro Raverii); 1608 (Venice: Alessandro Raverii); 1608 (Venice: Angelo Gardano); 1613 (Venice: Aere Bartolomei Magni); 1650 (Rome: Vitale Mascardi). I cannot attest to the accuracy of either list.

3. Ugo Boncompagni, the future Gregory XIII, was born in Bologna in 1502. After completing his studies in law, he came to Rome to serve Pope Paul III and remained there for the rest of his life, moving up the clerical hierarchy until his election to the papacy in 1572. He died in 1585. A strong defender of Catholicism, he held a procession to celebrate the St. Bartholomew Day massacre, "the destruction of the Huguenot sect." See J. N. D. Kelley, *The Oxford Dictionary of Popes* (Oxford: Oxford University Press, 1986), 269–71.

4. For a translation of the papal brief, see Oliver Strunk, *Source Readings in Music History* (New York: W. W. Norton, 1950), 357–59.

5. Giuseppe Baini, *Memorie storico-critiche della vita e delle opere di Giovanni Pierluigi da Palestrina* (Rome, 1828; repr., Hildesheim: Olms, 1966), 2:138: "Allo spuntar dell'anno 1584 si presenta il Pierluigi di persona al trono di Gregorio XIII e supplichevole gli domanda di grazia di accettare il mistico Cantico de' Cantici di Salomone posto in musica a bel disegno di nominarglielo. Sorrise il Papa a tai parole (così nelle memorie a penna sopraccitate) ed, accetto, disse, volentieri siffatta produzione, onde non mi sarà difficile di ravvisare nel dono l'animo del donatore. Voglia il cielo, rispose Giovanni, che, come studiato mi sono di esprimere con ardore gli amori divini di questo epitalamio, siasi anche nel mio cuore trasfusa una scintilla di carità. E, ricevuta dal Papa la benedizione, si partì ricolmo di contento" (At the begining of 1584, Pierluigi came in person before the throne of Gregory XIII and as a suppliant asked him to have the grace to accept the mystical Song of Songs of Solomon set to music with the intention of dedicating them to him. The pope smiled at these words, and said, "I accept willingly this production, for it will not be difficult for me to recognize in the gift the spirit of the giver." "May heaven grant," replied Giovanni, "that, as I have studied to express with ardor the divine loves of this epithalamion, there may be flowing even in my heart a spark of charity." And having received from the Pope the benediction, he left full of contentment).

6. There are two excellent English translations of this document: Strunk, *Source Readings*, 323–24 (complete) and Harold S. Powers, "Modal Representation in Polyphonic Offertories," *Early Music History* 2 (1982): 44–45 (partial). I quote Powers's translation in full (with two minor changes) and supply the rest myself.

7. For a broader view of the repudiation of the secular, see Christopher Reynolds, "Rome: A City of Rich Contrast," in *The Renaissance*, ed. Iain Fenlon (Englewood Cliffs, N.J.: Prentice Hall, 1989), 94–95.

8. Alfred Einstein, *The Italian Madrigal* (Princeton: Princeton University Press, 1949), 312.

9. Powers, "Modal Representation," 44. Lewis Lockwood, "Palestrina," *The New Grove Dictionary* rev. as *The New Grove High Renaissance Masters* (New York: W. W. Norton, 1984), drew the same conclusion about "già maturi." A careful study of the music and texts of this volume may provide further information about the date of composition. We can presume that at least some of Palestrina's other late publications also contained music composed earlier.

10. A year before his death in 1594, Palestrina was considering a return to his post as organist at the cathedral in Palestrina. See Raffaele Casimiri, "Memorie musicali prenestine del sec. XVI," *Note d'Archivio* 1 (1924): 15–16, 47–48.

11. I am grateful to Piero Gargiulo for reminding me of this fact. Karl Gustav Fellerer, *Palestrina: Leben und Werk* (2d ed., Düsseldorf: Schwann, 1960), 207–17, offers a chronological listing of Palestrina's music as it appeared in print. See also Michael Heinemann, *Palestrina und seine zeit* (Laaber: Laaber, 1994), 277–80.

12. For a useful overview and commentary, see Roland E. Murphy, *The Song of Songs: A Commentary on the Book of Canticles or the Song of Songs* (Minneapolis, Minnesota: Fortress Press, 1990).

13. Italics mine. The translation is from Einstein, *The Italian Madrigal*, 312, with emendation of the titles to conform to Zacconi's text. Lodovico Zacconi, *Prattica di musica seconda parte* (Venice: Alessandro Vincenti, 1622; repr. Bologna: Forni, 1983), 53–54: "Anzi lodai sempre il Palestrina, che così poco s'impiegò a far madrigali, havendolo fatto Iddio, acciò che ornasse la chiesa de canti suoi suavi come egli fece: ma se io li fossi stato vicino, e gli havessi potuto dire il mio parere, l'haverei disuaso anco à più potere che non si fosse impiegato a comporre, i motetti della Cantica come egli compose; poichè, hoggi giorno molti cantori si compiacciano di cantar soli: Quam pulchra es amica mea, quam pulchra es, Tota pulchra es amica mea, formosa mea, Fulcite me floribus quia amore langueo con altre cose che Dio sa con qual animo et intentione loro le cantano."

14. Robert L. Kendrick, "*Sonet vox tua in auribus meis*: Song of Songs Exegesis and the Seventeenth-Century Motet," *Schütz-Jahrbuch* 16 (1994): 99–118; I am grateful to Professor Kendrick for giving me a copy of his article in advance of publication and for sharing his insights about the interpretations of the Song of Songs.

15. Kendrick, "*Sonet vox tua*," 104, lists eight different levels of allegorical meanings found in the seventeenth century. For medieval interpretations, see E. Ann Matter, *The Voice of My Beloved: The Song of Songs in Western Medieval Christianity* (Philadelphia: University of Pennsylvania Press, 1990).

16. *Commentarii Michaelis Ghislerii Romani ex clericis regular. quos Theatinos nuncupant, in canticum canticorum Salamonis*. (Rome, 1609; 4th ed., Venice, 1617 [copy at Andover-Harvard Theological Library]).

17. *Biblia sacra vulgatae editionis Sixti Quinti Pont. Max*. (Rome: Typographia Apostolica Vaticana, 1592), 580–83. Kendrick, "*Sonet vox tua*," 104, drew attention to the extreme length of the commentaries, particularly in contrast to the brevity of the Song of Songs itself.

18. For a survey of Song of Songs settings used in Marian liturgy, see Shai Bursteyn, "Early 15th-Century Polyphonic Settings of Song of Songs Antiphons," *Acta musicologica* 49 (1979): 200–27.

19. Palestrina set the text a second time, for five voices, and included it in his 1569 motet print.

20. I am indebted to Don Randel for his essay, "Dufay the Reader," in *Studies in the History of Music, 1: Music and Language* (New York: Broude, 1983), 38–78.

21. For example, Harry B. Lincoln, *The Latin Motet: Indexes to Printed Collections, 1500–1600* (Ottawa: Institute of Mediaeval Music, 1993), located 24 settings of *Nigra sum* and *Tota pulchra es* in sixteenth-century printed anthologies.

22. He did set portions of the texts; for example, the opening words of Motet 11, *Sicut lilium*, appeared in his 1569 motet print.

23. Bibliographical control of the motet for this period is extremely limited. I base this observation on Lincoln, *The Latin Motet*. Ten of the incipits set by Palestrina had no other settings published in anthologies; only seven had more than five settings, but many of these will probably prove to be centonate texts different from the ones Palestrina used. One other composer who set the text continuously rather than as a series of excerpts was Leonhard Lechner, who probably composed *Das Hohenlied Salomonis*, a four-voice setting in six parts of chap. 1 and chap. 2:1–6 and 15–16 in about 1600. For a modern edition and commentary, see Walther Lipphardt, ed. *Newe gaistliche und weltliche Teutsche Gesang*, Leonhard Lechner Werke 13: (Kassel: Bärenreiter, 1973).

24. I have no idea why Palestrina chose the number 29.

25. The translations are by Matter, *The Voice of My Beloved*.

26. On tonal types, see Harold S. Powers, "Tonal Types and Modal Categories in Renaissance Polyphony," *Journal of the American Musicological Society* 34 (1981): 428–70. Many scholars have commented on the tonal organization of this print, including, for example, Raffaele Casimiri, ed., Giovanni Pierluigi da Palestrina, *Le opere complete* (Rome, 1939–), 11, p. xii.

27. Camillo Angleria, in *La Regola del Contraponto* (Milan: G. Rolla, 1622; facs. ed., Bologna: Forni, 1983), 81, describes the first motets of Palestrina's *Cantica* print as being in "il primo tuono." My thanks to Robert Kendrick and Marina Toffetti for this reference.

28. Powers, "Modal Representation," 46, described the music as being in five tonal types. On mode in Palestrina, see Powers, "Tonal Types," and "Modal Representation."

29. Cristle Collins Judd, "Modal Types and Ut, Re, Mi Tonalities: Tonal Coherence in Sacred Vocal Polyphony from about 1500," *Journal of the American Musicological Society* 45 (1992): 427–41.

30. Motet 22 (6:3–4): Pulchra es amica mea, suavis et decora sicut Ierusalem: *terribilis ut castrorum acies ordinata*. Averte oculos a me, quia ipsi me avolare fecerunt. Motet 23 (6:9): Quae est ista quae progreditur quasi aurora consurgens, pulchra ut luna, electa ut sol, *terribilis ut castrorum acies ordinata?*

31. For example, Motet 1 (Bride), Motet 2 (Chorus), Motets 3–4 (Bride), Motet 8 (Bride), Motet 14 (Bride), Motet 21 (Bride).

32. For example, Motets 6, 11, 13, 19, 28.

33. Sometimes a segment can consist of two subsections. For example, the beginning of Motet 25 has two subsections, "Quam pulchri sunt gressus tui" (how fair are your steps) and "in calceamentis" (in sandals); because both are repeated, I consider this a large segment with two subsections (a and b). Had only the second part been repeated, I would consider it two separate segments.

34. At 40 words, this is one of the longer texts, and at 69 measures one of the longer settings.

35. At one stage of my work, I considered "Dixi" and "Ascendam in palmam" to

be separate segments; I now think of them as a single segment, thanks in part to comments from Allan Keiler and Cristle Collins Judd.

36. For example, see the discussion of the patristic commentaries by Ghisleri, *Commentarii . . . in canticum canticorum Salamonis*, 950. I am grateful to Robert Kendrick for drawing my attention to this interpretation.

37. Charles T. Lewis and Charles Short, *A Latin Dictionary* (Oxford: Clarendon Press, 1879, repr. 1966), 79, define "alacer" as "lively, brisk, quick, eager; glad, happy, cheerful."

38. James Haar, "A Sixteenth-Century Attempt at Music Criticism," *Journal of the American Musicological Society* 36 (1983): 191–209, offers an interpretation of Zacconi's characterization of Palestrina's music as having "arte, contraponto, ottima dispositione, una sequente modulatione." Haar argues that "dispositione" means "Palestrina's preference for brightly voiced full triads wherever possible" (p. 209).

39. A cursory examination of a control group consisting of a number of motets, madrigals, and *madrigali spirituali* with F finals (one of the types represented in the Song of Songs collection, and the tonality of *Quam pulchra es*) suggests a kind of continuum. At one end are the liturgical or paraliturgical motets like *Sicut cervus* and at the other are the more pungent, colorful madrigals. The Song of Songs settings fall in between, comparable in color perhaps to the *Vergine* cycle. This topic clearly deserves further consideration.

40. Peter Ackermann, (in a paper on "Motette und Madrigal: Palestrinas Hohelied-Motetten im Spannungsfeld gegenreformatorischer Spiritualität" read at the conference "Palestrina Lassus Monteverdi: Musik in der Zeit des Umbruchs" (Duisberg, 1994), approached the issue of genre in Palestrina's Song of Songs motets by considering Pietro Pontio's remarks about genre in *Ragionamento di musica* (1588).

APPENDIX

Palestrina, Quam pulchra es

This edition is based on the 1588 edition, *Ioannis Petraloysii Praenestini motectorum quinque vocibus liber quartus nunc recens in lucem aeditus. Venetiis apud Iacobum Vincentium MCLXXVIII* (RISM P719). I consulted the altus, tenor, and quintus partbooks at the Houghton Library, Harvard University, and Professor Claudio Annibaldi kindly consulted the cantus and bassus partbooks at the Biblioteca di Conservatorio di Musica "Santa Cecilia," Rome. Vincenti, in his remarks to the reader, explained that fra Cypriano Venetiano had corrected the many errors the printers had made in the first edition ("ha emendato i detti mottetti da molti errori che erano occorsi per mancamento de stampatori nella prima impressione"); most of these in fact involve the use of accidentals. He also noted that the first edition could no longer be found in the bookshops, sufficient explanation for a new edition of "i frutti di questo gran musico." In this edition I retain original note values; I also give the accidentals exactly as they appear in the print, except that I have changed the "sharp" (Bmi) to the modern natural when it occurs in conjunction with B and E.

Palestrina, *Quam pulchra es*

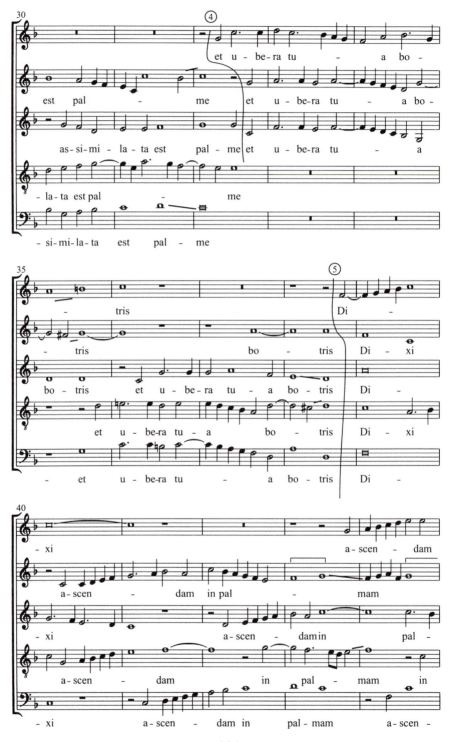

327

328

On William Byrd's
Emendemus in melius

Two texts, rather different in nature, may serve as prologue: the celebrated apologia from William Byrd's dedicatory letter in the *Gradualia:*

> In Sacred sentences (as I have learned from experience) there is such hidden and concealed power that to a man thinking about divine things and turning them over attentively and earnestly in his mind, the most appropriate measures come, I know not how, as if by their own free will, and freely offer themselves to his mind if it is neither idle nor inert.[1]

and a sorrowful, true confession by a reviewer, Imogene Horsley, of Wolfgang Boetticher's massive Lassus monograph:

> [we lack] analytical vocabulary in dealing with 16th-century music. We have analyzed closely the melodic and rhythmic structure of the single lines, the dissonance treatment in the combination of these lines, and the modal-tonal structure. But we have no way of summarizing in a few words the total polyphonic construction. It is in the small details, in the subtle and intricate combinations of the parts, that one finds the essence of the style and perceives the skill of the composer. The flux in the rhythm of the total complex of parts, the spacing of melodic climaxes of the different parts in the whole texture, the timing and spacing of successive entrances throughout the piece, the relative clarity of the text and emphasis resulting from the related rhythmic movements and melodic imitations among the parts—all these must be taken into consideration . . .[2]

The present "essay in musical analysis," then, is better an essay *at* musical analysis: a try.[3]

Texture

The music is grave, terse, reserved; yet even at first hearing, or at first reading, *Emendemus in melius* can hardly fail to move the listener by its highly expressive chordal declamation. In fact, Byrd never designed a more extensively homophonic motet. The basic plan is simple: accompanied soprano melody; but in this plan—so one feels after closer acquaintance—Byrd seems to have discerned a compositional problem of some subtlety, which occupied his first attention. This was the problem of texture, the modulation of accompaniment texture from block chords to some kind of contrapuntal activity, and back again.

The abbreviated score printed here has been designed to point up the gross contrasts in texture (see Example 15.1). Generally the inner voices are marked only when they move note-against-note with the outer parts; otherwise they have not been indicated, except in the last phrase. The score also includes a series of capital letters to facilitate reference to the phrases, some (anachronistic) harmonic indications, and a few other details that will be mentioned in due course.

Individual phrases begin with block chords, note-against-note in all voices, then turn to some sort of polyphony before the end, where of course the voices come together again in a chord. We are dealing with a phrase archetype: from stable texture to unstable texture and back, from rest to movement to rest, from calm to tension to resolution. Even the one truly imitative phrase in the motet, phrase L, of which there will be a great deal to say presently, first announces its subject in five-part block chords. Texture works together with dissonance, melody, harmony, and rhythm in tensing or complicating the middle of each phrase.

What our score cannot show are the delicate shades of half-homophony, half-polyphony in between the pliant chordal writing of, say, phrase D and imitative texture in all the voices as in phrase L. Indeed analysis of sixteenth-century music remains pretty helpless in the description or appreciation of mixed textures, though these often seem to hide tantalizingly the composer's highest art. As Horsley complains, Lassus is a prominent case in point. For Byrd, one of the most characteristic and problematic textures is exemplified by phrase J (Example 15.2). The essential line remains in the soprano; the other voices seem to stagger themselves, slightly, in haphazard manner, fitting in as best they can. Thus at "Deus" and "salutaris" the first tenor and alto respectively manage true imitations. At "Deus" none of the other voices resembles the main melodic line. At "salutaris" a second entry in the alto and one in the second tenor come somewhere close, while the bass contents itself with doubling the soprano in thirds.

There are motets by Byrd in which this style is employed almost throughout: a soprano melody half-harmonized by shadowy imitations, near-imitations, or non-imitative stirrings below. A work like *O Domine adiuva me*, from the *Cantiones sacrae* of 1589, must I think seem amorphous to us today, as (I believe also) it would have seemed to a Continental composer of Byrd's own time. This mixed style is less troublesome in *Emendemus in melius*, where to a greater or lesser extent it serves simply as a means of flexing the phrase in between the chordal beginning and the final chord. To a greater or lesser extent—but in any case just short of true thematic articulation in the accompa-

EXAMPLE 15.1 Byrd, *Emendemus in melius*

Example 15.1 (*continued*)

PART 2

EXAMPLE 15.2 *Emendemus in melius*, phrase J

nying parts. The briefer phrases are treated to the lightest interior movement. In the climatic phrase K, on the other hand, the lower voices whir and swell into considerable activity.

But a style that stakes so much on a melody and on the modulation of texture is bound to pinch the lower voices. They are not at all attractive to sing. Indeed many details make it seem that the lower parts were conceived in instrumental terms, as fill. Did Byrd originally plan the piece as pious chamber music for solo voice and accompanying viols—like the exquisite little "motet" *Adoramus te* printed in the *Gradualia?* One recalls his disposition of his first songbook, the *Psalmes, Sonets and Songs* of 1588: "heere are divers songs, which being originally made for Instruments to expresse the harmonie, and one voyce to pronounce the dittie, are now framed in all parts for voyces to sing the same."

Melody

To suggest that the control of texture was the key to Byrd's conception is not to minimize the craft with which he constructed the melody in the soprano. This shows the greatest sophistication.

In part 1 of the motet, for instance, but not in part 2, the melody molds itself like plainsong. The phrase-beginnings might almost paraphrase sections of some psalmody or litany, though the ends, where harmonic considerations come into play, generally draw away from a chant paradigm. The phrase-beginnings even look well in plainsong notation (Example 15.3). The descending semitone Eb–D stands out as the most striking single expressive factor in the motet: see phrases A, C, D, E, H^1, H^2, L. Semitones, however, must always be handled with care; overuse can result in a rather gross, exaggerated pathos. This Byrd escaped, perhaps, by boldly reiterating the steps D–Eb and D–F in such a way as to recall the characteristic and impassive inflections around a Gregorian reciting tone.

The general accents of Gregorian recitation are suggested—though not the comparatively rich Gregorian tune specified for the words *Emendemus in melius* (which may be seen on p. 524 of the *Liber usualis*). In other words, Byrd evokes the mood of plainsong, not its liturgical quality; in spirit he already stands far from his forebears in the medieval English Church. His chant-like

EXAMPLE 15.3   *Emendemus in melius*, phrase-beginnings in plainsong notation

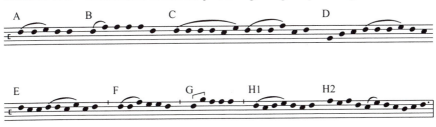

melody, furthermore, aims for climax in a thoroughly unmedieval fashion. After the opening segment of the text, the line dips to low *g'* at the first appeal "quaeramus," circling its way up an octave to the more intense appeal "miserere." Here phrase G expands the inflections *d''–e♭''* and *d''–f''* to the leap *d''–g''*; that amounts to no more than a fourth, but as the first fourth-leap so far it stands out. The details of the upward circling are worth noting:

> Phrase A dwells on *d''–e♭''*
> B enlarges this to *d''–f''*
> C absorbs both inflections
> D springs from low *g'* up to *d''–e♭''*
> E harps on the same
> F reinstates *d''–f''* and
> G finally calls up the leap *d''–g''*

But when in part 2 of the motet the same arc is traced for a parallel climax, the progress is significantly much more direct: from *g'* at the appeal "adiuva nos" up to *g''* at "propter honorem." Over the piece as a whole, the melody balances finely. The more intense climactic surge in part 2 is solidified in phrase K and discharged at phrase L by a longer, more profoundly relaxed continuation into the final cadence.

Whatever Byrd may have felt about the evocation of Gregorian accents in a motet, he seems to have possessed a lively sense of the contrast between such accents and the more functional, franker lines proper to the sixteenth-century style. In this connection the point about the melodic figures for "adiuva nos" and "libera nos," in part 2, is their decidedly un-Gregorian character, their clear sense of direction achieved by filling in a fourth stepwise, and springing it with dotted rhythm. In a modern style this might pass unnoticed, but after Byrd's part 1 with its uncertain melodic fluctuations, "adiuva nos" makes a point of urgency at once. Phrase J, starting on high *f''*, completes a double fourth, *g'–a'–b'–c''/f''*, the outlined seventh *g'–f''* is doubly urgent. When *b'–c''/f''* is followed by *c''–d''–g''* (phrase K), urgency grows into violence—or very nearly; but in retrospect, the jagged sequence is subtly balanced, controlled, and curbed by the identical fourth-leap in the previous climax, in phrase G. All 130-odd pitches of the melody, by the way, lie between *g'* and *g''*. All but five of them lie between *a'* and *f''*.

To the directional, un-Gregorian soprano figures of part 2, Byrd now joins similar material in the bass, which assumes new life. At "adiuva nos" the bass draws away from the soprano strongly, through a stepwise third (extended to a fourth); once again, no dazzling line in itself, but in appreciable contrast to the more fitful movements previously. For the climactic phrase K, the bass suddenly stirs itself to powerful action: sequential movement in fourths from *d* up to *b♭* imitating that urgent fourth in the soprano, and imitated also by a scattering of excited inner entries. The sequence ends by leaping up a sixth to *b♭*, the upper neighbor of the local dominant *a*; then the strong cadential patterns *b♭–a–d* and *e♭–d–g* recur under the imitations of phrase L. By dwelling on these semitones, the bass parallels the harping E♭–D of part 1, but in a context that we are bound to hear as more tonal.

The imitative motif for "libera nos," incidentally, must have been conceived as an inversion of the melodic figure for "adiuva nos" (the declamation "ádiuva" is what Byrd wants, both here and in the motet *O Domine ádiuva me*). The point of imitation includes a pair of inverted entries, no very common device of Byrd's, but one that serves quietly to point up the parallel meaning of the words, and the economy, the tautness of musical construction. It is curious to turn the page and see the next motet in the book begin with the very same motif, complete with inversion, on the same pitch, for the same word (Example 15.4). Perhaps the lineage of this idea can be traced back by way of Alfonso Ferrabosco, the emigré Italian composer whose connections with Byrd are well established, and who provided him with many models, to Lassus, who provided Alfonso with many models (Example 15.5).[4] Nobody had a monopoly on fourths in inversion, of course, and I expect we should not put too much stock in the assonance "laboravi–libera me." But it is a fact that opening imitations in inversion are quite common in Alfonso, quite uncommon at this time in Byrd.

Harmony

Very rarely does Byrd break away from what we would call root-position harmony. But he simply will not lead root-position triads by step in the bass; when a whole-tone bass progression is demanded, he smooths it along with an unobtrusive first-inversion chord (see the figures marked in Example 15.1). A few sixth chords that are rather less unobtrusive are used to provide semitone inflection in the bass, notably in phrases E and H[2]. These two phrases are parallel: H[2] intensifies the plagal cadence already sounded at the end of E, and expands that phrase by racking up more exposed semitones: soprano e''–f'', e^{b}''–d'', bass $c\#$–d, $B♮$–c. Not only the sheer density of semitones, but also of course the near cross-relations, make H[2] ("quia peccavimus tibi") the most excruciated phrase of the motet. So although part 1 ends on the tonic, and with a plagal cadence, it ends at a point of considerable anguish and only half-resolved melodic tension.

EXAMPLE 15.4   Byrd, *Libera me*, mm. 1–3

EXAMPLE 15.5　(a) Alfonso Ferrabosco, *Laboravi in gemitu*, mm. 1–2; (b) Lassus, *Domine ne in furore*, mm.1–2

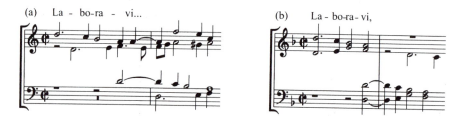

The whole motet is tinted with cross-relations once removed: phrases A, B, C, D, E, F, H¹, H², I, J, K, L. Direct cross-relations often appear in between—or articulate, or disjoin—the adjacent phrases. Perhaps Byrd was simply following convention, and perhaps he was taking a fresh look at convention for expresive or structural purposes of his own. B♮–B♭ disjoins phrases A and B and phrases H² and I (between parts 1 and 2); the latter progression, as all the voices subside, makes for an unusually strong articulation. F♯–F♮ disjoins phrases B and C; D and E; H¹ and H² (the disturbed phrase H² poised between cross-relations); and most strikingly—most dramatically—K and L. What is more striking yet, the progression F–F♯ is at one point forced into a phrase, at the start of K. This semitone, which could perfectly well have been omitted—there is no A–G step anywhere in sight—points to G in its own octave and also in the higher octave, throwing the music up gauchely toward the angular climax with its spilling resolution. The exact function of the semitone across the "dead" intervals escapes me, though Byrd would seem to have had more in mind than simply a contribution to the overall semitonal coloring.

Tonality

Emendemus in melius is in the Dorian mode on G. The clefs are treble, C₂, C₃, C₄, and F₃, accommodating a range from low A to high *g″* (though Byrd extends this with a single fine low G in phrase A). High *g″* mandates melodic climaxes on the finalis or tonic pitch, and low A is useful for cadences on D. In addition to the transposition accidental B♭, an E♭ appears in the signature; this mode rejoices in its flexibility with the sixth degree, and composers or scribes appear to have added the extra flat when they observed a preponderance of E♭s over E♮s in the music before them.[5] In *Emendemus*, indeed, things are so determinedly ad hoc that the second flat is absent from the signature of the second tenor part, and while duly marked at the beginning of the alto and first tenor parts, actually disappears from both before the end. It is astonishing to see notation of this kind so late in the sixteenth century, but we encounter other such anomalies in the 1575 *Cantiones sacrae*.

Despite the extra flats in the signatures, *Emendemus* is one of those Dorian compositions that lean in the "sharp" direction. Whereas the Phrygian alter-

EXAMPLE 15.6   (a) Byrd, *Tristitia et anxietas*; (b) *Haec dicit Dominus*

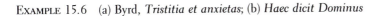

ation A♭ occurs only once, in an unimportant context (in phrase C, where it smooths a stepwise bass progression), E♮ with its attendant sharps ranges freely; all the full cadences on D are approached by C♯ or E♮ in the soprano, rather than by E♭ in the bass, for example. And in phrase K E♮ supports an E-minor triad, with B♮, under the climactic soprano note *g″*. All the other melodic Gs—the earlier climax at "miserere," the low notes at "quaeramus" and "ad-iuva"—had been harmonized by E♭. The harmonic intensification here, which grates harshly enough, contributes along with every other possible means to climax.

There is no question, I take it, that a composer writing a work of this kind is hearing harmonically. His harmonic hearing, though, is not necessarily or even very probably ours, and at our present state of imperfect aural sympathy with Renaissance music, I believe we should proceed most humbly in testing the Renaissance ear against our own, and vice versa. Tonic and dominant cadences, certainly, were in some sense complementary for Byrd: thus to con-clude part 1, the repetition of phrase H[1] (H[2]) settles to the tonic rather than to the dominant—a contrast that mirrors the tonal situation at the start, where phrase B should be heard as a loosely expanded version of phrase A, ending on the dominant rather than on the tonic. The expansion, as has been noted, comes about by a widening of the melodic semitone, which is a feature of a number of other Byrd motets with homophonic beginnings (Example 15.6).[6]

But besides tonic and dominant, part 1 admits only one other degree for cadences, the mediant B♭ (III). VI and VII, to say nothing of IV, are avoided. Now although the choice of B♭ in phrase G may simply have followed from the high F needed for the climactic melodic cadence, it certainly seems to link phrases C and G together. After the complementary tonic and dominant swings at the opening, the mediant in phrase C seems to move away rather sharply, especially in view of the emphatic cadence. But once the next phrases have returned to the tonic-dominant region, the next mediant (in phrases G) sounds instead like a climactic deflection from, or embellishment of, the dominant. It sounds more like a passing event than a goal—doubtless because the preceding dominant move in phrase F is so much more serious than that of phrase B. In other words, what I hear in part 1 is

a statement and answer:	A B	I V
a digression:	C	III
a return:	D E	(I) I
a differently stressed rehearsal of the tonal dynamic so far:	F G H¹ H²	V III (I) I

This interpretation seems to absorb the various phrases justly according to their rhythmic weight, to follow the cadential parallelisms, and to support the essential melodic span.

What is altogether clear, of course, is that Byrd could enhance the "Gregorian" quality of part 1 by limiting the cadence degrees as far as he dared. It is also excellently clear that part 2 strikes an instant contrast by aiming hard at a cadence on the subdominant C. To force this modulation, Byrd may have wanted the unusual clash between *b♮′, c″, and d″* (see Example 15.2)—a clash that I have seen bowdlerized in a contemporary MS copy.[7] With great ingenuity, this subdominant cadence is worked into a powerfully paced sequence of fifths in the bass: *f–B♭, g–c, a–d, b♭–*. As for the mediant B♭ that introduces the final phrase L so dramatically, the modern ear is bound to hear this and the succeeding prominent B♭ triads as a prolongation of the peak of the sequence. B♭ is finally resolved only when the soprano sings "libera nos," on a diminished fourth. This interval is in fact the most expressive in the whole piece (unless one counts the diminished fourth in phrase A); the complementary semitones soprano *d″–c♯″*, bass *b♭–a* seem to touch a spring to release the great climax. I say the modern ear, for we do need to be careful about begging the question of Renaissance tonal hearing. But there is some kind of evidence of this hearing in our immediate response to a passage of this kind, in the way it seems to dovetail into our own aural experience. At least I know no better kind of evidence.

Rhythm

A first instinct, perhaps, is to admire the free declamatory rhythm, which seems to rock delicately up to the point where a regular fourfold repetition takes hold in the bass, in phrase L. But this may be a lazy instinct. What we call "free" rhythm has doubtless been calculated minutely in order to achieve its irregularities; what is more, the declamatory patterns here are not so free. Four phrases in part 1 (B, D, G, the Hs) start with the identical rhythm— an irregular, shortbreathed idea. In poetic settings, this rhythm arises quite mechanically from an initial extension of the iambic foot (Example 15.7).[8]

The equally conventional but simpler dotted pattern at phrases A, I, and L (also at the word "salutaris" in J) becomes in this context also more purposeful. It can be no accident that a single rhythm opens both sections of the motet, and closes it. The rhythm at phrase E hurries, and echoes anxiously in the bass: a reflection, I believe, of the words "spatium . . . invenire non pos-

EXAMPLE 15.7   (a) Byrd, *I joy not in no earthly bliss*; (b) *Ambitious love*

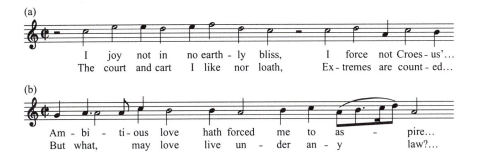

(a)

I   joy   not in   no earth - ly   bliss,   I   force   not Croes - us'...
The   court   and cart   I   like   nor   loath,   Ex - tremes   are count - ed...

(b)

Am - bi - ti - ous   love   hath forced   me   to   as   -   pire...
But   what,   may   love   live   un - der   an - y   law?...

sumus." (If I am right, these words may also explain why for once no gap
separates phrases D and E.) The arrangement of phrase C—eight times three—
seems to me whimsical, oddly dancelike, yet highly complex in the cross-
rhythms that it generates below. As for phrase K, it begins with a jagged, broad
rhythm; everything plays into this great climax.

Byrd moves rapidly from one phrase to the next, gaining a marked sense
of urgency for the piece as a whole. (You would never know it, however, from
recorded performances.) At first the cadence notes last for only a half note,
with the next phrase coming in after a quarter rest; later, after phrase E, he
allows the cadence to extend for another half note, or else he lengthens the
rest, so that the pause lasts for a whole note. Three phrases (D, J, and L) start
on the heels of their precedessors, without any rest at all. I have already spoken
of phrases D and E; the link between I and J is tight, as suits the syntax, and
as the relatively numerous short phrases of part 1 give way to just three large,
powerful periods in part 2. With phrase L, on the other hand, the slow dotted
rhythm on "libera nos" makes a sharp demarcation in spite of the syntax. The
rhythmic situation at the end of part 1 is interesting. Doubtless Byrd was obey-
ing a formal requirement here—both parts of the motet end with text repetition—and the fact that the repetition (phrases H[1] and H[2]) employs the identical
rhythm in the soprano ought to provide a measure of cadential stability. But
the rhythm feels so irregular—compare its seven beats to the six or eight shown
in Example 15.7—that the effect is less of stability than of repeated, emphasized instability. This is a warped, anxious cadence.

As for the end of part 2, the first appearance of the "libera nos" motif
provides an almost Baroque jolt, as the cross-accent and the cross-relation cut
in before the expansive, explosive phrase K has had time to settle. (There is a
poor sonority on the opening B-flat chord, however, and tired voice leading.)
The bass, it turns out, will serve as rhythmic control, but its next entry jolts
less, for a syncopated tenor entry precedes it by a quarter note, softening the
rhythmic anomaly and drawing attention away from the bass. Then a luminous
soprano entry, one further quarter note back, all but cancels the jar; now the
bass seems gravely to follow and complement the melody. Gradually, and very
beautifully, the bass has been won over to an easy fluidity. At the same time,

its quieting insistence lulls the composition, at last, into a regular repetitive meter such as had been only implicit in part 1.

This concluding phrase shows Byrd's most brilliant solution of the problem of texture (what I called his main compositional problem). He must have felt some concern about the justification of an imitative phrase after twelve non-imitative ones. So he took the unusual step of prefacing the point homophonically. But then he did not run off into amorphous contrapuntal accompaniments, as before; instead the melody was made to pause, half rhetorically, half in deference to the syncopated tenor an octave lower—one of several obvious places for it, but the one and only right place. For coming on the same pitch, but an octave lower, the tenor sounds like a meditative echo of the homophonic exclamation. And the rhythmic arrangement makes it sound as though the block chords are coming just slightly awry. Almost imperceptibly, the tottering homophonic structure loosens further under the stress of new imitations. The soprano, returning so expressively, reminds us that she (or choirboy he) carries "the first singing part," as Byrd describes it in the *Psalmes, Sonets and Songs.* Yet even this hegemony is weakened: further entries include two rather impressive inversions in the middle voices, and ultimately the soprano is blurred, by new syncopations. The space of a few bars sees a perfect flowering of imitative polyphony, grown with exquisite care out of coarser textures earlier in the composition.

Dissonance

Still more about this passage. So far, all strong authentic cadences (phrases B, C, J, K) employed a florid 4–3 suspension in the soprano. The cadence ending the motet is the first in which the soprano doubles the dominant degree of the bass, allowing a somewhat more dissonant web to unwind in the inner voices, instead. The top voice comes to rest on the *tierce de Picardie* (restful enough to Byrd, who concluded half of his motets in this way). For the extended final cadence, then, the melody is guided more serenely than before, while the inner voices assume more authority, in accordance with their newfound role in carrying through the imitations. Phrase L, furthermore, includes the only dissonant sevenths in the entire composition. They seem to murmur and caress, and they certainly help the "libera nos" motif to slip out of homophony into imitations.

As for the strong half-cadences (E, H^1, H^2), they all employ a fifth in the soprano, with the 4–3 resolving underneath, and resolving with an identical ornament which is in each case rhythmically anticipated (see the score). It is a commonplace that Byrd's part-writing lacks the cool disciplined elegance of, say, Palestrina's. ("If ther happen to be any iarre or dissonāce, blame not the Printer," Byrd mutters in one of his prefaces.) But for classical restraint, one could hardly ask for more than the treatment of the cadences in *Emendemus in melius.* Only in part 2 do the details of cadential dissonance depart from the most sober standards. A momentary augmented fifth jabs the cadence to phrase J (see Example 15.2). Within phrase K, passing notes clash, and so do major

EXAMPLE 15.8   *Emendemus in melius,* phrase K

and minor thirds above the first bass *a*—a little excruciation that Byrd liked (or needed) enough to repeat at once, in stronger note values, above the second bass *a* (see Example 15.8). "The vicious English taste for false relations," as Tovey jestingly called it, was at times a highly patrician taste.

Text

We may now be in a position to see what Byrd meant by the profound power of sacred words to suggest "the most appropriate measures." This is how he would appear to have read the text:

Part 1:   Emendemus in melius, quae ignoranter peccavimus: ne subito praeoccupati die mortis,
quaeramus spatium paenitentiae, et invenire non possumus.
Attende Domine, et *miserere*: quia peccavimus tibi.

Part 2: *Adiuva nos*, Deus salutaris noster:
   et propter *honorem* nominis tui libera nos.[9]

The marked break after "die mortis" is not exactly in accordance with the syntax. The opening three phrases are separated off as an exposition, introducing a central dramatic motif (conversion), an eternal truth as donnée (personal guilt), and an immediate scene (the deathbed). These phrases Byrd set more or less on a level, evoking the mood of Gregorian psalmody; yet the third element, death, causes the first harmonic wrench. Then he smelled action: at the first appeal, "quaeramus," the harmony starts to work its way back as the line sinks in abasement, moving up to the third appeal, "miserere," which is at once urgent yet inconclusive. Necessarily, after this outburst, sin is felt more keenly than before—in the disturbed chromaticism of melodic line and harmonic content, in the rhythmic contortion of the cadence. The repetition of "quia peccavimus tibi" (the word "tibi," by the way, introducing a new element) may obey a formal requirement, but it makes excellent rhetoric too. Certainly part 1 does not "resolve" very satisfactorily.

Doctrinally speaking, that would be because there has been no hint so far and therefore no experience of God's grace. When this thought appears in the text—the honor of His name—it then appropriately assumes the second climax, parallel but in every way greater, rougher, faster, and more assured than the first. In part 2, Gregorian recollections cede to the more dynamic melodic idiom of the Renaissance. "Libera nos," the final appeal, is conceived in quite a different spirit, after the reference to the possibility of salvation that the music has embraced so strongly. Unlike all the others, the final appeal is set to a descending line, many times imitated and repeated. Most beautiful of all, perhaps, is the sense of richness and I should say *consciousness* imparted by, at last, the full resource of imitative polyphony. A serenity, maturity, or balance denied to the cadence of part 1 can now be achieved; the conversion promised in the opening words has been accomplished musically, with all due responsibility, over considerable odds.

This reading of Byrd's reading of the text—what Kenneth Burke might have called a "dramatistic" reading—presupposes close attention to detail on the part of the composer. Even if Byrd had not admitted to attentive and earnest thinking, I do not know what else we should suppose sixteenth-century composers were up to, with that inbred, stereotyped, utterly refined idiom, if not refining it further. The interpretation, at all events, accounts for many facts: not only technical details, but also the overpowering primary fact of artistic impact. It does not often happen with Byrd (or any other composer) that a piece breathes such immediacy; however modest in style and scope, the piece is red hot, with its rush of phrases, its flux of melodic style, its brazen climax, and its amazing resolution doubly powerful and doubly solid because in the few bars infinite power seems held in reserve. Back of all is the composer's dramatic engagement with his text; which is what set everything into such passionate motion.

History

Emendemus in melius was William Byrd's first published work. It opens his first group of motets in the famous *Cantiones sacrae* of 1575, issued jointly with Thomas Tallis. Byrd was about 32, having arrived in London from Lincoln Cathedral only three years earlier.

He found the words in a foreign motet or else in a Roman service book, where they form one of the greater responds for Matins on the First Sunday in Lent. In 1575, the motet could hardly have been meant for liturgical use; and even under the old religion, English composers had rarely worked with Lenten texts. It is to Frank Harrison that we owe our comprehension of the text repertory set by English composers in the Middle Ages and also—thanks to his chapters in volumes 3 and 4 of *The New Oxford History of Music*—into the Renaissance. At the end of Henry VIII's reign and during Queen Mary's, composers set mostly the Mass Ordinary or hymns and responds proper to the most festive days, such as Christmas and Easter. The liturgy of Lent and other penitential occasions was marked by sobriety; sobriety meant restricted chants and little polyphony. Almost the sole Lenten items set by the older Sarum composers were *In pace* and *In manus tuas*, special texts that ended Compline—as though, perhaps, to provide a musical nightcap to days parched of polyphonic singing.

Only later did texts from Lent and the funeral services become favorites for polyphonic composition. Perhaps all, certainly some, of the great Tudor Lamentations for Holy Week date from the 1560s: two each by Tallis and Robert White, and one apiece by Osbert Parsley of Norwich and William Byrd of Lincoln. The two authors of the 1575 *Cantiones sacrae* seem to have vied in composing music for the First Sunday in Lent: Byrd's *Emendemus in melius*, Tallis's *Derelinquat impius* and *In ieiunio*—the latter confronting Byrd with real competition in the way of expressive text-setting. Robert Parsons, Byrd's predecessor in the Chapel Royal, set a group of three responds from Matins for the Dead. So did Byrd's friend Alfonso Ferrabosco. So did Byrd himself, publishing all three in 1575. Beside them are found *Libera me Domine et pone me juxta te*, a text carved out from one of the Job readings at that Martins, and *Memento homo*, the versicle sung while ashes are distributed on Ash Wednesday. In addition Byrd composed a Passion; two Lenten responds (*Ne perdas, Afflicti pro peccatis nostris*); a versicle from the Office for the Dead (*Audivi vocem*); and—following White—the Lenten Compline hymn *Christie qui lux es et dies*.

Anyhow, Byrd soon turned to nonliturgical texts for his motets, so that he could give full reign to his personal preference for sentiments of penitence and self-abasement, sometimes even unto despair. The words of *Emendemus in melius*, familiar as they were to every Catholic and to every Continental motet composer, are matched to Byrd's favorite and typical mood. This turn of mind has caused a certain amount of discomfort to those who prefer their Elizabethans to think positive. Charles Burney, living in a more sanguine time, would have explained it on grounds of contemporary fashion:

> There was, at this time, a kind of maudlin piety, which had seized Christians of all denominations; among Calvinists it exhaled itself in Psalmody; and in others, not less dolorous, in Lamentations. . . Even the Lute was to weep, and be sorrowful: for Dowland published about this time Lachrymae, or Seven Teares figured in seaven Passionate Pavins.[10]

Others including the present writer, have read into Byrd's motet texts something of the general distress of the Elizabethan Catholic community.

One should also not altogether rule out a technical consideration, especially in 1575, when the Catholic persecutions had not yet grown serious. Expressivity was the preoccupation of the musical avant-garde in the sixteenth century, and as everyone knows, musical expressivity works best with sentiments like depression and pathos. It has not been sufficiently emphasized how radical Byrd's motets must have sounded to Englishmen of the 1570s. In a dozen respects, his motets fairly defied comparison with the music of Taverner, Tye, White, Parsons, or even Tallis. Doubtless the moving declamatory accents of *Emendemus in melius* were most impressive of all; Byrd seems to have thought so, for he set this motet at the front of his publication. There it stands as a manifesto of a revolutionary new spirit in Elizabethan music.[11]

Revolutionary, that is, on the English scene; Continental music had taken such steps before. It seems clear that foreign influence must have been potent on Byrd, who had come down from the provinces in 1572 and almost at once established himself as London's leading composer. As with Sidney and Shakespeare, foreign models did not make Byrd into an "Englishman Italianated" or any other kind of musicological machiavel. Since the 1960s it has been known that Byrd owed much to the motets of Alfonso Ferrabosco, which have been preserved in some quantity in English manuscripts.[12] Among Alfonso's motets there is one and only one like *Emendemus in melius* (see Example 15.9). This is part 3 of an enormous full-scale setting of Ps. 104 in eleven parts; *Qui fundasti terram* takes care of verses 5–9 as briskly as is decent. Plainly the piece served Byrd as model. Besides adopting the quite individual texture, style, and form, he even duplicated its dimensions: 59 (original) breves divided among 12 phrases in Byrd (who has one extra semibreve), as against 13 phrases in Alfonso. Of the two composers, however, Alfonso maintains the musical texture much more rigorously, keeping his counterpoint prior to the cadences of the various phrases very unobtrusive, and attempting nothing like the final polyphonic burgeoning of Byrd's "libera nos." (To conclude, Alfonso simply repeats his last phrase in variation—as Byrd also did to conclude his part 1.) And in the matter of the harmony Alfonso does not venture further than the E♭ triad on one side and the A-major triad on the other. Byrd touches A♭ and E minor.

Qui fundasti terram, in fact, lacks all the subtlest features that we have admired in *Emendemus in melius*. The contrast between chant-like and Renaissance melody, the cunning modulation of texture, the finely controlled soprano line, the harmonic span and the sharp ear for harmonic effect, above all the dramatic reading—none of these is found with Alfonso. He provided Byrd with little more than the general strategy: expressive, pithy declamation

EXAMPLE 15.9 Alfonso Ferrabosco, *Qui fundasti terram* (3.p of *Benedic anima mea*)

with chordal accompaniment breaking down a little near the cadences. The rest we owe to Byrd's native genius.

It may not be superfluous to add, in conclusion, that an ear for "influences" is by all means worth cultivating, so long as the idea is to get a fulcrum outside the work of art to move analysis. Byrd says that musical ideas "come as if of their own free will, and freely offer themselves to the mind"; unfortunately, this does not much help the critic who is separated further than he knows from the mind and the ear of the sixteenth century. Professor Horsley says that we need analytical vocabulary, but one cannot analyze with any confidence in a vacuum. Comparison, and always comparison, is the critic's best help. Matched against Alfonso's composition, the intensity of Byrd's conception, his originality of means, his superb sense of shape, and his vital commitment to the sacred text stand out with especial clarity.

With more modern music, we have stored up from childhood an unconscious fund of comparative material, which has coalesced for us into a working norm for criticism and comparative analysis. We have a sense of style. With Lassus or Byrd, we lack this. It has to be painfully recovered, piece by piece, detail by detail, influence by influence, till hopefully we attain some modest plateau of understanding. And if this is the goal, I do not see that we are in a position to refuse any preferred tools: whether analogical, theoretical, musicological, phenomenological, imaginative, speculative, historical, anachronistic, liturgical, statistical. *Emendemus in melius.*

NOTES

This article first appeared in *Musical Quarterly* 49 (1963): 431–49. It is reprinted in revised form with the permission of Oxford University Press.

1. For the context of this remark, see the Preface to *Gradualia I (1605): The Marian Masses, The Byrd Edition* 5, ed. Philip Brett (London: Stainer and Bell, 1989), p. xvii; Brett's translation has been adapted here.

2. *Journal of the American Musicological Society* 12 (1959): 77.

3. Returning to this essay in 1994, I look askance at this opening toccata but resist the temptation to moderate it. The lack of a critical tradition for early music still agitates younger scholars, and rightly (for a notable example, see *Models of Musical Analysis: Music before 1600*, ed. Mark Everist [Oxford: Blackwell, 1992], the editor's introduction and passim). I am glad to have the opportunity to correct wrong statements about the mode of *Emendemus in melius*, fill in some elisions, and provide some updates.

More substantially, the section on rhythm has been rewritten, to reflect a change in conception and perception. This change is fundamental, even though it seems to leave the main outlines of the present reading undisturbed. What I was "essaying" in 1963 was a model of sixteenth-century rhythm predicated on the notion of the regular alternation of strong and weak semibreves, a model put forward forcefully by Edward E. Lowinsky in a 1960 essay, "Early Scores in Manuscript" (reprinted in *Music in the Culture of the Renaissance and Other Essays*, ed. Bonnie J. Blackburn [Chicago: University of Chicago Press, 1989], 803–40). But the evidence adduced in that article does not hold up to scrutiny, and Byrd's music tells otherwise. I now believe that this must be heard as generating its own fluctuating meter on the semibreve level as it goes along, making temporary triple meters as often or almost as often as duple meters (see, for example, part 2 of *Libera me*, the motet that follows *Emendemus* in the original publication). Certainly it is very hard—for me, impossible—to sense duple meter in part 1 of *Emendemus* . . . even with the help of the regular barring which has now become standard in editions of English Renaissance music (see *The Byrd Edition* 1, ed. Craig Monson [London: Stainer and Bell, 1977], 1–7). In the original article I sniped at the irregular barring in the old *Collected Vocal Works of William Byrd*, ed. E. H. Fellowes, and the even earlier *Tudor Church Music*, but I now prefer this to regular barring.

Those who believe in regular strong and weak semibreves will hear the cadence of part 1 of *Emendemus* (and the many others like it in the music of the time) as a syncopation. In this case I also (still) hear it as rhythmically odd, or aberrant, but not because of any sort of conflict with any sort of underlying duple meter.

4. *Alfonso Ferrabosco the Elder: Opera Omnia*, ed. Richard Charteris, Corpus Mensurabilis Musicae 96 (Stuttgart: Hänssler Verlag, 1984), 2:37; Lassus, *The Seven Penitential Psalms*, ed. Peter Bergquist, Recent Researches in the Music of the Renaissance 86–87 (Madison: A-R Editions, 1990), 10.

5. On this point and on mode in Byrd's motets in general, see Joseph Kerman, *The Masses and Motets of William Byrd* (Berkeley: University of California Press, 1981), 68–72.

6. *Cantiones sacrae I* (1589), no. 6, and *Cantiones sacrae II* (1591), no. 13.

7. St. Michael's Tenbury, MS 341, fol. 1v.

8. *Psalmes, Sonets and Songs* (1588), Nos. 11 and 18.

9. Let us amend what we have transgressed through ignorance, lest, should the day of death suddenly overtake us, we seek time for repentance and cannot find it. Harken, O Lord, and have mercy, for we have sinned against thee. Help us, O God of our salvation, and for the glory of thy name, deliver us.

10. *A General History of Music* (1789), III:135.

11. And *Emendemus in melius* evidently made an impact. Byrd himself took advantage of some of its features in the anthem *O God whom our offences* (*The Byrd Edition,* 11, no. 5), and the motet was more widely copied—that is, copied by more collectors—than any other of the 1575 motets (the motets *Laudate pueri,* no. 6, and *Attollite portas,* no. 11, top it only if their anthem versions are counted).

12. See Frank Ll. Harrison, "Church Music in England," *New Oxford History of Music,* 4, ed. Gerald Abraham (Oxford: Oxford University Press, 1968), Kerman, *The Masses and Motets of William Byrd,* and D. S. Humphreys, "Aspects of Elizabethan and Jacobean Music" (Ph.D. diss., Cambridge, 1976). For *Qui fundasti terram,* see the Ferrabosco *Opera Omnia,* 1:44–47.

Byrd, the Catholics, and the Motet

The Hearing Reopened

For Joseph Kerman, belatedly, on his seventieth birthday:
"Take well in worth, a simple toy."

Thirty years ago Joseph Kerman, following Edward Lowinsky's lead in discussing Clemens, first suggested that sixteen or so of Byrd's motets, employing metaphors such as the plight of Jerusalem, the Babylonian captivity, the Egyptian captivity, liberation, and the coming of God, or martyrdom, had been "politically" conceived, specifically to reflect the plight of persecuted English Catholics (see Table 16.1). Kerman took up this idea again in 1979, and in 1981 offered further refinements in a summation that has remained his last word on this intriguing issue.[1] More recently, in the course of editing Byrd's last great collection of Latin music, *Gradualia*, Philip Brett perceptively clarified the "political" character of that most overtly Catholic publication. Drawing upon revealing textual glosses in the Douai Bible to scriptural texts favored by Byrd, Brett reinforced the links to the Old Religion, and suggested alliances between the composer and the Jesuit mission to England.[2]

In this light, it no longer seems so surprising that Byrd should have been present at a major Jesuit event of the 1580s: the gathering at Hurleyford on 14 July 1586 to receive the Jesuits Henry Garnet and Robert Southwell, who had begun their mission in England only a week before. According to Southwell, the lengthy meeting was to include solemn Mass with voices and instruments on the feast of Mary Magdalene. In Father William Weston's description of this weeklong gathering and its elaborate services, "as if we were celebrating an uninterrupted octave of some great feast," the priest singled out one member of the company by name: William Byrd, who, he claimed (somewhat inaccurately) for the edification of his readers, "had sacrificed everything for the faith."[3]

In the Jesuits' view, the arrival of Garnet and Southwell had been long and eagerly awaited by the English Catholic community. For a year and a half William Weston had seemed the solitary Jesuit still at liberty in the realm.[4] As Southwell put it in a letter to Claudio Aquaviva, General of the Society of Jesus in Rome,

TABLE 16.1   Byrd's political motets

Plight of Jerusalem, Babylonian captivity, Egyptian captivity

Ne irascaris / Civitas sancti tui [Isa. 64:9–10]
Vide Domine afflictionem nostram / Sed veni Domine
Tribulationes civitatum audivimus / Timor et hebetudo mentis / Nos enim pro peccatis
Domine tu iurasti patribus nostris
Memento, Domine, congregationis tuae
Domine praestolamur adventum tuum / Veni, Domine, noli tardare
Quomodo cantabimus canticum Domini in terra aliena? [Ps. 136:4–7]
Plorans plorabit [Jer. 13:17–18]

The coming of God, liberation

Laetentur coeli / Orietur in diebus tuis
Vigilate, nescitis enim quando Dominus veniat [Mark 13:35–37]
Apparebit in finem [Hab. 2:3]
Exsurge, quare obdormis, Domine [Ps. 43:23–24]

Martyrdom

Deus, venerunt gentes / Posuerunt morticinia / Effuderunt sanguinem / Facti sumus opprobrium [Ps. 78:1–4]
Haec dicit Dominus: Vox in excelsis audita est lamentationis / Haec dicit Dominus: Quiescat
vox tua [Jer. 31:15–17]

Miscellaneous

Circumspice Hierusalem, ad orientem / Ecce enim veniunt [Baruch 4:36–37]
Unam petii a Domino [Ps. 26:4]

---

our coming has marvellously cheered and inspired Catholics; for previously they were complaining that they were practically deserted by the Society, and they were full of misgivings that their shepherds, dismayed by difficulties, were abandoning a flock that never stood in greater need of their care.

News of the two Jesuits' arrival quickly spread. Garnet remarked, in figures that also have a familiar ring, "We have to conceal the fact that we are members of the Society, lest the whole of Jerusalem be disturbed."[5]

I wonder if one of Byrd's "political" motets, one which he chose never to publish, could have been inspired by the arrival of these two Jesuit missionaries, already known to "the whole of Jerusalem":

Circumspice, Hierusalem, ad orientem et vide iucunditatem a Deo tibi ven-
ientem. *2.p.* Ecce enim veniunt filii tui, quos dimisisti dispersos, veniunt collecti ab oriente usque ad occidentem et verbo sancti gaudentes in honorem Dei.

(Jerusalem, look about you to the east and behold the joy that is coming to you from God. (Part 2) For behold your children are coming, whom you sent away; they are coming, gathered from the east and the west, at the word of the Holy One, rejoicing in the glory of God.)

The *secunda pars* opens with an unusual contrapuntal *tour de force* on the words "Ecce enim veniunt filii tui" (see Example 16.1). I suspect the main point of this interesting passage resides in the isolated, non-overlapping paired entries of the point in augmentation, carefully placed in the outer voices to make them more audible. These two stand out amidst the flurry of livelier entries in the other voices in diminution, and because of the solemnly portentious turn to the minor at this point. I would suggest that this brilliant six-part work in the cheerful Mixolydian mode (its only use in motets of this period) commemorates in the blatant pictorialism of part 2 the arrival of this particular pair of Jesuit missionaries, who would lead the Jesuit enterprise during the next two decades, which also witnessed the publication of Byrd's remaining Latin music, *Cantiones sacrae* I and II, the Masses, and finally *Gradualia* in 1605–7.[6]

Lately I have been playing the pursuivant amidst what Kerman once called "the murk of underdocumentation"[7] surrounding Byrd's other "political" motets. I have discovered that the tracts and pamphlets published by English Catholics—particularly Jesuits—help to dispel some of that Kermanesque gloom. Even if Byrd had not been a firm friend of Garnet and Southwell, as Jesuit martyrologists have liked to imagine,[8] he would certainly have known their words. The words of Byrd's "political" motets speak a language that turns out to have been much closer than previously realized to the rhetoric of other English Catholics, and especially of Jesuits such as Garnet and Southwell, both in their public and private communications. The existence of this common language helps explain how Byrd (or his priests or patrons) came to choose many of his texts, how others besides musicians could have known their sources, and also how such texts would have been "heard" by Byrd and his fellow Catholics.

This language is most apparent in books and pamphlets that had begun to appear in a trickle during the 1570s but grew to a sizeable stream immediately after Edmund Campion's execution in 1581. No fewer than 225 volumes were printed between Campion's martyrdom and Garnet's own death on the scaffold in 1606.[9] Several of these went through multiple editions, many ran to hundreds of pages, and some even spawned popular Protestant imitations. Writing in April 1596, ten years after the establishment of a secret press in London and shortly before its discovery, Garnet remarked to Aquaviva, "We have equipped at our expense a press which in a short space has filled the kingdom from the end to end with catechisms and other pious books." Papist books printed abroad were also smuggled into the country and sold by entrepreneurs such as the French ambassador's butler, who did a thriving business in the early 1580s (at the same time the embassy cook enjoyed a financial windfall by exporting used, now largely useless, English Catholic altar furniture).[10] Here we have time to dip into only the most obvious of these long forgotten and ignored "pious books."

Example 16.1 *(continued)*

Just as the most common themes of Byrd's "political" motets are the Babylonian captivity, the Egyptian captivity, and Jerusalem laid low, these are also the most frequently encountered allusions in Catholic writings, so common that after a while their use hardly even seems self-conscious, as the Catholic community becomes Jerusalem and individual Catholics Israelites. We have already seen one Jerusalem allusion in Garnet's private correspondence. In October 1588 he also wrote to Aquaviva:

> All our hopes turned precipitately into sorrow. All things are with us as they were with the Jewish people as they were about to go forth from Egypt. . . . Now with redoubled energy the chiefs and persecutors of Egypt have turned on us all the wrath they have conceived against Moses and Aaron.

Robert Southwell, on the other hand, might characterize the imprisoned Father William Weston as "a true Israelite, prudent as a serpent and simple as a dove."[11]

John Pibush, writing to Garnet three months before his own execution at Tyburn in February 1601, expressed it thus:

> The promised land of our Fathers has now for their children become a howling wilderness, over which the hungry fowlers have spread their nets of laws and statutes over the whole country. . . . God grant you and other poor Israelites a cloud to hide you from your enemies by day, and by night a column of fire in all your sudden flights.[12]

By contrast, when describing a reunion with Garnet and others at Baddesley Clinton early in 1590, Robert Southwell could rework the common Babylonian metaphor of Ps. 136 in a positive vein, together with a reference to Deut. 32:13:

> It was a delight to be all together for a few days, keeping our ancient customs, helping each other, and exchanging views. We opened our mouths and drew in the spirit. . . . We have sung the songs of Our Lord in a strange land; in this desert we have sucked honey from the rock and oil from the hardest flint.[13]

Three years earlier, in his *Epistle of comfort, to the reverend priestes, & to the Honorable, Worshipful, & other of the Laye sort restrayned in Durance for the Catholicke Fayth*, secretly printed in 1587 and reprinted in 1606 and 1616, Southwell had combined both Babylon and Egypt to characterize the harsh realities of the Catholic plight:

> For upon the fluddes of *Babilon*, what cause have we, but layinge a syde our myrth and musicke, to sitt & weepe, remembringe our absence, out of our heavenly *Sion:* In the vassalage and servilitye of *Egipt*, where we are so dayly oppressed with uncessante afflictions, & filthy workes.[14]

These all resonate in sympathy with Byrd's own Jerusalem, Babylon, and Egypt texts, especially Southwell's last, which recalls in particular the musical exchange between Philippe de Monte and Byrd, based upon Ps. 136, *Super flumina Babylonis/Quomodo cantabimus*, from a few years earlier.[15]

Many of Byrd's other "political" motets ring the changes on what turn out to have been other favorite rhetorical themes. The subject of the coming of God could represent either a veiled threat or a longed-for reward. When speaking "Of the Severe accounpte that we must yelde to God," in his immensely influential *First booke of the Christian exercise* (1582, reprinted in 1584, revised in 1585, and reprinted four more times), Robert Parsons directly quotes the text from Mark 13 that Byrd also adopted in his vigorous and vivid *Vigilate, nescitis enim quando Dominus veniat:*

> let us consider how easie a matter it is now for us (with a litle paine) to avoide the daunger of this daye; and for that cause it is foretolde us, by our most mercifull iudge and Savyour, to the end we should by our diligence avoyde it. For thus he concludeth after all his former threatenings: V*idete vigilate etc.* [Mar. 13.] *Looke aboute, watch and praye, for you know not when the tyme shalbe. But as I say to you, so I saie to all, be watchfull.* [16]

When Parsons employs another coming-of-God text shared with Byrd, *Apparebit in finem* (Hab. 2:3), in the widely circulated *An epistle of the persecution of Catholicks* (1582), he invokes precisely the sentiments Byrd himself probably had in mind:

> *I have once sworne in my holye, I will not lye, to David, his seed shall remayne for ever and ever.*
>   This is the promise, this is the firme protestation of god, to the seede of David, that is, to the Catholique churche of Christ, towchinge her everlastinge continuance, made by an othe, confirmed by his bloode, and established by the experience of manye ages. Wherefore we must not dispaire but confidentlie endure, [Ps. 24.] *for whoe so ever indureth our lorde, shall never be confounded. And if he do staie some what* [Abac. 2.] *longe, yet let us expect him, for that co[m]minge he will come, & will not forslowe it.* [17]

Byrd's most brutal "political" motet sets verses 1–4 from the singularly grim Ps. 78, *Deus, venerunt gentes / Posuerunt morticinia / Effuderunt sanguinem / Facti sumus opprobrium*, and has been linked to the executions of Catholic missionaries, who were customarily hanged, drawn, and quartered. [18] The horror of these notoriously grisly rituals was quickly conveyed to Catholics at home and abroad, not only in words, but also in vivid images. In 1583 Nicolò Circiniani adorned the walls of the chapel of the English College in Rome with scenes of English martyrs, intended to make or break the resolve of new recruits who worshiped there. In 1584 the newly completed frescoes were engraved by Giovanni Battista Cavalleri, the only record of them that still survives. Campion's own martyrdom barely two years earlier figured in several engravings (see Figures 16.1 and 16.2).

For his nine sixteenth-century English martyrs on the walls of the English chapel Circiniani drew upon six highly influential engravings from the 1582 Roman edition of Robert Parsons's *De persecutione anglicana*. These also provided inspiration for subsequent engravings by Richard Verstegan, who had probably begun his martyrological career as the printer of *A true reporte of the death and martyrdome of M. Campion Iesuite and preiste, & M. Sherwin, &*

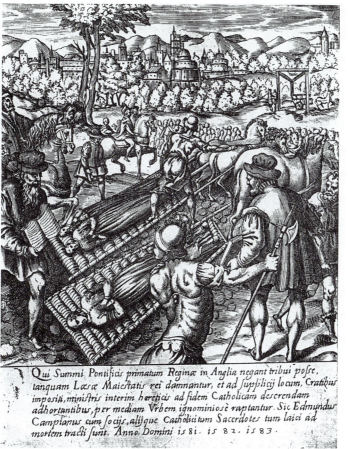

Qui Summi Pontificis primatum Reginæ in Anglia negant tribui posse,
tanquam Læsæ Maiestatis rei damnantur, et ad supplicij locum, Cratibus
impositi, ministris interim hæreticis ad fidem Catholicam deserendam
adhortantibus, per mediam Vrbem ignominiosè raptantur. Sic Edmundus
Campianus cum socijs, alijque Catholicitum Sacerdotes tum laici ad
mortem tracti sunt. Anno Domini 1581. 1582. 1583.

FIGURE 16.1 Nicolò Circiniani, *Ecclesiae anglicanae trophæa* (Rome, 1584), fol. 32.
Reproduced by permission of the Donohue Rare Book Room, Gleeson Library, University of San Francisco, San Francisco, California.

M. Bryan preistes, known to musicians as the source for the poem, "Why do I use my paper, ink, and pen," set by Byrd as a consort song, presumably in commemoration of Campion. Verstegan's *Theatrum crudelitatum hæreticorum nostri temporis* (1587), which went through eight editions in the next two decades, included among its 30 illustrations 12 large, detailed plates of English Catholic persecution (see Figure 16.3 for Verstegan's depiction of Jesuits' martyrdom).[19]

But Byrd probably needed no pictures. He also would not have been at a loss for words, for the brutal text of Ps. 78 turns out to have been frequently on the lips of papist pamphleteers, members of the Catholic community, and the martyrs themselves. The similarity between Byrd's detachable setting of Ps. 78:4, *Facti sumus opprobrium,* and Campion's speech from the hangman's

FIGURE 16.2   Nicolò Circiniani, *Ecclesiae anglicanae trophæa* (Rome, 1584), fol. 33. Reproduced by permission of the Donohue Rare Book Room, Gleeson Library, University of San Francisco, San Francisco, California.

cart, *Spectaculum facti sumus Deo* (1 Cor. 4:9) has not escaped modern scholars,[20] and may not have escaped Byrd:

> Facti sumus opprobrium vicinis nostris: subsonnatio et illusio his qui in circuitu nostro sunt.
>
> (We are become a reproach to our neighbours, scorn and derision to those who are around us.)

First Corinthians 4:9 echos and reechos as a staple in Jesuit tracts:

> With graue countenance, and sweete voyce, [Campion] stoutly spake as followeth. *Spectaculum facti sumus Deo, Angelus & hominibus,* Saying these are

8;

Perſecutiones aduerſus Catholicos à Prote-
ſtantibus Caluiniſtis excitæ in Anglia.

Sanguinis effuſi firmamus pignore Chriſti
Maiorúmque fidem, magni fundamina Petri,
Et tantum Latijs apicem veneramur in oris.
At gregis electi cuſtodia non cadet vnquam
In caput, ô Regina, tuum, regésque profanos,
Et minus in vilem fidei myſteria ſexum.

L 2   M A R I A

FIGURE 16.3   Richard Verstegan, *Theatrum crudelitatum haereticorum nostri temporis*
(Antwerp, 1587), p. 83. Reproduced by permission of the Donohue Rare Book Room,
Gleeson Library, University of San Francisco, San Francisco, California.

the wordes of S. Paule, Englished thus: *We are made a spectacle, or a sight*
unto God, unto his Angels, and unto men: verified this day in me, who am
here a spectacle unto my Lord, a spectacle unto his Angels, and unto you
men. [*A true reporte of the death and martyrdom of M. Campion* (1582)]

And yet behold when Campion made his end,
his humble hart was so bedewde with grace,
that no reproch could once his mind offend,
mildnes possest his sweet and cherefull face,
a pacient spectacle was presented then,
in sight of God, of angels, saints, and men.
["An other [poem] upon the same [death of Campion]," *A true reporte* (1582)]

Then he [Thomas Cottam] was turned backward to looke upon M. *Richardson*
who was then in quartering . . . once he [Cottam] said *Thy soule pray for me*
and at the last said, *O Lord, what a spectacle hast thou made unto me?* the

which he repeated twise or thrise." [Allen, A *briefe historie of the glorious martyrdome of xii. reverend priests* (1582)]

When he [Christopher Bailey] had mounted the scaffold he said, "Far be it from me to glory except in the cross of Our Lord Jesus Christ." Then lifting his eyes to heaven he made the sign of the cross as well as he could with his bound hands. "You have come," he said, "to see a man dying, a common spectacle; and that man a priest, a common spectacle too." [Letter of Robert Southwell, March 1590, quoted in Devlin, *Life of Robert Southwell*, 213]

In so muche [distress and persecution], as they may trulie say, . . . that same allso verye fytlie agreeth unto them, *we are made a spectacle to the worlde, to angels and to men: . . . we are accompted the parings of the worlde, and the refuse of all to this daye. . . .* I humblie beseche oure most mercifull and most mightie God . . . that they may finde mercie in the day of oure Lorde, who in their owne day, that is, in the daye of man, have showed no mercie to theire brethren [in margin:] Esa. 13. I. Cor. 4. [An *Epistle Towchinge the persecution of Catholics*]

Byrd sets "Facti sumus opprobrium" as a rare triple point, with three sepa-rate subjects treated together.[21] The word "opprobrium" stands out strikingly as tenor and soprano enter in stretto, with "opprobrium" as their first word, close upon its presentation in the lower voices (see Example 16.2); "spectaculum" might even be substituted for it without damage to sense or syntax. I would suggest that, just as in *Circumspice Hierusalem* Byrd may have used augmented entries in the outer voices to commemorate the arrival of Southwell and Gar-net, the rare triple point at "Facti sumus opprobrium vicinis nostris" was meant to commemorate Campion and his fellow martyrs, Alexander Brian and Raphe Sherwin, departing this world at Tyburn.

Psalm 78:2, *Posuerunt morticinia servorum tuorum*, served for part 2 of Byrd's large motet:

Posuerunt morticinia servorum tuorum escas volatilibus coeli: carnes sancto-rum bestiis terrae.

(The dead bodies of your servants have they given as meat to the birds of the sky; the flesh of your saints, to the beasts of the earth.)

William Allen must have had the text in mind when he described these execu-tions in A *briefe historie of the glorious martyrdome of xii. reverend priests* (1582):

yea even their bodies . . . though hanging on ports, pinnacles, poles & gib-bets, though torne of beasts and birdes: yet rest in peace, and are more honor-able, sacred, and soveraine: then the embaumed bodies of what worldly state soever in their regal sepulchers.[22]

At the conclusion of another similar tract from the same year, A *true reporte of the deathe and martyrdome of M. Campion*, beside Walpole's familiar "Why do I use my paper, ink, and pen," there appears another "Complainte of a Catholicke for the death of M. Edmund Campion." Here verse 2 of Ps. 78 clearly is transformed into the fourteeners of so-called "Drab Age Verse":[23]

EXAMPLE 16.2 Byrd, beginning of *Facti sumus opprobrium*

359

EXAMPLE 16.2 (*continued*)

O God from sacred throne behold
  our secret sorowes here,
Regard with grace our helplesse griefe
  amend our mournfull cheere.
The bodies of thy Saintes abrode
  are set for foules to feede,
And brutish birds devour the flesh
  of faithful folke in deede.

The text turned up just as blatantly yet again before the year was out in the form which was probably most widely seen, and probably most clearly associated with Catholic persecution: on the title page of Robert Parsons's *An epistle of the persecution of Catholickes.* Here Ps. 78 stands out as a kind of subtitle (see Figure 16.4).

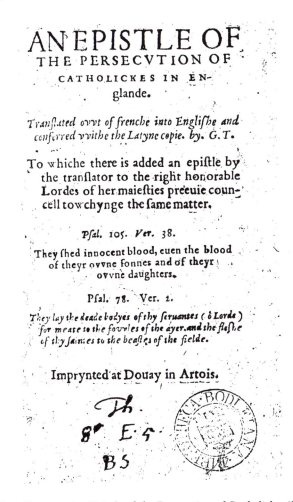

AN EPISTLE OF
THE PERSECVTION OF
CATHOLICKES IN EN-
glande.

*Tranſlated ovvt of frenche into Englishe and
conferred vvithe the Latyne copie. by. G. T.*

To whiche there is added an epiſtle by
the tranſlator to the right honorable
Lordes of her maieſties preeuie coun-
cell towchynge the ſame matter.

Pſal. 105. *Ver.* 38.

They ſhed innocent blood, euen the blood
of theyr ovvne fonnes and of theyr
ovvne daughters.

Pſal. 78. Ver. 1.

*They lay the deade bodyes of thy feruantes (ò Lorde)
for meate to the fovvles of the ayer, and the fleſhe
of thy ſaintes to the beaſtes of the fielde.*

Imprynted at Douay in Artois.

Th.
8° E. 5
B 5

FIGURE 16.4 Robert Parsons, *An Epistle of the Persecution of Catholickes* (1582), Title page. Reproduced by permission of the Bodleian Library, Oxford (8°. E. 5. Th. Bs.).

At least one English Catholic martyr, John Cornelius, executed on 4 July 1594, is reputed to have exclaimed "Posuerunt morticinia servorum tuorum," etc., on mounting the ladder of the gallows. Most remarkable, it turns out that at roughly the time Byrd's *Deus venerunt gentes* was composed, Garnet claimed the pope had granted an indulgence to "all those that did devoutlie for the conversion of England say that vearse w[hi]ch is in the hyme of Allhallow Day: *Gentem auferte perfidam*, &c. and the psalme 78, *Deus, venerunt gentes.*"[24] One wonders if the same indulgence would apply to the singing of Byrd's motet.

Byrd's setting of verses 1–2 of Ps. 50, *Miserere mei, Deus*, printed in the 1591 *Cantiones sacrae*, on the other hand, has never been singled out as "political"—not surprising, since any number of other composers, both Catholic and Protestant, also set various versions of this penitential psalm. But for Byrd and other Catholics from 1580 onward it must have carried a special meaning, for these were among the words most commonly uttered on the scaffold. According to William Allen's *A briefe historie*, John Paine and John Nelson both recited the *Miserere* at the last:

> After M. *Paine* told them that he said our lordes praier three times, and told them that he would say the psalme *Miserere*, and said it forth. . . . He himself [John Nelson] said [the Creed] in Latine, adding thereto the *Confiteor*, and the Psalmes *Miserere* and *De profundis*. [Allen, *A briefe historie*]

Alexander Brian said it twice, once when the hangman roughly removed him from the cart, and earlier during interrogation:

> they caused needles to be thrust under his nailes, wherat M. *Brian* was not moved at al, but with a constant mind and plesant countenance said the Psalme *Miserere*, desiring God to forgeve his tormenters.

Robert Southwell would also utter the *Miserere mei, Deus* at his execution in 1595.[25] Perhaps Byrd's particular preoccupation with setting this psalm, and so many other similar penitential texts, which rival in number the Jerusalem motets, may be explained by the fact that these motets were heard as gallows texts.

Even so unlikely a text as *Haec dies quam fecit Dominus*, especially familiar from Byrd's popular extrovert setting published in the 1591 *Cantiones sacrae*, could be turned into a gallows text. During a double execution at Tyburn on 27 February 1601, in the aftermath of the Earl of Essex's riot, Mark Barkworth, O.S.B. is reputed to have sung "with a joyful accent" *Haec dies quam fecit Dominus, exultemus*. He was joined by Roger Filcock, S.J. "in the same tone," at *Et laetemur in ea*. The association of Byrd, *Haec dies*, and this gallows tradition is made palpable by an early seventeenth-century recusant manuscript preserved in the Bodleian Library (MS Eng. th. b.2), where a description of Filcock's trials is followed by a four-voice musical setting of Filcock's last words, ascribed—inevitably—to "Mr Byrd." That the little motet sounds quite unlike Byrd is less significant than the fact that Catholics were prepared to believe it was by him.[26]

Fifteen years separate the *Cantiones sacrae* and *Gradualia*, which Kerman has seen as the product of Byrd's semiretirement to Stondon Massey near Sir John Petre's Catholic enclave at Ingatestone. Philip Brett has pointed to the significantly post-Tridentine spirit of Byrd's abandonment of Sarum texts in *Gradualia* in favor of the Roman forms authorized by Pius V in the Breviary of 1568 and the Missal of 1570. It may well have been Jesuits such as Jasper Haywood who fostered this specific practice in attempting to increase conformity between English Catholics and Rome. For a list of "Certain points of ecclesiastical discipline in England" of 1584, promoted by Haywood, includes as its fifteenth point, "It is wished with one consent, and greatly desired of worshipfull men, that all would follow the Romane use in their office and service as a thing commended to all the world by the Concell of Trent." Haywood's overly enthusiastic advocacy of such Roman innovations, at odds with traditional English Catholicism, met with such stiff opposition in some quarters that one Catholic layman threatened to denounce him to the privy council. Haywood was recalled from England in January 1585.[27] In such circumstances, Byrd's decision to adopt Roman practice looks even more like an acceptance of a position that could be perceived as Jesuitical.

The choice of the Propers in *Gradualia* I, consisting of Marian Masses, All Saints, and Corpus Christi, certainly seems politically motivated. Brett has suggested on codicological grounds that this volume's opening section of Marian and All Saints music, including all the five-part works, may have originally been intended as a separate publication. He concluded that "a fascicle that begins with the vision of a purified Catholic England and ends with a glorious commemoration of saints makes as strong a political as liturgical statement."[28] It may be useful, therefore, to examine in more detail how this political agenda is expressed and how it may have been "heard" within the Catholic community.

In the opening block of Marian music, Byrd provided not only for the four most important feasts of the Virgin directly, but also, by a more complicated route, for her minor feasts.[29] Such a Marian emphasis may in fact have been prompted by an upswing in Marian devotion consciously fostered by the Jesuits, and by Henry Garnet in particular. On 1 April 1573 Pope Gregory XIII had changed Pius V's recently instituted Feast of Our Lady of Victory to the Feast of Our Lady of the most Holy Rosary, whose widespread use, according to many, had brought victory over the Turks at Lepanto. Before coming to England, in the hope of fostering Marian devotion there, Garnet had even secured special permission from the General of the Dominicans to admit English Catholics to the Confraternity of the Rosary, and took pains to retain that concession under the subsequent General of the Order of Friars Preachers. In his first published work, *The societie of the Rosary*, secretly printed in 1593, Garnet pointed out that the confraternity had originally been instituted by St. Dominic against older heresies and would be comparably useful against modern ones.

> Sufficiente it is for oure purpose, that she is in speciall maner a rainbow against Heretickes: wher-as the Church generally singeth, she hath destroied

all heresies in the wholle world, and therefore is a perticuler signe and aboade of the ceassing thereof.

A new edition of *The societie of the Rosary* was brought out around 1596, copies of which were still available in 1609, when the Crown informer William Udall seized many from a Dutch priest at the house of the Venetian ambassador in London.[30] Beside an engraving of the Virgin and Child, the title pages of both editions proclaimed bluntly, "Rejoice Virgin MARY, since you alone have crushed all heresies through the world" (see Figure 16.5), a phrase also included in the recitation of the rosary. The same striking words also ring out in *Gradualia* at the opening of Byrd's *Gaude Maria Virgo*, the tract from the votive Mass of the BVM after Septuagesima.[31]

The presentation of the Corpus Christi Propers at the head of the four-part fascicle of *Gradualia* I (at one stage possibly conceived as the beginning of a separate volume) must have been designed as a comparably important statement, for it was their views of the Blessed Sacrament that distinguished English Catholics from their Protestant countrymen. In a very perceptive interpretation of the Corpus Christi music, Brett suggests:

> It is tempting to speculate that Byrd composed the votive Mass, the Corpus Christi antiphons, and the Litany of the Saints for some Jesuit enactment of the Forty Hours—there was certainly enough reason to conduct such a special devotion on behalf of the missionary priests and their congregations in the early years of the seventeenth century.[32]

Brett was right on the mark, for it can in fact be shown that the Forty Hours were being enacted by English Jesuits even earlier, and in the most extraordinary circumstances. In 1602 Fr. Giles Archer recounted that William Weston had fostered these same devotions even within the close confines of the Catholic prison at Wisbech Castle, during his imprisonment there, beginning in 1588:

> In all our devotional exercises he was the moving spirit. He introduced the practice of reciting litanies daily after dinner for the conversion of England and several times arranged for the Quarant'Ore before the Blessed Sacrament for the same intention . . . When we had the Quarant'Ore, he swept the place out, arranged the altar and polished the candlesticks as if he were a paid servant.[33]

The Mass for All Saints, on the other hand, appearing at the end of the five-part fascicle of *Gradualia* I, was less redolent with the sorts of doctrinal associations surrounding Mary or the Blessed Sacrament. Members of the English Catholic community can have been only too aware of the many who had lately joined the saints, who had suffered, and indeed, been encouraged to suffer, for the faith.[34] The English Jesuits, and Garnet in particular, were especially concerned with their dead, given the tenuous and precarious nature of the English congregation, which lacked the large communities of the European Provinces, prepared to pray for their own dead. In December 1596 Garnet had written to Aquaviva after the death of John Nelson:

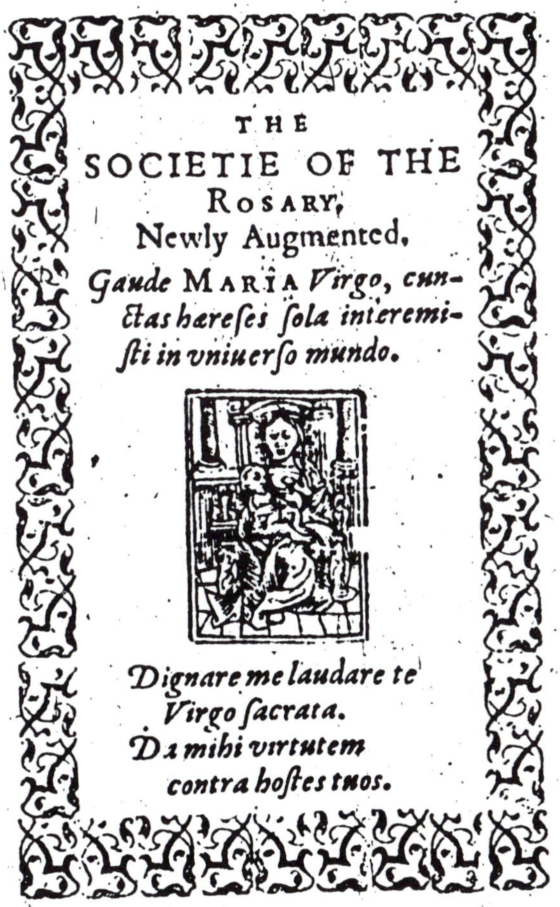
THE
SOCIETIE OF THE
ROSARY,
Newly Augmented.
Gaude MARIA *Virgo, cun-ctas hæreſes ſola interemi-ſti in vniuerſo mundo.*

Dignare me laudare te Virgo ſacrata.
Da mihi virtutem contra hoſtes tuos.

FIGURE 16.5 Henry Garnet, *The Societie of the Rosary* (ca. 1600), title page. Folger Shakespeare Library, Washington, D. C. (STC 19939a). Reproduced by permission.

> I beg your Lordship to remember him in your prayers and to commend his soul to the prayers of Ours. I hope they will be all the more generous to this fellow-warrior of theirs in proportion as we are fewer here and deprived of the fraternal assistance of our communities.[35]

In *The societie of the Rosary,* having pointed out that four anniversaries for the dead of the churches of the confraternity were stipulated after the four principal Marian feasts of the year (the ones set by Byrd), Garnet had lamented that this "cannot (as it is manifest) be performed in our country."[36]

This special concern with the dead once again clearly emerges from Catholic writers, who lapse into and out of the words of the propers for All Saints almost unconsciously:

> Doe not celebrate the daye of the Sayntes nativitye, which is an entrance of all griefs, and molestations, but the day of their death, which is a ridda[n]ce of their sorowes & a farewell to the deviles assaltes. We celebrate the daye of theire death because thoughe they seeme to dye, yet in deed they dye not.[37]

Here, in *An epistle of comfort*, Robert Southwell is less explicit about the connection with recent Catholic martyrs when he alludes to the offertory for All Saints, *Justorum animæ in manu Dei sunt*. William Allen, writing five years earlier in *A briefe Historie*, on the other hand, makes the point unequivocally:

> These Martyres are blessed, safe, free, past al mortal miseries, in the hands and garde of God, where the torment of malice can not touch them.[38]

These examples help to illustrate how even the liturgical texts Byrd set in *Gradualia* quietly spoke the language and reflected the concerns of Jesuit spirituality.

It is among the miscellaneous pieces from *Gradualia I*, however, that the most direct evocations of the Catholic cause found a place. Of these, the nonliturgical *Unam petii a Domino* is unusually direct in its plea for religious tolerance:

> Unam petii a Domino, hanc requiram: ut inhabitem in domo Domini omnibus diebus vitæ meæ. Ut videam voluntatem Domini, et visitem templum eius.
>
> (One thing I have asked of the Lord, this will I seek after: that I may dwell in the house of the Lord all the days of my life. That I may see the Lord's goodwill and visit his temple.)

Just how dangerously blunt this motet may have been is revealed by the cover of the Jesuit *First booke of the Christian exercise* (1582) (see Figure 16.6), where these very words stand out as a motto.

It was Brett who first observed the connection between another miscellaneous piece, the puzzling consort song included in *Gradualia*, *Adoramus te, Christe, et benedicimus tibi, quia per sanctam Crucem tuam redemisti mundum*, and the Little Office of the Holy Cross, and also remarked upon the special significance of the Cross for Jesuits.[39] From as early as Edmund Campion's famous Letter to the Lords of the Privy Council (1580), known as "Campion's Brag," the Holy Cross had become a primary symbol for the English Catholic community, and for the Jesuits in particular.

> And touchinge our Societie, be it known unto you that we have made a league . . . cheerfully to carry the cross that God shall lay upon us, and never to despaire your recoverie, while we have a man left to enjoy your Tiborne, or to be racked with your torments, or to be consumed with your prisons. The expense is reckoned, the enterprise is begun; it is of God, it cannot be withstood. Soe it was first planted, soe it must be restored.[40]

The Cross may even eclipse the Jerusalem/Babylon/Egypt allusions as the predominant symbol of the Jesuit mission, one at the same time emphatically

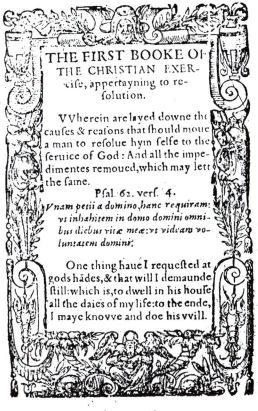

THE FIRST BOOKE OF
THE CHRISTIAN EXER-
cife, appertayning to re-
folution.

VVherein are layed downe the
caufes & reafons that fhould moue
a man to refolue hym felfe to the
feruice of God : And all the impe-
dimentes remoued,which may lett
the fame.

Pfal. 62. verf. 4.

*Vnam petii a domino,hanc requiram:
vt inhabitem in domo domini omnibus diebus vitæ meæ:vt videam vo-
luntatem domini.*

One thing haue I requefted at
gods hädes,& that will I demaunde
ftill:which is,to dwell in his houfe
all the daies of my life:to the ende,
I maye knovve and doe his vvill.

Anno. 1582.

VVITH PRIVYLEGE.

FIGURE 16.6 Robert Parsons, *The first booke of the Christian exercise* (1582), title page. Reproduced by permission of the Huntington Library, San Marino, California (RB 69058).

rejected by many English Protestants. As the Jesuit pamphleteer Richard Verstegan put it in "Of the Invention, or fynding of the Crosse of Christ," from *Odes in imitation of the seaven penitential psalmes,*

Somtyme the Crosse as sundry recordes tel,
Deryving vertue from our Saviours death,
Hath had the force, the divel to expel,
And by the same confirmed Christian faith,
But now it seemes, faith hath sustayned losse,
Because the divel hath chaste away the crosse.[41]

In *The first booke of the Christian exercise* Robert Parsons returns time and again to the Cross:

But now in the new testame[n]t, founded expresselie upon the crosse, the matter standeth much more playne, & that with great reason. [Luc. 24.] For yf Christ could not goe into this glorie, but by suffering, as the scripture sayeth: then by the most reasonable rule of Christ affirming, [Mat. 10.] *that the servante hathe not privilege above his master.* It must folowe, that all have to drinke of Christes cuppe, whiche are appointed to be partakers of his glorie. . . . Christ hathe geven this generall rule in the new testament: [Mat. 10.] *He that taketh not up his crosse and followeth me, is not woorthie of me.* By which, is resolved playnelie, that there is no salvatio[n] now to be had, but onelye for them that take up (that is doe beare willinglie) theyr proper crosses, and therwith doe folowe theyr captaine, walking on with his crosse. . . . To speake in one worde: God wolde make us by tribulation *crucified Christians:* Whiche is the most honorable title that can be geven unto a creature.[42]

Robert Southwell likewise repeatedly urged the persecuted to accept—indeed, to glory in—the Cross, in language increasingly vivid:

In vayne he claymeth the name of a christian, that doth not imitate Christe. . . . [Galat. 6.] Godd forbid that I shoulde glorye saving in the Crosse of our Lord Iesus Christ. . . . The author of lyfe hanging upon the Crosse made his will allotting to everyone workes of pietye, to his Apostles persecution . . . to the repentante Christians he commended the Crosse. Whereuppon *S. Maximus* well sayeth, that all the lyfe of a Christian, that will lyve agreeably to the Gospell, is a perpetuall crosse and martirdome. We must now acknowledge our profession, and not be ashamed of our inheritance, which Christ allotted unto us. We must saye with *S. Paule* [Galat. 6.] *Mundus mihi crucifixus est, & ego mundo* the worlde is crucified unto me and I to the world. . . . The Crosse is our inheryance, as *S. Ambrose* saythe, and therefore if you bringe us to the Crosse, or which is all one in effecte to the gallowes; we maye saye with *S. Andrew. O bona crux, accipe me ab hominibus, et redde me magistro meo, ut per te me recipiat, qui per te me redemit.* O good Cross take me from men and restore me to my maister, that by thee he may receive me, who by thee hathe redeemed me. For in this quarrell, *non maledictus,* not accursed, but [Deut. 21.] *benedictus homo qui pependit in ligno.* Blessed is the man that hunge uppon a tree. And therefore . . . Go on, you good magistrates, so much the better in the peoples eyes, if you sacrifyce unto them Catholikes, Racke us, torture us, condemne us, yea grinde us: youre iniquitye is proofe of our fayth.[43]

From the beginning the martyred priests, too, made the Cross perhaps their most prominent symbol, beginning with the martyred Campion:

His [Campion's] head set up so high doth call for mor
To fight the fight which he endured here,
The faith thus planted thus restored must be,
Take up thy crosse saith Christ and folow me.
["A Dialogue betwene a Catholike and Consolation" from *A true report of the death and martyrdom of M. Campion*]

Raphe Sherwin had headed his last letter to his uncle, "Absit ut gloriemur, nisi in CRUCE Domini JESU CHRISTI &c," words from Galatians also quoted by

FIGURE 16.7   Richard Verstegan, *Theatrum crudelitatum haereticorum nostri temporis* (Antwerp, 1587), title page. Reproduced by permission of the Donohue Rare Book Room, Gleeson Library, University of San Francisco, San Francisco, California.

Southwell, above, and likewise by Christopher Bailey from the scaffold in 1590. Alexander Brian and William Filbie both carried rude little handmade crosses in their tribulations. The discovery of Filbie's provoked the Protestant outcry "O what a villanous traitour is this, that hath a Crosse." Everard Haunse had ended his final letter to his brother, "Tolle crucem tuam & sequere me."[44] The centrality of the image of the Cross is demonstrated most graphically, however, by the cover illustration of Verstegan's *Theatrum Crudelitatum* (see Figure 16.7). Christ bearing his Cross leads a procession of Catholic priests taking up their own crosses.

Fifteen months after the publication of *Gradualia* I, on the Feast of the Invention of the Holy Cross in 1606, Henry Garnet, who for the two decades since his meeting with Byrd in 1586 had led the Jesuit mission in England, followed all these others to the scaffold. Among Garnet's last words were "Adoramus te, Christe, et benedicimus tibi, quia per sanctam crucem tuam redemisti mundum."[45]

Garnet had gone on to pray *In manus tuas* two or three times, and twice invoked the Blessed Virgin.[46] These acts raise the possibility that one more work from the miscellanies of *Gradualia* I carried a double meaning. The somewhat odd, four-part *In manus tuas*, a vocal adaptation of a string fantasy probably dating back to the 1570s or 1580s,[47] juxtaposes phrases from the Compline short responsory, here entirely directed toward the individual petitioner ("redemisti *me*, Domine, Deus veritatis"), with a portion of the *Ave Maria*:

> In manus tuas, Domine, commendo spiritum meum: redemisti me, Domine,
>   Deus veritatis.
> Sancta Maria, Mater Dei, ora pro nobis.
>
> (Into your hands, Lord, I commend my spirit:
> you redeemed me, Lord, God of truth.
> Holy Mary, mother of God, pray for us.)

This unliturgical combination, like the gallows text *Miserere mei, Deus* discussed earlier, may well have been intended to commemorate some of the same martyrs remembered on All Saints, whom Garnet was loathe to have forgotten. William Allen records in *A briefe historie* that John Short, William Filbie, and Cuthbert Maine all had prayed *In manus tuas*. Mary Queen of Scots had also uttered the prayer before her execution in 1587. In 1595 Garnet's most famous colleague, Robert Southwell, preceded Garnet to the scaffold. Southwell is reputed to have repeated *In manus tuas* no less than three times at Tyburn, as Garnet would do at St. Paul's churchyard ten years later. The majority of the martyrs also invoked the Blessed Virgin at the last. This may explain Byrd's textual conflation. To close his *In manus tuas* Byrd chose, not the opening angelic salutation of the *Ave Maria*, but part of the final petition ("Sancta Maria, Mater Dei, ora pro nobis"). "Nunc et in ora mortis" went without saying.[48]

> God knowes it is not force nor might,
>   nor warre nor warlike band,
> Nor shield & spear, nor dint of sword,
>   that must convert the land.
> It is the blood of martirs shed,
>   it is the noble traine
> That fight with word & not with sword
>   & Christ their capitaine.[49]

This rehearing of the "political" vocabulary of Byrd's motets reveals how regularly he marched in step with this "noble traine that fought with word and not with sword." Byrd's motets, like the Jesuit tracts whose words they echo, served to foster an English Catholic identity and ideology grounded in consensus, to sustain and strengthen communal stability within the households of the Catholic gentry, to whom they spoke most directly.[50] Word—and note—did not prove mightier than the sword, of course, as Byrd and the Jesuits may have hoped. But the works of *Cantiones sacrae* and *Gradualia* nevertheless offered a means of fostering a sense of membership in an old, continuing community at home and of affirming links to a larger, reclaimant Catholicism across the Channel.

NOTES

1. Joseph Kerman, "The Elizabethan Motet: A Study of Texts for Music," *Studies in the Renaissance* 9 (1962): 273–308; "William Byrd and the Catholics," *New York Review of Books* 26:8 (17 May 1979), 32–36; *The Masses and Motets of William Byrd* (London: Faber and Faber, 1981). Lowinsky's discussion appears in *Secret Chromatic Art in the Netherlands Motet*, trans. C. Buchman, Columbia University Studies in Musicology 6, (New York: Columbia University Press, 1946), esp. chap. 8, "Religious Background of the Secret Chromatic Art."

2. *The Byrd Edition* 5: *Gradualia I (1605) the Marian Masses*, ed. Philip Brett (London: Stainer and Bell, 1989), pp. vii–xx; *The Byrd Edition* 6a: *Gradualia I (1605) All Saints and Corpus Christi* (1991), pp. vii–xii. *The Byrd Edition* 6b: *Gradualia: Other Feasts and Devotions* (1993), pp. i–xxxiv. (I thank Prof. Brett for sharing much of this information before its publication.) Further putative Catholic sentiments among English musicians are also explored in David G. Mateer, "John Sadler and Oxford, Bodleian MSS Mus. e.1–5," *Music and Letters* 60 (1979): 281–95; Elizabeth Crownfield, "A Catholic Manuscript from Elizabethan England," *Abstracts of Papers Read at the Fifty-second Annual Meeting of the American Musicological Society, Cleveland, Ohio, November 6–9, 1986*, 21 (a discussion of Oxford, Christ Church MSS 979–83 as a possible recusant source). Byrd's early links to certain Catholic sympathizers, mentioned by E. H. Fellowes in *William Byrd*, 2d ed. (London: Oxford University Press, 1948), 39, may also have been strengthened recently by Christopher Harrison, who published excerpts from eight letters referring to Byrd, the Catholic Lord Thomas Paget, and music, in "William Byrd and the Pagets of Beaudesert: A Musical Connection," *Staffordshire Studies* 3 (1991): 51–63. (I should like to thank Joseph Kerman and Oliver Neighbour for bringing this article to my attention.) "Byrd" and "William" were common enough names at this period, of course, and an autograph letter among Harrison's documents (no. 1) clearly fails to match the hand of other unimpeachable autographs of the composer. The Mr. Byrd mentioned in Harrison's second letter, which specifically discusses musical issues, must be the composer. For now the interpretation of the eight letters remains uncertain.

3. For Southwell's reference to the feast of Mary Magdalene and Weston's description of Byrd, see William Weston, *An Autobiography from the Jesuit Underground*, trans. Philip Caraman (New York: Farrar, Straus and Cudahy, 1955), 77, n. 10 and 71, respectively. Southwell placed particular emphasis on the feast of Mary Magdalene, one of the two feasts of the year when he urged Catholics to make a general confession. See Thomas H. Clancy, "Spiritual Publications of English Jesuits," *Recusant History* 19 (1989): 441. On this meeting, see also Fellowes, *William Byrd*, 42; and Kerman, *The Masses and Motets*, 49–50.

4. Philip Caraman claimed that Weston was in fact the only Jesuit still at large in England after the expulsion of Jasper Heywood in January 1585. See Weston, *An Autobiography*, 17, n. 9.

5. Both quotations from Philip Caraman, *Henry Garnet, 1555–1606, and the Gunpowder Plot* (New York: Farrar, Straus and Cudahy, 1964), 32. English authorities had also been aware of the Jesuits' imminent arrival in England since 3 July. Ibid., 24n.

6. For Kerman's more general comments on the political implications of *Circumspice Hierusalem*, see *The Masses and Motets*, 153.

7. "William Byrd and the Catholics," 34.

8. See, for example, Weston, *An Autobiography*, 77, n. 11.

9. e.g., 4 in 1579, 7 in 1580, 8 in 1581, 10 in 1582, 6 in 1583, 7 in 1584, 3 in 1585, 1 in 1586, 6 in 1587, 4 in 1588, 4 in 1589, etc., with no fewer than 14 in 1599, 12 in 1600, 19 in 1601, and as many as 26 in 1605. See A. F. Allison and D. M. Rogers, "A Catalogue of Catholic Books Printed Abroad or Secretly in England, 1558–1640," *Biographical Studies* 33–34 (1956).

10. On Garnet's press, see Caraman, *Henry Garnet*, 44. On the business schemes of French embassy employees, see John Bossy, *Giordano Bruno and the Embassy Affair* (New Haven: Yale University Press, 1991), 12.

11. Caraman, *Henry Garnet*, 72–73; on Weston, ibid., 66.

12. Ibid., 270.

13. Christopher Devlin, *The Life of Robert Southwell, Poet and Martyr* (New York: Farrar, Straus and Cudahy, 1956), 209.

14. *An epistle of comfort* (Paris [false imprint—London?], 1587–88), fols. 42ᵛ–43ʳ.

15. On the exchange of motets, see Kerman, *The Masses and Motets*, 44–45, 180–81.

16. *The first booke of the Christian exercise, appertayning to resolution* ([Rouen], 1582), 63–64; here and in subsequent quotations, original italic is preserved. Bracketed sources appear in the margin in the original. Parsons's book was appropriated, cleansed of its popish elements by Edmund Bunny, and republished for Protestant use in a version that eclipsed its Catholic model, running to no fewer than twenty printings.

17. *An epistle of the persecution of Catholickes in Englande. Translated owt of frenche into Englishe and conferred withe the Latyne copie. by. G.T.* (Douay, [1582]), 49. The text was issued in Latin, German, French, Italian, and English editions.

18. Kerman, *The Masses and Motets*, 42, 44.

19. On the pictorial martyrologies, see A. G. Petti, "Richard Verstegan and Catholic Martyrologies of the Later Elizabethan Period," *Recusant History* 5 (1959): 65–67, and Thomas H. Clancy, *Papist Pamphleteers, the Allen–Persons Party and the Political Thought of the Counter-Reformation, 1572–1615* (Chicago: Loyola University Press, 1964), 128–129.

20. Kerman made the "opprobrium"–"spectaculum" connection in *The Masses and Motets*, 143n. Mateer ("John Sadler," 292–93), apparently independent of Kerman, remarked upon Campion's *Spectaculum facti sumus*, which he connected to miniatures of decapitated fools in the Sadler MSS because Campion became "'a fool for Christ's sake', in every sense of St. Paul's phrase." Mateer may have based his interpretation on the translation in the Authorized Version rather than the original Latin. His linking of the miniature and Jesuit martyrs may still be apt, for in 1597 Garnet wrote to Aquaviva that "Catholics here are called 'God's fools', since to their credit, they make themselves simpletons that they may become wise." Caraman, *Henry Garnet*, 236.

21. On the triple point, see also Kerman, *The Masses and Motets*, 143n.

22. William Allen, *A briefe historie of the glorious martyrdome of xii. reverend priests* ([Rheims: Jean Forgny], 1582), 43.

23. The characterization "drab age verse" was coined by C. S. Lewis in *English Literature in the Sixteenth Century excluding Drama* (Oxford: Clarendon Press, 1954).

24. On Cornelius, see *Records of the English Province of the Society of Jesus*, ed. Henry Foley, 4 vols. (London: Burns and Oates, 1877–78), 3:471. Edward Oldcorne testified on 5 March 1606 that Garnet had told him that the Pope had granted the

indulgence involving *Deus venerunt gentes* to Cardinal Allen. See *Records*, 4:224 and 231, where the quotation appears.

25. For Paine, Nelson, and Brian, see *A briefe historie*, 86–87, 137, 155; for Southwell, see Devlin, *The Life of Robert Southwell*, 323.

26. The execution is described in *Records*, 1:418–419. My thanks to Oliver Neighbour and Joseph Kerman for bringing the Bodleian *Haec est dies* to my attention.

27. For Brett's observation, see *The Byrd Edition* 5, p. vii. The Haywood document appears in *Records*, 4:681. On opposition to Haywood's innovations, see Christopher Haigh, "The Continuity of Catholicism in the English Reformation," *Past and Present* 93 (1981): 63.

28. Brett, *The Byrd Edition* 5, pp. xv and xix. See also Kerman, *The Masses and Motets*, 226.

29. Brett's exceedingly useful preface to *The Byrd Edition*, 5, pp. ix–xi clarifies this process.

30. Caraman, *Henry Garnet*, 143–45; *The societie of the Rosary. Newly augmented* [London, 1596–97], 54 and sig. A3ᵛ· See also P. R. Harris, "The Reports of William Udall, Informer, 1605–1612, Part I," *Recusant History* 8 (1966): 245 and 247.

31. "In universo mundo" does not appear in the tract. Of the Propers for the newly instituted Mass of the Holy Rosary, only the Introit could have been cobbled together from materials in *Gradualia* (using Byrd's setting of the Introit for the Assumption and the omnipresent verse, *Eructavit*). Brett has pointed out, however, that Gregory XIII had restricted the feast to churches (i.e., confraternities) of the Rosary; *The Byrd Edition* 5, p. ix, n. 6. The Virgin was invoked against heresy because she was traditionally believed to have taught the apostles how to subvert false doctrine. See Émile Mâle, *L'Art religieux après le Concile de Trente* (Paris: Librairie Armand Colin, 1932), 33.

32. *The Byrd Edition* 6a, pp. ix–xi. Quotation from p. x.

33. Weston, *An Autobiography*, 245–8.

34. Brett has observed the special meaning the Feast of All Saints must have had for English Catholics, and has eloquently described Byrd's own musical eloquence in underlining the words of the All Saints Propers in *The Byrd Edition* 6a, pp. vii–viii.

35. Caraman, *Henry Garnet*, 103. Caraman suggests that Garnet may have inspired the abiding devotion to its dead which came to characterize the English Jesuit community.

36. *The societie of the Rosary*, 25.

37. Southwell, *An epistle of comfort*, fol. 142ᵛ·

38. Allen, *A briefe historie*, 42.

39. *The Byrd Edition* pp. 6a, viii–ix.

40. *Records*, 3:631. "Campion's Brag" is most conveniently available in the appendix to Waugh, *Edmund Campion: Jesuit and Martyr* (Garden City, NY: Image Books, 1956), 191–96.

41. *Odes in imitation* (1601), 91–93. At the opening of the poem Verstegan had also been careful to point out that the Cross had even more venerable associations with Britain, since its rediscoverer, the empress Helena, had been a native of York.

42. *The first booke*, 244–45, 261.

43. *An epistle of comfort*, fols. 24ʳ–25ᵛ· 95ᵛ–96ʳ· 197ᵛ–198ʳ·

44. Allen, *A briefe historie*, 84, 88, 112, 145.

45. Brett observed Garnet's quotation of the text in *The Byrd Edition* 6a, p. ix.

46. Garnet's execution is also described in *Records*, 4:117–118.

47. Oliver Neighbour, *The Consort and Keyboard Works of William Byrd* (London: Faber and Faber, 1978), 92.

48. Allen, *A briefe historie*, 110, 113, 149. For Mary's last words, see "The Manner of the Queen of Scots' Death" in Philip Caraman, *The Other Face: Catholic Life under Elizabeth I* (New York: Sheed and Ward, 1960), 264. According to Henry Garnet, for example, before the three repetitions of *In manus tuas* Southwell said *Sancta Maria Mater Dei, et omni Sancti Dei orate et intercedite pro me*. See *Records*, 1:374–375.

49. "The complaint of a Catholicke for the death of M. Edmund Campion," *A true report*.

50. Christopher Haigh points out that the "book-based piety" of the landed Catholic gentry was not characteristic of English Catholicism as a whole, which was considerably more fragmented. See "The Continuity of Catholicism in the English Reformation," *Past and Present* 93 (1981), 37–69, esp. 66–69. Further details on the close connection between the Jesuit mission and the gentry appear in Christopher Haigh, *English Reformations: Religion, Politics, and Society under the Tudors* (Oxford: Clarendon Press, 1993), esp. 263–67.

Index of Names

Adam (canon of Saint Donatian, Bruges), 73

Adam de la Halle, 5, 28, 69, 73

Aesop, 268, 277, 284 n.36

Alber, Ferdinand, 305 n.19

Albrecht V (duke), 267

Alfonso of Aragon, 224

Allen, William, 358, 362, 366, 370

Ambros, August Wilhelm, 254

Anderson, Gordon, 21

Anonymous VII, 18

Anselm of Laon, 169

Anselm, Saint (archbishop of Canterbury), 222, 223, 225, 235, 236

Anthony Abbot, Saint, 6, 124–35, 138 n.13, 141 n.59

Antonio da Cividale, 119 n.15

Aquaviva, Claudio, 348, 350, 353, 364, 372 n.20

Arcadelt, Jacques, 164 n.23, 271

Archer, Father Giles, 364

Arlt, Wulf, 13

Astell, Ann, 153

Attaingnant, Pierre, 245, 246, 265

Aubry, Pierre, 28

Augustine, Saint, 173

Backus, Irena, 48 n.38

Bailey, Christopher, 358, 369

Bailli de Vermandois. *See* Tillay, Jamet de

Baini, Giuseppe, 307

Baltzer, Rebecca, 4, 7, 10, 46 n.26, 47 n. 30, 47 n. 36

Barbireau, Jacques, 164 n.23

Barkworth, Mark, 362

Barrè, Leonardo, 271

Baston, Josquin, 271

Battre, Heinrich, 107

Bauldeweyn, Noel, 164 n.23

Bayard, Samuel, 59

Beatrice of Aragon, 154, 214

Bede, 189 n.11

Beethoven, Ludwig van, 209

Belting, Hans, 41

Bennett, Adelaide, 49 n.43

Benoit, 105, 115

Bent, Margaret, 5–6, 10, 13, 105

Benthem, Jaap van, 162 n.6

Berg, Adam, 305 n.21

Berger, Anna Maria Busse, 243

Berger, Karol, 243

Bergquist, Peter, 305–6 n.21

Berichia, Giacomo, 307

Bernardino of Siena, Saint, 222–26, 224 Fig. 10.1, 237, 239 n.16, 240 n.34

Bernard of Clairvaux, 198

Besseler, Heinrich, 93

Biel, Gabriel, 129

Binchois, Gilles de, 143, 145, 151
Blackburn, Bonnie J., 192 n.35, 238
  n.12, 243
Blanchus, Ja., 227
Blosseville, 165 n.35
Bloxam, Jennifer, 7, 142, 145
Boen, Johannes, 57
Boethius, Anicius Manlius Severinus, 137
  n.2
Boetticher, Wolfgang, 266, 267, 273,
  275, 329
Böker-Heil, Norbert, 257 n.16
Bonaiuto di Corsino, 121 n.37
Boncompagni, Giacomo, 307
Bourdichon, Jean, 215
Boyde, Patrick, 102 n.17
Bragard, Anne-Marie, 246
Brant, Sebastian, 222
Brett, Philip, 348, 363, 364, 366, 373
  n.31 and n. 34
Brian, Alexander, 358, 362, 369
Brown, Howard Mayer, 243, 244, 245,
  248
Brownlee, Kevin, 13
Brumel, Antoine, 164 n.23, 226
Brunelleschi, Filippo, 104
Bruni, Leonardo (chancellor), 116
Bunny, Edmund, 372 n.16
Bureau, Jehan, 148
Burney, Charles, 286, 287, 343
Busnoys, Antoine, 4, 6–7, 11, 122–41,
  142–68, 266
Bustis, Bernardinus de, 222
Butterfield, Ardis, 28
Byrd, William, 4, 9, 10, 11, 329–47,
  348–74

Cavalcanti, Guido, 102 n.17
Campion, Edmund, 350, 354–57, 358,
  366, 368, 372 n.20
Canis, Cornelius, 223
Caracallus, Antoninus (Caracalla), 277,
  283 n.17
Carruthers, Mary, 37
Carver, Robert, 223
Cavalleri, Giovanni Battista, 354
Chabham, Thomas, 177, 182
Chafe, Eric, 305 n.16
Chaillou de Pesstain, 52, 72
Champion, Pierre, 147

Charles the Bold, 143
Charles the Fat, 132
Charles V, 267
Charles VII, 147, 149, 150, 152, 156,
  165 n.35, 224
Charles VIII, 240 n.31
Charles IX, 304 n.7
Chevalier, Etienne, 152
Cicero, Marcus Tullius, 270, 284 n.36
Ciconia, Johannes, 109
Cino da Pistoia, 102 n.17
Circiniani, Nicolò, 354, 355 *Fig. 16.1*,
  356 *Fig. 16.2*
Clemens non Papa, 164 n.23, 227, 269,
  270, 348
Clement VI (pope), 73
Clement VIII (pope), 300
Colonna, Giulio Cesare, 310
Compère, Loyset, 145, 214, 217, 232
Cook, James H., 23
Cordier, Jean, 241 n.45
Cornelius, John, 362
Corvinus, Matthias, 214
Cottam, Thomas, 357
Cowdery, James, 59, 62
Crecquillon, Thomas, 227, 271
Crook, David, 8–9
Cummings, Anthony M., 207

Damascene, Saint John, 48 n.38
Damian, Peter, 41
Daniel, Arnaut, 102 n.17
Dante, 102 n.17
Daser, Ludwig, 227
Denis, Saint, 56
Deschamps, Eustache, 69, 71
De Latre, Petit Jean, 223
De Silva, Andreas, 164 n.23, 226
Diogenes, 284 n.36
Domarto, Petrus de, 151
Dominic, Saint, 363
Donaes de Moor, 142
Dronke, Peter, 20
Du Chemin, Nicolas, 265
Duclos, Charles Pinot, 156
Du Fay (Dufay), Guillaume, 4, 6, 7, 8,
  10, 14, 68, 139 n.33, 104–21, 143,
  144, 145, 174, 189 n.11
Dunning, Albert, 267
Dunstable, John, 143, 144, 145

Egidius de Murino, 57, 73, 82
Einstein, Alfred, 310
Elders, Willem, 193, 194
Eleutherius, Saint, 56
Erasmus, Desiderius, 270, 284 n.36, 303
Ercole I d'Este (duke of Ferrara), 214, 234–235, 241 n.45
Essex, Earl of, 362
Eugenius IV (pope), 104, 117
Everist, Mark, 44 n.9

Fallows, David, 104
Fayrfax, Robert, 223
Ferrabosco, Alfonso the Elder, 335, 343, 344–45
Ferrante of Aragon (king of Naples), 234–35, 241 n.45
Festa, Costanzo, 164 n.23
Fétis, François-Joseph, 69
Févin, Antoine de, 164 n.23, 226
Fibonacci, 102 n.13
Filbie, William, 369, 370
Filcock, Roger, S.J., 362
Filleul, Jeanne, 148, 165 n.35
Finck, Hermann, 254
Finscher, Ludwig, 214, 232
Forest, 144, 145
Fouquet, Jean, 152, 152 *Fig. 7.1*
Fox, Michael, 150
Francis I, 240 n.31
Freud, Sigmund, 169, 188
Fuller, Sarah, 45 n.11, 46 n.22, 52, 103 n.21

Gaborit-Chopin, Danielle, 49 n.43
Gallus, 96
Gardano, Alessandro, 307
Gardano, Angelo, 307
Gardano, Antonio, 246, 307
Garnet, Henry, 348, 349, 350, 353, 358, 362, 363, 364, 365, 365 *Fig. 16.5*, 369–70, 372 n.20, 374 n.48
Gascongne, Mathieu, 227
Gautier de Coincy, 18
Geffroy de Paris, 101 n.10
Gennrich, Friedrich, 17
Gerard de Pes (archdeacon of Brabant), 68
Gerstenberg, Walter, 246
Gherardello da Firenze, 121 n.37
Ghiselin, Johannes, 164 n.23

Ghisleri, Michael, 311
Glarean, Heinrich, 226, 232, 303
Gombert, Nicolas, 164 n.23, 253–54, 268
Gond, Saint, 141 n.59
Gonzaga, Guglielmo (duke), 307
Good King René. *See* René d'Anjou
Gregory the Great, 172
Gregory XIII (pope), 307–8, 363
Grocheio, Johannes de, 12, 13, 172
Groß, Horst-Willi, 291
Guido d'Arezzo, 265, 266, 275, 293–94, 303
Guillaume de Deguileville, 139 n.33
Guisard de Cambrai, 73
Günther, Ursula, 93
Gumpelzhaimer, Adam, 293, 294 *Fig. 13.1*

Haar, James, 4, 8, 9, 10, 252–54
Haberl, Franz Xaver, 267, 275
Habsburg, 275
Haggh, Barbara, 68, 151
Haigh, Christopher, 374 n.50
Harrison, Christopher, 371 n.2
Harrison, Frank, 343
Haunse, Everard, 369
Haywood, Jaspar, 363
Helena (empress), 373 n.41
Henry (duke of Anjou), 305 n.21
Henry of Hesse, 177, 182
Henry VII, 223, 239 n.14
Henry VIII, 343
Hermelink, Siegfried, 287–88, 291, 292, 296
Higgins, Paula, 6–7, 136
Hiley, David, 67
Holford-Strevens, Leofranc, 101 n.10, 243
Hoppin, Richard, 73
Horsley, Imogene, 329, 330, 345
Howlett, David, 13, 85, 100 n.5, 102 n.12 and n.13, 103 n.21
Hughes, Andrew, 172
Hugh of St. Victor, 153
Hugo de Viteriaco, 71
Huot, Sylvia, 40, 50 n. 51, 50 n. 58

Isaac, Heinrich, 164 n.23, 226

Jachet, 164 n.23, 246, 268
Jacobus de Voragine, 126, 131
Jacqueline de Hacqueville, 164 n.27, 165 n.29
Jacques d'Arras, 73
James I (king of Scotland), 147, 149
Janequin, Clément, 271
Jean d'Estouteville, 165 n.35
Jeanne de Tasse, 147, 159
Jehan des Murs, 52
Jerome, Saint, 283 n.21
Joan of Aragon, 224
Johannes de Limburgia, 145
John the Baptist, Saint, 118 n.6
John, Saint, 269
John XXII (pope), 219, 221, 238 n.13
Joschino de Picardia, 134
Josquin des Prez, 4, 5, 7–8, 9, 10, 11, 107, 135, 142, 151, 162 n.6, 164 n.23, 189 n.11, 193–212, 213–42, 244, 247, 248, 249, 252, 253, 254, 265, 266, 268, 276, 300
Judd, Cristle Collins, 257 n.20
Juvenal, 270

Kellman, Herbert, 214
Kemp, Walter, 154
Kendrick, Robert, 311
Kerman, Joseph, 9, 255 n.2, 348, 350, 362
Kermer, Wolgang, 49 n. 46
Király, Peter, 214
Koechlin, Raymond, 49 n.43
Kotter, Bonifatius, 48 n.38

Lambertus, Magister, 18
Lantins, Hugo de, 113, 145
La Rue, Pierre de, 142, 164 n.23, 226
Lasso, Orlando di (Orlande de Lassus), 4, 8, 14, 223, 265–85, 286–306, 329, 335, 345
Lazarus, Saint, 269
Lechner, Leonhard, 322 n.23
Leech-Wilkinson, Daniel, 62, 73
Leonard of Pisa. *See* Fibonacci
Leoninus, 75
Leo X (pope), 194, 195
Lerch, Irmgard, 73
Le Roy, Adrian, 304 n.7
Le Roy and Ballard (publishers), 265

Leuchtmann, Horst, 305 n.14
Lewis, C.S., 154
Lewis, Mary, 256 n.9
Lhéritier, Jean, 164 n.23
Little, Charles T., 41, 49 n.43
Loach, Donald, 227
Long, Michael, 142
Lorimer, Nancy, 46 n.26, 46 n.29
Louis de Laval, 236
Louis X, 84
Louis XI, 6, 8, 147, 149, 151, 155, 156, 214, 215, 224, 225, 229–30, 234
Louis XII, 240 n.31
Lowinsky, Edward E., 243, 267, 270, 287, 346 n.3, 348
Ludwig, Friedrich, 17, 28, 47 n.35
Lupi, Johannes, 164 n.23, 227

Macey, Patrick, 7–8, 142, 276
Machaut, Guillaume de, 13, 14, 46 n.22, 52, 71, 74, 80 n.52
Maessens, Pieter, 268
Mahu, Stephan, 227
Maine, Cuthbert, 370
Manchicourt, Pierre de, 268
Mann, Nicholas, 103 n.32
Mantegna, Andrea, 196
Marenzio, Luca, 300, 319 n.1
Marie d'Anjou (queen), 152, 165 n.35
Margaret of Scotland, 6–7, 147, 149–52, 155–57
Margaret of York, 143
Marguerite d'Ecosse. *See* Margaret of Scotland
Marguerite de Hacqueville, 147, 159
Marguerite de Salignac, 148, 165 n.35
Marguerite de Vaux, 159
Marguerite de Villequier, 159
Marigny, Enguerran de, 84, 94, 101 n.11
Mary Magdalene, Saint, 348
Mary (queen of England), 223
Mary (queen of Scots), 370
Mattfeld, Jacquelyn, 196
Mechtilda of Bavaria, 267, 276
Medici, Catherine de', 305 n.21
Medici, Cosimo de', 116
Medici (family), 6, 116
Medici (party), 104
Meier, Bernhard, 266, 287, 291
Michaelangelo, 254

Michael (canon and archdeacon of Hainaut), 68
Michael, Saint, 131, 139 n.33
Molinet, Jean, 146
Monson, Craig, 9, 10
Monte, Philippe de, 223, 353
Monteverdi, Claudio, 243
Mouton, Jean, 8, 164 n.23, 226, 227, 244, 247, 248, 249, 252, 253

Natvig, Mary, 143, 145, 163 n.6
Nelson, John, 362, 364
Nino le Petit, 223
Nosow, Robert, 6, 7, 8, 10, 13

Obrecht, Jacob, 4, 7, 142, 145, 162 n.6, 169–92
Ockeghem, Johannes, 145, 162 n.6, 266
Oldcorne, Edward, 372 n.24
Ordelaffi, Giorgio, 119 n.15
Ordelaffi, Lucrezia, 119 n.15
Origen, 145, 152
Osthoff, Helmuth, 232, 234
Ovid, 84–89, 94, 95, 96, 98, 284 n.36
Owens, Jessie Ann, 8, 9, 164 n.23, 265–66

Page, Christopher, 50 n.54
Paine, John, 362
Palestrina, Giovanni Pierluigi da, 4, 9, 164 n.23, 223, 239 n.25, 253, 286, 291, 300, 307–28, 340
Pander, Lambertus, 73
Parmigianino, 253
Parsley, Osbert, 343
Parsons, Robert, 343, 344, 354, 361, *361 Fig. 16.4*, 367, 367 *Fig. 16.6*
Paul, Saint, 269
Payne, Thomas, 21
Perotin, 20, 25
Perrenot de Granvelle, Antoine, 267, 268
Pesce, Dolores, 13
Peter, Saint, 132
Petrarch (Francesco Petrarcha), 52, 96, 102 n.17, 115
Petre, Sir John, 363
Petrucci, Ottaviano, 256 n.6, 276
Philibert of Baden, 267, 276
Philip of Hesse, 270

Philip the Chancellor, 20–21, 24, 25, 40
Philip the Good (duke of Burgundy), 224, 239 n.14
Philip IV (the Fair), 84, 96, 98
Philip V, 84, 96
Philip VI of Valois, 56
Phinot, Dominique, 269
Pibush, John, 353
Piero di Mariano, 120 n.36
Piéton, Loyset, 195, 204
Pietrobono, 214
Pipelare, Matthaeus, 142
Pius V (pope), 223, 363
Planchart, Alejandro Enrique, 47 n.37
Plato, 284 n.36
Plummer, John, 145
Plutarch, 270
Pluto, 127, 128, 130
Pontormo, Jacopo da, 253
Power, Leonel, 144, 145, 151
Powers, Harold, 287, 291, 293, 310
Prégente de Melun, 148, 165 n.35
Prioris, Johannes, 226
Pythagoras, 284 n.36

Quidort, John, 138 n.25

Randall, Richard H., Jr., 49 n.43
Rankin, Susan, 74
Raphael, 252
Reginald de Bailleul, 73
Regis, Johannes, 145
Regnault de Dressay, 148
Reichert, Georg, 93
Rémi, Saint, 132
René d'Anjou, 8, 213, 224–26, *225 Fig. 10.2*, 229, 234, 240 n.34
René II (duke of Lorraine), 225
Rhau, Georg, 246
Richardson, M., 357
Rifkin, Joshua, 8, 13, 214
Robert of Artois (count), 79 n.42
Robert of Basevorn, 177, 182, 186, 187
Robertson, Anne Walters, 5, 10, 13, 51 n.63, 92, 103 n.30
Roch, Saint, 138 n.13, 141 n.59
Rochedieu, Charles, 101 n.10, 103 n.33
Roche, Jerome, 300
Roesner, Edward H., 100 n.6
Rokseth, Yvonne, 28, 44 n.6

Rore, Cipriano de, 8, 14, 164 n.23, 266, 268, 273, 286, 294
Rosso, Pietro, 116
Rubeus, Petrus. *See* Rosso, Pietro
Rupert of Deutz, 153
Rusch, Adolph, 169, *170 Fig. 8.1*
Rusticus, Saint, 56

Sanders, Ernest, 20, 73, 93
Sano di Pietro, 224 *Fig. 10.1*
Savonarola, Girolamo, 189 n.11
Schlötterer, Reinhold, 305 n.18
Schrade, Leo, 92, 103 n.21, 103 n.22
Schulenberg, David, 255 n.1
Scotto, Girolamo, 246
Sebastian, Saint, 141 n.59
Senfl, Ludwig, 227
Sforza, Galeazzo Maria (duke of Milan), 213, 214, 234, 241 n.44 and n.45
Shakespeare, William, 268, 344
Shearman, John, 252–53, 254
Sherr, Richard, 5, 7, 9, 10
Sherwin, Raphe, 358, 368
Short, John, 370
Sidney, Sir Philip, 344
Sirede, Benedictus. *See* Benoit
Socrates, 284 n.36
Solon, 268
Sorel, Agnes, 149, 152
Southwell, Robert, 348, 350, 353, 358, 362, 366, 368, 369, 370, 374 n.48
Sparks, Edgar, 142, 145
Spataro, Giovanni, 14
Starr, Pamela, 133, 238 n.7
Steinberg, Leo, 196
Storer, Walter, 101 n.10, 103 n.33
Strohm, Reinhard, 142
Sturges, Robert S., 189 n.6, 191 n.28
Susato, Tylman, 286

Tallis, Thomas, 343, 344
Tanneguy du Chastel, 165 n.35
Taruskin, Richard, 139 n.29, 142, 145
Taverner, John, 344
Thales, 270, 284 n.36
Thomas de Douai, 73
Thomson, George, 209
Tillay, Jamet de, 7, 147–50, 155–56, 159, 160

Tinctoris, Johannes, 123, 214
Tornieri, Giacomo, 307
Treitler, Leo, 58
Tschudi, Aegidius, 226
Tye, Christopher, 344

Udall, William, 364

Vaet, Iacobus, 227, 276
Vasari, Giorgio, 265
Vento, Ivo de, 223
Verdelot, Philippe, 164 n.23, 246, 269, 271
Verstegan, Richard, 354–55, 357 *Fig. 16.3*, 367, 369 *Fig. 16.7*, 369, 373 n.41
Vicentino, Nicola, 303
Vitry, Jacques de, 81 n.69
Vitry, Philippe de, 4, 5, 10, 11, 13, 14, 52–81, 96, 101 n.9, 102 n.18, 103 n.27
Volk, Robert, 48 n.38
Volquier de Valenciennes, 73

Wack, Mary, 149
Walpole, Henry, 358
Walther, H., 102 n.14
Warmington, Flynn, 139 n.29
Wathey, Andrew, 13, 101 n.9, 102 n.18
Weerbeke, Gaspar van, 145, 214, 217, 232
Wegman, Rob C., 6, 151
Wert, Giaches de, 269
Weston, Father William, 348, 353, 364
White, Robert, 343, 344
Wihelm IV (duke), 267
Willaert, Adrian, 4, 8, 10, 164 n.23, 243–64, 266, 268, 269, 300
Wittelsbach, 275
Wright, Craig, 188

Yudkin, Jeremy, 28

Zacconi, Lodovico, 310–11, 319
Zarlino, Gioseffo, 254, 283 n.18
Zenck, Hermann, 246
Zoilo, Annibale, 307